The Cosmopolitan Empire

An Alternative to Cosmopolitanism

Moses Hess, the 'red rabbi' who converted Engels and Marx to Communism, became a devotee of Spinoza, and also a Zionist. He was the first person to combine Zionism with Communism. He edited a newspaper called the Rheinische Zeitung.

Before meeting Hess, Marx and Engels were Young Hegelians, not Communists. Isaiah Berlin wrote in *Against the Current* (1979/81), "The first and fieriest German Hegelian to turn communist, Hess converted the young Friedrich Engels to his creed" (p. 224). Then Hess converted Marx to Communism. "In 1841 Hess fell under the spell of the brilliance and boldness of Karl Marx's views. He met Marx in August of that year, preached communism to him" (p. 227).

But Hess promoted nationalist socialism featuring class unity and harmony, just the opposite of Marxism. He advocated reform rather than revolution; he supported Saint-Simonian socialism in France (p. 217), and Lassalle's reformism in Germany (p. 230), both of which Marx attacked. Hess did not believe that class conflict is either desirable or inevitable (p. 220).

Marx also joined the Rheinische Zeitung as an editor, and discovered Babeuf there. By 1848, he and Engels had parted from Hess. In the *Communist Manifesto* of that year they poked fun at 'True Socialism', which he had advocated, as Utopian.

From 1862, with the publication of his book *Rome and Jerusalem*, Hess advocated a separate 'national socialism' for Jews. In 1867 he joined the International Working-men's Association, and he remained an active member of Marx's Communist factior of the First International; in 1868 and 1869, as a Marxist delegate, he fought the representatives of Proudhon and of Bakunin, despite admiring them (Berlin, p. 243).

In *Rome and Jerusalem*, Hess paid tribute to Spinoza: "The basic idea of the system of Spinoza, namely, that God is the only substance, the ground and origin of all being, is the fundamental expression of the Jewish genius, which has ever manifested itself in divine revelations from the time of Moses and the Prophets, down to modern days" (Hess, 1862/1918, p. 122).

Spinoza formulated a non-theistic version of Judaism; he even allowed for Zionism: "God may a second time elect them" (Spinoza, 1670/2021, TPT03-P31). Albert Einstein paid tribute to Spinoza's re-definition of God in non-anthroporphic terms. Other Jewish followers of Spinoza included Harry Waton and David ben Gurion.

Hess rejected cosmopolitanism, the cultural sameness enveloping the world, instead arguing that nations and national differences should be preserved. He thought that nations were the primary units in history, classes only secondary; and that Internationalism should unite, not abolish, nations. He rejected chauvinistic nationalism that subjugated others (Berlin, pp. 231 & 239), but disregarded the Palestinian presence.

Hess was the founder of Israeli nationalist socialism, the inspirer of the kibbutz movement, and of the Histadrut as a vehicle for public ownership of the economy.

The Cosmopolitan Empire

One World but Whose?

by Peter Gerard Myers

ISBN : 978-0-6458361-1-0

Polarity Press
381 Goodwood Rd
North Isis Qld. 4660
Australia
website: mailstar.net/PolarityPress
email: polaritypress@mailstar.net

Note on the Gaza War of 2023-4

This book was completed on Sept 21, 2023, just 2 weeks before the Hamas breakout of Oct. 7. I have made some corrections and updates to the text since then, but it does not cover the Gaza War; instead, I make some notes here.

Oct. 7 was a false-flag operation like 9/11. Mossad must have had spies in Hamas, who helped plan the Oct. 7 attack, selling it to gullible Hamas leaders. Evidence of LIHOP (Let it happen on purpose) includes:
- withdrawing IDF troops from the border. You saw the bulldozer opening the fence, but where were the IDF troops? They were stood down for 7 hours
- ignoring obvious Hamas training exercises in the weeks preceding the breakout
- ignoring repeated warnings from Egypt
- ignoring sensors which informed the IDF that the wall was breached
- NYT article says Israel knew Hamas' Attack Plan more than a year earlier
- Haaretz article says Despite Intel Warnings, IDF didn't inform the Nova Festival; it sacrificed them. To have warned them would have spilled the beans that IDF knew the breakout was coming: "Top defense officials held urgent consultations the night before October 7 about a possible Hamas attack. But no one in the IDF notified the the Nova festival organizers or the party-goers."
- Netanyahu planned to destroy Gaza, but needed to present this as self-defence; hence his need to get Hamas to attack first. Hamas had no idea that they were being used. For more detail see my webpage Foolish Hamas at mailstar.net/foolish-Hamas.html

A pdf of colour images from this book is at mailstar.net/book/Cosmo-Images-231222.pdf
A slide show with colour images from this book is at mailstar.net/book/Four-Factions.pptx
A clip of the **author's interview with Sean Stone, son of Oliver Stone**, is at https://youtu.be/_9t1v6eWXGE. The full interview 'The Illuminati Agenda' is at https://www.patreon.com/posts/illuminati-91521454.

Peter Gerard Myers, March 17, 2024

Origins of this Book

This book is based on my website https://mailstar.net/. It is fully archived at the Internet Archive; by double-clicking on the index page (index.html), you can run the site as it was in the past. I have always provided my real name, photo, address and phone number. I do not post using pseudonyms.

The name of my website is 'Neither Aryan Nor Jew'. *Aryan* is another name for *Indo-European*. The "neither Aryan" part means that the West should accept racial equality (but not open border immigration); the "nor Jew" part means that Jewish domination is equally unacceptable. I state on the index page, 'The name of this site is inspired by St. Paul's proclamation "There is neither Jew nor Greek".' F. Gerald Downing explained Paul's text at Galations 3:28 in *Paul and the Cynics* (1998).

Downing pioneered the study of the similarities between early Christianity and the Cynic philosophical movement; his main book is *Christ and the Cynics* (1988). Robert M. Price (2021) also counters the current promotion of Jesus as a conventional Jew and even a Zionist or Zealot, in his book *Judaizing Jesus*. The Cynics were independent thinkers in the mould of Socrates (who should be freed from Plato's use of him to present his own ideas), and advocates of the simple life; they had similarities with the early Taoists. Taoism, as a philosophy, might be called *Dialectical Idealism*.

Paul's "universal" Christianity had as its main rival the "Jewish" faction of Christianity, Jerusalem-based and led by James, which retained circumcision, the kosher food taboos and pharisaic legalism. James' faction disappeared after the Jewish uprising was put down by the Romans in 70AD (but they took four years to do it; it nearly brought down the Empire). However, some Zionists disparage Paul and are trying to make Christianity Jewish again, pro-James, pro-Zionist and pro-Third Temple.

Downing shows that the early Christianity of Paul's faction, far from being bigoted-fundamentalist or militant-zealot, was a broadminded movement grounded in universalist Hellenistic philosophy, on which it explicitly drew; Cynic philosophy is also comparable to the best of Chinese philosophy (early Taoism) as well.

This book is about conspiracies in high places. It touches all the live wires: the Globalists, the Deep State, the Jewish Lobby, the Gay Lobby, the Green Left, Freemasonry, the Illuminati, Big Brother, the Nanny State, and World Government.

Conspiracies it covers include the assassination of JFK, the attacks of 9/11, the Covid-19 Lockdown and Vaccine Mandates, and Malaysia Airlines MH370.

Anyone who disputes the narrative on such events is branded *Far Right* and ostracised; the public has been conditioned to have a Pavlovian reaction to 'Conspiracy Theories'. I began this project in 1994. For many years I wanted to produce a book covering these topics, but their broad scope and complexity delayed it until now.

Peter Gerard Myers
March 17, 2024

What other books call 'Cultural Marxism' is called 'Trotskyism' here

DISCLAIMER: Where this book discusses the LGBT issue, the author is not judging individuals on what they do in their own private lives—such judgment is up to God/the Divinity. The author is, instead, referring to the institutionalisation of LGBT material, in schools, academia, the media, government records (e.g. Birth Certificates), public discourse (e.g. mandatory pronouns) and law; and the exclusion of traditional viewpoints as 'hate'.

What other books call 'Cultural Marxism' is called 'Trotskyism' here. The form of Marxism which under Stalin became dominant in the Soviet Union, then China, Vietnam and other Soviet allies, rejected homosexuality; Stalin made it a crime. It is Trotsky's faction in the West which has promoted Gay Marriage and Sex Change. Those activists engaged in 'entrism', a tactic used by Trotskyists to infiltrate other groups of activists. Many of these latter Far Left activists are not card-carrying communists, so the term 'Trotskyoid' is preferred here. They may not even be aware that their movement was influenced or taken over by Trotskyists.

The Far Left promoted 'Multiculturalism', as a result of which one might have expected some normalisation of Polygyny and Polyandry in the West, to accomodate minorities and immigrants. Christian missionaries were unable to find anything in the Bible that outlaws them. Polygyny is a form of marriage common in tribal societies and in Islamic cultures, in which a small percent of men have more than one wife. Historically, warfare killed men more than women, so there were surplus women. The main risk of allowing polygyny is monopolisation of women by wealthy men; but in case of sex-imbalances e.g. caused by wars, it could be justified temporarily. Polyandry, where a woman has more than one husband, is less frequent, but was practised in Tibet and Nepal, where the husbands would often be brothers.

Both those practices are attested in the Anthropological record. Instead, the Far Left promoted Gay Marriage and Sex Change, neither of which had been attested in the Anthropological record (homosexuality, transvestism and genital mutilation *were* attested, but not same-sex marriage or sex change). Nero's depravity was not *marriage*. It had no legal sanction: Roman Law did NOT allow same-sex marriage.

Fabian socialism resulted in the Attlee Government in Britain and the Chifley Government in Australia, both of which introduced mixed economies with substantial public ownership. This book endorses those two governments. But in the wake of the 60s/70s movement, which was substantially Trotskyist, and of Margaret Thatcher's de-socialist movement in the service of the Mont Pelerin Society (the top-level think-tank of Capitalism), Fabians abandoned nation-based socialism and took up the Trotskyist culture-war and H. G. Wells' World State.

Apart from the Trotskyist component of the 60s/70s movement, there was a libertarian component, which was mostly beneficial. The author took part in it.

Political Correctness in Science Too

Halton Arp, an Astronomer, disproved the Big Bang theory (see pp. 280-1). Here are his comments on Peer Review and Paradigm Change, from his book *Seeing Red*:

Refereeing, or "peer review" as it is rather pompously called, is now unworkable. It has increasingly shown that it **lets in the bad papers and excludes the good ones**, exactly the opposite of what it is supposed to do. ... Is it reasonable then to send your ideas and data to **an anonymous competitor who can with impunity often steal, suppress or ridicule them**? What happens to the hallowed principle of jurisprudence that one has the right to confront one's accuser? (Arp, 1998, p. 270)

In the beginning there was an unspoken covenant that observations were so important that they should be published and archived with only a minimum of interpretation at the end of a paper. Gradually this practice eroded as authors began making and reporting only observations which agreed with their starting premises. The next step was that **these same authors, as referees, tried to force the conclusions to support their own and then finally, rejected the papers when they did not.** As a result more and more important observational results are simply not being published in the journals in which one would habitually look for such results. **The referees themselves, with the aid of compliant editors, have turned what was originally a helpful system into a chaotic and mostly unprincipled form of censorship.** (p. 271)

Their establishment science is the most blatant possible form of creationism. The claim is that not just humans, but the whole universe was created instantaneously out of nothing. So there is small debate about time scales, but the principle is carried much, much further in the Big Bang. ...
The greatly publicized theory is black holes where everything falls in. But the observations show everything falling out! (Can we count on conventional science always choosing the incorrect alternative between two possibilities? I would vote yes, because **the important problems usually require a change in paradigm which is forbidden to conventional science.**) (Arp, 1998, p. 228)

James Lovelock, writing in *The Ages of Gaia*, agrees:

In fact, nearly all scientists are employed by some large organization, such as a governmental department, a university, or a multinational company. Only rarely are they free to express their science as a personal view. ... they have traded freedom of thought for good working conditions, a steady income, tenure, and a pension. They are also constrained by an army of bureaucratic forces, from funding agencies to the health and safety organizations. Scientists are also constrained by the tribal rules of the discipline to which they belong. ... To cap it all, in recent years **the 'purity' of science is ever more closely guarded by a self-imposed inquisition called the peer review**. (Lovelock, 2000, Preface pp. xvii - xviii)

Table of Contents

Chapter 1: Introduction

The same Deep State which assassinated President John F. Kennedy in 1963 is responsible for causing the Ukraine war of 2022.

On January 17, 1961, in his farewell address, President Dwight Eisenhower warned against the establishment of a "military-industrial complex."

> We must never let the weight of this combination endanger our liberties or democratic processes. ... Yet, in holding scientific research and discovery in respect, as we should, we must also be alert to the equal and opposite danger that public policy could itself become the captive of a scientific-technological elite. (Eisenhauer, 1961)

Kennedy acknowledged that peoples around the world had supported communist movements out of genuine grievances, and he sought to ameliorate those grievances rather than wage a world war to destroy the communist regimes.

Yet he was no fellow traveller. Speaking in favour of Open societies and against Secrecy, he said, "we are opposed around the world by a monolithic and ruthless conspiracy that relies on covert means ... Its mistakes are buried not headlined. Its dissenters are silenced, not praised" (Kennedy, 1961).

The Deep State which overthrew him uses the same covert methods that JFK accused the Soviets of. This book is an attempt to expose those conspiratorial forces and identify their factions.

Announcing his candidacy for President almost 60 years later, JFK's nephew Robert F. Kennedy Jr. proclaimed the Ukraine war as the final collapse of the Neocons' "American Century":

> The collapse of U.S. influence over Saudi Arabia and the Kingdom's new alliances with China and Iran are painful emblems of the abject failure of the Neocon strategy of maintaining U.S. global hegemony with aggressive projections of military power. China has displaced the American Empire by deftly projecting, instead, economic power. Over the past decade, our country has spent trillions bombing roads, ports, bridges, and airports. China spent the equivalent building the same across the developing world. The Ukraine war is the final collapse of the Neocon's short-lived 'American Century.' The Neocon projects in Iraq and Ukraine have cost $8.1 trillion, hollowed out our middle class, made a laughingstock of U.S. military power and moral authority, pushed China and Russia into an invincible alliance, destroyed the dollar as the global currency, cost millions of lives and done nothing to advance democracy or win friendships or influence. (Kennedy, 2023)

Dollar Hegemony began when Richard Nixon removed Gold backing for the Dollar, in 1972, because U.S. Gold reserves were being drained by the combined expense of the Vietnam War and the Welfare State ('Great Society') inaugurated by JFK's successor, Lyndon B. Johnson. The removal of Gold backing allowed the U.S. to run Current Account Deficits without limit.

The above information might seem to endorse the 'Gold Bugs' who disparage fiat currencies. But the Gold Standard prolonged the Great Depression, by limiting the amounts that governments could spend on public works. It imposed austerity.

The term "Dollar Hegemony" was coined by Henry C. K. Liu; his associate, Economics Professor Michael Hudson explained how it worked in his book *Super Imperialism* (1972/2003). As world trade was largely conducted in U.S. Dollars, Central Banks were left holding Dollars rather than Gold. The only thing to do with those Dollars was to buy U. S. Treasury Bonds; this is a debt that U.S. authorities believe they will never have to repay, because repaying it would crash the Dollar. Nations which run trade surpluses with the U.S. are thus receiving (ultimately) useless Dollars in exchange. But they continue the game because it delivers jobs and skills to their economies, while draining them from the U.S. It's like Russian Roulette; at some point, the music will stop and the game will be up.

> Michael Hudson: Well, that is what my book, Super Imperialism, was all about, that I published in 1972. Dollar hegemony really began in 1972. Hegemony is a word that I can never really work into conversation very easily. It was actually Henry Liu that emphasized that term. He's a friend of mine and we were colleagues for many years. The dollar hegemony means the United States can issue dollar bonds, IOUs, and it never has to repay them. If we run a balance of payments deficit in the United States, the dollars end up in the foreign central banks. Most of the U.S. balance of payments deficits since the Korean war have been for military spending. (Hudson, 2022)

But Hudson says that, by seizing the Dollar Reserves of Russia during the Ukraine war, the U.S. unwittingly ended Dollar Hegemony in 2021:

> And amazingly enough, the end of dollar hegemony occurred last year when the United States itself said if any country pursues a policy that we don't like, we can grab all of the dollar reserves that they hold in the United States.

> We can grab all of the Treasury bonds they hold. We can just take them. All the bank deposits they have, we can grab. They grabbed that of Venezuela first. They grabbed that of Iran. They grabbed that of Afghanistan. And then they grabbed the $300 billion of Russia. So now the United States has told any country, if you do anything that we don't like, if you do not let our companies buy control of your economy, or if you try to sue

one of our oil companies that pollutes your land, we will grab all of your money and you'll be isolated.

Well, this ends other countries' ability to finance the American empire anymore. Other countries are terrified now. If they're all saying "Let's not denominate our trade in dollars. Let's not use the dollars. Let's use each other's currencies. We will finance other governments' treasuries." (Hudson, 2022)

Thus the Ukraine war is bringing down the U.S. Empire, and positioning China as rival and likely successor. And it is being blamed on the Neocons.

Philip Giraldi, a former CIA officer, reported, "It should be noted that the State Department top level is completely staffed by Jewish Americans who are politically-speaking neocons with close ties to Israel who also believe that the maintenance of total military dominance by the United State is good both for them and good for the Jewish state. All of them are Russo-phobes for various reasons often related to the history of Jews in Russia" (Giraldi, 2023).

Finance guru Zoltan Pozsar, in a dispatch just before he left Credit Suisse, took a similar line to Hudson's, arguing that

The U.S. dollar won't be de-throned overnight ... but on the margin, de-dollarization and digitization (CBDCs) by BRICS+ central banks will reduce dollar dominance and demand for Treasuries. (Pozsar, 2023)

In an earlier dispatch, Pozsar stated that Biden had weaponised the Dollar. He diagnosed the Ukraine War as quickly developing into an Economic War between the consuming West and the producing East:

Putin's frustration with the shifting balance of military power in Europe (NATO) then spilled over into a hot war in Ukraine on February 24th, which supercharged the economic war. Both sides went "nuclear" quickly, economically: the U.S. weaponized the U.S. dollar, and then Russia weaponized commodities.

Welcome to the war economy…

Think of the economic war as a fight between the consumer-driven West, where the level of demand has been maximized, and the production-driven East, where the level of supply has been maximized to serve the needs of the West… until East-West relations soured ... think of Russia as a "G-SIB of Commodities" and China as a "G-SIB of Factories" that are the world's biggest producers of commodities and consumer goods, respectively, providing two pillars of the low inflation world ... But now that the pillars of the low inflation world are changing. (Pozsar, 2022)

Ukraine, like Yugoslavia, was cleft between two civilisations. During World War II, Croatia and West Ukraine supported the Nazis, whereas Serbia and East

Ukraine were pro-Soviet. The bitter divisions of World War II are now sustaining the Ukraine war; but there would be no war if NATO had not promised to admit Ukraine. Despite all the Holocaust documentaries on TV, the West is now fighting alongside the Nazis' allies in Ukraine, against those who defeated the Nazis.

George Kennan warned (1997), "expanding NATO would be the most fateful error of American policy in the entire post-cold-war era". John J. Mearsheimer warned (2014) that the Ukraine Crisis is the fault of the West, not Russia.

Gene Sharp wrote a manual on how protest movements could bring down governments (Secor, 2005). In the background, the Soros Foundation, the National Endownment for Democracy (NED, the civilian arm of the CIA), and other US-backed NGOs funded and organised "Color Revolutions" in many countries, using Sharp's methods. With Antifa and Black Lives Matter, such tactics were used in the West itself—and backed by George Soros and other Left Billionaires.

Victoria Nuland admitted that the US had invested over $5 billion promoting "Democracy" in Ukraine (Nuland, 2013). Since 2014, NED spent $22 promoting anti-Russia groups in Ukraine (MacLeod, 2022).

The U.S. mounted the 2014 Maidan coup as a Color Revolution backed by NED using the script developed by Gene Sharp. It ousted a pro-Russia government and installed a pro-NATO, pro-EU one. One of its consequences would have been evicting the Russian Black Sea Fleet from Sevastopol naval base in Crimea; this would have destroyed Russia as a Great Power with access to the Mediterranean, the Middle East and Africa. That's why, just after the coup, Putin invaded Crimea. It had long belonged to Russia, before Khrushchev handed it back to Ukraine; and its population was Russian.

It's clear now that the Cold War did not end in 1991. The Soviet block stopped fighting, believing in a higher union of East and West, Gorbachev being an advocate of One World. But the U.S. block kept on fighting, picking off one Soviet ally after another (Milosevic, Saddam, Gaddafi, Assad), until Putin stood up to them over Ukraine and the expansion of NATO.

Those Soviet allies happened to be supporters of the Palestinians and ene-mies of Israel; hence the special interest of 'Neoconservatives' in sustaining the American Empire. They were former Trotskyists, the successors of those Stalin had overthrown in the 1920s and 30s. But they were not real conservatives at all, ra-ther they were Far Leftists; the only reason they were called 'conservative' is that they were anti-Soviet. At a time when the Democratic Party was seen as soft on Communism, the Neocons moved to the Republican Party, taking it over and oust-ing the real conservatives as 'paleoconservatives.'

However, in recent years some, e.g. David Horowitz and Norman Podhoretz, turned against Left extremism and supported Donald Trump. But all along, they remained Zionists, hostile to Iran and Israel's Arab neighbours. In Britain, the Revolutionary Communist Party (RCP) followed the same trajectory: they started out as (mainly Jewish) Trotskyists and ended up as the conservatives (but still Zionist) of Living Marxism (LM) magazine, then of Spiked Online. They are quite effective against Trotskyists and Greens, having been Far Leftists themselves.

The Neocons supported the candidacy of Ronald Reagan, and once elected he helped them move into cabinet positions. Dick Cheney appointed many, from which they later took over Foreign Policy.

Ronald Reagan was once seen as a hero of the 'Right'. However, he gutted the U.S. economy by cutting taxes on the rich; Donald Trump made the same mistake. Reagan also absolved Big Pharma of liability for damage caused by vaccines, at the same time as those vaccines were expanded and made mandatory for children—causing the epidemic of autism (Kennedy, Robert F., Jr., 2021, p. xxii).

Anthropologist Emmanuel Todd pronounced that, with the Ukraine war, the Third World War has begun—and that it is defined in Anthropological terms as LGBT (West) vs Patriliny (Rest of the World). But LGBT is also called Androgyny.

His interview of Jan. 12, 2023 with the French magazine Le Figaro was translated by Arnaud Bertrand and published at Moon of Alabama. Todd agreed with John Mearsheimer that the war has become 'existential' for both sides. Even though China is not a party to the Ukraine war, Todd sees it becoming involved:

> the conflict, which started as a limited territorial war and is escalating to a global economic confrontation between the whole of the West on the one hand and Russia and China on the other hand, has become a world war (Todd, 2023)

The Neocons, in conjunction with Zbigniew Brzeziński and the "mainstream" media, had long demonised Russia and sought to break it up as the Soviet Union had broken up. The Neocons ran Foreign Policy for George W. Bush, while Brzeziński's base was the Democratic Party of Barack Obama. Brzeziński channelled Polish hatred of Russia, while the Neocons funnelled Jewish revenge for pogroms of past centuries (and for Stalin's overthrow of Trotsky).

The Ukraine war started out as another "Afghan trap", which was intended to break Russia up as the Afghan war had broken up the Soviet Union. But the Russians saw what they were up against, and learned the lesson that Alexander Dugin imparted: don't trust the West; remember, it was Crusader armies, not Moslems, who devastated Constantinople. And his warning, "Carthago Delenda Est".

Thus the Neocons unwittingly forced Russia into alliance with China, forging the sort of Eurasian bloc that Halfold Mackinder warned against (but with Russia s resources going to China instead of Germany). Donald Trump, in calling for the abolition of NATO, tried to prevent this war from breaking out. The media retaliated with the Russiagate hoax. Trump's assassination of General Soleimani rendered him unfit for future office, but most Democrats, being the party of war, are worse.

Todd perceives that the war could lead to the collapse of U.S. financial hegemony, and the end of its empire:

> If the Russian economy resisted the sanctions indefinitely and managed to exhaust the European economy, while it itself remained, backed by China, American monetary and financial controls of the world would collapse, and with them the possibility for United States to fund their huge trade deficit for nothing. This war has therefore become existential for the United States. No more than Russia, they cannot withdraw from the conflict, they cannot let go. This is why we are now in an endless war, in a confrontation whose outcome must be the collapse of one or the other. (Todd, 2023)

He says that the defining difference between the blocks is LGBT (in the West) vs Patriliny (in the rest of the world):

> When we see the Russian Duma pass even more repressive legislation on 'LGBT propaganda', we feel superior. I can feel that as an ordinary Westerner. But from a geopolitical point of view, if we think in terms of soft power, it is a mistake. On 75% of the planet, the kinship organization was patrilineal and one can sense a strong understanding of Russian attitudes. For the collective non-West, Russia affirms a reassuring moral conservatism.

This looks like a battle that the West cannot win. Many parents in the West are fearful of LGBT propaganda targeting their children in schools and books; libraries hosting Drag Queen shows for young children are giving rise to parental protest groups. It's an election issue. And yet, the LGBT agenda is being pushed from on high, by the World Economic Forum—along with Transhumanism, eliciting fears that we humans will be overthrown by robots or cyborgs (Elliott, 2023).

In the 1950s, the West was still patrilineal. But in the late 1970s, divorce courts started awarding children to mothers, by default. The mother gained the children; then the house (because the children needed a home); then maintenance payments. The father was left without children or house, but obliged to pay the bills. This made divorce riskless for women, and it was nearly always women who initiated divorce in the next two decades. The man had to pay out so much money that, in many cases, he could hardly afford to establish another family or buy another house. Suicide by such fathers became a national scandal, one ignored by the Feminist media and politicians. Conservative politicians tried to make the law more even-handed, but 'Progressives' brought back the Feminist bias.

What it meant, in Anthropological terms, was that we had become matrilineal. But this was matriliny with Trotskyist venom built into it. Traditional matrilineal societies such the Trobriand Islanders did not punish men that way. Women were free to break the marriage, and they got the kids, but the man did not have to pay. The children were always considered part of the woman's clan, not his. It was the mother's brother who was considered their primary guardian, and his role was not affected by divorce. There is nothing wrong with matriliny, and patriliny works too, but changing horses midstream is traumatic.

Todd said "countries in the West often have a nuclear family structure with bilateral kinship systems, that is to say where male and female kinship are equivalent." But he is not quite right in calling Western descent "bilateral", at least where Divorce Courts are concerned. The West is increasingly not only LGBT but also matrilineal (the two go together, in Trotskyoid politics), and devoted to a sex war against hetero men and feminine women; and this represents a Culture War between the post-Christian West and the patrilineal Rest of the World.

This change was promoted by the Trotskyoid Left. Stalin made homosexuality a crime, but the Trotskyists promoted "Equal Love", and pursued Sex War as a variant of their Class War agenda. Trotsky set out the agenda in his book *The Revolution Betrayed* (see ch. 13 below).

The Far Left promoted "Multiculturalism", which, logically, might have resulted in the legalisation of Polygyny and Polyandry, to accomodate minorities and immigrants. Both these practices are well attested in the Anthropological record. Instead, the Far Left promoted Gay Marriage and Sex Change, which have never before been attested in the Anthropological record. Our ancestors, of only a few decades ago, would have been shocked at the LGBT values the West has adopted.

It's Trotsky's legacy. He must be laughing.

When Hitler was preparing for the invasion of the Soviet Union, the Russian people made it clear that they would not fight for Communism—which had inflicted the Red Terror, the Gulag and the Ukraine Famine on them. Stalin, reading the public mood, rehabilitated traditional Russian culture, religion and heroes; and so, Soviet Patriotism was born. Trotsky, in his book *The Revolution Betrayed*, accused him of rehabilitating God and the Family.

The West will have to do so too, dumping the LGBT/Androgyny agenda—or go down to China. Christians and Moslems in the West will not fight for the LGBT agenda. The U.S. military, which has honoured Drag Queens, already has a recruitment problem. The aircraft carrier Gerald R. Ford, commissioned in 2017, carries 5,000 sailors, mostly men, but has no urinals—catering for the Trans agenda.

Count Richard Coudenhove-Kalergi, one of the founders of the E.U., noted in his book *Practical Idealism* (1925/2019) that Feminism made women more masculine:

> The emancipation of women is also a symptom of the masculinization of our world, because it does not lead the feminine type to power, but the masculine. While in the past the feminine woman by her influence on the man participated in world leadership, today "men" of both sexes wield the scepter of economic and political power. The emancipation of women signifies the triumph of the "man-woman" over the real, feminine woman; it does not lead to the victory, but to the abolition of women. The "lady" is already extinct: the "woman" should follow her. (p. 112)

As women became more masculine, the dynamic between the sexes expressed as "vive la difference" changed. The loss of feminine women deprived men of the polarity which sustained heterosexuality; it contributed to the rise of homosexuality. Some Western men who had experienced the ravages of divorce sought wives from foreign countries, where women were still old-fashioned, feminine and religious; by this means, Feminism had a huge effect on the racial and cultural makeup of the West. Those women, and their Western husbands, sent money and goods to poor relatives back home (as do other migrants too). Their children have generally done well. A smaller proportion of Western women have also found spouses abroad.

Another notable leftist, Dr H. C. Coombs of Australian National University, expressed a similar view to Kalergi's:

> But although I sympathise fully with the women's movement I don't like to see the extremist women's groups wanting power and to be like men. I realise that they, like other oppressed groups, may see the holding of power as the only way to bring about changes, but I hope it is only a transitional phase. I would rather see more attention in our society paid to what might be called 'feminine' characteristics or values—tenderness, concern for others, kindness, sympathy—ideally found in both sexes. (Mayne-Wilson, 1974)

The reason that the West is pro-Androgyny, but the rest of the world is not, is that its traditional Christian civilization has been destroyed by Trotskyoid/Feminist culture warriors, based in the universities.

Chapter 2: Clash of Conspiracies

Conspiracies are the norm, not the exception. Other conspiracy writers allege that there is just one high-level conspiracy; but I maintain that there are four— British (Anglo-American Imperial), Globalist, Zionist and Green-Left. These four are forced to share power, and thus function as factions.

Sometimes, they clash; Globalist Jews and Zionist Jews have been clashing on the streets of Jerusalem and Tel Aviv. When Antifa and Black Lives Matter (Green Left) overturn statues (Anglo-American) with the support of Globalists (George Soros, the Economist magazine), that also demonstrates a Clash of Conspiracies.

This book covers three conspiracies done mainly by the Deep State:

- the assassination of JFK
- the hijacking of Malaysia Airlines flight MH370
- the Covid-19 Pandemic, Lockdown and Vaccine Mandates

and two done mainly by Zionists/Mossad:

- the 1967 attack on the U.S.S. Liberty
- the attacks of September 11, 2001.

Politically aware people know that President John F. Kennedy was murdered by the CIA; so was his brother Robert. A CIA agent, Robert D. Morrow, confessed his role, and the CIA's, in the assassination of JFK, but the media ignored his book, just as they ignored the deathbed confession of E. Howard Hunt.

9/11 and the Covid-19 Pandemic were preceded by practice sessions

Both 9/11 and the Covid-19 Pandemic were preceded by practice sessions, simulations where the actors could prepare their roles and how to manage the public reaction. The simulation before Covid-19 was called Dark Winter. The Covid-19 Pandemic was planned by the Elite, to get us to accept the Great Reset, taking control from governments and giving it to the W.H.O. (an unelected U.N. Agency, formerly funded by governments but now mostly funded by private Foundations), with loss of sovereignty and freedoms. The Elite suppressed safe treatments like Ivermectin, and forced lockdowns and dangerous vaccines on us; noncompliant doctors, nurses & teachers were sacked. The media were complicit.

David Gergen, one of the planners of Dark Winter, now has a seat on the Board of the Klaus Schwab Foundation, part of the World Economic Forum, which promotes the 'Great Reset.' The WEF says that it "penetrates the cabinets", but for an unelected body to do so is undemocratic and subversive. It implies Oligarchic rule—for the greater good, of course, because most people are Deplorables.

Globalists use Pandemics to get governments to cede sovereignty to UN

Vaccination has historically been beneficial, but natural immunity (from exposure to a disease, e. g. in childhood) gives better protection. From the time that Ronald Reagan gave Big Pharma companies freedom from prosecution for vaccine injuries, mass vaccination enforced by government has become dangerous.

Globalists realised that Pandemics could be a selling-point for getting governments to yield their sovereignty to a world body such as the U.N. The Covid-19 Pandemic had been planned for this end (and population reduction), but its actual timing was accidental— it leaked from a Chinese lab in Wuhan. In a 2016 c-span video, Peter Daszak of EcoHealth Alliance admits "my colleagues in China" develop "killer" Coronaviruses, funded by Tony Fauci and the U.S. Government. Daszak describes "insert[ing] spike proteins" into viruses to see if they can "bind to human cells" (Daszak, 2016). Youtube and the "mainstream" media censor this material.

Once the Pandemic was under way, Globalist media and governments adopted a propagandist approach. The Marxist Left and the Greens collaborated with them, but the Libertarian Left rebelled against Speech Codes and Vaccine Mandates; in Australia, they display the Eureka Flag, a libertarian flag.

Globalist attempt to implement the World State of H. G. Wells

The Globalists are attempting to implement the World State advocated by H. G. Wells. The concept goes back to Adam Weishauptzmon

it's Illuminist. Today's Globalists are not looking up Wells' books to see what to do next; rather, he developed his ideas via discussions with such people, and intuited their designs, allowing a special role for bankers. His books are the best guide to their plans.

Wells was the founder of the Green Left. Aldous Huxley's book 'Brave New World' and George Orwell's book *Nineteen Eighty-Four* are both warnings about what Wells' World State would be like. Huxley depicted dumbing-down with sex, drugs and entertainment; Orwell depicted Speech Codes and Thought Police. Both have turned out to be correct.

Four Factions of the Elite

There are four factions of the Elite:

- the "British" or Anglo-American Imperial; this refers to the secret society founded by Cecil Rhodes and led by Lord Alfred Milner. Carroll Quigley revealed its secrets in his book *The Anglo-American Establishment*. It aimed to create an imperial Anglosphere by getting the United States to rejoin the Empire, but the capital would be transferred across the Atlantic. The UKUSA secret treaty and the Five Eyes intelligence network are part of the Anglosphere.

Today, in Britain, the Rhodes/Milner society is called The Round Table or Chatham House; in the U.S. its partner is the Council on Foreign Relations (CFR). Although these bodies remain "British" with a unified foreign policy, the "British" have had to share power with the other three factions. Thus the structure of Anglosphere cohesion remains intact, but the content of their policies has been reversed from that of Rhodes and Milner. Margaret Thatcher, Boris Johnson and Donald Trump belong to the "British" faction.

- the Zionists (Jewish Lobby). AIPAC, the Neocons, and other supporters of Netanyahu belong in this faction. They brought about the Iraq War, and oppose the deal that Obama brokered with Iran.

Despite the efforts of the Rhodes/Milner conspirators, the reunion of the United States with the Anglosphere (Britain and its dominions) only occurred via the Balfour Declaration during World War I, when the Jewish Lobby (not representing *all* Jews) was promised Palestine in return for getting the United States into the war on the British side. David Lloyd George, Prime Minister of Britain at the time, explained this "Contract with Jewry" in his Memoirs. Whether the Jewish Lobby did get the U.S. into the war, and how it did so, are contentious issues even today; if it did *not* do so, why did it get Palestine anyway? It was through the Balfour Declaration that the Zionists became a faction of the Elite.

- the Globalists (Illuminati). If you are sceptical about the existence of the Illuminati, take a look at the Pyramid on the top of the Supreme Court of Israel: https://mailstar.net/illuminati.html. It has an All-Seeing Eye near the top, the same as on the back of the U.S. $1 bill. Readers can also find images of this Illuminati Pyramid via internet searches.

Didn't know it was there? That's because the "mainstream" media in the West have never mentioned it; they have been too busy publicising the sins of Catholic priests. Inside the building, there are 3 sets of 10 steps that lead to the Library beneath the Pyramid. The Library, for the use of Judges, has 3 levels, making a total of 33 levels beneath the Pyramid. Clearly, this is a link to the 33 degrees of Freemasonry; the illumination from the Pyramid guides the Judges. A plaque states that the Rothschild family designed and paid for the construction of the building; a painting at the entrance shows members of the Rothschild family with Shimon Peres, Yitzhak Rabin, and a model of the building.

George Soros and the Rothschilds belong to this faction, as do politicians they sponsor, e.g. Hillary Clinton, Barack Obama and Joe Biden. The Globalists opposed the Iraq War, and supported the deal that Obama brokered with Iran; they oppose Netanyahu. The Economist magazine, part-owned by the Rothschilds, is the best—although imperfect—guide to Rothschild policy.

- the Green Left. They are the Left faction of the Globalists. Both promote Open Borders, Net Zero, Speech Codes, LGBT and the Culture War. During the Covid-19 Plandemic, both were pro-Vaccine and pro-Lockdown. But they differ over Palestine, the War on Terror, and public ownership of industries. The Globalists and Zionists had Jeremy Corbyn banned from standing as a Labour candidate at the next election, but the Green Left support him. Alexandria Ocasio-Cortez, Bernie Sanders, Trotskyists and the Greens belong in this faction.

There's a clash of conspiracies; that's what overturning statues, by Antifa & Black Lives Matter, is all about. The Globalists (Illuminists) and their Green Left allies have been overthrowing the "British". When activists burned down churches in Canada, and when they sought to change the Australian constitution so that they could dominate through Aboriginal proxies, these events show that the "British" order has been overthrown. By what? By another order, the Illuminist one.

Margaret Thatcher belonged to the "British" conspiracy; but the European Union (EU) is an Illuminist project, as is the Trans Pacific Partnership (TPP). These bodies, rather than being a policy agenda of the "British", submerge Britain (on the one hand) and the United States (on the other) in Globalist blocks which would end their economic independence, terminate their sovereignty, flood them with immigrants, and do away with their Constitutions.

Bill Clinton signed the U.S. up to join the International Criminal Court ('Rome Statute') in 2000; but George W. Bush "unsigned" the treaty, stating that the US would not ratify it. Clinton's action was Illuminist, whereas Bush's was "British". The Illuminists want rule by United Nations Agencies (e.g. the W.H.O., now mainly funding byprivate Foundations), U. N. Committees and the I.C.C., bodies they control or aspire to control, whereas the "British" want rule by the Anglosphere.

Cartoon Wars—Clash between Globalists and Zionists

Zionist Jews have their own Illuminati-Communist-CFR Conspiracy Theory. They see a revamped Communist movement behind Feminism, Gay Marriage, the World Court, the Kyoto Protocol etc. Being anti-Stalinist, it does not wear the Communist label, and instead disguises itself behind a multitude of single-issue lobbies. And they're right.

Where they're wrong, is that Zionism—the push for Greater Israel, and for the Third Temple—is another conspiracy. There's a Clash of Conspiracies. Each side— the Globalists and the Zionists—published cartoons lampooning the other; these cartoons were branded 'antisemitic' by the other side.

In 2014, Netanyahu's Jewish opponents used antisemitic tactics to stop him from launching more wars, this time against Iran. Gideon Rachman in the Financial Times opined, "Obama needs to take on the Israel lobby over Iran". No longer invisible, the New York Times of January 14, 2014 mentioned AIPAC's lobbying of Congress on the Iran bill. But where was Noam Chomsky? Still in denial of the Lobby's power.

Economist cartoon depicts Jewish Lobby stopping Peace Deal with Iran

The Economist magazine of January 16, 2014 (print edition) featured a cartoon depicting the Jewish Lobby stopping a Peace Deal between Obama & Iran. The cartoon depicts the leaders of the United States (Obama) and Iran (Ayatollah Khomeini) as willing to

do a deal, but hardliners on both sides are holding them back. The Lobby has control of Congress, as shown by the Star of David on the shield. The Anti-Defamation League said the cartoon depicts the "anti-Semitic canard of Jewish control".

Yair Netanyahu publishes Soros 'Illuminati' cartoon

On September 9, 2017, Yair Netanyahu, the son of Bibi, published (on Facebook) a cartoon portraying George Soros as the

All-Powerful Jew who controls the world. It shows Manny Naftali, former superintendent of the Prime Minister's Residence, being bought by Eldad Yaniv, who is bought by Ehud Barak, who is bought by the money of the Illuminati, who are bought by a Reptilian—a codeword for Jewish bankers?—who control the world for George Soros. The Soros 'Illuminati' cartoon was also published by Haaretz, by other Israeli newspapers, and by JTA (Jewish Telegraph Agency). Liberal or Progressive Jews were outraged.

NYT depicts Netanyahu leading Trump; and Netanyahu as Moses

On Thursday April 25, 2019 the New York Times international print edition published a cartoon in the opinion pages. It shows Israeli Prime Minister Netanyahu as a dog on a leash leading

a blind U.S. President Donald Trump around. Netanyahu has a Star of David around his collar, and Trump wears a skullcap.

On Saturday April 27, 2019, the weekend edition of the Times international edition published a second cartoon, depicting a blind Netanyahu as Moses bringing from the mountain, not the Ten Commandments but the Israeli flag—i.e. not a universal moral law, but Zionism.

9/11 was a Mossad job with CIA complicity

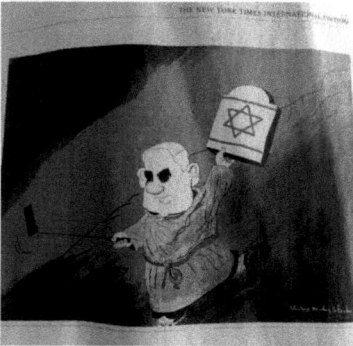

The attack on the World Trade Center of September 11, 2001 (9/11) was a Mossad job with CIA complicity. The payoff for Mossad was getting the U.S. to fight Israel's enemies; the payoff for the Deep State was the War on Terror and the Patriot Act, by which liberties were curtailed and a surveillance regime introduced.

The Anthrax attacks at the time of 9/11 were blamed on Moslems, until it was revealed that the samples of Anthrax came from U.S. labs. Francis Boyle said that tracking down who sent the Anthrax would be a good way of discovering who really did 9/11 (Boyle, 2005, p. 47).

On October 30, 2014, Haaretz, an Israeli newspaper, published a cartoon showing Netanyahu flying a plane into the World Trade Center. The Jewish Daily Forward also published the cartoon on October 30. It depicts Netanyahu as "the" 9/11 Terrorist, the mastermind behind the whole operation. The name "Israel" on the plane implies that 9/11 was a Mossad operation, to get the U.S. to fight

Israel's enemies. This would mean that 9/11 was a False Flag attack, and that Osama bin Laden and the "Arab hijackers" were patsies. This cartoon is closer to reality than the fake news put out by the "mainstream" media and history books about 9/11. Readers can find this cartoon (in colour) with internet searches.

Former Mossad Officer Victor Ostrovsky revealed that Mossad's motto is "By Way of Deception, thou shalt do war" (Ostrovsky & Hoy, 1990, p. 53).

He said that Mossad trained BOTH SIDES in the Sri Lankan civil war. In the Foreword to the book, Claire Hoy wrote,

"The Mossad—believe it or not—has just 30 to 35 case officers, or katsas, operating in the world at any one time. The main reason for this extraordinary low total, as you will read in this book, is that unlike other countries, Israel can tap the significant and loyal cadre of the worldwide Jewish community outside Israel. This is done through a unique system of sayanim, volunteer Jewish helpers" (p. xi).

In a follow-up book, *The Other Side of Deception*, Ostrovsky disclosed that Mossad provoked the U.S air strike on Libya in 1986 by making it appear that terrorist orders were being transmitted from the Libyan government to its embassies around the world. But the messages originated in Israel and were re-transmitted by a special communication device—a "Trojan horse"—that Mossad had placed inside Libya. (Ostrovsky, 1994, pp. 113-7).

Mossad next moved against Saddam, drawing the U.S. to make war on him. Ostrovsky (1994) also revealed that Mossad murdered Robert Maxwell; that it supported Moslem fundamentalists, to derail the peace process; and that it planned to kill George H. Bush in Madrid, in payback for the peace process he initiated. For his revelations, Ostrovsky received death threats, and was branded "the most treacherous Jew in modern Jewish history" (Ostrovsky, 1995).

Former Australian PM said Israel sank the Liberty, deliberately

Another conspiracy is Israel's attack on the U.S.S. Liberty in 1967, and the subsequent cover-up. Elements of the U.S. Government wanted to publicise Israel's attack, but the Jewish Lobby warned them that this would be 'antisemitic'; so they hushed it up (U.S.S. Liberty, 2014). Former conservative Australian Prime Minister Malcolm Fraser, who was Jewish, said in an interview with Jon Faine on ABC Radio (Australia), that Israel deliberately sank the Liberty:

Faine: Bob Carr has managed to upset a lot of people... with his memoir, saying that he thought that the pro-Israel... lobby* in Australia wielded too much power. What does Malcolm Fraser think of that?

Fraser: They certainly do.

Fraser: The Jewish community seek to get Australia to support policies as defined by Israel. Look, Israel years ago, during one of the wars, killed 30 or 40 Americans on a spy ship [the USS Liberty*] in the Western [sic] Mediterranean.

Faine: That was a mistaken missile hit, if I remember correctly, or an air strike. I can't remember.

Fraser: Well, the Americans tried to cover it up. It wasn't a mistake. It was deliberate. (Fraser agrees with Carr on Lobby, 2014)

Australian Foreign Minister: policy "subcontracted" to Jewish Lobby

Bob Carr, Australian Foreign Minister in the Labor government of Julia Gillard, wrote in his memoirs *Diary of a Foreign Minister*, that Australia's Mideast foreign policy had been "subcontracted" to Jewish donors (Taylor, 2014).

In the U.K., the ouster of Jeremy Corbyn from the Labour leadership gave precedence to a tiny Jewish minority over the majority of Labour members—the ones who had elected Corbyn as leader in a popular vote. The lobbyists' grievance was that Corbyn sided with the Palestinian victims of Israel's apartheid policies. No less a figure than Jimmy Carter had called it 'apartheid', and for that his book *Peace Not Apartheid* was likened to both *Mein Kampf* and the *Protocols of Zion*.

The same lobby which defamed Carter is also behind the attack on Corbyn. An Al Jazerra documentary showed that the campaign against Corbyn was orchestrated by the Israeli Embassy. When the media taunt Corbyn for mixing with Antisemites, they mean Paul Eisen, but they never mention that he is Jewish (Myers, 2020, Nov. 4). He's called 'antisemitic' because he publicises Israel's massacre of Palestinians in 1948, three years after the liberation of Auschwitz (see p. 316).

The disappearance of MH370 also involved a conspiracy—probably by the Deep State, not by the pilots. If one of the pilots had wanted to suicide, he would not have flown for five hours, as per the official theory, but got it over quickly.

Akhenaten's Universal God vs. Jehovah the Tribal God

Freemasonry has several incompatible themes/goals: Androgyny, Ancient Egypt, and building the Third Temple (Albert Pike wrote that it was the Templars' real goal). Yet there is no connection between the Temple of Solomon and Ancient Egypt—except, perhaps, via Akhenaten, whom Sigmund Freud depicted as the true founder of Judaism. But Akhenaten was a heretic Pharaoh, founder of the Aton (Aten) religion, and the enemy of the Ancient Egyptian religion.

Freud wrote in *Moses and Monotheism*, "The Jewish people had abandoned the Aton religion which Moses had given them and had turned to the worship of another god {Jehovah} who differed little from the Baalim of the neighbouring tribes. All the efforts of later distorting influences failed to hide this humiliating fact" (Freud, 1967, p. 87).

For Akhenaton, Aton was not the *chief* god, but the *only* god; and there were no statues to him (or it). Akhenaton's hymn to Aton, tr. James H. Breasted, reads

O thou sole god, whose powers no other possesseth,
Thou didst create the earth according to thy desire

While thou wast alone. (Mackenzie, 1907/1978, p. 336)

Jews, the most Internationalist and yet the most Nationalist (chauvinist) of peoples, are riven by this oscillation between Akhenaten's Universal God and Jehovah the Tribal God. It manifests as the struggle between Illuminism and Zionism; the clashes in Israel over Netanyahu's attempt to muzzle the Supreme Court are part of that struggle If Netanyahu wins, he might deport the Palestinians. The Illuminati Pyramid on the top of the Supreme Court building is a statement of the difference. One might surmise that the struggle is between Illuminist/Masonic Judaism and Talmudic Judaism. (Myers, 2018/2023).

Globalists, Zionists and National Jews

Any book dealing with Communism and Globalism inevitably covers Jewish factions and lobbies. It's safe to blame Freemasons, Jesuits, the "British" or the Vatican, but anyone who writes about Jewish power is attacked. However, I am calling the shots as I see them, Masonic and Jewish both. I must also steer wide of the shoals of Communism (now wearing a 'Progressive' guise) and Nazism. I have chosen to be up front and address these matters directly here. But I am trying to avoid the unsupported allegations that plague conspiracy literature.

I believe that Winston Churchill (1920) was correct in locating Jews in three camps. Today, the first two operate collectively as lobbies—Globalist and Zionist—and the third comprises individual Jews who protest against the other two (and against the Deep State). The Globalists backed Obama, Hillary Clinton and Biden; the Zionists backed Trump. Of course, the Globalist Jews are a bit Zionist too, but they support United Nations Security Council resolutions against Israeli settlements and the wall fencing off the Palestinians; it is a matter of degree. I do not class Trotskyist or Progressive Jews who operate collectively in mainly Jewish movements, in the third camp, but rather count them among the Globalists.

The leadership of Globalism is partly Jewish and partly Masonic; but the Masonic part is Illuminised Masonry, which features the Pyramid and All-Seeing Eye.

Eight Jewish holidays, but only two Christian ones

Zionism is part-Jewish and part-Christian Fundamentalist. However the Calendar of the U.S. House for Representatives for 2017 listed eight Jewish holidays, but only two Christian ones (Myers, 2019b).

The Jewish holy days listed were Passover, Rosh Hashanah, Yom Kippur and Hanukkah—the start and end of each, a total of 8. The Christian holy days listed were Easter Sunday and Christmas (but Christmas is increasingly secularised). Good Friday was not listed. Calendars for other years are similarly distorted. This is conclusive evidence that it's Jews rather than Christians who are dominant.

The third camp of Jews do not co-ordinate their efforts as the other two do—they have no central bodies, they do not own or manage the media, and few have Foundations—but operate individually. They work with non-Jews, and are not separatists. These are the Jews I admire, and among this camp I have found some friends. During the Covid-19 Pandemic, Jews in this third camp played an important role in the dissident movement.

The persons of Jewish ethnicity I admire for their efforts (apologies to any who consider themselves ex-Jews) include:

Anti-Covid-Vax, pro Ivermectin, Hydroxychloroquine: Drs Vladimir Zelenko, Simone Gold, Thomas Levy, Peter Breggin and David Brownstein.

Anti-Covid-Vax, Anti-Lockdown, Anti-Genocide and Anti-police-State: Francis Boyle, Steve Kirsch, Ezra Levant, Avi Yemini, (ex-Jew) Gilad Atzmon, Naomi Wolf, Max Blumenthal, Joel Kotkin.

Expose 9/11 Conspirators: (part Jewish) Alan Sabrosky, Aaron Russo, Alex Jones, Steve Pieczenik.

Oppose Feminist war against Men: Bettina Arndt (of part-Jewish heritage).

Oppose Neocon Wars: Jeffrey Sachs, Seymour Hersh.

Under a dramatic headline "Ukraine Is the Latest Neocon Disaster", Professor Jeffrey D. Sachs impaled the Neocons who have run U.S. Foreign Policy for the past 30 years (Sachs, 2022). He listed the leaders of the Neocons as

HOUSE CALENDAR — September 2017
MAJORITY LEADER KEVIN McCARTHY — 115th Congress, First Session
@GOPLeader — MajorityLeader.gov

HOUSE CALENDAR — April 2017
MAJORITY LEADER KEVIN McCARTHY — 115th Congress, First Session
@GOPLeader — MajorityLeader.gov

HOUSE CALENDAR — December 2017
MAJORITY LEADER KEVIN McCARTHY — 115th Congress, First Session
@GOPLeader — MajorityLeader.gov

Leo Strauss, Donald Kagan, Norman Podhoretz, Irving Kristol, Paul Wolfowitz, Robert Kagan (son of Donald), Frederick Kagan (son of Donald), Victoria Nuland (wife of Robert), Elliott Cohen, Elliott Abrams and Kimberley Allen Kagan (wife of Frederick).

Every one of them is Jewish. As is Sachs himself. Yet he could not mention this fact. This is the most extraordinary aspect of Jewish power—it cannot be mentioned, and those who do mention it are branded 'Nazi'. Even Israel Shamir was branded 'Fascist'; surely this will be my fate too—and I am non-Jewish.

The "mainstream" media did not report Sachs' comments, despite his prominence; only the "dissident" media did so. Henry Kissinger, a Realist like Sachs, is Jewish as well; it's not as if they are ALL "bad guys". So why not highlight their commonality—might not outing it induce more responsibility?

Israeli columnist Ari Shavit wrote in Haaretz, "The war in Iraq was conceived by 25 neoconservative intellectuals, most of them Jewish, who are pushing President Bush to change the course of history. Two of them, journalists William Kristol and Charles Krauthammer, say it's possible. But another journalist, Thomas Friedman (not part of the group), is skeptical" (Shavit, 2003).

NYT published stmt by Israeli journalist: U.S. is "in our hands"

In an Oped published by the New York Times on May 27, 1996, Shavit admitted to Israel's wanton killing of more than a hundred Lebanese civilians in April, and said that Israel got away with it because the United States is "in our hands":

NYT Op-Ed page, May 27, 1996, p. A21
How Easily We Killed Them
by Ari Shavit

We killed 170 people in Lebanon last month. Most were refugees ... How easily we killed them—without shedding a tear, without establishing a commission of inquiry, without filling the streets with protest demonstrations ...

We killed them out of a certain naive hubris. Believing with absolute certitude that now, **with the White House, the Senate, and much of the American media in our hands**, the lives of others do not count as much as our own. (Shavit, 1996)

On the Holocaust issue, after reading literature from both sides, in 2009 I conducted an intensive debate which lasted three weeks. I concluded that the Nazi Holocaust had occurred; the debate is online (Myers, 2009/2011).

Does one Holocaust justify Another?

I have never been a 'Holocaust Denier', but I do reject Holocaust Exceptionalism. What's the difference between being killed in a Gas Chamber, and being killed in the Red Terror? Or the Gulag? Or the genocide of the Kulaks (the collectivist famine in Ukraine & Russia)? Or the Great Leap Forward? Or in Israel's massacres in Gaza and Jenin? Or by white phosphorus in the U.S. invasion of Iraq?

A woman called Victoria, who assailed me with Hasbara-like propaganda, wrote, "an entire people was subject to a campaign of methodic genocide that was premeditated. ... To ethnically cleanse an entire group of people and expel them from their homelands is genocide too".

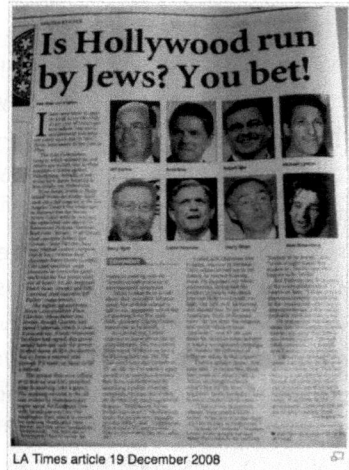

Is Hollywood run by Jews? You bet!

LA Times article 19 December 2008

I replied as follows:

The Nazis attempted to get rid of Jews within the regions they conquered. But they made no attempt to get rid of Jews in other countries. So it did not apply to "an entire people".

In the same way, Israel is conducting a genocide of the Palestinians. But only the ones living in Palestine, not those living in the West. So not "an entire people".

Further, Israel and its Lobby have lobbied for the West to attack Arab/Islamic countries—Iraq, Libya, Syria. That cost a million lives in Iraq alone, plus ongoing disasters.

Many people regard Netanyahu as akin to Nazis. The "holocaust exceptionalism" argument breaks down.

Nazi mass killing of Jews would not have happened if Jews had not been the predominant leaders of the Bolshevik Revolution.

In Ch. 16 of The Last Days of the Romanovs, Robert Wilton named the Jews running all the revolutionary parties: https://mailstar.net/wilton.html

Admittedly Stalin turned the tables on them, and gave them a taste of their own medicine. But first they had imposed the Red Terror, and a genocide of the "Great Russian" people. The term "genocide" includes destruction of a people's culture. The "holocaust exceptionalism" argument breaks down.

Finally, Nazi mass killing of Jews would not have happened if Zionists had not swayed the outcome of World War I via the Balfour Declaration—which was regarded as a contract between Britain and World Jewry.

Theordor Herzl, the founder of Zionism, wrote:

"When we sink, we become a revolutionary proletariat, the subordinate officers of all revolutionary parties; and at the same time, **when we rise, there rises also our terrible power of the purse."** (The Jewish State, p. 91) https://mailstar.net/herzl.html

In his Complete Diaries, Vol. II. p. 711, Theodore Herzl, the founder of Zionism, says that the area of the Jewish State stretches: "From the Brook of Egypt to the   Euphrates": https://mailstar.net/tmf.html

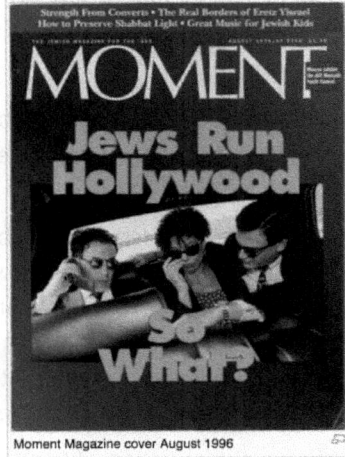

Moment Magazine cover August 1996

Leonard Stein writes in his book The Balfour Declaration (Vallentine-Mitchell, London, 1961):

"Herzl describes in his diaries an interview with Chamberlain in April 1903, when the El Arish scheme was again discussed. He told Chamberlain, he says, that 'we shall get [Palestine] not from the goodwill but from the jealousy of the Powers. And if we are in El Arish under the Union Jack, then our Palestine will likewise be in the British sphere of influence.' This suggestion, Herzl writes, was not at all ill-received.89" (p. 25) https://mailstar.net/balfour.html

If all such details are kept out of the picture, "holocaust exceptionalism" seems plausible. But when the missing details are included in the total picture, the "holocaust exceptionalism" argument breaks down. All sides have blood on their hands, and none are morally superior. (Myers, 2018a)

Contrary to the Marxist materialist view that economic forces (the "base") determine the mental "superstructure", I maintain that ideas are causative (as a Final Cause, in Aristotle's sense). There would have been no French Revolution without decades of revolutionary writing beforehand; one does not start to build a house without first having a plan.

Kevin MacDonald (1998) depicts Jews as an ethnic group "posturing as a religion" (p. 27). Yet he agrees that the Jewish ethnic group has been created by the Jewish religion. He is unaware that there is an atheistic variant of that religion: he pays no attention to Spinoza. Traditionally, Jews were defined as a nation (Jews a Nation); and even now, some diaspora Jews operate as a dispersed nation, as Victor Ostrovsky revealed (pp. 14-5 above). Of their two main factions—Globalist (Left) and Zionist (Right), only the Zionist Right operate as a nation. In the past, the Irish diaspora operated as a nation, and the Chinese government is currently encouraging the Chinese diaspora to do so too—but other Chinese resist.

Being Jewish is a matter of ethnicity, but also involves consent, i.e. self-identification, which is subjective but evidenced by participating in Jewish groups and projects, including covert ones. Some Jews break the ethnic bond and become 'national Jews' or ex-Jews.

Before the Exile, Israelites/Hebrews/Jews were a race. Judaism was polytheistic, and similar to Canaanite religion; Yahweh had a wife, the goddess Asherah. In Babylon, Jewish leaders encountered the Zoroastrian religion; they incorporated changes to Judaism, making it monotheistic, moralistic and messianic. Ezra invented the Exodos as a precedent to motivate a Return to Palestine. He created the Torah, blending diverse earlier stories into one.

After the destruction of Carthage by Rome, many Carthaginians and Phoenicians converted to Judaism. Spain had been a Carthaginian colony; this conversion is the likely origin of the large Jewish communities of Spain and North Africa.

At times, the Jewish religion has been missionary, taking in large numbers of converts. That happened in the Roman Empire and in medieval Khazaria. Most Jews today are Ashkenazi, descendants of Khazar converts (with Semitic admixture). The original Mizrahi (Eastern) Jews are just Arabs who follow the Jewish religion.

Spinoza invented a non-theistic version of Judaism; he even allowed for Zionism: "God may a second time elect them" (1670/2021, TPT03-P31). When Orthodox Jews became Bolsheviks, switching to atheistic Judaism, they were staying within Judaism, and united in political action for a this-worldly utopia. No other religion defines itself in terms of iconoclasm of tradition. Bolshevik Jews were still Jews: Spinoza and Marx were just newer prophets giving a higher revelation.

In Catholic Spain, and even in Protestant countries without any persecution, some Jews (*conversos* or *marranos*) pretended to be Christians. Jewish crypsis facilitated covert action against Christianity. Other Jews warned of a Jewish culture-war against Christianity; some become 'national Jews' or even ex-Jews. Leo Amery, who helped draft the Balfour Declaration, was an example of a secret Jew; after his son John became a Nazi, Leo repudiated him.

Chapter 3: Androgyny and the LGBT Attack on the Family

The Family is an enemy, sexual identity is an enemy—Giorgia Meloni

Giorgia Meloni became Prime Minister of Italy, with a speech in which she laid bare the Woke (Green Left, Trotskyoid) agenda. They promote LGBT and immigration, but she promotes motherhood and the traditional family, stopping the boats, and wants to stop same-sex couples from being registered as parents:

> Now they're talking about getting rid of the words "father" and "mother" on documents. Because the family is an enemy, national identity is an enemy, sexual identity is an enemy... It's the old groupthink game: they've got to get rid of everything that we are, because when we no longer have an identity and we no longer have any roots, we will be deprived of awareness and incapable of defending our rights. That's their game. They want us to be Parent 1, Parent 2, gender LGBT, Citizen X: code numbers. But we are not code numbers, we are people and we will defend our identity. I am Giorgia! I am a woman! I am a mother! I am Italian! I am Christian! You will not take that away from me! You will not take that away from me! (Farrell, 2023)

Androgyny in place of Complementarity between the Sexes

One of the tenets of the Illuminists is Androgyny—the idea that there is only one sex, or that sexuality is a continuum rather than a polarity. This idea is behind Gay Marriage, Unisex toilets, and the 'Trans' movement.

The idea that there are six or seven "genders", rather than two "sexes", is a way of saying that sexuality is a continuum, linear rather than binary or a polarity.

The Androgyny concept holds that the individual human contains both sexual poles, instead of just one. June Singer defined it thus:

> androgyny ... in its broadest sense can be defined as the One which contains the Two; namely, the male (andro-) and the female (gyne). (Singer, 1989, p.5)

She called Androgyny the "guiding principle of the New Age" (p. 3).

Dennis Altman, Professor of Politics at Latrobe University in Melbourne, said that Gay Liberation aims not just at freedom for Gays to live as they wish, but to change the majority culture, in recognition that we are all androgynous.

> Liberation, then, in the restricted context with which we are primarily concerned implies freedom from the surplus repression that prevents us recognizing our essential androgynous and erotic natures. (Altman, 1972, p. 83)

No longer is the claim made that gay people can fit into American society, that they are as decent, as patriotic, as clean-living, as anyone else. Rather, it is argued, it is American society itself that needs to change. (Altman, 1972, p. 106)

Further, he says, Gay Liberation wanted to overthrow the heterosexual nuclear family model.

Gay liberation demanded not just civil liberties for homosexuals, but rather a change in the social ordering of sexuality and an end to the dominance of the heterosexual nuclear family model. (Altman, 1980, p. 168)

Compare this with Ancient Egyptian art, which depicts male and female figures in conjunction—unity obtained through the coming together of two sexes. Here, Pharaoh Menkaure, of the Old Kingdom, is shown with his Queen.

Or the Taoist Yin-Yang symbol on the Korean flag: it expresses the idea that sexual polarity is fundamental to the universe, like electromagnetic polarity. The two poles are complementary. Only together do they make a whole; but each contains the seed of the other.

Anthropologist David Maybury-Lewis wrote,

"The ancient Egyptians believed that a totality must consist of the union of opposites. A similar premise, that the interaction between yin (the female principle) and yang (the male principle) underlies the workings of the universe, is at the heart of much Chinese thinking. The idea has been central to Taoist philosophy from the fourth century B.C. ... Peoples all over the world, in Eurasia, Africa and the Americas, have come to the conclusion that the cosmos is a combining of opposites and that one of the most important aspects of this dualism is the opposition between male and female. (1992, p. 125)

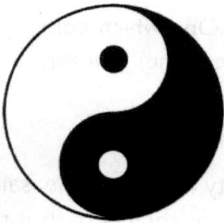

No Urinals on the Gerald R. Ford

The aircraft carrier U.S.S. Gerald R. Ford, commissioned in 2017, has no urinals, in order to be 'gender neutral'. All its toilets are Unisex cubicles. Yet over 80% of the 5,000 sailors are men; their views, it seems, were not consulted. This decision was made by Gender Warriors behind closed doors.

The new aircraft carrier Gerald R. Ford has all sorts of high-tech gear equipped for 21st century naval warfare. But there is one thing that male sailors will notice is no longer available: Urinals.

For the first time, every bathroom on the Ford — known throughout military circles as a head—is designed to be "gender-neutral," meaning all of the urinals have been replaced with flush toilets and stalls, Navy officials say.

The vast majority of the 5,000-plus sailors who will deploy aboard the carrier Ford are men, as women account for only about 18 percent of sailors in the Navy.

Bathroom design experts say water closets with seated toilets are less sanitary and take up far more space than wall-mounted urinals.

Nevertheless, the Navy says there are advantages to eliminating urinals.

It will allow the Navy to quickly and efficiently change a head's assigned gender, so depending on the ship's demographics at the time, berthing areas can be switched between male and female to accommodate the crew's needs. ...

It's a decision that comes as a surprise to many professionals who design restrooms.

"[A toilet is] by far a less clean environment than a urinal. By far," said Chuck Kaufman, president of the Public Restroom Company, an organization that specializes in designing bathrooms.

For men, traditional seated toilets are farther away, making them harder targets to accurately focus on. Thus, men who use a water closet are more likely to miss the bowl and hit the floor, says Kaufman. He says that when men are obligated to pee in water closets, urine tends to build up on the floor, leaving an abysmal stench.

"A urinal is a target," said Kaufman. "What is a problem is [with a water closet] you have a very big target and we can't aim very quickly."

The only way to ensure men accurately aim into a toilet bowl is to force men to sit down, which is unlikely to happen, said Kaufman. (Rathmell, 2017)

When I visited Sweden in 2018, I noticed that there were no urinals at Stockholm airport. When I was about to leave, I fell into conversation with a Swedish woman in the departure lounge, and mentioned this. She defended it, and said that her own father sits down to urinate, "out of respect for women". "You're castrating the men," I replied.

The Unisex movement arose from the Communist movement, even though Marx and Engels themselves saw homosexuality as bourgeois decadence, a product of alienation between the sexes. Since Stalin made homosexuality a crime, the Gay movement can be identified with the anti-Stalin faction, with Trotskyism.

Don't say "Ladies and Gentlemen"

During the 1980s & early 1990s, I worked as an I.T. specialist in Canberra. But I moved around the industry, and eventually became an expert on software for which there was not much demand. Finding myself out of the industry, I decided to take up teaching, which I had earlier done in Catholic schools.

In 1997, I enrolled in the Dip. Ed. course at the University of Canberra. On March 26, in a lecture on Gender policy, the lecturer stated that it was wrong to say "good morning, ladies and gentlemen" or "good morning, boys and girls"; instead one must say, "good morning, people".

The lectures were recorded on audio cassette, for the benefit of absent students. I obtained the tape, recorded it, transfered it to computer, and produced a transcript. The lecturer stated, in answer to questioning from me, that the reason it is wrong to say "good morning, ladies and gentlemen" is because "the Education Department has a policy on gender inclusive language". He further stated, "I am saying that if I said, 'good morning, ladies and gentlemen', that a number of people would complain about it, and have previously."

Nobody mentioned the Five (or 6 or 7) Genders, but everyone in the class of 200 presumably knew that the Lecturer was thinking of the rights of the Other Three (or 4 or 5) Genders. If only I had thought to ask him whether, on his logic, schools need more than two kinds of toilets.

Unable to endure this indoctrination for nine months, I quit the course, and sent the tape to The Canberra Times; one commentator mentioned it in his column, noting that the tape bore out my account. I also sent a copy of the tape to Paul Sheehan of the Sydney Morning Herald, who commented, "they're brainwashing our teachers". Of what value, then, is a degree or diploma in Education?

Some months later, when I returned to the campus, I met one of the students, an older one like me; she said to me, "You were our salt!"

I was not naive; I guessed that such "Gender" policy was being imposed in all Education Departments and universities. Deprived of a job, I remained unemployed, but not on welfare; better poverty with dignity. I developed my website; but my children blamed me.

The Canberra Times published a letter from me attesting the above, on Sunday July 6, 2002. I checked its Letters page every day for the next week, but the University did not reply, even though its reputation was on the line. Clearly, the University could not reply, because my account was true.

I placed the first 6 minutes 41 seconds of the lecture on the internet, where I draw out from the lecturer the reasons for his prescription. You can hear for yourself how new schoolteachers are being brainwashed in Trotskyism.

Many who have been to university before will be shocked to discover how they have changed; it's a clear example of the Thought Police in action. You can listen to the lecture at https://mailstar.net/gender.mp3.

The Rulers in George Orwell's dystopian novel *Nineteen Eighty-Four* say:

We have cut the links between child and parent, and between man and man, and between man and woman. No one dares to trust a wife or a child or a friend any longer. But in the future there will be no wives and no friends. Children will be taken from their mothers at birth, as one takes eggs from a hen. The sex instinct will be eradicated. Procreation will be an annual formality like the renewal of a ration card. We shall abolish the orgasm. (Orwell, 1954, p. 215).

... a heretical thought - that is, a thought diverging from the principles of Ingsoc - should be literally unthinkable, at least so far as thought is dependent on words ... excluding all other meanings ... This was done partly by the invention of new words, but chiefly by eliminating undesirable words and by stripping such words as remained of unorthodox meanings. (p. 241).

When the U.S. invades other countries for 'regime change', it claims the high moral ground, a "Right to Protect" some minority; in the case of Afghanistan, "Women's Rights" was the mantra used to justify destroying the country.

'Breastfeeding' is replaced with 'Chestfeeding'

But that was before the LGBT movement went so far as to get rid of the term 'woman'. Since, in Woke countries, one can now legally change one's sex, the term 'woman' is discouraged in Woke circles; instead, 'person who menstruates'. 'Breastfeeding' is replaced with 'chestfeeding,' to allow for "Trans women".

The Gender Institute at Australian National University (ANU) in Canberra issued a Gender-Inclusive Handbook, which encouraged academics and other staff to stop using the terms 'mother' and 'father', and instead use "gender inclusive" language, such as 'chestfeeding' instead of 'breastfeeding' and 'human milk' rather than 'mother's milk':

Australia's leading university has encouraged staff to use "parent-inclusive language", such as "chestfeeding" instead of "breastfeeding" and "human milk" rather than "mother's milk".

Similarly, the terms "mother" and "father" should be replaced with "gestational" and "nongestational" parent, according to the Australian National University's Gender-Inclusive Handbook.

Published last year by the Canberra university's Gender Institute, the handbook describes itself as a guide intended for "any ANU student or staff member involved" in teaching.

It offers recommendations to "uplift female and gender minority students". (Chung, 2021).

Men who redefine themselves as women, i.e. 'trans women', are now allowed to enter womens bathrooms, prisons and sporting teams, in many states. Schools and hospitals are changing the sex and name of 'trans' children without parents' consent; the parents are accused of hate and bigotry—see a real-life case on p. 378.

Androgyny is Cosmopolitan, but a sign of Decline—Camille Paglia

Camille Paglia, an expert on classical civilisation and also on gender politics, warned that a similar Androgynous movement preceded the fall of the Roman Empire. On 22 October 2016, she spoke at the 'Battle of Ideas' conference:

I've always been fascinated and attracted to the subject of androgeny... exploring history, but the more I explored it, the more I realised that, historically, the movement towards androgeny occurs in late stages of culture, as a civilisation is starting to unravel. You find it again and again and again in history.

People who live in such periods... whether it's the Hellenistic era, whether it's the Roman Empire, whether it's the Mauve decade of Oscar Wilde in the 1890s, whether it's Weimar Germany ... people who live in such times feel that they are very sophisticated, they're very cosmopolitan, and homosexuality, heterosexuality, so what, anything goes and so on. But, from the perspective of historical distance, you can see it's a culture that no longer believes in itself and then what you, invariably, get are people who convinced of the power of heroic masculinity on the edges, whether they are the Vandals and the Huns, or whether they are the barbarians of ISIS. You see them starting to mass on the outside of the culture. And that's what we have right now.

So there is a tremendous and rather terrifying disconnect between the infatuation with the transgender movement in our own culture and what's going on out there ... I'm concerned, I feel it's ominous ... What concerns me is when well-meaning adults believe that they're helping people by making easier some permanent change in the body from which there is no going back. For example, Brown University, one of the elite Ivy League schools in the United States, put sex-reassignment surgery on its insurance programme so that they can get a sex change in college ... I feel that's evil. (Paglia, 2016)

Who is "on the edges" today? The rest of the world—East Asia (China, Korea, Japan, Singapore), Islam, India, and Russia. All these rising economies are patrilineal, as the West used to be until, via the Trotskyist/Illuminist influence of the 60s/70s movement, it discarded its traditions and became matrilineal/LGBT.

Freemasonry, the Templars, and Androgyny

Aleister Crowley, a 33º Freemason, proclaimed himself "Baphomet XI", after Baphomet, the god of Androgyny. The Templars were accused of worshipping Baphomet and practising homosexual relationships with one another.

Barbara Frale (2004/2009) says that the Templars practised homosexual initiation; and were also required to spit on the cross during the initiation:

Then the preceptor gave him the kiss of monastic brotherhood—on the mouth. Often this kiss, common to all religious orders, was followed by two more kisses on the belly and the posterior, which was usually covered by the tunic, but at times there were officiators who exposed their bottoms and, according to some witnesses, even obscenely proposed kisses on the penis. Most postulants obeyed without arguing when the request was moderately humiliating, such as a kiss on the behind, and refused in more extreme cases. While the preceptors demanded that a postulant at least deny Christ or spit on the cross, they usually overlooked a refusal of kisses, and unwilling candidates were not forced to comply.

Finally, the preceptor exhorted the new Templar not to have sexual relations with women, inviting him. should he absolutely not be able to live chastely, to unite with his brothers and not to refuse them should they request sexual favors from him. ... In practice, all the candidate had to do was submit to those words in silence with no signs of rebellion, as proof of his obedience.

The surviving trial testimony consists of approximately one thousand depositions with only six attesting to homosexual relations, all of which were described as long-term relationships that almost always had a dimension of affection. In the Temple, such relationships involved a small number of individuals. ...

At the end of the ceremony, the "victim" of all these impositions was invited to report to the chaplain of the order to confess the sins he had just committed and ask for forgiveness. The priests of the Temple comforted these penitents by telling them that they had not committed grave offenses and that if they demonstrated remorse and shame, they would be absolved. Often, however, the brothers confessed to priests outside the Temple, generally Franciscans or Dominicans, who, naturally, were dumbfounded and amplified the brothers' moral disquiet by telling them they had committed mortal sins, sometimes encouraging them to leave the order. (pp. 169-70)

Freemasonry appears to perpetuate the Templar order, even though the chain of transmission is unclear and disputed. Albert Pike wrote,

"The secret movers of the French Revolution had sworn to overturn the Throne and the Altar upon the Tomb of Jacques de Molai. When Louis XVI. was executed, half the work was done; and thenceforward the Army of the Temple was to direct all its efforts against the Pope" (Pike, 1871/2011, p. 630).

What was that "Army of the Temple" if not the Freemasons?

Knights Templar degrees are included in Masonic rites, and there is an explicit focus there on rebuilding the Jewish Temple—something that the Christian New Testament does not countenance; there is thus an implicit Zionism as well. The Masonic club for boys is called Demolay International; it boasts being the biggest club in the world for young men aged 12 to 21. Why give it this name, if the Templar connection is incidental?

The Anti-Defamation League, a Jewish branch of Freemasonry, argued in a brief to the Supreme Court that Christian groups should not be able to provide after-school religious instruction unless Satanic groups are allowed to do so as well. The ADL says so on its own site:

https://www.adl.org/blog/key-supporter-of-after-school-religious-clubs-ironically-says-satanic-temple-can-be-barred

Key Supporter Of After-School Religious Clubs Ironically Says Satanic Temple Can Be Barred

August 9, 2016

Recently, The Satanic Temple announced that it plans starting after school clubs for the coming school year and sent letters to a number of public school districts advising them of its intentions.   Under a 2001 U.S. Supreme Court ruling, K-12 public schools must allow these clubs if they allow secular community groups to use their facilities. ...

Firmly believing that providing after-school access to religious organizations constitutes unconstitutional endorsement of religion, ADL in 2000 filed a friend-of-the-court brief with the U.S Supreme Court opposing such access. ... Liberty Counsel, a self-described Christian ministry... erroneously claims that public schools can bar The Satanic Temple clubs.

The Satanic Temple contains a statue of Baphomet.

A statue of the Baphomet, in a Satanic temple, is shown making the Devil's Horns sign. The Inverted Cross on the wall is also a Satanic symbol.

William Schnoebelen spent nine years as an active Freemason (both York and Scottish rites), attaining the 32º. He also spent sixteen years as a high-level teacher of witchcraft, spiritism and ceremonial magic.

He says that the lower degrees of Freemasonry teach salvation through good works, but the upper degrees teach salvation through Luciferian doctrine. That means that its claim to represent the religion of ancient Egypt is a deception, because that religion was anti-Seth, meaning anti-Satanic.

On Baphomet, Schnoebelen writes (1991),

"Also frequendy mentioned is the allegation that the Templars worshiped a mysterious idol called Baphomet. This idol was described in various ways: a man with the head of a goat, a head with three faces, or a head with a beard, which taught the knights of the Order magical secrets" (p. 165).

"The Freemason, Satanist and pervert Aleister Crowley took the name Baphomet when he assumed leadership of the occult/Masonic organization, the O.T.O. (Order of Eastern Templars)" (p. 167).

Schnoebelen says that the Baphomet Cross, worn by Aleister Crowley, is also on the hat of the Sovereign Grand Commander of all 33° Masons in a very slightly modified form:

"A Masonic symbol seen less frequently is the 33° cross because it appertains only to the highest degrees. It is more commonly called the Crusader's Cross or the Jerusalem Cross. It was supposedly worn by the first Grand Master of the Knights Templar, Godfrey de Bouillon, after he liberated Jerusalem from the Muslims. This symbol is on the hat of the Sovereign Grand Commander of all 33° Masons in a very slightly modified form. it is part of the magical signature of Aleister Crowley, the supreme satanist of this century" (p. 119).

Christian women are enticed into a Masonic Order called the Eastern Star, imagining it to be the star of Bethlehem to which the Magi came. Schnoebelen warns:

> But the symbol of the Star is an inverted, five pointed star, with the two points facing upwards—known in witchcraft and Satanism as a pentagram. The inverted pentagram is the official symbol of the two largest Satanic churches, the Church of Satan and the Temple of Set. This inverted star, with the goat's head within it (called "Baphomet") is on the cover of The Satanic Bible, and found on the albums of Satanic rock groups. (Schnoebelen, p. 97)

> The phrase "Eastern Star" has a specialized meaning in occultism. It refers to the star Sirius, which is the most significant star in Satanism! It is sacred to the god Set. Remember Set as the evil Egyptian god who killed Osiris? Set is probably the oldest form of Satan! The Eastern Star is the star of Set. (p. 99)

The Eastern Star of Freemasonry   **Goat Pentagram, Sabbatic Goat, Baphomet**

The center of the Lodge is a "blazing star" which supposedly symbolizes Divine Providence. The illustration on the next page shows the prominent place given the pentagram in the Lodge room.

However, we can dig yet deeper into the meaning of this star. In Albert Pike's commentary on this degree, we find the usual duplicity found elsewhere in the Lodge. He explains:

> To find in the BLAZING STAR of five points an allusion to Divine Providence is fanciful; and to make it commemorative of the Star that is said to have guided the Magi, is to give it a meaning comparatively modern. Originally, it represented Sirius, or the Dog-star, the forerunner of the inundation of the Nile (p. 100)

> Sirius is magically regarded as the most dangerous star in the sky. The Egyptian people suffered the most during its time of ascendancy. It reached

its apogee in the Egyptian sky on July 23. This was the hottest, driest time of year for the civilization, when the Nile was at its lowest ebb—the Nile, upon which Egypt depended for irrigation.

Thus, Sirius was a star of scorching, blasting evil. It was the most dreaded omen in the heavens. Its association with the dog or hyena, is ancient. Oddly enough, we carry in our modern language a reference to this scorched time of year. The time of great heat and humidity from mid-July to mid-August is often called the "Dog-days." The reference is to the Dog-star, Sirius.

In identifying Sirius, we have come very close to identifying the true deity of Masonry by yet another of his many masks. (Schnoebelen, 1991 , pp. 101-2)

This affinity with Set (Seth) and the star Sirius shows that Freemasonry is pro-Seth, not pro-Osiris as it pretends. And Seth is connected to the Androgyny theme.

Despite the affinity to Ancient Egypt claimed by Crowley and the Freemasons, the ancient Egyptians despised Androgyny; they associated it with Seth, the enemy of Horus. Seth murdered Osiris, took over as king, and later attempted to sodomise his son Horus, to deprive him of the kingship—because being sodomised was considered unmanly. This is the only clear case of homosexuality in the literature of Ancient Egypt. Seth was the god of Disorder, the equivalent of Satan in Egyptian religion.

The Masonic claim to perpetuate the Egyptian religion is thus fake. That religion actually has more in common with Christianity, with Christ being a figure like Osiris, resurrected from the dead, then becoming Judge of the Dead. Mary and Jesus are Madonna and Child, like Isis and Horus.

Postmodernism is Atheist Existentialism—a philosophy of Nihilism and Despair

Postmodernism, coupled with Deconstruction, is a kind of Atheistic Existentialism that emerged in French Trotskyoid circles and was used for a Gramsciist March through the Institutions. LGBT activists adopted it, asserting that the Gay Family is as natural as the Heterosexual Family. They are engaged in a calculated attempt to see how far they can go in defying Nature. So much for Charles Darwin: this philosophy, emphasising the unlimited freedom of the human will, the human Will Over Nature, is non-Darwinian. They 'deconstruct' conventional history as a 'meta-narrative', but uphold their own Social Justice/Woke meta-narrative.

The accusation levelled at all opponents, that they create 'essences' (reifications) is the trademark of Existentialists, and suggests an extreme Nominalism. However, they have created their own 'essence', namely Patriarchy. Ecofeminism is a form of Radical Feminism that equates Men with the destruction of Nature. Yet even though it identifies with Nature, it repudiates *Human* Nature. It supports Trans and the Gay Family, and institutionalised childcare a-la-Plato rather the more natural childcare by the family, such as one finds in tribal societies.

There are different sorts of atheism. Religious non-theism rejects the anthropomorphism of traditional religions but affirms an impersonal divinity. Thus Albert Einstein said,

> I cannot then believe in this concept of an anthropomorphic God who has the powers of interfering with these natural laws. As I said before, the most beautiful and most profound religious emotion that we can experience is the sensation of the mystical. And this mysticality is the power of all true science. If there is any such concept as a God, it is a subtle spirit, not an image of a man that so many have fixed in their minds. In essence, my religion consists of a humble admiration for this illimitable superior spirit that reveals itself in the slight details that we are able to perceive with our frail and feeble minds. (Bucky, c1992)

Einstein was a religious non-theist and a follower of Spinoza. Spinoza formulated non-theistic Judaism, the religion of Jewish Communists such as Moses Hess. Religious non-theism deleveped in India about 600BC and in China c. 500BC.

Jainism was founded c. 550 BC, by Mahavira. Gautama tried Jain asceticism but found it too extreme; he formed Buddhism as "the middle path". One group of ascetics, the Ajivikas, founded by Gosala, allowed their members to engage in sex. The Ajivikas may have been like the early Taoist philosophers of China, and the Cynic philosophers of Greece. Like original Buddhism, the Jain religion is non-theistic. It sees all living beings as souls, the human being no more valuable than the non-human. Therefore, no living being, even a mosquito, can be killed.

Reg Little, co-author of *The Confucian Renaissance* (1989), commented to me that "The East thinks of Divinity as Impersonal, but Civil Law as Personal; whereas the West thinks of Divinity as Personal, but Civil Law as Impersonal" (personal communication).

Having a religion (a non-fanatical one), even if the religion is non-theistic, helps one's mental health. It helps because it involves submission to, and faith in, a higher authority, something outside oneself. But Postmodernism has no such faith; the only meaning it imparts to its adherents is political struggle; as a result, it amounts to Nihilism, and leads to drug-addiction, despair and suicide—because of the meaninglessness of life.

Chapter 4: Rousseau, Natural Man, and Human Rights

Karl Marx is well known for the saying, "Workers of the World Unite. You Have Nothing To Lose But Your Chains." Less well known is that Marx' word 'chains' refers to the first sentence in Chapter 1 of Jean-Jacques Rousseau's book *The Social Contract*: "Main was born free, and he is everywhere in chains" (Rousseau, 1762/1968, p. 49).

Article 1 of the Universal Declaration of the Rights of Man, made by the United Nations in December 1948, comes straight from Rousseau. It begins, "All human beings are born free".

Rousseau placed all five of his children into an orphanage

Yet in his Confessions, Rousseau admits that he placed all five of his children (born to his defacto wife Therese, whem he married later in life), into an orphanage, one by one at birth, without even giving them a name, and never saw any of them again. So much for them being "born free". In fact, nobody is born free: everybody is born into particular circumstances he/she does not choose.

Voltaire attacked Rousseau for abandoning his children; in reply, he set down his life-story in his autobiography, The Confessions of Jean-Jacques Rousseau.

Rousseau justifies his action as follows: "in handing my children over for the State to educate ... I thought I was acting as a citizen and a father, and looked upon myself as a member of Plato's Republic" (Rousseau, 1781/1953, p. 333). He describes handing over the successive babies on pages 322, 333, 334, and 385-7. There can be no greater indictment of Plato's Republic.

Rousseau drew a blueprint for the New Order. He used the concept of "natural man", inspired by idyllic reports of the life of the native peoples of North America, to de-legitimate the dovernments, religions and institutions of Europe: they were all wrong. Marx and Engels noted the revolutionary impact of the New World upon the Old, in *The Communist Manifesto*.

The modern communist movement began with Thomas More's book *Utopia*, written in 1515, just after Columbus' discovery of America in 1492. In her book *Utopia fact or fiction?*, Loraine Stobbart argues that More's book, far from mere fiction, was based on reports of actual Maya communities.

But Jared Diamond (2005) dispelled that illusion:

Archaeologists for a long time believed the ancient Maya to be gentle and peaceful people. We now know that Maya warfare was intense, chronic, and unresolvable. ... Captives were tortured in unpleasant ways depicted clearly on the monuments and murals (such as yanking fingers out of sockets, pulling out teeth, cutting off the lower jaw, trimming of the lips and fingertips, pulling out the fingernails, and driving a pin through the lips), culminating, sometimes years later, in the sacrifice of the captive in other equally unpleasant ways such as tying the captive up into a ball by binding the arms and legs together, then rolling the balled-up captive down the steep stone staircase of a temple. (p. 172)

The Maya, like the Aztecs, removed the still-beating hearts of captives

They also practised Human Sacrifice; and, like the Azecs, they removed the still-beating hearts of captives:

The present study is based on a systematic taphonomic assessment of five Classic period skeletal series from which we collected three or four primary interments showing anthropogenic marks suggesting either heart extraction or evisceration. ... Human heart sacrifice was conceived as a supreme religious expression among the ancient Maya. The amputation of the still-beating heart, the annihilation of human life, and the offering of this vital organ, considered the essence of life and nourishment for the divine forces, allowed for the ultimate communication with the sacred and compensation to the gods (Tiesler & Cucina, 2006).

The revolutionary 'First Nations' movement in Canada, Australia and Chile is one front in the "Culture War" that began in the 1960s and 70s. It's led by the Trotskyists and their allies, the same people who have given us Gay Marriage and Trans-women (other fronts in the culture war). It's Communism by the back door.

Amazon tribesmen: constant wars, mainly over Women

Napoleon Chagnon, an Anthropologist who spent much of his life living with previously uncontacted Yanomoto tribes of the Brazilian rainforest, over a period of 30 years, refuted the Noble Savage concept. The various groups were constantly warring with one another, mainly over women. Tribesmen would kill men in other tribes or groups, then acquire the widowed women as additional wives. Men who killed other men had more children and thus, in Darwinian terms, were more successful; and also had higher status. Death was believed to be caused, not by nature but by sorcery, leading to payback killings. Surprise attacks in the early morning wiped out whole villages. Chagnon's findings upset the Marxist Anthropologists—who, he said, were devotees of the Marxist "religion"—and led to a major split in the profession (Chagnon, 2013).

Claudio Villas-Boas repported the same of the Panara (Kreen-Akrore):

"The Kreen-Akrore are hard, he said with feeling. "Truly hard." And he went on to describe their attitude to prisoners. In the jungle, women are the deciding factor in war. If you capture the wives, you not only eliminate your enemies' battalions of the future, but, with a little application, can double your own force in a generation. And so most Indian raids are for women, and this serves the—unconscious—purpose of bringing new genes into an isolated group. For instance, when Orlando and Claudio contacted the Txukahamei, they had found half a dozen white captives, and roughly a dozen children taken from other tribes. The white women had taught the Txukahamei to load and repair their captured guns, and thus, for tribes isolated in the jungle, captives represent a vital window on the outside world. (Cowell, p. 93)

The Yanomoto and the Panara, having been protected from intruders, are now civilised and function successfully as part of the Brazilian state.

Australian Aborigines: 3 Migrations, Late Ones Forced Early Ones South

William Buckley was a white convict in south-east Australia, who escaped and spent decades living amongst uncontacted Aborigines, in a number of tribes. He learned their languages, lived as an Aboriginal, learned to hunt and to trap fish, had an Aboriginal wife for a while, and forgot English and even his own name. Later, when Melbourne was established by John Batman, he gave himself up, and was pardoned, serving as an interpreter and helping to keep the peace between the Aborigines and the whites. His first-person story was later published, and became a best-seller. He reported constant wars, mainly over women. Aborigines, used to killing game for food, had no qualms about killing people too. They engaged in ritual cannibalism, to acquire the victim's strength (Buckley, 1852/2002, pp. 61, 87, 117, 197). Alice Duncan-Kemp, who grew up with Aborigines in the Channel Country of S.W. Qld, also reported sacred/ceremonial cannibalism (1961, p. 84; 1968, p. 96).

Daisy Bates, who spent a lifetime living among Aborigines of Western and South Australia, who spoke their languages and was adopted into their kinship system—as Kabbarli (Grandmother)—reported many cases of cannibalism:

> In one group, east of the Murchison and Gascoyne Rivers, every woman who had had a baby had killed and eaten it, dividing it with her sisters ... I cannot remember a case where the mother ate a child she had allowed, at the beginning, to live. (Bates, 1967, p. 107-8)

> Every one of the natives whom I encountered on the east-west [railway] line had partaken of human meat, with the exception of Nyerdain, who told me it made him sick. (p. 195)

Deserts and droughts probably contributed to the cannibalism. Pastoralists impacted Aborigines' water sources and hunting grounds. The British had their flaws too. But it was not a clear-cut case of Good vs Bad, as Rousseau imagined.

Aboriginal Law gave young women in marriage to old men. After whites arrived, young men began to flout the Law, forming illicit relationships. Bates reported, "Irregularity crept over until there was not one straight marriage among the thousands I encountered" (p. 106). As traditional Law broke down, the High Culture was lost. But in some areas the Law is being revived, at least on marriage.

Anthropolgist W. E. H. Stanner lived with Aborigines of northern Australia, and even learned to hunt using their methods. He noted the difficulty:

> The life of a hunting and foraging nomad is very hard even in a good environment. Time and again the hunters fail, and the search for vegetable food can be just as patchy. A few such failures in sequence and life in the camps can be very miserable. The small, secondary foodstuffs—the roots, honey, grubs, ants, and the like, of which far too much has been made in the literature—are relished tidbits, but not staples. The aborigines rarely starve but they go short more often than might be supposed when the substantial fauna—kangaroos, wallaby, goannas, birds, fish—are too elusive. (Stanner, 1960, pp. 69-70)

Consequently they "came in" to settlements to obtain government rations, or obtained jobs on farms etc. Stanner continued:

> I appreciated the good sense of the adaptation only after I had gone hungry from fruitless hunting with rifle, gun, and spears in one of the best environments in Australia. (p. 70)

Bates stated that circumcised tribes were later arrivals, and forced the uncircumcised tribes further south (1967, pp. 30, 59 & 119). Duncan-Kemp noted the same (1961, p. 204); the uncircumcised tribes were matrilineal and practised Woman Law, but the circumcised tribes were patrilineal and practised Male Law (1961, pp. 80, 206). Late arrivals came from India (1968, p. 25). There were 3 or 4 migrations (1968, pp. 45-6, 146-7). The First Nations Lobby deny multiple arrivals.

DNA studies by Mark Stoneking of the Max Planck Institute showed that a migration from India reached Australia about 4,000 years ago, and brought more advanced tool-making techniques and the dingo (Yong, 2013). Tindale and Lindsay (1963) identified 3 migrations: Negritos (Tasmania & Cape York), Murrayians (southern Australia) and Carpentarians from India (northern Australia).

The Marxist Left's veneration for primitive societies is superficial. The primitives practised polygyny (they had multiple wives), whereas the Left promotes LGBT and Gay Marriage. The primitives insisted on respect for elders, whereas the Left promote youth rebellion. Aboriginal Law punished illicit relationships by death; and homosexuality by death. Anthony Mundine said, "That ain't in our culture and our ancestors would have their head for it." (Henderson, 2013).

Inca Communism—a well-ordered society, but with Child sacrifice

Inca civilisation was a model kind of Communism. Although lacking wheeled transport, horses and cattle, it nevertheless established an unsurpassed road system, which collapsed under Spanish rule. The society was divided into classes, and extremely well-ordered; the equality within each class and the stable family life impressed those Spanish with eyes to see. Yet the Incas practised child sacrifice on mountain-tops. Inca society did not allow much freedom.

Rousseau did not use "natural man" as a model for his new society. The Social Contract is peppered with references to Sparta and Classical Rome, and draws on Plato's *Republic*, rather than American Indian society, to design the New Order.

Rousseau was the "father" of the French Revolution, patron of the new methods of education in our schools, and architect of the "Human Rights" ideology.

To undermine the Old World Order, the Revolution chose to use the same dirty tricks that the Old Order used to maintain itself, which Machiavelli had described in *The Prince*. That is, it adopted the ethic that the end justifies the means. This is clearly stated by Rousseau in *The Social Contract*: "Machiavelli's *Prince* is a handbook for Republicans" (Rousseau, 1762/1968, p.118). Even Babeuf appealed to Machiavelli, in his defence at the High Court of Vendome (Babeuf, 1797/1967).

Rousseau endorsed Machiavellian methods and violent means

Rousseau explicitly endorses violent means:

In ancient times, Greece flourished at the height of the cruellest wars; blood flowed in torrents, but the whole country was thickly populated. 'It appeared,' says Machiavelli, 'that in the midst of murder, proscription and civil wars, our republic became stronger than ever; the civil virtue of the citizens, their morals, and their independence, served more effectively to strengthen it than all their dissensions may have done to weaken it.' A little disturbance gives vigour to the soul, and what really makes the species prosper is not peace but freedom. (Rousseau, 1762/1968, note on p.131)

Although Rousseau did not rear even one child, his book *Emile* has been acclaimed by Left educators and many of its precepts (e.g. against rote learning) are followed in our schools today. Similarly, Plato, the originator of the idea that children should be communally reared by the State (in creches, daycare centres etc), rather than by the family, was himself a bachelor. Celibate Catholic priests were for centuries the arbiters of family policy; and childless Radical Feminists, and LGBT or Trans advocates, have been such in recent times. The West prizes theory-builders in ivory towers over experience and trust in "Mother Nature".

Do rights belong primarily to the individual or to the community?

The West's discourse about Human Rights avoids the big questions:

- Where do Rights come from? God? Evolution? The generosity of a Ruler? Decision by "experts"? Decision by plebiscite? How could Darwinian evolution lead to

Rights? Why is a social contract "implicit" in human but not in animal communities—baboons, kangaroos, seals? Can parties have a contract without knowing it?

- If rights are not "natural" but "positive", then who decides them? A U.N. Committee? If so, on what basis? Perhaps by reference to some other U.N. document akin to a secular Bible?

- Do rights belong primarily to the individual or to the community (tribe, family, nation etc.)? If to the individual, then they cut across all communities and threaten all traditions. Traditional societies are based on the primacy of the group—the individual must fit in, the Common Good takes precedence. Rousseau had it both ways, asserting, on the one hand, natural individual human rights (by birth), and on the other, the primacy of the General Will over individual choice.

Rights are often Zero-Sum. For example, Children's Rights can reduce Parents' Rights. Who decides whether to allow an underage girl to have a sex-change? Teachers, or her parents? Many tomboys would have lost their breasts if today's Social Engineers had been around in years past; Camille Paglia calls it Child Abuse. Who decides whether to allow Drag Queen Story Time performances to young children of ages 1 to 6? And why do they want to expose such young children to sexualised adult content? Parents are fighting back, reclaiming their Rights.

If someone is allowed to change the 'Sex' field on his/her Birth Certificate, is a prospective partner entitled to know what the originally registered sex was? If not, surely this infringes that partner's rights.

Individual Human Rights are incompatible with indigenous authority structures. Most initiation ceremonies, the basis of traditional authority and discipline, involve the endurance of pain, fear and bodily mutilation, and infringe the initiates' "rights".

"Progressive Left" thinking treats the family as "the locus of oppression", and therefore tries to destroy it, wrongly harming the main source of nurturance and protection in a harsh world. This has been especially harmful in Black and Indigenous communities.

In place of Christianity, Rousseau felt that a Civil Religion was required, as a belief-system (ideology) and also as a form of devotion. He advocated Deism, reminiscent of the impersonal God of Plato—an impersonal concept of divinity comparable to the Brahman of Hinduism, the Law-of-Karma of Buddhism, and the Heaven or Tian of China.

Based on Rousseau's Deism, the French Revolution desecrated churches, installed a prostitute as Goddess, and held a 'feast of the Supreme Being'. The present Postmodernist ideology, however, is based on Atheism, asserted as a dogmatic principle. This is not just a denial of a personal divinity or an impersonal one;

it is a denial that there is anything greater than Man. And that there is any Human Nature, which might constrain us. It is a statement that Man Makes Himself, unconstrained; that Man is the Measure of All Things. God cannot exist, because otherwise Man's Freedom would be constrained. Reports of UFOs unsettle the Elite, because of the implication that we humans are not in control.

It is commonly thought that a society based on "Human Rights" would be tolerant. Yet although Rousseau on the one hand declares the natural rights and freedoms of all citizens of the state, on the other hand he idolises Sparta under the tyranny of Lycurgus, and recommends the use of Machiavellian methods once the New Order is in power.

Towards the end of *The Social Contract*, he explains that the state he proposes would have a 'Civil Religion', with secular dogmas obliging compliance: "Without being able to oblige anyone to believe these articles, the sovereign can banish from the state anyone who does not believe them; banish him not for impiety but as an antisocial being" (Rousseau, 1762/1968, p.186).

Thus the Enlightenment, the culmination of a centuries-long struggle for freedom from the Inquisition of the Church, ends up endorsing an Inquisition of its own: firstly on paper, in *The Social Contract*, and later in the French and Bolshevik Revolutions. The unity-of-thought-and-action, called "praxis" in Marxist jargon, requires that incorrect thought cannot be tolerated. In Rousseau's Civil Religion the one thing that would not be tolerated is intolerance:

"As for the negative dogmas, I would limit them to a single one: no intolerance. Intolerance is something which belongs to the religions we have rejected" (Rousseau, 1762/1968, p. 186). Anyone who proclaims "outside the church there is no salvation" would be expelled from the state (p.187).

But if we do not tolerate the intolerant, are we ourselves not intolerant? Such are the contradictions of creating "heaven on earth". In a one-world-society constructed along Rousseau's lines, the dissidents could not be exiled —they would have nowhere to go!

Marx & Engels envisaged Heaven on Earth

Marx himself used the expression "heaven on earth", in describing his goal:

"Someday the worker must seize political power in order to build up the new organization of labor; he must overthrow the old politics which sustain the old institutions, if he is not to lose heaven on earth, like the old Christians who neglected and despised politics" (Marx, 1872/1971, p. 64).

Engels explained the Communist heaven thus:

"The history of early Christianity has notable points of resemblance with the modern working-class movement. Like the latter, Christianity was originally a movement of oppressed people: it first appeared as the religion of slaves and emancipated slaves, of poor people deprived of all rights, of peoples subjugated or dispersed by Rome. Both Christianity and the workers' socialism preach forthcoming salvation from bondage and misery; Christianity places this salvation in a life beyond, after death, in heaven; socialism places it in this world, in a transformation of society." (Engels, 1894/1975, p. 56).

Marx and Engels present an interesting divergence from Rousseau and Babeuf here. They lauded classical Rome, and lamented the Christian overthrow of it; but Marx and Engels said that the Christian overthrow did not go far enough.

Our "liberated" society is following Plato rather than Darwin, in determining early childhood policy. In his book *The Subversive Family*, Ferdinand Mount points out that the attack on the family, begun by Plato, was continued by the Church, which for 1500 years disparaged family life as inferior to celibacy.

Marx says that Luther liberated Christianity from monasticism, by making Conscience a tyrant. Luther "freed man from outward religiosity while he made religiosity the innerness of the heart. He emancipated the body from its chains while he put chains on the heart" (Marx, 1844/1974, pp. 35-37). Note that word 'chains' again. Marx saw himself as completing the attack on authority Luther had begun: "As the revolution then began in the brain of the monk, so now it begins in the brain of the philosopher" (Marx, 1844/1974, pp. 35-37).

Like the Church, the Marxist movement regarded the family as a threat, a rival source of loyalty and sustenance to the all-powerful state it sought, and which Rousseau had designed in accordance with Machiavellian principles.

Marx, Freud & Nietzsche banish God/divinity

Although Spinoza's formulation of Judaism retained divinity, Marxists, mainly the Trotskyoid kind, have banished God and divinity from public life and education, and the traditional Conscience and Morality too. Freud's followers similarly worked to diminish the Superego (Conscience), unleashing the forces of Id. Nietzsche, rejecting moralism and proclaiming the Death of God, likewise undermined Conscience. In the West, the conjunction of these forces has wrecked Christian civilisation by blocking its transmission from the older generation to the younger. Yet it is thriving in the Third World, which has rejected the Culture War.

Chapter 5: Nietzsche, the Jews and the Origins of Christianity

When Nietzsche blames "the Jews" for the destruction of classical civilisation, he means the Christians. The real Jews (of the Old Testament) he admires for their lack of pity or mercy or empathy with non-Jews; he admired the same aristocratic qualities in the *Laws of Manu*, which justifies the caste system of India. Yet, the real Jews fought the Roman Empire (which Nietzsche admired for its nobility) in 66-70 A.D., and came close to defeating it; the Romans took four years to regain control.

Nietzsche wrote, calling the Christian Church "Jews" and "Israel":

> The Romans were the strongest and most noble people who ever lived. ... The Jews, on the contrary, were the priestly, rancorous nation par excellence, though possessed of an unequaled ethical genius ... Remember who it is before whom one bows down, in Rome itself, as before the essence of all supreme values ... three Jews and one Jewess (Jesus of Nazareth, the fisherman Peter, the rug weaver Paul, and Maria, the mother of that Jesus). This is very curious: Rome, without a doubt, has capitulated. It is true that during the Renaissance men witnessed a strange and splendid awakening of the classical ideal ... But presently Israel triumphed once again, thanks to the plebeian rancor of the German and English Reformation, together with its natural corollary, the restoration of the Church ... In an even more decisive sense did Israel triumph over the classical ideal through the French Revolution ... And yet, in the midst of it all, ... Napoleon appeared, most isolated and anachronistic of men, the embodiment of the noble ideal. (Nietzsche, 1974, pp. 185-6)

But Santaniello (1997) noted that Nietzsche's target was Christians rather than Jews, and that he upheld the superiority of the (Jewish) Old Testament:

> it is seldom noted that Nietzsche is not attacking contemporary Jewry but priestly Judea, which he believes gave rise to (anti-Semitic) Christianity. ... Nietzsche ... reiterates that ... ressentiment lurks within the "antisemites where it has always bloomed"; that he contrasts the superior Old Testament with the New; and that his overall wrath is unleashed upon the entire history of Christianity. (p. 31)

> Nietzsche attributes the slave revolt in morality to the priestly caste of Judea that reaches its fruition with Christianity ... The point here is simply that Nietzsche is describing Christianity's inheritance of priestly Judea, as distinct from original Israel. (p. 32)

> Nietzsche derided priestly Judea, all the while upholding contemporary Jewry and original Israel. (p. 33).

Nietzsche agrees that Christianity originated with the Book of Isaiah:

"Renan located the origin of Christianity with the prophet Isaiah, discarded original Israel and held nineteenth-century Jews, Israel's remnants, responsible for the death of Jesus. Nietzsche's position is the exact reverse. Although Nietzsche concurs with Renan that Christianity originated with the prophet Isaiah, he disagrees that this represents spiritual progress, but rather, the origin of Israel's demise which has culminated in the (anti-Semitic) Christianity of ressentiment" (p. 36).

The Book of Isaiah (specifically Deutero-Isaiah) begins the transition from the real Jews to the Christians; with Deutero-Isaiah, the Baptising Sects are born.

Most commentators say that Deutero-Isaiah wrote Isaiah 40-55; but he also rewrote other parts of Isaiah. Deutero-Isaiah is the first Semitic announcement of the Zoroastrian doctrine of the Saoshyant or "World Savior" and the beginning of an alternate school of Judaism which became the Essenes (Glasse, 2014).

Two kinds of Judaism emerged from the Zoroastrian influence on the exiles in Babylon. Ezra's kind led to Pharisaism; Deutero Isaiah's kind became the Essenes, who evolved into the Christians (personal communication from Cyril Glasse).

Here is Deutero-Isaiah's attack on the Jewish religion—from The Book of Isaiah, chapter 1 (NIV). Note the rejection of animal sacrifices (which are still planned for the Third Temple), and the exhortation to ritual washing (baptism)—(personal communication from Cyril Glasse):

10 Hear the word of the Lord,
    you rulers of Sodom;
listen to the instruction of our God,
    you people of Gomorrah!
11 "The multitude of your sacrifices—
    what are they to me?" says the Lord.
"I have more than enough of burnt offerings,
    of rams and the fat of fattened animals;
I have no pleasure
    in the blood of bulls and lambs and goats.
12 When you come to appear before me,
    who has asked this of you,
    this trampling of my courts?
13 Stop bringing meaningless offerings!
    Your incense is detestable to me.
New Moons, Sabbaths and convocations—
    I cannot bear your worthless assemblies.
14 Your New Moon feasts and your appointed festivals
    I hate with all my being.
They have become a burden to me;

I am weary of bearing them.
15 When you spread out your hands in prayer,
    I hide my eyes from you;
even when you offer many prayers,
    I am not listening.
Your hands are full of blood!
16 Wash and make yourselves clean.
    Take your evil deeds out of my sight;
    stop doing wrong.
17 learn to do right!
Seek justice,
encourage the oppressed.
Defend the cause of the fatherless,
plead the case of the widow.

Cyril Glasse, author of *The New Encyclopedia of Islam*, offers this explanation (personal communication):

Actually, Isaiah, Deutero Isaiah, and Trito Isaiah are the wrong way to look at the text. They are the result of a historically developing attitude but the attitude is mistaken in its assumptions. The Book of Isaiah is the work of a School of Prophecy which has absorbed Zoroastrianism into Babylonian religion and put it through the wringer of Hellenism. There are many different pieces of material in Isaiah. A number of different authors. But it is a school of thought, which is new and powerful and which changed the whole world.

I started reading Isaiah and I was struck at section 8 or so where Yahweh says that he is sick and tired of burnt sacrifices and says stop sacrificing animals and go do ceremonial ablutions *a la Perse*. Wash yourselves and take care of orphans and widows. This is modern talk, and the modernists did not notice this is modernism because they did not realize that they themselves were the results of the profound innovations which are in Isaiah.

Andre Dupont Sommer who translated and deciphered the sense of the DDS scroll "mystical commentary on Habakkuk," said, in a footnote that Isaiah is written in 200 BC style Hebrew language.

After Zoroastrianism percolated through Babylonia as a result of Cyrus the new synthesis was Zurvanism. The name "I am that I am" which Ezra has Yahweh mouth in Exodus is actually a name of God in Zoroastrianism. The Jewish translator James Darmesteter of the Yasna, which lists the names of Ahura Mazda, left this name out in his translation because then everyone would have known that Ezra copied this from the Persians and put it into the mouth of burning bush. *Get it, Burning Bush?* In Zurvanism, it must be noted, Ahura Mazda is not supreme god but the good brother twin of the bad brother Ahriman who is the elder, having ripped his way out their mother's womb and their father is Zurvan or "boundless time."

Then came Hellenism, and Aristotle and rational thinking. Isaiah is the founding document of the Baptists and that is why Jesus, the Teacher of Righteousness, quotes from it when he is reading in the Synagogue in Luke. The Koran is full of Isaiah. ...

The school that produced the finished document of Isaiah also wrote the Psalms ...

Ezekiel dates himself to the destruction of the second Temple, but he contains ideas from Plato. ... Daniel was written around 167 BC, as propaganda for the Maccabees and ... Ezekiel was also written as Maccabean propaganda around 167 BC and post dated back to 587 BC.

When it comes to the Bible, Jesus, and Islam, quote me all you want.

So, Nietzsche was not wrong to posit Zoroaster (Zarathrustra) as the first Moralist.

The asceticism in Christianity—celibacy and self-denial—which Nietzsche detested, came not from Judaism or Zoroastrianism but from the Ahimsa tradition of India, where it was pioneered by the Jains and Buddhists. Naked Jain monks were known to the Greeks as 'gymnospohists', and considered philosophers. Travel between Greece and India was via the Royal Road, begun by the Assyrian Empire and completed by the Persian. Emperor Ashoka of India sent Buddhist missionaries in all directions, including to Bactria (then a Greek kingdom) and to Alexandria, where they influenced Jewish sects such as the Therapeutae and Essenes.

Clement of Alexandria, who lived c.150-215 A.D., wrote (c.200/1954),

the Brahmans neither eat animal flesh nor drink wine. ... They despise deaths and reckon life of no account. For they are persuaded that there is a regeneration. ... And the Indians who are called Holy Men go naked throughout their entire life. They seek for the truth, and predict the future, and reverence a certain pyramid beneath which, they think, lie the bones of a certain god. Neither the Gymnosophists nor the so-called Holy Men have wives. They think sexual relations are unnatural and contrary to law. For this cause they keep themselves chaste. The Holy Women are also virgins.

Norman Cohn shows how the Essenes (at Qumran) and Christians diverged from Judaism: "On the other hand, the Pharisees never accepted the notion of a great supernatural power hostile to God—they had no use for even a qualified dualism, any more than present day Judaism has. Belief in the Devil, his power and his eventual overthrow, remained the preserve of certain groups which deviated more widely from the central tradition of Judaism. Two of these groups are known to history: the Qumran sect and the Jesus sect" (Cohn, 1993, p. 224).

In that light, Christianity might be summed up as a form of Zoroastrianism. Which might explain Nietzsche's hostility to both.

Revilo P. Oliver (2001) wrote, "The Zoroastrian cult and all the cults derived from it can be summarized in one sentence. They replace race with a church" (Oliver, p. 152). Ken Freeland replied, "The fascist's quip that **Zoroastrians replaced race with a church** (as do both Christianity and Islam) can be turned on its head by saying that **Jews turn a church into an ethnicity**" (personal communication).

Cyril Glasse notes that the Gospel story of the Three Wise Men, following a star and visiting the newborn Jesus in Bethlehem, has a Zoroastrian theme. The Three Wise Men are Magi, Zoroastrian priests. In the story, they are attesting that the child Jesus is indeed the promised saviour:

'MAJU.S. ... The visit of the Magi, or Zoroastrian priests, in the Christian story of Jesus, refers to the accomplishment of the Zoroastrian prophecy. This prophecy in Zoroastrianism says that a virgin will bathe in a lake in which the seed of Zoroaster is preserved and that she will conceive the "world savior (Saoshyant)." It is only one of so many Zoroastrian elements in Christianity, that the latter can be considered as a prolongation of Zoroastrianism with a Semitic catalyst. The inclusion of the Magi story in the Bible was intended to show that the Zoroastrian prophecy, at the time still well known in Palestine, had been fulfilled in the birth of Jesus' (Glasse, 2009).

Robert M. Price points out that Zoroaster, like Jesus, underwent a Baptism and a Temptation by the Devil:

"According to Zoroastrian scripture, the founder was the son of a Vedic priest. One day Zoroaster, having immersed himself in a river for ritual purification, comes up from the water only to behold the archangel Vohu Mana offering him a cup to drink. He then commissions him to preach the unity and supremacy of the Wise Lord Ahura Mazda. At once who should appear but the evil anti-God Ahriman? He tries to persuade Zoroaster to abandon this path, though he spurns the offer. Let's see: a cleansing rite in the river, the appearance of a heavenly messenger, a call to ministry, temptation by a devil, and the prophet's successful resistance. Is there an echo in here?" (Price, 2017, p. 23).

Mary Boyce provides the story of Zoroaster's initiation in a river—in effect a baptism:

Finally revelation came to him (according to the tradition in his thirtieth year, which was conventionally the time of full and sage maturity). Allusions to the manner of it, in Y. 43, are amplified in one Pahlavi account.

Here it is said that Zoroaster was attending a gathering met to celebrate the spring festival (Maidhyoi.zarama) ; and that he went at dawn (according to ancient ritual practice) to fetch water from a river nearby for the haoma-ceremony. He waded deep into the current to draw the purest water; and it was as he returned to the bank—himself necessarily in a state of ritual purity, emerging from the pure element, water, in the freshness of a spring dawn—that he had a vision. He saw standing on the bank a shining being clad in a garment like light itself, who, tradition says, revealed himself as Vohu Manah, Good Intention. By him Zoroaster was brought into the presence of Ahura Mazda and the other five Immortals, before whom "he did not see his own shadow upon the earth, owing to (their) great light". And it was at that moment that spiritual enlightenment came to him. (Boyce, 1975, pp. 184-5)

Price details the Temptation of Zoroaster:

Zoroaster was also tempted as he embarked on his mission. He began as a priest of the old Vedic religion. One day when he was thirty years old (Luke 3:23) he waded out into a river to obtain water for the haoma ceremony. Returning to the riverbank in a state of ritual purity from having immersed himself in the sacred element of water, he beheld in a vision the archangel Vohu Mana (Good Thought) sent from Ahura Mazda. The angel instructed him concerning the true God (Ahura Mazda, "Wise Lord," was apparently the same as Varuna, who had been the high god of the Aryan pantheon before the warrior Indra displaced him) and commissioned him prophet of the new Zoroastrian faith (Dinkard 3.51-61). The archangel swept him up into heaven to confer with Ahura Mazda. Later, after a period of study and meditation in the countryside, Zoroaster found himself face to face with the evil Ahriman, seeking to avert him from his mission: "Do not destroy my creatures, O holy Zarathustra! Renounce the good law of the worshippers of Mazda, and thou shalt gain such a boon as the murderer gained, the ruler of the nations." Zoroaster's reply: "No! Never will I renounce the good law of the worshippers of Mazda, though my body, my life, my soul should burst!" (Fargard 19.1.6-7). (Price, 2003, p. 125).

Robert Eisenman depicts Jesus as a zealot (revolutionary) and his followers as participants in the Jewish war against Rome of 66-70. But S. G. F. Brandon argues that the war prompted Christians to distance themselves from Jews, and led to the triumph of Paul's faction over the pro-Jewish one of James. Eisenman and Hyam Maccoby target Paul as the "inventor" of Christianity; they resent his "Universalism" in opposition to Jewish "Particularism". Brandon wrote (1968),

The non-Jewish Christians must have found themselves in a dangerous and difficult position as a result of the Jewish revolt against Rome ... Gentile Christians ... had no leaders capable of resisting the Jerusalem claims, and many doubtless submitted, accepting a version of Christianity that was essentially Jewish in its ideas and outlook. A version, too, that assumed the spiritual superiority of Israel; for part of the offence of Paul's 'gospel', for the Jerusalem Christians, was its equation of Jew and Gentile in a common need of salvation. ... Paul's eclipse probably lasted for about a decade, from AD 55 to 66; it was terminated, in turn, by the eclipse of Jewish Christianity which ensued from Israel's defeat by Rome. (pp. 60-2)

But many verses in the Gospels suggest parallels with Cynic texts advocating simple living. F. Gerald Downing (1988) collects those verses together and shows that the early Christians were followers of the Cynic philosophy.

If the first Christian missionaries obeyed instructions of the kind recorded in Mt. 9.35-10.16, Mk 6.6-11, Lk. 9.1-5, 10.1-12, they would have looked like a kind of Cynic, displaying a very obvious poverty. Not all Cynics wore exactly the same dress; not all of them even carried the staff that for some was symbolic. But a raggedly cloaked and outspoken figure with no luggage and no money would not just have looked Cynic, he would obviousiy have wanted to. (p. vi)

Socrates was an enigmatic character like Diogenes of Sinope, one of the founders of the Cynic movement. The words that Plato puts into the mouth of Socrates are likely to be Plato's, not Socrates'. Socrates was known for pithy aphorisms not easily put into the form of propositions—which Plato favoured. Socrates acknowledged his own ignorance, whereas Plato fostered the "Platonic Illusion" of knowledge, namely that Reality can be fully grasped intellectually and expressed in words.

Denis McCormack drew my attention to Marcus Eli Ravage's articles (Jan. and Feb., 1928) taunting Christians with having been the unwitting dupes of Jews in the destruction of Roman Civilisation. On the one hand, he (wrongly) depicts Jesus as a Zealot, and Christians as supporters of the Jewish uprising against Rome in 66-70; on the other, he credits Judaism, via Christianity, with introducing the pacifism and self-renunciation which destroyed Rome's pagan civilization: "Our tribal customs have become the core of your moral code" (Ravage, 1928, Jan.).

But Ravage was wrong; scholarship has since revealed that, prior to the Exile, Judaism was a pagan religion, polytheistic and much the same as Canaanite religion. Francesca Stavrakopoulou revealed that Yahweh originally had a wife, Asherah, who was later edited out of the Bible—by translating the name 'Asherah' as 'Sacred Tree'—and that child sacrifice played a central role in ancient Judahite religious practice (Stavrakopoulou, 2004). The gods formed a Divine Council (like a parliament, whereas monotheism is like an absolute monarchy).

During the Exile in Babylon, under the Persian Empire, Judaism was recast. The pagan elements were removed or disguised, and Judaism adopted Monotheism, Messianism and Moralism from Zoroastrianism, an Aryan religion.

Ending paganism was a Zoroastrian project; it had already reformed, in Iran, the traditional Aryan religion expressed in the *Rig Veda* books I-IX, which records the Aryan invasion of Pakistan and northern India (Myers, 2002/2023). Book X of the *Rig Veda* records a different reform in India, a reflectiveness which led to the Upanishads, Jainism and Buddhism. Both reforms led to the development of conscience. Nietzsche opposed both reforms (the moralism of Zoroaster, and self-renunciation from Buddhism), when they later joined up in Christianity.

The Persian Emperor Darius I left an inscription stating

> A great god is Ahuramazda, who created this earth, ... I am Darius the great king, king of kings, king of countries containing all kinds of men, king in this great earth far and wide, son of Hystaspes, an Achaemenid, a Persian, son of a Persian, an Aryan, having Aryan lineage. (Darius, c.521BC).

What we now know as Judaism was recast from an Aryan religion! Christian morality derives not from Judaism but from Zoroastrianism. For more info on the influence of Zorostrianism on Judaism see mailstar.net/zoroaster-judaism.html.

Another Aryan religion, Buddhism, led to the pacifism and self-renunciation in Christianity. Nietzsche, like Ravage, blamed (Second-Temple) Judaism for those practices, but they came (via the Therapeutae of Alexandria) from Ashoka's India.

Harry Waton revealed a Jewish program to re-convert Christians to Judaism (see pp. 163-4). If the Third Temple be built, after the Zealots pull down the Dome of the Rock, and they announce their Messiah, Christianity could split over it, Evangelicals becoming Jewish again, the rest severing the Jewish tie completely.

Despite the Old Testament as a commonality between Judaism and Christianity, Marcion assessed that they are two very different religions; Arthur Schopenhauer thought so too. Marcion formulated a Christianity without the Old Testament; similarly, Mani formulated Manichaeism as a blend of Zoroastrianism, Buddhism and Christianity—but without the Old Testament.

Although the Persian Empire upheld the Zoroastrian religion—as seen in texts repudiating "the Lie", a reference to Ahriman—the Emperors did not allow fundamentalists to gain control, as happened in the Roman Empire when Christians took over (they banned all religions but their own and Judaism). In the Persian Empire, the religions of subject peoples were tolerated, except when they rebelled. Mithra and the goddess Anahita re-appeared with Mazda, as a sort of trinity, in the pantheon of the later Persian Empire.

Chapter 6: The Illuminati from Weishaupt to Lenin

It will be shown here that Bolshevism emerged from Illuminised Freemasonry.

Freemasonry is not a single entity; the Blue Lodges (degrees 1-3) are not conspiratorial, but are used as a cover by revolutionary Masons of high degree. Beginning at the Council of Wilhelmsbad in 1782, Illuminists penetrated some branches of Freemasonry and 'Illuminised' them.

Illuminised Freemasonry was cosmopolitan and revolutionary. Some conservative Christian political leaders belong to English Masonry, despite claims by others that it is anti-Christian. Masonry seems to show different faces like a chameleon, according to whether it assesses members as amenable to its revolutionary program. Christian members may be shielded from it, and never discover it.

Adam Weishaupt founded the Order of Illuminists on May 1, 1776. It espoused Rousseau's noble savage concept: civilisation was deemed to have corrupted an original happy stateless society. But whereas Rousseau's followers in the French Revolution were nationalists, Weishaupt was an internationalist who sought worldwide regime change leading to a World State.

The Illuminists were not merely a Masonic-type secret society with rituals and advancement through degrees, but operated like a militia (Billington p. 943). One might liken them to the underground communist parties.

Abbe Augustin Barruel (1798/1995) produced a detailed account of the Masonic and Illuminist roles in the French Revolution, but it bears his conservative Catholic perspective. Nesta Webster's *World Revolution* (1921/2013) is still relevant, a century later. It is the best book for the novice researcher to start with. James H. Billington's *Fire In The Minds Of Men* (1980) covers the Illuminist movement from Weishaupt to Lenin. The author was Librarian of Congress, and is not polemical. This is the best book to show sceptics that the Illuminati did not die out in the late 1700s.

From its inception in 1776, Jews and ex-Jesuits were banned from the Order (Barruel, p. 416). The ban on Jews was lifted during the Masonic congress at Wilhelmsbad in 1782 (Webster, 1921/2013, p. 20).

Unlike Rousseau and the Philosophes, Weishaupt did not publicise his ideas, but rather kept the Order's goals, strategy and very existence, secret; what we know about it came from accidents, splits which led some members to disclose what they knew, and court cases where members were forced to testify.

Barruel based his analysis on a number of documents he had obtained. The first is a collection of Original Writings of the Sect of Illuminees, discovered on

October 11-12, 1786, in the House of Zwack, a member (p. 394). Additional Original Writings were found in a search at Sandersdorf castle in 1787.

Other documents include *The Last works of Spartacus and Philo*. It contains two important degrees, and the laws laid down for the adepts (p. 395).

The Discourse of the Hierophant (Instructor) for the Degree of Priest (Epopt) is very revealing. The text says,

"Nature drew men from the savage state and re-united them in civil societies ... New associations present themselves to these wishes, and by their means we return to the state whence we came ..." (p. 477). "At the formation of states and nations, the world ceased to be a great family, to be a single empire; the great bond of nature was rent asunder. ... Nationalism, or the love for a particular nation, took place of the general love. ... Then it became a merit to extend the bounds of states at the expense of the neighbouring ones. ... Diminish, reject that love of the country, and mankind will once more learn to know and love each other as men" (p. 478).

The Hierophant, for the instruction of the proselyte, discourses on the origin of Masonry: "The rough stone of Masonry becomes the symbol of the primitive state of man, savage but free. The stone split or broken is the state of fallen nature, of mankind in civil society, no longer united in one family, but divided according to their states, governments, or religions. The polished stone represents mankind reinstated in its primitive dignity, in its independence". But he then says, "The Freemasons, like Priests and chiefs of nations, have banished reason from the earth. They have inundated the world with tyrants, impostors, spectres, corpses, and men like to wild beasts" (p. 490).

Weishaupt thereby dismisses the Great Architect of English Masonry with the God of the Christians (p. 491). And later brands all other religions also superstitious (p. 506). However, Grand Orient Masonry was atheistic.

The Illuminizing Legislator instructs his pupils "to seize upon the public education, the ecclesiastical government, the chairs of literature, and the pulpit" (p. 537).

Barruel concludes that Illuminati principles "under the pretence of rendering human nature more happy and united in one family, aim at nothing less than destroying every Religion, every title to property, every town, every fixed residence, and every nation" (p. 538).

Webster (1921/2013) sums up Weishaupt's goals:

Reduced to a simple formula the aims of the Illuminati may be summarized in the following six points:

Abolition of Monarchy and all ordered Government.

Abolition of private property.

Abolition of inheritance.

Abolition of patriotism.

Abolition of the family (i.e. of marriage and all morality, and the institution of the communal education of children).

Abolition of all religion (pp. 22-3).

How Weishaupt and Bode took over Freemasonry

Johann Bode was a Freemason who joined the Bavarian Illuminati, taking the name *Amelius*, and helped them take over Freemasonry, introducing Illuminati features into Masonic rituals.

Barruel details how they did it:

Bode was thoroughly convinced that Illuminism, so far from being an invention of Jesuits and Priests, was no other than a most determined conspiracy against Princes and the Priesthood, which he equally hated ... Bode introduced its laws into the new Masonic Ritual. It was on seeing these laws that the Mason who best foresaw their consequences exclaims, in the bitterness of his heart: "Oh my Brethren! At what point shall I begin, or where shall I end, when I speak to you of that Bode known among the Illuminees by the name of Amelius? He acted where Knigge could not gain admittance. It was through his means that the Illuminees gained their ascendancy in the new system that was to have been established at Wilhemsbaden; that they gained admittance into our Directories; and that they succeeded in fraternizing with the greater part of our Brethren of the Strict Observance. His Insinuator Knigge had left him no alternative but to bring over Freemasonry to this unfortunate alliance, or to crush the Brotherhood. To the astonishment and grief of every true Mason, it was by the combined efforts of Bode and Knigge, that the greater part of the Lodges throughout Germany were tainted and infected with this baneful Illuminism." (Barruel, p. 671)

One strategy was to make the Freemasons believe that their Orders were secretly being run by Jesuits—the hated enemy. Many left their lodges, and joined those under Illuminati control:

Bode at length made a collection of every thing that could be said on the subject, and sent the whole of these materials to the Brother Bonneville at Paris. He soon published his work, entitled *The Jesuits expelled from Freemasonry*; and this production, sent to all the regular Lodges, was supposed to be the death-blow to this terrible phantom.

On investigating these different productions, we observe, that their drift was to make the Free-masons believe that all their Lodges were secretly under the direction of the Jesuits; that each Mason, without suspecting it, was but the slave and instrument of that society which had long since been looked upon as extinct, but whose members, though dispersed, still preserved an ascendancy disgraceful to Masonry, and dangerous to nations and their rulers. The result of all this tended to persuade the brethren, that true Masonry was not to be sought for either among the Rosicrucians or the Scotch Knights, and still less among the English Masons, or those of the Strict Observance; but solely among the Eclectic Lodges that were under the direction of the Illuminees. (Barruel, p. 706)

The Masonic Brethren of the ordinary Lodges heard so much of their being the dupes of the Jesuits, that they abandoned the Strict Observance and the Rosicrucians, and flocked to the Eclectic Masons, then under the direction of the Illuminees. The Masonic Revolution was so complete and so fatal to ancient Masonry, that its zealous Masters and Venerables declared this fiction of Jesuits Masonry to be a conspiracy truly worthy of a Danton or a Robespierre. (p. 706)

Bode converted Nicholas Bonneville to Illuminism; Bonneville and Mirabeau introduced Illuminati ideas to France. Bonneville was a book publisher whose *Cercle Social* had 8,000 members including Condorcet, Marechal, Restif, Cloots and Babeuf. Bonneville became a Freemason in 1786, then came under the influence of Bode, who sent him materials about Jesuits secretly running Masonic Orders, which Bonneville published in 1788 in a book titled *Jesuits Expelled from Masonry*. In the same year he also published another book, *Dagger Shattered by the Masons*, in which he accused the Jesuits of having introduced into Masonic degrees the myths of the Templars and their doctrine of revenge (Tsatsarounos, 2014).

Many Masons such as Albert Pike state that the execution of Louis XVI was revenge, by Freemasons, for the execution of Jacques de Molay.

Bonneville introduced Babeuf to Illuminism; he and Buonarroti then perpetuated it. During the French Revolution, Bonneville's group were influential in the Girondins, but they came under attack from Robespierre, a nationalist and deist.

Babeuf and Buonarroti transmit the Illuminist Legacy

After the fall of Robespierre during the French Revolution, the Directory took over. François-Noël Babeuf, who renamed himself 'Gracchus', conspired to overthrow it and institute 'equality' with the abolition of private property. Babeuf is the only person that Marx and Engels praise in *The Communist Manifesto*.

Philippe Buonarroti, from an Aristocratic family, studied law at the University of Pisa, then became a Freemason. During the French Revolution he was arrested and sent to a prison at Paris, where he met other revolutionaries, including Babeuf. Together they worked out a program for Communist revolution, based on the principles of Weishaupt.

Babeuf's conspiratorial group, the Society of the Pantheon, included "some extraordinary men, Darthe, Sylvain Marechal, Germain, and Buonarroti, who was to survive them all and to be their historian" (Laski, p. 88).

On May 27, 1797, the High Court at Vendome sentenced Babeuf to death and Buonarroti to deportation.

Harold J. Laski deemed Babeuf's conspiracy the first detailed plan for a communist regime: "a definite programme and an equally definite method of moving towards its realization" (p. 68). These conspirators were called Babouvistes. They were the first to advocate that communist rule should operate as a Dictatorship: "when the political State had been captured, a period of rigorous dictatorship would be necessary as the prelude to communist democracy" (Laski, p. 93).

"An assembly was impossible since it left the success achieved to the hazard of a popular vote. The revolution had not been made merely to change the form of administration; its object was to change the nature of society itself. This could not be left to the people who had been trained to habits which ignored the natural order of things. The revolutionary Government must therefore act on behalf of the people. ... It is the doctrine of permanent revolution by dictatorship in the name of the proletariat".

"Parliamentarianism and democracy are impossible because they risk the whole purpose of the insurrection ; the people are not yet fit to be entrusted ... Liberty must be denied at the outset lest it be lost for ever. ... The dictatorship was thus, in effect, the general will of the proletariat." (Laski, p. 94).

Lenin put such a regime into practice, drawing on the ideas of Babeuf and Buonarroti: "Lenin, so to say, is the Babouvistes writ large" (Laski, p. 99).

Billington traces the succession from Buonarroti to Lenin: "Seen from above the revolutionary tradition is a story of elite, intellectual leaders: a thin line of apostolic succession from Buonarroti to Lenin" (Billington, 1980, p. 16).

Babeuf's movement lived on through the book Buonarroti wrote, which "became a textbook for the communist movement in the 1830's and fourties in France" (Lehning, 1956, p. 112). After Buonarroti's death in 1837, leadership passed to Louis Auguste Blanqui.

Buonarroti's secret society used a cell-type structure: "certain aspects of the organisation, of the leadership, the methods and the ultimate aims were only known to some of the members belonging to the most inner circle of the society.

In other words, the essence of a secret society as defined by Adam Weishaupt" (Lehning, p. 116).

Billington says, "Buonarroti sought to work through existing Masonic lodges: to recruit through them, influence them, use them as a cover" (p. 91). "Only those in the inner circle were told that the organization sought radical social change as well as a republican constitution" (p. 92). Billington sums up: "the Masonic milieu seems the essential starting point for any serious inquiry into the occult roots of the revolutionary tradition" (p. 92).

Buonarroti's organizational plan "was simply lifted from the Bavarian Order of Illuminists. This radical and secular occultist movement was organized on three levels in a secret hierarchy: church, synod, and areopagite." (Billington, p. 93)

The "church" was the local cell; its leader was alone linked with the regional "synod." Synods were headed by a "territorial deacon," who supervised all "churches" in the region. The highest "areopagite" grade sent out its own "mobile deacons" to enforce control (p. 93).

"Babeuf's secret, hierarchical organization resembled that of the Illuminists and of Bonneville" (Billington, p. 97).

Buonarroti's companion Joachim de Prati revealed some details in his memoirs. Lehning reports that in Milan, 'he became initiated in 1810 in a secret society "a masonry in a masonry, unknown to the very grand-masters and deputy-grandmasters" and from that moment, Prati relates, he became connected with all the secret societies, which afterwards assumed different names, in Germany, Italy and France. The society in Milan was "a section of that "directing committee", which afterwards caused so much uneasiness to Napoleon, the Holy Alliance and to Louis-Philippe". This committee was the "Great Firmament" of the "Philadelphes"' (Lehning, p. 118).

The Philadelphes were organised on Masonic lines, with symbols and grades, but also drew on Weishaupt's Illuminati. Novices were admitted using Masonic ritual, but the lower grades (first and second) had no idea of the existence of the third grade.

Prati published an English translation of the "professions of faith" of all three grades. The credo of the third grade reveals the secret revolutionary programme. Lehning notes, 'That this third grade was called the Areopagus is revealing. This was the name of the "conseil", the highest grade of Weishaupt's "Illuminati"' (Lehning, p. 124).

The Carbonari were a Masonic order which mobilised Italians against the Austrians, the French and the Church. Those belonging to higher grades and certain lodges sought to overthrow monarchs and despots. "The most radical wing of the

Carbonari society and probably the members of the upper grades dedicated themselves to liquidating all existing governments and to establishing a republican regime in the united Italy that they aspired to create" (Rath, p. 367). Some of the ultraradicals held egalitarian views like the Jacobins (p. 368).

Having been a Mason himself, Napoleon III knew their revolutionary proclivities, and placed his own officials at the head of official Masonic organizations; but there was also an underground masonic movement which sought to overthrow him (Nicolaevsky, 1966).

Napoleon III crushed the revolution in France, but it broke out again after his fall:

'Blanqui remained in prison; and the last great popular uprising of the era (of one hundred thousand rebels against Napoleon III's proclamation of dictatorship) in December 1851, was crushed with five hundred killed and twenty thousand convicted. There was no major upheaval in France and no further mention of the "dictatorship of the proletariat" anywhere until the Paris Commune twenty years later' (Billington, p. 285).

The revolutionary Masons made many attempts to kill Napoleon III: "... all the secret societies of the era were filled with people who were more or less sympathetic to terrorism ... Mazzini not only considered Napoleon III the most dangerous political opponent of Italian unification but personally regarded him as a traitor, and consequently sent to France group after group of terrorists whose mission was to assassinate Napoleon III" (Nicolaevsky, 1966).

Louis Blanc was thought to be a reformist, but recent publications show his connections with revolutionary masonry. "Outwardly, these groups had the form of a masonic organization and bore a masonic name, the Lodge of the Philadelphians (Loge des Philadelphes). ... All the outstanding leaders of the Commune were apparently members of the Lodge ... acting behind the scenes, the Philadelphians helped to found and organize the Commune" (Nicolaevsky, 1966).

Communists praise the Paris Commune of 1871, but they omit to mention the death and destruction. The Communards shot the Archbishop of Paris, Georges Darboy, killed other clergymen, and set fire to much of Paris.

During the Commune, John Leighton witnessed 'eight or ten thousand members of Parisian free-masonry who are crowding along the Rue de Rivoli' in support of the Commune. 'A patriarchal Freemason, wearing his collar and badges, has arrived in a carriage; they help him to alight with marks of the greatest respect. The court is by this time full to overflowing, an enthusiastic cry of "Vive la Franc Maconnerie! Vive la Republique Universelle!"' (Leighton, 1871/2019, pp. 220-1).

Debate over the Jewish Role

Adolphe Cremieux belonged to the Lodge of Mizraim, to the Scottish Rite, and also to the Grand Orient (Queensborough, 1933/2013, p. 417).

At a general assembly of Alliance Israelite Universelle, on May 31 1864, Cremieux said: "The Alliance is not limited to our cult, it voices its appeal to all cults and wants to penetrate in all the religions as it has penetrated into all countries. Let us endeavour boldly to bring about the union of all cults under one flag of Union and Progress. Such is the slogan of humanity" (p. 419).

Cremieux was the link between Alliance Israelite Universelle and Freemasonry. Masonic writers have asserted that the 18th degree, conferred by the Grand Orient, makes the initiate, if not a member, at any rate a supporter of the Alliance (Queensborough, 1933/2013, p. 487).

Nesta Webster noted, "It has several times been stated that Weishaupt was himself a Jew. I cannot find the slightest evidence to this effect" (Webster, 1924/2000, p. 128n1).

Yet Jewish author Bernard Lazare wrote (1894/1995), "There were Jews in the circle around Weishaupt, and a Jew of Portuguese origin, Martinez de Pasquales, established numerous groups of illuminati in France" (p. 154).

"... the Jews were the most active, the most zealous of missionaries. We find them taking part in the agitation of Young Germany; large numbers of them were members of the secret societies which constituted the fighting force of the Revolution; they made their way into the Masonic lodges, into the societies of the Carbonari, they were found everywhere in France, in Germany, in England, in Austria, in Italy. ... Many of the Jewish members of the International took part subsequently in the Commune, where they found others of their faith" (Lazare, pp. 155-6).

A common refutation of the above is the claim that many lodges were closed to Jews. But Gougenot des Mousseaux explains:

"Many lodges are, or rather were, closed to the Jew, because he was unpopular in Masonry as elsewhere. But what is true for the plebs of the Order is by no means true for its real leaders, who are the friends, the auxiliaries, the lieges of the Jew, and who always welcomed him as a sovereign lord" (des Mousseaux, 1869/2022, p. xxiv. footnote 2).

Des Mousseaux says he received a letter from a Protestant statesman revealing the Jewish role in the 1848 revolutions:

"Statesman in the service of the Great Germanic Power, and as clairvoyant as sagacious, one of our friends—one of those rare Protestants who remained faithful to the divinity of Christ—wrote to us in December 1865:

"For in the present times, I believe that the Jews are very active in destroying the foundations of our society and in preparing for revolutions. They belong to an admirably well endowed race, which produces geniuses in all fields and in all tendencies; I mean original men, of high intelligence and great power of action. ... Since the revolutionary upsurge of 1848, I have found myself in touch with a Jew who, out of vanity, betrayed the secrets of the secret societies with which he had joined, and who warned me eight to ten days in advance of all revolutions which were going to explode anywhere in Europe."

"I owe him the unshakeable conviction that all these great movements of oppressed peoples, etc., etc., are combined by half a dozen individuals who give their orders to secret societies all over Europe!"

"The ground is completely mined under our feet, and the Jews provide a large contingent to these miners ... The Jewish bankers will soon be, by their prodigious fortunes, our masters and lords."

"I am finally told 'that all of the great radical newspapers of Germany are in the hands of the Jews'" (pp. 365-7).

Blue Lodge Masons are a cover for the Masons of Higher Degree

Albert Pike wrote in *Morals and Dogma*, dubbed the 'Masonic Bible', that Blue Lodge Masons (of degree 1 to 3) are deliberately deceived by those of high degree:

"The Blue degrees are but the outer court or portico of the Temple. Part of the symbols are displayed there to the Initiate, but he is intentionally misled by false interpretations. It is not intended that he shall understand them; but it is intended that he shall imagine he understands them. Their true explication is reserved for the Adepts, the Princes of Masonry. ... It is well enough for the mass of those called Masons, to imagine that all is contained in the Blue Degrees" (Pike, 1871/2011, p. 626).

Dealing with the 30th Degree—Knight Kadosh—Pike admits that the Templars' real agenda had been rebuilding the Jewish temple. Their model was Zorobabel, an Old Testament character; they have no truck with the New Testament.

"The avowed object of the Templars was to protect the Christians who came to visit the Holy Places: their secret object was the re-building of the Temple of Solomon ... The Templars, or Poor Fellow-Soldiery of the Holy House of the Temple intended to be re-built, took as their models, in the Bible, the Warrior-Masons of Zorobabel, who worked, holding the sword in one hand and the trowel in the other. Therefore it was that the Sword and the Trowel were the insignia of the Templars, who subsequently, it will be seen, concealed themselves under the name of Brethren Masons. [This name, Freres Masons in the French, ... was corrupted in English into Free-Masons]" (Pike, 1871/2011, p. 624).

The Templars maintained two doctrines, to hide their real agenda from the Christians. The Freemasons likewise pretended fealty to Essenism (John the Baptist), but hid the centrality of the Kabalah in their cult, which by implication is Jewish:

"The Templars, like all other Secret Orders and Associations, had two doctrines, one concealed and reserved for the Masters, which was Johannism ; the other public, which was the Roman Catholic. Thus they deceived the adversaries whom they sought to supplant. Hence Free-Masonry, vulgarly imagined to have begun with the Dionysian Architects or the German Stoneworkers, adopted Saint John the Evangelist as one of its patrons, associating with him, in order not to arouse the suspicions of Rome, Saint John the Baptist, and thus covertly proclaiming itself the child of the Kabalah and Essenism together" (Pike, 1871/2011, p. 625).

The Freemasons achieved their first major goal with the execution of Louis XVI; their next goal was to overthrow the Church:

"The secret movers of the French Revolution had sworn to overturn the Throne and the Altar upon the Tomb of Jacques de Molai. When Louis XVI. was executed, half the work was done; and thenceforward the Army of the Temple was to direct all its efforts against the Pope" (Pike, 1871/2011, p. 630).

Connection between the 'Fallen Angels' and Freemasonry/Theosophy

Although the Marxist movement was atheistic, and the Grand Orient was atheistic too, other orders of Freemasonry spawned the 'New Age' or 'Green' religion. It, too, features the idea of "illumination", and looks to the "fallen angels" not as devils but as Enlightened.

In the story of Adam and Eve, did not God lie when he said they 'would surely die' if they ate the forbidden fruit? Did not the serpent tell the truth when he said they would be enlightened?

But this misunderstands the real meaning of the story. The story of Adam and Eve is based on the Epic of Gilgamesh, from ancient Sumeria about 3000 years B.C., about the connection between sex and death. Through having sex, we give birth to children. As they grow up, the older generation must die off, to make room for new generations. If they did not, the earth would become overpopulated. That's why the gods made the Great Flood. The authors of the Book of Genesis reworked the earlier Sumerian/Mespotamian origin stories, reversing their meaning to create a counter-myth overthrowing Sumerian civilisation, and instead portraying Jews as the founders of civilisation. In the Epic, Gilgamesh is a priest-king living in the city, and Enkidu is a wild man, living in a state of nature (did Rousseau read this?). His companions are the animals, and he lives in harmony with them—but without sex. Gilgamesh sends a sacred prostitute to seduce him. Enkidu falls in love with her, after which the wild animals flee his company; he then moves to the city. The bottom line of the story is that, in his original state, he was immortal, but after the sex he became mortal, that is, subject to death.

In the same way, Adam and Eve did not die on the spot when they ate the fruit, but they became mortal. Before that, they had been immortal—but without sex, they were virginal. Sex and Death are intimately connected (Myers, 2002/2012).

Discussing the 19th Degree—Grand Pontiff—Albert Pike praises Lucifer:

"The Apocalypse is, to those who receive the nineteenth Degree, the Apotheosis of that Sublime Faith which aspires to God alone, and despises all the pomps and works of Lucifer. LUCIFER, the Light-bearer! Strange and mysterious name to give to the Spirit of Darkness! Lucifer, the Son of the Morning! Is it he who bears the Light, and with its splendors intolerable blinds feeble, sensual, or selfish Souls? Doubt it not! for traditions are full of Divine Revelations and Inspirations: and Inspiration is not of one Age nor of one Creed. Plato and Philo, also, were inspired" (Pike, 1871/2011, p. 248).

Manly P. Hall, another leading authority on Freemasonry, also attests the role of Lucifer:

"When the Mason learns that the key to the warrior on the block is the proper application of the dynamo of living power, he has learned the mystery of his Craft. The seething energies of Lucifer are in his hands and before he may step onward and upward, he must prove his ability to properly apply energy. He must follow in the footsteps of his forefather, Tubal-Cain, who with the mighty strength of the war god hammered his sword into a plowshare" (Hall, 1923/2020, pp. 50-1).

Aleister Crowley, the magician who adopted the title 'Baphomet XI', and whom John Lennon admired, was also a 33° Freemason.

The Theosophical Society has a strong connection to Freemasonry. Helena Blavatsky was allegedly a Freemason; her successor Annie Besant certainly was. Alice Bailey, a leading Theosophist, was married to Foster Bailey, a 33° Mason in the Scottish Rite. Bailey's publishing company was called Lucifer Publishing Company; it was later changed to Lucis Publishing Company. Her organisation Lucis Trust is a registered NGO with the United Nations, promoting One World.

Bailey's Lucis Trust views Lucifer as one of the 'solar angels', a light-bearer:

The Esoteric Meaning of Lucifer

... for a brief period of two or three years in the early 1920's, when Alice and Foster Bailey were beginning to publish the books published under her name, they named their fledgling publishing company "Lucifer Publishing Company". By 1925 the name was changed to Lucis Publishing Company and has remained so ever since. Both "Lucifer" and "Lucis" come from the same word root, lucis being the Latin generative case meaning of light. The Baileys' reasons for choosing the original name are not known to us, but we can only surmise that they, like the great teacher H.P. Blavatsky, for whom they had enormous respect, sought to elicit a deeper understanding of the sacrifice made by Lucifer. Alice and Foster Bailey were serious students and teachers of Theosophy, a spiritual tradition which views Lucifer as one of the solar angels, those advanced Beings Who Theosophy says descended (thus "the fall") from Venus to our planet eons ago to bring the principle of mind to what was then animal-man. In the theosophical perspective, the descent of these solar angels was not a fall into sin or disgrace but rather an act of great sacrifice, as is suggested in the name "Lucifer" which means light-bearer (Lucis Trust).

The magazine of the Theosophical Society was originally named 'Lucifer': 'in 1887 the magazine of the Theosophical Society took "Lucifer" as its name in an effort to bring clarity to what it regarded as an unfairly maligned sacrificing angel' (McKechnie, 1989).

St. Paul gave the Christian response: "And no wonder, for Satan himself masquerades as an angel of light. It is not surprising, then, if his servants masquerade as servants of righteousness. Their end will be what their actions deserve" (2 Corinthians, 11: 14-5, NIV).

The Book of Genesis contains two main origin stories: chapter 2 (Adam and Eve) and chapter 1 (Creation). The story in chapter 2 is Semitic, but chapter 1 is derived from the Zoroastrian religion (of Persia, via Babylon). The Zoroastrian religion has a Fall, but it's very different from the Semitic story. In the Zoroastrian religion, the Fall occurs in Heaven with the rebellion of the Fallen Angels. Their leader is Ahriman, from which the Christian Devil comes.

Theosophists say that the Book of Isaiah 14:12, referring to a falling star, Venus or Lucifer, has mistakenly been connected to the Fall of the rebellious angels:

How you have fallen from heaven,
    morning star, son of the dawn!
You have been cast down to the earth,
    you who once laid low the nations! (NIV).

Their argument is that Lucifer, far from being the Devil, is the Enlightener of humanity. Yet, their Masonic associates (e.g. many rock musicians) feature the Baphomet, inverted crosses, the Pyramid and the All-Seeing Eye, whose demonic character is hostile to Christianity, associated with witchcraft (the bad kind), and harmful to traditional culture.

The Bible says very little about the Rebellion in Heaven; it's a Christian-Zoroastrian idea, not a Jewish one. It's mainly found in the Book of Enoch, which, although influential among the Essenes (a copy was found at Qumran), is not accepted as 'revealed' in the Jewish Canon or the Christian Canon. Even so, it is quoted in the New Testament at Jude 1:14-5, and was widely used in the early Church (Book of Enoch, 2023). Enoch himself is mentioned in the Book of Genesis (4.17 to 5.24), at 1 Chronicles 1.3, Sirach 44.16 and 49.14, and, in the New Testament, at Lk 3.37, Heb 11.5 and Jude 14.

The Jewish religion makes very little of the story of Adam and Eve; it does not regard this as marking a Fall. In Jewish terms, the Fall is the destruction of the ancient kingdoms of Israel and Judah; and the Redemption is their restoration and the imposition of a Pax Judaica on the world.

In Christian terms, there are two Falls—that of Adam and Eve, and the Fall in Heaven, i.e. the war between the rebellious angels and the good ones. Evolution theory renders the Fall of Adam and Eve somewhat problematic. But the Fall in Heaven remains relevant, because demonic evil is always a pressing problem, not least with the current Culture War against Western culture and religion.

The attack on the family, Satanism in Hollywood and in rock music, Satanic temples, the Baphomet, the Pyramid and the All-Seeing Eye—these have a demonic component. Christianity is still a form of Zoroastrianism, and resistance to the occult movement is growing.

Maurice Strong, founder of the U. N.'s Green Religion, said "It is the responsibility of each human being today to choose between the force of darkness and the force of light" (Melanson, 2001). He wasn't thinking of Darkness & Light in Christian terms, but in Masonic/Theosophical terms—the 'force of darkness' being Christianity, and the 'force of light' the New Age religion.

Hannah Newman runs a Hasbara-type campaign proclaiming that the New Age movement, which she says is based on Theosophy, is Nazi.

Newman's webpage is called "The Rainbow Swastika". She routinely calls opponents 'Nazi', as writers of the Larouche network used to. Her main complaint is that the New Age movement, which she connects to the Globalist-Green movement, isn't Jewish. She alleges that it is Aryan (White), and launching an assault on Judaism: "in the process singling out Judaism—and eventually the Jewish people—for destruction" (Newman, 5761=2001). In that webpage, she does not even give the Western date (2001), but only the date in the Jewish Calendar, 5761 years since Creation.

Newman ignores the Masonic connection to the New Age religion—Scottish

Freemasonry in the U. S. published a magazine called 'The New Age'—because it would not fit her case that the Globalist conspiracy is White, not Jewish. Freemasonry has close ties to Globalist Jews: there is an Illuminati pyramid on top of the Supreme Court of Israel, and a plaque states that the building was designed and funded by the Rothschild family.

The University of Pennsylvania library (n. d.) maintains archive listings for the Masonic magazine titled The New Age. It states, "The New Age was a Masonic magazine published by the Supreme Council of the Thirty-Third Degree Ancient and Accepted Scottish Rite of Freemasonry for the Southern Jurisdiction of the United States. The New Age began in 1904."

The Freemasonry Watch website (https://freemasonrywatch.org/) published Newman's material and follows her line. A lot of other conspiracy websites follow her line too; they can't get into trouble blaming Globalism on Whites instead of Jews.

This despite the mass immigration into Western countries for which Jewish lobbies can take much of the credit.

This despite Ari Shavit's statement, published in the New York Times, "We killed them out of a certain naive hubris. Believing with absolute certitude that now, with the White House, the Senate, and much of the American media in our hands, the lives of others do not count as much as our own" (Shavit, 1996).

This despite the Illuminati pyramid on the top of Israel's Supreme Court.

Saying that Congress, the president and the media are Jewish-controlled—as Shavit did—is now deemed antisemitic in some places, and illegal as in the early Soviet Union. The First Amendment is a barrier—for so long as the U. S. Constitution holds.

This chapter has shown that Illuminism, as a network of revolutionaries using goals and methods pioneered by Adam Weishaupt, continued up to the time of Lenin. But Illuminists do not disclose themselves as such.

Surely Trotsky was an Illuminatus, not in terms of Degrees he might have passed through, but in terms of his alignment with Weishaupt's goals. His high-level backers would probably, in many cases at least, be Freemasons; but they too hide such allegiance, or only indicate it via symbols, such as the hand-in-the-vest hand sign. Stalin is well-attested making that sign; he even had statues cast of himself making it. There is also a photo of Trotsky making it; the UK Daily Mail has it at http://i.dailymail.co.uk/i/pix/2008/10/08/article-0-02DEDC910000044D-377_233x423.jpg. Tony Fauci made it, and Xi Jinping made the same sign at the opening of the Wuhan Military Games in 2019 (Myers, 2021/2022).

During the Cold War, the CIA did not regard Trotskyists as a security risk, because they opposed the Soviet Government. Saunders (2000) exposed the tacit alliance between Trotskyists and the CIA against the Soviet Union.

But the "Far Right" in the United States habitually bundled all kinds of Communists together, failing to see significant differences between Stalinists and Trotskyists, on the one hand, and Stalinists and Maoists on the other. Joseph McCarthy, for example, made no distinction between Stalinists and Trotskyists; and the 'Far Right' denied the reality of the Sino-Soviet split until Nixon went to China. The war between China and Vietnam made it clear to all but fanatics.

Trotskyists, presenting an anti-Soviet visage, often escaped the same sort of scrutiny that Stalinists underwent. The Reece Committee, investigating the subversive activities of the tax-free Foundations—Rockefeller, Carnegie, Ford et. al.—failed to identify the Trotskyists as equally subversive.

But Rene Wormser, in his study of the Reece Committee and the Foundations, noted that Trotsky's followers were equally dangerous and more widespread:

> The emphasis on a search for organized Communist penetration of foundations absorbed much of the energy of the investigators and detracted somewhat from the efficacy of their general inquiry into "subversion." There are varieties of Communist sectarian programs and propaganda of a dissident nature, aside from those directed from Moscow. A follower of Trotsky's brand of communism may be no less a danger to our society because he opposes the current rulers of Russia. It is likely that there are more Trotsky followers in the United States than followers of the Kremlin. Even among the formerly orthodox supporters of the Party line, there has occurred a mass conversion to a domestic form of the Communist theory and method. (Wormser, 1858/2014, p. 177)

The left-wing billionaires promoting the Culture War, such as George Soros, are not Stalinist, but are rather in Trotsky's camp, not card-carrying members but 'Trotskyoid'.

Left-wing Oligarchs such as David Rockefeller and George Soros can also be imputed to be Illuminati, because their actions accord with Weishaupt's goals (see p. 53 above). They support the Marxist (Trotskyist) Culture-War but also support Capitalism (private ownership of the economy) and Free Trade.

Despite this apparent contradiction, there is a logic to it. Their stance on both cultural issues and economic issues is anti-nationalist. The culture-war destroys religion and the family, while Free Trade destroys small business and the family farm, and open-border immigration keeps wages low and replaces the working class. First Nations movements threaten to split the nation. The Illuminism of Weishaupt was an elite movement among professionals and aristocrats. Marx gave it a 'proletarian' bent, but it has since returned to its elite roots.

It's alleged by some conspiracy writers, e.g. Lady Queensborough, that Lord Palmerston, Secretary of War, Foreign Secretary, and Prime Minister, was a Free-mason, a Grand Master, and even the head of English Freemasonry, and that he ran revolutionaries in Continental Europe while holding office in Britain. Yet none of those details are mentioned in standard biographies. That omission, however, is not a disproof; after all, Freemasonry is a secret society.

Margaret Jacob notes that academics often omit mentioning a person's Masonic membership:

Despite the importance of Freemasonry for the Enlightenment, of whatever variety, this originally British institution has received scant attention from British academic historians. Even one of the finest, most comprehensive biographies produced by the current generation of English scholars, J. H. Plumb's *Sir Robert Walpole* (London, 1956-61), never once mentions that Walpole was a Mason or that important servants of his government and some of his diplomatic agents were also. (Jacob, 2006, pp. 91-2)

Whether Palmerston did have the alleged Masonic and revolutionary involvement is outside the scope of this book. But the point is that revolutionaries are not all working class; Bankers and Freemasonry have established connections to social revolution, as George Soros and David Rockefeller show.

Benjamin Disraeli also discoursed on that topic, but cast his books as 'novels' because, sometimes, the truth just cannot be stated openly. As George Orwell said, it can be a major struggle to express what you see right in front of your face.

Chapter 7: Cecil Rhodes' "British Conspiracy" cf. the Illuminists

A "conspiracy" can be defined as a lobby which operates over a long period of time, partly in the open but partly covertly, and engages in agenda-setting.

It's common for conspiracy analysts to argue that there is just one high-level conspiracy; I argue, instead, that there are several, but, because they have had to share power with one another, they operate as factions.

Stanley Monteith, in *Brotherhood of Darkness*, listed several candidates for a single overarching conspiracy: the Bankers, the Central Bankers, the Jewish Bankers, the Council On Foreign Relations (CFR), the Bilderbergers, the Trilateral Commission, the Club of Rome, Communism, Socialism, Secular Humanism, Tax-Exempt Foundations, the (Demonic) Hierarchy, the Illuminati, the Jews, the Jesuits, the Masons, the New Age, the Order of the Quest, the Rosicrucians, Skull and Bones, the Theosophical Society, and UFO Believer (Monteith, 2000).

The "British" Conspiracy

But his final choice is Cecil Rhodes' secret society, known as the Rhodes Group, the Milner Group (in the years when Lord Milner led it), Chatham House or the Round Table. Carroll Quigley disclosed its inner workings in his books *The Anglo-American Establishment* (written in 1949, published in 1981) and *Tragedy and Hope* (1966). Quigley claimed that the CFR was the American branch of the Round Table, but others maintain that it's independent but allied.

Rhodes relied on funding from Lord Rothschild and other Jewish financiers; they were part of his Group. Lord Rothschild was executor of some of Rhodes' wills, and owned more shares in Rhodes' companies than Rhodes did himself.

Cecil Rhodes' first will (dated 1877) endowed a secret society with the goals being "the extension of British rule throughout the world, ... emigration from the United Kingdom,... the ultimate recovery of the United States of America as an integral part of a British Empire ... and finally the foundation of so great a power as to hereafter render wars impossible and promote the best interests of humanity" (Quigley, 1981, p. 33).

The Rhodes Group, Quigley wrote in *Tragedy and Hope*, sought 'to free Britain from Europe in order to build up an "Atlantic bloc" of Great Britain, the British Dominions, and the United States' (Quigley, 1966, p. 582). The means they used were the Rhodes Scholarships, the Round Table groups, and the Chatham House organisation, which set up Royal Institutes of International Affairs in all the dominions and a Council on Foreign Relations in New York.

The Group, per Quigley, functioned as an informal secret government within a formal "democracy". One of its methods was agenda-setting, i.e. anticipating problems and formulating solutions before they arose, then intensively marketing their solution when the problem did arise. They controlled the banks and most of the media.

Quigley portrays the Group as operating like a lobby:

"After the election of 1935, the Milner Group took a substantial part in the government, with possession of seven places in a Cabinet of twenty-one seats. By the beginning of September of 1939, they had only five out of twenty-three, the decrease being caused, as we shall see, by the attrition within the Group on the question of appeasement. In the War Cabinet formed at the outbreak of the war, they had four out of nine seats" (Quigley, 1981, pp. 229-30).

But the Group had little sway over the British Labour Party. The election of the Government of Clement Attlee gave the Group "a rude jolt in August 1945, when the General Election removed the Conservative government from power and brought to office a Labour government. The influence of the Group in Labour circles has always been rather slight" (Quigley, 1981, p. 309).

They had some influence in the unity governments headed by Ramsay MacDonald, but those Governments had split the Labour Party—with the connivance of the Group. Two Labour MPs, Malcolm MacDonald (son of Ramsay) and Godfrey Elton, became closely associated with the Group.

In the United States, the CFR regularly populates the Government, whether Democratic or Republican; but has at times faced stiff competition from other think-tanks, e.g. the American Enterprise Institute, and the (Neocon) Project for a New American Century (PNAC).

Given that Quigley's two books are about exposing a secret society, one organised on Masonic lines, it is surprising that the words 'Mason', 'Freemason' and 'Masonry' do not occur in either book.

Yet both Rhodes and Milner were Masons—a fact that Quigley omits.

Cecil Rhodes was Master at Apollo lodge No. 357, and also joined a Scottish Rite Lodge at Oxford, Prince Rose Croix Lodge No. 30.

Alfred Milner became Master at Anglo-Colonial Lodge (O'Brien, 1979, p. 247).

Masonic networks spread across the British Empire, under the authority of British Grand Lodges; they formed a cultural bond, and played an important role in consolidating the Empire.

Rhodes' Secret Society was organised on Masonic lines, having two tiers: within the 'Elect', power was held by the leader (Rhodes) and a junta of three (Stead, Brett and Milner).

However it was not officially masonic, not being subject to any Grand Lodge.

Quigley says that the society allowed him to examine its records. Given the Masonic orientation of the society, it would be reasonable to guess that Quigley was only permitted such access because he himself was a Freemason.

Many conspiracy analysts, including the present author, got a start from Executive Intelligence Review, a weekly anti-Establishment news magazine with its own global intelligence network, during its hayday in the 1990s. The writers at EIR constituted a cult centred on the guru, Lyndon H. Larouche, Jr. He had been a Trotskyist in the 1930s, who later announced that he would form a 'Fifth International'. Ex-Larouche writers later founded Asia Times, and still write there.

The Larouche view says that there is a single worldwide conspiracy controlled from Britain—meaning the Cecil Rhodes movement, the British Monarchy, the Fabian Society and the City of London, all operating as one unified conspiracy. Even though the British Empire is officially dead, Larouche literature speaks of "the new British Empire".

Note that this goes beyond Quigley. Quigley never bundled the Fabian Society into the Rhodes Group; nor did he depict Bertrand Russell or H. G. Wells as part of it, whereas Larouche literature depicted them as eminent propagandists for "The British". The Larouchites claimed that H. G. Wells and the Fabians were part of the "British" conspiracy, members of the Round Table. I reject that claim, because Wells and the Webbs were supporters of Trotsky, not Rhodes. Wells was Illuminist, not "British."

I later broke with Larouche literature because it blamed everything on "the British" and dodged the Masonic/Illuminist issue and the Jewish issue. To comprehend the conspiratorial forces at work today, the first task is to correct the errors of the Larouche movement. They were right about a "British" conspiracy—the UKUSA secret treaty and the Five Eyes intelligence network attest to it— but wrong to deny the Illuminist one.

The City of London shows up in Quigley's books as the Economist magazine, which Quigley claims for the Rhodes Group. In Larouche literature, the City shows up as the Rothschild bankers, with George Soros their affiliate in the United States.

The Nov. 13 2020 issue of Executive Intelligence Review features a headline on its front cover "Defeat the British Coup In the United States". That issue of EIR (vol. 47, #46) is at https://larouchepub.com/eiw/public/2020/2020_40-49/2020-46/eirv47n46-20201113-hi-res.pdf.

David P. Goldman, a Larouche writer who wrote for Asia Times under the pseudonym 'Spengler', spilled the beans when he broke with Lyndon Larouche. In his article Confessions Of A Coward, he revealed his Jewish identity and that of other Larouche writers, and came out as a born-again Zionist:

We were all about thirty, and most of us were Jewish. ... I had grown up as a red-diaper baby in a secular Jewish household ... I joined the left-wing Zionist youth organization Hashomer Hatzair and spent a summer on a kibbutz in Israel where the Israeli flag flew underneath the red flag of international socialism. ...

During the 1960s, LaRouche was a one-man Trotskyite splinter group, teaching free-lance courses on Marxist economics at whatever venue would have him. He culled student radicals with an intellectual bent who were repelled by the mindlessness endemic on the left in the late 1960s. ... But, Godless and faithless, we were all possessed by a fear of being Jewish, and LaRouche offered us a rock to hide under. LaRouche feigned a sort of philo-Semitism ... LaRouche's anti-Semitism was rarely in the open, but it often lurked just beneath the surface. (Goldman, 2009)

The economist Michael Hudson revealed "LaRouche cultivated Jewish followers who were breaking away from their parents (usually CP members, I think) and replaced them" (Myers, 2020/2023). Hudson helped send Laruche to prison because, he said, Larouche plagiarised his Ph. D. thesis. They were both Trotskyists; Lyndon was a devotee of Michael's father Carlos, who took part in the Minneapolis general strike of 1934. Carlos used to visit Trotsky in Mexico, driving him to Frida Kahlo's place and back. Michael Hudson says that he is Trotsky's godson.

Larouche never publicly revealed that he was a Grand Orient Freemason, or that his private war against the "British" was, in fact, against English Freemasonry.

That Lyndon Larouche was a Grand Orient Freemason is stated by John Daniel—a Larouche supporter—in his book *Scarlet and the Beast: A History of the War between English and French Freemasonry*. He writes, in a footnote: "Personal interviews with the Lyndon LaRouche campaign over a period of six years" (Daniel, 1993, p. 558, fn 2072); and in another footnote, "Personal interviews with the Lyndon LaRouche campaign. LaRouche is a Grand Orient Freemason, who claims there are good Masons and bad Masons. Ben Franklin was a good Mason, says LaRouche. LaRouche also recognizes both Freemasonries, and says that the French style is good and the British wicked. He is bent on the destruction of English Freemasonry. See dossier on LaRouche in Appendix 1" (Daniel, 1993, p. 558, fn 2073).

Andrea Bosco takes a line similar to Quigley's, in his book on the Round Table Movement:

Chatham House and the Council on Foreign Relations played, in fact, a hegemonic role in the process of formation of British and American foreign policies in the inter-war period. On the initiative of Curtis, the Round Table achieved "the strategic object" of the strengthening of Anglo-American relations "with a necessary tactical change," namely with the creation of an Anglo-American 'institutionalized' foreign policy elite. (Bosco, 2017, p. 464)

After World War II, the United States inherited the British Empire, but operated it with indirect rule rather than direct rule as Britain had done. After the end of the Cold War, it tried to extend its empire to enmesh the whole world.

Larouche literature reacted by exposing the Anglo-American ascendancy, and retrospectively took a pro-Soviet line, denying the Ukraine Famine. After Tiananmen 1989, EIR at first proclaimed it a massacre, but later reversed course and took a pro-China line. In domestic policy, Larouche literature opposed Privatisation, Deregulation, and Austerity; it stood for a National Bank funding publicly-owned infrastructure without usury, tax havens, or foreign debt; and for traditional Christian (especially Catholic) social teaching. To sum up, Left (socialist) economics and Right (conservative) social policy.

Michael Hudson's economic line is similar to Larouche's because, he says, Larouche plagiarised his Ph.D. thesis on Peshine Smith (1814—82), a pre-Civil War protectionist economist. Despite his emotional ties to Trotskyism, Hudson seems to be a protectionist.

Many EIR writers, such as F. William Engdahl, David P. Goldman ('Spengler' at Asia Times) and Pepe Escobar, later broke away but retain much of the EIR orientation, so are called 'ex-Larouche' writers. One sign that they broke away is that Engdahl writes of 'CIA' operations rather than 'British' operations, and Escobar writes of the 'U.S. Empire' not the 'British' one. Escobar did an interview with Michael Hudson, Larouche's sworn enemy.

The Jewish issue has always been the most risky for Larouche writers. Whitney Webb followed up earlier Larouche investigations of drug networks and the MEGA spy ring. She exposed Jeffrey Epstein's Mossad operation (arranging sex with underage girls for American political leaders, recording it, then blackmailing them). Her material is at unlimitedhangout.com. Ann Coulter (2022) said that the FBI found photos and CDs at Epstein's New York mansion, but did not seize them because "they only had a warrant to search the house, but not to remove evidence—evidence at the heart of the entire sex trafficking scheme".

Matthew Ehret still propagates the Larouche line today. Most people think that there's an American empire, not a British one, these days. Engdahl and Escobar agree about that; but Ehret still thinks it's the 'British' empire. Ehret spreads other Larouche errors too, which I expose below.

There are 800 American bases worldwide, including 6 American air force bases in Britain. There are no British bases in the U.S.A. There IS a way to connect the American empire to Cecil Rhodes and the Round Table, because Rhodes said he didn't mind if the capital of the Anglosphere crossed the Atlantic to the U.S.A., and if the movement was republican not monarchist. The UKUSA secret treaty and the Five Eyes intelligence network are expressions of this Anglosphere—so there IS a British conspiracy of sorts, except that now it's an American conspiracy.

Larouche writers insisted that the United States was being colonised by Britain; but Robert F. Kennedy, Jr. wrote that, after World War II, the United States dismantled the British Empire, and instead imposed its own "soft colonization":

> In August 1941, President Franklin Roosevelt forced Winston Churchill to sign the Atlantic Charter as a condition for U.S. support of the Allied effort in World War II. The Charter—a heartening emblem of American idealism—required the European allies to relinquish their colonies following the war. ... The continent, however, quickly reopened to "soft colonization" by multinational corporations and their state sponsors. During the Cold War, the U.S. military and intelligence agencies largely replaced Europe's colonial armies in those regions, supporting virtually any tinhorn dictator who proved his "anti-Communist" bona fides by rolling out red carpets for U.S. multinationals. (Kennedy, Robert F., Jr., 2021, p. 293)

If one subtracts the 'reptilian' theme from David Icke's writings, his line is very similar to Larouche's. Dr John Coleman's line is also similar to Larouche's. Larouche publications call the Green movement 'Nazi' (they say Hitler was a Green) or brand it a 'British' conspiracy. They oppose the Club of Rome's de-industrialisation agenda, and promote nuclear power, especially new types of reactors.

Living Marxism Magazine, renamed LM Magazine and now Spiked Online, takes a line very similar to Larouche publications. LM grew out of the (Trotskyist) Revolutionary Communist Party, and was substantially Jewish, like the early Larouche movement. But the two groups differ in that LM/Spiked is pro-Zionist, and Spiked writers have been published in the Times of London and Rupert Murdoch's The Australian—both being strongly Zionist.

Against Larouche, I maintain that the Communist movement comes from Adam Weishaupt's Illuminati, not from the British. It participated in the French Revolution, the Revolution of 1848, the Paris Commune, and early Bolshevism. H.G. Wells' campaign for a Cosmopolitan World State is Illuminist, not British.

Stalin overthrew the Jewish Bolsheviks, and took Communism in a different direction, which China under Xi Jinping has inherited. The anti-Stalin 'Trotskyoid' Left, which Stalin defeated in Russia, has consolidated in the West and largely overthrown the Christian order via the so-called Culture War. That Culture War is Illuminist, not British.

I define 'Trotskyoid' as follows:

Trotskyoids are Communists or Communist fellow-travellers in Trotsky's camp but not necessarily orthodox and not necessarily members of a Trotskyist organisation, who repudiate Stalin and who support a Gramsciist strategy of cultural subversion, that is, a "march through the Institutions" to destroy Western civilisation from the inside, using the Universities as seminaries of subversion, or the Media, Courts or other cultural instruments. This Gramsciist strategy follows Gramsci's unconventional Marxism in attacking the "infrastructure" (in Marxist terminology) rather than the economic "base".

Isaac Deutscher is an example of a Trotskyoid writer. He is Trotsky's leading interpreter in the West; his 3-volume biography of Trotsky calls him a 'Prophet'. Deutscher was an original thinker, not someone who followed a party line. He is sometimes erroneously called a 'Stalinist' because he credited the Soviet Union with achieving some sort of socialism, even though it was "deformed", whereas hardline Trotskyists refuse to say anything good about it at all.

But Deutscher kept hoping and predicting that it would abandon Stalinism {"vulgar Marxism") and return to Trotskyism ("classical Marxism"). In the same way, Trotsky, defending the Soviet Union as a "deformed workers' state", hoped to return as leader after Stalin's clash with Hitler, during which, he envisaged, both would be overthrown; this may be why Stalin had him killed.

On December 4, 1939, Trotsky published in his Bulletin of the Opposition an article The Twin-Stars: Hitler-Stalin, in which he noted that in the event of war between Hitler and Stalin, both might be swept away by revolutions. He quoted the French ambassador's comment to Hitler, "In case of war the real victor would be Trotsky" (Volkogonov, 1996, p. 342). Volkogonov comments, "he believed that the world war might end in world revolution, and then the sixty-year-old revolutionary might get his last historical chance" (p. 343).

Deutscher was employed by the Economist magazine during the 1930s and 40s. Given that the Gramsciist attack is cultural, not targeting capitalists *per se*, some capitalists have been in league with it, such as David Rockefeller and George Soros; the Economist magazine of recent decades is also on board.

The Deutscher Prize is awarded annually for an innovative book in the Marxist tradition; its winners are announced in the London Review of Books, and the recipient presents the Deutscher Memorial Lecture at the London School of Economics. Deutscher lectures often are published in New Left Review, which is a Trotskyoid publication; authors regularly published in New Left Review, given its clear pro-Trotsky stance, are also Trotskyoid by this definition.

The Frankfurt School's synthesis of Marx and Freud was pioneered by Trotsky himself. They are not Trotskyist in the narrow 'party' sense, but they are Trotskyoid in the wider culture-war sense. Most were Jewish; and also Zionists (see p. 108). Trotsky's book *The Revolution Betrayed* berates Stalin for restoring God and the Family, whereas he (Trotsky) aspired to turn wives against husbands and children against parents. The destruction of the Family in the West has Trotskyist pedigree.

Putin, meanwhile, has re-established Christianity in Russia. The new Cold War is between the atheistic, LGBT, Trotskyoid, Cosmopolitan West, and a coalition of Christian-socialist Russia and Confucian-Stalinist China.

Two Conspiracies—British and Illuminist

What about Antifa and Black Lives Matter and affiliated groups, toppling statues of American founding fathers and even calling for Cecil Rhodes' statue to be removed?

These are not done by "the British", but by Trotskyists and Anarchists (not to be confused with the Libertarian Left) funded by George Soros. Don't be fooled about Antifa: behind those black masks are many Trotskyists.

In this video, Antifa masked protestors chant "Soros, Soros, where's our Money? Soros, Soros, where's our Money?" Watch the video at https://mailstar.net/Antifa-Soros-Where-is-Money.mp4. Could the sound have been dubbed? No, because two of the Antifa protestors are moving their hands in sync with the music. It was originally uploaded at truthseeker, August 18, 2017. This video has been deleted from a num-

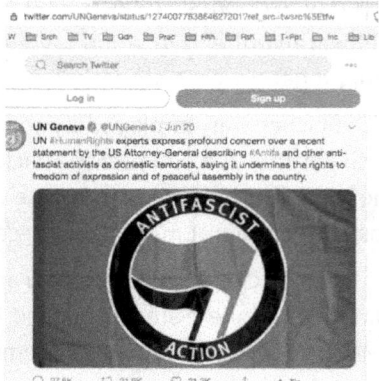

ber of sites. I found it at https://www.youtube.com/watch?v=UBmuDDm_CuM, and uploaded it to my website on July 7, 2019. Just as well, because Youtube has since deleted it.

Amidst the riots following the death of George Floyd, the Economist magazine, part Rothschild-owned, welcomed the toppling of the statue of Edward Colston, commenting, "Its toppling helps to redress Britain's selective historical memory":

https://www.economist.com/britain/2020/06/11/the-colston-statue-and-britains-legacy-of-slavery

Black Lives Matter protests
The Colston statue and Britain's legacy of slavery
Its toppling helps to redress Britain's selective historical memory Britain

Jun 11th 2020 edition Jun 11th 2020

... Other historical figures were soon under attack. The authorities removed the statue of Robert Milligan, another slaver, from London's docklands. Graffiti on Winston Churchill's plinth in Parliament Square accused him of being a racist. The long-running campaign to remove the statue of Cecil Rhodes from outside Oriel College, Oxford, roared back to life. The Labour Party announced on June 9th that the councils it controls in England and Wales will reassess the "appropriateness" of their monuments.

A Leader (editorial) opined that the statue of Cecil Rhodes should be removed from outside Oriel College, Oxford, and placed in a museum:

https://www.economist.com/leaders/2020/06/11/how-to-handle-racists-statues

Reckoning with the past
How to handle racists' statues
Should they stay or should they go?

Leaders Jun 11th 2020 edition Jun 11th 2020

Statues become flashpoints at times of social change because they honour the values, and reflect the hierarchies, of the times in which they were erected. ... As a rule, someone whose failings were subordinate to their claim to greatness should stay, whereas someone whose main contribution to history was baleful should go. ...

Cecil Rhodes is a harder case. He was not the worst imperialist, but he drove many black people off their land. He left a huge, grubby fortune to charity. His statue is on private property, so the choice rests with Oriel College, Oxford. It ought to put him in a museum.

The Economist's casting out of Rhodes calls to mind the 'British Conspiracy' theory of the Larouche movement. If the British Imperialists are behind the woke movement, then they are casting themselves out. But if the Illuminati Globalists are behind it, it means that there are TWO conspiracies—the British one and the Illuminist one; and that one is overthrowing the other. It is not Rhodes, but Rothschild, who rules.

American Blacks are often bundled with Jews as fellow victims of discrimination. But they also experience Jews as landlords, and in Black organisations partly run by Jews. Friction led to the formation of a group called Blacks and Jews. They published historical surveys stating that Jews were among the most important slave dealers. In response, Jewish apologists wrote angry rebuttals.

One thing the Economist seems not to have called for, is an apology for the role of Jewish banking families in forcing China to accept imports of opium. The Sassoons, for example, were known as the 'Rothschilds of the East' (Kienholz, 2008, p. 6).

Nor has the Economist acknowledged the Jewish role in early Bolshevism; instead, it has denied it.

Matthew Ehret follows Larouche in treating H. G Wells, Bertrand Russell and the Fabians as members of the Round Table, all equally part of the Rhodes conspiracy. In his article H. G. Wells' Dystopic Vision Comes Alive With The Great Reset Agenda, he wrote:

> H. G Wells, Russell and other early social engineers of this new priesthood organized themselves in several interconnected think tanks known as 1) the Fabian Society of Sidney and Beatrice Webb which operated through the London School of Economics, 2) the Round Table Movement begun by ... Cecil Rhodes ... and finally 3) the Co-Efficients Club of London.

> As noted by Georgetown Professor Carol Quigley, in his 1981 The Anglo-American Establishment, membership in all three organizations was virtually interchangeable. (Ehret, 2020)

Ehret's statement "As noted by Georgetown Professor Carol Quigley, in his 1981 The Anglo-American Establishment, membership in all three organizations was virtually interchangeable" is not borne out by the text.

Searches of the index of the print version of The Anglo-American Establishment (Quigley, 1981), and text searches of the online version (https://archive.org/details/carrollquigley_angloamericanestablishment) show that

(1) the only occurrence of the word 'coefficient'—actually 'Coefficients'—is on pp. 137-8 (print), p. 118 (pdf)

Quigley states there that Milner attended dinners of the Coefficients, but in a private capacity. He does not say that the Coefficients were members of the Round Table:

> Milner was the creator of the Round Table Group (since this is but another name for the Kindergarten) and remained in close personal contact with it for the rest of his life. In the sketch of Milner in the Dictionary of

National Biography, written by Basil Williams of the Kindergarten, we read: "He was always ready to discuss national questions on a non-party basis, joining with former members of his South African 'Kindergarten' in their 'moot' from which originated the political review, The Round Table, and in a more heterogeneous society, the 'Coefficients,' where he discussed social and imperial problems with such curiously assorted members as L. S. Amery, H. G. Wells, (Lord) Haldane, Sir Edward Grey, (Sir) Michael Sadler, Bernard Shaw, J. L. Garvin, William Pember Reeves, and W. A. S. Hewins (Quigley, 1981, p. 137).

(2) Nowhere does Quigley mention the Fabian Society. The only occurrences of the word 'Fabian' relate to Sir Fabian Ware.

But 'Webb, Sidney' has an entry on p. 131 (print), where Quigley says, 'On 12 September of the same year, he wrote to his son, the present Viscount Esher: "There are things that cannot be confiscated by the Smillies and Sidney Webbs. These seem to me the real objectives."' (Quigley, 1981, p. 131).

The statement Ehret made does express Larouche's view, but not Quigley's view.

In an article titled The Origins of the Deep State in North America Part 1: The Round Table Movement , Ehret wrote that the Round Table movement "worked in tandem with the Coefficients Club, the Fabian Society, and the Rhodes Trust, all of whom witnessed members moving in and out of each others ranks":

The Round Table movement ... worked in tandem with the Coefficients Club, the Fabian Society, and the Rhodes Trust, all of whom witnessed members moving in and out of each others ranks. The historian Carrol Quigley, of Georgetown University wrote of this cabal in his posthumously published "Anglo-American Establishment" (6):

"This organization has been able to conceal its existence quite successfully, and many of its most influential members, satisfied to possess the reality rather than the appearance of power, are unknown even to close students of British history. This is the more surprising when we learn that one of the chief methods by which this Group works has been through propaganda." (Ehret, 2019)

In footnote 15, Ehret states "fn. 15: (15) Notable Coefficients who were also be Fabians: Lord Alfred Milner, Sir Arthur Balfour, Lord Robert Cecil, Lord Bertrand Russell, H.G. Wells (protégé of Thomas Huxley), Leo .S Amery and Sir Edward Grey."

The history of the Fabian Society is covered in McBriar (1966).

Russell resigned from the Fabian Society in 1903 (Clarke, 1984); Wells left the Fabian Society in 1908 (McBriar, 1966, p. 322). The others listed by Ehret as members of the Fabian Society do not show up in McBriar (1966). But, since they were prominent people, this surely indicates that they were never members of the Fabian Society.

In the above quote, when Quigley refers to "this organization", he means the Round Table Group, which he calls the Anglo-American Establishment. He does not include the Fabian Society in it; nor the Coefficients Club.

Russell resigned from the Coefficients Club in 1903, complaining that Edward Grey's policies would lead to war. Russell was in the Coefficients Club for less than 2 years; he was never a member of the Round Table.

Quigley (1981), in his history of the Round Table (Milner group), does not list Wells as a member of the Round Table, but only lists him as a member of the Coefficients Club, which operated 1902-1909.

The Round Table groups began in 1909. Neither Wells nor Russell were members of the Fabian Society at that time.

Matthew Ehret also claims that Lord Milner, head of the Round Table, helped create Bolshevism:

> https://matthewehret.substack.com/p/why-putin-criticized-the-bolshevik
>
> Why Putin Criticized the Bolshevik Counter Revolution: Trotsky, Parvus and the War on Civilization
> Matthew Ehret
> Nov 2, 2021
>
> Leon Trotsky, who Lord Milner, Schiff, Paul Warburg etc always intended to be the leader of the movement that would take control over the dead bodies of the Romanovs, was fortunately ousted by the saner forces around Joseph Stalin in 1927.

Here, Ehret says that Lord Milner funded the Bolsheviks:

> https://canadianpatriot.org/2022/09/13/why-putin-criticized-the-bolshevik-counter-revolution-trotsky-parvus-and-the-war-on-civilization-2/
>
> Why Putin Criticized the Bolshevik Counter Revolution: Trotsky, Parvus and the War on Civilization
> By Matthew Ehret
> Posted On September 13, 2022
>
> Upon deeper analysis conducted by historians like Anthony Sutton, Kerry Bolton, and Robert Cowley, both organizations which eventually merged into a singular force, enjoyed vast financial patronage of western imperial powerhouses such as Paul Warburg, Jacob Schiff (head of Kuhn, Loeb & co.) and even Lord Alfred Milner—head of the newly formed Round Table Movement.

Ehret is wrong about Milner supporting the Bolsheviks. In early 1917, Milner had supported the February Revolution, but later he supported an attempted coup by General Korniloff (Gollin, pp. 550-1). This backfired, because Alexander Kerensky released the Bolshevik prisoners, including Trotsky, to fend off the coup (Volkogonov, 1996, p. 74). Kerensky opposed the Whites more than he opposed the Reds.

Kerensky (1927/2008) revealed that Lord Milner, Minister in the Lloyd George government, had encouraged the coup by Korniloff: :

> On the streets of Moscow pamphlets were being distributed, entitled "Korniloff, the National Hero." These pamphlets were printed at the expense of the British Military Mission and had been brought to Moscow from the British Embassy in Petrograd in the railway carriage of General Knox, British military attache. At about this time, Aladin, a former labor member of the Duma, arrived from England, whither he had fled in 1906, after the dissolution of the first Duma. In London this once famous politician lost his entire political baggage and became an extremely suspicious adventurer. This discredited man brought to General Korniloff a letter from Lord Milner, British War Minister, expressing his approval of a military dictatorship in Russia and giving his blessing to the enterprise. This letter naturally served to encourage the conspirators greatly (p. 315).

Bruce Lockhart was pro-Trotsky, but in his *Memoirs Of A British Agent* (Lockhart, 1933) he states clearly that Milner was not pro-Bolshevik. Milner opposed the Bolshevik government, but endorsed having contact with their leaders. Lockhart and Raymond Robins functioned as unofficial ambassadors of Britain and the U.S.A.; both were pro-Trotsky, and had unfettered access to Trotsky. Lockhart wrote of Milner:

> "I find it hard to write of Lord Milner in anything but superlatives. ... He believed in the highly organised state, in which service, efficiency, and hard work were more important than titles or money-bags. He had little respect for the aristocrat, who was effete, and none at all for the financier, who had made his money not by production but by manipulation of the market" (Lockhart, 1933, p. 207).

> "He had arranged my Russian mission, not because he had anything but a profound abhorrence of Bolshevism, but because he believed that I understood the Russian situation better than most Englishmen. He was probably disappointed when I seemed to go over body and soul to the Bolsheviks" (p. 208).

Illuminists come out into the open

Manly P. Hall wrote that "Freemasonry is a fraternity within a fraternity—an outer organization concealing an inner brotherhood of the elect ... two separate yet interdependent orders, the one visible and the other invisible" (Hall, 2018, p.

1). A comparison would be the relationship between the underground Communist Party and the above-ground one. The visible Masonic groups were the Blue Lodges (degrees 1-3), which were not conspiratorial, and unaware that they were being used as a cover by the invisible lodges—the Red Lodges, one might call them.

During the nineteenth century, Illuminists operated through invisible Masonic lodges to overthrow Church and State. But as Globalisation took hold, their movement has operated openly through bodies such as the CFR, the Club of Rome, the Bilderberger Group, the Trilateral Commission, the World Economic Forum, Tax-free Foundations, and United Nations committees and courts. They do not control the U.N. General Assembly, or the Security Council (because of the veto); however they do control some important U.N. officials and committees. The W.H.O. is now funded by the Gates Foundation and the Rockefeller Foundation.

That the Globalist movement is Illuminist is ascertained by comparing its values and goals with those of Adam Weishaupt. His goals (see p. 53) were:

- the destruction of religions (i.e. atheism, ridicule of religions, satanism, luciferianism)
- the destruction of the family (i.e. marriage, parental rights, LGBT)
- the destruction of nation states (free trade, immigration, a borderless world)
- One World (rule by unelected U. N. Committees).

'Anacharsis' Cloots pursued such goals during the French Revolution.

Illuminism had some influence during the French Revolution, but it was not the dominant influence. Robespierre was a deist (following Rousseau), and inaugurated the Cult of The Supreme Being. He executed Cloots, partly on account of his atheism, and partly because Cloots was an internationalist, who favoured extending the war to other European countries—something which Marx praised. Robespierre was a nationalist, and this sums up the difference between the French Revolution and the Illuminists; but their time was coming.

Babeuf followed Weishaupt's strategy, and developed the first communist organisation in the late part of the French Revolution. One indication of Weishaupt's disciples is their name-change to a 'classical' name. Weishaupt changed his name to 'Spartacus', Cloots changed his to 'Anacharsis', Babeuf changed his to 'Gracchus'.

Buonarroti wrote the history of Babeuf's struggle, and transmitted the legacy. Marx and Engels took it up. Trotsky continued the same goals. H. G. Wells continued them. George Soros continued them in recent times. And Klaus Schwab sounds if they are his goals too.

Adam Weishaupt was not 'British'; the Kalergi Plan is not 'British'; Klaus Schwab is not British. Therefore, better see them as Illuminist rather than 'British'.

This does not mean that they passed through numerous Masonic degrees. There is no proof that they have joined a secret society. That they are Illuminist can reasonably be imputed (inferred), but not proven. Why should Ockham's Razor be allowed use of, to refuse this appellation, given that the Illuminati did in the past operate as a secret society, and Freemasonry still does so, and these modern 'Illuminati' match Weishaupt's goals? They are Globalist in their ideas, their aspirations, and their loyalties, and they also support Weishaupt's anti-family policy.

Weishaupt was based in Frankfurt, Germany. That was also the base of the Rothschilds—their name means "Red Shield". And it was the base of the Frankfurt School, which has demolished our universities. May Day, on May 1 each year, celebrates the founding of the Illuminati.

There WAS a British Conspiracy: it created the British Empire, but exists today only as the Anglosphere.

Speaking about Immigration, Joe Biden said in a youtube video of Feb 2015:

https://www.youtube.com/watch?v=UgrliuQW_-Q .

"the wave still continues. It's not going to stop. Nor should we want it to stop. As a matter of fact, …um It's one of the things we are most proud of. There is a second thing in that black box, an unrelenting stream of immigration. Non-stop. Non-stop. Folks like me who are Caucasian or European descent, for the first time in 2017, we will be an absolute minority in the United States of America. Absolute Minority. Fewer than 50% of the people in America from then and on, will be White European stock. That's not a bad thing; that's the source of our strength."

Biden's policy is not 'British'; it's Illuminist.

It is not racist to oppose Open-Border immigration; even migrants want limits to immigration. Mass immigration harms the wages and job security of the working and middle classes. I uploaded the Biden video to https://mailstar.net/mailstar.net/Biden-immigration-nonstop.mp4.

Cecil Rhodes wrote in his "Confession of Faith" of 1877:

"I contend that we are the finest race in the world and that the more of the world we inhabit the better it is for the human race. Just fancy those parts that are at present inhabited by the most despicable specimens of human beings … I contend that every acre added to our territory means in the future birth to some more of the English race" (Flint, 1976, pp. 248-9).

Yes, it's shockingly racist. But Zionism is no less racist. You can criticise some but not others; critics of Israel are branded 'antisemitic', and ostracised. The WOKE crowd want to remove statues of Rhodes—with the approval of The Economist.

The Deep State is Illuminist too. The CFR and other "British" institutions were originally set up as British, but they've been taken over by Illuminists. Rothschild, not Rhodes, calls the tune.

On top of the Supreme Court building in Israel is an Illuminati pyramid with an all-seeing Eye, just like on the back of the U.S. $1 bill. This pyramid is not visible from the street, but it can be seen from the tops  of surrounding buildings, and from planes. Under the pyramid is a staircase with 3 flights of 10 stairs each, making 30. Then there are 3 levels of the Library, making 33 levels beneath the pyramid, matching the 33 degrees of Freemasonry. The Library is for the use of the Judges; the pyramid ostensibly channels enlightenment down to them. Thanks to Roy Tov (now deceased) for this photo.

At the bottom of the building is a plaque stating that the Rothschild family designed and funded the building. A painting at the entrance shows members of the Rothschild family with Shimon Peres, Yitzhak Rabin, and a model of the building. The pyramid has never been shown in the mainstream media. Thanks to Vigilant Citizen for the photo.

THE UK Supreme Court also features an All-Seeing Eye, but the symbolism is less blatant. In both cases, it's Illuminist—not "British".

George Soros appears to be a Freemason of 33rd Degree, indicated by the address of Soros Fund Management at 888 7th Avenue, 33rd Floor, New York, NY

10106. The company address was given in this profile: https://mailstar.net/Soros-888-33rd-Floor.png.

Soros is wealthy enough to have chosen any address. The fact that he chose an address on the 33rd floor is probably a sign to Masons that he is a Mason of 33º, the moreso because the 888 also has Masonic significance. Amazon lists a "888 Graphics Masonic Freemason Compass Golf Hat Clip"; 888 Graphics also sell, at Amazon, a 888 skull hat clip and a Baphomet Lucifer Devil Golf Hat Clip. 888 Graphics sell, at Sears, a Baphomet winestopper (Myers, 2022). Once again, a connection between Freemasonry and Baphomet, the god of Androgyny.

Soros' address should be connected to the Illuminati pyramid on the Supreme Court of Israel, designed and funded by the Rothschilds.

Soros created the European Council of Foreign Relations—it's not British, it's Illuminist. So are the Kalergi Plan and the E.U. You can topple statues of Rhodes, but talking about Rothschild power or that of other Jewish bankers is taboo.

Stalin stole the Jewish Bolsheviks' conspiracy, and gave the Old Bolsheviks a taste of their own medicine. A century later, after Soros and Gorbachev got rid of Stalinism, the Green Left is taking us back towards Old Bolshevism.

H. G. Wells—Illuminist not 'British'

William Engdahl shows his Larouche pedigree when he misquotes H. G. Wells on Cecil Rhodes, making Wells out to be a racist:

http://www.williamengdahl.com/englishNEO3Apr2017.php

Brexit: Securing a New English-speaking Union?
By F. William Engdahl
3 April 2017

Agreeing with Cecil Rhodes, the founder of the Round Table's fraternity, H.G. Wells stressed that the coming world order must be based on cooperation, "between all the western peoples and, more particularly, between all the Nordic peoples," by which he meant Anglo-Saxon and racially kindred peoples.

The above statement by Engdahl implies that "between all the western peoples and, more particularly, between all the Nordic peoples," was written by Wells as his own view. But Wells was saying that this was *Rhodes'* view. Wells agreed in part, but Wells' comment that Rhodes was "warped by prejudices and uncritical assumptions" is omitted by Engdahl.

This is what Wells actually wrote of Rhodes, in *Experiment in Autobiography, volume 2*:

A man I never met, who must have been a very curious mixture of large conceptions and strange ignorances, was Cecil Rhodes. ... Much the same ideas that were running through my brain round about 1900, of a great English-speaking English-thinking synthesis, leading mankind by sheer force of numbers, wealth, equipment and scope, to a progressive unity, must have been running through his brain also. He was certainly no narrow worshipper of the Union Jack, no abject devotee of the dear Queen Empress. The institution of the Rhodes scholarships which transcended any existing political boundaries and aimed plainly at a sort of common understanding and co-operation between all the western peoples and more particularly between all the "Nordic" peoples—he was at just about the level of ethnological understanding to believe in Nordic superiority—indicates a real greatness of intention, though warped by prejudices and uncritical assumptions (Wells 1934/1969, pp. 759-60).

Writing during a period of Nordic dominance, Wells was trying to persuade the Nordics to give up their empires, and acquiesce in a World State. If he had told them that there would be mass immigration into Europe from the third world, they would have rejected his ideas. He had to disguise them; he did the same when encouraging the Germans to surrender during World War I, and when preaching 'Convergence' to Stalin in 1934.

His son Geoffrey Wells, writing under the name Geoffrey West, attests to this strategy during World War I:

He also followed Wilson in urging the official declaration of Allied war-aims, and this was one of the first points he brought forward when, early in 1918, at Lord Northcliffe's invitation, he joined the Enemy Propaganda Committee established at Crewe House. At the beginning of May he became first director of propaganda policy against Germany ... As Director of Propaganda he was willing to promise whatever would bring Germany to surrender. (West, Geoffrey, 1930, pp. 223-4)

Wells, like Trotsky, advocated Open Borders and envisaged mass immigration

The bottom line is that Wells, like Trotsky, advocated Open Borders and envisaged mass immigration. Wells claimed that, once borders were opened, people would most likely stay where they were; but of course this is not what happened. The Great Replacement of European populations neutralises all of Wells' assurances, but fits Trotsky's vision perfectly.

Wells spelled out what Open Borders would mean in terms of migration, in his book *After Democracy*:

Given peace on earth and abundance for all, will there not be a rapid and indeed a frightful increase of population and a great clash of races? Here again I must answer in a sentence or so. As World dictator I should see to it that the kind of knowledge which leads to a restriction of population is spread throughout the whole world. That secured, I do not think mankind need fear over-population. Nor do I think the races of mankind are going to devour one another. There is not going to be any great overrunning of peoples. The climatic regions of the earth determine the character of their human populations. The negro did not capture tropical Africa; tropical Africa made him and gave herself to him: for keeps, I think. The brownish peoples again hold the sub-tropical world by virtue of their superior adaptation to that world; similarly the whites the rainy temperate zone, and the Mongols dry Asia. So it seems to me. There may be a lot of marginal admixture; there may be replacement with altered conditions: but my World Dictatorship at any rate will be untroubled by the nightmare of racial swarmings. Men in the coming future will find that when they are free to move wherever they choose about our planet they will for the most part stay in the habitats congenial to them. When they know how to limit their increases they will limit them. The great migrations of the past have been hunger marches, and my economic controls and my population controls will have put an end to such disturbances. (Wells, 1932a, pp. 200-201)

In an interview with the Jewish Telegraphic Agency on January 18, 1937, Trotsky canvassed the possibility of mass migration:

Socialism will open the possibility of great migrations on the basis of the most developed technique and culture. It goes without saying that what is here involved is not compulsory displacements, that is, the creation of new ghettos for certain nationalities, but displacements freely consented to, or rather demanded, by certain nationalities or parts of nationalities. The dispersed Jews who would want to be reassembled in the same community will find a sufficiently extensive and rich spot under the sun. The same possibility will be opened for the Arabs, as for all other scattered nations. National topography will become a part of the planned economy. This is the great historic perspective as I see it. To work for international Socialism means to work also for the solution of the Jewish question. (Nedava, 1972, p. 205).

Illuminists pushed for World Government at the Peace Conference of Versailles, but British opposed it

The Treaty of Versailles, in 1919, was an opportunity to launch a World Government. That was the policy of the Left, including H. G. Wells, but it was NOT the policy of Milner or the Round Table.

Wells put this proposal for the League of Nations:

His plans for a League of Free Nations had been bold and far-reaching. Britain would have had to give up her Empire and her navy, and become a republic. Every nation in the world would have been admitted, and the League would in effect have controlled the world's armed forces, and would have been public trustee for the world. (Dickson, 1969, p. 322)

Wells' son Geoffrey Wells, under the name Geoffrey West, reported:

Wells conceived a League genuinely controlling all armed forces, to be, in fact, public trustee for the world. Inevitably it would supersede the British Empire, and he urged his countrymen to face and accept the fact. (West, Geoffrey, 1930, p. 222)

When the League did not turn out that way, "His conclusion was that a League of Nations leading to a World State could grow to reality only out of a soil of world-history." (West, Geoffrey, 1930, p. 225) And so, Wells wrote a history of the world; however, it was largely ghost-written by experts he enticed to join the project.

By 1920, Wells turned against the League, because "one wanted not a League of Nations, but a league to suppress nationalism. The League stood for nationalism, he for the World State" (West, Geoffrey, 1930, p. 231).

Wells was calling on ALL NATIONS to surrender—not just Germany. He made this explicit in 1918: "Three years and a half ago a few of us were saying this was a war against the idea of imperialism, not German imperialism merely, but British and French and Russian imperialism, and we were saying this not because it was so, but because we hoped to see it become so. To-day we can say so, because now it is so." (Wells, 1918/2003, p. vi).

They would all surrender, and a World State would emerge in their place. But what it would be like, no-one can say. It might save us from disasters, but it might be a tyranny. What do promises matter, once there is total monopoly of power and news, and nowhere to escape to?

Wells accused Sir Edward Grey of precipitating World War I, not in a 'Make it happen' way but a 'Let it happen' way: "It is charged against him that he did not definitely warn Germany that we should certainly come into the war, that he was sufficiently ambiguous to let her take a risk and attack, and that he did this deliberately. I think that charge is sound" (Wells, 1934/1969, p. 770).

He despaired of Grey's presence at Versailles: "When I was working for the creation of a League of Nations Union, it was with a sort of despair that I found that everyone in the movement was insisting on the necessity of having Grey for our figurehead. For him a League of Nations was necessarily a League of Foreign Offices" (Wells, 1934/1969, p. 771}.

Compare this with the position of the Milner Group, per Quigley: 'In the leading article of the September 1920 issue, The Round Table took up the same problem and repeated many of its arguments. It blamed Wilson for corrupting the Covenant into "a pseudo world-government'" (Quigley, 1981, p. 256).

Quigley says that the Group did not want the League of Nations to be a World Government, with its own army and able to command the governments of its member states. Instead the Round Table view was that their consent would be required for League actions.

"The Milner Group never intended that the League should be used as an instrument of collective security or that sanctions should be used as an instrument by the League. From the beginning, they expected only two things from the League: (1) that it could be used as a center for international cooperation in international administration in nonpolitical matters, and (2) that it could be used as a center for consultation in political matters" (Quigley, 1981, p. 248-9).

Yearwood (2009) examined British policy on the League at the Conference of Versailles. G. N. Barnes, a Labour member of the War Cabinet, was chairman of the League to Abolish War. In May 1918 he gave a speech in honour of Karl Marx, calling for an Allied conference at which workers would participate.

"For many on The Left the league was to embody the universal will for peace, which had been betrayed, and would continue to be betrayed, by governments controlled by elite interests. Therefore it must not be left in the hands of governments. It had instead to be a popular institution ... representative not of cabinets but of peoples" (Yearwood, 2009, p. 100).

But they knew that the Elite "would not create a super-state capable of overriding national governments in the interest of some general will of all humanity" (p. 100).

One Left proposal was for a popular assembly; another was for international courts "to replace, as much as possible, the political process by a judicial one ... Therefore the road to peace lay in requiring states to submit disputes to tribunals which could make and enforce decisions on the grounds of justice or equity" (pp. 100-101).

But "the British government firmly opposed it. London's own plans centred on conferences or councils, not on courts ... compulsory arbitration had no place in British plans for the league ... they would not commit themselves to go to war to impose a judgement the justice or expediency of which they doubted" (Yearwood, 2009, p. 101).

France wanted the League to have a standing army and a general staff, but David Lloyd George argued that the League 'must not be constituted as a body with executive power' (p. 105). Lord Robert Cecil headed the British delegation, and took the Foreign Office view of the league as a diplomatic instrument, not an executive body.

Andrea Bosco, citing Lionel Curtis, says this was the Round Table position:

The Round Table always opposed the League as an instrument of collective security through sanctions, and envisaged it as a centre for multilateral diplomacy and international co-operation on the basis of voluntary agreements. Curtis pointed out even more clearly that the Peace Conference did not have the mandate "to produce a written constitution for the globe or a genuine government for mankind," and that "if the burden of a world government" was placed on an association of sovereign nations, it would "fall with a crash." On the base of national sovereignty it was not possible to establish more than "a permanent annual conference between foreign ministers ... with a permanent secretariat ... in which all questions at issue between States can be discussed and, if possible, settled by agreement." (Bosco, 2017, p. 371)

The Second International held a conference at Berne, calling for the League

to be parliamentary rather than governmental; it should include the defeated powers from the start, with equal rights and duties for all nations; it should protect peoples who had not yet achieved independence, ... should abolish standing armies, and eventually achieve complete disarmament—until that was done, it should have use of the remaining armed forces, as well as of economic means of pressure; it should settle disputes by mediation, and by the arbitration of an International Court; it should control tariffs, promote free trade, and control also the production and distribution of foodstuffs and raw materials. (Yearwood, 2009, p. 122)

Was this what Wells was advocating? He did not seek parliamentary rule, but something like early Bolshevism, or rule by U. N. Committees of Experts. Wells wanted the World State to be unitary, not federal. He thought that the only way to unite humanity was to get rid of countries altogether; therefore a federation of countries would not work. W. Warren Wagar, a supporter of Wells' plan for Cosmopolis, also opposed World Federalism. Its only merit, he said, is that is easier to 'sell' to those fearful of giving up their sovereignty:

'Federalism itself is something of a myth. This is the constitutional formula by which "minimal" powers will be delegated to the world authority, and all others reserved to the self-governing states' (Wagar, 1971, p. 33).

In proposing that the League of Nations be a World Government, Wells was not speaking for the Round Table or for the British Government. Rather, this proposal was a Left position in keeping with Weishaupt's goal of replacing countries and governments with One World. The One World movement comes from Weishaupt and the Illuminati, not from the British.

Wells' Open Conspiracy is an Illuminati program

Wells' Open Conspiracy is an Illuminati program. It does not come from the Rhodes movement; but the Rhodes movement has been infiltrated by the Illuminati. George Soros and the Rothschilds are Illuminati, no longer in the Rhodes camp. Soros funded Antifa, and the Economist applauded the toppling of statues.

Bill Clinton signed up to join the International Criminal Court, just before he left office; George W. Bush cancelled the initiative. The former is Illuminati, the latter consistent with Rhodes' values.

The E.U. is an Illuminist project—not British, but Illuminati. Brexit is in keeping with Rhodes's values. The Illuminati are partly Jewish and partly Masonic; calling them 'British' only muddies the waters. Globalist politicians toe the Illuminati line.

Larouche literature mostly portrays the Jewish lobby as a tool of the British. It does not talk about the Balfour Declaration, because that's a case where the Zionist tail wags the British dog. But there's one place where Larouche literature treats the Lobby as an independent and powerful body, in their book *The Ugly Truth about the Anti-Defamation League*. They accuse the ADL, an Order of Jewish Freemasonry, of uprooting Christianity and fostering the New Age religion:

> While the ADL has concentrated upon uprooting the traditions of Western Christian civilization from public life—e.g. by throwing Christianity out the front door of schools—it has not protested as "New Age religion" has been ushered in the back door, now to permeate society. (Executive Intelligence Review, 1992, p. 105)

They note Masonic penetration of the Supreme Court:

> During the period of time when the attention of the Court seemed to focus on religion-clause cases, roughly 1949-56, seven members of the Craft served on the Court along with a former Mason, Justice Sherman Minion. Masons continued to dominate the Court, while most of the decisions to uproot Christianity were made, until 1971. The Southern Jurisdiction of Scottish Rite Freemasonry, to which the preponderance of Supreme Court justices belonged from the period of 1939 to 1971, is the self-described "New Age" Jurisdiction. (p. 106)

and they also tackle the Jewish lobby:

> unless the power of the Zionist lobby is cut down to size, any newly elected Congress will be like lambs walking to the slaughter. (p. 122)

The Balfour Declaration was NOT a matter of the British creating the Jewish lobby. Rather, that lobby was playing off the two sides, German and British, to exact the best price for its financial support; the sought price being Palestine.

David Lloyd George wrote of the Balfour Declaration, in his book *Memoirs of the Peace Conference*, Volume II, chapter XXIII:

> Russian Jews had been secretly active on behalf of the Central Powers from the first; they had become the chief agents of German pacifist propaganda in Russia; by 1917 they had done much in preparing for that general disintegration of Russian society, later recognised as the Revolution. It was believed that if Great Britain declared for the fulfilment of Zionist aspirations in Palestine under her own pledge, one effect would be to bring Russian Jewry to the cause of the Entente.
>
> It was believed, also, that such a declaration would have a potent influence upon world Jewry outside Russia, and secure for the Entente the aid of Jewish financial interests. In America, their aid in this respect would have a special value when the Allies had almost exhausted the gold and marketable securities available for American purchases. Such were the chief considerations which, in 1917, impelled the British Government towards making a contract with Jewry. (Lloyd George, 1939, p. 726)

The Conclusion is that there are a number of conspiracies in elite circles—but they operate as a number of factions:

- the British
- the Zionist
- the Globalist/Illuminist
- the Green Left (Progressives, in effect the Left wing of the Globalists).

Divergence between the Rhodes and Rothschild factions

The Economist magazine's casting its lot with Antifa and Black Lives Matter against Rhodes highlights a divergence between Rothschild and Rhodes that goes back right to the early days of the Rhodes movement.

Rothschild's biographer Derek Wilson pointed out that Lord Nathanael ("Natty") Rothschild was not committed to Cecil Rhodes' goal of imperial expansion. He even floated a loan for the Boer government:

> When, therefore, Rhodes came home in July 1887 and approached Natty personally for financial backing, Lord Rothschild ... guaranteed De Beers one million pounds ... This did not prevent Barnato competing for the company's assets but the combination of De Beers and Rothschilds was too much for him ... and De Beers emerged triumphant. Soon afterwards the two concerns amalgamated.
>
> One reason why Barnato held out so long was his opposition to expansionism. Rhodes made it clear that the funds of the new company—De Beers Consolidated Mines Limited—would be used for the northward march of imperialism. There was never any distinction in his mind between making money and carrying the British flag into newly conquered territory.

And Rhodes persuaded himself that Lord Rothschild shared his simple idealism.

He was wrong. Lord Rothschild was not an unreserved imperialist, as Rhodes gradually discovered. In 1888 he made a will, nominating Natty to administer the bulk of his estate for financing a sinister secret society for promoting the extension of British power. Over the next few years Rhodes wrote a stream of letters to New Court on the subject of British politics in southern Africa. He found his correspondent clear-headed, firm and quite unprepared to confuse the roles of banker and politician. In response to Rhodes' suggestion that company funds be used to finance territorial expansion, his banker advised: "if ... you require money for that purpose, you will have to obtain it from other sources than the cash reserve of the De Beers Company. We have always held that the De Beers Company is simply a diamond mining company." And Rhodes cannot have been very pleased to learn, in 1892, that Rothschilds had floated a loan for the Boer government of the Transvaal. The bank had considerable investments in South African mines, railways and general development. They were, therefore, on the side of peace and stability. Any influence they exercised as the decade wore on was towards the end of preventing Britons and Boers drifting into war. The turbulent Rhodes, by contrast, was implacable in his opposition to the Johannesburg regime and, in 1895, organised an (unsuccessful) uprising to topple it—the notorious Jameson Raid. Rhodes had gone much too far. He was censured by the British government and was forced to resign the premiership. By this time he had long ceased to have close and cordial relations with Natty. Probably he never really grasped the fact that, though the Rothschilds disliked Gladstone's policy of colonial retrenchment, they were not advocates of unbridled imperialism for its own sake. (Wilson, 1994, pp. 304-5)

In the 1930s, the Round Table Movement promoted Appeasement, but Lord Victor Rothschild (1910-1990, 3rd Baron Rothschild) was a Communist. He was the successor to Nathanael ("Natty", 1840-1915, 1st Baron) and Walter (1868-1937, 2nd Baron); the current Lord Rothschild, Jacob (1936-), is the 4th Baron Rothschild.

Perry (1994) claims that Victor Rothschild was the "Fifth Man" in the Cambridge spy-ring. He was a Cambridge Apostle, and shared an apartment in Bentinck St. with homosexual spies Guy Burgess and Anthony Blunt.

In 1940, Blunt and Burgess were living in Rothschild's leased three-storey maisonette as was his assistant at MI5, Tess Mayor, whom he later married, and Patricia Parry (later Baroness Llewellyn-Davies. the Wilson-appointed Labour peeress), both left-wing Cambridge graduates. ... Bentinck Street became a facility for the analysis and of espionage material including microfilm and documents. (Perry, 1994, p. xxv)

When the lease ran out, the four permanent occupants and Victor all pooled their resources to take it over. The meticulous Blunt handled the details of managing the household accounts and the five shared a common kitchen and sitting room, which was used for much entertaining.. Blunt had a boyfriend installed, whereas, true to long-term form, Burgess had homosexual parties with friends and boys. ... Yet that life and the partying went on and attracted many visitors who were often too drunk to leave. Maclean, Philby and Guy Liddell were frequent guests. ... After these drunken forays, Tess often found herself assisting an inebriated Blunt or Burgess from the front door of the maisonette to bed. (p. 93)

Perry implies that **Victor Rothschild preferred Trotsky** (this is the meaning of the reference to Stalin's Jewish pogroms, below), **but was prepared to help Stalin to defeat Hitler**. Otto was the name of his handler:

While making his assessment, the ever gracious Otto delivered his polished lines of enticement. Philby, Blunt and Burgess had warned him that Rothschild had to be reeled in on the Jewish, anti-Hitler line. Too much clap-trap about the 'rightness' of the communist view might cause his eyes to glaze over with uncertainty and boredom. He had heard and comprehended all the theory but was unconvinced. **He knew too much about Stalin's Jewish pogroms** in Russia.

Rothschild judged Stalin and Hitler to be about equal in their appalling treatment of Jews. A dictator was a dictator, and a dead, starving or tortured human was the same on either side of the Eastern border. ... Victor would not be seduced like Burgess and Philby by ideology and the panacea of a perfect communist world with a post-Stalinist figure astride East and West. (p. 54)

Perry casts Victor Rothschild as a Zionist and Progressive, more devoted to those causes than to the British Establishment:

The Third Lord Rothschild was camouflaged as the Fifth Man by virtue of his powerful position in the Establishment. The vast wealth of his banking dynasty embedded him in the power elite more than the other members of the Ring of Five. It was a perfect cover and served to shield him. He seemed the epitome of the ruling class of twentieth-century Britain, and therefore the least likely to be a traitor. Yet a closer scrutiny showed that he had other allegiances, which over time and on specific occasions ran contrary to British interests.

Rothschild was more loyal to his Jewish heritage than anything English. He showed this in his long commitment to his race's problems. After his political awakening at Cambridge in 1930 he supported refugees from Soviet and German pogroms. In the war, he feverishly fought the Nazis. Once Hitler was defeated, Rothschild assisted in the creation of a homeland for the Jews who had been dispossessed. When the new nation was established he again helped in guiding Israeli leaders to the people, technology and weaponry which would defend it. (p. xl)

The Round Table Movement condoned Appeasement, not because they were Nazis, but to "kill two birds with one stone" by setting Germany and Russia against each another, much as the United States and Israel supplied weapons to both sides in the Iran-Iraq war. Quigley explains (Lord Lothian was Philip Kerr, leader of the Round Table Movement at that time):

> This event of March 1936, by which Hitler remilitarized the Rhineland, was the most crucial event in the whole history of appeasement. ... And by this date, certain members of the Milner Group and of the British Conservative government had reached the fantastic idea that they could kill two birds with one stone by setting Germany and Russia against one another in Eastern Europe. In this way they felt that the two enemies would stalemate one another, or that Germany would become satisfied with the oil of Rumania and the wheat of the Ukraine. It never occurred to anyone in a responsible position that Germany and Russia might make common cause, even temporarily, against the West. Even less did it occur to them that Russia might beat Germany and thus open all Central Europe to Bolshevism. (Quigley, 1981, p. 265)

> This idea of bringing Germany into a collision with Russia was not to be found, so far as the evidence shows, among any members of the inner circle of the Milner Group. Rather it was to be found among the personal associates of Neville Chamberlain, including several members of the second circle of the Milner Group. (p. 269)

> Lord Lothian's speech of 5 December 1934 in the House of Lords is, at first glance, a defense of collective security, but a second look shows clearly that by "collective security" the speaker meant appeasement. (p. 271)

> It goes without saying that the whole inner core of the Group, and their chief publications, such as *The Times* and *The Round Table*, approved the policy of appeasement completely and prodded it along with calculated indiscretions when it was felt necessary to do so. (p. 271)

Andrea Bosco says that Kerr (Lord Lothian) came to blame the Round Table Movement, which he had been part of, for precipitating World War I. With its alliances and secret treaties, it had laid a trap, which Germany had fallen into by giving Austria license to make war on Serbia for allowing the assassination of Archduke Ferdinand.

> During the twenty months spent next to Lloyd George as a war leader, Kerr developed a sense of guilt for having been involved, through The Round Table, in the wild anti-German press campaign, which played such a

crucial role in building widespread popular consent to British entry into the war. (Bosco, 2017, pp. 376)

As a result, Kerr supported Appeasement, in order to head off a second world war. His motivation was different from those seeking to play off Germany and Russia against one another:

Great Britain could have prevented [World War I], and Lothian spent all his intellectual and moral energies in the years to come developing the theory and practice of appeasement in order to prevent its repeat on a larger scale. Here is the key to understanding Lothian's complete severance from Milnerism.

Bosco says that before WWII, Kerr (LordLothian) pursued a policy diametrically opposed to that of Milner before WWI:

Aware that the Great War had been an unnecessary carnage, in which he lost his brother David, Lothian made of his desperate attempt to prevent the Second World War a personal matter. He brought into play all the extraordinary fire-power accumulated meanwhile by the Round Table, especially at the Royal Institute of International Affairs—better known as Chatham House—and with the Round Table's stable connections in the City and with the property of The Times and The Observer. In the implementation of a policy diametrically opposed to that of Milner, appeasement, Lothian actually contributed to paving the way to Hitler's supremacy in Central and Eastern Europe, exactly what Milner and the Liberal League had denied to the King's cousin. It is interesting to note how the architects of those diametrically opposed policies towards Germany belonged to the same organization, and how those policies were in any case unable to prevent the outbreak of two world wars. Indeed, they accelerated the drift towards catastrophe. (Bosco, 2017, pp. 376-7)

Chapter 8: The Cosmopolitan Empire, its Factions and Alternatives

Ancient Greeks thought of the tribal world they had left behind as "barbarian"; however Diogenes of Sinope (the Cynic) proclaimed himself, not "Greek" but "a citizen of the world." That's where the word "cosmopolitan" comes from.

When Alexander met him, Diogenes, lying on the footpath, asked him to move: "Please get out of my sunlight." Calling themselves 'cosmopolitan', today's Globalists pretend to play the part of the ascetic Diogenes, but actually envisage themselves as Alexander, ruler of the world.

We are all Citizens of the World, but do we want to be Citizens of *their* World State?

Carroll Quigley called it the Anglo-American Establishment. Lyndon Larouche called it the New British Empire. Alain Soral calls it the American Empire. The Saker calls it the Anglo-Zionist Empire. I venture to call it the Cosmopolitan Empire.

Factions in that empire include the Anglo, the Zionist, the Globalist, and the Green Left (the Left wing of Globalism).

The Anglo one refers to the Anglosphere of Britain, its dominions, and the United States, based on British and Irish ancestry. The Anglo-American Establishment refers to the governing regime centred in New York and London, and in Canada, Australia, and New Zealand.

The Zionist one refers to Zionist domination of the United States, e.g. in the Laval Affair, the attack on the U.S.S. Liberty, the Neocons, the Lobby, 9/11, the War on Islam, the Calendar of the House of Representatives, and Noahide Law. A Catholic abbot was recently told to cover his cross at the Western Wall (Joffre, 2023).

The Globalist one, which preaches Cosmopolitanism, is based in the financial centres of London and New York. Its premier publication is The Economist magazine, and its best known activist, after David Rockefeller, is George Soros.

The Green Left one functions as the Left wing of Globalism. It supplies Progressive activists in Academia, the Media, the Bureaucracy, the Judicial system, and on the street, like Antifa and Black Lives Matter.

On Jan. 9, 1988 the Economist magazine published an article 'Get Ready for the Phoenix' advocating a global currency, and predicting its arrival by 2018.

THIRTY years from now, Americans, Japanese, Europeans, and people in many other rich countries, and some relatively poor ones will probably be paying for their shopping with the same currency. Prices will be quoted not in dollars, yen or D-marks but in, let's say, the phoenix. ...

The phoenix zone would impose tight constraints on national governments. There would be no such thing, for instance, as a national monetary
policy. The world phoenix supply would be fixed by a new central bank,
descended perhaps from the IMF. The world inflation rate—and hence,
within narrow margins, each national inflation rate—would be in its
charge. Each country could use taxes and public spending to offset temporary falls in demand, but it would have to borrow rather than print money
to finance its budget deficit. ... This means a big loss of economic sovereignty, but the trends that make the phoenix so appealing are taking that
sovereignty away in any case. ... Pencil in the phoenix for around 2018,
and welcome it when it comes. (World Currency)

One can see parallels with the Euro; it too was designed by bankers. Within
the Eurozone, the countries of the periphery (Italy, Greece, Portugal, Spain) have
been impoverished by the loss of their own monetary policy. This is part of Globalisation; another part is Open Borders.

From the 1970s, the Globalists forced the Anglo-Zionist Empire to undergo a
Great Replacement. Open Border immigration diluted its European heritage, and
the Culture War destroyed its Western Civilisation. Such policies are not consistent
with Anglo domination. Anglo domination continued until the 1960s, but from
the 1970s, Cosmopolitan forces usurped it. They belong in two camps— Globalist
finance, as represented by the Economist magazine (part-Rothschild-owned) and
Project Syndicate (owned by George Soros), both of which set political agendas
and the limits of discourse—and the Trotskyoid/Progressive/Green Left activist
movements in Academia, the Media, the Bureaucracy and the Judicial system, together constituting the Deep State.

The Globalists and the Progressives operate in alliance, e.g. on the Covid-19
Plandemic and its intended outcome, the Great Reset; and on the Ukraine War.
Together, they disparage and undermine all the dissident groups which resist One
World goals (e.g. the UN's Agenda 21).

Yet, the Progressives do not operate as a unified party as the Communist Party did. Rather, they operate as networks of activists. Their Left-wing Communism
and their broad adherence to the anti-Stalin camp make 'Trotskyoid' a suitable
descriptor. These are the people that Stalin overthrew. Gay Marriage and the Trans
movement come from the Trotskyoid camp—as per Trotsky's 1937 book *The Revolution Betrayed*, where he sets forth his revolutionary social policies to smash God
and the Family.

Alternatives to Capitalism and Communism

Prior to the Privatisation and Deregulation brought about by Margaret
Thatcher, Britain and Australia were reckoned as socialist countries. There was a

clear distinction between 'socialism' and 'communism'. But since the fall of the Soviet Union, Trotskyist concepts have taken over. They do not call the Britain or the Australia of those days 'socialist', but instead brand them 'capitalist', 'racist' and 'sexist'. Nor do they call the Soviet Union of the postwar years 'communist', but only 'State Capitalist'.

To escape from rule by the Bankers, we need to reject Trotskyist terminology, and examine alternatives to Capitalism, to see if we can find one that suits. That means socialism—but not the Green Left socialism favoured by the Bankers.

Socialism can be state-based or anti-state; revolutionary or reformist; religious or atheistic; and national or international.

During the Covid-19 Plandemic, the Economist magazine noticed that anti-Lockdown protests were uniting the Anarchist Left (meaning the Libertarian Left, not Antifa, which is Trotskyoid) and the anti-Establishment Right:

https://www.economist.com/britain/2021/07/03/the-anti-lockdown-movement-is-still-going-strong

The anti-lockdown movement is still going strong
It has united the anarchist left and anti-establishment right
Jul 3rd 2021

Throughout the pandemic opponents of lockdowns have held hundreds of protests, many motivated by a conspiracy theory also popular in America: that covid-19 was faked to provide an excuse for systematic regime change. ...

The protests attract both anarchist left and anti-establishment right. ... Many want their movement to grow into a libertarian opposition to the "Great Reset".

But the Marxists and the Green Left were overwhelmingly pro-Lockdown. In the mainstream media, the Anti-Vax and anti-Lockdown protestors were commonly called 'Far Right', 'Nazi' or 'Fascist'. Yet I noticed a strong Anarchist/Libertarian Left streak in the protest I attended at Bundaberg, and the same was obvious in video footage from Melbourne. The Economist was correct.

In the 1970s, I was one of those who left the city to take up an Alternative Lifestyle in a rural area. I learned to build a house from hippies—we all built our own homes, and had babies at home too. Now, some decades later, laws have been passed which make building your own home much more difficult; and home birth has been persecuted too—for example, it is difficult for homebirth midwives to get insurance. Those laws have a 'Left' provenance—but the Left that promotes them is the Marxist Left, while the Left that opposes them is the Libertarian Left (some call them Anarchist, but they are not the violent kind of Anarchist).

The distinction goes back to the battle between Marx and Proudhon in the mid-nineteenth century; and then to the battle between Marx and Bakunin in the 1860s & 70s. Proudhon opposed violence, but Bakunin condoned it.

The Anarchist Left distrusts the state; it builds co-operatives instead. The kibbutz movement was Anarchist; Bill Mollison's Permaculture communities too. Anarchists oppose the authoritarianism in Marxism. De-platforming and Cancel Culture are examples of that; they were begun by Trotskyists. Shane Burley, an 'anti-fascist' who de-platforms anti-Zionists (Norman Finkelstein, Gilad Atzmon, David Rovics) appears to be a closet Trotskyist, using entrism to influence Anarchists.

That's the distinction between state-based socialism and anti-state socialism.

Another distinction is between revolutionary socialism, which endorses violence to overthrow the state; and reformist socialism, which shuns violence and seeks to gain incremental changes.

The chain of revolutionary socialism led from Weishaupt to Babeuf and Buonarroti, to Auguste Blanqui, to Marx and Lenin; also to Bakunin and the Russian nihilists. James H. Billington traces the connections in his book *Fire In The Minds Of Men: Origins Of The Revolutionary Faith*. He shows that Illuminism continued throughout the nineteenth century, contrary to the claim that it died out.

Kolakowski (1978) derived revolutionary socialism from Babeuf, and reformist socialism from Saint-Simon :

> Blanqui believed in the allconquering force of the revolutionary will embodied in an armed conspiracy, while Blanc trusted that gradual reform by the state would abolish inequality, exploitation, crises and unemployment. The former doctrine is derived from Babouvism; the latter from Saint-Simon, with some attenuation as regards democracy and the take-over of all means of production by the state. Blanqui's ideas were adopted by Tkachev and afterwards by Lenin; those of Blanc by Lassalle and the modern social democrats. (p. 216)

Blanc has since been identified as a covert revolutionary (Nicolaevsky, 1966).

Proudhon was shocked at the violence of the Jacobins during the 'June Days' of the 1848 revolution. Bakunin endorsed violence but rejected Buonarroti's hierarchical organisation aimed at revolutionary dictatorship. His approach was like that of the Anarcho-Syndicalists during the Spanish Civil War. Like them he was militantly hostile to the Church.

Proudhon advocated a peasant socialism, like the Socialist Revolutionary (SR) Party in Russia at the time of the Bolshevik Revolution; however he opposed violence, whereas they engaged in assassination. Proudhon, like the SRs, wanted the peasants (family farmers) to have their own land and a good deal of autonomy, rather than being subject to a totalitarian state as per Marxism. Despite strong language against unearned wealth, Proudhon was a reformist.

Reformist socialism begins with Saint-Simon (1760-1825); in his scheme, private property would be subordinated to the common good and not left to the owner's whim. Unlike Marx, Saint-Simon rejected Class War. He saw no essential antagonism between workers and employers; they were both part of the 'industrial class'. His socialism would use the State to foster class unity between them for the common good.

"Saint-Simon did not look to the oppressed workers to carry out his plans, but believed that society would be transformed for their benefit by manufacturers, bankers, scholars, and artists, once they had been convinced by the new doctrine" (Kolakowski, 1978, p. 189).

The chain of reformist socialism then passes to Emperor Napoleon III, who implemented Saint-Simon type socialism in France; and to Lassalle, then, through him, to Bismarck, who implemented socialism in Germany, where it was called 'State Socialism' or 'Christian Socialism'. The Webbs and the Fabian Society were reformist too.

Socialism can be religious or atheistic. Clement Attlee, who created the socialist regime in Britain in 1945 and gave India its independence, was a Christian; Ben Chifley, who created the socialist regime in Australia, likewise. Freemasonry, Theosophy and the New Age movement are religious but anti-Christian, and some elements of them are satanic (but that's still different from atheism). Robespierre, following Rousseau's deism, inaugurated the Cult of The Supreme Being. Trotsky was a militant atheist, and the early Bolsheviks set about destroying Christianity.

Finally, socialism can be nation-based or internationalist. Nation-based socialism operates in nation-states which want to retain their national sovereignty; International Socialists want a World State which does away with nation-states. The national versions of socialism are known variously as State Socialism, Christian Socialism and Agrarian Socialism; the international versions are Communist, Illuminist or Masonic.

Napoleon III crushed the Communists, but introduced Reformist Socialism

Louis Napoleon (Emperor Napoleon III) came to power in the wake of the violent Communist Revolution of 1848; and after his fall, the Paris Commune of 1871 unleashed a similar bout of violence, in which the revolutionaries burned parts of Paris. Louis Napoleon was elected President of France, but the Constitution allowed only one term. On Dec. 2, 1851, he mounted a coup d 'etat, promising to submit his program to a plebiscite.

"The results of the plebiscite, which were in no way rigged, were startling. Over seven million voted their approval of the project, and by implication of the coup itself, while the 'No' votes were a mere six hundred thousand. Louis Napoleon considered himself 'absolved' of his illegal coup by this vote, though all observers agreed that he never overcame his unhappiness at the necessity for it." (Smith, 1985, p. 11).

Elie Halevy characterised Napoleon III's regime as socialist, based on class unity rather than class war: 'the socialist Revolution of 1848 led in the end to the dictatorship of 1851, which was strongly influenced by Saint-Simonian theory. The Second Empire was both a reaction against "socialist anarchy" and a further development of that principle of organisation which is an inherent part of Socialism' (Halevy, 1941).

Napoleon III kept the Communists at bay, but implemented socialist policies. He had been a Freemason himself, but constrained the revolutionary faction of Masonry. David Labaree (2021) shows that the Left's dismissive opinion of him is unwarranted:

> His most visible gift was the complete remaking of the city of Paris, which at the time he took power was a collection of medieval villages with narrow, filthy streets, no sanitation or running water, and an appalling death rate. He turned it into the magnificent modern city that we all love, with broad boulevards, expansive squares, and stunning buildings. He made Baron Haussmann prefect of Paris, and the rest is history.

> By the time Haussmann stepped down in January 1870, he had overseen the demolition of 19,722 buildings, which had been replaced by some 43,777 new structures, all with running water and sanitary facilities. He had designed and overseen the construction of ninety-five kilometers of broad new gas-lit streets, including most of the great thoroughfares of the capital.

> And the improvements were not just to the physical environment; he also had a big impact on social welfare.

> The last vestiges of the eighteenth century were carried away with the rubble from the demolished medieval buildings. A fresh breeze wafted across the French capital, transforming not only the avenues and architecture but the entire attitude and outlook of the people liberated from the restraining values and ideas of the past. Thanks to Louis Napoléon's emphasis on public education, the working classes were finally taught to read and write, and new book publishers, new newspapers, reviews, and magazines multiplied, bringing literary creation as well as news from across the world and the ever expanding empire.

The living and working conditions of the working class—totally ignored by Napoléon—became a lifelong preoccupation with Napoléon III. ... At the same time, the vast rebuilding of the capital put many tens of thousands of the unemployed to work. Louis Napoléon also introduced farsighted job-creation and old-age pension schemes for the working class, not to mention mandatory education at the primary school level. (Labaree, 2021)

Lassalle accepted the Prussian state, whereas Marx had sought to destroy the State via revolution. Henry C. K. Liu wrote, 'Lassalle rejected the idea of Marx that the state was a class-based power structure with the function of preserving existing class relations and destined to "wither away" in a future classless society. Instead, Lassalle saw the state as an independent entity, an instrument of justice essential for the achievement of the socialist program' (Liu, 2011).

Elie Halevy (1941) noted that Bismarck got his socialism from Lassalle:

Lassalle was the first man in Germany, the first in Europe, who succeeded in organising a party of socialist action. Yet he viewed the emerging bourgeois parties as more inimical to the working class than the aristocracy ... This created a strange alliance between Lassalle and Bismarck. When in 1866 Bismarck founded the Confederation of Northern Germany on a basis of universal suffrage, he was acting on advice which came directly from Lassalle. And I am convinced that after 1878, when he began to practise "State Socialism" and "Christian Socialism" and "Monarchial Socialism," he had not forgotten what he had learnt from the socialist leader.

In the 1860s, Marx and Bakunin duelled over the nature of the state. Bakunin accused Marx of promoting totalitarian dictatorship, the rule of a small elite of intellectuals in the name of the proletariat. Bakunin, instead, advocated self-rule of the peasants and the workers in something like the soviets (workers' councils) developed in Russia prior to the Bolshevik Revolution—before their capture by the Bolsheviks. Bakunin was advocating the withering of the state, and to compete with him, Marx postulated a two-stage process: an interim regime of centralised dictatorship, called 'Socialism', followed by a stateless society called 'Communism'.

Soviet leaders kept extending the 'Socialist' period, saying that they had not yet reached the 'Communist' stage. In reality, it's unlikely that the stateless phase would ever be reached; better to call a spade a 'spade' and admit that the two-stage plan was phony. We should describe the U.S.S.R., Maoist China, and their satellite regimes, as 'Communist'; and leave the word 'Socialist' to describe reformist regimes with a mixed economy, part nationalised by the state, part owned by private corporations. Postwar Britain and Australia (before Thatcher) were of this type; and so are Putin's Russia and China post-Deng. However, postwar Britain and Australia were democracies, whereas China is still totalitarian.

Crises as the Excuse for World Government

Today in the United States, the regime is called a 'Democracy', but it's actually an Oligarchy. Donors buy Politicians. Business and political leaders meet at the World Economic Forum to set the agenda for the next year. The WEF was founded by David Rockefeller, and the Rockefeller Foundation and Soros' Open Society Foundation have regularly awarded large grants to it. The WEF is 'woke': it endorses Gay Marriage, LGBTQ, gender-gap Feminism, and anti-racism—the whole Left side of the Culture War. And it allows no debate—it operates by 'consensus', but this is very much driven by those at the top.

Bill Moyers said of David Rockefeller: "The unelected if indisputable chairman of the American Establishment ... one of the most powerful, influential and richest men in America ...[he] sits at the hub of a vast network of financiers, industrialists and politicians whose reach encircles the globe" (Moyers, 1990).

For many years he was chairman of the Board of the Council On Foreign Relations (CFR). He founded the Trilateral Commission, and the Club of Rome was founded at his mansion in Italy. He joined Edmund de Rothschild of the European banking empire to fund 'Debt for Nature'. In 1974 a Club of Rome publication endorsed the statement, 'The Earth has cancer and the cancer is Man' (Mesarovic and Pestel, p.1). The Rockefeller Foundation promoted the Copenhagen Climate-Change conference, and the Earth Charter—drafted by Maurice Strong, Mikhail Gorbachev, and Steven Rockefeller.

Speaking to a Bilderberger meeting in Baden, Germany, in June, 1991, David Rockefeller said, 'It would have been impossible for us to develop our plan for the world if we had been subjected to the lights of publicity during those years. But, the world is more sophisticated and prepared to march towards a world government. The supranational sovereignty of an intellectual elite and world bankers is surely preferable to the national autodetermination practiced in past centuries' (Maxwell, 2000, pp. 15-16).

Most conspiracy theorists, especially the Larouche writers from Executive Intelligence Review, attributed this plan to the Cecil Rhodes 'British Conspiracy'. But Rhodes envisaged domination by the British race, whereas the Globalists are inundating western societies with mass immigration, and destroying its civilisation via the Culture War.

Rhodes' British Conspiracy has been subverted by another conspiracy, the Illuminati. A leading culture warrior, Herbert Marcuse of the Frankfurt School, was brought to the United States by the Rockefeller Foundation.

But the Cosmopolitan Empire is not merely the "American Empire". The Globalists have plans to develop NAFTA into a region state of 'North America', as the E.U. is a region state. This would be the end of the U.S. Constitution; there is a mighty struggle within the U.S. Supreme Court between the Originalists and the Liberals, which will determine whether the Constitution survives.

Region states are an intermediate form between nation-states and a world-state.

Another startling comment attributed to David Rockefeller is 'We are on the verge of a global transformation. All we need is the right major crisis and the nations will accept the New World Order' (Rockefeller, 1994).

The threat of crises which can only be solved on a world scale, by a World Government—it would be the only means of dealing with them—was long a feature of the writing of H. G. Wells.

Although he never went to university, he was one of the most influential intellectuals from 1900 to 1940. His seeded his dramatic novels with political themes, stressing the need for a World State. He commonly depicted wars—of Aliens from Mars invading Earth (*The War of the Worlds*, 1897); of humans using planes for bombing—and he was the first writer to envisage an Atomic Bomb. The whole point of all these scary novels about future wars, was that we would destroy ourselves unless all nations united in a World State. Not a federation of nation states, but a unitary World State.

Wells was the first writer to envisage aircraft being used in war, in his novel *The War of in the Air* (1908). When this did happen during World War I, he was co-opted into War Propaganda, and produced a book called *The War to End War*, setting out war aims. "Ending War" meant World Government—a permanent Peace; and Wells sought this outcome at the Peace Conference of Versailles. Yet was no pacifist. During the war, Wells encouraged the British to fight: his novel *Mr Britling Sees It Through* was a best seller.

After the war, he produced books covering the whole of History, natural as well as human, and embedded his philosophical outlook in them—for example, sympathy for Communism. His model was the *Encyclopedie* of Denis Diderot, which had helped pave the way for the French Revolution. Like Diderot, Wells was militantly hostile to the Church. To produce these historical books, Wells gained the contribution of a number of specialists, although only Wells was listed as the author. The main book, *The Outline of World History*, sold 2 million copies; the smaller one, *A Short History of the World*, was used as a textbook in British schools. These books, although historical, read like story books, such was Wells' skill as a writer. Several editions were produced.

Larouche writers like Matthew Ehret, and even ex-Larouche writers like F. William Engdahl, wrongly brand Wells a member of Cecil Rhodes' British Conspiracy.

They confuse the Coefficients Club—a dinner circle hosted by Beatrice Webb—with Rhodes' Round Table. Wells was a member of the former but not the latter.

At the Coefficients Club Wells met Lord Milner (head of the Round Table), Sir Edward Grey, and other members of the elite, as well as Bertrand Russell. Russell later wrote that he and Wells were the only anti-Imperialists in the Club. The Club began during the division caused in Britain by the Boer Wars; the Webbs and most other Fabians had supported the war; Russell strongly opposed it.

Nesta Webster connected Wells' advocacy of a World State with earlier advocacy by members of the Illuminati. In her book *World Revolution* (1921/2013) she wrote:

> M. Louis Blanc is no doubt right in pronouncing Babeuf to have been an Illuminatus, a disciple of Weishaupt, and it was thus in accordance with the custom of the sect that he had adopted a classical pseudonym, renouncing his Christian names of Francois Noel in favour of Gracchus, just as Weishaupt had assumed the name of Spartacus, the Illuminatus Jean Baptiste Clootz had elected to be known as Anacharsis, and Pierre Gaspard Chaumette as Anaxagoras. The plan of campaign devised by Babeuf was therefore modelled directly on the system of Weishaupt, and on his release from prison ... he gathered his fellow-conspirators around him and formed an association on masonic lines by which propaganda was to be carried on in public places, the confederates recognizing each other by secret signs and passwords. At the first meeting of the Babouvistes—amongst whom were found Darthe, Germain, Bodson, and Buonarotti—all swore to "remain united and to make equality triumph," and the project was then discussed of establishing a large popular society for the inculcation of Babeuf's doctrines. (p. 55).

> The conspiracy of Babeuf was thus the expiring effort of the French Revolution to realize the great scheme of Weishaupt. ... (p. 73)

> Yet another witness to the persistence of this theory is Mr. H. G. Wells, whose visions of the future expounded in the concluding chapters of his Outlines of History and articles on Russia are simply a compound of Rousseau, Weishaupt, Clootz, and Babeuf. ... What else is the "World State" now being advocated by Mr. Wells in the Sunday Times but Clootz's "Universal Republic," or his idea of union between all peoples regardless of nationality but Clootz's "solidarity of the human race". (p. 291)

Wells and the Fabians were enthusiastic about the Bolshevik Revolution. But they had no interest in the gory details of the Red Terror, the destruction of churches and the priesthood, the Kronstadt massacre, the Gulag, or the Ukraine Famine. Their only interest was in the rebuilding from a blank slate, which occurred after these bloody events.

Wells, the apostle of Cosmopolitanism, presented his plans for a World State in his book *The Open Conspiracy* (1928 and 1933); a 1931 edition was called *What Are we To Do With Our Lives?*.

Wells wrote in the 1933 edition: 'The idea of reorganizing the affairs of the world on quite a big scale, which was "Utopian," and so forth, in 1926 and 1927, and still "bold" in 1928, has now spread about the world until nearly everybody has it. It has broken out all over the place, thanks largely to the Russian Five Year Plan' (p. 15).

Wells and the Webbs admired Trotsky, but turned a blind eye to the blood on his sword. Stalin's victory disconcerted them. Wells had sided with Trotsky, but he hid his dislike for Stalin when they met for an interview in 1934, just after Wells had similarly interviewed Roosevelt. Wells' goal, as ever, was to see if he could get them to coalesce into a World State.

An earlier draft of Wells' World State was in his book *Anticipations* (1901 and 1914), in which he proposed an elite group of 'Samurai' modelled on Plato's Guardians, who would take over the world and impose a World State. However, Plato's Republic, as envisaged in *The Laws*, is a community of only 5,040 households. To adapt it to a world scale involved additional concepts, sourced from Judaism, Freemasonry, or Illuminism. There is no evidence that Wells was a Freemason, or joined an Illuminist group; but their ideas were current in the milieu Wells inhabited. He was an armchair revolutionary, a middle-class intellectual who disliked both the Aristocracy and the working class; the income from his books, both fiction and non-fiction, allowed him to lead a life of leisure.

In Wells' Introduction to the 1914 edition of *Anticipations* he used the term 'open conspiracy' for the first time:

> That conception of an open conspiracy of intellectuals and wilful people against existing institutions and existing limitations and boundaries is always with me; it is my King Charles's head, and it forms the substance of the longest novel I have ever written-that is, if ever the war will let me get it written -the novel I am still writing. I admit that after fourteen years this open conspiracy still does not very definitely realize itself, but in that matter I have a constitutional undying patience. That open conspiracy will come. It is my faith. It is my form of political thought. (Wells, 1914/1999, pp. xiv-xv)

In *Anticipations*, Wells envisages overthrowing the U.S. Constitution: "The American constitution and the British crown and constitution have to be modified or shelved at some stage in this synthesis," (Wells, 1902/1999, p. 148).

Having joined the Fabian Society, Wells tried to take it over, to turn it into his 'samurai'. However, Shaw and the Wells refused to cede control, so he left. Nor did he have any success mobilising such a movement during the turbulent 1930s; the Left were busy fighting in the Spanish Civil War. Their goals were limited to defeating Franco, Mussolini and Hitler. They were divided about Stalin; this was the time of the Purges.

But after World War II, Wells' ideas came to fruition in the 1946 Baruch Plan for International Control of Nuclear weapons and materials, proposed to Stalin by Truman.

It had been drafted by Bernard Baruch, a Jewish banker, and David Lilienthal, Jewish head of the Atomic Energy Commission. Baruch had earlier been associated with Wilson's attempt to have the League of Nations created as a World Government, with a World Army and a World Court. The *Encyclopaedia Judaica* says that Baruch "served on the Supreme Economic Council at the Conference of Versailles, where he was President Wilson's personal economic adviser" (Bernard Baruch, 1971). Baruch was also a Zionist; Benjamin Freedman said that he headed the Jewish delegation obtaining Palestine at the Peace Conference in 1919.

David Lilienthal had written, in 1918, of the Jewish Mission to unite the World:

> But the establishment of monotheism is not the only mission of the Jew. ... His concept of God's Unity implied the Unity of Man; his Sacred Book declared it; his Prophets taught it. But monotheism necessitated stern aloofness. Later, persecution yielded social clannishness. ... Concepts of ideals leap far beyond tribal limitations to identify themselves with the deepest passions of universal man! Brotherhood, once held for those of the blood alone, is now comprehended as the object of his abiding but repressed yearning for all men! (Lillienthal, 1918).

In 1946, the atomic scientists who had created the Nuclear Bomb, alarmed by U.S. military leaders who wanted to use nuclear weapons to bomb Russia, proposed a worldwide Atomic Energy Commission to control both military and civilian aspects of the nuclear industry. Their plan was developed in the pages of the Bulletin of the Atomic Scientists. A number of the articles in that journal explicitly canvassed World Government, meaning that the proposed Commission would control world armaments and have a monopoly on the use of force. This would impact the sovereignty of both the United States (the Senate would have to ratify it) and the Soviet Union (for which the abolition of the veto was a major threat).

Then they issued a book *One World Or None*. The high-profile backers of the Baruch Plan also contributed chapters in the book. Most of them were Jewish (and International Socialists): Albert Einstein, Robert Oppenheimer, Leo Szilard, Walter Lippmann, Niels Bohr, James Franck, Eugene Rabinowitch, Hy Goldsmith, Hans Bethe, and Harold Urey. For more details on the Baruch Plan see Myers (2019a).

The slogan 'One World Or None' sums up the catch-22 we face: form a World Government, or wars using Nuclear Weapons or Bioweapons (Pandemics) will wipe us out. Save the Environment (from Global Warming, or Resource Depletion, or loss of Biodiversity), or the Earth dies and, ultimately, we do too.

Leo Szilard, father of the Bomb and one of the drivers of the Baruch Plan, got some of his ideas from Wells' novel envisaging an Atomic Bomb. He also supported Wells' Open Conspiracy for World Government; and visited Wells.

Wells' ideas helped to convert Labour politicians in Britain and Australia from the postwar Christian Socialism of Clement Attlee in Britain and Ben Chifley in Australia, to Thatcherite-Reaganite privatisation and deregulation as a prelude to some sort of International Socialism. Which kind, we won't know until it's too late: once a World Government exists, there will be nowhere to escape to, and our rulers will be able to impose whatever regime they choose.

Klaus Schwab's statement about the Great Reset, "Whatever you need, you will rent", suggests Agenda 21 and also Wells' Open Conspiracy.

"You will own nothing, but you will be happy" would have been more convincing if he had said, "We will own nothing, but we will be happy."

The point being, that he seemed to promise a 2-class society: an elite eho owned everything, and a proletariat who owned nothing.

The United Nations has proposed an "emergency platform" which it wants nations to agree to, granting it the right to takle charge of world affairs during emergencies such as the Covid-19 Pandemic.

https://www.un.org/sites/un2.un.org/files/our-common-agenda-policy-brief-emergency-platform-en.pdf

Our Common Agenda Policy Brief

Strengthening the International Response to Complex Global Shocks - An Emergency Platform

March 2023

The Emergency Platform would not be a standing body or entity but a set of protocols that could be activated when needed.

It could be triggered by climatic or environmental events, pandemics, events involving a biological agent, disruptive activity in cyberspace or outer space. This is World Government by the back door.

If we don't want World Gov't, we must reject Laissez-Faire Capitalism

If we don't want it, if we have any choice, we need to escape from the current economic system. And that requires rethinking Capitalism and Socialism.

Despite the One World aspirations of the Globalists, half the world is not in their pocket. They planned their moves in the 1990s and early 2000s, when they thought that China was theirs and Russia weak. As a result, they have forced Russia into the arms of China. Now, Russia, China, Iran and other sanctioned countries form a 'block of the sanctioned'. Oil sheiks are selling oil for non-$ currencies; Africa and South America are also somewhat independent.

Some politicians are on our side; we need to support them by countering the forces behind the Culture War. Which groups coalesced into the Trotskyoid/Progressive/Green Left movement?

- The original Trotskyists, supporters of Trotsky against Stalin.

- Communists who broke with Soviet Union over the Moscow Purges, the Pact with Hitler, the Doctors' Plot, the Slansky Trials, Hungary 1956, or Czechoslovakia 1968. Some became Zionists; others formed the New Left.

- The Frankfurt School, who were supporters of Old Bolshevism but opponents of Stalin. Their brief was to combine Marx with Freud (this was also Trotsky's policy). They were also Zionists. In December 1971 Marcuse visited Israel, where he met Moshe Dayan:

> Horkheimer recited Kaddish over his parents' graves, attended synagogue on high holy days, and in 1971 made a special request to the Jewish community of Stuttgart in the region where he was born, to see if the Hebrew name which he was given at birth could be found. (Ivry, 2015).

- The 60s /70s movement, which was part Anarchist/Libertarian, part Maoist, part Trotskyist. The Anarchists/Libertarian Left 'dropped out'; the Marxists stayed in the system to change it from the inside. The Trots used entrist methods to take over Feminist groups, Gay groups, Indigenous groups, Black movements etc., shifting them from moderate to extremist positions.

- Foundations funded by left-wing billionaires, e.g. the Rockefeller Foundation, which funded Herbert Marcuse. This an example of Globalists funding Communists.

- H. G. Wells, prophet of the Cosmopolitan movement; his influence is on political parties, academics, and bankers.

On the role of Bankers and the Wealthy in forming the World State, Wells wrote in *Anticipations* :

"this effective New Republic may begin visibly to shape itself out and appear. It will appear first, I believe, as a conscious organization of intelligent and quite possibly in some cases wealthy men". (Wells, 1902/1999, p. 147).

Compare that with David Rockefeller's statement "The supranational sovereignty of an intellectual elite and world bankers is surely preferable to the national autodetermination practiced in past centuries." (Maxwell, 2000, pp. 15-16).

Wells continued in *The Open Conspiracy* (1933a):

"And when we come to the general functioning classes, landowners, industrial organizers, bankers, and so forth, who control the present system, such as it is, it should be still plainer that it is very largely from the ranks of these classes, and from their stores of experience and traditions of method, that the directive forces of the new order must emerge." (Wells, 1933a, p. 46)

The term 'socialism' has acquired a bad name from the totalitarianism of Stalin and Hitler, but also from Trotskyist misuse of this term to mean Gay Marriage, Trans rights, Open-Border immigration, and rights for minorities over the majority.

Rene Wormser (1958/2014), despite noting that Trotskyists were different from Stalinists, went ahead and bundled all types of socialists together:

Moreover, it is difficult to mark the line beyond which "socialism" becomes "communism." The line may be between methods of assuming power, communism being distinguished from other forms of socialism by its intent upon establishing a dictatorship of the proletariat. But this line is by no means clear. Socialism has the same ends as communism, though with an allegedly democratic approach, The Communist Manifesto of 1848 is the basis of all socialist parties the world over. (pp. 177-8)

That statement is wrong. Emperor Napoleon III crushed the Communists who had mounted the 1848 revolution, and who tried again in 1871, but he instituted a socialist economy inspired by Saint Simon. Karl Marx was bitterly oposed to Louis Napoleon, as he was to Proudhon, Saint Simon, Lassalle and Bakunin. Bundling them all together, as Wormser does, traps us in the current Capitalist despotism.

The reformist socialists of the nineteenth century were national socialists, in that they aspired to transform their own economy but retain national sovereignty; they did not envisage submitting to World Government or Open Borders. They sought class unity rather than class warfare, and Reform rather than Revolution.

When Lord Milner took over Britain's war economy after the fall of the Asquith Government in late 1916, at a time when Britain had been losing World War I badly, he replaced laissez-faire management with socialist co-ordination. He had grown up in Germany, and introduced German efficiency to Britain. He spared agricultural workers from conscription, gave them a minimum wage, and a floor price for wheat and oats (Gollin, pp. 416-9).

William Pember Reeves was born in Christchurch, NZ, but moved to Britain, where his 2-volume book (1902/1969) on state-led development in Australia and

New Zealand found favour in Fabian circles; they saw it as an exemplar for Britain. He was appointed Director of the London School of Economics.

Reeves noted, "Free trade had conquered England, though it was not to conquer her colonies" (v. I, p. 233). Australia is mainly composed of deserts, and even the fertile areas are beset by droughts and floods; the Outback was alluring but threatening. Whereas Americans expressed "distrust of a strong, interfering central authority", Australians looked to the state for help and development (p. 61).

> The State took up the work of providing transport and, of borrowing great sums to build railways, roads, and bridges, the die was cast. Government, with a partial grip of the soil and a complete grip of the land-transport, held a position too commanding for any private capitalists to challenge. It could borrow money much cheaper in London than any colonial financiers ... the colonists, acting through their Governments, resolved to be their own exploiters, and to build railways and lay telegraph lines for themselves. (p. 62)

The colonial governments of Australia and New Zealand also led the way, worldwide, in progressive socialist legislation: votes for women, wages boards to fix minimum wages, the 48 hour week (8 hour day), Industrial Arbitration courts, and Old Age Pensions (v. I, pp. 138-9; v. II pp. 18, 281). At Federation in 1901, Australia's *Colonial* Socialism became *National* Socialism (thanks to Denis McCormack for that insight). Australia was known as the Workers' Paradise (Outlander, 1911).

After the Depression and World War II, Australia's Chifley Labor government of 1945-9 embarked on extensive nationalisation. The conservative government of Robert Menzies (Liberal Party) and John McEwen (Country Party) maintained that mixed economy after 1949. Australia's socialism was called 'Country Party Socialism', because it was maintained by both Labor and the Country Party.

The socialist regimes of Britain and Australia after World War II were Christian, but can also be described as varieties of national socialism—based on class unity, not class war. In the 1960s and 70s, Communist militants in the unions wore Britain's Labour governments down. Those Communists had no brief for class unity; only for class war. Margaret Thatcher responded with class war from the side of Capital. The postwar regime of class unity gave way.

It was only in the wake of Thatcherism that Fabians dumped the national socialism introduced by Attlee and Chifley, and took up International Socialism and Wokeness instead, allowing Trotskyists to lead them by the nose.

Apart from Britain and Australia, postwar Israel had a national socialist economy. Zeev Sternhell explained it:

Nationalist socialism, properly understood, appeared in Europe in the last years of the nineteenth century and the beginning of the twentieth as an alternative to both Marxism and liberalism. ... The uniqueness of European nationalist socialism, whose origins can be traced to the pre-Marxist socialism of Proudhon, in relation to all other types of socialism, lay in one essential point: its acceptance of the principle of the nation's primacy and its subjection of the values of socialism to the service of the nation. ... This form of socialism preached the organic unity of the nation and the mobilization of all classes of society for the achievement of national objectives. ...

Nationalist socialism sought to manifest a natural solidarity between productive national wealth and the worker; between the owners of capital, who provide jobs, and the native born-workers. ... Class warfare was obviously out of the question.(Sternhell, 1998, pp. 7-8).

That is the kind of socialism that Clement Attlee and Ben Chifley established, under which I grew up in Sydney. What a wonderful economy it was; what a tragedy that we abandoned it. King O'Malley, Denison Miller, Jack Lang and Ben Chifley established and/or defended Australia's publicly-owned Commonwealth Bank, which was the Reserve Bank (the bank of issue) as well as a Savings and Trading bank; these heroes took Australia back from the private bankers.

Miller, the first head of the bank said, "This bank is being started without capital, as none is required at the present time, but it is backed by the entire wealth and credit of the whole of Australia" (Lang, 1962, p. 21). He stepped in to provide cheap loans, replacing expensive loans from London. Asked where his bank had raised all that money, Miller replied, "On the credit of the nation. It is unlimited" (p. 22). During World War I, Miller funded the establishment of the Australian Shipping Line, by issuing cheques (drawn on the Commonwealth Bank) to buy a fleet of 30 ships. Miller also funded the Transcontinental Railway Line from the West Coast to the East. That is what true Socialism is—not Gay Marriage. These days, we are in hock to private bankers; in the United States, Ellen Brown is waging a valiant campaign for Public Banking (Brown, 2013).

Dr H. C. "Nugget" Coombs was Governor of the Commonwealth Bank from 1949, and of the Reserve Bank (split off in from it in 1960) to 1968. He was a Taoist; his book *Trial Balance* contains many quotes from Lao Tzu (Coombs Taoist).

From the 1940s to the 1980s, Australia had strong centralised government, of the protectionist nation-building type, working with the private sector rather than stifling it. The Government did not issue myriads of rules, and did not control private lives, e.g., after World War II, migrants could build a garage, then live in it while building their own house; that is now illegal. The family and the churches were supported; there were no Speech Codes and no thought crimes.

Governments owned banks (Reserve, Saving, Trading, Rural & State), 99% of the railways, airlines (Qantas & TAA), the national shipping line, universities, the Post Office (including Telecom), ABC Radio (& later TV), the CSIRO research body, the Grain Board and other marketing boards, infrastructure projects e.g. the Snowy Mountains Authority, which built the biggest hydro-electric scheme and diverted the Snowy River west to water the desert (growing citrus, grapes, wheat, rice etc.), and the Hydro Electric Commission, Tasmania's electricity authority. Wages were high, taxes were high, and there was full employment. We did not know how well off we were.

The split in Labor of the 1930s, pitting Jack Lang (Labor Premier of N.S.W.) against Ted Theodore (Labor Federal Treasurer) was caused by James Scullin (Labor Prime Minister). Scullin approved the proposal of Sir Robert Gibson that Sir Otto Niemeyer of the Bank of England visit Australia to advise on banking policy. Ross Fitzgerald wrote, "It is astonishing that Scullin approved the request. Apparently he kept the decision secret because he feared to tell his Labor colleagues. It is not clear how far Theodore approved or was even consulted. " (Fitzgerald, 1994, p. 241). Niemeyer was responsible for Britain's disastrous return to the Gold Standard, and insisted that Australia follow deflationary policy during the Depression, whereas both Lang and Theodore advocated credit expansion. If the Labor Party had made Theodore leader in 1929 in place of Scullin, and gone for a Double Dissolution election to get control of the Senate—as advocated by Frank Anstey (Fitzgerald, p. 229)— the 1930s Split could have been averted or minimised.

In the 1950s Split, Bob Santamaria tried to save the Labor Party from the fellow-travellers, who were Stalinist then. Communists controlled major unions, and used strikes (e.g. the Coal Strike) as a political weapon to try to bring down the system, even though Chifley's government was socialist. Santamaria's Industrial Groups worked to counter Communist control of the unions, but rather than support him, Chifley and Dr. Evatt branded him an enemy.

It was Evatt, not Santamaria, who split Labor over the Communist issue. Evatt chose to represent the Communist-led Waterside Workers Federation at the High Court; then he took a pro-Soviet line when Vladimir Petrov, a Soviet spy, defected in 1954. KGB couriers later forcibly escorted Petrov's wife Evdokia across the tarmac at Mascot Airport, Sydney, to return her to Moscow. When the plane landed in Darwin, Australian intelligence agents boarded it and allowed Evdokia to ring her husband, after which she decided to defect too. The dramatic photo of Evdokia being escorted by KGB couriers kept Labor out of power until 1972.

The A.L.P. still honours Evatt with a Foundation named after him, and refuses to admit that it was wrong about the Petrov Affair, just as the British Labour Party has still not admitted that the Zinoviev Letter was genuine.

Chapter 9: How the Economist became Left wing, and the Trots betrayed the People

In recent decades, the Economist magazine has been advocating policies generally regarded as 'left-wing': Feminism, the Gay and Trans movements, Indigenous movements, anti-Racism, Refugees, Open-border immigration, and 'Human Rights'.

They are all part of the Culture War against the Christian religion, Western civilisation and nation states. This Culture War is akin to that waged by the Freemasons and Illuminati in the eighteenth and nineteenth centuries.

Before Margaret Thatcher came to power, however, The Economist was regarded as a right-wing newspaper, because it opposed the Socialist state created by Clement Attlee.

Just after her death on April 8, 2013, the Economist ran several articles lauding her counter-revolution:

https://www.economist.com/blogs/blighty/2013/04/margaret-thatcher-0

Margaret Thatcher A cut above the rest
Margaret Thatcher transformed Britain and left an ideological legacy to rival that of Marx, Mao, Gandhi or Reagan
Blighty

Apr 8th 2013

by A.W. and R.C.

Judged from the grand historical perspective, Mrs Thatcher's biggest legacy has to do with the spread of freedom—with the defeat of totalitarianism in its most vicious form in the Soviet Union, and with the revival of a liberal economic tradition that had gone into retreat after 1945.

The Economist sided with Thatcher's branding the socialist Britain created by Attlee an 'evil empire' along with the Soviet Union:

http://www.economist.com/news/briefing/21576081-margaret-thatcher-britains-prime-minister-1979-1990-died-april-8th-age

No ordinary politician
Margaret Thatcher, Britain's prime minister from 1979 to 1990, died on April 8th at the age of 87. We assess her legacy to Britain and the world

Apr 13th 2013

For Mrs Thatcher, her system was moral as much as economic. It confronted the "evil" empires of communism and socialism. Many things caused the collapse of the Soviet Union in 1991, but the clarity of Mrs Thatcher's beliefs was a vital factor. ...

The country shifted significantly to the left during the second world war, leading to a landslide victory for Clement Attlee's Labour Party in 1945. Building on the forced collectivism of the war years, the Attlee government embarked on industrial nationalisation and introduced the welfare state. To a generation of politicians scarred by the mass unemployment of the 1930s, full employment became the overriding object of political life. ...

It was, as Mrs Thatcher's favourite intellectual guru, Friedrich Hayek, had warned in 1944, "the road to serfdom". ...

In 1984 began the great round of privatisations, in which behemoths such as British Telecom, British Gas and British Airways were sold off. Individuals were encouraged to buy shares, thus creating the image, at least, of "popular capitalism". ...

After vanquishing the enemy in the South Atlantic, she rounded on the "enemy within" at home: in the BBC; the universities; and in local government ...

Mrs Thatcher's privatisation revolution spread around the world. Other E.U. countries followed her example, if not her rhetoric: in 1985-2000 European governments sold off some $100 billion-worth of state assets, including national champions such as Lufthansa, Volkswagen and Renault. The post-communist countries embraced it heartily: by 1996 Russia had privatised some 18,000 industrial enterprises. India part-dismantled the licence Raj, and unleashed a cavalcade of successful companies. Across Latin America governments embraced market liberalisation. ...

Margaret Thatcher's counter-revolution was not merely her own doing. Behind her was the Mont Pelerin Society, which, despite a deliberately-chosen low-key name, functioned as the 'Comintern' of Capitalism. It was a lobby founded by Friedrich Hayek, which met at Mont Pelerin in Switzerland, to which Big Business and its hired economists belonged, and which spawned numerous think-tanks promoting privatisation. The Economist explains:

https://www.economist.com/christmas-specials/2016/12/24/how-vienna-produced-ideas-that-shaped-the-west

How Vienna produced ideas that shaped the West
The city of the century

Dec 24th 2016 | VIENNA

But Hayek was not just a dry theorist. He was also a relentless circus-master for the liberal cause. ...

To organise the fightback he founded the Mont Pelerin Society (MPS) in 1947. Named after the Swiss mountain where the first meeting was held (simply because the founding members couldn't agree on a more appropriate alternative), the MPS was Hayek's own Circle for liberalism. It fused the Viennese liberals in exile, including Karl Popper, who had just published The Open Society and its Enemies, with their embattled fellow-travellers from Germany, France, Britain and America, most notably Milton Friedman. Over the next decades the MPS spawned scores of think-tanks around the world dedicated to spreading the word of the Austrian school. Politicians often attended their meetings. The "Chicago school" of economists was made up largely of MPS members. After decades of quiet campaigning, Hayek's ideas were taken up again by a subsequent generation of politicians in the mid-1970s, including Margaret Thatcher and Ronald Reagan.

When Milton Friedman died in 2006, the Economist magazine lauded him as "a giant among economists":

https://www.economist.com/special-report/2006/11/23/a-heavyweight-champ-at-five-foot-two

Special report | Milton Friedman

A heavyweight champ, at five foot two

The legacy of Milton Friedman, a giant among economists

Nov 23rd 2006

Mr Friedman brought about profound changes in the way his profession, politicians and the public thought of economic questions ... {he opposed} price supports for farming; tariffs and import quotas; rent control; minimum wages ...

Trots betray the People

In 1979, about the same time as Thatcher came to power, Australia's main Trotskyist party, the Socialist Workers Party (SWP), published a book entitled *Socialism or Nationalism?: Which Road for the Australian Labor Movement?*, by Jon West, Dave Holmes and Gordon Adler, which argued for Free Trade, for the abandonment of tariffs, and against the 1950s economic model. The book condemned all the other Communist parties as Stalinist and Nationalist.

The SWP has since renamed itself Socialist Alliance; it is the publisher of Green Left Weekly.

This book argued for the Thatcherite agenda, but from left-wing arguments, aiming to persuade Labor politicians. It came at a time when Labor was desperately looking for a new policy which might bring it to government. Three years later, Gough Whitlam and Ralph Willis (who later became Treasurer) co-authored Fabian Society Pamphlet No. 37, called *Reshaping Australian Industry: Tariffs and Socialists*, in which they put the same Free Trade line.

The Preface of the SWP book says, "Many of the most important of these debates have taken place over the question of internationalism and nationalism. ... This book is a further defence of Marxist internationalism and reflects the views of the Socialist Workers Party, the Australian Trotskyist organisation" (West et al, pp. 9-10).

Jon West, in his chapter Nationalism and the Labor Movement, calls for aboriginal self-determination: "The one policy which Australian governments have steadfastly refused to adopt is the right of Blacks to decide their own fate, i.e. Black self-determination. ... If we are to have one single united Australian nation, clearly an independent Black nation cannot be allowed to exist. ... In the clash between Black nationalism and white Australian nationalism, it is Black nationalism which is progressive and Australian nationalism which is reactionary" (West, Jon, 1979, p. 19).

Arguing against Tariff Protection, Jon West writes, "Perhaps the most obvious strategic conception which flows from the nationalist outlook for the labor movement is protectionism. ... Protectionists argue that the big problem facing workers is the competition from foreign goods on the Australian market; the development of industry overseas, primarily in Asia, which is supposed to take jobs from Australian workers; and a running down of Australian manufacturing industry" (West, Jon, 1979, p. 27).

Jon West also condemns Left-Nationalists for rejecting Foreign Investment:

The left-nationalists have proposed a variety of arguments to demonstrate that foreign-owned corporations are more damaging to the interests of Australian working people than corporations owned in Australia. Some of these arguments deserve attention.

It is often argued that foreign investment slows Australia's economic growth because foreign companies ship home their profits instead of plowing them back into the Australian economy. Two replies are possible to this argument. Firstly, there is no evidence to suggest that Australian companies re-invest a higher proportion of their profits than foreign corporations ...

Another argument is that foreign corporations tend to shut down, to lay off workers more frequently because large multinationals can transfer their operations to other countries if Australian wages are too high. However, Australian companies are just as susceptible to shifts on the international and domestic markets as multinationals ...

A further argument is that foreign corporations are tending to invest in raw materials, primarily mining industries, and are thus turning Australia into a quarry for U.S. imperialism. ... (West, Jon, 1979, p. 67)

All of these things have happened since Free Trade was introduced in the 1980s; but the argument West does not mention, is that without Protection, our government—the one we intend to represent us—cannot manage the economy, since under Free Trade it has no control of exports, imports, and foreign capital flows i.e. foreign investment and foreign debt.

While the Trotskyists say that Australian workers should not co-operate with Australian-owned business, they themselves are co-operating with Foreign Capital.

On August 19, 1998, I attended a meeting of Politics in the Pub at Olims Hotel in Canberra, on the subject of Globalisation. It was organised by the (Trotskyist) International Socialist Organisation; various union leaders were there. ISO leader Rick Kuhn, of the Australian National University, put the view on Tariffs presented above: he said that employers want to restore Tariffs, but encouraged workers to resist such a move. "We support Globalisation," he said, "because it draws people from different societies together; what we oppose is the exploitation that can follow." If I were a worker listening to such advice, I would wonder if the speaker were really on my side.

Trotskyist Jon West's most salient point was that "Perhaps the worst aspect of the adoption of protectionism as a policy for fighting unemployment is that it is seen as a substitute for a class-struggle approach" (West, Jon, 1979, p. 29). In other words, a Protected economy fosters class unity; without antagonism between the classes, sexes, and races, the Trotskyists are out of business.

Australia's postwar Christian Socialist economy was inaugurated by the Labor Government of Ben Chifley. But Communists in the unions mounted a strike in the Coal industry which helped bring Chifley's government down in 1949. Even today, the Trotskyists play up their role in bringing down the best government Australia ever had. Fortunately, the conservative parties maintained the socialist economy until Thatcherism arrived in the mid 1980s.

Similarly in Britain, Communists in the unions, such as Arthur Scargill of the National Union of Mineworkers, fomented strikes which weakened the Christian Socialist economy and paved the way for Margaret Thatcher's rise, undermining the fairest economy Britain ever had.

With the abandonment of the postwar Socialist regimes, we are now in the throes of class war, sex and gender war, race war, and war over environment policy. There has never been less unity.

Just as the Economist became 'left-wing' after Thatcher's counter-revolution, George Soros was deemed 'left wing' after his Foundations helped bring down the Soviet Union and Yugoslavia.

Soros helped precipitate the 1997 Asia Crisis, then gave an interview to the Sydney Morning Herald, in which he said,

"If there was ever a man who would fit the stereotype of the Judeo-plutocratic Bolshevik Zionist world conspirator, it is me" (Hewett, 1997).

Given that his Foundations had helped bring down the Stalinist Soviet Union, which kind of Bolshevik would he be? Why a Trotskyoid, of course. He funds Trotskyist causes, e. g. Antifa.

The Economist magazine was a staunch opponent of the Corn Laws, by which British agriculture was protected with tariffs. Karl Marx also applauded the Repeal of the Corn Laws, but for different reasons: "But, generally speaking, the Protective system in these days is conservative, while the Free Trade system works destructively. It breaks up old nationalities and carries antagonism of proletariat and bourgeoisie to the uttermost point. In a word, the Free Trade system hastens the Social Revolution. In this revolutionary sense alone, gentlemen, I am in favor of Free Trade" (Marx, 1848/1976, p. 450).

Karl Marx advocated Free Trade, i.e. Laissez-Faire Capitalism, because (a) whereas Protectionism builds up the nation-state, Free Trade breaks it down, as a prelude to the creation of a world-state by the Capitalists (b) Free Trade breaks down traditional cultures, as a prelude to the creation of a world culture (c) Free Trade exacerbates class warfare, and through this the Capitalists will lose control of the world-state—they will be defeated by the impoverished classes, with the help of their backers in the higher classes.

Marx' speech welcoming Free Trade was translated into English by Florence Kelley, and published, with an Introduction by Frederick Engels, in *Wage-labor and Capital*. Engels wrote in the Introduction:

> That was the time of the Brussels Congress, the time when Marx prepared the speech in question. While recognising that Protection may still, under certain circumstances, for instance, in the Germany of 1847, be of advantage to the manufacturing capitalists; while proving that free trade was not the panacea for all the evils under which the working class suffered, and might even aggravate them; he pronounces, ultimately and on principle, in favour of free trade. (Engels, 1902, p.6)

So Marx and Engels clearly knew that Free Trade might worsen the lot of the lower classes, but advocated it anyway, as a means to achieving a World State. They were prepared to endorse an evil means, to achieve what they saw as a worthy end.

Trotsky's biographer Dmitri Volkogonov noted "At the Third Comintern Congress on 23 July 1921, Trotsky declared: 'Only crisis can be the father of revolution, while a period of prosperity is its gravedigger'" (Volkogonov, 1996, p. 474.)

Sir James Goldsmith (1994) argues against Free Trade, in his book *The Trap*. The front cover asks, "How is it that humanity's greatest leap forward in material prosperity has resulted in extreme social breakdown?" It also presents the case against modern Agriculture, the E.U., and the homogenization of the sexes.

In Australia, Thatcherite privatisation and deregulation began in the mid-1980s. Its leader was John Howard of the Liberal Party, but the Labor Government of Bob Hawke and Paul Keating implemented identical policies; the electorate was not presented with a choice, since both main parties had the same policies.

One voice in Australia warned that privatisation and deregulation would lead to 'Big Brother' laws of social control. Rick Farley, director of the National Farmers Federation (NFF), said that governments, no longer running much of the economy themselves, would interfere with our private lives instead:

> The electorate should be warned of cynical moves by government into "big brother" social regulation, the director of the National Farmers Federation (NFF), Mr Rick Farley, said yesterday. Mr Farley told the conference that as government progressively withdrew from the area of industry regulation, it was seeking new areas of social regulation to provide a basis for political debate and an appearance of activity (Cribb, 1988).

When the hippies and alternative lifestylers left the cities in the later 1970s, they went to rural areas and built their own houses without regulation; and had babies at home, without being coerced into doing it the hospital way. I was one of them.

The new social regulation that began in the 1980s, now called the Nanny State, suppresses these basic rights. Despite the high cost of housing, you cannot legally build your own home independently of bureaucratic Building Codes, meddlesome Inspection regimes, and hefty Council fees—even if you live in a rural area.

Yet, many of the hippie-build homes were well built, artistic, and economic. Although Building Codes claim to enforce higher standards, it is only the building industry that was cutting corners, not those building their own homes out of love.

Australian house frames are now built from flimsy Radiata Pine, 70mm x 35mm, or very thin steel frames prone to rust (and steel is energy-intensive and non-renewable). Before the Building Code, and before the Greens turned most of the hardwood State Forests into National Parks, Australian hardwood house frames were much stronger, 4" x 2" in the southern states, and 3" x 2" in Qld, because Qld hardwoods are more dense. Eucalypt is much stronger than pine.

The building industry now builds expensive, monotonous, soul-less housing developments with no space for trees or gardens. Such housing estates are heat sinks relying on air-conditioning. Hippie-build houses were unique, designed by the owner, and hand-crafted—made of mudbrick, rammed earth, stone, weatherboard, log cabins etc., and no two the same.

What Building Codes are really about is centralised control. Insurance laws have been amended to deny insurance to those who do it their own way.

You can no longer look for parts for your washing machine in a recycling yard; they bear signs saying 'No Scavenging', the excuse being that you might sue them for stubbing your toe.

With the proliferation of litigation, homebirth midwives find it difficult (and expensive) to get insurance.

Ivan Illich (1977) perceived that the dominance of the Professions (including specialists and experts in all the Trades) was disabling ordinary people from making decisions in the own lives:

> The Age of Professions will be remembered as the time when politics withered, when voters, guided by professors, entrusted to technocrats the power to legislate needs, renounced the authority to decide who needs what and suffered monopolistic oligarchies to determine the means by which these needs shall be met. (pp. 11-12)

> ... the bodies of specialists that now dominate the creation, adjudication and implementation of needs are a new kind of cartel. They are more deeply entrenched than a Byzantine bureaucracy ... and equipped with a tighter hold over those they claim as victims than any mafia. (p. 15)

> The disabling of the citizen through professional dominance is completed through the power of illusion. Religion finally becomes displaced, not by the state or the waning of the faith, but by professional establishments and client confidence. (p. 27)

Chapter 10: George Soros and the 1997 Asia Crisis

Japan's postwar economy was a kind of National Socialism pursuing neither guns nor butter but accrual of capital. It was admirable in many ways, and has since been adopted, with variations, by Singapore, Taiwan, Korea and China.

However, this system was not so good for those on the other end. It destroyed jobs in many other countries, and led to economic colonialism.

Kinhide Mushakoji, an author published by the Trilateral Commission as well as UNESCO, wrote that the Asian Tigers were Japan's occluded (i.e. secret, hidden) East Asia Co-Prosperity Sphere.

Daniel Burstein sounded the alarm in 1988 with his book *Yen: Japan's new Financial Empire and its Threat to America.*

George Soros wrote, in his 1987 book *The Alchemy of Finance*, "Japan has been accumulating assets abroad, while the United States has been amassing debts. ... President Reagan ... pursued the illusion of military superiority at the cost of rendering our leading position in the world economy illusory; while Japan wanted to keep growing in the shadow of the United States as long as possible. ... Japan has, in fact, emerged as the banker to the world" (Soros, 1987/1994, p. 350).

Usurping Soros' own role, perhaps? Soros continued, " ... the prospect of Japan's emerging as the dominant financial power in the world is very disturbing, not only from the point of view of the United States but also from that of the entire Western civilization. ... The United States and Britain are members of the same culture. This is not true of Japan. ... The Japanese think in terms of subordination. Contrast this with the notion that all men are created equal ... Japan is a nation on the rise; we have become decadent" (pp. 353-4).

ASEAN was another target. Its decision to admit Burma was seen as defiance of the U.S. Soros and fellow speculators depicted themselves as champions of "human rights". They objected to Burma's joining ASEAN, but not to Vietnam's joining.

Burma (Myanmar) is important to them partly because it's a satellite of China; it gives China access to the Indian Ocean. Western leaders touting 'Human Rights' tried to isolate the Burmese government, as they later isolated the Sri Lankan government during the Tamil Tigers' civil war, driving both regimes into the arms of China.

Just as Japanese methods were covert, so were Jewish methods. Soros and other hedge-fund managers, with the help of leading Jewish figures within World Finance, brought down the "Asia Model" in 1997.

At the time:

- Alan Greenspan was head of the Fed

- James Wolfensohn was head of the World Bank

- Stanley Fischer was running the IMF (as Chief Economist)

- Madeline Allbright was U.S. Secretary of State

- Robert Rubin was Secretary of the Treasury (Treasurer)

- Lawrence Summers was his Deputy

- Mickey Kantor was Secretary for Trade (in charge of GATT and WTO)

- William Cohen was Secretary for Defence

- Sandy Berger was National Security Adviser

all being Jewish.

And Paul Wolfowitz, also Jewish, played a role in the ouster of President Suharto.

George Soros, Jewish too, was heavily involved in the "Asia Crisis". The currencies of Indonesia and some other Asian countries had been pegged to the yen prior to the "Asia Crisis", suggesting a "yen block". As the U.S. dollar fell, those currencies rose with the yen. Those who exonerate Soros say that the "Asia Crisis" was caused by those currencies rising too high, and by China's devaluing its currency 33% in 1994, undercutting ASEAN exports. Yet, subsequently, the whole "Asia model" was discredited, suggesting ideological motives.

And the "yen block" was destroyed as well. In the Sydney Morning Herald, economist Max Walsh commented, "A little-noticed but significant feature of the Asian crisis has been the demise of the yen bloc" (Walsh, 1998).

Chalmers Johnson, writing in the Australian Financial Review of November 18, 1998, said that Western Financiers caused the Asia Crisis:

Globalisation: creed of greed

If the APEC leaders fail to deal with the real cause of the Asian financial crisis—the preservation of American global hegemony—then this week's summit will fail to accomplish anything substantial, argues Chalmers Johnson.

After all the endless mouthing off in the pages of The Wall Street Journal, The Economist of London and The Australian Financial Review about East Asia's "crony capitalism", the lack of "transparency" in Asian stock exchanges, the "no pain, no gain" logic of the International Monetary Fund, and how the Asian economic challenge to Anglo-American capitalism had fizzled, we now know that none of these things had anything at all to do with the Asian—now global—economic crisis. ...

Here's the new explanation as it is developing in seminar rooms from Seoul to Kuala Lumpur: with the end of the Cold War, the United States decided it had to launch a rollback operation in East Asia if it were to maintain its global hegemony.

The high-growth economies of East Asia had become the main challengers to American power in the region, and it was time they be brought to heel. The campaign worked in two phases.

First, a major ideological barrage from the Jagdish Bhagwatis and Ross Garnauts of this world was launched to soften up the Asians. These famous tenured professors of economics, who never once faced a "market force" in their own lives, were hired to preach the beauties of "globalisation', in this case meaning American economic institutions.

Concretely, these include total laissez-faire, destruction of unions and social safety nets, staffing of regulatory agencies with retired financiers, indifference to pay differentials between CEOs and the ordinary labor force, moving manufacturing to low-wage areas regardless of the social costs, and totally unregulated flows of capital in and out of any and all economies.

Then came phase two. Once the Asian economies had begun to open themselves up and were standing in the world marketplace more or less naked, the "hedge funds" were let loose on them. These funds are actually huge concentrations of capital owned by very wealthy Western white men, who manipulate bewilderingly complex financial instruments called "derivatives". They usually locate their offices in offshore tax havens like the Cayman Islands and do everything in their power to avoid regulators or tax collectors in the so-called "free market democracies".

The funds easily raped Thailand, Indonesia and South Korea and then turned the shivering survivors over to the IMF, not to help the victims but in order to ensure that any Western bank was not stuck with "non-performing" loans in the devastated countries.

An article 'How To Kill A Tiger' in the Asian edition of Time Magazine, dated November 3, 1997, tells how the Speculators did it:

How To Kill A Tiger
Speculators Tell The Story Of Their Attack Against The Baht, The Opening Act Of An Ongoing Drama
By Eugene Linden
TIME magazine Asia
November 3, 1997 Vol. 150 No. 18

The description was brutally honest: "We are like wolves on the ridgeline looking down on a herd of elk," said one of the currency speculators who helped trigger the cascading devaluations that eventually led to the stock-market tumbles that swept the globe last week. Late last year, eight months before Thailand finally succumbed and devalued the baht, the wolves had been on the prowl. ... Unable to resist, each predator began to plan his attack. "By culling the weak and infirm, we help maintain the health of the herd," said the trader. ...

The Thai economy had become one big bulging bubble, and late last year the wolves took notice. ...

Sensing that their prey had been cornered by their own venality, the wolves began to circle in early 1997. ... Drawing from multibillion-dollar war chests, hedge-fund operators such as George Soros and Julian Robertson intensified their attack on the baht. One way the speculators bet against the currency was by entering into contracts with dealers who would give dollars in return for an agreement to repay a specific amount of bahts some months in the future. If the baht rose in value, the seller of

How to Kill a Tiger

Speculators tell the story of their attack against the baht, the opening act of an ongoing drama

the contract made money; but if it fell, the buyer profited because he could repay the contract with cheaper bahts. Demand for such contracts started to drive up interest rates, and the Bank of Thailand began issuing many of these so-called forward contracts itself. ...

Now speculators had access to an estimated $15 billion in forward contracts issued in February and March that they would not have to cover for as much as a year. An estimated 80% to 90% of these forward contracts ended up in the hands of speculators. By May the central bank realized it was contributing to the baht's undoing and abruptly stopped issuing any more forward contracts.

Sensing blood, traders began moving in for the kill and in mid-May flooded the market with orders to sell bahts. ...And on July 2, the baht was devalued, setting off a chain reaction throughout the region's currency markets and then, last week, around the world's stock exchanges. While no hard number is available, the wolves who started all this turmoil were very well fed, probably with profits in excess of $3 billion.

The Time article came with graphs showing the collapse of the currencies of Thailand, the Philippines, Malaysia and Indonesia.

Those graphs have been deleted, but I uploaded them to https://mailstar.net/Time-kill-Tiger.jpg. They show that whereas all four currencies plummeted, only the Baht went up in the weeks before, because Soros et. al. were borrowing Baht to pay for forward contracts—to short it, betting that it would fall.

The graphs show that the plunge began in mid June 1997. The ASEAN Foreign Ministers, meeting at Kuala Lumpur on May 31, 1997, had agreed to admit Burma , in defiance of Soros, Al Gore, and Madeline Albright.

The Asia Crisis led to the fall of Indonesia's President Suharto, crafted by Paul Wolfowitz:

> Long before Iraq, Paul Wolfowitz's neo-conservative idea was successfully applied in the Philippines and Indonesia, claims Steve Hanke
> The Australian
> April 29, 2003
> MOST people think the overthrow of Saddam Hussein resulted from the U.S. Government's embrace of a new policy. This particular policy may be new, but the regime change idea and its use are not.

> U.S. Deputy Defence Secretary Paul Wolfowitz and a small group of like-minded neo-conservatives developed the regime change idea some time ago and have been promoting it since. The Iraqi dictator was not the first to fall in the crosshairs of that policy. When the U.S. government concluded that Philippines president Ferdinand Marcos was illegitimate, he had to go. Consequently, Washington assisted in his removal from power in 1986. The point man who engineered the overthrow of Marcos was Wolfowitz, an assistant secretary of state at the time.

> During Wolfowitz's tenure as the U.S. ambassador to Indonesia from 1986 to 1989, he planted the regime change idea once again. This time president Suharto was in the crosshairs. He was deemed to be corrupt and undemocratic, and had to be overthrown. The U.S., with the help of the International Monetary Fund, eventually accomplished its goal in 1998, when Suharto was toppled in May that year. ...

> Australia's former prime minister Paul Keating arrived at a similar conclusion: "The [U.S.] Treasury quite deliberately used the economic collapse as a means of bringing the ouster of president Suharto."

Chapter 11: Karl Marx' writings on Jews & Finance—censored as Anti-Semitic

Many readers of Karl Marx's book *Capital* have wondered why it says nothing about the role of Jewish Bankers. In fact, Marx did write several items on that topic: firstly in German, *An Der Juden Frage* (1843), translated as *On the Jewish Question*, and then two opinion pieces in English for the New York Daily Tribune (1855 & 1856).

On the Jewish Question has two parts. The first part, which was often quoted in books about Marx during the Cold War, is relatively innocuous. The second part, which is much more incisive, is hard to find. But I have spared you the trouble, dear reader, by providing the best bits below.

The two opinion pieces for the New York Daily Tribune are explosive. But they have been censored from Marx literature— except for *The Karl Marx Library*. You can also look them up at libraries in New York.

In the 1850s, Karl Marx had no qualms about exposing the Rothschilds. This was the time of the Crimean War, and Marx accused them and other Jewish bankers of helping to fund it, by buying Russian bonds. The Czarist regime was a pet hate of Marx; it had helped stem the tide of revolution in Europe.

A decade later, when Marx and Bakunin were competing to control the First International, Bakunin, in his 1869 article Polémique contre les Juifs, accused Marx's circle of being heavily Jewish, and even claimed that the Rothschilds were in league with Marx. Left-wing Jews, he said, had one foot in the communist movement and the other in the bank.

Anarchist (Libertarian Socialist) Ulli Diemer supplies the following translation:

Bakunin on Marx and Rothschild

"Himself a Jew, Marx has around him, in London and France, but especially in Germany, a multitude of more or less clever, intriguing, mobile, speculating Jews, such as Jews are every where: commercial or banking agents, writers, politicians, correspondents for newspapers of all shades, with one foot in the bank, the other in the socialist movement, and with their behinds sitting on the German daily press — they have taken possession of all the newspapers — and you can imagine what kind of sickening literature they produce. Now, this entire Jewish world, which forms a single profiteering sect, a people of bloodsuckers, a single gluttonnous parasite, closely and intimately united not only across national borders but across all differences of political opinion — this Jewish world today stands for the most part at the disposal of Marx and at the same time at the disposal of Rothschild. I am certain that Rothschild for his part greatly values the merits of Marx, and that Marx for his part feels instinctive attraction and great respect for Rothschild.

This may seem strange. What can there be in common between Communism and the large banks? Oh! The Communism of Marx seeks enormous centralization in the state, and where such exists, there must inevitably be a central state bank, and where such a bank exists, the parasitic Jewish nation, which. speculates on the work of the people, will always find a way to prevail ... ." (Bakunin, 1871/1924, pp. 204-216)

To modern ears, this sounds antisemitic as well as an overstatement. But Theodore Herzl, one of the main founders of Zionism, confirmed the connection between Jewish Bankers and Revolution in his book *The Jewish State*: "When we sink, we become a revolutionary proletariat, the subordinate officers of all revolutionary parties; and at the same time, when we rise, there rises also our terrible power of the purse" (Herzl, 1896/1988, p. 91).

Another decade later, after Marx' death in 1883, Engels welcomed the extensive Jewish support for the Communist movement, and warned against antisemitism, in a letter titled On Anti-Semitism (in which he also states that he is not Jewish):

...But whether you might not be doing more harm than good with your anti-Semitism is something I would ask you to consider. For anti-Semitism betokens a retarded culture, which is why it is found only in Prussia and Austria, and in Russia too. Anyone dabbling in anti-Semitism, either in England or in America, would simply be ridiculed ...

 where production is still in the hands of the farmers, landowners, craftsmen and suchlike classes surviving from the Middle Ages — there, and there alone, is capital mainly Jewish, and there alone is anti-Semitism rife.

Furthermore, we are far too deeply indebted to the Jews. Leaving aside Heine and Börne, Marx was a full-blooded Jew; Lassalle was a Jew. Many of our best people are Jews. My friend Victor Adler, who is now atoning in a Viennese prison for his devotion to the cause of the proletariat, Eduard Bernstein, editor of the London Sozialdemokrat, Paul Singer, one of our best men in the Reichstag — people whom I am proud to call my friends, and all of them Jewish! After all, I myself was dubbed a Jew by the Gartenlaube and, indeed, if given the choice, I'd as lief be a Jew as a 'Herr von'!

London, April 19, 1890
Frederick Engels (Engels, 1890/1934)

By the time of the Bolshevik Revolution, 50% of Russian revolutionaries were Jewish, and they had a number of Jewish bankers in their camp. Contrary to the official line that Communists were proletarians, Lenin's Bolshevik party was mainly composed of intellectuals. Disclosing the Jewish role in Finance might jeopardise their support, so Lenin censored it—even though Marx himself had written about it.

Encyclopaedia Judaica (2007) states that Lenin censored Marx' essay "On the Jewish Question":

Bolshevik Theory (1903-1917)

[Moshe Mishkinsky]

Although generally relying on Marx on questions of fundamental importance, Lenin did not resort to Marx's famous essay "On the Jewish Question" when dealing with Jewish affairs, because of its anti-Jewish implications. He rejected outright any suggestion that the Bolsheviks should ignore anti-Jewish policy and propaganda in czarist Russia, let alone make use of its popular appeal. Lenin regarded the czarist anti-Jewish hate campaign as a diversionary maneuver, an integral part of the demagogic campaign against "the aliens" conducted by henchmen of the czarist regime. (Mishkinsky, 2007)

Leninist regimes denied the Jewish role in creating Communism, just as they denied the Jewish role in Finance; and they equally denied that Stalin overthrew the Jewish Bolsheviks. Many of those he overthrew ended up as Zionists; others became Neocons.

A century later, Marx' writings on the preponderance of Jews in Banking and Finance remain suppressed.

Abram Leon (1918—1944), a Jewish Trotskyist, did write a candid expose, *The Jewish Question: A Marxist Interpretation*. But since that time, most Trotskyists have hidden the Jewish role in Usury.

Marx' two essays of the 1850s, The Jewish Bankers of Europe and The Russian Loan, are excised from his writings in Trotskyist circles, and are unknown elsewhere. My website was the first place on the internet where the text was online.

The Marxists Internet Archive (marxists.org) is a Trotskyist site; Trotskyists downplay the 'antisemitic' content in Marx's writings.

On the Jewish Question has two parts. In the first part, Marx is commenting on Bruno Bauer's paper Die Judenfrage (The Jewish Question). In this second part, Marx is commenting on Bruno Bauer's paper Die Fahigkeit der heutigen Juden und Christen frei zu werden (The capacity of the present-day Jews and Christians to become free).

The following text of On the Jewish Question is from *The Marx-Engels Reader*, ed. Robert Tucker (Norton & Company, New York, 1972 and 1978). The online version (https://genius.com/Robert-c-tucker-chapter-i-annotated) is the 1978 edition; but my quotes below are from the 1972 edition:

> Let us consider the real Jew: not the sabbath Jew, whom Bauer considers, but the everyday Jew. Let us not seek the secret of the Jew in his religion, but let us seek the secret of the religion in the real Jew. What is the profane basis of Judaism? Practical need, self interest. What is the worldly cult of the Jew? Huckstering. What is his worldly god? Money. Very well: then in emancipating itself from huckstering and money, and thus from real and practical Judaism, our age would emancipate itself. ...

> We discern in Judaism, therefore, a universal antisocial element of the present time, whose historical development, zealously aided in its harmful aspects by the Jews, has now attained its culminating point, a point at which it must necessarily begin to disintegrate. In the final analysis, the emancipation of the Jews is the emancipation of mankind from Judaism.

> The Jew has already emancipated himself in a Jewish fashion.

> "The Jew, who is merely tolerated in Vienna for example, determines the fate of the whole Empire by his financial power. The Jew, who may be entirely without rights in the smallest German state, decides the destiny of Europe. While the corporations and guilds exclude the Jew, or at least look on him with disfavour, the audacity of industry mocks the obstinacy of medieval institutions." (Marx, 1843/1972, pp. 46-7)

Marx is here quoting from Bauer's Die Judenfrage (The Jewish Question). He continues:

> This is not an isolated instance. The Jew has emancipated himself in a Jewish manner, not only by acquiring the power of money, but also because money has become, through him and also apart from him, a world power, while the practical Jewish spirit has become the practical spirit of the Christian nations. The Jews have emancipated themselves in so far as the Christians have become Jews. (Marx, 1843/1972, p. 47)

Various translations from the German original have appeared, including one by Dagobert Runes that imputed a genocidal motive to Marx: "A World Without Jews".

Marx was NOT genocidal, He was saying that Jews should stop being Jewish, i.e. change their cultural practices—which he saw as arising from their religion.

In the 1850s, Marx wrote opinion pieces in English for the New York Daily Tribune, for which he was paid $5 each. Among them were two pieces on Jewish bankers: 'The Loanmongers of Europe' (also published as 'The Jewish Bankers of Europe'), published on Nov. 22, 1855, and 'The Russian Loan', published on Jan. 4, 1856. They can be inspected at libraries in New York. They were reproduced in *The*

Karl Marx Library, Volume 5 On Religion, arranged and edited by Saul K. Padover (1972).

The Trotskyist site marxists.org has a list of the articles of Marx and Engels published in the New York Daily Tribune; but these two pieces are missing (censored):   https://www.marxists.org/archive/marx/works/subject/newspapers/new-york-tribune.htm .

Here is part of The Loanmongers of Europe, from The Karl Marx Library, Volume 5:

The Jewish Bankers of Europe*

* From "The Loanmongers of Europe," published in the New York Daily Tribune, November 22, 1855.

TAKE Austria, for instance—a country which suffers from chronic scarcity of cash. What is she doing at this moment? She proposes to raise money by negotiating the mortgage bonds of the landowners of the Austrian dominions. But how is such an operation possible?

Through the Jewish houses, who, shut out from all more honorable branches of business, have acquired in this an inevitable degree of aptitude. There are in Vienna the Rothschilds, and Arnsteins, and Eskeles, and the Jew-Greek house of Seria, for whom the management of a loan of $100,000,000 is a matter of most easy accomplishment. The way they start at the loan is to get all their correspondents to canvass their business constituencies, and with the allurements of a particular commission, their correspondents of course do their best to ensnare their customers. (Padover, 1972, p. 219)

Here is the remainder of The Loanmongers of Europe, from the 1855 New York Daily Tribune of November 22, 1855:

The broad facts we have pointed out have naturally produced all over Europe, especially in its northern, western, and central portions where the indolence which prevails in the southern part (as Italy, Spain, and Portugal) is modified by climate, all manner and kinds of capitalists, speculators, and jobbers, who have no other business beyond that of dealing in money. Now there are posted in every point of Europe Jewish agents who represent this business and who are the correspondents of other leading Jews. It must here be borne in mind that for one big fish, like Rothschild, there are thousands of minnows. These make play and find food chiefly in Amsterdam, London, Frankfurt, Vienna, Berlin, Hamburg, Paris, and Brussels, and, as a general thing, loans are distributed among them in the following proportion:

Amsterdam, say $25,000,000 London $25,000,000 Frankfurt $15,000,000 Vienna $10,000,000 Berlin $10,000,000 Hamburg $5,000,000 Paris $5,000,000 Brussels $5,000,000 Total $100,000,000

Beside the regular agents every one of these places swarms with Jews who aid in placing the stock. All over Germany and Holland, in Hanover, Brunswick, Cassel, Carlsruhe, Mannheim, Cologne, Rotterdam, The Hague, Antwerp, and again in Poland and the adjoining countries, in Breslau, Gacow, Warsaw, and so almost throughout Europe, there are to be found in almost every town a handful of Jews who deem it an honor to take a little of the new stock on speculation if the Rothschilds or any other of the great Jewish houses are connected with the negotiation. It is this business Free Masonry among the Jewish bankers which has brought the barter trade in government securities to its present height.

It remains to be seen, and the time is not distant, how the chief houses connected with this barter trade will stand when distrust makes their customers disgorge the securities which have been forced down their throats and the markets become overglutted with unsalable bonds. Bearing in mind the havoc which the first Napoleon's wars created among these loanmongers, we have heretofore pointed out the smash, which from a knowledge of their financial position and connections we have no hesitation in predicting as sure to happen as a consequence of the present war to the representatives of this particular race.

That very compact machinery which is their greatest power of success in times of prosperity is their greatest cause of danger in time of adversity. Let the confidence in the Rothschilds be only once slightly shaken, and the confidence in the Foulds, the Bischoffsheims, the Stieglitzes, the Arnsteins and Eskeles is gone. The results of despotism and monopolism are precisely similar. Let Louis Napoleon be chopped off, as he may be any moment by some Pianori, and France is in confusion. Let Lionel Rothschild of London, James of Paris stagger under any clever combination of disasters, and the whole loanmongering fabric of Europe will perish. (Marx, 1855)

An image of the article is at https://mailstar.net/NY-Daily-Tribune-18551122p4.jpg.

As for the Russian Loan: I uploaded a pdf of page 4 of the 1856 New York Daily Tribune issue of January 4, featuring "The Russian Loan" to https://mailstar.net/NY-Daily-Tribune-18560104p4.pdf.

The whole issue (including the front page) is at https://mailstar.net/NY-Daily-Tribune-18560104.pdf .

Here is the first part of The Russian Loan, from *The Karl Marx Library, Vol. 5*:

The Russian Loan*

THE issue of a new Russian loan affords a practical illustration of the system of loanmongering in Europe, to which we have heretofore called the attention of our readers.

This loan is brought out under the auspices of the house of Stieglitz at St. Petersburg. Stieglitz is to Alexander what Rothschild is to Francis Joseph, what Fould is to Louis Napoleon. The late Czar Nicholas made Stieglitz a Russian baron, as the late Kaiser Franz made old Rothschild an Austrian baron, while Louis Napoleon has made a Cabinet Minister of Fould, with a free ticket to the Tuileries for the females of his family. Thus we find every tyrant backed by a Jew, as is every pope by a Jesuit. In truth, the cravings of oppressors would be hopeless, and the practicability of war out of the question, if there were not an army of Jesuits to smother thought and a handful of Jews to ransack pockets.

* Published in the New York Daily Tribune, January 4, 1856. (Padover , 1972, p. 221)

Here is the remainder of The Russian Loan, from the New York Daily Tribune (January 4, 1856, p.4):

The loan is for fifty millions of rubles, to be issued in 5-percent bonds, with dividends payable at Amsterdam, Berlin, and Hamburg, at the exceedingly moderate price of 86 rubles—that is to say, in consideration of paying 86 rubles, in several installments, the payer is entitled to 5 rubles dividend per year, which amounts to nearly 6 percent, and to a bond of 100 rubles endorsed by the Russian Government, as security for his capital, which is redeemable at some remote period between this and doomsday. It is worthy of notice that Russia does not appeal, as Austria has recently done, to the moneyed enthusiasm of her own subjects, stirred up by the stimulus of bayonets and prisons; but this shows only the greater confidence which she has in her credit abroad, and the greater sagacity which she possesses in raising money without embarrassing and therefore without disappointing the people at home. Baron Stieglitz does not propose to retain one single kopeck of the fifty millions for the Greek, Sicilian, American, Polish, Livonian, Tartarian, Siberian, and Crimean sympathizers with Russia, but distributes seventeen millions of the loan to Hope & Co. of Amsterdam, the same share to Mendelssohn & Co. of Berlin, and sixteen millions to Paul Mendelssohn-Bartholdy of Hamburg. And although British and French houses do not, for obvious reasons, court a direct participation in the loan, we shall presently show that indirectly they contribute largely to furnishing their antagonists with the sinews of war.

With the exception of a small amount of five and six percent Russian bonds negotiated at London and Hamburg, and of the last Russian loan which was taken up by the Barings, Stieglitz of St. Petersburg in connection with Hope & Co. of Amsterdam, have been the principal agencies for Russian credit with the capitalists of Western and Central Europe. The four-percent Hope certificates, under the special auspices of Hope, and the four-percent Stieglitz inscriptions, under the special auspices of Stieglitz, are extensively held in Holland, Switzerland, Prussia, and to some extent even in England. The Hopes of Amsterdam, who enjoy great prestige in Europe from their connection with the Dutch Government and their reputation for great integrity and immense wealth, have well deserved of the Czar for the efforts they have made to popularize his bonds in Holland. Stieglitz, who is a German Jew intimately connected with all his co-religionists in the loanmongering trade, has done the rest. Hope commanding the respect of the most eminent merchants of the age, and Stieglitz being one of the Free Masonry of Jews which has existed in all ages—these two powers combined to influence at once the highest merchants and the lowest jobbing circles, have been turned by Russia to most profitable account. Owing to these two influences, and to the ignorance which prevails about her interior resources, Russia, of all the European continental governments, stands highest in the estimation of 'Change, whatever may be thought of her in other quarters.

But the Hopes lend only the prestige of their name; the real work is done by the Jews, and can only be done by them, as they monopolize the machinery of the loanmongering mysteries by concentrating their energies upon the barter trade in securities, and the changing of money and negotiating of bills in a great measure arising therefrom. Take Amsterdam, for instance, a city harboring many of the worst descendants of the Jews whom Ferdinand and Isabella drove out of Spain, and who, after lingering awhile in Portugal, were driven thence also, and eventually found a safe place of retreat in Holland. In Amsterdam alone they number not less than 35,000, many of whom are engage in this gambling and jobbing of securities. These men have their agents at Rotterdam, The Hague, Leyden, Haarlem, Nymegen, Delft, Groningen, Antwerp, Chent, Brussels, and various other places in the Netherlands and surrounding German and French territories. Their business is to watch the moneys available for investment and keenly observe where they lie. Here and there and everywhere that a little capital courts investment, there is ever one of these little Jews ready to make a little suggestion or place a little bit of a loan. The smartest highwayman in the Abruzzi is not better posted up about the locale of the hard cash in a traveler's valise or pocket than those Jews about any loose capital in the hands of a trader.

These small Jewish agents draw their supplies from the big Jewish houses, such as that of Hollander and Lehren, Konigswarter, Raphael, Stern, Sichel, Bischoffsheim of Amsterdam, Ezekiels of Rotterdam. Hollander and Lehren are of the Portuguese sect of Jews, and practice a great ostensible devotion to the religion of their race. Lehren, like the great London Jew, Sir

Moses Montefiore, has made many sacrifices for those that still linger in Jerusalem. His office, near the Amstel, in Amsterdam, is one of the most picturesque imaginable. Crowds of these Jews assemble there every day, together with numerous Jewish theologians, and around its doors are congregated all sorts and manners of Armenian, Jerusalem Barbaresque, and Polish beggars, in long robes and Oriental turbans. The language spoken smells strongly of Babel, and the perfume which otherwise pervades the place is by no means of a choice kind.

The next Jewish loanmongering concern is that of Konigswarter, who came from a Jewish colony in Furth in Bavaria, opposite Nuremberg, whose 10,000 inhabitants are all Jews with some few Roman Catholic exceptions. The Konigswarters have houses at Frankfurt, Paris, Vienna, and Amsterdam, and all these various establishments will place a certain amount of the loan. Then we have the Raphaels, who also have houses in London and Paris, who belong, like Konigswarter, to the lowest class of loanmongering Jews. The Sterns come from Frankfurt, and have houses at Paris, Berlin, London, and Amsterdam. One of the London Sterns, David, was for some time established at Madrid, but so disgusted the chivalrous Spaniards that he was compelled to quit. They have married the daughters of one of the rich London Goldsmiths, and do an immense business in stock. The only man of ability in the family is the Paris Stern.

The Bischoffsheims are, next to the Rothschilds and Hopes, the most influential house in Belgium and Holland. The Belgian Bischoffsheim is a man of great accomplishments and one of the most respected bank directors and railway magnates. They came from Mayence, and owing to the genius of this Belgian Bischoffsheim, have attained to their present eminence. They have houses at London, Amsterdam, Paris, Brussels, Antwerp, Frankfurt, Cologne, and Vienna, and have recently sent a clerk or agent to New York. They have intermarried with a Frankfurt Jew of the name of Goldschmidt, who, however, is not distinguished either for wealth or genius, although pretending to both. One of these Goldschmidts—and the most insignificant of the firm—presides over the London concern, while one of the Bischoffsheims rules over that of Amsterdam, and the other over those of Brussels and of Paris.

As far as the seventeen million rubles assigned to Holland are concerned, although brought out under the name of Hope, they will at once go into the hands of these Jews, who will, through their various branch houses, find a market abroad, while the small Jew agents and brokers create a demand for them at home. Thus do these loans, which are a curse to the people, a ruin to the holders, and a danger to the governments, become a blessing to the houses of the children of Judah. This Jew organization of loanmongers is as dangerous to the people as the aristocratic organization of landowners. It principally sprang up in Europe since Rothschild was made a baron by Austria, enriched by the money earned by the Hessians in fighting the American Revolution. The fortunes amassed by these loanmongers are immense, but the wrongs and sufferings thus entailed on the people and the encouragement thus afforded to their oppressors still remain to be told.

We have sufficiently shown how the Amsterdam Jews through their machinery at home and abroad, will absorb in a very little time the seventeen millions of rubles put at the disposal of Hope. The arrangements attendant on the placing of the amount in Berlin and Hamburg are of a similar nature. The Mendelssohns of Berlin are descended from the good and learned Moses Mendelssohn, and count among the more modern members of the family the distinguished musical composer. In their case, as in that of the Lessings and a few other Frankfurt, Berlin, and Hamburg families, owing to some peculiar literary tradition or some peculiar influence of refinement, their houses are far superior in character to those of the general clique of loanmongers. Their representative in Hamburg too, Mr. Beschutz, is a man of high character, and there is little doubt that under their auspices the thirty-three millions put by Stieglitz at their disposal will soon be taken. But, as in the case of Hope of Amsterdam, the part taken by the Mendelssohns will only be nominal, and to lend the prestige of their name. Rothschilds' special agent at Berlin, Simon Bleichroder, and their occasional agents, the Veits, will very likely take a portion on speculation, and sell it with a profit to the small Jew fry of Berlin, Hanover, Magdeburg, Brunswick, and Cassel, while the Frankfurt Jews will supply the small fry of Darmstadt, Mannheim, Carlsruhe, Stuttgart, Ulm, Augsburg, and Munich. This small fry again distribute the stock among still smaller fry, until eventually some honest farmer of Swabia, some substantial manufacturer of Crefeld, or some dowager Countess of Isenburg has the honor of becoming the permanent creditor of the Czar by locking the stock up as a permanent investment. The Jew jobbers of Breslau, Ratisbor, Cracow, and Posen, the Frankels of Warsaw, Benedick of Stockholm, Hambro of Copenhagen, Magnus of Berlin, with his extensive Polish constituency, Jacobson of the same city, and Ries and Heine of Hamburg—both houses of great influence in Jew financial circles, especially Heine—will each and all disseminate a goodly amount among their multitudinous customers and bring the stock within the reach of all the northern section of Europe. In this wise any amount, however large, is soon absorbed. It must be borne in mind that besides the local and provincial speculations, there is the immense stock-jobbing machinery between the various European gathering points of the loanmongering confederation now all connected by telegraph communication, which, of course, vastly facilitates all such operations. Moreover, almost all the Jew loanmongers in Europe are connected by family ties. At Cologne, for instance, we find the principal branch house of the Paris Foulds, one of whom married a Miss Oppenheim, whose brothers are the chief railway speculators of Rhenish Prussia and, next to Heistedt and Stein, the principal bankers of Cologne. Like the Rothschilds and the Greeks, the loanmongering Jews derive much of their strength from these family relations, as these, in addition to their lucre affinities, give a compactness and unity to their operations which insure their success.

This eastern war is destined at all events to throw some light upon this system of loanmongers as well as other systems. Meantime the Czar will get his fifty millions and, let the English journals say what they please, if he wants five fifties more, the Jews will dig them up. Let us not be thought too severe upon these loanmongering gentry. The fact that 1855 years ago **Christ drove the Jewish moneychangers out of the temple**, and that **the moneychangers of our age enlisted on the side of tyranny happen again chiefly to be Jews**, is perhaps no more than a historical coincidence. The loanmongering Jews of Europe do only on a larger and more obnoxious scale what many others do on one smaller and less significant. **But it is only because the Jews are so strong that it is timely and expedient to expose and stigmatize their organization.** (Marx, 1856)

'Philosemitic' Marxists deny the authenticity of 'The Loanmongers of Europe', and 'The Russian Loan'.

Kevin B. Anderson (2010) wrote , 'Padover has created a convenient digest of the problematic discussions by Marx on Judaism and Jews (KML 5, 169-225). Padover errs, however, when he attributes to Marx "The Russian Loan," a particularly noxious Tribune article about Jewish bankers published on January 4, 1856 (KML 5, 221-25). In "Die Mitarbeit von Marx und Engels an der 'New York Tribune' " (2001), an illuminating essay that forms part of the apparatus to MEGA I/14, the volume's editors (Hans-Jürgen Bochinski and Martin Hundt, with Ute Emmrich and Manfred Neuhaus) write that the earlier attributions of "The Russian Loan" to Marx can "definitely be ruled out," this on the basis of a close textual analysis (903). Ledbetter' (Anderson, 2010, footnote 18 on p. 262, in Notes to Pages 52-62).

Anderson displays his philosemitism elsewhere in the book too:

Unfortunately, not all of Marx's discussions of Jews show as much sympathy. A considerable number of anti-Semitic characterizations crop up in his writings. For example, in the important "first thesis" on idealism and materialism in the "Theses on Feuerbach" (1845), Marx attacks Feuerbach not only on philosophical grounds as a crude materialist, but also for having developed a notion of praxis that was "defined only in its dirty-Jewish [schmutzige jüdischen] form of appearance" (MECW 5,6). This text was not intended for publication, and elsewhere in the unpublished material, such as Marx's letters to Engels, even more virulent references to Jews can be found. Marx also made some extremely problematic comments on Jews in his published work.18 Such references marred his otherwise penetrating critique of liberal democracy in the 1843 essay, "On the Jewish Question" (Marx [1843] 1994; see also MECW 3, 146-74), and can also be found in some of his later work, especially Herr Vogt (1860). Several Marx scholars have argued with some justice that similar references abound in the writings of nineteenth-century secular radical intellectuals, including others of Jewish origin such as the poet Heinrich Heine (Rubel in Oeuvres); see also Draper 1978). Others have pointed to the limitations of the secular and assimilationist perspective shared by Marx and many other pre-twentieth-century writers, both Jewish and non-Jewish, who, while supporting political and civil rights for Jews, nonetheless continued to make very troubling pejorative comments about Jewish life and culture (Traverso 1994, Jacobs 1998). None, not even Marx's strongest defenders on this issue, however, have suggested that Marx made a significant positive contribution on the issue of Jews and anti-Semitism.

Marx's references to Judaism and Jews were certainly problematic. They showed the downside of a universalistic secular outlook that, by condemning all religion, sometimes failed to distinguish between the impact of such attacks on a dominant religion and those on a persecuted minority one. These remarks, as problematic as they were, were for the most part occasional ones that were not typical of Marx's overall discussions of nationalism and ethnicity. (I leave aside the psychological issue of Marx's possible personal ambivalence toward his own Jewish origins.) (Anderson, 2010, pp. 51-2)

Anderson is more concerned about offending Jewish sentiment, than examining whether Marx' analysis of Jewish Power—the nexus between Money and Power—was actually correct. Anderson's somewhat grovelling tone undermines his case.

If Marx did not write The Loanmongers of Europe and The Russian Loan, who did? Only he had the required combination of expertise on Capitalism, inside information about Jewish practice, and his incisive style of writing. Anderson did not bother to disclose the name of any alternative author.

Saul K. Padover was a reputable author. Wikipedia has this on him:

"Saul Kussiel Padover (April 13, 1905 — February 22, 1981) was a historian and political scientist at the New School for Social Research in New York City who wrote biographies of philosophers and politicians such as Karl Marx and Thomas Jefferson" (Saul Padover, 2022).

Wikipedia has this on *The Karl Marx Library*:

"The Karl Marx Library is a topically-organized series of original translations and biographical commentaries edited by historian and Karl Marx scholar Saul K. Padover (1905-1981) and published by academic publisher McGraw-Hill Books" (Karl Marx Library, 2019).

Lenin never mentioned—i.e. censored—Marx's materials on Jews. Those who reject 'The Loanmongers of Europe' and 'The Russian Loan' belong in that camp too.

A book of selections of Marx' essays in the New York Tribune also excludes 'The Loanmongers of Europe' and 'The Russian Loan', among others. However, it makes no claim to be complete.

That book is *Dispatches for the New York Tribune: Selected Journalism of Karl Marx, Selected and with an Introduction by James Ledbetter, Foreword by Francis Wheen* (Ledbetter, 2007).

James Ledbetter was deputy managing editor of CNNMoney.com. Given the nexus of Money, Power and Media, it would be surprising if Ledbetter is not a philosemite.

The cover of *Dispatches* states that "Francis Wheen is a journalist, author and broadcaster. ... His biography of Karl Marx ... won the Isaac Deutscher Memorial Prize".

But Deutscher was a Trotskyist who called Trotsky a "Prophet".

I asked Bruce Brown, of New York, to look up the original articles at New York Public Library. Here is his report:

Bruce Brown <address withheld> 2 May 2017 at 12:20

Peter -

Your long wait has been handsomely rewarded. Indeed, you've hit the jackpot!

In a nutshell, I found both articles in the original New-York Daily Tribune on the dates you gave.

First the librarian at the front desk searched for articles in the Daily Tribune by Karl Marx. She found seventeen and printed out the search results, but Loanmongers and Russian Loan were missing.

Then, by searching for the articles by title only, she found the missing two.

Then I went to the microfiche room. The librarian there was able to access the two issues in question from a computer database. I will forward his e-mail containing the complete Nov 22, 1985 issue (Loanmongers).

Here's what shocked both of us. NONE OF THE ARTICLES IN THE N-Y DAILY TRIBUNE WERE BY-LINED! ZERO ATTRIBUTION OF AU-

THORSHIP! Not just on that page, but on all pages. We then looked up the New York Times issue of the same date and discovered that none of their articles were by-lined either.

The resourceful librarian found a history of by-lining in U.S. journalism. There we discovered that by-lining was not practiced until ordered by Gen. Hooker, a Union general in the Civil War, in 1863. Prior to that, it was simply "not done."

Meaning that, with rare exceptions, NO ONE CAN PROVE AUTHORSHIP OF ANY ARTICLE PUBLISHED IN THE U.S. PRESS BEFORE 1863. Attribution of articles to Karl Marx -- or anybody else, for that matter -- is ENTIRELY CONJECTURE IF BASED ON THE PUBLICATION ALONE!

The librarian then found a whole book about the articles of Karl Marx in the N-Y Daily Tribune, which he included as a link.

That "book about the articles of Karl Marx in the N-Y Daily Tribune" is *Dispatches*, as I have discussed above.

Marx's analysis of Jewish Finance—and the nexus between Money and Power—deals with the Big End of Town, the Ruling Class, what we now call the 1%. He showed that the old landed Aristocracy has been displaced by a new class of Financiers, predominantly Jewish. To suppress that information is a betrayal of the People. To hide it or disown it, on the ground that Jews might be offended, is cowardly. But given that Lenin censored 'On the Jewish Question', one can expect no better of the philosemites today.

Karl Marx wrote 'The Loanmongers of Europe' and 'The Russian Loan' in 1855 and 1856 respectively. The Trotskyists claim to be the true descendants of Marx— but what have they added to our knowledge on that topic, in the last 165 years? Perhaps they accept funding from George Soros?

The Trots have changed the meaning of the word "Left". Today, the author of the above articles would be branded "Far Right". But we don't have to let the Trots be the arbiters.

As the Ruling Class (the 1%) has become increasingly Jewish, it has adopted Jewish ideologies and tastes, and even Yiddish words. Jews have championed 'Minority' causes—but mainly in the Diaspora, where they are a minority, not in Israel-Palestine with regard to the native Palestinians, Bedouin etc. Our Ruling Class now promote Gender Feminism, Gay Marriage, and Trans-Sexualism. The old landed aristocracy would never have done so—it was Christian (Anglican)—but the increasingly dominant Jewish Financial Aristocracy promotes such 'Left' causes. These policies are Post-Christian.

It's widely called 'Cultural Marxism'; but Karl Marx himself would not have recognised this as either 'Marxist' or 'Left'. It's his Trotskyist, largely Jewish, disciples who have foisted these changes on us. These stances are called 'Left', but this is a Fake Left.

Marx wrote, in 'On the Jewish Question' (see above): "Even the species-relation itself, the relation between man and woman, becomes an object of commerce. Woman is bartered away". No hint of Gay Marriage there. This is traditional Complementarity between the sexes.

Marx's revelations corroborated by J. A. Hobson

Marx's revelations about the dominance of Jews in finance were corroborated by J. A. Hobson, who observed the Jewish role at Johannesburg during the Boer war, in the period 1900-1903:

> If one takes the recent figures of the census, there appears to be less than seven thousand Jews in Johannesburg, but the experience of the streets rapidly exposes this fallacy of figures. The shop fronts and business houses, the market-place, the saloons, the "stoeps" of the smart suburban houses, are sufficient to convince one of the large presence of the chosen people. If any doubt remains, a walk outside the Exchange, where, in the street "between the chains," the financial side of the gold business is transacted, will dispel it. So far as wealth and power, and even numbers are concerned, Johannesburg is essentially a Jewish town. Most of these Jews figure as British subjects, though many are, in fact, German and Russian Jews who have come to Africa after a brief sojourn in England. The rich, vigorous, and energetic financial and commercial families are chiefly German Jews. (Hobson, 1900, p. 11)

> Before I went there, the names of Beit, Eckstein, Barnato, &c., were of course not unknown to me; the very ship in which I crossed bore many scores of Jewish women and children. But until I came to examine closely the structure of industry and society upon the Rand I had no conception of their number or their power. I thus discovered that not Hamburg, not Vienna, not Frankfort, but Johannesburg is the New Jerusalem. (p. 189)

> It is not too much to say that this little ring of international financiers already controls the most valuable economic resources of the Transvaal. The first and incomparably the most important industry, the gold-mines of the Rand, are almost entirely in their hands. (pp. 190-1)

In his book *Imperialism* (1902), he noted that Jewish financial networks form the 'central ganglion' of international capitalism; and that their wealth gives them the means to force governments to enact their preferred policies:

These great businesses—banking, broking, bill discounting, loan floating, company promoting—form the central ganglion of international capitalism. United by the strongest bonds of organisation, always in closest and quickest touch with one another, situated in the very heart of the business capital of every State, controlled, so far as Europe is concerned, chiefly by men of a single and peculiar race, who have behind them many centuries of financial experience, they are in a unique position to control the policy of nations. (Hobson, 1902/1905, pp. 57-9)

Jeremy Corbyn wrote the Foreword for a new edition of Hobson's *Imperialism*, for which he was branded an antisemite by a certain Lobby:

Jewish groups hit out at Jeremy Corbyn on Wednesday after it emerged that the Labour party leader had written a foreword for a century-old book containing several anti-Semitic tropes. A Labour spokesman defended Mr Corbyn's decision to praise the "wider issues" raised in Imperialism: A Study, written by John A Hobson in 1902, which argued that capitalism was the main driver of western imperialism in the Victorian era.

The book, which Mr Corbyn in 2011 described as a "great tome", has been criticised as anti-Semitic because it argues that European finance was driven "by men of a singular and peculiar race who have behind them many centuries of financial experience". (Pickard, 2019)

The 1% include the Rothschilds and Rockefellers, but they don't show up in the Forbes Rich List. Very wealthy people want privacy; they use their money to suppress media scrutiny by—for example—withdrawing advertising from media that expose them. They use Trust Funds to minimise tax by imputing the income amongst family members. The most wealthy people hide their wealth from tax authorities, and from the public.

"Every year Forbes' Rich List crowns billionaires and offers them the title of 'world's richest people,' but names such as Rothschild and Rockefeller are never listed, although the combined wealth of these two families is estimated to be over a trillion dollars. These two families, who are believed to be the world's only trillionaires, are excluded from Forbes' Rich List every year, along with royal families" (Motroc, 2015).

Why? Because they are so wealthy that Forbes dare not risk offending them by publicising that wealth. The 1% operate as a mafia. We can't identify them, because Tax records are fraudulent.

In October 1994, the Spectator magazine published an article by William Cash, titled Kings of the Deal: William Cash investigates Hollywood's new Jewish Establishment.

It stated that the East-coast WASP Establishment had been displaced by a new Jewish establishment. On November 5 the Spectator published letters critical of Cash—including one from The Board of Deputies of British Jews—and Cash's reply.

The editor, Dominic Lawson, who is Jewish, later wrote that Advertisers had threatened to withdraw their business. Conrad Black, owner of the Spectator, was assailed, and his media empire threatened. Lawson wrote, in the UK Telegraph:

"Once Tom Cruise, Steven Spielberg, Barbra Streisand and Kevin Costner had written letters to Conrad denouncing me as the new Torquemada the row caught the imagination of the entire North American media, and then ricocheted into Israel, where Conrad Black was immensely vulnerable through his ownership of the Jerusalem Post. Advertisers threatened to withdraw their business across the length and breadth of Conrad's empire. But again he never gave me any sense of the pressure he was under; still less did he rebuke me" (Lawson, 2004).

For the same reason, Forbes dare not publish the wealth of the Rothschilds and Rockefellers, and, no doubt, other super-rich people.

But there is a way to counter their piracy: Tax Havens should be treated as the Pirate Dens they are.

The site https://missingprofits.world/ states that close to 40% of multinational profits are shifted to Tax Havens each year, thereby depriving governments of the funds with which to pay their debt, build infrastructure, and look after their citizens. The site also provides a map of the tax havens around the world (Tørsløv, 2022). In effect, Tax Havens are the new "surplus value", the way that Capital cheats Labor out of its wages. The Australian government caved in to business pressure, and scaled back a law which would have curtailed profit-shifting: "Multinational firms have won a reprieve from a new law that would have forced them to publicly disclose the taxes they pay around the world" (Kenner , 2023).

Nicholas Shaxson examined how Tax Havens operate, in his book *Treasure Islands: Tax Havens and the Men Who Stole the World*. The cover states that Tax Havens cause poverty:

Tax havens are the most important single reason why poor people and poor countries stay poor. They lie at the very heart of the global economy, with over half the world trade processed through them. They have been instrumental in nearly every major economic event, in every big financial scandal, and in every financial crisis since the 1970s, including the latest global economic downturn. (Shaxson, 2011, cover)

Shaxson says that the tax haven network is the new British Empire:

Nobody disagrees that London sits, spider-like, at the centre of a vast international web of tax havens, hoovering up trillions of dollars' worth of business and capital from around the world and funnelling it to the City of London. (Shaxson, 2011, p. vii)

The modern offshore system did not start its explosive growth on scandal-tainted and palm-fringed islands in the Caribbean, or in the Alpine foothills of Zurich. It all began in London, as Britain's formal Empire gave way to something more subtle. (Shaxson, 2011, p. 89)

The Financial Aristocracy promotes the Fake Left; anything but the real Left. The True Left would remove the Tax-Free status of Foundations funded by big business, abandon Free Trade Agreements, tax financial trades , simplify Double Taxation Agreements and ensure that they do not scam branch-office economies at the expense of headquarters ones, stop Transfer-Pricing, abolish Tax Havens and nullify debt owed to entities based in them as well as socialise assets owned anywhere in the world by entities based in them.

The abolition of Tax Havens could be done by international conferences declaring them corrupt and a criminal enterprise, one based on two sets of books—one for shareholders, one for tax authorities.

Economist Michael Hudson says that this practice is routine; he disclosed how Tax Havens work in an interview with Standard Schaefer (Schaefer, 2004). The interview was titled An Insider Spills the Beans on Offshore Banking Centers: an Interview with Michael Hudson for Counterpunch. https://michael-hudson.com/2004/02/an-insider-spills-the-beans-on-offshore-banking-centers/.

Chapter 12: Karl Popper vs. Arnold Toynbee on the interpretation of Karl Marx

The differences between Karl Popper and Arnold Toynbee over the interpretation of Karl Marx's philosophy turn out to be a surprisingly fruitful way of opening up all three.

Popper's attack on Toynbee over Marx occurs in Volume II of *The Open Society and Its Enemies*. In justifying his position, he refers to shorter background material from Volume I.

Toynbee's critique of Marx is in *A Study of History, Volume V* (Oxford University Press, London, 1939), pp. 178-189, and the Annex on pp. 581-7.

The debate raises the questions: should Karl Marx be viewed as a social scientist, or as the prophet of a religion? Did the totalitarianism and iconoclasm of the Soviet Union derive from Plato's Republic, or from Judaism?

Nietzsche, like Rousseau and Babeuf, looked to ancient Rome as a model. On the other hand, Weishaupt—founder of the Illuminati—and Marx rejected Rome. Weishaupt adopted the name 'Spartacus', leader of a slave rebellion against Rome; and Marx wrote that Rome, far from a model of inspiration, represented nothing but slavery. In The Holy Family, he wrote,

> Robespierre then explicitly calls the Athenians and Spartans "peuples libres". He ... quotes its heroes as well as its corrupters—Lycurgus, ... Brutus, ... Caesar ... . In his report on Danton's arrest ... Saint-Just says explicitly: "The world has been empty since the Romans, and only their memory fills it and still prophesies liberty." ... Robespierre, Saint-Just, and their party fell because they confused the ancient ... commonwealth based on real slavery with the modern ... commonwealth based on emancipated slavery, bourgeois society. (Marx, 1845/1975, pp. 121-2)

Weishaupt's hostility to Rome could be an indication that he was Jewish, even though Nesta Webster found no evidence of that (Webster, 1924/2000, p. 128n1). The Spartacus League, founded by Rosa Luxemburg and Karl Liebknecht, suggests a connection with Weishaupt and Illuminist networks; Weishaupt had adopted the name 'Spartacus'.

This divergence between the Jewish and non-Jewish revolutionaries shows the uneasy coalition between them. Similarly, Stalin came to concede some merit in pre-Revolutionary Russian culture, but Trotskyists see none. In Australian Universities, Humanities faculties were captured during the 1980s by academics who not only wished to recount Australia's sins and display its dirty washing, but who could see no merit at all in the Australia of earlier decades.

Does this iconoclasm, this attempt to obliterate the past, come from Plato, or from Judaism?

As theorised by Rousseau and Babeuf, the New Order is nationalist: socialism in one country. However, as theorised by Weishaupt and later Marx, it is internationalist: on a world-wide scale.

The divergence between the nationalist and internationalist forms of the New Order appears in the confrontation between the Stalinist and Trotskyist traditions. Stalin's purges diluted the Jewish dominance of the Bolshevik administration.

Michael Higger explains in his book *The Jewish Utopia* that whereas Plato's Republic "is chiefly concerned with what will hold the ideal city together ... The rabbis, on the other hand, are mainly interested in that ideology which would hold the whole world, or the Universal State, together." (Higger, 1932, p. 5).

Popper, in *The Open Society and its Enemies*, sourced Plato as the inspiration of the Communist movement, and ridiculed Arnold Toynbee for arguing that Marxism was mainly inspired by Judaism. Popper, in effect, writes out any Jewish contribution to Communism, sourcing it all to elements deriving from Western Civilisation itself. Yet, Plato, in his *Republic* and the later *Laws*, makes it clear that he is only thinking of a small community—the *Laws* envisages a city of 5,040 households as its ideal experimental community (for which Plato is drafting the laws or scheme).

Michael Higger shows that ideas of a world-wide utopian community are central in the Jewish religion. Higger writes that "A Jewish Utopia begins where Wells leaves off" (Higger, 1932, p. 6). This is a reference to H. G. Wells' "Open Conspiracy" blueprint for a World State.

Popper, a non-theistic Jew, was an Anti-Communist who nevertheless paid tribute to Marx, sharing some Marxist Anti-Communist traits, while Toynbee was an advocate for Christian Socialism.

Popper insisted on treating Marx as a social scientist and humanitarian; Toynbee maintained that he was the prophet of a new religion.

Marx laid himself open to such a view, when he said in a speech, "Someday the worker must seize political power in order to build up the new organization of labor; he must overthrow the old politics which sustain the old institutions, if he is not to lose heaven on earth, like the old Christians who neglected and despised politics" (Marx, 1872/1972).

Norman Cohn (1957/1970) agreed on the religious aspect of Marxism: "For what Marx passed on to twentieth-century Communist movements was not the fruit of his long years of study in the fields of economics and sociology but a quasi-apocalyptic phantasy which as a young man, unquestioningly and almost uncon-sciously, he had assimilated from a crowd of obscure writers and journalists" (p. 287).

Cohn's obituary in The Guardian summed up his insight: "Cohn claimed that Joachim of Fiore, a 12th-century Calabrian abbot, anticipated Marxism, with Joa-chim's successive ages of the Father, the Son and the Spirit reappearing as primi-tive communism, class society and the final withering away of the state" (Lay, 2007).

This insight was explicated by Cohn in *The Pursuit of the Millennium*. Christian theology used a twofold division of time: the Era of the Father (The Fall to Re-demption by Christ), then the Era of the Son (the Kingdom of God, i.e. Christen-dom). Joachim of Fiore (1145-1202) added a third era, an Era of the Holy Spirit, doubting that the Kingdom of God had been realised in Christendom, and imply-ing that Church rule was just another evil to be overcome. Joachim's dialectic of the three stages of spiritual fulfilment led to the Marxian dialectic of the three stages of primitive communism, class society, and final communism.

Marx's three stages of History are: an initial paradise of Tribal Communism; a time of class war (called Civilisation, but in reality it was slavery—overt in classical times and covert under Capitalism); and a future paradise (inaugurated by the Communist Party in place of the Church), which is a return to the original paradise but at a higher technological level and on a worldwide scale. Marx dismisses the Ancient Civilsations as slave societies, and our 'bourgeois' era as covert slavery.

This three-fold division of Time is characteristic of religions derived from the Zoroastrian. Whereas earlier religions were oriented to preserving the past, or se-curing Order in the face of Chaos, religions in the Zoroastrian mould are future-oriented, depicting History as progressive and as Salvation History. The first stage—the paradise—is the inspiration for the faithful of the second stage to strive to achieve the (predestined) third stage.

Toynbee assessed the apocalyptic element in Marxism as religious—and de-rived from Judaism:

> The distinctively Jewish (or perhaps originally Zoroastrian) element in the traditional religious inspiration of Marxism is the apocalyptic vision of a vi-olent revolution which is inevitable because it is the decree, and irresisti-ble because it is the work, of God himself, and which is to invert the pre-sent roles of Proletariat and Dominant Minority in a tremendous peripe-teia—reversal of roles which is to carry the Chosen People, at one bound, from the lowest to the highest place in the Kingdom of This World. Marx has taken the Goddess 'Historical Necessity' in place of Yahweh for his omnipotent deity, and the internal proletariat of the modern Western

World in place of Jewry; and his Messianic Kingdom is conceived as a Dictatorship of the Proletariat. But the salient features of the traditional Jewish apocalypse protrude through this threadbare disguise, and it is actually the pre-Rabbinical Maccabaean Judaism that our philosopher-impresario is presenting in modern Western costume; for it is of the essence of the Marxian apocalyptic doctrine that the Messianic Kingdom is not only to be a material kingdom in This World but is also to be won by a victorious stroke of violence. (Toynbee, 1939, pp. 178-9).

Similar to Toynbee's position that Marxism is a religion, Bertrand Russell wrote on Marx's eschatology:

To understand Marx psychologically, one should use the following dictionary:
Yahweh = Dialectical Materialism
The Messiah = Marx
The Elect = The Proletariat
The Church = The Communist Party
The Second Coming = The Revolution
Hell = Punishment of the Capitalists
The Millennium = The Communist Commonwealth

The terms on the left give the emotional content of the terms on the right, and it is this emotional content, familiar to those who have had a Christian or a Jewish upbringing, that makes Marx's eschatology credible. A similar dictionary could be made for the Nazis, but their conceptions are more purely Old Testament and less Christian than those of Marx, and their Messiah is more analogous to the Maccabees than to Christ (Russell, 1946, p. 382).

The militant atheism of Communism was a "clearing of the deck", a jealous purging of all other religions, similar to that initiated by Akhenaten and later commanded by Yahweh; but Yahweh himself, as the transcendent god outside the creation, was replaced conceptually by Spinoza's immanent god.

Zoroastrianism, not Plato or Heraclitus, is the source of Historicist thinking. But Heraclitus may have been influenced by the clash of opposites depicted in Zoroastrian thinking; Zoroastrianism was the religion of the Persian elite, within the Persian empire. Lawrence H. Mills, an Avesta scholar, derives Heraclitus' metaphysics—the cosmic war of opposites, and Logos (an underlying unity) as Reason embedded in Nature—from Zoroastrian inspiration (Mills, 1903-4, pp. 89-95 and 100-106).

Zoroastrian thought articulates antagonistic polarity, in which one pole (the evil) must be destroyed. In contrast, Taoist thought is based upon complementary (yin/yang) polarity. Heraclitus articulates a mix of antagonistic polarity (in which strife prevails between the poles) and complementary polarity (both poles being essential parts of the whole).

Thomas C. McEvilley presented a detailed case for mutual influence between India and Greece in the ancient world. The Persian Empire included both Ionia in the west (i.e. the Ionian Greeks) and parts of India in the east. The Persians adopted from the Assyrians the strategy of deporting troublesome communities to remote areas; they deported Ionian Greek rebels to the far east, where they later formed Greek kingdoms in Bactria (Afghanistan). The western Greeks and the eastern Greeks maintained contact for hundreds of years across the Persian Empire. At times, the influence was from India to Greece; at other times, the reverse.

He wrote, "The period of unimpeded contact through the medium of Persia lasted approximately from 545 till 490. These dates include the heart of the brief moment of pre-Socratic philosophy. The work of Pythagoras, Heraclitus, Empedocles, Parmenides, and others falls between them. Only the work of Thales seems clearly to have preceded this period, and even before the conquest trade routes between Greece and India were open and in use" (McEvilley, 2002, p. 18).

Joseph Needham (1961) showed that there had been early contact between China and the West, and mutual cultural exchange by 1600BC. Victor H. Mair, in his book *Contact and Exchange in the Ancient World,* shows that knowledge and ideas spread both ways across the Silk Road, from around 2000BC. Heraclitus' philosophy is similar to Taoism, and he too took to the hills. The discovery of the Tarim Mummies proved the reality of east-west contact in the last two millennia BC.

Popper's interpretation of the trial of Socrates is an important contribution. Sparta, having won the Peloponnesian War (431-404), forced Athens to grant an amnesty which prevented it from punishing traitors (supporters of Sparta) among its own citizens. The leaders of Athens saw Socrates as such a traitor. If they had wanted to prosecute him for attacking the traditional religion, they would have done it decades earlier, rather than waiting until he was aged 70 or 71.

The critical fact about Socrates, which discredits the view that he was martyred for subverting morality, is his age at his trial. Surely he had been challenging tradition for many decades; why then leave it so late to bring charges against him?

Popper wrote, "But if Socrates was, fundamentally, the champion of the open society, and a friend of democracy, why, it may be asked, did he mix with anti-democrats? For we know that among his companions were not only Alcibiades, who for a time went over to the side of Sparta, but also two of Plato's uncles, Critias who later became the ruthless leader of the Thirty Tyrants, and Charmides who became his lieutenant. ... But these connections were to cause his death. When the great war was lost, Socrates was accused of having educated the men who had betrayed democracy and conspired with the enemy to bring about the downfall of Athens" (Popper, 1966, pp. 191-2).

Popper goes on to say that Plato betrayed Socrates, by depicting him as a critic of Athenian democracy and a supporter of the closed tribal society, of which Sparta was the model. But in solely blaming Plato for modern totalitarianism, Popper lets Judaism off the hook completely.

J. L. Talmon wrote two studies of the revolutionary tradition. The first, *The Origins of Totalitarian Democracy*, omits any mention of Jewish involvement, tracing Totalitarianism to Rousseau's 'General Will', with Plato as one of the ancestors.

In the second, *Israel Among the Nations*, he writes Judaism back in as an agent of revolution: "It has for a long time been almost an axiom ... that the Jews were the natural standard-bearers of the revolution" (Talmon, 1970, pp. 1-2). "Jews everywhere looked upon the French Revolution as a date comparable to the exodus from Egypt, and to the issuing of the Law from Mount Sinai, this time not to the Jews alone, but to all the nations" (p. 9). "The great wave of revolutions in 1848 ... was greeted by very many Jews as proof that all nations were about to enter into a revolutionary world association" (p. 21).

Talmon quotes Disraeli: "Had it not been for the Jews ... the uncalled-for outbreak would not have ravaged Europe. But the fiery energy and the teeming resources of the Children of Israel maintained for a long time the unnecessary and useless struggle ... everywhere the Jewish element. ... And all this because **they wish to destroy that ungrateful Christendom** which owes to them even its name, and whose tyranny they can no longer endure" (p. 24).

And Talmon quotes J. L. Bernays in the New York German-Jewish journal Israels Herold in 1849: "In order to obtain their emancipation, **the Jews had first to destroy the Christian essence of the state, the 'Christian State'. ... The Jew is not only an atheist, but a cosmopolitan, and he has turned men into atheists and cosmopolitans**; he has made man only a free citizen of the world" (pp. 24-5).

More evidence for the connection between Jews, Jewish Bankers, and Revolution is supplied by Theodore Herzl, one of the main founders of Zionism, in his book *The Jewish State*: "**When we sink, we become a revolutionary proletariat**, the subordinate officers of all revolutionary parties; and at the same time, **when we rise, there rises also our terrible power of the purse**" (1896/1988, p. 91).

Israel Shahak (1994) disclosed the Totalitarian elements in Judaism:

In May 1993, Ariel Sharon formally proposed in the Likud Convention that Israel should adopt the 'Biblical borders' concept as its official policy. There were rather few objections to this proposal ... It is not only the belief itself, however dogmatic, but the refusal that it should ever be doubted, by thwarting open discussion, which creates a totalitarian cast of mind. Israeli-Jewish society and diaspora Jews who are leading 'Jewish lives' and organised in purely Jewish organisations, can be said therefore to have a strong streak of totalitarianism in their character. (p. 10)

However, once the modern state had come into existence, the Jewish community lost its powers to punish or intimidate the individual Jew. The bonds of one of the most closed of 'closed societies', one of the most totalitarian societies in the whole history of mankind were snapped. (p. 15)

So one will not find in Hannah Arendt's voluminous writings whether on totalitarianism or on Jews, or on both, the smallest hint as to what Jewish society in Germany was really like in the 18th century: burning of books, persecution of writers ... Nor can one find in the numerous English-language 'Jewish histories' the elementary facts about the attitude of Jewish mysticism (so fashionable at present in certain quarters) to non-Jews: that they are considered to be, literally, limbs of Satan, and that the few non-satanic individuals among them (that is, those who convert to Judaism) are in reality 'Jewish souls' who got lost ... (p 16)

There were no Jewish comedies, just as there were no comedies in Sparta, and for a similar reason. (p 18)

Also, many Jews who appear to be active in defending human rights and who adopt non-conformist views on other issues do, in cases affecting Israel, display a remarkable degree of totalitarianism and are in the forefront of the defence of all Israeli policies. (pp. 101-2)

It should be recalled that Judaism, especially in its classical form, is totalitarian in nature. (p. 103)

I suggest that the totalitarian elements in Communism came not from Russian tradition or Chinese tradition, but from the totalitarian streak in Judaism disclosed by Shahak. The Jewish religion's harsh condemnation of pagans (goyim or "the nations"), its insistence on separation from them, its depiction of God's People's unending battle with its opponents—these are the origin of the hardness.

Bolshevism was much more ruthless than Czarism had been. In Czarist prisons, prisoners could write books (Trotsky did so, in Odessa), and it was easy to escape; in Bolshevik prisons, both were almost impossible.

In *The Black Book Of Communism*, Stephane Courtois et. al. (1999) refute the claim that the cruelty of Bolshevism derives from Russian tradition:

First, we should consider the possibility that responsibility for the crimes of Communism can be traced to a Russian penchant for oppression. However, the tsarist regime of terror against which the Bolsheviks fought pales in comparison with the horrors committed by the Bolsheviks when they took power. The tsar allowed political prisoners to face a meaningful justice system. The counsel for the defendant could represent his client up to the time of indictment and even beyond, and he could also appeal to national and international public opinion, an option unavailable under Communist regimes. Prisoners and convicts benefited from a set of rules governing the prisons, and the system of imprisonment and deportation was relatively lenient. Those who were deported could take their families, read and write as they pleased, go hunting and fishing, and talk about their "misfortune" with their companions. Lenin and Stalin had firsthand experience of this. ... True, riots and insurrections were brutally crushed by the ancien regime. However, from 1825 to 1917 the total number of people sentenced to death in Russia for their political beliefs or activities was 6,360, of whom only 3,932 were executed. This number can be subdivided chronologically into 191 for the years 1825-1905 and 3,741 for 1906-1910. These figures were surpassed by the Bolsheviks in March 1918, after they had been in power for only four months. It follows that tsarist repression was not in the same league as Communist dictatorship. (pp. 13-4)

James Billington (1980) agrees: "For all their use of provocateurs, the tsarist Okhrana never engaged in the counterassassinations abroad that the Soviet secret police were to attempt. Indeed, the growing concern for due process at trials and relatively humane treatment in prison and exile made the Okhrana's campaign against the revolutionaries far less severe and effective than that of its Soviet successors. There were only four mass arrests by the Okhrana in the early twentieth century, and Lenin like many others enjoyed relatively good conditions for reading and writing during his far-from-arduous exile in Siberia" (p. 480).

Stalin's cruelty is legendary, but he overthrew the Jewish Bolsheviks, who had initiated that cruel system, by using their own covert methods against them. When Russian emigrants went to Palestine and established the state of Israel there, they brought with them both socialism (the kibbutzes being a benign kind) and the totalitarianism disclosed by Israel Shahak. Their treatment of the Palestinians and of their neighbours bears comparison with Soviet precedents.

As for the 'Open Society', could there be anything more 'Closed' than the Jewish Bible's mindset in its depiction of Goyim/'the Nations'?

I supplied evidence on p. 81, that George Soros is a Freemason; the Rothschilds admit that they are. What's so 'Open' about that secret, closed society?

John F. Kennedy was a rare non-Freemason among U.S. Presidents. In a speech at the Waldorf-Astoria Hotel in 1961 he said, 'The very word "secrecy" is repugnant in a free and open society; and we are as a people inherently and historically opposed to secret societies, to secret oaths and to secret proceedings' (Kennedy, 1961). Two years later, Grand Master Earl Warren handed the (cover-up) report on his assassination to President Lyndon Johnson, also a Freemason.

Chapter 13: Bolshevism, the Exodus story, and the Jewish Mission to transform the world

Many writers deny the special role of atheistic Jews in Bolshevism; but other writers affirm it. Jewish writers who do so include Harry Waton, Leonard Schapiro, Jacob Talmon, and Yuri Slezkine. In this chapter, when covering this contentious topic, I draw exclusively on Jewish authors.

When Theodor Herzl visited Russia in 1903, he met the Minister of Finance, Count Witte. Leonard Schapiro (1961) noted that "Witte duly pointed out to Herzl that while the Jews formed only seven million out of a total population of 136 million, about fifty percent of the members the revolutionary parties was Jewish" (Schapiro, 1961, p. 148).

Jacob (J. L.) Talmon expands on this:

In his famous interview with the Tsarist Minister Witte, Herzl was faced with the question why the Jews who constituted only 3 per cent of the population of Russia supplied 50 per cent of its revolutionaries. In an ill-tempered note jotted down at the time of the famous Second Congress of the Social-Democratic Party in Brussels and London, which saw the split into Bolsheviks and Mensheviks, Lenin refers to the fact that a third of all the delegates were Jews.

But absolute figures do not tell the whole story. The qualitative aspects were more significant. Through their concentration in the two capitals of Russia, in the other large cities, and in the more advanced Western provinces, like Vilna, Minsk, Kiev, Kharkov, not to speak of Warsaw and other purely Polish cities, the Jews were able to play a role out of all proportion to their numbers. (Talmon, 1970, pp. 28-9)

Yuri Slezkine, whose book *The Jewish Century* won the 2005 National Jewish Book Award, affirms "the special relationship between Bolsheviks and Jews or rather, between the Bolshevik and Jewish revolutions" (Slezkine, 2004, p. 180).

After the creation of Israel in 1948, Soviet Jews had loyalties to an external homeland allied to the United States. Slezkine observes,

The great alliance between the Jewish Revolution and Communism was coming to an end as a result of the new crusade against Jewish Communists. What Hitler could not accomplish, Stalin did, and as Stalin did, so did his representatives in other places. In the fall of 1952, a large show trial was staged in Czechoslovakia. Eleven of the accused, including the general secretary of the Communist Party of Czechoslovakia, Rudolf Slansky, were identified as ethnic Jews and accused of being agents of international Zionism and American imperialism. ...

In Hungary, Romania, and Poland, a high proportion of the most sensitive positions in the Party apparatus, state administration, and especially the Agitprop, foreign service, and secret police were held by ethnic Jews ...

All three regimes resembled the Soviet Union of the 1920s insofar as they combined the ruling core of the old Communist underground, which was heavily Jewish, with a large pool of upwardly mobile Jewish professionals, who were, on average, the most trustworthy among the educated and the most educated among the trustworthy. (Slezkine, 2004, pp. 313-4)

In 2015, Francis Boyle, Professor of Law, was asked during an interview with Pravda.ru, why the United States was hostile to Russia.

He explained that two factions had gained power in foreign policy. Zbigniew Brzezinski, a die-hard Russia-hater from Poland, ran all the foreign affairs and defence policies of the Obama presidential campaign, and stacked the administration with his acolytes. The neo-conservatives were the second faction: "I went to school with large numbers of these neoconservatives at the University of Chicago, Wolfowitz and all the rest of them. Many of them are grandchildren of Jewish people, who fled the pogroms against Jews, and they have been brainwashed against Russia and the Russians" (Boyle, 2015).

Their forerunners, the atheistic Jews who manned the Old Bolshevik regime and especially the Cheka, were partly motivated by a feeling of revenge for those pogroms (which in some cases were reprisals for assassinations conducted by Jewish revolutionaries).

But there were other motivations uniquely Jewish. Hostility to Christianity was one. Jewish separatism was another. Slezkine (2004) noted that, prior to 1917, Jews spoke Yiddish not Russian:

... the majority of Russian Jews continued to live in segregated quarters, speak Yiddish, wear distinctive clothing, observe complex dietary taboos, practice endogamy, and follow a variety of other customs that ensured the preservation of collective memory, autonomy, purity, unity, and a hope of redemption. The synagogue, bathhouse, heder, and the home helped structure space as well as social rituals, and numerous self-governing institutions assisted the rabbi and the family in regulating communal life ... Non-Jews almost never spoke Yiddish, and very few Jews spoke the languages of their Ukrainian, Lithuanian, Latvian, Moldovan, or Belorussian neighbors. (Slezkine, 2004, p. 105-6)

Jewish political action was motivated by the Exodus myth

In effect, Jews were maintaining a different civilisation, whose foundation myth was the Biblical story of the Exodus. They identified the Tsar with Pharaoh:

The history of the people of Israel relived by every Jew on every Sabbath had nothing to do with his native shtetl or the city of Kiev; his sea was Red, not Black, and the rivers of his imagination did not include the Dnieper or the Dvina. "[Sholem Aleichem's] Itzik Meyer of Kasrilevke was told to feel that he himself, with wife and children, had marched out of Egypt, and he did as he was told. He felt that he himself had witnessed the infliction of the ten plagues on the Egyptians, he himself had stood on the farther shore of the Red Sea and seen the walls of water collapse on the pursuers, drowning them all to the last man—with the exception of Pharaoh, who was preserved as an eternal witness for the benefit of the Torquemadas and the Romanovs. (p. 106)

Hyam Maccoby (1982) stated that Jewish political action was motivated by the Exodus myth: "The basic myth of the Jewish civilization was of the liberation of a nation of slaves, pitted against all the oppressive regimes of the world" (p. 182).

This refers not merely to Egypt, but to all 'pagan' governments worldwide. Thus Pharaoh = Hitler; or Pharaoh = Stalin. This is the basis of the Jewish revolutionary spirit.

Michael Walzer, a Jewish Trotskyist, former editor of the progressive Dissent magazine, and a Zionist, wrote, "Indeed, revolution has often been imagined as an enactment of the Exodus and the Exodus has often been imagined as a program for revolution" (Walzer, 1985, p. ix).

Yet archaeology has since found that the Exodus never happened; even Israel Finkelstein, the Archaeologist, says so. The story was concocted in Babylon, to motivate the "Return" to Palestine by providing a precedent.

Despite claiming that Israelites spent hundreds of years in Egypt, the Bible makes no reference to the Pyramids. Ashraf Ezzat noted, "Have you ever wondered **why are the Egyptian Pyramids and temples not mentioned in the Bible?** Do you know that Egypt is mentioned in the Bible around six hundred times? The number is phenomenal and perplexing at the same time, for no one can revisit Egypt that too many times and never refers to one of its ancient icons; the Pyramids" (Ezzat, 2016).

One even finds the 'Pharaoh' concept in the mind of George Soros—he equated Stalin to Pharaoh. In his book *Underwriting Democracy*, Soros said of the Soviet Union's heavy-industry sector: "We may view the gigantic hydroelectric dams, the steel plants, the marble halls of the Moscow subway, and the skyscrapers of Stalinist architecture as so many pyramids built by a modern pharaoh" (Soros, 1990).s

Egyptologist Donald B. Redford (1992) wrote:

There is perhaps no other scriptural tradition so central to the reconstruction of Israel's history that Deuteronomy presents us with than the
Exodus of the Hebrews from Egypt. It has become a prototype of salvation, a symbol of freedom and the very core of a great world religion. Yet
to the historian it remains the most elusive of all the salient events of Israelite history. The event is supposed to have taken place in Egypt, yet Egyptian sources know it not. On the morrow of the Exodus Israel numbered
approximately 2.5 million (extrapolated from Num. 1:46); yet the entire
population of Egypt at the time was only 3 to 4.5 million! (p. 408)

One final irony lies in the curious use to which the Exodus narrative is put
in modern religion, as a symbolic tale of freedom from tyranny. An honest
reading of the account of Exodus and Numbers cannot help but reveal that
the tyranny Israel was freed from, namely that of Pharaoh, was mild indeed
in comparison to the tyranny of Yahweh to which they were about to
submit themselves. (p. 422)

Exodus story confuses Expulsion of Hyksos with the building of Amarna

The Exodus story in the Bible is largely fictitious, but based on memories of
two historical events, the Expulsion of the Hyksos and the building of the City of
Akhetaten at Amarna; these events were centuries apart.

Redford shows that Manetho, the Egyptian historian who wrote in Greek, also
mixed up the two events. (p. 415).

That mistake was easy to do, because after the end of Amarna period—
comprising four pharaohs in 13 years—most records of Akhenaten were erased.

The Hyksos were a mixed group, Canaanites/Hebrews from Palestine and
probably Aryan chariot officers. Cyrus Gordon said that the Hyksos had horses and
war chariots, which would have helped them defeat Egypt. Later pharoahs had
them, and Yahweh is depicted, in the Bible, sitting on a Merkabah (Merkavah),
which means "throne-chariot".

The influx of Indo-European immigrants into the Near East during the second millennium B.C. revolutionised the art of war. The newcomers introduced the horse-drawn war-chariot, which gave a swift striking power
hitherto unknown in the Near East.

The elite charioteer officers, who bear the Indo-European name of maryannu, soon became a new aristocracy throughout the entire area, including Egypt. With them appears also a new type of royal epic, which we may
call the Indo-European War Epic. Embedded in it is a motif that has become commonplace in world literature: the Helen of Troy theme, whereby a hero loses his destined bride and must wage a war to win her back.
Greek and Indic epic illustrate this theme {The Indian one is the Ramaya-
na}, and it is from the Iliad that it has become popular in the modern

West. However, it is completely absent from the romantic literatures of early Mesopotamia and Egypt, and it appears in the Semitic World only in the wake of the Indo-Europeans with their maryannu aristocracy. The Helen of Troy theme first appears at Ugarit of the Amarna Age, in a community where the Indo-European elements are present, including a firmly entrenched organisation of maryannu. As we shall note later, the theme permeates the early traditions of Israel, particularly the saga of Abraham. (Gordon, 1962, pp. 25-6).

Martin Bernal (1991) agrees:

"Thus, there would seem no reason to deny the inherently plausible notion that horses and chariots came in with the Hyksos, and that the Hyksos 'invasion' was directly or indirectly connected to the Hurrian expansion and further that there may have been Indo-Aryan speakers involved in the movement" (p. 322).

Israelites did not build the Pyramids, but helped build Amarna

Rosenberg (2015) connects the "Children of Israel" with the building of the City of Akhetaten at Amarna. The vital clue is the Book of Exodus, Chapter 1 verse 14, where it says that the Egyptians "made their lives bitter with hard service in brick and mortar" (NIV).

Rosenberg explains:

In other words, the Children of Israel were unskilled or semi-skilled makers of, and workers in, mudbrick. They could well have made millions of bricks out of the Nile mud, but then, what is it that they built with them? They did not build the pyramids, or any temples or palaces as these were all built with stone. And the peasants' houses, which were made of mudbrick, were built by the fellahin themselves. So what project needed millions of bricks and thousands of mudbrick-layers? The Bible tells us that there were six hundred thousand Israelite adult males at the Exodus, but even if there were only 6,000 or 600, what project needed so many mudbrick-layers? There was indeed only one project that we know of that was so large and built in mudbrick, and that was the city of Akhetaten, which was later called el-Amarna.

Akhenaten had fallen out with the priesthood of Amun-Ra at Thebes (Luxor). Breasted (1951) noted that

One of Amenhotep III's High Priests of Amon had also been chief treasurer of the kingdom, and another, Ptahmose, was the grand vizier of the realm; while the same thing had occurred in the reign of Hatshepsut, when Hapuseneb had been both vizier and High Priest of Amon. Besides these powers, the High Priest of Amon was also the supreme head of.the organization including all the priests of the nation. Indeed, the fact that such extensive political power was now wielded by the High Priests of Amon must have intensified the young king's desire to be freed from the sacerdotal thrall which he had inherited. (p. 362)

Akhenaten turned to the traditional sun-god, Ra, whose cult was based at Heliopolis in the north. At Thebes (Luxor), he had been merged with Amun as Amun-Ra. Akhenaten used the new name Aton (Aten) for Ra, and built a temple to Aton at Thebes, which upset the Amun priesthood. The falling-out worsened, and Akhenaten decided to create a new capital further north, at Amarna, which would be dedicated solely to the Aton. Rosenberg continues,

> So he had to build it quickly, and indeed it was built, according to Egyptian records, within two years by many slaves and the Egyptian army, and it was constructed in mudbrick for speed. It was this great project that was most likely built by the Israelites, under the direction of taskmasters from the Egyptian army, who were both cruel and pressing because it had to be done so quickly. We have a plan of it; it was built for perhaps 20,000 people and all in two years. But Akhenaten and his ideas were not popular. He did wonderful things and even gave women rights to worship and own property, but the people disliked his innovations and the priests hated him, and when he died just 16 years after building the city, it fell apart.

Manetho's account, reported by Redford, includes a priest called Osarsiph, who others have identified with Moses.

> A. 1. The King (Amenophis/Hor) desires to see the gods. 2. Amenophis son of Paapis the seer declares he may if he cleanses the land of lepers. 3. The King sends all lepers to the quarries east of the Nile. 4. Amenophis the seer predicts an invasion of thirteen years. ... 7. In Avaris the lepers choose as their leader Osarsiph, priest of Heliopolis. 8. Osarsiph makes monotheistic and racially exclusive laws. (Redford, p. 414)

Redford shows that Manetho's "lepers" are connected with Akhenaten:

> The dispatch of the impure ones to quarries east of the Nile is an etiological explanation of the whirlwind of quarrying and construction that went on during the reigns of Amenophis III and Akhenaten ... the devotees of Akhenaten's sun cult are the historical reality underlying the "lepers," and this is confirmed by the iconoclastic nature of the lepers' legislation and the figure of thirteen years for the occupation, which corresponds to the period of occupation of Amarna. Osarsiph moreover is remembered as a priest of Heliopolis, where sun worship was endemic. (pp. 415-6)

So Freud was not wrong in connecting Moses to Akhenaten. The "lepers" probably left Egypt during the turbulent times at the end of the Amarna period. But the numbers are a tiny fraction of those alleged in the Bible, the route is wrong, and Redford shows that the place-names in the Bible story reflect the reality of the 6th & 5th centuries B.C. rather than earlier times. Further, the mummy of

Ramesses II is in the Egyptian museum at Cairo, and shows no signs of having been drowned in the Red Sea or a Sea of Reeds.

Redford shows that archaeological and historical records do not support the Exodus stary: "the post-Exilic compiler of the present Biblical version had no genuinely ancient details. He felt constrained to supply them from the Egypt of his own day and, significantly perhaps, cited several places where Asiatic elements and especially Judaean mercenaries resided in the sixth and fifth centuries" (p. 410).

No large-scale Return from Babylon

As for the "Return" from Babylon, Israel Finkelstein (2018) used Archaeology to assess the books of Ezra, Nehemiah, and Chronicles on this matter. He found that Charles Torrey was correct to deny that any large-scale Return took place in the Persian period.

On the list of returnees at Ezra 2:1-67 and Neh 7:6-68, Finkelstein wrote,

"five of the fifteen identifiable sites that appear in the list were uninhabited in the Persian period and an additional six were sparsely populated, while all sites were inhabited in the late Hellenistic period most of them providing evidence for strong settlement activity at that time. In addition, important Persian-period places are not mentioned in the list. All this leads me to suggest that the list of returnees depicts Hasmonean realities in the second century BCE." (2018, pp. 159-60).

Exodus story was unknown to Israelites of Elephantine

Cowley (1923) published a collection of Jewish papyri from a garrison of Jewish soldiers employed by the Persian Empire at its southern boundary, Elephantine.

The texts, written in Aramaic, cover practically the whole 5th century B.C. There is no evidence that Hebrew was used by the community. These are the earliest Jewish texts known, pre-dating all extant manuscripts of the Hebrew Bible. The community have no knowledge of a written Torah, or of the Passover ritual. They were polytheistic, honouring Yahweh (Ya'u) and other gods too ('Anath, Bethel, Ishum, Herem).

Cowley commented:

What precisely constituted a kahen [priest] at Elephantine does not appear. One of their prerogatives, we might suppose, would be to possess the Law of Moses and to administer it. Yet there is no hint of its existence. We should expect that in 30 25 they would say 'offer sacrifice according to our law', and that in other places they would make some allusion to it. But there is none. So far as we learn from these texts Moses might never have existed, there might have been no bondage in Egypt, no exodus, no monarchy, no prophets. There is no mention of other tribes and no claim to any heritage in the land of Judah. Among the numerous names of colonists, Abraham, Jacob, Joseph, Moses, Samuel, David, so common in later times, never occur (nor in Nehemiah), nor any other name derived from their past history as recorded in the Pentateuch and early literature. It is almost incredible, but it is true.

Again, that essentially Jewish (though also Babylonian) institution, the Sabbath, is nowhere noticed. (p. xiii)

Most Zionist commentators miss Cowley's point—Judaism as we know it (Ezra's kind) had not been invented then. They practised an earlier kind.

A "Passover letter" of 419 BC from Persian Empire Darius II 423-404 gives detailed instructions for keeping Passover. The instruction to hold a Passover shows that the Elephantine Jews knew nothing of the Passover ritual or the Exodus story.

A letter to the priests of the temple of Jerusalem requests approval for the rebuilding of a Jewish temple at Elephantine; centralisation of worship in Jerusalem is unknown.

Gmirkin (2006) comments:

The Elephantine Papyri consist of approximately 80 papyri in Aramaic discovered at Aswan in Egypt and originating from the Jewish military colony at Yeb (Elephantine), at the second cataract of the Nile, guarding the Egyptian-Ethiopian border. Many of the Elephantine Papyri were dated in terms of the regnal years of the Persian kings who then ruled Egypt. The collection as a whole came from the period 494-ca. 400 BCE. Most of these were letters, legal documents, supply accounts and the like, but one (no. 21) contained an order from Darius II in 419 BCE to the Jews at Elephantine enjoining them to observe the Days of Unleavened Bread, while a second series (nos. 27, 30-34) documented the Egyptian destruction of a Jewish temple at Yeb in 411 BCE and the fruitless efforts of the colonists during the years 410-407 BCE to secure permission to have it rebuilt. ...

Yet when the Elephantine Papyri are scoured for evidence of the existence of the Pentateuch or any portion thereof, the results are emphatically negative. There is no evidence that the priests at Yeb were of Aaronide descent. Indeed, there is no mention of Aaron or Levites in the papyri. Of over 160 Jews at Elephantine mentioned in the papyri, not one name comes from the Pentateuch. Nor is there any reference in the papyri to the Exodus or any other biblical event. Reference to laws of Moses or other authoritative writings is entirely absent. ...

The extraordinary absence of any reference to the contents of the Pentateuch in the Elephantine Papyri is ail the more remarkable given the friendly contacts between the Jews of Elephantine and the priests of the temple of Jerusalem. (pp. 29-30).

Robert M. Price (2017) explains:

The Book of Ezra plainly states that Ezra, an official of the Persian Empire, journeyed from Persia to Jerusalem "with the law of your God which is in your hand" (Ezra 7:14), a document which formed the basis for the subsequent reorganization of Judea and the building (rebuilding?) of the Temple. Part of this agenda was to reinstitute the celebration of the Passover, supposedly long "neglected" (1 Esdras 1:17-21).

More than likely, the Passover was an innovation, and the Exodus accounts which mention it were cooked up for the occasion to give the rite an ancient-seeming pedigree. As we will soon see, a great number of the anecdotes in Exodus, Leviticus, and Numbers serve in this manner to retroactively legitimatize later Jewish ritual practices. (Price, 2017, pp. 59-60).

Deuteronomy is dead set against syncretism and polytheism. ... There is considerable railing against "Canaanite" and "Amorite" polytheism (Deut. 12:2-3). Deuteronomy 20:16-18 has God direct Israel to displace (massacre) the Canaanite nations because of their polytheism, idol-worship, and fertility rites (sex magic). ...

So what are we to make of all the condemnation of "Canaanite" idolatry and polytheism? It is part of a drastic rewriting of history. What really happened was that at some point (retrospectively placed variously in the reigns of Hezekiah and Josiah), a group of scribes, prophets, and priests engineered a massive, systematic reform of traditional Hebrew religion, eliminating all deities but Yahweh, outlawing the former Israelite gods and goddesses, and then denying that Israel had ever worshipped them except insofar as their ancestors had mixed true, monotheistic Judaism with "Canaanite" polytheism. in fact, the heathen "Canaanites" whose reputation they blackened were their own Israelite forbears (Price, 2017, p. 75).

Price endorses the statement by Niels Peter Lemche that "The Old Testament ... came into being in a post-exilic Jewish society, presumably during the Hellenistic Age" (p. 91). Price concludes that the Old Testament was written only shortly before the New.

His books shred the traditional understanding of both Judaism and Christianity. But religion still plays an important role for individuals and for community life. Understanding the human origins of the holy books leads to a redefinition of the religion. Direct contact with clairvoyance, seances, Tarot readings, witchcraft, psychic surgery, Near-Death Experiences, telepathy, exorcism and the like—perhaps miracles too—convinces many people (including me) that there is another dimension, one that we cannot understand. Alfred Russel Wallace thought so too. It is on account of this mysterious side of life that religion remains part of our lives.

A Sense of Mission—Messiah ruling the world from Jerusalem

Non-Jews need to know the ideas that drive Jews, because they have a sense of Mission that affects everybody.

Religious Judaism is based on the concept of a Messiah ruling the world from Jerusalem, imposing Noahide laws and centralising worship in the Third Temple. Quite possibly, all other religions would be outlawed.

US Ambassador to Israel, David Friedman, posed with this poster of the Temple Mount, in which the Dome of the Rock and Al-Aqsa Mosque were missing. The Times of Israel reported on May 22, 2018, that Friedman was visiting the Bnei Brak headquarters of the Achiya organization, an ultra-Orthodox NGO, when one of the group handed him a large poster showing the Temple Mount in Jerusalem, but with the Jewish Third Temple standing in place of the Muslim Dome of the Rock and Al-Aqsa Mosque. Friedman later claimed that he had been unaware that the Dome and the Mosque were missing.

The Zionists want to pull down the Dome of the Rock, because they wrongly believe that it is the site of the First and Second temples. The Romans built a fortress, the Tower of Antonia, to house a legion, 5,500 troops. It's now wrongly called the Temple Mount. Six hundred feet south, Herod built a new temple, which Romans could view, and go down to, from the Antonia. Ernest Martin proved, in his book *The Temples that Jerusalem Forgot*, that Herod's temple (the 2nd Temple) was near the Spring of Siloam (Gihon), in the City of David. The temple required 'living water' from an underground spring, not from a reservoir; it used water from Gihon Spring; no such spring water was available at the Dome of the Rock.

George Wesley Buchanan agreed. He produced the map shown here, and wrote,

Suddenly, I remembered Ezekiel 47 and realized that the temple at Jerusalem had to have been located right there near the Spring of Siloam and not up the hill in the heavily walled area about 600 feet to the north where the Dome of the Rock and Al-Aqsa Mosque are now located. ...

The Dome of the Rock (Roman Fortress of Antonia)

Northern boundary of the City of David

Spring of Siloam (Gihon)

Temple Mount (Mount Ophel)

Watchtower of Siloam

David's Citadel (used by Syrians)

From the death of Herod until the end of the Jewish-Roman war in Jerusalem (AD 70), thousands of Jews fought thousands of Romans. In AD 66, Jews grew so skillful, militarily, that they massacred the Romans in the Antonia and took over the fortress. **The Romans brought in four legions of foot soldiers and hundreds of cavalry and spent 4 years in siege to regain control of the Antonia. The Antonia is the only place in Jerusalem where that many soldiers could have been quartered.** ...

It is because of the mistaken notion that the Haram was the former temple area that **Jews today come from all over the world by the thousands to worship at the western wall**. They believe that God will listen to their prayers, because his presence is just on the other side of the wall. Now, **the evidence informs us that on the other side of that wall dwelt Mars, the Roman god of war**. (Buchanan, 2014)

A sense of Mission—World Peace (World gov't) & a this-worldly paradise

Secular Judaism—non-theistic Judaism—is based on a sense of Mission to save the world and human society, in a material sense. Jewish messianism has been secularised as the Jewish mission to institute a this-worldly paradise. It's the unspoken background to Bolshevism and also, perhaps, to the Green movement.

Ben-Ami Shillony's book *The Jews and the Japanese: the Successful Outsiders* is intended to explain Judaism to Japanese readers. Professor Shillony (1991) calls himself 'a Jew, an Israeli' (p. 10). He writes, "'Judaism was the first religion to make world peace a central element in its eschatology" (p. 31).

Actually Judaism borrowed it from Zoroastrianism, as Norman Cohn admitted (see below). Shillony continues,

'Yet quite often peace implies domination, and in many languages the word "pacify" also means "conquer". King Solomon could afford to be a king of peace because he ruled "over all the kings from the Euphrates to the land of the Philistines, and to the border of Egypt' (p. 32).

This quote, from 1 Kings 4:21, may not be historically accurate, yet it is the basis of promises that Jews will rule those lands again—at Genesis 15:18; Exodus 23:30-31; Deut 11:24; Josh 1:4—and is a major motivator of modern Zionism.

Harry Waton, a Jewish Communist, wrote (1939) that Christians will become Jews. Communism, he said, is Judaism's project for the world. All other religions are other-worldly; only Judaism lives for this world, and specifically for a political program which unifies and equalises mankind:

> The Jews differ from all other races and peoples because of Judaism; ... Judaism concerns itself only about this earth and promises all reward right here on this earth. The Kingdom of God is to be realized right here on this earth. The immortality which men are to enjoy, they will enjoy right here on this earth. (Waton, 1939, p. 52)

> Since the Jews are the highest and most cultured people on earth, the Jews have a right to subordinate to themselves the rest of mankind and to be the masters over the whole earth. ... The Jews will become the masters over the whole earth and they will subordinate to themselves all nations, not by material power, not by brute force, but by light, knowledge, understanding, humanity, peace, justice and progress. Judaism is communism, internationalism, the universal brotherhood of man, the emancipation of the working class and the human society. It is with these spiritual weapons that the Jews will conquer the world and the human race. The races and the nations will cheerfully submit to the spiritual power of Judaism, and all will become Jews. ... (pp. 99-100)

> The communists are against religion, and they seek to destroy religion; yet, when we look deeper into the nature of communism, we see that it is essentially nothing else than a religion. ... (p. 138)

> Christianity was a regression from Judaism. ... a Christianity which was nothing else than paganism ... Christianity is only a preparation for Judaism. (pp. 171-2)

> The time will come when all Christians will become mature, they will all embrace Judaism, and they will all justify themselves by deeds. Then the Christians will become Jews. (p. 174)

David Ben-Gurion was an atheist who admitted that the Bible's claim that God had chosen the Jews was wrong; rather they chose themselves. Yet he still based the Jewish Mission on the Bible. In his book *Recollections*, he formulates Non-Theistic Judaism. He declares that there's no Chooser, but still a Chosen People:

> Everything we are as Jews, including our drive occasionally to grope beyond traditional bounds, comes directly from the Bible. (Ben-Gurion, 1970, p. 16)

> Of course, speaking personally as one who is non-religious, I believe that theology reverses the true sequence of events. To me it is clear that God was 'created' in the image of man as the latter's explanation to himself of the mystery of his own earthly presence. More of that in another chapter. ... From the Bible, therefore, stems Jewish man's concept of himself, an image he has passed on to the whole of western civilization through the daughter religions of Islam and Christianity. (pp. 18-9)

> Are our faith and our suffering unrelated? I think not. One appears to grow from the other. By the metaphysical nature of the Biblical ethic, the Jews developed a universal conscience. ... With a code of conduct resolutely loftier ... worshipping a God who was universal ... this small people remained apart ... disdainful even in dispersion of its surroundings. (p. 20)

> How can the Lord be universal, asked Spinoza, and have a Chosen People? I won't argue the metaphysics of the point. But the message of the Chosen People makes sense in secular, rationalist and historical terms when turned around to describe an act of selection by Abraham and his successor of a God they had formulated. In other words, first came man, then his gods. This does not decrease the power of the Jewish God to work for good nor the validity of the Bible's message of righteousness. The Jews in their Book, according to the secularist idea, set down an accomplished fact by saying: 'It is our duty as a people to be a model to the God we have chosen, to conform to His ways as we have defined them and to devote ourselves to making the land we have settled and attributed to His gift to us a prosperous land run along our moral precepts.' In that sense, the Jews can be considered a self-chosen people. (pp. 124-5)

> The Bible endowed the Jews with a self-appointed mission as thinkers, questioners, formulators. (p. 127)

Douglas Rushkoff defines Atheistic Judaism by a sense of Mission

In an article in the New York Times, Douglas Rushkoff (2002) defined Atheistic Judaism (yes, a religion can be atheistic) in terms of a sense of Mission: "Judaism is founded in iconoclasm, a principle especially relevant to a world so hypnotized by its many false idols. ... Judaism is ultimately enacted through the very real work of social justice." The Forward called him a "latter-day Baruch Spinoza" (Forward 50).

One of the 'false idols' atheistic Jewish iconoclasts have attacked is heterosexuality; thus the Trans movement has sought to install 'trans women' (men by birth) in women's sports, women's toilet, and women's prisons. Those who fought back were said to be motivated by 'hate'; this reduction of their viewpoint to a malicious motive is a new kind of totalitarianism, with ancestry in early Bolshevism.

Trotsky promised "Paradise on Earth":

> But you, workers of the other countries, ... overthrow the bourgeoisie, take the power into your hands, and then we shall turn the whole globe into one world republic of Labour. Al the earthly riches, all the lands and all the seas—all this shall be one common property of the whole of humanity, whatever the name of its parts: English, Russian, French, German, etc. We shall create one brotherly state: the land which nature gave us. This land we shall plough and cultivate on associative principles, turn into one blossoming garden, where our children, grand-children, and great-grand-children will live as in a paradise. Time was when people believed in legends which told of a paradise. These were vague and confused dreams, the yearning of the soul of the oppressed Man after a better life. There was the yearning after a purer, more righteous life, and Man said: "There must be such a paradise, at least, in the 'other' world, an unknown and mysterious country." But we say, we shall create such a paradise with our toiling hands here, in this world, upon earth, for all, for our children and grand children and for all eternity! ... (Trotsky, 1918/1920, pp. 19-20)

Jewish religion adopted such ideas from the Zoroastrian religion

Even though such ideas are 'secular', they are still derived from the Jewish religion; what is less known is that the Jewish religion adopted such ideas from the Zoroastrian religion, when Jews were living in Babylon under the Persian Empire and later under the Greek and Parthian Empires.

The Persian Empire was the first multicultural empire. Its rulers had a religion universal yet exclusive—the Zoroastrian religion—whose god Mazda (Light) was so to influence Jewish thinking, that Yahweh was changed from a tribal God into a universal one; and, like Mazda, depicted as Creator of the world. The moralism, the messianism and the millennialism which are so central to Judaism are derived from the Zoroastrian religion.

Zoroastrianism was a revealed religion, like the Judaism reconstructed by Deutero Isaiah (II Isaiah, Second Isaiah). It had a prophet (Zoroaster), and revealed scriptures—the Avesta its Bible, the Gathas its Psalms, and the Zend its Talmud (commentary). All these things, Judaism copied.

One major difference remained. In Zoroastrianism, Mazda was creator only of what is good, while Anra Mainyu, the Devil, was creator of bad things. But in Judaism, Yahweh is the "author alike of prosperity and trouble" (Boyce, 1982, p. 120). In this respect, Yahweh is like Shiva or Kali.

Mary Boyce (1982), citing a study by Morton Smith, presents striking evidence of Isaiah II's copying from Zoroastrianism:

> Striking testimony to the religious import of some of their propaganda comes from the verses of Second Isaiah, that is, from chapters 40-48 of the Book of Isaiah ... (p. 43)

> The particular Gatha which provides striking parallels for Second Isaiah is Yasna 44. This is formed as a series of questions addressed to Ahura Mazda, each with an expected answer of 'I am' or 'I do'. 'Not only is the use of such rhetorical questions a conspicuous peculiarity of the style of II Isaiah, but almost all of those particular questions which make up the cosmological part of the Gatha (vss. 35) are either asked or answered in II Isaiah, with Yahweh taking the place of Ahura Mazda'. Thus Y 44.3.1-2: 'This I ask Thee, tell me truly, Lord, who in the beginning, at creation, was the father of justice?' is echoed by Is. 45.8: 'Rain justice, you heavens ... this I, Yahweh, have created.' For Y 44.3.3-5: 'Who established the course of sun and stars? Through whom does the moon wax, then wane?' there is Is. 40.26: 'Lift up your eyes to the heavens; consider who created it all, led out their host one by one.' Y 44,4.14 runs: 'Who has upheld the earth from below and the heavens from falling ? Who (sustains) the waters and plants? Who yoked swift (steeds) to the wind and clouds?'; and it is matched by Is. 40.12, 44.24 'Who has gauged the waters in the palm of his hand, or with its span set limits to the heavens? ... I am Yahweh who made all things, by myself I stretched out the skies, alone I hammered out the floor of the earth.' Further, the question to Ahuramazda, Lord of Wisdom, in Y 44.4.5: 'Who, O Mazda, is the Creator of good thought?' has for counterpart Is. 40.13: 'With whom did [Yahweh] confer to gain discernment? Who taught him how to do justice or gave him lessons in wisdom?'; and the demand in Y 44.5.13: 'What craftsman made light and darkness?' is matched by Is. 45.7: 'I am Yahweh, there is no other, I make the light, I create darkness'. ...

> That Ahura-Mazda is the Creator of all things good is a major Zoroastrian doctrine and 'Creator' is his most constant title, which on occasion replaces his proper name. It would seem, therefore, ... that Second Isaiah, rooted in the traditions of his own people, accepted the message of hope and the new concept of God, but saw the Supreme Being in his own terms as Yahweh. (pp. 46-7)

Boyce sums up, "Among all the subjects of the Achaemenians and Macedonians it is the Jews who appear to have absorbed most from Zoroastrianism" (Boyce, 1991, p. 367).

Herodotus wrote in his *Histories* (c. 430 BC/1860) that the Persians "have no images of the gods":

> The customs which I know the Persians to observe are the following: they have no images of the gods, no temples nor altars, and consider the use of them a sign of folly. This comes, I think, from their not believing the gods to have the same nature with men, as the Greeks imagine. (1.131)

Herodotus also said that they abhor telling lies (the Lie being one of their names for Ahriman, the Devil): "The most disgraceful thing in the world, they think, is to tell a lie; the next worst, to owe a debt: because, among other reasons, the debtor is obliged to tell lies" (1.139).

Features that Judaism copied from Zoroastrianism (see Magee, 2009) include:
* a Chosen people
* messianism and redemption
* revealed scriptures
* Purity laws
* separatism
* endogamy
* a sacred fire kept burning
* no images of the gods
* baptism or ritual baths
* even the skull cap
* a corpse is ritually impure
* the word "Pharisee" means "Parsee".

Leviticus 6:12 says, "The fire on the altar must be kept burning; it must not go out. Every morning the priest is to add firewood and arrange the burnt offering on the fire and burn the fat of the fellowship offerings on it" (NIV).

This perpetual fire is a feature of Zoroastrian fire-temples.

In the Zoroastrian religion, corpses were deemed particularly polluting. The Jewish religion seems to have copied some features; they are detailed at Numbers 19: 9-13.

The Circle of Ancient Iranian Studies website hosts a book *Persia & The Creation Of Judaism*, by Dr M D Magee, of which Book 2 is titled *How Persia Created Judaism*. Chapter 5 is titled Zoroastrian Influences on Judaism and Christianity Part III. It states: "The basis of the Zoroastrian purity laws is the battle between Good and Evil. ... The Zoroastrian purity laws permitted people to be 30 or more paces from a corpse without being polluted by the demon of corruption. ... Curiously, the ritual for making cleansing water, in Numbers 19, involves the burning of an unblemished red heifer, the ashes of which were kept to make the "water of impurity, for the removal of sin". When someone is polluted from a dead body, the water had to be sprinkled over him. Despite the differences from Zoroastrian practice, the association of the purification ritual with a cow and poured water seems remarkable in a society where sheep were normally the sacrificial animal of choice" (Magee, n. d.; also see Magee, 2009).

The Book of Numbers, chapter 19, in the Bible, tells how the red heifer is to be prepared. Verse 9 states (NIV): "A man who is clean shall gather up the ashes of the heifer and put them in a ceremonially clean place outside the camp. They are to be kept by the Israelite community for use in the water of cleansing; it is for purification from sin."

Verses 11-13 (NIV) give the Jewish law on touching corpses: "Whoever touches a human corpse will be unclean for seven days. They must purify themselves wit the water on the third day and on the seventh day; then they will be clean. But if they do not purify themselves on the third and seventh days, they will not be clean. If they fail to purify themselves after touching a human corpse, they defile the Lord's tabernacle. They must be cut off from Israel. Because the water of cleansing has not been sprinkled on them, they are unclean; their uncleanness remains on them."

Magee (2009) has more on this topic.

Norman Cohn, in his last book, dealt with Jewish millennialism, and conceded its Zoroastrian origins. In *Cosmos, Chaos and the World to Come: The Ancient Roots of Apocalyptic Faith*, he wrote, "the similarities between Zoroastrianism and the notions that one finds in the Jewish apocalypses are too remarkable to be explained by coincidence" (Cohn, 1993, p. 222). He concedes that religions based on a linear concept of Time, i.e. Time as Salvation History, derive from Zoroaster. That means Judaism, Christianity, Islam, Marxism, and the Green religion.

He refutes claims about the 'universalism' of II Isaiah: "Much has been written about Second Isaiah's 'universalism' ... The main thrust of Second Isaiah's argument leads in a very different direction. All nations that oppose the people of Israel are to be destroyed ... Other nations will be permitted to serve the Israelites by bringing them back to their homeland" (Cohn, p. 154).

And he explains how Jews came to borrow from Zoroastrians: "For some two centuries Judaea formed part of the vast Achaemenian empire, while the large Jewish diaspora also lived within the bounds of that empire. Achaemenian rule was relatively benign, and was recognised by the Jews to be so: whereas there is plenty of Jewish propaganda against Babylon and Greece and Rome, there is not a single Jewish text, biblical or rabbinic, directed against the Persians" (p. 223).

Like Zoroastrians, Jews saw themselves as a people chosen by God: 'It was not simply that, like Zoroastrians, Jews saw themselves as a people chosen by God to implement his intention for the world—Second Isaiah and his successors had taught them to look forward with confidence to a time when, under God, they would be lords of a fertile, prosperous and peaceful world, and when their enemies would be finally subdued, never to rise again. Relatively modest though it was, this prospect will have prepared at least some Jews to sympathise with the far more grandiose Zoroastrian notions about the 'making wonderful' (Cohn, p. 223).

After Alexander conquered the Persian Empire in 330 BC, Zoroastrian prophecies of a future Messiah mobilised Iranians and inspired similar thoughts in Jews:

> In the Hellenistic period the descendants of Iranian colonists of Achaemenian times are known to have dwelt side by side with Jewish settlers in many towns in Babylonia, in the area around Damascus, in Lydia and Phrygia. Both groups produced distinguished citizens, who served together on town or provincial councils—and, as Greek was now a common language of the educated, they will have communicated with one another more easily than before. And wherever Iranians lived there were Zoroastrian priests, many of whom will have been impressively devout and zealous. ...
>
> By that time what Zoroastrian priests had to tell will have been very much what some Jews wanted to hear. The overthrow of the Achaemenian empire was a truly traumatic experience for Iranians. It was not simply that a dispensation that had been perceived as divinely ordained and everlasting was abruptly and totally obliterated —it was replaced first by the miseries of defeat, then by generations of warfare between the successor states. Iranians and Jews were no longer rulers and ruled but fellow-sufferers in an uncertain and tormented world.
>
> In such circumstances the eschatological promises enshrined in Zoroastrian teaching must have taken on a new urgency. (Cohn, 1993, pp. 223-4)

Eight decades after the fall of Persia, Iranians regained independence from the Greek empires with the rise of the Parthian Empire (247 BC to 224 AD). It was the enemy of Rome, and the natural ally of Jews.

> The attraction of Zoroastrianism will have been reinforced when, in the second century BC, Iranian power revived under the Parthians. When, in the first century, Judaea came under the harsh rule of Rome, Jews looked to Parthia as Rome's most formidable enemy. ... and when, in 40 BC, they invaded Syria Palestine, entered Jerusalem, and installed a Jewish king in place of the hated Roman nominee Herod, they could be regarded as champions of the Jews against the Romans. And though Herod was reinstated by the Romans two years later, the Parthians persisted with their efforts to move west and to oust the Romans. These developments can

only have made Zoroastrian prophecies of salvation from tyranny and of the coming of the kingdom of God sound still more convincing.

Contacts between Parthians and Jews—including, later, Christian Jews—continued also outside Palestine. Babylon, with its important Jewish community, was under Parthian rule. ... Thus the Pharisees, though they belonged to mainstream Judaism, felt no difficulty in 'interpreting' the scriptures in the light of new doctrines which they believed to be truly Jewish, but which were really of Zoroastrian origin. (Cohn, 1993, pp. 224-5)

Isaiah's vision of a United World at Peace

The Book of Isaiah is often cited for its Jewish 'universalism' and vision of a united world at peace. But this is what it actually says (NIV):

https://biblehub.com/niv/isaiah/1.htm

The Book of Isaiah, chapter 2, verses 1 to 4—The Mountain of the Lord

1 This is what Isaiah son of Amoz saw concerning Judah and Jerusalem:
2 In the last days
the mountain of the Lord's temple will be established
as the highest of the mountains;
it will be exalted above the hills,
and all nations will stream to it.
3 Many peoples will come and say,
"Come, let us go up to the mountain of the Lord,
to the temple of the God of Jacob.
He will teach us his ways,
so that we may walk in his paths."
The law will go out from Zion,
the word of the Lord from Jerusalem.
4 He will judge between the nations
and will settle disputes for many peoples.
They will beat their swords into plowshares
and their spears into pruning hooks.
Nation will not take up sword against nation,
nor will they train for war anymore.

The Book of Isaiah, chapter 14

2 And Israel will take possession of the nations
and make them male and female servants in the Lord's land.
They will make captives of their captors
and rule over their oppressors.

The Book of Isaiah, chapter 60—The Glory of Zion

10 "Foreigners will rebuild your walls,
and their kings will serve you.

Though in anger I struck you,
in favor I will show you compassion.
11 Your gates will always stand open,
they will never be shut, day or night,
so that people may bring you the wealth of the nations—
their kings led in triumphal procession.
12 For the nation or kingdom that will not serve you will perish;
it will be utterly ruined.

H. G. Wells commented on this Zionist agenda in his book *The Fate of Homo Sapiens*:

Almost every community with which the orthodox Jews have come into contact has sooner or later developed and acted upon that conspiracy idea. A careful reading of the Bible does nothing to correct it; there indeed you have the conspiracy plain and clear. It is not simply the defensive conspiracy of a nice harmless people anxious to keep up their dear, quaint old customs that we are dealing with. It is an aggressive and vindictive conspiracy. People are apt to catch up and repeat phrases about the nobility of the Book of Isaiah on the strength of a few chance quotations torn from their context. But let the reader take that book and read it for himself straightforwardly, and note the setting of these fragments. Much of it is ferocious; extraordinarily like the rantings of some Nazi propagandist. The best the poor Gentile can expect is to play the part of a Gibeonite, a hewer of wood and a drawer of water for the restored elect. It is upon that and the like matter that the children of the orthodox have been fed. It is undeniable. There are the books for everyone to read. It is not tolerance but stupidity to shut our eyes to their quality. (Wells, 1939, pp. 128-9)

The U. S. edition, titled *The Fate of Man*, lacks the above paragraph on the Book of Isaiah. Wells was no Zionist, but after World War II he apologised to Chaim Weizmann for not appreciating the Jewish people's need of a homeland. Despite not being a Zionist, his support for the Globalist movement made him a close ally of the Globalist Jewish Left.

On account of Wells' anti-Zionist statements such as the above, Hannah Newman, a Zionist Jew, accused him of being a Nazi promoting—as part of the New Age movement— "a kinder, gentler Final Solution" (Newman, 5761=2001). She says, "Key NA disciples have released additional how-to books, such as H.G. Wells' "The Open Conspiracy" (Newman, 5761=2001). That the agenda is "a kinder, gentler Final Solution" is claimed in Newman, 1997/2006. She erred in classing Wells as "New Age". Far from being religious, he was a materialist, atheist and Communist (or 'Illuminist'—that would be a more exact descriptor for him).

Chapter 14: Stalin overthrew the Jewish Bolsheviks

Russians now see the early Soviet period as a time of Jewish domination. The Bolshevik leadership was only about half Jewish, but those atheistic Jews controlled it, and had a fanatical hatred of everything Russian.

A Bolshevik Postcard, issued in 1918 and shown here, listed Leaders of the October Coup: all are Jewish except Lenin, but he had a paternal Jewish grandfather and identified as Jewish. Stalin is not among them. From the hardback edition of Trotsky's biography of Stalin (Trotski, 1947), between pages 260 & 261.

In the preceding years, many Jews had abandoned Orthodox Judaism and become atheists. They joined all the revolutionary parties, in particular the Menshevik Party, but also the Bolshevik Party, the Socialist Revolutionary Party, and the Anarchists.

Russian Minister of Finance Sergius Witte told

17. A Postcard widely circulated on the first anniversary of the Bolshevik coup, entitled "The Leaders of the Proletarian Revolution," showing (1) Lenin,(2) Trotsky (3) Zinoviev, (4) Lunacharsky, (5) Kamenev, (6) Sverdlov

Theodore Herzl that "while Jews made up only some 5% of the population they comprised 50% of the revolutionaries" (Spence, 2017, p. 16).

Leonard Schapiro gave more exact numbers: "Witte duly pointed out to Herzl that while the Jews formed only seven million out of a total population of 136 million, about fifty percent of the members the revolutionary parties was Jewish" (Schapiro, 1961).

After the February Revolution, Prince Lvov headed an interim government largely composed of Freemasons, in which Kerensky, a minister, proclaimed Jewish rights. Kerensky later became Prime Minister. Many Jews supported his regime, which proclaimed a Republic and organised the first free election in Russian history.

Kerensky was Jewish, a Freemason (in the Grand Orient of the Peoples of Russia), and a member of the Socialist Revolutionary Party.

The GOPR was irregular, co-Masonic (admitted women), dispensed with most rituals, and did not use mystic symbolism. Kerensky became Chairman of the Council (equivalent to Grand Master) in 1916.

Ludwig Hass (1983) traced the role of Freemasons in preparing the February Revolution:

"an information office for the left groupings ... was comprised exclusively of masons: Nekrasov, Kerensky, and Chkheidze. The office was to gradually prepare public opinion for the coup, and then to offer the latter support."

Masons populated the cabinets of the Provisional Government after the fall of the Czar. The first such 10-person Cabinet was composed of at least five masons, including Kerensky, Nekrasov, Shingarev and Tereshchenko. Succeeding cabinets included Yefryemov, Pereverzhev, Prokopovich, Skobelev and V. N. Stepanov.

"Deputy ministers for certain periods were Savinkov, Urusov and Volkov; Chkheizde was president of the Petrograd Soviet of Workers' and Soldiers' Deputies. Teplov, already a general, commanded the Petrograd military district during the Kornilov period. One could come across many an adept in other responsible positions" (Hass, 1983).

Kyrkunov (2022) wrote,

Political figures such as Alexander Kerensky, Alexander Guchkov, Nikolay Chkheidze or Nikolay V. Nekrasov are considered to be members of the Grand Orient of the Peoples of Russia, and their role in the February Revolution was very important. Their names were known before, but the actual participation in the GOPR was not, they were not seen as conspirators, the organization itself was not that well known, and generally even if there were some talks, those were considered to be rumors. Eventually, closer to the 1960s more materials began to come out, letters, interviews, some were produced by Boris I. Nikolaevsky, a Menshevik, who was supposedly a Freemason himself and could freely talk to his 'brethren'. After all, more information became available when Alexander Kerensky himself began to recall the days when he was a Freemason in the GOPR, many activities became clearer after the issue of his memoirs.

The Bolsheviks banned Freemasonry in 1922, but Stalin was clearly a Freemason during his later years in power, probably a member of a different Masonic order. He even had statues cast of himself making the Masonic 'hidden hand' hand sign (Myers, 2021/2022). The frontal photo of Stalin shown here is a still I made from a video, in which Stalin makes this Masonic handsign.

His left hand is in his coat pocket—no doubt, it was cold. His right hand is not in his right pocket, but making the sign. What is the meaning of this? Was he signalling to Freemasons in the West? They certainly have a lot to explain.

Stalin's mother seems to have had a Masonic funeral (arranged by Beria, because Stalin was busy). Her upright funerary shroud has a Jewish appearance, but it is probably Masonic instead.

In 2021, a website showed a photo of the grave of Stalin's mother, in Tlibisi, Georgia, and pronounced it 'Jewish'. This was because of the cup on the top, and the full-length shroud over the body; graves at Jewish cemeteries

were shown for comparison. The site is zet09.livejournal.com/232250.html. It's in Russian, but Google Translate will translate it into English for you. A photo of the grave   is   at

https://upload.wikimedia.org/wikipedia/commons/6/65/Grave_of_Ekaterine_Gior
gis_asuli_Geladze.jpg.

I asked Israel Shamir to check. He got his contact in Tlibisi to investigate this grave; that person said it's genuine—the grave of Stalin's mother. Shamir pointed out that one commentator at the above link, Martini09, disputed the claim that this style of grave is Jewish. He said that it's Masonic; and that Jews copied this

Masonic fashion, considering themselves 'supermasons'. He showed photos of some non-Jewish graves with a cup on the top and a small shroud, including Pushkin and V. V. Andreev. However Stalin's mother's grave has a full-length shroud, like the Jewish graves shown (Myers, 2021/2022).

At Yalta, when Stalin made a pact with Roosevelt and Churchill, all three were Freemasons.

Xi Jinping made the Masonic 'hidden hand' hand sign at the opening of the Wuhan Military Games on October 18, 2019. Note that this is on Xinhua video.

During the Covid-19 pandemic, Anthony Fauci, the highest-paid official in the United States, made

the same Masonic hand sign at a press conference on April 5, 2020 (Myers, 2021/2022). The media, probably Masonic themselves, did not report it. the scene is on video. Who was Fauci signalling to?

Kerensky had scheduled elections to a Constituent Assembly for Nov. 25, 1917, but the Bolshevik Revolution occurred on Nov. 7 (Oct. 25 old date). The Bolsheviks let the vote go ahead, but they lost badly to the Socialist Revolutionary Party.

The SR Party represented the peasants, who were 90% of the population. The Bolsheviks claimed to represent the 'proletariat', by which they meant the urban workers, just a small percentage of the population. However, the leading Bolsheviks were all intellectuals—intelligentsia.

Of 767 seats, the Bolsheviks won 183 seats, the Mensheviks 18 seats, the Socialist Revolutionary Party 324 seats, the Ukrainian Socialist-Revolutionary Party 110 seats, and minor parties took the remaining seats.

The assembly met on 18—19 January 1918, but the Bolsheviks forcibly dispersed it after only 13 hours. The SR party then split into Left and Right factions. The Left SRs accepted Bolshevik rule, while the Right SRs (by far the majority) opposed it.

The Left SRs entered a coalition government with the Bolsheviks, until the Treaty of Brest-Litovsky (March 3, 1918), which ceded Ukraine to Germany. The Right SRs opposed the Bolsheviks for dispersing the Constituent Assembly; the Left SRs opposed ceding Ukraine. By August 1918 the Bolsheviks had banned all the other parties, including the Left SRs.

In the meantime, the Left SRs had helped Trotsky destroy the Anarchists.

In prior decades, some SR members had assassinated Tsarist officials. Leonid Kannegisser took part in the assassination of Vyacheslav von Plehve, the Russian Minister of Interior. Fanny Kaplan attempted to assassinate a Tsarist official in Kyiv.

On August 30, 1918, Leonid Kannegisser assassinated Moisei Solomonovich Uritsky, Chief of the Petrograd Cheka; and on the same day, Fanny Kaplan shot Lenin three times, wounding him seriously.

Both Kannegisser and Kaplan were SRs. Kaplan made this statement to the Cheka:

"My name is Fanya Kaplan. Today I shot Lenin. I did it on my own. ... I had resolved to kill Lenin long ago. I consider him a traitor to the Revolution. I was exiled to Akatui for participating in an assassination attempt against a Tsarist official in Kyiv. I spent 11 years at hard labour. After the Revolution, I was freed. I favoured the Constituent Assembly and am still for it" (Fanny Kaplan., 2023).

Here's the punchline: both Kannegisser and Kaplan were Jewish.

Bruce Lockhart, the unofficial British liaison to the Bolsheviks, was imprisoned with Kaplan, because the Bolsheviks suspected that he was implicated in the assassination attempt. He records of Kaplan:

> At six in the morning a woman was brought into the room. She was dressed in black. Her hair was black, and her eyes, set in a fixed stare, had great black rings under them. Her face was colourless. Her features, strongly Jewish, were unattractive. She might have been any age between twenty and thirty-five. We guessed it was Kaplan. Doubtless, the Bolsheviks hoped that she would give us some sign of recognition. Her composure was unnatural. She went to the window and, leaning her chin upon her hand, looked out into the daylight. And there she remained, motionless, speechless, apparently resigned to her fate, until presently the sentries came and took her away. She was shot before she knew whether her attempt to alter history had failed or succeeded. (Lockhart, 2002, p. 320)

Although atheistic Jews had been members of many revolutionary parties, in the years after the October Revolution they abandoned factional differences and joined the Bolshevik bureaucracy in large numbers; and the government explicitly called them to do so. They played the same role in administering the state, that Germans had played in the Tsarist regime. They were the new intelligentsia, and one of their jobs was to eliminate the old, patriotic Russian intelligentsia. And so, in the Politburo, in the ministries (Commissariats), and in the bureaucracy, the regime came to be seen as 'Jewish.' Making anti-semitism a capital crime only confirmed this in the eyes of Russians.

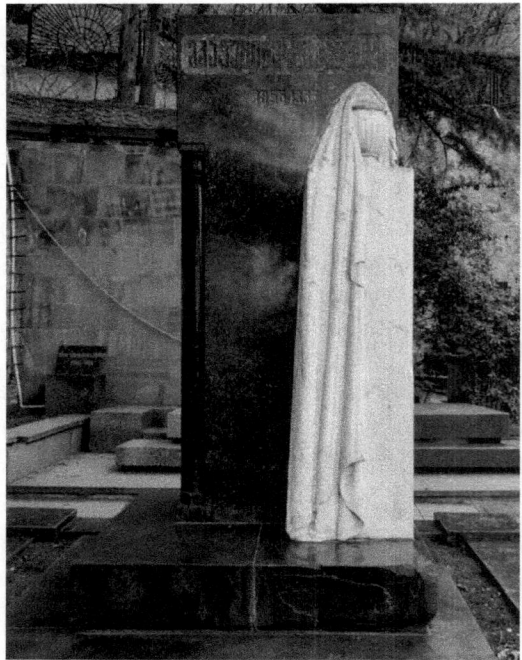

Photo of the grave of Stalin's mother at Tbilisi, Georgia. Taken by Reda Kerbouche; from Wikimedia Commons. https://commons.wikimedia.org/wiki/File:Grave_of_Ekaterine_Giorgis_asuli_Geladze.jpg. Some say that the shroud is Jewish; others say it's Masonic

Enzo Traverso stated (1994), "In the course of the civil war, the Jewish population rallied massively to the Red Army (often the only existing defense against the

pogroms), and its intelligentsia was recruited en bloc to the Soviet State apparatus" (p. 7). "The revolution transformed the Jewish intelligentsia, this layer of
pariahs, humiliated and persecuted by the former regime, into an elite called upon to play a role of the highest importance in the construction of socialism. The
Jews entered the state apparatus, universities, and liberal professions on a massive scale" (p. 153).

Ran Marom wrote (1979), "Since the end of 1917, the Bolsheviks had faced the
problem of running a system with no professional bureaucrats and specialists.
Without support from the Tsarist bureaucracy, they had to turn to the Jewish intelligentsia which saw in the Bolshevik Revolution an opportunity to achieve full civil
rights. Many Jewish figures suddenly appeared in the Bolshevik administration, in
the highest echelons of the bureaucracy, and especially in education, justice,
banks, commerce, foreign affairs, and the secret police" (pp. 22-3).

The Bolsheviks allied with minorities (Latvians, Poles, Jews) to overthrow the
Whites (Great Russians). Arkady Vaksberg attests the prominence of Jews in the
Cheka (Secret Police):

> The Soviet political police had "aliens" in its makeup from the start, partic-
> ularly Latvians, Poles, and Jews. It is important to note that "aliens" (includ-
> ing Armenians and Georgians) formed a very large percentage of all Soviet
> departments and ministries-for obvious reasons. Oppressed, or at least
> discriminated against, second- and even third-class citizens in the old Rus-
> sia, they felt a new energy in the new regime and with fanatical dedication
> launched themselves on revolutionary careers. But their presence was
> most visible (again for obvious reasons) in the activities of the vicious
> Cheka-GPU, noticed by both the public at large and the leaders who paid
> attention to the national question. ... And therefore if someone named
> Rabinovich was in charge of a mass execution, he was perceived not simply
> as a Cheka boss but as a Jew ... (Vaksberg, 1994, pp. 36-7)

On the murder of the Tsar's family, Vaksberg says that "the first violins in the
orchestra of death of the tsar and his family were four Jews—Yanker Yurovsky,
Shaia Goloshchekin, Lev Sosnovsky, and Pinkus Vainer (Pert Voikov). The concert
master and conductor was Yakov Syerdlov." (p. 37)

Vaksberg names the Jews at the head of the Cheka:

> As fate would have it, the people who surrounded Stalin and who had
> rendered him services in the twenties and thirties were mostly Jews.
> Among the first leaders of the repressive apparat created almost immedi-
> ately after the revolution to terrorize the whole country, first in the form
> of the VChK, or Cheka ... the man who was closest to Stalin and worked
> totally on his behalf was Genrikh Yagoda. (p. 35)

Those with a talent for executions were rewarded:

Along with Trilisser, and with similar formulations, this glorious battle order was awarded to many other famous Chekists who were part of Stalin's
entourage and who had already distinguished themselves with a talent for
execution—Yakov Agranov, Matvei Berman, Karl Pauker, and other representatives of the Jewish proletariat. ... Even closer to Stalin than Trilisser
were two high-ranking figures at Lubyanka—Yakov Agranov, Yagoda's first
deputy, and Karl Pauker, head of the operative department. (pp. 39-40)

And Jews ran the Gulag too:

And Koltsov allegedly had access to "corresponding circles" inside the
Commissariat of Foreign Affairs through his good friend Matvei Berman,
chief of the GULAG and later Deputy Commissar of Foreign Affairs. (p.
89)

When Lenin died, the U.S.S.R. was run by a triumvirate—Kamenev, Zinoviev &
Stalin. Of these, Stalin was the only non-Jew. This is the other critical fact which
shows Jewish dominance.

Bertrand Russell attested the Jewish role in creating Bolshevism, in a letter he
wrote in 1920 just after visiting the U.S.S.R. He published the letter in his autobiography:

To Ottoline Morell
Hotel Continental Stockholm 25th June 1920
Dearest O

... the time in Russia was infinitely painful to me, in spite of being one of
the most interesting things I have ever done. Bolshevism is a close tyrannical bureaucracy, with a spy system more elaborate and terrible than the
Tsar's, and an aristocracy as insolent and unfeeling, composed of Americanised Jews. No vestige of liberty remains, in thought or speech or action
(Russell, 1920/1975, volume 2 p. 172; in the paperback it's on p. 354).

Stuart Kahan, Jewish himself and a nephew of Lazar Kaganovich, wrote (1987)
in his biography of Lazar:

After all, wasn't the revolution prepared and fashioned by Jews? Both of
Karl Marx's grandfathers were rabbis, and Lenin's grandfather was also
Jewish. And wasn't Yakov Sverdlov, the first chief of state, a Jew, as was
Trotsky himself? But most people believed the Jews could be dealt with, as
they always had been dealt with before.

That Trotsky, unquestionably the most outstanding man among the Bolsheviks, was a Jew did not seem an insuperable obstacle in a party in which
the percentage of Jews, 52 percent, was rather high compared to the percentage of Jews (1.8 per cent) in the total population.

Lazar would have to keep a close eye on this. Would the people accept the revolution orchestrated by the Jews, or would they accept only one aspect and discard the other? (p. 81)

Not that ALL Communists were Jews. Communism had non-Jewish precedents: Plato's Republic/Laws as a community of 5,040 households; Inca Communism; and the Utopia of Thomas More, which may have been based on reports of Maya civilisation (Stobbart, 1992).

What Judaism contributed was the world-wide scope: the plan for a Bolshevik world-state was a Jewish idea, expressed in Trotsky's "Permanent Revolution". The leaders in the early years of Soviet Russia were about 50% Jewish; but the non-Jews were initially less important.

The same applied in the creation of Christianity. Its early leaders were Jewish; it was divided into a "Jewish" faction, led by James, and a "Hellenistic" faction, led by Paul. In the Stalin-Trotsky split, the Trotskyists were the "Jewish" faction.

Stalin's opportunity to take over arose because (1) Lenin died (2) Kamenev and Zinoviev feared Trotsky, even though all three were Jewish, and allied with Stalin (the junior member of the three) against him.

Kamenev and Zinoviev later joined Trotsky's 'Opposition' grouping; this marked the coalescence of the anti-Stalin Communists around Trotsky as leader. The word "Trotskyist" applies to formal members of Trotskyist sects; 'Trotskyoid' is a more generic term, indicating support but not necessarily formal membership.

Trotsky, in his article Thermidor and Anti-Semitism noted that Stalin was depicting the Opposition as a Jewish camp:

Between 1923 and 1926, when Stalin, with Zinoviev and Kamenev, was still a member of the "Troika," the play on the strings of anti-Semitism bore a very cautious and masked character. Especially schooled orators (Stalin already then led an underhanded struggle against his associates) said that the followers of Trotsky are petty bourgeois from "small towns" without defining their race. ... at the time of the expulsions of the Opposition from the party, the bureaucracy purposely emphasized the names of Jewish members of casual and secondary importance. This was quite openly discussed in the party, and, back in 1925, the Opposition saw in this situation the unmistakable symptom of the decay of the ruling clique.

After Zinoviev and Kamenev joined the Opposition the situation changed radically for the worse. At this point there opened wide a perfect chance to say to the workers that at the head of the Opposition stand three "dissatisfied Jewish intellectuals." (Trotsky, 1937/1941)

Joseph Nedava conceded that the identification of the Opposition with Jewishness had some justification in fact:

Nevertheless, the fact is that Jews were all along conspicuous among the Opposition, very few were to be found in the Stalin entourage, and fewer still in the rightist faction of Bukharin. Being mainly urban, they moved in the comparatively small intellectual circles and, marked by their "Jewish" characteristics, could be easily pointed at. Also, they were by their very nature and revolutionary upbringing closer to Trotskyism than to Stalinism. They repudiated the idea of "socialism in one country" as too small a prize to fight for. They would accept nothing less than world revolution. Thus the Stalinist identification of the Opposition with Jewishness had some justification in fact. In later years the designations "Opposition" and "the Evreskaia" were almost interchangeable. (Nedava, 5732/1972, pp. 174-5)

NOTE: The publication date 5732 (of Nedava's book) means the year 5732 in the Jewish Calendar—implying a date from Adam. This is the official dating (Calendar) used in Israel. It's also the dating system used in Freemasonry—e.g. in Masonic publications. Non-theistic Jews, who object so much to religious fundamentalism in the West, have not campaigned against this religious dating-system in Israel. The Jewish Calendar is, in fact, the Babylonian Calendar of old.

Benjamin Ginsberg, Professor of Political Science at John Hopkins University, wrote that Jews "formed the largest and most important group of victims of the Stalinist purges":

Stalinist Russia is a notable example of a regime that had been closely identified with Jews, whose non-Jewish leadership turned to anti-Semitism ... As we saw earlier, in the aftermath of the Bolshevik revolution, Jews played an extremely prominent role in the Soviet regime. During the struggles that followed Lenin's death in 1924, however, anti-Semitic appeals to the Communist Party's rank and file were among the weapons used by Stalin to defeat Trotsky, Zinoviev, and Kamenev and seize the party's leadership.

Indeed, much of the invective used by Stalin in the intraparty battles of this period was designed to appeal to anti-Semitic sentiment inside and outside the party. For example, the label, "left oppositionist," used by Stalin to castigate his enemies, was a euphemism for Jew. ...

During the 1930s, Stalin moved to consolidate his power by intimidating or eliminating all potential sources of opposition within the Communist party, the army, the secret police, and the administrative apparatus. Jews exercised a great deal of influence within all these institutions and, as a result, formed the largest and most important group of victims of the Stalinist purges. Jews constituted about 500,000 of the ten-million purge victims of the 1930s and comprised a majority of the politically most prominent victims.

In a series of show trials, during this period, the key Jewish officials of the Communist party and Soviet state were accused of plotting against the revolution and were systematically killed. These included Kamenev, Zinoviev, Radek, and Rykov. Important Jewish military commanders such as Yakir and Schmidt were also liquidated. The secret police forces used to implement these purges often were led by Jews who were killed in their turn, until the influence of Jews within the secret police was substantially diminished. Those liquidated included Yagoda, Pauker, Slutsky, and the Berman brothers. (Ginsberg, 1993, pp. 53-4)

In the Soviet Union, the Party (CPSU) controlled the Government (Council of People's Commissars); and the highest level of the Party was the Politburo. Within the Politburo, Jews predominated in the early years of the Soviet Union: this single fact shows that Jews created the Soviet Union.

Only after Stalin's rise to power did this situation change.

The membership of the Politburo on 22 March 1921 after the 10th Party Congress was: Lenin, Trotsky, Zinoviev, Stalin, and Kamenev.

These details are from Leonard Schapiro's book *The Communist Party of the Soviet Union* (1960, p. 606). Schapiro himself was Jewish, and, although providing these names, did not draw attention to their Jewishness.

Three of the five members of the Politburo (Trotsky, Zinoviev, and Kamenev) were Jewish by birth. Lenin identified with the Jewish part of his ancestry, as Volkogonov (1996) showed (p. 9). Stalin was the only non-Jew.

The Politburo, the inner group of the Central Committee, with authority to make policy, was set up in 1919, and replaced by the Praesidium in 1952. Schapiro (1960) lists the Members and Candidate Members of the Politburo and the Praesidium from 1917 to 1958.

This list of names is a guide to who was running the U.S.S.R. Note the changes in the 1920s, as Stalin edged his opponents out, and in the 1950s, after the death of Stalin. CC = Central Committee (of CPSU); CCC = Central Control Commission (disciplinary body within CC).

Membership in Oct. 1917 was:

1. Bureau for the political guidance of the insurrection. Elected at the C.C. meeting 10 (23).10.17—V. I. Lenin, G. E. Zinoviev, L. B. Kamenev, L. D. Trotsky, I. V. Stalin, G. Ia. Sokol'nikov, A. S. Bubnov. (Schapiro, 1960, p. 606)

Zinoviev, Kamenev, Trotsky and Sokol'nikov were Jewish. Lenin identified with the Jewish part of his ancestry.

2. Elected in March 1919 after the 8th Congress—Members: Lenin, Kamenev, Trotsky, Stalin, N. N. Krestinskii; Candidates: Zinoviev, N. I. Bukharin. (p. 606)

Kamenev, Trotsky and Sokol'nikov were Jewish; Lenin identified with the Jewish part of his ancestry.

3. Elected 22 March 1921 after the 10th Congress—Members: Lenin, Trotsky, Zinoviev, Stalin, and Kamenev; Candidates: V. M. Molotov, M. I. Kalinin and Bukharin. (p. 606)

Three of the five members of the Politburo were Jewish. Lenin identified with the Jewish part of his ancestry. Stalin was the only non-Jew.

4. Elected 3 April 1922 after the 11th Congress—Members: Lenin, Kamenev, Trotsky, Stalin, Zinoviev, A. I. Rykov, M. M. Tomskii; Candidates: Bukharin, Molotov, V. V. Kuibyshev, Kalinin.

5. Elected 26 April 1923 after the 12th Congress—Members: Lenin, Kamenev, Trotsky, Stalin, Zinoviev, Rykov, Tomskii; Candidates: Bukharin, Molotov, Kuibyshev. (p. 606)

From the death of Lenin to the expulsion of Trotsky:

6. Elected 2 June 1924 after the 13th Congress—Members: Kamenev, Trotsky, Stalin, Zinoviev, Rykov, Tomskii, Bukharin (Lenin died 24 January 1924); Candidates: Molotov, Kuibyshev , Kalinin , F. E. Dzerzhinskii.

7. Elected 1 January 1926 after the 14th Congress—Members: Bukharin, K. E. Voroshilov, Zinoviev, Kalinin, Molotov, Rykov, Stalin, Tomskii, Trotsky; Candidates: Ia. E. Rudzutak , Dzerzhinskii, G. I. Petrovskii, N. A. Uglanov, Kamenev.

8. C.C. plenary session 14-23 July 1926—Zinoviev expelled and replaced by Rudzutak
Elected Candidates: Petrovskii, Uglanov, G. K. Ordzhonikidze, A. A. Andreev, S. M. Kirov, A. I. Mikoyan, L. M. Kaganovich, Kamenev (Dzerzhinskii died 20 July 1926). (pp. 606-7)

9. C.C. plenary session 23 October 1926—Trotsky and Kamenev expelled. (p. 607)

Andrey Diky (1967) says that Jews constituted the "ruling class" for the first 30 years of the Soviet Union (p. 5). In tables at the back of his book, he names the personnel running various ministries, showing that most were heavily Jewish.

After the assassination of Uritsky and the attempt on Lenin, the Red Terror was officially launched; but it had been proceeding unofficially ever since the Bolsheviks took power.

Stalin continued the Terror that they instigated, but, in his overthrow of Trotsky, put many of the Old Bolsheviks to the sword. Jews still dominated the ministries which ran the country, but the Purges of 1937-8 were "a holocaust of Jewish Bolsheviks", in the words of Leonard Schapiro:

"Or again, take the elimination of Trotsky, Zinov'yev, and the countless Jewish bolsheviks who fell with them during the 1920s, and the great holocaust of Jewish bolsheviks which took place in 1937 and 1938" (Schapiro, 1961).

This is not because Stalin was targeting Jews at the time; the Jewish toll was only a side-effect of his struggle with Trotsky. It happened because so many of Trotsky's supporters were Jewish.

Just before World War II broke out, Litvinov was removed as Commissar of Foreign Affairs, replaced with the non-Jewish Molotov. This was so that the Pact could be made with Hitler.

Such changes, Diky says, only applied to a few Jews in conspicuous positions. The rest remained in place.

The Pact was made to buy time. But Hitler's invasion of Western Europe was quick and relatively bloodless, so it bought less time than had been expected.

Once Germany attacked the U.S.S.R, it issued a lot of propaganda about Jews running the regime. This was true, and Russians and Ukrainians knew it, but they could not say so or do anything about it. They were resentful, because Jews had largely administered the instruments of terror and the famine of the 1930s, while Russians and Ukrainians had been the victims.

Nevertheless, apart from West Ukrainians, they did not rally to the Nazis. Instead, Soviet Patriotism was born. The Russian people would not fight for Communism, but for Russia. The regime, although heavily Jewish, had to rehabilitate Russian history, including its military heroes. As Diky puts it,

The medals of Alexander Nevsky, Suvorov and Kutuzov were instituted, and, soon after, titles that were known in pre-revolutionary Russia and golden shoulder straps which were so much hated by those who created the U.S.S.R., were also introduced.

The spirit of the past, against which various Goublemans, Apfelbaums, Suritzmans and their fellow tribesmen had fought to their utmost to eradicate it from the memory of the nation during quarter of a century and to deprecate it in every possible way, was let out from the bottle. As soon as this spirit got loose it found such response among those who had staunchly, with their blood, defended their Motherland, the land and the heritage of their ancestors, it was impossible to drive it back.

The international-Cosmopolitan mist had disappeared and in its place life had returned to the seemingly dead patriotism of the Russian people and the patriotism of the whole population of the U.S.S.R., people who realized their own strength and their right to rule their own country. (Diky, 1967, p 272)

During the war, Jews knew they faced certain death from the Nazis, so many retreated to the east, leaving Russians to do the fighting. This was noticeable to all, and did not go down well, given the savage losses at the front. Robert Robinson, a black American living in Moscow, wrote about it:

> However, it was not rumor but newspaper accounts of the Nazis' treatment of Jews in already conquered territory that set off a mass exodus of Jews from Moscow. As soon as word was out that Moscow's factories were being dismantled and shipped to the east, thousands of Jews began to flee. If the Kremlin was abandoning Moscow they did not intend to be left unprotected in the path of the Germans. They walked away from their jobs and homes, leaving their apartment doors open.

> Jews held a significant number of the professional jobs in Moscow. They occupied the very highest positions at my factory; in fact, at times both the chief engineer and the head administrator were Jewish. As far as I knew, only four Jews were regular workers in my factory while hundreds of others held managerial positions. Many of the leading journalists, numerous high ranking officials at the Ministry of Foreign Affairs, and the majority of physicians, professors, teachers, jurists, economic planners, and finance managers were Jewish.

> As we drove toward Gorky, we saw those thousands and thousands of Jews who had been unable to make rail connections flooding the roads. As a result of this exodus, the Jews quickly came to be resented by other Russians, who accused them of abandoning Moscow rather than staying behind and resisting the Germans. After the exodus of Moscow's Jews in 1941 I frequently heard anti Semitic remarks, whereas in my previous eleven years in the Soviet Union I had never heard even one. (Robinson, 1988, pp. 162-3)

After the war, Russians and Ukrainians no longer submitted to Jewish domination. This was something not created by Stalin, but recognised by him. Diky says:

> And when Zhdanov, the communist and follower of the Third International, said, "Cosmopolitans without kith or kin", no one, besides the foreign Jews, protested against these words.

> And when the words "Cosmopolitans without kith or kin" were pronounced, people interpreted them as the recognition by the power itself that the loyalty of those who spoke and acted in their name was taken under doubt. This corresponded exactly to what people thought and wanted, and whose national feelings after the victorious war were aggravated in the light of all of what they had seen and had suffered during the war.

Stalin, who was well-informed about these feelings, took this circumstance into consideration and in every possible way always underlined the sacrifices and merits of the "Russian" people during the war, recalling nowhere either the Jewish people or its sacrifices and merits, the presence of which were doubted by the population of the whole country.

All the population of the country still well remembered the millions of sacrifices during the collectivization, famine and camps in which no Jews were seen. Moreover, these sacrifices were not the result of brutality inflicted by some invading enemy, but were inflicted by the ruling class which consisted mainly of the Jewish ethnic group. (Diky, 1967, p. 276)

As Jews lost their privileged position, most turned against the U.S.S.R.:

In the U.S.S.R. itself the Jewish ethnic group started gradually to lose its privileged position and to get equal rights and opportunities with the rest of the population. This was interpreted by the Jewry of whole Diaspora as "discrimination". ... And the larger part of the world's Jewry changed from advocates of the U.S.S.R. to its opponents. (p. 271)

The Jewish Anti-Fascist Committee, an alliance of leading Soviet and American Jews, proposed turning Crimea into a Jewish republic.

Crimea hosts the Sevastopol naval base, which gives Russia access to the Mediterranean. Without it, Russia is no longer a great power. The proposal for a Jewish Crimea was deemed a military risk by Stalin and Khrushchev. By the late 1940s, they sensed that Jews were aligning with the United States. The Soviet Constitution provided for Union and autonomous republics to enter into direct relationship with foreign countries, and even to secede.

In reaction to Hitler's draconian measures, Zionist Jews lobbied for the creation of Israel. In the postwar years, Russians were rejecting Cosmopolitanism, while Russian Jews were rallying to the newly created state of Israel. After the 1967 and 1973 mid-East wars, many emigrated.

When Golda Meir arrived in Moscow in October 1948 as ambassador of Israel, she was mobbed by a crowd of 50,000 ecstatic Jews. Thousands subsequently applied to emigrate to Israel; the government sensed the unreliability of the Jews.

Orlando Figes (2007) stated that Stalin had supported the creation of Israel, but came to see Jews as potentially a fifth column:

Stalin became increasingly afraid of pro-Israeli feeling among the Soviet Jews. His fears intensified as a result of Golda Meir's arrival in Moscow in the autumn of 1948 as the first Israeli ambassador to the U.S.S.R. Everywhere she went she was cheered by crowds of Soviet Jews. On her visit to a Moscow synagogue on Yom Kippur (13th October), thousands of people lined the streets, many of them shouting 'Am Yisroel Chai' ('The

People of Israel live!')—a traditional affirmation of national renewal to Jews throughout the world but to Stalin a dangerous sign of 'bourgeois Jewish nationalism' that subverted the authority of the Soviet state. (p. 493)

Soviet spymaster Pavel Sudoplatov wrote (1995), "The tragedy was that in a closed society like the Soviet Union, the establishment of the state of Israel in 1948 made the Jews appear to be the only significant national group with a foreign-based homeland. This automatically placed the whole national group under suspicion of potential divided loyalties, especially after Israel defeated the Arabs in the 1948 war of independence. The pride that followed the Jewish military victory revitalized the cultural consciousness of Soviet Jews, which had been destroyed in the twenties" (p. 309).

In the postwar years, Jews retained high positions in the professions and in cultural ministries, but were moved aside from diplomacy, foreign affairs, external politics and defense matters.

After the war, there was a housing shortage in Kyiv; much of the city was in ruins. Jews wanted to return to their homes, but Khrushchev said:

> Jews in the past have committed many sins against the Ukrainian people. The people hate them for this. In our Ukraine we do not need the Jews. And, I think that for the Ukrainian Jews who survived Hitler's attempts to destroy them, it would be better if they did not try to return here. It would be better for them to go to the Birobidzhan. You see, here we are in the Ukraine. Do you understand? This is the Ukraine. And we are not interested that the Ukrainian people would interpret the return of Soviet power as the return of the Jews. (Diky, 1967, p. 256)

In the end, many Jews did return. But West Ukrainian Nazis, who had participated in the holocaust against the Jews during the war, made a pact with the Zionists in 1966. Henceforth, these Nazis and Zionists would work together to bring down the U.S.S.R.:

> In May of 1966 in New York, the fraternization of the Zionists and the men of the Petlura occurred along and again with a joint vow to destroy "Russian Communism", without referring to the Jews this time. The details of this fraternization were published in the Ukrainian weekly "Our Fatherland" in May 1966. The comparison of these two vows given by the Petlura men shows that they changed from Jewish destroyers into their allies in their common business of liquidating the united U.S.S.R. ... (Diky, 1967, p. 14)

That alliance has been on display from the 2014 Maidan coup to the war of 2022.

Diky has some differences from Solzhenitsyn. After 1948, when Jewish dominance finished in the Soviet Union, Diky advocated for Soviet Patriotism. He supported the Soviet Union, whereas Solzhenitsyn opposed it. Diky did not raise the Gulag or the religious question—the destruction of the Orthodox Church—whereas for Solzhenitsyn, spiritual matters were very important.

Stalin's Purges reduced the dominance of the Jewish intelligentsia which had rallied to the Bolsheviks during the civil war, and manned the bureaucracy for the first 30 years. These atheistic Jews had replaced the Germans, who provided similar professional and administrative services in Czarist Russia.

After the Purges of 1936-8, Jews continued to support the Soviet Union, because Hitler was deemed the main threat. Jews participated heavily in the International Brigades during the Spanish Civil War of 1936-9, in support of the Republican government allied to the Soviet Union.

From the mid 1930s, Stalin reversed the earlier Affirmative Action policy favouring minorities, and initiated a policy of Russification.

Many Jewish communists initially stayed with the Stalin camp, because it was running the U.S.S.R., and before World War II Jews had many leading positions, e.g. as ambassadors and in the Cheka.

But over the years, more and more swung over to the anti-Stalin camp. Events which led to this included:

• Stalin's Purges of mid 1930s were aimed at weeding out closet or suspected Trotskyists (including from the Army—Trotsky had been War Minister, and appointed its senior commanders—and from the Comintern). The numbers of victims multiplied as suspects implicated others (sometimes wantonly) to save themselves

• Stalin's alliance with Hitler (it was the last straw for Arthur Koestler)

• Soviet rehabilitation of Russian tradition during World War II, to enlist patriotic feelings

• The Jewish lobby overplayed its hand towards the end of World War II, promoting a plan for a Jewish republic in the Crimea, with strong ties to American Jews and thus somewhat independent. Stalin later turned against its sponsors

• The creation of Israel in 1948 provided Jews with a rival centre of loyalty

• The Doctors Plot of 1953 was actually about a Zionist conspiracy. It grew out of a plan to make Crimea an autonomous Jewish republic funded by American Jewish plutocrats; this plan was proposed by American Jews during World War II. Stalin intended to purge leaders closely involved with that scheme: Beria, Molotov, Mikoyan, Voroshilov and Voznesensky; this was the genesis of the Doctors

Plot. Beria was the main target, but evidence indicates that he killed Stalin first. Stalin died within 2 months of the Doctors Plot being announced. For evidence that he was murdered, see Appendix 5.

Stalin was likely murdered on or about Purim, March 1. The Doctors Plot was announced by Tass on January 13, 1953. On February 11, 1953: the U.S.S.R. severed diplomatic relations with Israel. On March 5, 1953, Stalin was declared dead. The imprisoned Doctors were freed by Beria, on taking power.

• Jews overwhelmingly sided with Israel in the 1967 and 1973 Middle-East wars; but the Soviet Union was allied to the Arabs

• Subsequently, Jewish ties to Israel and the U.S. made them appear untrustworthy; as a result, they were kept out of sensitive positions, and reacted by emigrating from the U.S.S.R.

The Baruch Plan of 1946, proposed by Truman to Stalin, aimed at joint management of atomic energy and nuclear weapons, with the U.S. retaining a veto. But discussions in the Bulletin of the Atomic Scientists also portrayed it as a potential World Government; Stalin rejected it. He noted that Jews were at the top of nuclear matters in both the U.S.A. and the U.S.S.R., and was determined to lessen that reliance.

The significance of Stalin is, not that he was a "good guy", but that he gave to Jewish Bolsheviks a taste of their own medicine, and, over time, made Communism a less Jewish and more Russian system, reflected in the name for World War II, "the Great Patriotic War". In view of the Trotskyists in the West promoting Gay Marriage and LGBT, Stalin can be seen as a defender of tradition.

Many people who believe that we need a world based on common ownership of major parts of the economy (and this is my own view) were deceived by the Bolsheviks and their supporters in the West, who hid the terrible stifling of freedom of thought in the new regime. Further, they hid the fact that at the start, Bolshevism was based not on equality of classes, but on Jewish domination (in league with other aggrieved minorities) of the majority Russians.

Western sympathisers were particularly attracted to Trotsky and deceived by him, because of his skill in writing the story of the Revolution. His version became the accepted account for many Fellow-Travellers in the West. In their view, Stalin "buggered it up"; but, in truth, he stole the Jewish conspiracy.

His cruelty was, in part, aimed at the Jewish forces he had ousted; but the Soviet Union tried to keep its Jews IN, unlike Nazi Germany, which tried to get them OUT.

Today, the Western media is hostile to Stalin and the post-Soviet governments in Russia. To what extent is that hostility retaliation for Stalin's overthrowing the Jewish Bolsheviks?

Benjamin Ginsberg, in his book *The Fatal Embrace: Jews and the State* (1993) documents how Jews dominated one regime after another over a period of centuries. He also shows that the wealth and power they attained made them vulnerable to being evicted. Major evictions were from Spain in 1492 and from Germany in the 1930s. A list of expulsions and other countermeasures against Jews, from 250AD, (thanks to Denis McCormack for it) is at https://www.simpletoremember.com/articles/a/HistoryJewishPersecution/.

During the Roman Empire, there were riots against Jews in Alexandria, and Jewish uprisings in Cyrenaica, Cyprus, Egypt and Jerusalem. Jewish rebels slaughtered Roman garrisons, but the rebels were subsequently crushed by Roman legions. The fanatical resistance at Masada motivates Zionists even now; Netanyahu's allies want to deport the Palestinians (in breach of the Balfour Declaration, which was a contract between Britain and Jewry) and tear down the Dome of the Rock and Al Aqsa mosque, igniting a world war with Islam. Unnecessarily, because they have the wrong site (see p. 162).

Ginsberg also documents Jewish dominance of the United States. Writing in 1993, he says:

> Today, though barely 2% of the nation's population is Jewish, close to half its billionaires are Jews. The chief executive officers of the three major television networks, and the four largest film studios are Jews, as are the owners of the nation's largest newspaper chain and most influential single newspaper, the New York Times. In the late 1960s, Jews already constituted 20% of the faculty of elite universities and 40% of the professors of elite law schools; today, these percentages doubtless are higher. (p. 1)

> That fully three-fourths of America's foreign aid budget is devoted to Israel's security interests is a tribute in considerable measure to the lobbying prowess of AIPAC and the importance of the Jewish community in American politics. (p. 2)

What does that say about "Jewish Internationalism"—that trademark Jewish concern for the underdog?

Ron Unz, at unz.com, has documented the declining proportion of non-Jewish white students (*Aryans*, one might say) at Harvard and other Ivy-League universities.

Racial statistics lump Jewish whites and non-Jewish whites together, producing a 'whites' tally, which hides the Jewish dominance and the non-Jewish white decimation. Yet this is the ethnic group that founded the United States. What pos-

sible reason could there be for this decline? Is it Harvard's affirmative-action policies? Perhaps it's the WOKE hostility to whites? Perhaps the Feminist undermining
of white males? Is there a Jewish campaign against the white race, as some say,
pointing to Noel Ignatiev's call to "abolish whiteness" (White Genocide, 2002), and
the defence of, or only mild criticism of, the "Kill the Boer" chant, by the New York
Times and the ADL? Of the call to violence, the NYT commented 'historians and
the left-wing politician who embraces it say it should not be taken literally'
(Elignon, 2023); the ADL said 'baseless claims of "white genocide" have been made
by right-wing extremists ... ADL is the leading anti-hate organization in the world'
(Greenblatt, 2023). Were these the sorts of people that Stalin overthrew?

Auditing Stalin's ledger-book, the record of his crimes on one side and his accomplishments on the other, is quite a political task. What proportion of those
who highlight his crimes, also deny that the early Soviet Union was created by
Jews, and that Jews remained dominant as Diky showed (see pp. 185-9), until Stalin overthrew them?

Chapter 15: Trotsky accuses Stalin of rehabilitating God and the Family

Leon Trotsky was one of the bloodiest mass murderers of the Twentieth Century. Yet in the West his crimes have been airbrushed, and he has been normalised, depicted sympathetically as a family man, a lover of Frida Kahlo, and a victim of Stalin's brutality.

The Soviet Union was supposed to be based on workers "taking control" of the workplace, but the Kronstadt Massacre, ordered by Trotsky, put an end to that illusion.

Erich Fromm sought to normalise Trotsky: "In whatever way one may disagree with Marx, Engels, Lenin, Trotzky, there can be no doubt that as persons they represent a flowering of Western humanity. They were men with an uncompromising sense of truth" (Fromm, 1958/2002, pp. 271-2).

George Weigel, writing (2021) in a 'progressive' Catholic journal titled First Things, also sought to normalise Trotsky: "Trotsky actually had ideas, however misshapen, and something vaguely resembling a conscience. Stalin was pathologically power-mad and had no discernible conscience whatsoever."

Stalin overthrew the Trotskyists during the purges of the 1930s. But the Revolution had turned on itself as early as the Kronstadt Massacre of 1921, during which Trotsky ordered the massacre of the sailors who had helped bring Bolshevism to power.

The uprising threw off Communist rule and proclaimed the slogan "Soviets without Communists". Pitirim Sorokin described protests he witnessed in St Petersburg just before the Kronstadt revolt:

By 1921 the destructive consequences of the Communist program became clear to even the dullest peasants. Their fields lay untilled and weed-grown. The peasants had no seeds to sow and they had no incentive to industry. In the towns everything was slowing down to a death sleep. Nationalized factories, having no fuel, stopped operating. Railways were broken down. Buildings were falling in ruins. Schools had almost ceased to function. The deadly noose of Communism was slowly choking the people to death. But Russia did not want to die, and in one sudden, desperate uprising the whole system for a time was smashed. (p. 263)

On the Nicolaevsky Bridge the demonstration met Communist troops, which opened fire and dispersed the workmen. The next days the riots were renewed. The crowds were larger and more defiant, and it was plain that the people were trying to get together. Many were arrested or killed. But the movement grew, and as Russians in the Red army refused to act, the Government brought up the ever-faithful forces, principally Lettish,

Bashkirian, and International troops, and restrained the mobs. On February 26 a great demonstration occurred in the center of the town, on the Nevsky Prospekt, and this time so many people were killed that it seemed that the Government had completely suppressed the uprising.

The next day, February 27, we heard that the Kronstadt sailors, formerly ardent supporters of Communism, had revolted. This turned out to be true, and had that revolt succeeded, had we had even one free newspaper to support their revolt, it would have been the end of the Soviet Government. Plainly we heard the cannonade from Kronstadt, and plainly we saw the panic of the Government. Within twenty-four hours a proclamation appeared announcing the New Economic Policy (NEP). According to the proclamation, requisitions from peasants were to be replaced by definite taxes; trade and commerce were to be re-established; many factories would be denationalized; people would be allowed to buy and sell food; special conferences of non-Communist workers would be organized to improve living standards. In this way Communism was liquidated and "NEP" was established. (Sorokin, 1924, pp. 265-6)

Dmitri Volkogonov described (1996) Trotsky's crushing of the revolt:

The Red Army's crushing of the Kronstadt revolt, which occurred during the Tenth Party Congress of March 1921 when the once-loyal garrison rebelled against Bolshevik policies, gave a perfect illustration of Trotsky's capability in this sphere. When he was told about the uprising, he at once dictated an address:

{quote} To the population of Kronstadt and the rebellious forts. I order all those who have raised their hand against the socialist Fatherland to lay down their arms immediately. Recalcitrants must be disarmed and handed over to the Soviet authorities. Commissars and other representatives of the regime who have been arrested [by the insurgents] must be released at once. Only those who surrender unconditionally can count on the mercy of the Soviet Republic. I am simultaneously issuing instructions to prepare to crush the insurgency and the insurgents with an iron hand. {end quote}

The address was signed by Trotsky, as People's Commissar, S.S. Kamenev, as commander-in-chief of the armed forces, commander of 7th Army Tukhachevsky, and chief-of-staff Lebedev. (p. 130)

Decades later, two Soviet defectors met in New York, and reflected on the meaning of the Kronstadt Massacre. Whittaker Chambers describes his 1952 meeting with Walter Krivitsky:

I met Krivitsky with extreme reluctance. Long after my break with the Communist Party, I could not think of Communists or Communism without revulsion. I did not wish to meet even ex-Communists. Toward Russians, especially, I felt an organic antipathy.

But one night, when I was at Levine's apartment in New York, Krivitsky telephoned that he was coming over. There presently walked into the room a tidy little man about five feet six with a somewhat lined gray face out of which peered pale blue eyes. ... By way of handshake, Krivitsky touched my hand. Then he sat down at the far end of the couch on which I also was sitting. His feet barely reached the floor. ...

Krivitsky ... said ... "Kronstadt was the turning point." I knew what he meant. But who else for a thousand miles around could know what we were talking about? Here and there, some fugitive in a dingy room would know. But, as Krivitsky and I looked each other over, it seemed to me that we were like two survivors from another age of the earth, like two dated dinosaurs, the last relics of the revolutionary world that had vanished in the Purge. Even in that vanished world, we had been a special breed—the underground activists. There were not many of our kind left alive who still spoke the language that had also gone down in the submergence. I said, yes, Kronstadt had been the turning point.

Kronstadt is a naval base a few miles west of Leningrad in the Gulf of Finland. From Kronstadt during the Bolshevik Revolution in 1917, the sailors of the Baltic Fleet had steamed their cruisers to aid the Communists in capturing Petrograd. Their aid had been decisive. They were the sons of peasants. They embodied the primitive revolutionary upheaval of the Russian people. They were the symbol of its instinctive surge for freedom. And they were the first Communists to realize their mistake and the first to try to correct it. When they saw that Communism meant terror and tyranny, they called for the overthrow of the Communist Government and for a time imperiled it. They were bloodily destroyed or sent into Siberian slavery by Communist troops led in person by the Commissar of War, Leon Trotsky, and by Marshal Tukhachevsky, one of whom was later assassinated, the other executed, by the regime they then saved.

Krivitsky meant that by the decision to destroy the Kronstadt sailors, and by its cold-blooded action in doing so, Communism had made the choice that changed it from benevolent socialism to malignant fascism. Today, I could not answer, yes, to Krivitsky's challenge. The fascist character of Communism was inherent in it from the beginning. Kronstadt changed the fate of millions of Russians. It changed nothing about Communism. It merely disclosed its character. (Chambers, 1952/2001, pp. 459-60)

The lesson is that this 'fascist' character began not with Stalin, but with Trotsky and Lenin.

Trotsky was the instigator of the Bolshevik coup known as the October Revolution. Then he and Lenin jointly launched the Red Terror, and both wrote books defending it when Karl Kautsky criticised it.

The Red Terror sought to destroy the Russian Orthodox Church, killing its priests and destroying its churches, and to crush the spirit and the civilisation of the Russian people.

During the Civil War against the anti-Communists, Trotsky positioned special "blocking" troops in the rear, behind his front-line troops, to shoot deserters and stop the front line retreating from battle. That's how he won.

In his autobiography *My Life* (1930), Trotsky wrote, "So long as those malicious tailless apes that are so proud of their technical achievements—the animals that we call men—will build armies and wage wars, the command will always be obliged to place the soldiers between the possible death in the front and the inevitable one in the rear" (Trotsky, 1930/1975, p. 427).

Whereas Hitler's supporters are in jail for Holocaust Denial, and most of Stalin's supporters in the West disappeared after 1991, Trotsky's heirs and supporters are entrenched in Academia, university campuses, Foundations, the Media, the Public Service, and the Judiciary.

They have dominated university campuses for decades. They regularly march in city centres—marches organised by Socialist Alliance, Socialist Alternative, or other Trotskyist sects. Green Left Weekly is a mainly Trotskyist newspaper.

Radical Feminism, Sex Change and Gender Ideology have come out of the Trotskyist camp.

The narrow definition of "Trotskyist" is one who acknowledges Trotsky over Lenin as the true leader of the revolution. A broader definition is one who sides with Trotsky rather than Stalin in their split, and promotes Trotsky's "ultra-left" cultural revolution rather than Stalin's conservative reaction. On that basis, the Feminist, Gay, Green and Black liberation movements have substantial Trotskyist ancestry. One may call it "Trotskyoid" to emphasise that these movements are independent networks rather than centrally controlled.

Formerly Trotskyist "neocons", such as Robert Kagan and Victoria Nuland, run U.S. Foreign Policy on Russia, turning Trotsky's 'Permanent Revolution' into 'Permanent War.'

Max Shpak showed that 'Neoconservatism' is actually a kind of Marxism coupled with Zionism. It's only called 'conservative' on account of its opposition to Stalinism. It demonises the Russian people because of their resistance to Jewish domination. Shpak wrote (2002):

It is a well-established fact that many of the early luminaries of neoconservatism (most famously Irving Kristol in the 1940's, a more recent famous example being David Horowitz) came from Marxist backgrounds, and that neoconservatism (like Marxism itself) began and continues to be a largely a phenomenon of Jewish intellectualism. ...

More important for the purposes of this analysis, however, are the practical reasons for Jewish sympathy with Bolshevism. European and American Jews alike carried deep-seated hatreds for the traditional regimes and religions of the European continent, particularly Czarist Russia and various Eastern European nations due to (real and imagined) "persecution" and "pogroms" that occurred there. Thus, when the Bolsheviks overthrew the Czar, destroyed the hated Orthodox Church, rendered powerless the landed religious peasantry, and replaced traditional Russian authority with a largely Jewish Commissariate, world Jewry (including alleged "capitalists" like the Schiffs and Rothschilds) embraced the Revolution and Marxist ideology alike.

With Russia becoming an effective Jewish colony where "anti-Semitism" was an offense punishable by death and the native gentile culture was effectively stamped out (thanks to a leadership consisting mainly of Jews such as Trotsky, Zinoviev, Kamenev, and Severdlov, held together under the stewardship of the obsequious philosemite Lenin), Jews throughout the world put their hopes in the possibility of similar revolutions elsewhere. Indeed, their comrades in arms were hard at work affecting similar changes in Hungary (Kuhn), Austria (Adler) and Germany (Eisner). The rise of Fascist and Nazi movements only served to further polarize Jewish support in favor of international communism. (Shpak, 2002).

That support declined with Stalin's purges, his pact with Hitler, and his accommodation to Russian tradition and nationalism.

When Hitler invaded the Soviet Union, it became clear the Russian masses would not fight for the sake of Bolshevism, an ideology that brought them so much misery, but rather for the sake of Russian blood and soil. From then on, the Soviet leadership had to court the very Russian nationalist elements that the early Bolsheviks had worked so hard to stamp out. This lead to an increasing tolerance towards the Russian Orthodox Church and a decreased Jewish presence in the Soviet politburo and KGB. Thus, the U.S.S.R. was "betraying" the very elements that made it attractive to the Jewish establishment to begin with. (Shpak, 2002).

After the creation of Israel in May 1948, Jewish Marxists who opposed nationalism for Russians sought a way to justify Zionism.

Jewish leftists who once advocated internationalism for gentile nations were forced to come to terms with the implications of this ideology for their own nationalist sentiments. Thus, they needed an ideology which would let them have their cake (opposing gentile nationalism) and eat it too (by supporting Israel), and they found just such a worldview with neo-conservatism. (Shpak, 2002).

During the Cold War, Neocons turned against the Soviet Union; after the Cold War ended, they continued their war against Russia.

While paleoconservative leaning Cold Warriors such as Pat Buchanan have pushed for normalized relations with Russia, the neocons continue to fight on the Cold War, enthusiastically supporting Chechen separatists as "freedom fighters" and advocating NATO expansion. The reasons for this difference are entirely obvious: the Old Right's enemy was Communist ideology, while neoconservative Jews nurtured a hatred for Russian nationalism. (Shpak, 2002).

Perceptions of the Left have been largely shaped by Isaac Deutscher, a Jewish Trotskyist prominent in New Left Review.

Despite New Left intellectuals' thinking of themselves as "outsiders", Deutscher's material was published by The Economist and the BBC. The winners of the Deutscher Prize are announced in the London Review of Books, and the Deutscher Memorial Lecture is presented at the London School of Economics.

The New Left movement is broadly 'Trotskyoid', meaning pro-Trotsky is a broad sense without implying party membership or doctrinal orthodoxy.

Trotskyist organisations such as the International Socialist Organisation, the Socialist Workers Party, the Democratic Socialist Party, Resistance and Socialist Alliance, using entrist methods, spread Trotskyist ideology within universities, the political parties, the education system, and the legal system.

The 60s/70s movements mounted a Cultural Revolution which had libertarian elements that 'dropped out', but the Marxist (Trotskyist) elements wrought a 'long march' through the institutions. They were inspired by Antonio Gramsci, but also implementing the "Open Conspiracy" of H. G. Wells.

The Frankfurt School was Trotskyoid. Herbert Marcuse wrote an anti-Stalin book, *Soviet Marxism: A Critical Analysis*, based on his research at the OSS (predecessor of the CIA).

Feminist writers of the late 1960s and early 1970s were lambasting the Soviet Union for betraying its early revolution, while they were continuing that revolution in the West.

Trotsky explicitly promoted Radical Feminism, Youth Rebellion, Communal Childrearing and the Destruction of the Family, in his book *The Revolution Be-*

trayed. It was written in 1936, when Trotsky was living in Norway, and was first published in 1937. The English translation is by Max Eastman.

Trotsky there describes the attack on all tradition launched by the Bolsheviks, and Stalin's reversal of its extremes. I hope that many Trotskyist sympathisers will be shocked to see how extreme he really was—something meaningful to us in the West now that our own family life has been shattered by the same forces.

His campaign is ironic because his own family life, with his second wife Natalya Sedova, was quite normal, as was that of Karl Marx. The only unusual thing is that Trotsky's son Leon Sedov took his mother's surname.

Chapter 7 of *The Revolution Betrayed* deals with Family, Youth and Culture. In the section titled 'Thermidor in the family', Trotsky attacks Stalin's winding back of the Old Bolshevik attempt to destroy the family:

1. Thermidor in the family

The revolution made a heroic effort to destroy the so-called "family hearth"—that archaic, stuffy and stagnant institution in which the woman of the toiling classes performs galley labor from childhood to death. The place of the family as a shut-in petty enterprise was to be occupied, according to the plans, by a finished system of social care and accommodation: maternity houses, creches, kindergartens, schools, social dining rooms, social laundries, first-aid stations, hospitals, sanatoria, athletic organizations, moving-picture theaters, etc. The complete absorption of the housekeeping functions of the family by institutions of the socialist society, uniting all generations in solidarity and mutual aid, was to bring to woman, and thereby to the loving couple, a real liberation from the thousand-year-old fetters. ...

During the lean years, the workers wherever possible, and in part their families, ate in the factory and other social dining rooms, and this fact was officially regarded as a transition to a socialist form of life. There is no need of pausing again upon the peculiarities of the different periods: military communism, the NEP and the first five-year plan. The fact is that from the moment of the abolition of the food-card system in 1935, all the better-laced workers began to return to the home dining table. ... The same conclusion must be extended to the social laundries, where they tear and steal linen more than they wash it. Back to the family hearth! But home cooking and the home washtub, which are now half shamefacedly celebrated by orators and journalists, mean the return of the workers' wives to their pots and pans that is, to the old slavery. (pp. 144-6)

... the revolutionary power gave women the right to abortion, ... the state makes a sharp change of course, and takes the road of prohibition. ... The triumphal rehabilitation of the family, taking place simultaneously—what a providential coincidence!—with the rehabilitation of the ruble, is caused by the material and cultural bankruptcy of the state. ... the leaders are forcing people to glue together again the shell of the broken family, and not only that, but to consider it, under threat of extreme penalties, the sacred nucleus of triumphant socialism. It is hard to measure with the eye the scope of this retreat.

... the same arguments which were earlier advanced in favor of unconditional freedom of divorce and abortion—"the liberation of women," "defense of the rights of personality," "protection of motherhood"—are repeated now in favor of their limitation and complete prohibition. (Trotsky, 1937/1967, pp. 149-153)

Trotsky applauds the Old Bolshevik attack on parental authority, and indoctrination of children against parents; and decries Stalin's rolling back of this too:

While the hope still lived of concentrating the education of the new generations in the hands of the state, the government was not only unconcerned about supporting the authority of the "elders", and, in particular of the mother and father, but on the contrary tried its best to separate the children from the family, in order thus to protect them from the traditions of a stagnant mode of life. Only a little while ago, in the course of the first five-year plan, the schools and the Communist Youth were using children for the exposure, shaming and in general "re-educating" of their drunken fathers or religious mothers with what success is another question. At any rate, this method meant a shaking of parental authority to its very foundations. In this not unimportant sphere too, a sharp turn has now been made. ...

The denial of God, his assistance and his miracles, was the sharpest wedge of all those which the revolutionary power drove between children and parents. Outstripping the development of culture, serious propaganda and scientific education, the struggle with the churches, under the leadership of people of the type of Yaroslavsky, often degenerated into buffoonery and mischief. The storming of heaven, like the storming of the family, is now brought to a stop. (Trotsky, 1937/1967, pp. 153-4)

Clearly, the 'Culture War' in the West was derived from Old Bolshevism—mainly via Trotskyists. Germaine Greer wrote (1984) in *Sex and Destiny*:

The received idea of the ultra-left is that Soviet moves to weaken the family, by the institution of state nurseries, the facilitation of divorce, the ideology of free love, and the legalisation of birth control and abortion, were modified because the family was found to be the necessary training ground for the submissive citizen, and so it is, but not in quite the way that revolutionary Marxist orthodoxy sees it. What state capitalism realised was that the nuclear family is the most malleable social unit; houses were built for it, social services catered to it, and its descendants were drawn off into training institutions and its parents into state care. State capitalism and monopoly capitalism necessitate the same patterns of consumption, mobility and aspiration. The idea is simple and irrefutable; if all men are to be brothers, then nobody can be anybody else's brother. It is as true for Western Europe and America as it is for those parts of the Soviet Union where Family has been shattered. The operation of the process in the Soviets may be cruder, more brutal than in, say, Australia, but it is only therefore slightly less likely to succeed. ... Rooted in territoriality, self-defensive, disciplined in aggression, the Family is resistant to any authority but its own. (pp. 228-9)

However, Trotskyists did not learn from the Soviet Union's experience, because they deemed Stalinism a 'betrayal' of True Communism. Instead, they are bringing the Culture War begun by Old Bolshevism to the West; but, as David Horowitz noted, in the West it is called 'Feminism' rather than 'Marxism'.

The connection between Feminism and Marxism goes back to Frederick Engels' book *The Origin Of The Family, Private Property And The State*.

Engels says there that all women must enter the workforce, and that the State will replace parents as the guardian of children. The government, not parents, would be in charge of children; there would be no full-time mothers, and the occupation of 'housewife' would be abolished:

> The modern monogamous family is founded on the open or disguised domestic slavery of women, and modern society is a mass composed of molecules in the form of monogamous families. In the great majority of cases the man has to earn a living and to support his family ... In the family, he is the bourgeois, the woman represents the proletariat. ... the emancipation of women is primarily dependent on the re-introduction of the whole female sex into the public industries. To accomplish this, the monogamous family must cease to be the industrial unit of society. (Engels, 1884/1908, p. 89)

> Monogamy arose through the concentration of considerable wealth in one hand—a man's hand—and from the endeavor to bequeath this wealth to the children of this man to the exclusion of all others. This necessitated monogamy on the woman's, but not on the man's part. Hence this monogamy of women in no way hindered open or secret polygamy of men. (p. 91)

Communism would abolish this secret polygamy of men. It would force men to be monogamous like women; and when one tired of the other, the partnership would be easily dissolved. In effect, the 'boyfriend-girlfriend' relationship would replace Marriage:

For with the transformation of the means of production into collective property, wagelabor will also disappear, and with it the proletariat and the necessity for a certain, statistically ascertainable number of women to surrender for money. Prostitution disappears and monogamy, instead of going out of existence, at last becomes a reality—for men also. At all events, the situation will be very much changed for men. But also that of women, and of all women, will be considerably altered. With the transformation of the means of production into collective property the monogamous family ceases to be the economic unit of society. The private household changes to a social industry. The care and education of children becomes a public matter. Society cares equally well for all children, legal or illegal. This removes the care about the "consequences" which now forms the essential social factor—moral and economic—hindering a girl to surrender unconditionally to the beloved man. Will not this be sufficient cause for a gradual rise of a more unconventional intercourse of the sexes and a more lenient public opinion regarding virgin honor and female shame? (Engels, 1884/1908, pp. 91-2)

However, in their own private lives, the leading Communists did not practice what they preached. The men were polygamous, and their children were reared by stay-at-home mothers.

Karl Marx had a child with the family's maid, Helene Demuth; he was polygamous, but his wife Jenny was monogamous and a stay-at-home mother. Frederick Engels lived with two Irish working-class sisters, Mary and Lizzie Burns. Initially, Engels called himself a bachelor, even though Mary was his partner; after Mary died, he married her sister Lizzie—contravening the communist ban on marriage. But while Mary was alive, and Lizzie was ostensibly their housekeeper, it looks like a polygamous relationship: polygamy for Engels, but monogamy for the women.

Lenin did not have children, but Trotsky did. He left his first wife and children when he took up with Natalya; she reared their children as a stay-at-home mother. Later, Trotsky had an affair with Frida Kahlo. So, Trotsky was polygamous, but Natalya was monogamous.

H. G. Wells, who preached the state taking over the role of parents, was also a polygamist, but his women were monogamous while they were with him. He wanted the state to take control of the rearing of children from parents, but his own children were reared by their mothers.

These people would have us destroy the family, although they themselves had normal family lives.

Plato, the originator of the whole scheme, was a bachelor who did not have children.; yet his ideas about child-rearing were followed on a large scale in the twentieth century—in the Soviet Union, in Israeli kibbutzim, and in the West.

His book *The Republic* (c. 360 BC) envisages an ideal state, ruled by philosophers or Guardians. Among the Guardians there is community of wives and children. They do not have private residences, but live communally.

There are many similarities with the Soviet Union (the Nomenklatura being the Guardians). But also with the way Feminism is taking the West.

In Plato's Republic, the Sexual Division of Labour is done away with. Instead, women do the same jobs as men; they also exercise naked in the gym with men, and fight in the army with men. Children are bred as dogs are bred: the best men and women are mated, and their children raised by the state. Defective children are quietly put away. Children are reared by child-care workers; the parents do not know whose child is whose.

In BOOK V, section 460 Plato writes (tr. Benjamin Jowett):

> The proper officers will take the offspring of the good parents to the pen or fold, and there they will deposit them with certain nurses who dwell in a separate quarter; but the offspring of the inferior, or of the better when they chance to be deformed, will be put away in some mysterious, unknown place, as they should be.

> Yes, he said, that must be done if the breed of the guardians is to be kept pure.

> They will provide for their nurture, and will bring the mothers to the fold when they are full of milk, taking the greatest possible care that no mother recognizes her own child; and other wet-nurses may be engaged if more are required. (Plato, c. 360 BC/1901)

Jean-Jacques Rousseau is also widely influential in the education system today. Although, like Plato, he did not rear even one child, his book *Emile* has been acclaimed by Left educators, and many of its precepts (e.g. against rote learning) are followed in our schools today. This shows the extent to which Western intellectuals are prepared to elevate theory over practice.

Marx envisaged his Proletarian State as an implementation of Plato's Republic along the lines sketched out by Rousseau in *The Social Contract*. Marx's state would be ruled, not by manual workers but by intellectuals—academics, theory-trained professionals and scientists, playing the role of Philosopher Kings.

In Russia, this was clear by 1920; Alexandra Kollontai drew attention to it. As Paul Johnson points out in his book *Intellectuals*, we intellectuals—I am one too—are just as liable to make mistakes as are non-intellectuals, and we are dangerous when we band together to control a movement in the Leninist style. It is when intellectuals speak in a babble of discordant opinion, rather than in a chorus of similitude, that intellectual life is flourishing.

Radical Feminists, like Plato and like Catholic priests and Buddhist monks, have no children themselves (except, perhaps, from a male partner they discarded when they turned lesbian), but guide the rest of us on this topic.

The Trotskyist / H. G. Wells version of Communism is alive and well

Behind Feminism, Gay Marriage, the World Court, Agenda 21 and the Earth Charter lies a revamped Communist movement. Being anti-Stalinist, it does not wear the Communist label, and instead disguises itself behind a multitude of single-issue lobbies.

There IS a need for Environmental Limits, but the One Worlders are using this as an excuse—a surrogate issue—to push World Government.

The Trotskyist / H. G. Wells version of Communism is alive and well. Open-border immigration, casual relationships treated as equivalent to marriage, sex war, parents afraid of being "dobbed in" to the government, children equal to parents and the property of the state ... the wreckage of family life was brought to the West from the pre-Stalin period of the Soviet Union. We did not recognise it as Communist simply because we identified Stalin's modifications as Communism.

In the early (Old Bolshevik) period of the Soviet Union, marriage was abolished, polygamy was abolished (this mainly affected the Islamic cultures of Central Asia), and homosexuality was legalised. Stalin restored marriage, gave advantages to married women over unmarried women, and made homosexuality a crime.

The Marxist Cultural Revolution, begun in the West in the late 1960s, has taken the West down the path pioneered by the early U.S.S.R. This change was engineered by the New Left, which had substantial atheistic Jewish leadership; one must distinguish between the theistic and atheistic versions of Judaism. David Horowitz, former Editor of Ramparts magazine, acknowledged the Jewish role in the New Left, but later turned against it. Jewish authors at Spiked online, likewise abandoned their Trotskyist role when they were members of the Revolutionary Communist Party.

To understand the change wrought by New Left, one needs to know the Marxist theory of the history of relations between the sexes. It may be expressed as follows (my words):

> Marriage as we know it arose only a few thousand years ago, when men
> enslaved women, making them their private property. Before that, descent
> was matrilineal, and a woman's children were supported by her relatives,
> no matter who the fathers were. Generally, the fathers were unknown. A
> woman had one or more husbands or lovers at a time, discarding them as
> she tired of them or fell out with them (or as they died). When this sys-
> tem was restored in the Soviet Union, the state took over the role of the

relatives, in looking after a woman's children. The woman joined the workforce, and the children were looked after in childcare centres.

H. G. Wells, a closet Trotskyist and advocate of One World, wrote of Marriage and the Family, in his book *Experiment in Autobiography, volume II*:

> Socialism, if it is anything more than a petty tinkering with economic rela-tionships is a renucleation of society. The family can remain only as a bio-logical fact. Its economic and educational autonomy are inevitably doomed. The modern state is bound to be the ultimate guardian of all children and it must assist, place, or subordinate the parent as supporter, guardian and educator; it must release all human beings from the obligation of mutual proprietorship, and it must refuse absolutely to recognize or enforce any kind of sexual ownership. It cannot therefore remain neutral when such claims come before it. It must disallow them. (Wells, 1934/1969, p. 481)

Likewise Bertrand Russell. He wrote, in his book *In Praise of Idleness*:

> All this would be changed if it were the rule, and not the exception, for married women to earn their living by work outside the home. ... The problem is to secure the same communal advantages as were secured in medieval monasteries, but without celibacy ... The separate little houses, and the blocks of tenements each with its own kitchen, should be pulled down. ... There should be a common kitchen, a spacious dining hall ... All the children's meals should be in the nursery school ... From the time they are weaned until they go to school, they should spend all the time from breakfast till after their last meal at the nursery school. (Russell, 1935/1973, pp. 35-7)

Teenagers in the West are totally turned against religion, and their parents, by the music and Hollywood TV shows that fill their minds. Schoolteachers teach them about sex & contraception, and even sex-change, but not about marriage (except Gay Marriage). Many begin to have sex around the age of 16 or 17, and seek to leave home around 18 to 20, especially to escape parental control. Even if they are still at their parents' home, they occasionally have a boyfriend or girl-friend sleep the night with them. Their parents can do nothing to stop this.

To treat "relationships" as the equivalent of marriage is, in effect, to abolish marriage. As social breakdown proceeds, desperation will force us back to the es-sentials of life. We'll be looking for ways to re-establish family ties, and the bonds between men and women. That will mean, in part, re-institutionalising marriage. Traditional marriages are based on the sexual division of labour—distinct roles for each sex.

Marriage is a relationship where each sex dominates yet serves the other, in a relatively secure arrangement short of ownership of the other person. The security of the arrangement has meant that marriages may survive an affair, while de-facto relationships (based on more possessive boyfriend-girlfriend ideas) do not.

The sexes exist in relation to each other—we live for each other: we are each other's delight. The delight is suggested by the old euphemism for sex, as "knowing" another person. The pornography and prostitution industries distort that delight. Out of respect for the personality behind the body, the depiction of sex should not be too explicit. Even the sculptures in the Temple of Surya at Konark leave much to the imagination. Pornography, on the other hand, is explicit, crude, demeaning or commercial, e.g. delivering viewers up to advertisers.

The public want to protect children from pornography, but "SafeSearch" filters also censor politically incorrect content, labelling it "hate speech" or "fake news". For example, information defending Ivermectin or exposing the risks of Coronavirus vaccines, or the Lockdown, might be filtered out as "Disinformation". The United Nations has promoted such "Misinformation" legislation.

Such censorship of public information and debate is a threat to Democracy, so the definition of "Free Speech" becomes crucial. It means allowing viewpoints critical of the Government line. Primarily, it is about text, which appeals to the intellect; secondarily about graphics, e.g. cartoons, and thirdly music or video, which appeal to the emotions. Text is essential to free speech. "Free Speech" should not include violent actions such as burning the Koran, although Denmark and Sweden allowed it on "Free Speech" grounds (Free Speech burn Koran). Why don't they prosecute such actions as "Hate Crimes" or "Hate Speech"? When the distinction between speech and actions is blurred, free discussion is at risk.

Conservatives face a Catch 22: if they support censorship of pornography and LGBT literature aimed at children, their pro-censorship stance may undermine their opposition to censorship in political and medical matters. But the 1940s and 50s provide a model for the first kind of censorship and rejection of the second.

Each culture produces its own male and female personalities. For each to take delight in the other, we must pay much more attention to the way we prepare boys and girls for their later lives as husbands and wives, fathers and mothers.

Under Lenin & Trotsky, the Soviet Union abolished marriage—that's the situation we're in now, and we should learn from the Soviet experience. Stalin brought marriage back in, and gave married women privileges over unmarried ones.

Before Radical Feminism and the LGBT movement, there were two sexes (male, female), and two genders (masculine, feminine). Now, we are told that despite what nature gives you, you can remake yourself as any sex/gender you wish. You can be gay, or lesbian, have a sex-change to become a man or a woman. Your chromosomes can't be changed, but everything else can.

So, we are told, sex and gender are no longer a polarity but a continuum. There is only one sex—we are all androgynous.

Bronislaw Malinowski was one of the pioneers of fieldwork Anthropology, famous for his studies of the matrilineal Trobriand Island people of Papua New Guinea, who allow unmarried girls sexual freedom, but still institutionalise marriage and fatherhood. He wrote in his book *The Father in Primitive Psychology* (1927):

> In all this the role of the husband is strictly laid down by custom and is considered indispensable. A woman with a child and no husband is therefore, in the eyes of tradition, an incomplete and anomalous group. The disapproval of an illegitimate child and of its mother is, then, a particular instance of the general disapproval of everything which goes against custom. ... The family, consisting of husband, wife, and children, is the standard set down by tribal law, which also prescribes to every member a rigidly defined part to play.

> Paternity, unknown in the full biological meaning so familiar to us, is yet maintained by a social dogma which declares: "Every family must have a father; a woman must marry before she may have children; there must be a male to every household." (pp. 84-5)

E. E. Evans-Pritchard was another pioneer Anthropologist. He wrote in his book *The Position of Women in Primitive Society and Other Essays in Social Anthropology* (1965):

> Now, I suppose that among those things that first strike a visitor to a primitive people is that there are no unmarried adult women. Every girl finds a husband, and she is usually married at what seems an unusually early age. ... in a society with a primitive technology and economy, running the home is a whole-time occupation, to which is added the care of small children ... The primitive woman has no choice, and, given the duties that go with marriage, is therefore seldom able to take much part in public life. But if she can be regarded as being at a disadvantage in this respect from our point of view, she does not regard herself as being at a disadvantage, and she does not envy her menfolk what we describe as their privileges. She does not desire, in this respect, things to be other than they are; and it would greatly puzzle her if she knew that in our society many women are unmarried and childless. (p 45)

The above quotations from leading Anthropologists show just how great is the Trotskyist revolution against human nature, wrought in the West through its Radical Feminist and Gay arms. This does not mean that women can't have careers and jobs, but it does suggest natural limits to "modernist" social-engineering. Third-world feminists have rejected the lesbian separatists from the West. In the

Anglican Church, Africans and Asians defeated the push by Bishop John Spong to equate homosexuality with heterosexuality. People in third-world countries, less brainwashed by the Trotskyists and their NGOs, are increasingly defeating the latter in world forums, e.g. U.N. conferences.

The 'Stalinist' Governments of China, Vietnam, Cuba, Zimbabwe et. al. have no truck with the Trotskyists, seeing them for what they are. China's isolating of the Trotskyist NGOs at the 1995 U.N. World Women's Conference in Beijing was an important defeat for them.

Trotskyism is deeply connected to the Unisex Movement.

The Unisex (Androgyny) Movement ultimately denies that there are TWO sexes; it's really saying that there is only ONE, that the apparent differences between the sexes are superficial or illusory; this is the meaning of its promotion of sex-changes. The idea that there are five or six "genders", rather than two "sexes", is a way of saying that sexuality is a continuum, a linear thing, rather than a polarity.

The Unisex movement arose from within the Communist movement, even though Marx and Engels themselves saw homosexuality as bourgeois decadence, a product of alienation between the sexes. Given that Stalin made homosexuality a criminal offence, the Gay movement can be identified with the anti-Stalin faction, with Trotskyism. The Trotskyist sects Socialist Alliance, Socialist Alternative et. al., make 'Gay liberation' a core part of their ideology.

Dennis Altman, a Gay Jewish academic who made a name for himself when a Lecturer at Sydney University, does not explicitly call himself a Trotskyist, but in his book *Homosexual: Oppression and Liberation* (1972) he writes:

> Women's, gay and now men's liberation are embarked on a revolution that is so unlike our traditional concept of revolution that we tend not to recognize it for what it is. It is hardly surprising that old and large sections of the new left fail to relate to these developments. I quote from a mimeographed sheet distributed during the Washington convention by a group called the International Socialists whose views are typical of many: "Newer movements like Women's Liberation and Gay Liberation are growing fast—but big sections of both are more and more into consciousness-raising. Nothing wrong with this in itself—but it isn't matched by a real growing power of these movements." (p. 213)

As a Lecturer in Politics, Altman must have known that the International Socialists were Trotskyist. The divide in the Left between the Old Left and the New, is basically that between Stalin and Trotsky. So deep and bitter is it, that no Stalinist quotes Trotskyist literature approvingly, or lists any of Trotsky's books in a bibliography; any politically knowledgeable person who quotes Trotskyist literature approvingly or authoritatively can be assumed to be a Trotskyist sympathiser, even if not a member of a Trotskyist organisation.

To identify a Trotskyist writer, one must know the tell-tale clues, in particular the accusation that during the 1930s the U.S.S.R was lapsing into fascism, sexual repression or counter-revolution. Such accusations are made, for example, by Wilhelm Reich in his book *The Mass Psychology of Fascism* (1991), where he writes, "In 1935 it was clear that the development of the Soviet Union was about to be stricken with a severe misfortune. ... They failed to go back to the genuinely democratic efforts of Engels and Lenin ... " (p. 209).

The back cover of Alix Holt's book *Selected Writings of Alexandra Kollontai* reads "Alexandra Kollontai—the only woman member of the Bolshevik central committee and the U.S.S.R.'s first Minister of Social Welfare—is known today as a historic contributor to the international women's movement, and as one of the first Bolshevik leaders to oppose the growth of the bureaucracy in the young socialist state" (Kollontai, 1977). Decoded, this "opposition to bureaucracy" means that she was on Trotsky's side.

Numerous New Left writers, claiming allegiance to a synthesis of Marx with Freud, make statements like those above. The New Left is so Trotskyist, and its brand of Communism so pervades our minds and culture in the West today, that we cannot see that the fall of the U.S.S.R was not the fall of "Communism" at all, but only the fall of Stalinism—and to the hardcore Trotskyists, he was just another Hitler, the one who stole their conspiracy from them.

Germaine Greer came under Trotskyist influence during her formative years in Sydney, but later grew out of it. In her first book *The Female Eunuch* she wrote (1971), "Hopefully, this book is subversive ... the oppression of women is necessary to the maintenance of the economy ... If the present economic structure can change only by collapsing, then it had better collapse as soon as possible. ... The most telling criticisms will come from my sisters of the Left, the Maoists, the Trots, the I.S., the S.D.S., because of my fantasy that it might be possible to leap the steps of revolution and arrive somehow at liberty and communism without strategy or revolutionary discipline." (pp. 21-2).

The I.S. are the International Socialists, a Trotskyist group; by "the Trots", she probably meant the Socialist Workers' Party, since renamed the Democratic Socialist Party, and now Socialist Alliance.

John Lennon donated money to a Trotskyist group. The following report, dated March 2, 2000, is from the wsws Trotskyist website: "A former agent for the British Security Service (known as MI5) has alleged in a sworn statement that the agency received reports from a high-level spy inside the Workers Revolutionary

Party during the late 1960s. The ex-agent, David Shayler, is currently living in exile in France, where he has fled to escape prosecution for his exposure of state secrets. In his February 18 affidavit, Shayler asserts that the spy provided MI5 with reports of financial support given by John Lennon to the WRP" (North, 2000).

John Lennon's philosophical song Imagine can thus be assumed to reflect Trotskyist utopianism:

Imagine, the Trotskyist anthem by John Lennon

{my comments thus}
Imagine there's no heaven {no religion}
It's easy if you try
No hell below us
Above us only sky
Imagine all the people
Living for today...
Imagine there's no countries {world government}
It isn't hard to do
Nothing to kill or die for
And no religion too {i.e. official Atheism—suppression of religion}
Imagine all the people
Living life in peace... {peace = world government}
You may say I'm a dreamer
But I'm not the only one
I hope someday you'll join us
And the world will be as one {world government}
Imagine no possessions {communism; or the Great Reset}
I wonder if you can {John certainly had plenty}
No need for greed or hunger
A brotherhood of man
Imagine all the people
Sharing all the world... {open borders, one world government}
You may say I'm a dreamer
But I'm not the only one {A whole generation has been led astray}
I hope someday you'll join us
And the world will live as one {world government}

Lennon's philosophy may sound idyllic, but he led young people astray with his advocacy of "living for the present". The story of Pinocchio illustrates the outcome.

However, in his last public performance, on April 18, 1975, Lennon sang a different version of Imagine. In place of "And no religion too", he sang, "No immigration too". Thanks to Denis McCormack for pointing this out. Watch it at https://www.reddit.com/r/beatles/comments/t9qczp/imagine_john_lennons_final_public_performance/.

That line is at 1m19s; but at 0m53s he sang "Imagine there's no countries".

If there are no countries, then borders are open to immigration and imported goods (the sort which destroy our industries). Lennon, in rejecting immigration, was belatedly turning against the Cosmopolitanism that marked the earlier version. He was finally waking up to the Trotskyist agenda.

I do agree that he was a great musician—the Beatles, the Beach Boys and the Bee Gees made beautiful music, from which heights, sadly, rock music descended to the depths of punk, heavy metal, rap, and Satanism.

The album cover for Sgt. Pepper's Lonely Hearts Club Band (1967) included sorcerer Aleister Crowley at John Lennon's insistence:

> "Do what thou wilt shall be the whole of the law," was the personal motto of Aleister Crowley (1875-1947), once known to the headline writers as "the Great Beast" and "the Wickedest Man Alive". It was a philosophy that would endear him to the counterculture of the 1960s and make him a hero for rock stars such as Jimmy Page and Jim Morrison. Perhaps the sealer for Crowley's second coming was his inclusion on the album cover for Sgt. Pepper's Lonely Hearts Club Band (1967), at John Lennon's insistence. (McDonald, 2013)

John Lennon stated that Crowley was included because of his "Do what thou wilt" philosophy:

Aleister Crowley inspired the counterculture movement of the 1960s.

> Most people are quite aware of Aleister Crowley's censored appearance on the cover of Sgt. Pepper among the Beatles' other heroes. Few, though, have gone on to ask why Aleister Crowley made the cut. John Lennon made the connection clear in an interview with Playboy when he said that "The whole Beatle idea was to do what you want, right? To take your own responsibility." Lennon was paraphrasing "Do what thou wilt," which is one of the central precepts of Thelema, the religion founded by Aleister Crowley. Thelema is the Greek word which means "will" and teaches that we each must discover our individual inmost nature, described as the "True Will." (ac2012, 2012)

The Beatles were only the first of many counterculture rock musicians in the 1960s-70s to openly cite Aleister Crowley as an influence, and to turn to Satanism. The photo shows the album cover for the Beatles singles CD Yellow Submarine and Eleanor Rigby. Paul McCartney is making the 666 sign, and John Lennon is making the Devil's Horns. Both are Satanic. Also shown is Anton LaVey, founder of the Satanic Temple, making the same handsign. Note the Pentagram too.

The annual Hollywood Emmy Awards (for actors, directors, producers etc.) are awarded by the National Academy of Television Arts and Sciences (NATAS). Written in reverse, that spells SATAN.

What kind of sex happened in the rock scene? Drunken sex with strangers. Drugged sex. Mindless sex. Non-volitional sex. Sex one regretted in the morning. Unplanned pregnancy. Marriages made in Hell, which spawned a new generation of orphans. Marriages made on the basis of fleeting sexual attraction, rather than long-term suitability.

Marriage is for children, not parents; parents sacrifice themselves for their children. Marriage is for lineages over time, by which society is structured; this is why arranged marriages often work. Abolishing marriage, we stopped shaping our boys and girls in preparation for it. Girls grew up witnessing neither birth nor death. In childcare, we replaced parental love (or the love of a relative or mammy) with 'professional' expertise, taught via courses.

The New Left's idea that through rock music a superior kind of sex was available, was an infantile delusion. The 'Stalinist' governments branded the rock scene 'bourgeois'; along with jeans and other Western exotica, it became part of the underground movement undermining those regimes in the name of 'freedom'. But once they had 'freedom', they wished they had some order as well.

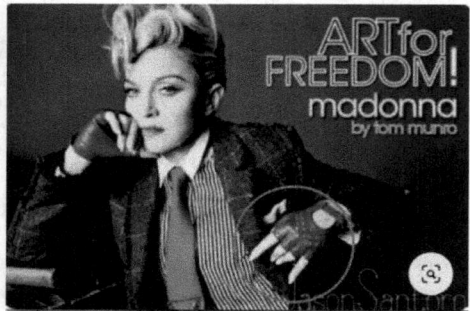

Today's rock music has a frenetic quality; and in rock dancing, the partners do not touch each other. Whereas rock music is jarring, folk music and folk dancing are melodic and graceful; they are traditional, i.e. they look to the past (whence they come), whereas rock music lives only in the present.

Millions of children have been deprived of their fathers by Radical Feminism's attack on the family. Trotskyists had a big influence on that movement; it's the "stolen generation" we dare not mention.

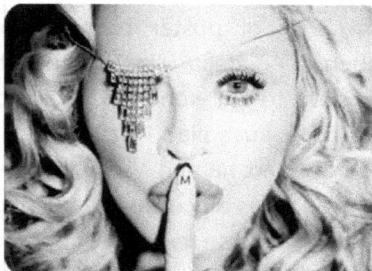

Ex-Freemason Altiyan Childs revealed the secrets of Freemasonry in a 5-hour video, titled Freemasonry Unveiled (2021). He says that Christian trappings hide an anti-Christian interior; Freemasonry is Satanism in disguise. However, 90% of Freemasons don't know who they're serving; those deemed too Christian are not invited into the secret religion, so they're not aware of it.

He shows photos of many rock stars making Masonic signs, e.g. covering one eye, and placing a finger across the lips, in reference to the vow of silence.

The photos of Madonna and Anton LaVey here are from his documentary film.

One photo shows Madonna making the Devil's Horns sign; in another, she covers one eye and holds a finger to her lips (meaning not to disclose secrets). Altiyan Childs says these are Masonic symbols. In another, she wears a jacket featuring the Masonic (Illuminati) pyramid and all-seeing Eye.

Also shown is one of three 20 metre high Inverted Crosses displayed by the Museum of Old and New Art (MONA) on the waterfront in Hobart, Tasmania, in 2018. The Inverted Cross is as a Satanic symbol. The Museum promoted this Satanic display in an appeal to Progressives.

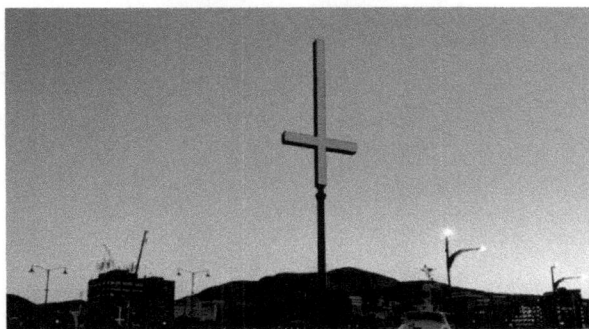

Tasmania used to be a very Christian place; not any more. The state government contributed $2.1 million to Dark Mofo each year. It refused to do anything about the blasphemous images, because it might impact the tourist industry. Some Christian bishops made statements, but many had been cowed by the constant attacks on Christianity.

An election poster from a shopping centre in Canberra, Australia, shows what the Trotskyists have done to our women. The Democratic Socialist Party (DSP), Australia's Trotskyist political party, had formerly been named the Socialist Workers Party (SWP), and has since been renamed Socialist Alliance. They publish the newspaper Green Left Weekly.

PUBLIC FORUM:

FIGHT THE BACKLASH AGAINST WOMEN'S RIGHTS!

Panel of Speakers from & ACT Pro-Choice Campaign. incl. LARA PULLEN, activist in the ACT Pro-Choice Campaign, and Resistance Youth Movement; and Democratic Socialist Party candidate at the last ACT Elections.

Room 1, Griffin Centre, Bunda St., Civic.
7-30 pm Tuesday 30 June

DEMOCRATIC SOCIALIST PARTY

John Lennon, no doubt, liked beautiful , feminine women. He would have been appalled that Feminism would have made them like this.

Trotskyist websites have censored the correspondence of Marx and Engels on homosexuality.

The letter from Engels to Marx of 22 June 1969, which condemned homosexuality, used to be at

https://www.marxists.org/archive/marx/works/1869/letters/69_06_22.htm

but the Marx-Engels Archive now says "File No Longer Available!"

The same letter used to be at

http://marxists.anu.edu.au/archive/marx/works/1869/letters/69_06_22.htm

but that link now returns "File No Longer Available!"

Why did the Trots remove it? Because they promote LGBT, and do not want their followers to know that Marx and Engels opposed it. The letter they removed is at pp. 297-8 below.

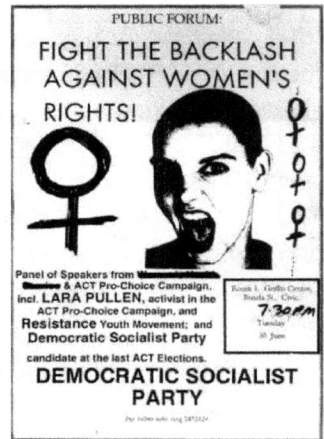

Chapter 16: Trotsky and the Jewish Bankers

In two of her writings, Trotsky's widow Natalia Sedova calls Trotsky "the leader of the October revolution". And if she thought so, then he no doubt did too. Both of these writings are at marxists.org, a Trotskyist site.

> Stalin feared most the revelations of **the leader of the October revolution** and, therefore, wanted to silence him at all costs. Fully cognizant of the fact that the press of the entire world was paying attention to Trotsky's opinions, Stalin had to find some way of preventing him from defending himself. (Trotsky, Natalia Sedova, 1942)

> The tumultuous crowd set up **a large portrait of the leader of the October Revolution** on one of the cars, cheered enthusiastically, and halted the train as it started moving. **But Trotsky was not on it.** (Trotsky, Natalia Sedova, 1947)

The notion that Trotsky, not Lenin, was the leader of the Bolshevik Revolution is also implicit in George Orwell's books *Animal Farm* and *Nineteen Eighty-Four*. Christopher Hitchens (2010) pointed out that there is no 'Lenin pig' in Animal Farm. Orwell must have picked up this notion when fighting with the Trotskyist P.O.U.M. in Spain.

World War I destroyed much of the Russian economy, and the Civil War destroyed the rest. The Reds under Trotsky killed off a large part of the aristocracy, the professionals, managers and businessmen, and the clergy—these were all on the 'Right'.

They also killed off opponents on the 'Left': SRs, Anarchists and Mensheviks.

The result was that the experts and managers needed to run industries were no longer available. And the Bolsheviks were committed to exterminating them as a class.

This policy was officially inaugurated after the assassination of Uritsky and the attempt on Lenin, on August 30, 1918, ironically both acts done by Jews, even though the Red Terror was focused on anti-Semites.

On September 1, Krasnaya Gazeta (The Red Gazette) proclaimed: "For the blood of Lenin and Uritsky, let streams of blood be shed—more blood, as much as possible" (Red Terror, 1918).

On September 5, the Council of People's Commissars issued a decree on the "Red Terror."

Martyn Latsis, a member of the board of the Cheka, issued a printed instruction in the KGB weekly Red Terror:

"We are not waging war against individuals. We are exterminating the bourgeoisie as a class. ... Do not look for evidence that the accused acted in word or deed against Soviet power. The first question should be to what class does he belong. ... It is this that should determine his fate." (Melgunoff, 1927).

When Karl Kautsky (also Jewish) criticised the Red Terror in 1920, Trotsky wrote a book to justify it. This book was titled *The Defence of Terrorism*; it was also published as *Dictatorship Vs. Democracy*, and also as *Terrorism & Communism: A Reply to Karl Kautsky*. Trotsky wrote:

> But terror can be very efficient against a reactionary class which does not want to leave the scene of operations. Intimidation is a powerful weapon of policy, both internationally and internally. War, like revolution, is founded upon intimidation. A victorious war, generally speaking, destroys only an insignificant part of the conquered army, intimidating the remainder and breaking their will. The revolution works in the same way: it kills individuals and intimidates thousands. In this sense, the Red Terror is not distinguishable from the armed insurrection of which it is the direct continuation. (Trotsky, 1920, p. 58; in DvD it's on p. 55)

Trotsky had no compunction about the shedding of blood—until he himself was the victim hunted by Stalin:

> As for us, we were never concerned with the Kantian-priestly and vegetarian-Quaker prattle about the "sacredness of human life". We were revolutionaries in opposition, and have remained revolutionaries in power. To make the individual sacred, we must destroy the social order which crucifies him. And that problem can only be solved by blood and iron. (Trotsky, 1920, p. 63; in DvD it's on p. 60)

Here is the irony: the Bolsheviks were exterminating the Russian bourgeoisie (professional and business class), but they reached out to the American bourgeoisie to help rebuild Russia's economy. And, American bankers and businessmen participated willingly.

This was first documented by Antony C. Sutton is his 1981 book *Wall Street and the Bolshevik Revolution*, and in his trilogy *Western Technology and Soviet Economic Development* (Sutton, 1973; see Myers, 2013/2019).

American bankers and businessmen were happy to build Communism in Russia, as long as they made money out of it.

Similarly, in the period 1990-2020, they happily built up Red China, while making pots of cash. They were happy to jettison America's own workforce, for low-paid workers abroad. And in the process China copied, bought or stole the secrets of Western Technology, the Golden Goose.

During the 1920s, over 350 foreign "concessions" enabled foreign companies to operate in Russia without gaining property rights. Foreign capital and skills were introduced in all sectors of the economy. Soviet oil drilling acquired the American rotary technique; refineries were built by foreign corporations. A.E.G., General Electric. and Metropolitan-Vickers were the major operators in the machinery sectors.

In the 1930s, 'technical-assistance agreements' operated in place of 'concessions'. Soviet imports from the West included machine tools and complete industrial plants: three tractor plants (which also produced tanks), three major automobile plants, oil refining units, and aircraft plants.

Standard Oil bought huge quantities of Russian oil; General Electric built hydroelectric generators. Other businesses with Soviet operations were General Motors, International Harvester, John Deere, Caterpillar Tractor, and banks including Chase National, National City, and Equitable Trust.

Sutton's work has been revised and corrected by Richard B. Spence in his 2017 book *Wall Street And The Russian Revolution, 1905-1925*.

In that book, Spence also corrects his own earlier writings on Trotsky; and on Sidney Reilly—who was actually Jewish, born Sigmund Saloman Rosenblum. Spence shows that Reilly, nominally a British spy, actually double-crossed the British, and was part of a clique of pro-Trotsky Jewish bankers and businessmen. Others in the clique included Abram L'vovich Zhivotovsky—Trotsky's uncle Abram, who was a Wall street banker—and Sir William Wiseman, the chief of Britain's intelligence service in New York. He, too, was pro-Trotsky rather than pro-Britain, and ended up working at Kuhn Loeb, the Jewish bank.

Spence, having uncovered much material that contradicts what was previously taken to be fact, is the most authoritative writer on these controversial matters; I have therefore taken his position against contrary ones.

He tip-toes around matters Jewish, and disperses his information; but by carefully putting the pieces together, the reader can assemble the jigsaw.

The American businessmen wanting to invest in Russia were generally not supportive of the Czar. Many preferred a constitutional republic, the sort Kerensky tried to establish; but others were sympathetic to the Bolsheviks—some to Trotsky in particular.

Charles R. Crane exemplified the pro-Kerensky, anti-Bolshevik faction. His company made air brakes for railway cars; he gained exclusive rights to supply air brakes to Russian passenger trains, for which he formed a joint venture with Westinghouse. He was also a banker, but anti-Jewish.

Elihu Root, a former Senator and Secretary of War who led the Root mission to Russia, was also pro-Kerensky.

The American Red Cross mission to Russia was led by William Boyce Thompson, a banker and mining engineer who operated copper mines in the American west. He donated $1 million to the Kerensky government but, when the Bolsheviks took over, he let them have this money; they used it to flood Germany and Austria with revolutionary propaganda. Thompson advocated for them back in the U.S.A.. In the Washington Post of Feb 2, 1918, Thompson wrote that he gave money to the Bolsheviks to undermine the militarist regimes of Germany and Austria.

Both of these missions (Root and ARC) were clandestine intelligence operations, connected to Wall Street and the U.S. Government.

Thompson's offsider, Raymond Robins, took over the Red Cross Mission after Thompson left. Robins was pro-Bolshevik, and a great fan of Trotsky. Robins favoured recognition of the Bolshevik regime, but Ambassador David Rowland Francis opposed recognition.

John Silas Reed was another fan of the Bolsheviks, especially Trotsky; Robins put Reed on the Red Cross payroll. Spence (2017) notes of Reed that "in January 1918, he was the warm-up act for Comrade Trotsky at the Third Congress of Soviets" (p. 184). Then, on 29 January, Trotsky made Reed the new Soviet consul in New York.

None of the above Americans—Crane, Root, Thompson, Robins and Reed—were Jewish. Bruce Lockhart was another non-Jewish fan of Trotsky.

In January 1919, the Civil War was raging between Trotsky's Red Army and the Whites. Wilson wanted to bring the two sides together, and have them participate at the Peace Conference of Versailles. Wilson's adviser, Col. Edward M. House, had published in 1912 a political tract in the guise of a novel titled *Philip Dru: Administrator*, in which he advocated "Socialism as dreamed of by Karl Marx" (House, 1912, p. 45). House was born Mandell Huis; John Coleman says he was a Dutch Jew.

House, and non-Jewish Socialist writer Lincoln Steffens, urged Wilson to send an American Mission to Moscow. He did so, appointing William Bullitt to lead it, accompanied by Steffens and a military intelligence officer, Walter W. Pettit. All were pro-Bolshevik; Bullitt's mother was Jewish.

Bullitt returned saying that the Bolsheviks agreed to the proposal. But others saw that recognition was involved, at a time when the Bolsheviks were instigating revolutions in other countries.

E. J. Dillon (1919) wrote in *The Peace Conference*:

Another glaring instance of the lack of straightforwardness which vitiated the dealings of the Conference with the public turned upon the Bullitt mission to Russia. Mr. Wilson, who in the depths of his heart seems to have cherished a vague fondness for the Bolshevists there, which he sometimes manifested in utterances that startled the foreigners to whom they were addressed, despatched, through Col. House, some fellow-countrymen of his to Moscow to ask for peace proposals which, according to the Moscow Government, were drafted by himself and MM. House and Lansing, and presented to Lenin by MM. Bullitt, Steffens and Petit. Mr. Bullitt, however, who must know, affirms that the draft was written by Mr. George's secretary, Mr. Philip Kerr, and himself. If the terms of this document should prove acceptable the American envoys were empowered to promise that an official invitation to a new peace conference would be sent to them as well as to their opponents by the 15th April. (p. 112)

Philip Kerr (Lord Lothian) was a leading member of Cecil Rhodes' Round Table group, which Viscount Alfred Milner (Lord Milner) headed from 1902 to 1925. From 1925 to 1940, Kerr succeeded him as leader; Lionel Curtis also played a leading role.

Henry Wickham Steed, editor of the Daily Mail, which was published in Paris during the Peace Conference, raised the alarm. He single-handedly blocked a secret push for World Government at the Peace Conference. In his memoirs (1924), he wrote:

Mr. Philip Kerr and, presumably, Mr. Lloyd George knew and approved of this mission. Mr. Bullitt was instructed to return if possible by the time President Wilson should have come back to Paris from the United States. Potent international financial interests were at work in favour of the immediate recognition of the Bolshevists. Those influences had been largely responsible for the Anglo-American proposal in January to call Bolshevist representatives to Paris at the beginning of the Peace Conference—a proposal which had failed after having been transformed into a suggestion for a Conference with the Bolshevists at Prinkipo. The well-known American Jewish banker, Mr. Jacob Schiff, was known to be anxious to ensure recognition for the Bolshevists, among whom Jewish influence was predominant; and Tchitcherin, the Bolshevist Commissary for Foreign Affairs, had revealed the meaning of the January proposal by offering extensive commercial and economic concessions in return for recognition. At a moment when the Bolshevists were doing their utmost to spread revolution throughout Europe, and when the Allies were supposed to be making peace in the name of high moral principles, a policy of recognizing them, as the price of commercial concessions, would have sufficed to wreck the whole Peace Conference and Europe with it. At the end of March, Hungary was already Bolshevist; Austria, Czechoslovakia, Poland, and even Ger-

many were in danger, and European feeling against the blood-stained luna-
tics of Russia ran extremely high.

Therefore, when it transpired that an American official, connected with
the Peace Conference, had returned, after a week's visit to Moscow, with
an optimistic report upon the state of Russia and with an authorized Russian proposal for the virtual recognition of the Bolshevist regime by April
10th, dismay was felt everywhere except by those who had been privy to
the sending of Mr. Bullitt. (Steed, pp. 301-2)

In the Paris Daily Mail of March 27th, Steed strongly opposed recognition of
the Bolshevik government. House deplored his criticism of recognition.

'That day Colonel House asked me to call upon him. I found him worried both
by my criticism of any recognition of the Bolshevists and by the certainty, which
he had not previously realized, that if the President were to recognize the Bolshevists in return for commercial concessions his whole "idealism" would be hope-
lessly compromised as commercialism in disguise.' (Steed, p. 302)

Steed argued that, with Bolshevik revolutions under way in many European
countries, recognition would undermine the forces resisting them.

I pointed out to him that not only would Wilson be utterly discredited but
that the League of Nations would go by the board, because all the small
peoples and many of the big peoples of Europe would be unable to resist
the Bolshevism which Wilson would have accredited. I insisted that, unknown to him, the prime movers were Jacob Schiff, Warburg, and other
international financiers, who wished above all to bolster up the Jewish Bolshevists in order to secure a field for German and Jewish exploitation of
Russia.

Colonel House argued, however, that without relations of some kind with
the Bolshevists it would be impossible to prevent the utter ruin of Russia
and the starvation of thousands of the best Russians who were without
food; and that, if supplies could be sent to Russia under proper control,
the needy might be relieved and the Allied and Associated Governments
might get trustworthy information of the true position in Russia. He asked
me therefore to meet him and Auchincloss next morning to see if some
sound line of policy could not be worked out. This I agreed to do; but,
shortly after leaving Colonel House, information reached me that Mr.
Lloyd George and President Wilson would probably agree next morning
to recognize the Bolshevists in accordance with Mr. Bullitt's suggestions.
Feeling that there was no time to lose I wrote, forthwith, a leading article
for the Paris Daily Mail of March 28th, called "Peace with Honour." (Steed,
pp. 302-3)

Steed's editorial pre-empted Wilson's intended announcement of recognition, and Wilson had to abandon it. House reported his anger to Steed.

I had hardly sent this article to the printers when an American friend, Mr. Charles R. Crane, who had been dining with President Wilson, called to see me. He showed great alarm at the turn things were taking. "Bullitt is back," he said, "and the President is already talking Bullitt's language. I fear he may ruin everything. Our people at home will certainly not stand for the recognition of the Bolshevists at the bidding of Wall Street." He urged me to point out the danger clearly in the Daily Mail. I reassured him and told him that what I could say was already said and that he would find it in the Daily Mail next morning.

Before I was up next day, Colonel House telephoned to say that he wished to see me urgently. Apparently, to use an Americanism, my article "had got under the President's hide." When I reached the Crillon, House and Auchincloss looked grave. I told them that, had I waited to discuss policy with them before writing my article, the chances were that there would have been no policy to discuss because the President and, possibly, Lloyd George would have committed themselves to recognition of the Bolshevists that very morning. The Colonel begged me, however, in view of the delicacy of the situation to refrain from further comment until it could be seen how things would go; and I consented, on the understanding that nothing irrevocable would be done unless I were informed beforehand. (Steed, pp. 304-5)

Wall Street was divided over recognition. Together with Crane and Root, other American businessmen opposing recognition included John D. Rockefeller, William Rockefeller and Herbert Hoover. They formed the Committee on the Study of Bolshevism, which attacked both the Martens Bureau and the Bullitt Mission.

Only a year after the Peace Conference, Trotsky proposed taking the Revolution to the whole world; his goal was "the World Soviet Federation".

The Manifesto of the Comintern's Second Congress (1920), composed by Trotsky, stated:

The Communist International has proclaimed the cause of Soviet Russia as its own. **The international proletariat will not sheathe its sword until Soviet Russia has been made a link in the federation of Soviet republics of the whole world.** (Volkogonov, 1996, p. 202)

In an article on the idea of the 'United States of Europe', intended for Pravda, Trotsky wrote, "We are of course talking about **a European socialist federation as a component part of a future world federation** ..." (Volkogonov, 1996, pp. 208-9)

This is what Steed was concerned about.

After Stalin took over, Bullitt became anti-Communist.

The Bolsheviks tried another means to gain recognition: business and international trade. What could not be obtained politically would be achieved via influential American businessmen. They set up the Soviet Bureau, led by Ludwig C. A. K. Martens, who operated as unofficial Soviet ambassador to the United States.

Martens formed a committee to operate the Bureau, with former Novy Mir manager Gregory Weinstein and socialist businessman Julius Hammer, son of Armand. Both were Jewish. Spence comments that "Julius arranged an array of front companies and deals to assist the Soviet cause" (Spence, 2017, p. 95).

They recruited thirty full-time employees, mostly of Russian or Russian-Jewish origin. The Bureau leased the entire third floor at the World Tower Building, 110 West 40th St in New York.

Mahoney and Mahoney (1998) state that Martens was not Lenin's man, but Trotsky's. They wrote:

> In 1921 Trotsky replaced Nyberg (Nuorteva) as Director of the Soviet Bureau with Ludwig C.A.K. Martens. Trotsky had finally succeeded in placing one of his most trusted men in America. ... Martens promoted trade between American businesses and Soviet commerce despite the fact the United States had an embargo against such trade. Although trade may have been the ostensible justification for the creation of the Soviet Information Bureau, Martens at the same time was providing covert financial support to the newly formed C.P.U.S.A. This covert funding to a domestic communist party was part of Trotsky's program to support continuous international revolution and the world spread of communism. (pp. 122-3)

Trotsky spent two months in New York before and during the February Revolution.

Spence upends the claims of his poverty: "The Trotskys' immediate lodging was the swank Hotel Astor near Times Square. Not only was this one of the most expensive hostelries in the city, it had a reputation as a gathering place for the Wall Street elite" (Spence, 2017, p. 136).

When Trotsky and Natalya stepped off their boat, "The Novy Mir crowd was there in force; Bukharin rushed up to give the arrival a bear hug and Kollontai hovered nearby. Someone alerted the press, and the New York Times had a reporter on scene" (Spence, 2017, p. 137).

Julius Hammer met Trotsky on arrival, arranged his expensive accommodation, and provided him with a car and chauffeur:

> Trotsky joined the staff of Novy Mir next day. The paper's manager, Gregory Weinstein was also "closely associated with [Trotsky] while the

latter was in this country." Also present at this gathering were Julius Hammer and Gregory Chudnovsky, later described as Trotsky's "right hand man" at Novy Mir. Only a short time before, Chudnovsky had been working with Parvus in Switzerland and Copenhagen.

Trotsky cryptically referred to one of his benefactors in New York as "Dr. M.," a man further identified by his wife as "Dr. Mikhailovsky." Among other things, he supposedly lent his car and chauffeur to shuttle the Trotskys around town. There was, indeed, a Dr. Michael Michailovsky ... He undoubtedly met Trotsky in New York. However, again Trotsky either misremembered or deliberately misstated the part about the car and chauffeur. Michailovsky ran a modest practice on the Upper West Side. The man with the car and driver was another doctor—Julius Hammer. It also was Hammer who found the Trotsky's their apartment conveniently close to his own home in the Bronx. (Spence, 2017, p. 145)

One of Trotsky's aims in New York was to obtain money for the intended Bolshevik Revolution: "Everywhere Trotsky turned in New York he was surrounded by persons willing and able to give him money. ... The many threads connecting Trotsky, Lenin, Parvus, Reilly, Schiff and the Germans, all came together in the early months of 1917." (Spence, 2017, p. 146).

Jewish banker Jacob Schiff, who funded the Japanese side in the Russo-Japanese war of 1905, was ecstatic at the fall of the Tsar, announced while Trotsky was in New York. Did he give money to Trotsky? According to Spence, Charles Crane said yes:

Some years later, Charles Crane shared his private thoughts on the "Trotsky money" question ... In a 1921 letter to his friend Dr. Charles Eliot, Crane asserted that Jacob Schiff "had given Trotsky fifty thousand dollars when he started to Russia." The source of this information Crane laid to "the head of our State Department Secret Police in New York." ... Thirteen years further on, Crane elaborated on this in a letter to his son John, saying Schiff had handed the $50,000 to Trotsky at Lillian Wald's house the night before he sailed. Indeed, in Crane's view Wald was the mastermind of the whole affair. Crane proclaimed that "Trotsky was always in touch with her and followed her orders" and "she could always get any amount of money from the Schiff Warburg family." (Spence, 2017, pp. 147-8)

Important Trotsky supporters who turned up while he was in New York included Sidney Reilly, who returned to 120 Broadway, and Antony Jechalski.

Trotsky returned to Russia via Christiania (Oslo) in Norway. Spence says that he immediately sent a telegram to his uncle Abram, a banker:

His first stop, however, was the Christiania telegraph exchange were he fired off a terse message to Petrograd: "After a month of English captivity, I come to Petrograd with family 5/18 May." The message's recipient was one Abram L'vovich Zhivotovsky. (Spence, 2017, p. 5)

Abram Zhivotovsky did business in Vladivostok with another Jewish businessman, Moisei Akimovich Ginsburg, and his local agent, Sidney Reilly.

Reilly's banker buddy McRoberts was friends with Olof Aschberg, the (Jewish) Red Banker, who helped transfer funds to the Bolsheviks; Aschberg was Zhivotovsky's representative in Stockholm. (Spence, 2017, p. 118)

Reilly was close to Antony Jechalski, and to Alexander Weinstein, who had been Zhivotovsky's agent in London before switching to work for Reilly. In London, Weinstein mixed with Ludwig Martens, Maxim Litvinov (later Commissar for Foreign Affairs), and Benjamin Sverdlov (brother of Yakov, the first President of Soviet Russia). All were Jewish Bolsheviks (Spence, 2017, p. 114).

Spence uncovered a letter from Uncle Abram to Trotsky when he was in internal exile at Alma Ata. The letter was dated 3 October 1928:

It purported to be from an American follower who provided the Old Man with call-number information for his books in the New York Public Library. A long string of numbers followed, none of which had anything to do with library locations. Rather, the numbers none-too-cleverly concealed a coded message. It acknowledged that Trotsky's proposed plan for "active struggle" against "Kinto" (a disparaging name for Stalin) would be adopted, and that an unnamed country (the U.S.?) had guaranteed Trotsky a visa and diplomatic protection if he could secure his release from the U.S.S.R. Most intriguing, the message noted that "the material side of the project is completely secured" and "the money sent has been deposited," presumably meaning deposited in New York. The message was signed, "your Abram." (Spence, 2017, p. 254-5)

Apart from Uncle Abram, another of Trotsky's close relatives was a banker. Mahoney & Mahoney (1998) wrote,

A discernible link between Trotsky and the funding of the Bolshevik cause by the international bankers was through Abram Givatovzo, Trotsky's cousin. Givatovzo was a private banker in Kiev before the Bolshevik revolution. After the revolution he became a leader in the private banking community in Stockholm. From Sweden he continued to channel financial assistance to the Bolsheviks. (p. 116)

On Trotsky's Left Opposition, which began in 1923, the same authors wrote,

Trotsky's Left Opposition from the beginning had functioned on two levels. Openly, on the public platforms, in its own newspapers and organized cadre. It also operated behind the scenes in small clandestine conferences led by Trotsky and his cohorts who planned the underground strategy and tactics. Trotsky built a secret conspiratorial opposition organization. By 1923, this underground apparatus was extensive and powerful—using codes, recognition signals, danger signs and advanced tradecraft techniques. There were secret printing presses throughout Russia with Trotskyite cells in the army, diplomatic corps, Soviet state governments and Party institutions. (Mahoney & Mahoney, 1998, p. 115)

Sidney Reilly was executed by Stalin's OGPU, as a dangerous Trotskyist agent, after he crossed the border from Finland to Russia on September 25, 1925.

It was done via the Trust, a bogus White anti-Soviet organisation set up to trap opponents of the regime. It was a false-flag operation.

But Reilly knew about the Trust. Spence suggests that the Trotskyist Opposition used it as "a cover to channel support and funds to a real opposition—the Trotskyist opposition" (Spence, 2017, p. 248).

"Reilly wasn't walking into a trap, he was walking into the arms of people he believed to be his comrades. Some of them were, but somewhere along the line the secret of Reilly's mission had been blown" (Spence, 2017, p. 249).

"The deciding factor was Stalin, who monitored the situation closely, demanding updates every half-hour. Why would he have taken such keen interest in the arrest of a single British spy? A dangerous Trotskyist agent, of course, would have been another matter" (Spence, 2017, p. 249).

Two months before Reilly's death, two other Trotskyist agents, Isaiah Khurgin and Efraim Sklyansky, both Jewish, had died in a 'boating accident' in upstate New York.

Sklyansky had been Trotsky's deputy running the Red Army during the civil war. In 1924 Stalin removed Sklyansky from the military commissariat, and on January 6, 1925 the Politburo removed Trotsky as head of the Red Army. In May 1925 Trotsky was appointed head of the Main Concession Committee; this was a demotion, but it gave him the opportunity to follow up his connections with foreign bankers in New York.

Boris Berlatsky and Abram Fineberg, Moscow 'bankers,' arrived at Wall Street on August 24, 1925, the same day as Sklyansky; all headed to Amtorg, the American Trading Organization. Amtorg succeeded the Martens Bureau, which had been shut down.

Spence infers that Sklyansky and Khurgin were intending to establish a Trotskyist headquarters beyond Stalin's control, near Wall Street (Spence, 2017, p. 244).

Long Lake was intended as the venue for a secret Trotskyist meeting; but Stalin got wind of it. Khurgin and Sklyansky, rowing a canoe, drowned in choppy waters less than 100 yards from shore. A briefcase was retrieved from the lake; that briefcase seems to have ended up in Stalin's hands, providing him with further details of the plot (Spence, 2017, p. 247).

Their funeral in New York was attended by 500 mourners; a wreath from Trotsky was prominent, and there were many wreaths from American businessmen and bankers who had ties with Amtorg.

In Moscow, the pair received a final send-off, attended by Trotsky but not Stalin.

Sir William Wiseman, the chief of Britain's intelligence service in New York, was also a Trotskyist agent closely involved with Reilly. Spence notes:

"Professor Gottheil also was one of British intelligence chief William Wiseman's stable of informants. So, too, was Sidney Reilly. Wiseman even had a spy right in Schiff's board room at Kuhn Loeb—Otto H. Kahn" (Spence, 2017, p. 140).

"What Wiseman likely realized … was that Reilly was never really working for them. He was still serving the Revolution, or at least Trotsky's Revolution" (Spence, 2017, p. 192).

After leaving British Intelligence, Wiseman took a job at Jewish bank Kuhn Loeb:

"Wiseman's big opportunity came in September 1920 when Jacob Schiff died. The new dominant figure at Kuhn Loeb was his old collaborator Otto Kahn. The following year, Kahn latter invited him into the firm. … In early 1922, Kuhn Loeb organized its own spin-off to capitalize on East European opportunities, the New York & Foreign Development Corporation. Wiseman became its head. For much of that year he was in Czechoslovakia, Poland and Romania, where he employed Reilly as an agent" (Spence, 2017, p. 220).

'In January 1925, Reilly wrote to ex-partner Edward Spears that "I am in excellent connection with Kuhn, Loeb & Co., the Metropolitan Trust Co., the National City Bank, Blair & Co., and several other minor banks." His connection to Kuhn Loeb surely ran through Wiseman. In December 1924, precisely the time Reilly founded Trading Ventures, State Department Special Agent Sharp determined that Wiseman not only was au courant with Reilly's whereabouts, but also actively involved with him in various foreign business deals' (Spence, 2017, p. 239).

Henry Wickham Steed, editor of the Daily Mail, alleged that the prime movers behind Bolshevism "were Jacob Schiff, Warburg, and other international financiers" (Steed, 1924, p. 302).

Archives of the U.S. State Department, Office of the Historian, provide documentary evidence of transactions involving the financing of Bolshevism. The Swedish bank Nya Banken in Stockholm handled many of the transactions. The Max Warburg bank opened an account for Trotsky; the notes here are from the State Dept. historian.

https://history.state.gov/historicaldocuments/frus1918Russiav01/d371

PAPERS RELATING TO THE FOREIGN RELATIONS OF THE UNITED STATES, 1918, RUSSIA, VOLUME I
File No. 862.20261/53
The Ambassador in Russia (Francis) to the Secretary of State
[Telegram]
PETROGRAD , February 9, 12 p.m., to February 13, 1918, 1 a.m. 1
[Received February 13, 8.22 a.m., to February 16, 7.55 a.m.] 2354. Following prepared by Sisson and myself from documents we have seen whose authenticity I do not doubt and the originals of which we are endeavoring to procure.

DOCUMENT NO. 9

MR. RAPHAEL SCHOLNICKAN, HAPARANDA.

Dear Comrade: The office of the banking house M. Warburg has opened, in accordance with telegram from the Rhenish Westphalian Syndicate, an account for the undertaking of Comrade Trotsky. The attorney [?] purchased arms and has organized their transportation and delivery track Lulea and Vardö to the office of Essen & Son in the name Luleå receivers and a person authorized to receive the money demanded by Comrade Trotsky.

J. FÜRSTENBERG

Note: This is the first reference to Trotsky. It connects him with banker Warburg and with Fürstenberg. Luleå is a Swedish town near Haparanda.

DOCUMENT NO. 10

LULEÅ, October 2, 1917.

MR. ANTONOV, HAPARANDA.

Comrade Trotsky's request has been carried out. From the account of the syndicate and the Ministry (probably Ministry of Foreign Affairs in Berlin, press division) 400,000 kroner have been taken and remitted to Comrade Sonia who will call on you with this letter and will hand you the said sum of money.

J. FÜRSTENBERG

Note: Antonov is the chief military leader of the Bolsheviki. He was in command of forces that took St. Petersburg. He is now in field against Kaledin and Alexeev. At the date of this letter Trotsky was already at the head of Petrograd Soviet and the Bolshevik revolution was only a month away.

More State Dept. documents on Bolshevism are at https://history.state.gov/historicaldocuments/frus1918Russiav01/d621.

Max Warburg of Hamburg had brothers Paul and Felix at Wall Street: Paul was the brother-in-law of Jacob Schiff, and Felix was the son-in-law of Jacob Schiff. All were Jewish bankers.

An undated, anonymous article Trotsky And The Jews Behind The Russian Revolution, whose author calls himself "A Former Russian Commissar", alleges that the February revolution, which installed Prince Lvov (and then Kerensky), was Rothschild-backed; but the October revolution, led by Trotsky, was backed by the Schiff and Warburg banks.

Trotsky And The Jews Behind The Russian Revolution

by A Former Russian Commissar

[...] There has long existed an old, but purely financial rivalry between forces surrounding the Rothschilds and the so-called German-American Jewish banking block. The latter was at this time under the control of the late Jacob Schiff, an international Jewish banker of Wall Street, closely allied with the Warburgs of New York and Hamburg, Guggenheim, Hanauer, Kahn, and others.

Jointly, the two rival groups had financed the preparatory work by assisting revolutionary groups of intellectuals, and by deliberately spreading propaganda all over the world, which later was to create an hostile attitude toward the Russian Empire. Jacob Schiff was especially active in all attempts to undermine the Czarist government. As early as 1904-5 he, as head of Kuhn, Loeb and Company, floated the Japanese war loans which brought about the defeat of Russia in the conflict of those years, and which struggle was followed by the revolution in Russia of 1905.

It was the Zionists and the Rothschilds who succeeded in dethroning Czar Nicholas II in 1917. They may have surprised their German-American rivals by the March coup of the Russian Duma; but Jacob Schiff and those allied with him, namely the Warburgs of New York and Hamburg; the German-Jewish Westphalian-Rheinland Syndicate; the Lazare brothers of Paris; the Ginzburgs of Petrograd, Tokyo and Paris; Speyer and Company of London, New York, and Frankfurt on the Main; and the Nya Banken of Stockholm—these forces were not caught unprepared for an eventual coup by their European Jewish rivals.

For them the "exiled" Trotsky-Bronstein was just the man to frustrate the efforts of the Rothschilds. If the latter could finance a Kerensky-Ruthenberg combination, Jacob Schiff and Company could very well counter such moves by causing discord in the revolutionary forces. Trotsky-Bronstein, the unscrupulous advocate of international mutiny and former head of the 1905 St. Petersburg Soviet, would be the one efficient, capable plotter to undermine the young Republic created by the Rothschilds.

In other words, there were Jews behind Kerensky; but there were more powerful Jews behind Trotsky! Although they represented two rival groups of bankers, fighting among themselves for power, yet both were agreed as to the ultimate destruction of Russian individualism. (A Former Russian Commissar, 1980).

In his autobiography *My Life*, Trotsky admits that the oppressive Bolshevik dictatorship was all the more terrible because of his opposition (the 'trio' is the triumvirate which succeeded Lenin: Kamenev, Zinoviev and Stalin):

The weaker the trio felt in matters of principle, the more they feared me—because they wanted to get rid of me—and the tighter they had to bolt all the screws and nuts in the state and party system. Much later, in 1925, Bukharin said to me, in answer to my criticism of the party oppression: "We have no democracy because we are afraid of you'". (Trotsky, 1930/1975, p. 508)

Richard Spence shows that Stalin defeated the Jewish bankers' conspiracy to enthrone Trotsky.

From 1928, Stalin replaced 'concessions' with 'technical-assistance agreements'; this changed the status of foreign companies from partners of the Soviet Government to mere employees (Spence, 2017, p. 253).

Chapter 17: Even in exile, Trotsky kept inciting Insurrection

At first, Stalin treated Trotsky mildly. He was exiled to Alma Ata in Kazakhstan (in the east of the U.S.S.R.) on January 31, 1928. But after he kept mobilising the Left Opposition, with intent to overthrow the Soviet Government, he was expelled from the Soviet Union to Turkey in February 1929.

To Stalin's surprise, Trotsky then became a worldwide celebrity; many supporters visited him at his home on Büyükada island, one of the Prince's Islands (Prinkipo) near Istanbul. Sidney and Beatrice Webb dropped in during May 1929.

From Turkey he applied for asylum in Britain and other countries. The Webbs, H. G. Wells, and other leftists appealed to the British Government to let him in. Marjorie Wells, the daughter-in-law and secretary of H.G. Wells, organised two petitions to Home Secretary Clynes. She was the wife of Wells' son George Philip Wells.

Signatories included Beatrice Webb, G. B. Shaw, J. M. Keynes, C. P. Scott and Harold Laski. Isaac Deutscher gave the details in *The Prophet Outcast*:

> Shaw ... wrote to Clynes, the Home Secretary ... 'But Mr. Trotsky cannot be silenced. His trenchant literary power and the hold, which his extraordinary career has given him on the public imagination of the modern world, enable him to use every attempt to persecute him. ... He becomes the inspirer and the hero of all the militants of the extreme left of every country. Those who had 'an unreasoning dread of him as a caged lion' should allow him to enter Britain 'if only to hold the key of his cage'. ... Other European governments were no more willing to 'hold the key of his cage'. ...

> The truth is that even in exile Trotsky inspired fear. Governments and ruling parties made him feel that no one can lead a great revolution, defy all the established powers, and challenge the sacred rights of property with impunity. Bourgeois Europe gazed with amazement and glee at the spectacle, the like of which it had not seen indeed since Napoleon's downfall— never since then had so many governments proscribed one man or had one man aroused such widespread animosity and alarm. ...

> The Social Democratic parties, especially those which were in office, felt somewhat disturbed in their democratic conscience, but were no less afraid. When George Lansbury protested at a Cabinet meeting against the treatment of Trotsky, the Prime Minister, the Foreign Secretary, and the Home Secretary replied: 'There he is, in Constantinople, out of the way— it is to nobody's interest that he should be anywhere else. We are all afraid of him.' (Deutscher, 1970, pp. 17-20)

In her diary, Beatrice Webb wrote of her visit to Trotsky on Prinkipo:

We were alone with the great revolutionary for a couple of hours. He is a charming and accomplished man; looks more like an intellectual musician than an organizer of war and revolution. He opened with in polished French with a suave and deferential claim to being one of our disciples who had strayed away from our teaching! (Webb, 1943/1985, pp. 165-6).

After Britain rejected Trotsky's request for asylum, she wrote to him:

My husband and I were very sorry that you were not admitted into Great Britain. But I am afraid that anyone who preaches the permanence of revolution, that is carries the revolutionary war into the politics of other countries, will always be excluded from entering those other countries. (Deutscher, 1970, p. 21)

But she gave another side of Trotsky, during the Moscow Trials of 1936, in a letter to Madame E. Halevy:

We saw Trotsky in 1929 and we thought that he was in a state of megalomania, ready to do anything against Stalin and his associates, partly for personal reasons, but perhaps mainly because in his giving up promoting revolutions in other countries, Stalin and his friends were betraying the revolution in Russia. (Webb, 1936/1978, p. 414)

In volume II of their book *Soviet Communism: A New Civilisation?*, Sidney And Beatrice Webb cover the contest between Stalin and Trotsky:

Stalin, in the autumn of 1924, launched the slogan of "Socialism in a Single Country"; meaning that, in view of the failure of the world revolution to break out, the duty of the U.S.S.R. was to make itself into a successful and prosperous socialist state, which would serve as an example and a model for the proletariat of the world. ...

But there was a substantial issue in debate, at any rate until it was finally and authoritatively decided by the Plenum of the Central Committee of the Party in April 1926 ; a decision ratified, after more discussion, by the Fourteenth and Fifteenth Party Conferences of October 1926 and December 1927. (Webb & Webb, 1935, pp. 1099-1100)

Trotsky refused to accept these decisions of the Party, and continued to campaign against it. That's why he was expelled and exiled:

After these decisions, Trotsky persisted in his agitation, attempting to stir up resistance ; and his conduct became plainly factious. It was this persistence in faction after the Party had definitely decided that led to his banishment to Alma Ata at the beginning of 1928, and to Constantinople at the beginning of 1929. (Webb & Webb, 1935, fn. 2, p. 1100)

The debate was conducted on religious lines:

The difficulty of discovering "what it was all about" is increased by the characteristic method of controversy adopted by both sides. The question was not put as "which policy would be likely to be most advantageous or most successful". It was perpetually argued as "what was the view taken by Marx and Engels, and by Lenin himself ; and what exactly did these authorities mean by this or that text discovered among their voluminous writings". (pp. 1100-1)

The Webbs list Four Arguments of the Trotskyists:

The final objection that we can disentangle from the controversy of 1924-1927 is that the pursuit of socialism in a single country meant the betrayal of the world proletariat, to whom the hope had been held out of a world revolution. It was, so Trotsky alleged, the policy of a narrow nationalist egoism, unworthy in the successors of Lenin, Engels and Marx. Better far, it was said, devote all the energies of the U.S.S.R. to the tasks of the Comintern. The proper communist policy, it was urged, was to promote actively a proletarian insurrection in every country, by fomenting strikes, inciting colonial rebellions, subverting the troops, and eventually seizing power by a forcible revolution in one state after another. (Webb & Webb, 1935, p. 1103)

But the Webbs come out on Stalin's side:

The answer was plain. Five years' experience had shown in 1924 that there was little promise, in Western Europe or the United States, of any early success along such a road. ... The building-up of socialism in a single country was, in fact, in itself the most promising method of causing proletarian revolutions elsewhere; and of propagating communist theories in a way to which the capitalist governments would find it difficult to take exception. (pp. 1103-4)

However, the Webbs note their sympathy for Trotsky and hostility to Stalin, in a footnote:

We are unable, in this exposition of the constitutional structure and trends of progress in the Soviet Union of the present day (1935), to do justice to the lifelong revolutionary career, and the considerable services, of Leon Trotsky, which have been, for the past seven years, obscured by the malevolence of those by whom he was opposed and defeated. In the main controversy of 1925-1929 he may be deemed to have had the advantage over his adversaries in the citation of texts, even if, judged by subsequent experience, he was incorrect in his forecasts and unstatesmanlike in his particular recommendations. (fn. 1, p. 1100)

Britain's 'national unity' Government was headed by Ramsay MacDonald of the Labour Party, but most Labour MPs were in the Opposition. Intellectuals such as the Webbs, G. B. Shaw and H. G. Wells had little influence.

MacDonald advocated Class Unity, not Class War. He had already been burnt by Communists and fellow-travellers in 1924, when the Zinoviev Letter help bring down his similar 'national unity' Labour Government.

So despite pressure in the House of Commons, Cabinet refused entry to Trotsky. Hansard records the efforts of his supporters to obtain entry: https://hansard.parliament.uk/commons/1929-07-24/debates/8e398d2e-7f7f-49f6-b35d-46487fd8001f/MTrotsky.

Trotsky wrote about it in Chapter 45 of his autobiography *My Life* (1930).

Trotsky's fellow-traveller supporters, in their questions and statements in the House of Commons, appealed to England's tradition of admitting asylum-seekers, and spoke of him as if he were a mere philosopher, who might benefit from experiencing English democracy at first hand.

In contrast, Winston Churchill (1930) commented, "Trotsky, whose frown meted death to thousands, sits disconsolate, a bundle of old rags, stranded on the shores of the Black Sea".

Only two years earlier, when he was still free in Russia, Trotsky (1927) had written in support of the English General Strike of 1926, which he had hoped would lead to a Communist revolution: "The defeat of the revolution in China, following the defeat of the English General Strike, has filled the imperialists with the hope that they may succeed in crushing the Soviet Union."

In the summer of 1933, Trotsky moved from Prinkipo to France; the government of Édouard Daladier gave him asylum, in the provinces, using a pseudonym.

After Hitler's election in January 1933, Comintern policy, which was followed by Stalinist parties in Europe, was to ally with 'bourgeois' parties against Fascist parties. These alliances were called 'Popular Fronts'.

In France, the Popular Front led by Léon Blum won the election of May 1936; Communist (Stalinist) parties became part of the government.

The Trotskyist position, in view of the rise of the left and the mass strikes in 1934 and 1936, was to proceed with a General Strike in order to bring down the Left Government and replace it with a Workers Revolutionary government. Trotsky himself announced and promoted this policy in 1934. He called it the "Action Program for France".

While the Spanish Civil War was under way, Trotsky repeatedly incited mass insurrection in France, i.e. mass strikes to install a Trotskyist government, both when he was living there (1933-35) and when in Norway (1935-6). The Trotskyist site wsws.org explains:

Leon Trotsky, who between 1933 and 1935 lived in exile in France, followed events closely and sought to influence the outcome. Even later, after being forced to leave France for Norway, he took great interest in developments in France and remained in close contact with his French comrades. (Schwarz, 2006)

After mass protests by the Right on February 6, 1934 and by the Left on February 9, at which more than 20 people were killed, the Leftist French Government signed an order to deport Trotsky for his role. However, no other country would take him. He was moved to a tiny village, kept in isolation, and placed under strict surveillance. Trotsky (1935) wrote about it in "An Open Letter to the French Workers: Stalinist Betrayal and the World Revolution".

In May 1935, after the Franco-Soviet Treaty of Mutual Assistance was signed, Trotsky was informed that he was no longer welcome in France. He applied to move to Norway.

Norway gave him permission to move there. He took up residence from June 10, 1935.

But the following year, French newspapers complained about his role in inciting the mass strikes of May-June 1936 with his articles; the Norwegian government became uneasy about having him.

On 14 August 1936, the Soviet Press Agency TASS announced a 'Trotskyist—Zinovievist' plot to kill Stalin, and the imminent start of the Moscow Trials. Norway then imposed conditions on Trotsky: to stop writing about politics, not to give interviews, and to have his correspondence vetted by the police. Trotsky refused.

On 19 December 1936, Trotsky and his wife were deported from Norway on a ship bound for Mexico. The *Ruth* arrived in Mexico on 9 January 1937; the Mexican president welcomed him and arranged transport in his own special train.

After the Moscow Trials, Trotsky sought opportunities to denounce the Soviet persecution of his movement. In 1939 he agreed to testify before the U.S. House of Representatives committee, chaired by Martin Dies Jr., the forerunner of the House Un-American Activities Committee (HUAC).

But they found out that he "intended to use the Committee as a forum … and would call the workers of the world to turn world war into world revolution" (Deutscher, 1970, p. 482).

They then rescinded his invitation to appear, and he was denied a visa.

P.O.U.M., in Spain, wanted Trotsky to move to Catalonia. If Trotsky's allies had gained power in any European country, they would have invited him to move there, and he would have established a rival Communist government to that in Russia. Alternatively, if Stalin had lost the war with Hitler, Trotsky could have hoped to return to Russia triumphant. That prospect is probably the main reason that Stalin had him killed.

Deutscher hoped that Destalinisation would lead to the rehabilitation of Trotsky in Russia. But in 1961 Leonid Brezhnev honoured Ramon Mercader with the title 'Hero of the Soviet Union'.

Gorbachev dared not rehabilitate Trotsky directly, although he did rehabilitate his son Sergei Sedov in 1988—but not his other son Leon—and allow the publication of Trotsky's books in 1989. Russians, however were once bitten, twice shy.

After Western advisers caused the collapse of Russia during the Yeltsin years, Stalin returned somewhat to favour: partly for overcoming the Jewish Bolsheviks (because they hated Russia), partly for defeating Hitler, and partly for building a strong state able to resist American Imperialism.

Chapter 18: H. G. Wells keeps the Dream alive

Freda Utley, a friend of Bertrand Russell, narrates a story of hope and disillusion, as she tells how she became a Communist, and how she lost the faith.

She first visited the U.S.S.R. in 1927, when the New Economic Policy (NEP) was still operating. Life was much improved after the years of civil war and forced requisitions (War Communism). The peasants now owned their own land, were producing for profit, and the rural economy was booming: "The market places of Moscow and other towns were overflowing with vegetables, dairy produce, milk, and other foods. New apartment houses and office buildings built in the severe but pleasing style introduced after the Revolution were much in evidence. There were no queues for bread and other foods at the state and co-operative shops" (Utley, 1940, p. 15).

Back in London, she joined the Communist party, and married a Russian Jew, Arcadi Berdichevsky, who worked at the Soviet Trade Mission. She took a job with the Comintern, and in September 1930 they moved to Moscow.

Collectivisation ended the NEP, and brought a drastic drop in rural living standards. The peasants were turned into serfs again, and their work was appropriated by the government for capital accumulation. Rural exports paid for machinery purchased from abroad; the cost was the 6 million lives of the Ukraine Famine (which also occurred in parts of Russia).

Despite having worshipped Trotsky as the greatest leader, she came to see that his campaign against the NEP destroyed the good old days:

> Preobrazhensky, the most honest of the Left opposition group, stated openly that only by treating the Russian countryside as a colonial area could the necessary super-profits be obtained to finance the industrialization of the U.S.S.R. Such plain speaking was too much even for the Left opposition and brought ruin to the author once Stalin was in control and busy carrying out Preobrazhensky's policy in an extreme form. (p. 47)

> There began that terrible murder of the Kulaks by the state, which is almost unparalleled in history for its cruelty. I use the word murder deliberately, for although the Kulaks were not lined up and shot, they were killed off in a manner far more cruel. Whole families, men, women, children, and babies, were thrown out of their homes, their personal possessions seized, even their warm clothing torn off them; then, packed into unheated cattle trucks in winter, they were sent off to Siberia or other waste parts of the Soviet Union. (p. 51)

Western intellectuals fell for Soviet propaganda:

Communists and fellow travelers, many of whom at home had never seen the inside of a factory or a power station, journalists and authors, school-teachers and "intellectuals" of all kinds, went on conducted tours of the Soviet Union and worshiped before the shrine of the machine. ... Yet for the Russian people the much-admired "gigantic successes on the industrial front" meant only hardship, undernourishment, and overwork. (pp. 196-7)

But everyone in Russia who had anything to do with industry or trade knew that jerry-building, poor materials, incompetent or skimped work, hidden defects, made the factories and power stations erected at the cost of so much sweat and misery incapable of producing more than a fraction of what they had been planned to produce. The machines imported in exchange for the food and manufactures so sorely needed by the Russian people, or in exchange for the timber produced by the wretched prisoners of the O.G.P.U., deteriorated rapidly and soon became defective or unworkable. These defects and shortcomings were, in fact, often referred to in the Soviet Press. But they were always ascribed to the sabotage or the ignorance or the inefficiency of individuals, never to the system which was in fact responsible. Yet it was the system to force engineers and technicians, all the qualified experts, to work under Party bosses who knew nothing about the enterprises of which they were in charge, and could always put the blame on the non-Party specialists when things went wrong. ... the concentration camp awaited them in the short or the long run, so they tried to make the run as long as possible. (pp. 197-8)

During the Great Purge of 1936, her husband was arrested by the OGPU:

On the night of April 10-11, Arcadi wakened me saying, "We have visitors." I sprang out of bed to see a soldier in the passage. Two O.G.P.U. officers in uniform were in our sitting room, together with the janitor of the block of flats. The O.G.P.U. officers told us we must not speak to each other, and started on a methodical search of the whole flat. ... As the hours passed and the search went on, I said to myself over and over again, "They will find nothing and then they will go. They will find nothing and then they will go." ...

When Arcadi went to the toilet, the soldier went with him, presumably to see that he should destroy no papers. ... They took all my letters from Arcadi, preserved through the years. They took my address book. ... At seven o'clock Jon wakened, and we gave him breakfast. At eight o'clock they told Arcadi they were taking him away to be examined, but the search was not yet completed. I made him coffee. My mind now was filled with only one purpose: to strengthen him for the ordeal before him. I knew he was innocent, but I also knew of the terrible, long, exhausting examinations to which the O.G.P.U. subjects its victims. Arcadi had been up all night, and might be confused, too tired to think clearly. By this time they allowed us to talk a little. Jon was around the place, and him they could not silence. ...

At about nine o'clock they took him away. We kissed for the last time. At the door I said, "What can I do; shall I go to R?" He shrugged his shoulders. "No one can help," he said.

No words of love passed between us; they were not needed. Reserved to the last and calm to the last, he gave me a gentle smile and was gone.

I never saw him again. ...

Others shunned me. Friends were afraid to speak to me. When someone is arrested in the U.S.S.R., it is as if the plague had struck his family. All are afraid of any contact, afraid to be seen talking to the stricken family. I was comparatively lucky. Several friends stuck by me. The R's told me to come to their flat, in the same block as ours, whenever I felt like it. They had lived for years in the United States and had not lost all their decency and courage. ...

One man at the Institute whom I had known years before in London tried to console me by showing me mine was the lot of all. He said, "I don't suppose there is a family in Moscow which has not lost one member in the past years either through arrest or through typhus." (pp. 261-2)

She blamed Stalin and was inclined to become a Trotskyist. But Bertrand Russell persuaded her otherwise: 'Bertie would bang his fist on the table and say, "No! Freda, can't you understand, even now, that the conditions you describe followed naturally from Lenin's premises and Lenin's acts? Will you never learn and stop being romantic about politics?"' (p. 11).

Like H. G. Wells, Russell had visited Soviet Russia in 1920. He went there as a Marxist, and came back disillusioned.

Russell described Bolshevism as tyrannical, even in 1920, well before Stalin's rise: "Bolshevism is a close tyrannical bureaucracy, with a spy system more elaborate and terrible than the Tsar's, and an aristocracy as insolent and unfeeling, composed of Americanised Jews. No vestige of liberty remains, in thought or speech or action" (Russell, 1920/1975, v. 2 p. 172; in the paperback it's on p. 35).

H. G. Wells also noted the role of Jews, but explained it away: "there came flowing back from America and the West to rejoin their comrades a considerable number of keen and enthusiastic young and youngish men ... It is these young men who constitute the living force of Bolshevism. Many of them are Jews, because most of the Russian emigrants to America were Jews; but few of them have any strong racial Jewish feeling. They are not out for Jewry but for a new world" (Wells, 1920, p. 74).

On his return, Russell (1920/1962,) dispelled myths about Communism, in his book *The Practice and Theory of Bolshevism*:

> Bolshevism is not merely a political doctrine; it is also a religion, with elaborate dogmas and inspired scriptures. When Lenin wishes to prove some proposition, he does so, if possible, by quoting texts from Marx and Engels. (p. 8)

> [Bolshevism is] a slavery far more complete than that of capitalism. A sweated wage, long hours, industrial conscription, prohibition of strikes, prison for slackers, diminution of the already insufficient rations in factories where the production falls below what the authorities expect, an army of spies ready to report any tendency to political disaffection and to procure imprisonment for its promoters--this is the reality of a system which still professes to govern in the name of the proletariat. (p. 86)

Pitirim Sorokin was present during the visit of H. G. Wells to Russia in 1920; he describes a dinner given for Wells:

> The English Labor Delegation, H. G. Wells and Bertrand Russell, like other foreigners, saw principally what the Communists wanted to show them; they came in touch with few non-Communists, nor would they have been able to speak with many such had they so desired. They simply swallowed what ever bait the Soviet leaders offered them and went home impressed with the dictatorship of the proletariat, "endless Communist enthusiasm," and the devotion of the people to the Soviet Government. I did not meet Bertrand Russell, but friends of mine did meet him and made what efforts they could to enlighten him as to the true condition of affairs.

> I was present at the meeting in the Palace of Labor, from which most real laborers were excluded, and I saw something of H. G. Wells who, from his arrival, was placed under the constant guardianship of Gorky. Wells visited the Academy of Science, but he could not talk with J. Pavlov or other distinguished academicians. Gorky did not take him through the University, but showed him only its one decently equipped building, the physical laboratory.

> A dinner was given Wells in the House of Arts, with clean table cloths, clean dishes, and better food than any of the intellectuals had seen in years. There was even meat on that table. But to give it a proletarian appearance, the spoons were of wood. To create a truly liberal atmosphere, a number of University professors and literary men were invited, although most of the guests were Communists, and two Chekhists were on hand to watch the counter-revolutionaries. Indignant at the betrayal of truth by these men, I decided to make a speech, although I could not then use the English language. Addressing Wells, but really speaking to the Communists, I explained the real situation and the appalling campaign of murder which

was being carried on in the name of liberty. I spoke moderately, for one does with the hangman in the room, but I must have spoken to the point, for Gorky suddenly interrupted, saying that such speeches were inadmissible.

"Then why are we here?" I asked. "Are we invited only to assist in deceiving this great English writer?" At this several celebrated Russian writers, to show their indignation, rose and left the room, crying: "We refuse to be classed with liars." Amphitheatroff, an eminent novelist, remained, saying to me: "I am going to try to finish your speech." He did manage to speak briefly, but Gorky made him take his seat, declaring that what he was saying was "improper." Gorky's own speech was a sweeping defense of the Communist Government, and made him very popular with them. But it cost him the respect of the intellectuals, many of whom after that evening would never take his hand. As for me, even before the dinner to Wells was over, I left the hall and once more, for my "health's sake," disappeared. (Sorokin, 1924, pp. 243-5)

Wells blamed the civil war for the chaos he saw, and drew lifelong inspiration from the Communist experiment. He sought the creation of a World State, along Soviet lines but centred in the English-speaking world.

He rejected Marx's advocacy of Class War and rule by the proletariat; in Wells' view the new society could only be built by experts in the various professions, by managers and by bankers. Marxism denigrated those people as 'bourgeois'.

In his book *Anticipations* (serialised in 1901, published as a book in 1902, and with a new Preface in 1914), Wells envisaged rulership by a caste of intellectuals, the Samurai, on the model of Plato's *Republic*. This book was Wells' first best-seller. In the Preface to the 1914 edition, Wells used the term 'Open Conspiracy' for the first time:

The general idea of the "New Republic," the onslaught on "Democracy," the manifest dislike for such partizan and particularist things as trade unionism and nationalism are as much a part of me as those intonations of my voice or the shape of my nose. That conception of an open conspiracy of intellectuals and wilful people against existing institutions and existing limitations and boundaries is always with me ... That open conspiracy will come. It is my faith. (Wells 1902/1999, pp. xiv-xv)

Lenin's Bolshevik Party was quite similar to Wells' Samurai in its early years, before the masses were invited to join.

The young revolutionaries who set up the Soviet regime were not workers, but intellectuals; not proletarians, but ruling in the name of the proletariat.

Wells' viewpoint is like Weishaupt's Illuminism. Weishaupt advocated the abolition of Nations (a World State), the abolition of Religions, and the abolition of the Family. Wells concurred on all three.

Marxism is a variant of Illuminism, and is closely associated with Grand Orient Freemasonry. Wells' philosophy has been called 'Marxism for the Elite'. The Trotskyist site marxists.org classifies Wells as a Utopian Socialist, and hosts some of his books, e.g. *A Modern Utopia* (1905).

In *Anticipations* (1902/1999), Wells pitches his line at the Elite, trying to persuade them to push for a World State—and even override the U.S. Constitution:

> ... this effective New Republic ... will appear first, I believe, as a conscious organization of intelligent and quite possibly in some cases wealthy men, ... confessedly ignoring most of the existing apparatus of political control ... (p. 147)

> The American constitution and the British crown and constitution have to be modified or shelved at some stage in this synthesis ... (p. 148)

> In its more developed phases I seem to see the New Republic as ... a sort of outspoken Secret Society, with which even the prominent men of the ostensible state may be openly affiliated. A vast number of men admit the need but hesitate at the means of revolution, and in this conception of a slowly growing new social order organized with open deliberation within the substance of the old, there are no doubt elements of technical treason, but an enormous gain in the thoroughness, efficiency, and stability of the possible change. ... The New Republicans will constitute an informal and open freemasonry. (pp. 154-5)

> If the surmise of a developing New Republic—a Republic that must ultimately become a World State of capable rational men, developing amidst the fading contours and colours of our existing nations and institutions— be indeed no idle dream, but an attainable possibility in the future, and to that end it is that the preceding Anticipations have been mainly written, it becomes a speculation of very great interest to forecast something of the general shape and something even of certain details of that common body of opinion which the New Republic, when at last it discovers and declares itself, will possess. (p. 157)

In *The Open Conspiracy* (1928), Wells envisages a role for bankers—left-wing bankers like George Soros, David Rockefeller, and the Rothschild family (part-owners of The Economist magazine):

> And when we come to the general functioning classes, landowners, industrial organizers, bankers, and so forth, who control the present system, such as it is, it should be still plainer that it is very largely from the ranks of these classes, and from their stores of experience and traditions of meth-

od, that the directive forces of the new order must emerge. The Open Conspiracy can have nothing to do with the heresy that the path of human progress lies through an extensive class war. (p. 57)

But there remains a residuum of original and intelligent people in banking or associated with banking or mentally interested in banking, who do realize that banking plays a very important, interesting part in the world's affairs, who are curious about their own intricate function and disposed towards a scientific investigation of its origins, conditions, and future possibilities. Such types move naturally towards the Open Conspiracy. Their enquiries carry them inevitably outside the bankers' habitual field to an examination of the nature, drift, and destiny of the entire economic process. (pp. 57-8)

Martin Gardner pointed out (1999), in his Introduction to the Dover Edition of *Anticipations*, that Wells' World State would be a police state:

For a short time Wells viewed Lenin's revolution in Russia as not far from his notion of a great state taken over by an efficient elite. When he visited Russia and met Lenin—a visit he recorded in *Russia in The Shadows* (1920)—he found fault with many aspects of communism, but there is no hint that he deplored its total absence of democracy. Indeed, to put it bluntly, the world state outlined here and in A Modern Utopia is a police state. Wells never made it clear whether his Samurai would take power gradually or by a bloody revolution. (pp. vi-vii)

Gardener said that *Anticipations* launched Wells' career as a Futurist—a social engineer:

Anticipations was Wells's first best-seller. The book had an enormous impact on British intellectuals and their European counterparts. George Bernard Shaw, Sidney and Beatrice Webb, William and Henry James, and Arnold Bennett were among a raft of eminent writers who highly praised the book. (p. iii)

Wells made no secret of being opposed to Democracy. He was a Totalitarian of sorts, but which sort?

This is not of a mere 'academic' interest, because the New World Order currently being implemented seems to draw on Wells' blueprint. Whether it is Communist or Fascist makes a great deal of difference, and is matter of urgency.

It's not that Globalist leaders are poring over Wells' books to learn what to do next; rather, he seems to have formed his views by discussions with the Progressive elite, including bankers, over many years. So, the views he articulates are not just his, but theirs too. After the fall of the Soviet Union, they have had an opportunity to put their ideas into practice. The phenomenon of 'Left-wing billionaires' like George Soros has put paid to the idea that Capital always supports conservative social policies.

The view that Wells was a 'Liberal Fascist', not a Communist, was put by Philip Coupland:

> The relationship between these two sides of Wellsism is well illustrated by the 'Liberal Fascism' which Wells called for in his addresses to the Young Liberals at their Summer School in Oxford in July 1932. The reason why he was there, Wells stressed, was to 'assist in a kind of "Phoenix Rebirth" of Liberalism'. 'Central' to this reborn 'Liberalism' would be what Wells called a 'competent receiver', by which he meant 'a responsible organisation, able to guide and rule the new scale human community'. The ' competent receiver' was also, Wells carefully explained, 'flatly opposed' to the norms of 'parliamentary democracy', being a 'special class of people' of the type anticipated in 'the Guardian of Plato's Republic' (Coupland, 2000, pp. 172-3).

An alternative view is that what Wells advocated was 'Marxism for the Elite'. He repeatedly bagged Marx, but praised the early Soviet Union—the regime of the Old Bolsheviks, who later coalesced around Trotsky.

Wells criticised Marx's claim that the New Order would be led by the working class, i.e. the uneducated proletariat. Instead, Wells envisaged leadership by the same class that led the French Revolution—the progressive intellectuals and professionals. This time, however, instead of establishing a national state, they would create a World State.

Did not Trotsky try to do the same? Wells often praised him, and tried to have him given asylum in Britain. How could Wells be a Nazi or Fascist, if he was pro-Trotsky?

The Old Bolshevik leaders themselves were mostly intellectuals, not workers; they were like the Jacobins, and so, fit Wells' model rather than Marx's. Could it be, then, that Wells was just 'calling a spade a spade'?

An alternative way of looking at it is that the Marxist movement of the nineteenth century was using Buonarroti's textbook, which itself was based on principles worked out by Adam Weishaupt. In this light, the Marxist movement is seen as Illuminist, and the fall of the Soviet Union marks only the end of the Stalinist deviation.

Real Illuminism was pro-Trotsky. And like Weishaupt's movement in its early years, it was led by intellectuals and professionals—not workers (they are now deemed 'Deplorables'). So Marx's proletarian formulations are a deviation, from which true Illuminism has re-emerged. Rather than calling Wells' policies 'Marxism for the Elite', they should be called 'Illuminist'.

From its foundation in 1776, Weishaupt's Illuminist movement was cosmopolitan and atheistic; Cloots pursued the same internationalism and atheism during the French Revolution, for which he was executed by the nationalist and deist Robespierre.

Wells, too, applied the word "cosmopolitan" to his World State; this was the very word Stalin used in the anti-cosmopolitan campaign of 1946-7. And The Open Society of Karl Popper and George Soros would be "cosmopolitan". And Gorbachev embraced cosmopolitanism.

Before we consider Coupland's case, let us get some facts on the ground.

Firstly, Wells' World State would not be Capitalist. In *A Modern Utopia* he says that the State would be the sole landowner, and would provide goods and services through local authorities, which would have a feudal relationship to the central government (Wells, 1905, p. 89).

Wells' son Geoffrey West attests Wells' position that there would be no private ownership of the economy in the World State:

Wells had long ago rejected the simple opposition of Capital and Labour ... 'In an organized world there will be no organized labour, as such, because everyone will play his or her part in the common task and no one will toil, and there will be no capitalists, because capital, the accumulated resources of mankind, will be administered for the common good. Or if you like to put it in another way, Humanity will be one labour organization and the only capitalist in the world. In such a state questions of wages and dividends disappear. They will give place to the question of the "fair share". Of everyone we shall ask what is the fair share of effort he or she shall contribute to the commonweal and what is the fair share of consumable goods he shall take from the commonweal. The amount of the fair share in each case depends entirely upon the applied science in the world. ... I think the future welfare of mankind depends ... upon the supersession of private ownership in economic affairs.' (West, Geoffrey, 1939, pp. 237-8)

Wells repeatedly deprecates peasants, i.e. small family farmers. He advocates a "get big or get out" policy; that is one reason he supported Collectivisation in the Soviet Union.

In his *Outline of World History*, he discusses the three economic periods in the Soviet Union: "Thus in thirteen years Russia underwent three revolutions while remaining under the control of the same group of leaders; she sought in turn to realize the ideas of communism, of a liberal socialism, and of a rigidly disciplined state capitalism, and so she remains" (1931 & 1940, pp. 1136).

The first period, which he calls "communism", was the time of War Communism and the Requisitions of food.

The second period, which he calls "liberal socialism", was the time of the New Economic Policy (NEP), in which private businesses operated freely.

The third period, which he calls "state capitalism", was the Collectivisation under Stalin (which Trotsky had demanded, but Wells overlooks that).

The 1931 and 1940 editions of *The Outline of History* praise Lenin and Trotsky. Text & page#s are the same in both editions:

> At the head of the Bolshevik dictatorship, which now set itself to govern Russia, was Lenin, a very energetic and nimble-witted man who had spent most of his life in exile in London and Geneva, engaged in political speculations and the obscure politics of the Russian Marxist organizations. He was a quite honest revolutionary, simply living and indefatigable, with no experience whatever of practical administration. Associated with him was Trotsky, an exile from New York, who was presently to develop considerable practical military ability. (Wells, 1931 & 1940, p. 1130)

And disparage Stalin:

> In 1924 Lenin died. He was succeeded by Stalin, a dour-spirited Georgian who broke, expelled or executed many of his former colleagues and in particular that able saviour of the Soviet republic in its direst military need, Trotsky. (Wells, 1931 & 1940, p. 1136)

The 1961 edition, revised by Roman Postgate from Wells' papers, brands Stalin a counter-revolutionary devoid of original thought:

> Communism, in the days of Stalin, was no longer "the revolution" in the old-fashioned Socialist phrase; it was much more like a counter-revolution. ... Throughout Stalin's rise to power, and even afterwards, the old slogans were used, the old institutions (even if powerless) preserved, and Stalin, himself, the man for whose advantage the revolution was first arrested and then turned back, used throughout all his murderous career the same language as Lenin. His verbose works, which his followers had to master and admire, are derivative, and void of any original thought." (Wells, 1961, pp. 1192-3)

The 1931 and 1940 editions of *The Outline of History* ridicule Mussolini. Text & page#s are the same in both editions:

> The slide towards communism continued during 1921 in the face of a gathering opposition ... the Fascisti ... met violence with violence, they carried it to new extremes, they established an anti-socialist terror. ... The shadow of communism was replaced by the reality of brigand rule. (Wells, 1931 & 1940, p. 1107)

Wells' 1939 book *The Fate of Homo Sapiens* speaks of "Hitler's insanity ... shouting, frothing and orating in a madhouse":

Hitler's insanity would have had little effect upon the world if it had not slotted very easily into certain essential needs of the German situation. But for that he might be shouting, frothing and orating in a madhouse at the present time. But it happened that he supplied just the inflexible spearhead, the inhuman pertinacity, required to give extreme expression to the feelings of a humiliated and outrageously treated people. (Wells, 1939, p. 181)

During World War II, Wells urged the allies to bomb Rome. The Sydney Morning Herald reported on Jan 20, 1941: 'Mr. H. G. Wells, in a remarkable article in the "Sunday Dispatch" asks: "Why don't we bomb Rome?"' (Bomb Rome).

And David C. Smith reports, in his biography of Wells, that he often had lunch at the Soviet Embassy:

"In January 1940, as an example, he advocated the bombing of Berlin" (p. 451). "... he simply called for all-out attacks on Rome and other Axis cities ... Wells constantly urged the U.S. to enter the war" (p. 452). "Just before Wells left for the U.S.S.R. he again had lunch with Maisky {the Soviet Ambassador}; they discussed which questions he should put to Stalin" (p. 310). "Wells continued to remain sympathetic to the ideals of the Soviet Union, as did the Webbs and many other English intellectuals. He congratulated the Webbs on their mammoth book, Soviet Communism ... Wells even sent a letter (with others) to celebrate the twenty-first anniversary of the Revolution" (p. 311). "Throughout 1941, Wells continued to attend luncheons and other occasions. ... He did occasionally venture out to preside over an anti-fascist meeting of one sort or another, and he and Maisky often had lunch, usually at the Soviet Embassy" (p. 471). "He also continued a little political activity, and apparently got out to vote in 1945. ... He also told the Daily Worker that he would support a regenerate Communist Party if there were one in his Marylebone district". (Smith, 1986, p. 476)

The Daily Worker was a Communist newspaper, since renamed The Morning Star. Here is Wells saying that he would vote Communist in 1945 if there was a candidate, rather than for Clement Attlee's Labour Party; 'regenerate' might mean 'Trotskyist'. Attlee went on to create a national-socialist state in Britain, and gave India its independence.

Wells' son Anthony West says that his lover Moura Budberg was a Soviet spy:

Moura had been in Moscow not just once since 1931, but several times. She was visiting Russia annually, and sometimes getting there at intervals of as little as three months. All that she had told my father about her situation vis-a-vis the Russian authorities had to be untrue. She was crossing the Soviet frontiers all the time, and circulating with impunity when on Russian soil. There was only one circumstance in which anyone with her record could move between the two worlds and within Russia as openly as she was doing: her movements had to be made with the knowledge and consent of the secret police. She had to be a Russian agent in good standing. ... As soon as he came within sight of this conclusion my father was compelled to consider its implications. The most obvious of them had to be that she had been planted on him just as she had been planted upon Gorky. She would almost certainly have been under the orders of her controller when she came to seek him out in England after Gorky had decided to go home. (West, Anthony, 1984, p. 144).

Wells knew she was a spy, but could not tear himself away:

But when my father at last came face to face with Moura in Estonia, the hardest thing for him to deal with was that she could still work that magic. Spy or no, Moura was Moura, and in spite of all that he had learned about her double dealing, her physical and emotional holds upon him were as strong as ever. ...

If he wanted to go on being her lover, he would have to take her on her own terms, the first of which was that all her skeletons should stay in the dark in the cupboards in which she had put them.

Long before they left Estonia it had become apparent to my father that he would indeed have to break with Moura if he was to prevent his private life from becoming an ongoing refutation of all that he publicly stood for. What was truly appalling to him about this realisation was that it was as clear to him that he couldn't even contemplate actually doing such a thing—no matter what Moura might have done, no matter what she might still be doing, it was quite simply not a possibility that he should give her up. (pp. 145-6).

Wells' biographer David C. Smith states that he was living with Moura during World War II:

"It was during the three periods of greatest stress that he produced the most work. ... the third, although he was now living comfortably with Moura, is the period of the Second World War" (Smith, p. 451}.

In view of the above evidence, it is ludicrous to claim that Wells was a Fascist or Nazi. But how did those claims, articulated by Philip Coupland (2000), arise?

In the wake of the Great Depression of the 1930s, laissez-faire policies were no longer tenable, and Western societies polarised into Far Left and Far Right. In Britain, this was the time of Mosely's Blackshirts. Wells and Mosely sounded each other out, but nothing came of it.

Wells' novel *The Shape of Things to Come* (1933) depicts a movement which overthrew governments and established a World State. He called this movement the 'Modern State' Movement. A movie of the book, called *Things to Come*, was produced in 1936.

In the story, the Air Dictatorship of the World Council shuts down the Catholic Church, then Islam and Hinduism too. It introduces a new religion, and cosmopolitan schools:

'There was a definite hunt for medicine men, sorcerers, priests, religious teachers, and organizers of sedition; they would be fined or exiled, and parents and others would be fined for "impeding" the education of their children at the cosmopolitan schools' (Wells, 1933/1979, p. 400).

Wells wrote that 'millions of young men who began Fascist, Nazi, Communist ... became Modern State men in their middle years' (Wells, 1933/1979, p. 474).

Similarly, F. A. Hayek wrote (1940),

"The relative ease with which a young communist could be converted into a Nazi or vice versa was generally known in Germany, best of all to the propagandists of the two parties. Many a University teacher in this country in the 1930's has seen English and American students return from the Continent, uncertain whether they were communists or Nazis and certain only that they hated Western liberal civilisation" (Hayek, 1944, p. 22).

Wells derived both sides from Plato's Republic:

"This Communist Party, like the Italian Fascisti, owes its general conception to that germinal idea of the Modern State, the Guardians in Plato's Republic. For if anyone is to be called the Father of the Modern State it is Plato" (Wells, 1933/1979, p. 154).

The film, *Things to Come*, depicted the Modern State revolutionaries in black shirts like Mosley's supporters. This led to allegations that Wells was a 'Liberal Fascist'.

However, Nick Cooper, writing at Wikipedia, says:

'Wells is sometimes incorrectly assumed to have had a degree of control over the project that was unprecedented for a screenwriter. Posters and the main title bill the film as "H. G. Wells' Things to Come", with "an Alexander Korda production" appearing in smaller type. In fact, Wells ultimately had no control over the finished product, with the result that many scenes, although shot, were either truncated or not included in the finished film' (Cooper, 2012).

Malcolm Pollack noted that Wells, like other leftists, approved of the economic reforms made by the Fascists and Nazis in the 1930s before the war. Pollack mentions FDR as an admirer; another was David Lloyd George.

'Like most Progressive thinkers of the era, Wells approved of the Leftist social reforms that swept Europe in the early years of the 20th century under the banners of the Fascists and Nazis, and he called, in a speech to the Young Liberals at Oxford in 1932, for a "'Phoenix Rebirth' of Liberalism," a kind of "enlightened Nazism" that he proposed be called "Liberal Fascism." He was a friend and admirer of FDR (who, before the war, shared Wells' high opinion of Fascist ideals), and was a frequent visitor to the White House' (Pollack, 2009).

In 1932, Wells addressed the Young Liberals, as both Coupland and Pollack mention, and told them, "I am asking for liberal Fascisti, for enlightened Nazis".

In the same year, Wells published a book titled *After Democracy*, in which he repeated the above statement: "Liberalism, then, means the progressive, world State; that is its spirit and objective, even if Liberalism has not always realized the full implication of its thoughts and feelings. For Catholicism also was once a feeble giant. I am asking for a Liberal Fascisti, for enlightened Nazis; I am proposing that you consider the formation of a greater Communist Party, a Western response to Russia. ... the Liberal world-state" (Wells, 1932a, pp. 20-5).

And Wells notes, as he did in 1920, that Communism is run by Russian Jews: "That, you may say, is grandiose. It is not more grandiose than the Communist conception. At times recently I have asked myself, Are we really as much the intellectual and moral inferiors of that band of Russian Jews as we seem to be? Are we indeed, by comparison, nit-wits, feeble wills, and shysters?" (p. 26).

The above statements do not mean that Wells supported Mussolini or Hitler, but that he saw their movement as a recruiting-ground for his own. An 'enlightened Nazi' is not a Nazi, but someone who has converted from Nazism to the Modern State Movement. A 'liberal Fascist' is not a Fascist, but a former Fascist who converted to the Modern State Movement. The fact that he also called the organisation he hoped to build "a greater Communist Party" shows that he was not converting to Fascism or Nazism.

The above sentence of Wells, where he says that Bolshevism is led by Russian Jews, is cited by Coupland as evidence of Wells' antisemitism: "Strong hints to Wells's antisemitism were also apparent in his description of the Communist Party as 'that band of Russian Jews'" (Coupland, 2000, p. 79).

That is a ridiculous claim by Coupland, in view of the fact that Bolshevism WAS created by Jews; it only shows Coupland's own unreliability. Wells wrote reams of adulation for the Early Bolsheviks, and only mentioned their Jewishness in two places, and then fleetingly, whereas Bertrand Russell, who noticed the Jewishness in 1920 as did Wells, made a much stronger statement in his autobiography (Russell, 1920/1975, v. 2 p. 172).

A number of authors have wondered whether Wells supported a violent revolution, or only a peaceful one. They need only have consulted *The Outline of History*, where Wells condones the Kronstadt Massacre. He did not feel it necessary to devote more than a few words to it, making out that the Bolsheviks had no choice but to execute the sailors who, a few years earlier, had installed them in power. The 1931 and 1940 editions have the same text and the same page#s:

'In March, 1921, the Bolshevik government had to suppress, and did suppress, an insurrection of the sailors in Kronstadt, "'the Pretorian Guard of Bolshevism"' (Wells, 1931 & 1940, p. 1134).

Wells' *Outline of History* (1931 & 1940) makes no mention of the Ukraine Famine, or of the Concentration Camps—which were inaugurated by Lenin—or of the Red Terror, except where he says, "The old inquisitorial and tyrannous Tsarist police was practically continued under the new government" (Wells, 1931 & 1940, p. 1133). In fact, Bolshevik rule was much more ruthless than the Czar's had been.

Wells interviewed both Roosevelt and Stalin in 1934. The published transcript of the Stalin interview (Wells & Stalin, 1934/2008) makes no mention of the Ukraine Famine, or the Gulag, or the Terror.

But Wells' goal was to coax Stalin to accept fusion with the United States, so any probing questions would have been counter-productive.

In her book *My Life With Nye* (1980), Jennie Lee describes meeting H. G. Wells at a dinner party in 1929. He had no interest in the problems of ordinary people, but kept harping on about the teaching of history:

H. G. Wells was one of the bright guiding stars of my youth. I read avidly everything he wrote. That day in Parliament there had been a violent debate about all the issues that meant most to me—the cruelty and indignities of the Means Test, failure to get on with the building of urgently needed houses, schools and hospitals, and all this against a background of hundreds of thousands of unemployed building workers. I arrived at Great College Street brimming over with indignation. H. G. Wells brushed aside anything I tried to say, returning obsessively to the teaching of history in schools. We began glaring at one another with growing hostility. So this was H. G. Wells, this dumpy little man with the squeaky voice, totally indifferent to the problems that concerned the great mass of ordinary people . (Lee, 1980, p. 85)

Wells is best seen as a solitary Illuminatus who, by keeping his readers guessing about his true allegiance, was able to shape generations of 'Progressive' intellectuals. His novels reached even wider sectors of the reading public, and the films made from them are still shown today.

He seems to have divined the intent of the Left Billionaires and Progressives leading us toward One World today. At present we have a sort of 'Liberal Communism', Communism without public ownership, in which billionaire plutocrats such as George Soros and Larry Fink (chairman and CEO of Blackrock) impose Communist (read 'Trotskyist') social values with an increasing totalitarianism. It's Green Communism, not Red Communism.

Many people were deceived about Wells' agenda, but George Orwell was not one of them. His book *Nineteen Eighty-Four* is a response to Wells' World State.

Wells advocated a World Encyclopedia available to everyone for free

In 1936-38 Wells advocated a free World Encyclopedia available to everybody; he called it the World Brain. His initial model was Diderot's *Encyclopedie*; Wells' own *The Outline of History* (which sold 2 million copies) was an updated version of Diderot. It had the same goal as Diderot: indoctrination; Wells' own material was seeded with his atheistic, cosmopolitan values (Wells World Brain).

Wikipedia and Google implement that World Brain. They purport to provide unbiased knowledge, but censor views and persons they deem politically incorrect. Larry Sanger, co-founder of Wikipedia, described it as biased towards left-liberal policies (Flood, 2020). Interviewed by journalist Glenn Greenwald, Sanger that the CIA and FBI have been editing Wikipedia since 2008 (Durden, 2023).

Two Israeli Zionist groups run courses on Wikipedia editing to counter anti-Zionist viewpoints. Yesha Council, representing the Jewish settler movement, has thousands of members who post to Youtube, Facebook and other social media (Shabi and Kiss, 2010). As part of its hasbara strategy, the Israeli Foreign Ministry monitors foreign news and asks stations to change unfavourable news (Jones, 2001; thanks to DMcC).

Chapter 19: Stalin was Murdered within 2 months of the Doctors Plot

From the Bolshevik Revolution on, the Communist movement was polarised into two camps: a camp of covert Jewish domination—by atheistic Jews, followers of Spinoza's atheistic variant of Judaism—and a camp rejecting the idea that Jews represent the Working Class, or however else "the People" is defined.

The Bolshevik Jews did not represent "all Jews", any more than the Catholic destroyers of Inca South America represented "all Catholics"; but they *were* Jews.

There is nothing in Marxist theory that says that Jews will lead the Revolution and run the new government. Yet that is what happened in Soviet Russia; but the knowledge of this was suppressed. This camp became the Trotskyist camp. Even though the Trotskyist camp make anti-Zionist noises, and oppose the extremes of Zionism (e.g. Likud), they are nevertheless secretly pro-Zionist.

Stalin gained power using similar covert methods to his opponents—not announcing his intentions but just implementing them. He saw the Jewish domination as an alien coup, and saw himself as representing the genuine Russians in their quest for socialism.

Yet, he relied heavily on Jewish party members, both cabinet members like Beria and Lazar Kaganovich, and field workers like the Jews staffing the Cheka. Stalin's third and last wife was Rosa Kaganovich, sister of Lazar (and Jewish).

Stalin had Trotsky killed; yet Stalin himself was later killed in turn. He was intending to purge leaders closely involved in the scheme to make Crimea an autonomous Jewish republic funded by American Jews—Beria, Molotov, Mikoyan, Voroshilov and Voznesensky; they constituted the 'Zionist' faction in the leadership. This was what the Doctors Plot was about.

While Stalin was in power, the Trotskyists in the Soviet Union had to lie low. After Stalin's removal, Beria released many political prisoners, Trotskyists among them.

Anatoliy Golitsyn, in his book *New Lies For Old*, explains that Beria had a new policy: he wanted to let East Germany reunite with West Germany. In his early months of power, there was a flood of refugees from East Germany to the West, panicking the Party leaders. In consequence, they deposed him and installed Khrushchev, who had Beria executed.

Khrushchev denounced Stalin in 1956 to justify his murder and implicate his rivals in the Politburo (on which, see Appendix 5); but the denunciation backfired, leading to uprisings in Hungary and Poland, as a result of which Khrushchev partially returned to Stalinist methods.

Beria's policy can be seen as a forerunner of Gorbachev's.

Soviet Russia had been created by atheistic Jews, but Stalin overthrew them, stealing their conspiracy and developing a Russian (non-Jewish) kind of Communism. In the same way, the first Christians had been Jews, but through Paul (as against James) a non-Jewish kind of Christianity developed.

The Jewish Bolsheviks belatedly coalesced around Trotsky as leader of the "Left Opposition". Its three leaders, Trotsky, Kamenev and Zinoviev, were Jewish: Stalin said the Left Opposition was led by three "dissatisfied Jewish intellectuals" (Trotsky, 1937/1941).

Stalin was obsessed with Trotsky's challenge to him from abroad, via his books and his popularity amongst intellectuals, and feared that he might one day return to claim the leadership. His purges of the 1930s were directed primarily against Trotsky and his supporters; but many innocent people were dragged into the successive rounds of denunciations.

With the rise of Hitler, Stalin was seen as the lesser evil, so Jews continued to support the U.S.S.R. The creation of Israel, however, presented Jews with a rival loyalty; this began a Cold War between Moscow and Jerusalem. When Stalin observed how Soviet Jews rallied to Israel, Jews were gradually removed from the top positions they had held.

This struggle led to the murder of Stalin in 1953. The U.S.S.R. severed diplomatic relations with Israel on February 11 that year. Stalin was aware that a group of people was out to get him, but they got him before he could discover who they were. He died within 2 months of the Doctors' Plot being announced. His murderers were in two factions: a 'Zionist' one (Beria, Molotov, Mikoyan, Voroshilov and Voznesensky) and a 'Russian' one (Khrushchev, and probably Kaganovich, according to Stuart Kahan's biography *The Wolf of the Kremlin* (1987)). The 'Zionist' one seized power, but was overthrown a few months later by Khrushchev. For evidence that Stalin was murdered, see Appendix 5.

Mao saw himself as the 'Stalin' of China. He did not know that Stalin had been murdered, but when he saw how Stalin was repudiated, fearing that the same could happen to him, he inaugurated the Let 100 Flowers Bloom campaign to draw his enemies out.

Rejecting Khrushchev's moderate policies, which he branded 'Revisionist', he moved to the extreme Left, launching the Great Leap Forward. Its failure led to Mao's demotion; he was removed from the running of the economy, and left with a purely ceremonial role.

Liu Shaoqi and Deng Xiaoping opposed the Great Leap Forward; the party placed Liu in charge of the economy. To regain his power and unseat Liu and

Deng, Mao promoted the disastrous Cultural Revolution, mobilising young people into the Red Guards. Liu was a particular target. Finally, having wrecked China, Mao accepted Nixon's olive branch, delivered by Kissinger; the U.S.S.R. thus gained Vietnam (by winning the Vietnam war), but lost China, a much bigger prize.

In 1979, with Vietnam invading Cambodia (which China regarded as its back-yard), China invaded Vietnam (to force it to withdraw). Vietnam had just renewed a defence treaty with the U.S.S.R., a treaty from which China was excluded; China was testing that treaty. The U.S. warned the U.S.S.R. not to intervene—thus taking China's side. In the 1980s, China allowed the CIA to monitor Soviet nuclear tests from Xinjiang (Lardner & Smith, 1989).

After Mao's death, Deng Xiaoping visited Japan, and decided to move to-wards the Japanese economic model. But Japan's hierarchic society, culminating in the Keiretsu, was different from China's; China later found the South Korean chaebol a better model for it to follow. It also used Lee Kwan Yew's Singapore as a model, and invited overseas Chinese to help build the new China.

Simon Leys, a sinologist who studied China's Cultural Revolution, observed that the West itself is undergoing its own Cultural Revolution:

'A similar evolution seems to be taking shape in the West. In universities, the commissars of tomorrow question the legitimacy of disinterested research (the crime is to consider that an objective fact is more respectable than all ideologies), any study that cannot serve the dogmas of their propaganda is now condemned for being "irrelevant." ' (Leys, 1974/1977, p. 138).

"Almost certainly **we are moving into an age of totalitarian dictator-ships—an age in which freedom of thought will be** at first **a deadly sin** and later on a meaningless abstraction. The autonomous individual is going to be stamped out of existence" (p. 140).

"One can see what is wrong with the left-wing movement by the ugliness of their women" (p. 196).

Many of Leys' descriptions of the Cultural Revolution in China sound like the West's own cultural revolution—the Radical Feminism, Gay Pride, Children's Rights (which amounts to a diminution of parents' rights over their children), dumbing down, Political Correctness, "Hate Speech" laws. These mobilisations of various "minorities" are akin to Mao's use of the Red Guards in China. Ours is less intense but lasting longer:

"denouncing and tracking down beauty, grace" (p. 27);

"humiliations inflicted by children on their elders" (p. 47);

"young members of the new ruling elite have less culture than many illiterates or semiliterates under the old regime" (p. 141);

"deleting most of the history, language, and literature that are the foundations of culture" (p. 149);

"cretinizing the most intelligent people on earth" (p. 167);

"prefabricated jargon that is a substitute for thought" (p. 167).

Chapter 20: No Celebrations in 2017, but regret at Fall of U.S.S.R.

In 2017, there were no official ceremonies in Russia for the Centenary of the Bolshevik Revolution. That year, Russians avidly watched an antisemitic television series, 'Trotsky,' which depicted Trotsky as the instigator of the October Revolution (Trotsky TV Series).

Yet Putin had called the collapse of the Soviet Union "the greatest geopolitical catastrophe of the century." NBC News reported:

> Russian President Vladimir Putin told the nation Monday that the collapse of the Soviet empire "was the greatest geopolitical catastrophe of the century" and had fostered separatist movements inside Russia." (Soviet collapse, 2005)

And Putin also said, "Whoever does not miss the Soviet Union has no heart. Whoever wants it back has no brain." The Wall Street Journal said he made this statement in 2010:

> "Whoever does not miss the Soviet Union has no heart," Russian President Vladimir Putin famously said in 2010. But he quickly added, "Whoever wants it back has no brain." (Miller, 2010)

How to reconcile this apparent contradiction?

Gorbachev rehabilitated the victims of Stalin, including Sakharov and Trotsky's son Sergei Sedov but not Solzhenitsyn, and allowed the remaining Zionist Jews to leave. He removed the totalitarian aspects of Communism, leaving the good aspects—full employment, free education, free medical care, social equality, and a strong state able to resist American hegemony. This is what Russians remember when they mourn the fall of the Soviet Union.

The Soviet Ruble had been strong too. The New York Times reported on Sep 6, 1971 that 1 Ruble exchanged for U.S.$1.11:

> LONDON, Sept. 1—The Soviet Union took note of monetary upheavals in the capitalist world today with a token devaluation of the ruble against the Western currencies that have floated up to higher rates. ... Fifteen currencies were affected by the changes. The dollar was left unchanged at 90 kopecks to the dollar. From the standpoint of the ruble, the rate is one ruble (100 kopecks) equals $1.11. (Lee, 1971)

Official exchange rates of the sixth Soviet ruble (1961-1991) per U.S.$ were:
1982 1R = $1.4124
1984 1R = $1.2642
1987 1R = $1.4925 (Soviet Ruble, 2023).

After the fall of the Soviet Union, the Ruble plummeted:

"The ruble's exchange rate versus the U.S. dollar depreciated significantly from U.S. $1 = 125 RUR in July 1992 to approximately U.S. $1 = 6,000 RUR when the currency was redenominated in 1998." (Russian ruble, 2023).

Life expectancy plummeted too. Millions of Russians died in the new times of insecurity brought about by American advisers. That's why Russians feel betrayed by the West. In the wake of the betrayal of Eastern Europe—its impoverishment through bad economic advice (from the West) after the fall of Communism, and the West's opportunism in re-establishing Empire—a good side of Communism is once again being seen.

Valdas Anelauskas, a Lithuanian dissident in the late Soviet Union, moved to the United States, and discovered (1999) that he'd been duped:

> Today, after all these years of living here in the United States, I understand very well that all the bad things which Soviet propaganda told us about America were not, in most cases, lies at all. ... We heard about poverty, homelessness and unemployment, about consumerism and "trash culture," about violent crime and racial conflicts, but their manner of conveying the information was neither believable nor affective. ...
>
> Three times, I myself saw people shot on the subway. In fact, somebody was shot sitting almost next to me. In Brooklyn, the area where we lived—not the worst neighborhood, nothing to compare with Harlem or South Bronx—we could hear gunfire outside on the street almost daily. ... If you compare New York to European or even Canadian cities, it's like a hell on earth. All the big cities in the Soviet Union of twenty years ago— Moscow, Leningrad, Kiev—were completely safe at any time. I remember I could walk safely anywhere at night in Moscow. ... Before coming to the United States, I never could even imagine that a human society could be so thoroughly soaked with shameless deception and greed. (pp. 23-4)

Of course, his memories are of the late Soviet Union, after Gorbachev had got rid of the totalitarian features.

The year 2009 marked the 20th anniversary of the Fall of Communism in Eastern Europe. But there were no celebrations. Most people felt worse off. Industries had been shut down, unemployment had soared, insecurity was rife. Western companies saw the Eastern zone as an export market. As they brought their products in, local production fell. To pay for the imports, these countries sold assets, e.g. Latvia is largely owned by Western banks and other countries.

Chapter 21: Wells, Sakharov, Gorbachev and Convergence to World Government

H. G. Wells was the 20th Century's leading exponent of One World Government, which he also called The New World Order

He was a champion of minorities, yet his New World Order is totalitarian. He was a militant rationalistic atheist; religious people he deemed less mentally evolved, and therefore their ideas do not count. Whilst campaigning for Peace—by which he meant One World Government—he advocated any violent means necessary. His system would be run by an elite, which would attempt to make its rule eternal by suppressing all dissent and rival educational systems. He supported Communism as an ideal system, but criticised its implementation in the U.S.S.R. His Internationalism is really Trotskyism in a disguised form.

British Labour MP Michael Foot wrote (1995) a biography of Wells which omits to mention Wells' advocacy of World Government; nor is this term listed in the index of Foot's book. Foot, like Wells, gives the impression that Wells opposed Soviet Communism, but it would be more accurate to say that he opposed the Stalinist faction, but supported Trotsky. In 1929, when Stalin expelled Trotsky from the U.S.S.R., Wells and the Webbs sent him messages of support, and then lobbied to have him admitted to Britain; the Webbs even visited him.

Wells spelled out his ideas most clearly in the 1933 edition of *The Open Conspiracy*.

His aim is "a single world commonweal, preventing war" (Wells, 1933a, p. 30). But it may be "systems of world control rather than a single world state" (p. 32).

The method is "The Open Conspiracy, the world movement for the supercession or enlargement or fusion of existing political, economic, and social institutions ... a movement aiming at the establishment of a world directorate" (pp. 32-3).

It would not lead to a parliament of mankind, but rule by committees of experts:

"in a polyglot world a parliament of mankind or any sort of council that meets and talks is an inconceivable instrument of government. The voice will cease to be a suitable vehicle. World government, like scientific process, will be conducted by statement, criticism, and publication that will be capable of efficient translation. ... we should have the collective affairs of the world managed by suitably equipped groups of the most interested, intelligent, and devoted people" (p. 31).

The movement would be cosmopolitan: "We have to make an end to war, and to make an end to war we must be cosmopolitan in our politics" (p. 28). The early

U.S.S.R. gave high place to cosmopolitanism, but in Stalin's later years, 'cosmopolitan' became a codeword for Jews.

Eugenics is a core part of it: "Intelligent control of population is a possibility ... later, directed breeding will come" (p. 34).

The profit motive would cease: "removing credit and the broad fundamental processes of economic life out of reach of private profit-seeking and individual monopolization" (p. 44).

Despite the Marxist creed, Wells says the U.S.S.R. is run by an oligarchy. "In Russia, ... Marxism has been put to the test ... beneath this creed a small oligarchy ... has attained power" (p. 45).

Wells supports their grand plans, but thinks he can do it better: "The Five Year Plan is carried out as an autocratic state capitalism" (p. 45). The description of Stalin's system as "state capitalism" is a classic Trotskyist formulation.

Wells' Open Conspiracy is based in the West, and bankers are the leaders:

"And when we come to the general functioning classes, landowners, industrial organizers, bankers, and so forth, who control the present system, such as it is, it should be still plainer that it is very largely from the ranks of these classes, and from their stores of experience and traditions of method, that the directive forces of the new order must emerge" (p. 46).

More tribute to bankers:

"there remains a residuum of original and intelligent people in banking or associated with banking or mentally interested in banking, who do realize that banking plays a very important and interesting part in the world's affairs, who are curious about their own intricate function and disposed towards a scientific investigation of its origins, conditions, and future possibilities. Such types move naturally towards the Open Conspiracy" (Wells, 1933a, p. 46).

The Open Conspiracy will introduce the Millennium: 'the nearer draws its uprising, its constructive "dictatorship," and the Millennium' (p. 44).

Wells anticipates the decolonisation movement, freeing nations from the European empires. But then they will be swept up into the One World movement:

India, China, Russia, Africa present melanges of social systems ... the social traditions to which they will try to make the new material forces subservient will be traditions of an Oriental life ... They will have their own resistances to the Open Conspiracy ... To a number of the finer, more energetic minds of these overshadowed communities ... the Open Conspiracy may come with an effect of immense invitation. At one step they may go from the sinking vessel of their antiquated order, across their present conquerors, into a brotherhood of world rulers. They may turn to the problem of saving and adapting all that is rich and distinctive of their inheritance to the common ends of the race. But to the less vigorous intelligences of this outer world, the new project of the Open Conspiracy will seem no better than a new form of Western envelopment, and they will fight a mighty liberation as though it were a further enslavement to the European tradition. They will watch the Open Conspiracy for any signs of conscious superiority and racial disregard. Necessarily they will recognize it as a product of Western mentality. (Wells, 1933a, pp. 58-9)

Or should that be Jewish, perhaps? A replacement of Aryan rule with Jewish rule, as Harry Waton envisaged (see p. 164)? He wrote,

The Aryans will enlarge and beautify the earth; but they will settle to enjoy the world which they created only in the tents of the Jews. These tents are communism, internationalism, the universal brotherhood of man, the emancipation of the working class and the human society—a society of free and morally autonomous rational human beings. The destiny of the Aryans is to become Jews. (Waton, 1939, p. 102)

Wells claimed that the Bolsheviks had no interest in a World State:

"Marxism never had any but the vaguest fancies about the relation of one nation to another" (Wells, 1933a, p.60). But Lenin and Trotsky did advocate a world-state, which they called "a workers' republic".

The likening of Stalin's system to Czarism is a standard Trotskyist strategy: "the new Russian government, for all its cosmopolitan phrases, is more and more plainly the heirs to the obsessions of Tsarist imperialism, using the Communist Party, as other countries have used Christian missionaries, to maintain a propagandist government to forward its schemes" (Wells, 1933a, p. 60).

Soviet propaganda may be overpowered by Western propaganda:

Nevertheless, the Soviet government has maintained itself for more than twelve years, and it seems far more likely to evolve than to perish. It is quite possible that it will evolve towards the conceptions of the Open Conspiracy, and in that case Russia may witness once again a conflict between new ideas and Old Believers. So far the Communist party in Moscow has maintained a considerable propaganda of ideas in the rest of the world and especially across its western frontier. Many of these ideas are now trite and stale. The time may be not far distant when the tide of propaganda will flow in the reverse direction. It has pleased the vanity of the Communist party to imagine itself conducting a propaganda of world revolution. Its fate may be to develop upon lines that will make its more intelligent elements easily assimilable to the Open Conspiracy for a world revolution. (Wells, 1933a, p. 60)

If the Soviet government can be induced to join the Open Conspiracy, that can only come from the top, via a Gorbachev-type figure:

> Russia is a land of tens of millions of peasants ruled over by a little band of the intelligentsia who can be counted only by tens of thousands. It is only these few score thousands who are accessible to ideas of a world construction, and the only hope of bringing the Russian system into active participation in the world conspiracy is through that small minority. (Wells, 1933a, p. 61)

Yet Wells argued that his One World will be ruled by "an elite of intelligent, creative-minded people" (p. 45). So what's the difference from the Soviet system? Wells' target appears to be Stalin; he is a Trotskyist, despite calling his system "constructive liberalism".

Another smear likening Stalinism to Czarism:

> Marxism lost the world when it went to Moscow and took over the traditions of Tsarism ... Entrenched in Moscow from searching criticism, the Marxist ideology may become more and more dogmatic and unprogressive ... until the rising tide of the Open Conspiracy submerges, dissolves it afresh, and incorporates whatever it finds assimilable. (Wells, 1933a, p. 61)

This "dissolving afresh" represents the Trotskyist hope of destroying "socialism in one country", as happened under Gorbachev.

Wells anticipated the Activist groups of the 1960s-70s Culture War (Green, Gay, Feminist, Ethnic, Animal Rights):

> There should be many types of groups. Collective action had better for a time—perhaps for a long time—be undertaken not through the merging of groups but through the formation of ad hoc associations for definitely specialized ends, all making for the new world civilization. Open Conspirators will come into these associations to make a contribution. (Wells, 1933a, p. 72)

They will be cosmopolitan:

> "In this book we are not starting something; we are describing and participating in something which has started. ... its cosmopolitan character becomes imperatively evident" (p. 73).

A connection with the Illuminati movement?

> "Whenever possible, the Open Conspiracy will advance by illumination and persuasion" (p. 88).

The Open Conspiracy fights for Open Borders:

> the movement is bound to find itself fighting for open roads, open frontiers, freedom of speech, and the realities of peace in regions of oppres-

sion. The Open Conspiracy rests upon a disrespect for nationality, and there is no reason why it should tolerate noxious or obstructive governments because they hold their own in this or that patch of human territory. It lies within the power of the Atlantic communities to impose peace upon the world and secure unimpeded movement and free speech from end to end of the earth. (Wells, 1933a, p. 89)

It will take control of Education; but a Resistance will develop:

While the Open Conspiracy is no more than a discussion it may spread unopposed because it is disregarded. As a mainly passive resistance to militarism it may still be tolerable. But as its knowledge and experience accumulate and its organization becomes more effective and aggressive, as it begins to lay hands upon education, upon social habits, upon business developments, as it proceeds to take over the organization of the community, it will marshal not only its own forces but its enemies. A complex of interests will find themselves restrained and threatened by it, and it may easily evoke that most dangerous of human mass feelings, fear. ... The establishment of the world community will surely exact a price—and who can tell what that price may be?—in toil, suffering, and blood. (Wells, 1933a, pp. 90-1)

In 1934, Wells interviewed both Roosevelt and Stalin. He was trying to persuade them to coalesce into a World State; he described the encounter thus:

Stalin is an exceptionally unsubtle Georgian. ... I not only attacked him with the assertion that large scale planning by the community, and a considerable socialization of transport and staple industries, was dictated by the mechanical developments of our time, and was going on quite as extensively outside the boundaries of Sovietdom as within them, but also I made a long criticism of the old-fashioned class-war propaganda ... I said that ... technicians, scientific workers, medical men, skilled foremen, skilled producers, aviators, operating engineers, for instance, would and should supply the best material for constructive revolution in the West, but that the current communist propaganda, with its insistence upon a mystical mass directorate, estranged and antagonised just these most valuable elements. Skilled workers and directors know that Jack is not as good as his master. Stalin saw my reasoning, but he was held back by his habitual reference to the proletarian mass ... I tried to get back to my idea of the possible convergence of West and East upon the socialist world state objective, by quoting Lenin as saying, after the Revolution, "Communism has now to learn Business," and adding that in the West that had to be put the other way round. Business had now to learn the socialization of capital—which indeed is all that this Russian Communism now amounts to. It is a state-capitalism with a certain tradition of cosmopolitanism. (Wells, 1934/1969, pp. 806-7)

Wells elaborated the scenario for drawing the U.S.S.R. back in, in his book *The Shape of Things to Come* (1933/1979). In that book he called his movement the 'Modern State' Movement:

> The method of treaty-making and a modus vivendi was already in operation in regard to Russia. There indeed it was hard to say whether the Communist party or the Modern State Movement was in control, so far had assimilation gone. And the new spirit in the old United States was now so 'Modern' that the protests of Washington and of various state governors against the Controls were received hilariously. Aeroplanes from Dearborn circled over the capital and White House and dropped parodies of the President's instructions to dissolve the Air and Food Trust of America. All over that realist continent, indeed, the Controls expanded as a self-owned business with a complete disregard of political formalities. But the European situation was more perplexing. (p. 364)

Wells wrote (1933a, p. 61) that the Soviet Union could only be changed from the top. Mikhail Gorbachev told interviewer Daniel Yergin in 2001 that this is exactly what happened: "Starting reforms in the Soviet Union was only possible from above, only from above. Any attempt to go from below was suppressed, suppressed in a most resolute way" (Yergin, 2001/2022).

Well's One World ideas bore fruit in 1946, when the U.S. Government proposed the Baruch Plan to the Soviet Union. On the surface, it was merely about a body to limit Nuclear Weapons; but discussions in the Bulletin of the Atomic Scientists also portrayed it as a potential World Government. Stalin turned it down (Myers, 2019a).

David Ben-Gurion claimed that 'uniting the world', which he advocated and predicted, was a particularly Jewish idea. Invited in 1962 to predict what the world would be like in 25 years' time, he wrote in Look Magazine of January 16, 1962:

> The image of the world in 1987 as traced in my imagination: the Cold War will be a thing of the past. ... continents will become united in a world alliance, at whose disposal will be an international police force. All armies will be abolished, and there will be no more wars. In Jerusalem, the United Nations (a truly United Nations) will build a shrine of the Prophets to serve the federated union of all continents; this will be the scene of the Supreme Court of Mankind, to settle all controversies among the federated continents, as prophesied by Isaiah. Higher education will be the right of every person in the world. A pill to prevent pregnancy will slow down the explosive natural increase in China and India. And by 1987, the average life-span of man will reach 100 years. (Ben-Gurion, 1962)

Note that he predicted that Eastern Europe would be torn from the Soviet sphere and joined with Western Europe in a body like the E.U. Ben-Gurion was a Communist but obviously not a Stalinist, hence in Trotsky's camp. His policy is called 'Convergence'; that is, to One World.

Convergence to One World was a Zionist/Trotskyist idea which influenced Gorbachev, and which destroyed the Soviet Union. The aim was to seize control of the U.S.S.R. from the Stalinists, while securing the West for 'Marxist' values of the early Bolshevik period: Gay Rights, Feminism, the abolition of Marriage, cultural revolution, minorities against the majority.

Andrei Sakharov put a

David Ben-Gurion (Prime Minister of Israel) : "The image of the world in 1987 as traced in my imagination : The Cold War will be a thing of the past. Internal pressure of the constantly growing intelligentsia in Russia for more freedom and the pressure of the masses for raising their living standards may lead to a gradual democratization of the Soviet Union. On the other hand, the increasing influence of the workers and farmers, and the rising political importance of men of science, may transform the United States into a welfare state with a planned economy. Western and Eastern Europe will become a federation of autonomous states having a Socialist and democratic regime. With the exception of the USSR as a federated Eurasian state, all other continents will become united in a world alliance, at whose disposal will be an international police force. All armies will be abolished, and there will be no more wars. In Jerusalem, the United Nations (a truly United Nations) will build a Shrine of the Prophets to serve the federated union of all continents; this will be the seat of the Supreme Court of Mankind, to settle all controversies among the federated continents, as prophesied by Isaiah. Higher education will be the right of every person in the world. A pill to prevent pregnancy will slow down the explosive natural increase in China and India. And by 1987, the average life-span of man will reach 100 years."

similar Convergence scenario to that articulated by Ben-Gurion, in books published in the West in the late 1960s and early 1970s, gaining a reputation as one of the Soviet Union's leading dissidents. Yet there was a great difference between his view and that of Alexander Solzhenitsyn.

Solzhenitsyn repudiated the entire regime, from the time of Lenin on, denouncing Lenin as the originator of all the evils; whereas Sakharov proclaimed himself a Marxist, and shielded Lenin from blame. He seems to make no mention of Trotsky, but it can be inferred that he was in the Trotskyist camp.

Sakharov was officially pardoned on December 9, 1986, soon after Gorbachev gained power. The New York Times reported on Dec. 20, 1986:

"Andrei D. Sakharov, the physicist who was banished to the city of Gorky for his support of human rights causes, is free to return to Moscow, the Soviet Union announced today. At the same time, Dr. Sakharov's wife, Yelena G. Bonner, a human rights campaigner who was convicted of anti-Soviet activities in 1984, was pardoned" (Taubman, 1986).

But treason charges against Solzhenitsyn were only dropped in September 1991, a month after Gorbachev fell in August 1991. Subsequent to the dropping of charges, Solzhenitsyn announced that he would return to Russia. The New York Times reported on September 18, 1991:

"The chief prosecutor of the Soviet Union said today that he was dropping treason charges against Aleksandr I. Solzhenitsyn, removing the last legal obstacle for the Russian writer to return to his homeland after 17 years in exile. Mr. Solzhenitsyn, living in exile in Vermont, has said he will return after charges were dropped. But he indicated today that he would not return to Russia immediately" (Rosenthal, 1991).

During Yeltsin's eight years of chaos, Solzhenitsyn came to side with the upholders of order, and approved Putin; and Putin, on winning the Presidential election, visited him, in what amounted to a mutual endorsement.

Sakharov, like Ben-Gurion, worked for Convergence between the Soviet Union and the West, resulting in World Government. This meant seizing control of the U.S.S.R. from the Stalinist faction, and restoring it to the Trotskyist faction.

But for the U.S.S.R. to dock with the West, the U.S. had to have a Government brimming with Fabian World Federalists—such as the Clinton Government. Just before leaving office, Bill Clinton signed the U.S. up to join the Interational Criminal Court, which George W. Bush annulled on taking power.

When the U.S.S.R. fell in 1991, however, the United States was run by the Republican Party, and Britain by the Tories, who were in no mood to share power. From the time when Zbigniew Brzezinsky was National Security Adviser in the late 1970s, the United States had pursued a policy of covert guerilla war against the U.S.S.R., organising the Moslems in Afghanistan and the Catholics in Poland in their conflicts with the U.S.S.R.

What of Gorbachev? He pursued many of Sakharov's policies, condemned Stalin, spoke highly of Lenin, wrote repeatedly about a World Civilisation, allowed Jews to emigrate, allowed George Soros' Foundations to operate, and attended Shimon Peres' 80th birthday party. This suggests that he is in the Zionist/Globalist/Trotskyoid camp.

Early in his Presidency, he rehabilitated Bukharin, to be a model for his pro-Market reforms as well as his anti-Stalinism.

He allowed Trotsky's books to be published, and rehabilitated Trotsky's son Sergei Sedov, but gave an anti-Trotsky speech on November 2, 1987, to mark the 70th anniversary of the Bolshevik Revolution. However, Gorbachev could not come out publicly as a Trotskyist. Russians regarded Trotskyism as a heresy; even in 2017, the centenary of the Revolution, there was no support for Trotsky. Russians know that Stalin defeated the Bolshevik Jews who imposed the Red Terror, even though such facts are suppressed in the West.

Admittedly, Gorbachev allowed more freedom than one would expect of a Trotskyist, and was a gentler, kinder person. He was not DIRECTLY a Trotskyist, but INDIRECTLY he was, via Sakharov. It is Sakharov's defence of early Bolshevism, rejection of Stalin, and aspiration for World Government, which marks him as a Trotskyist. Gorbachev followed his line.

Gorbachev followed Andrei Sakharov's ideas on East-West Convergence towards World Government. Anatoliy Golitsyn garbled the story; he thought that the Convergence idea emanated from Moscow; in fact it was brewed up in the West.

Gorbachev said that his aim was to "transfer power to the Soviets". This meant taking power from the Communist Party (CPSU) and giving it to the soviets (councils elected by workers in a show of hands). It's what Daniel Cohn-Bendit called for in 1968, in his book *Obsolete Communism: the Left-Wing Alternative*.

Gorbachev got rid of the totalitarian aspects of Communism, leaving the good side, e.g. full employment and a publicly owned economy (no oligarchs). But, anticipating a deal with the West to form a World Government along the lines of the Baruch Plan (World Peace, a nuclear-free world), he dismantled the Soviet Union. The West betrayed him, sending advisers who destroyed the Russian economy.

Sakharov (1968/1976) bundled Mao with Hitler and Stalin:

Mankind can develop smoothly only if it looks upon itself in a demographic sense as a unit, a single family without divisions into nations other than in matters of history and traditions. (p. 42)

The salvation of our environment requires that we overcome our divisions and the pressure of temporary, local interests. (p. 44)

An extreme reflection of the dangers confronting modern social development is the growth of racism, nationalism, and militarism and, in particular, the rise of demagogic, hypocritical, and monstrously cruel dictatorial police regimes. Foremost are the regimes of Stalin, Hitler, and Mao Tse-tung ... (p. 45)

Sakharov mapped out a four stage plan for Convergence between East and West, leading to World Government. Note that 'leftist Leninist Communists' means 'Trotskyists':

> In the first stage, a growing ideological struggle in the socialist countries between Stalinist and Maoist forces, on the one hand, and the realistic forces of leftist Leninist Communists ...

> In the second stage, persistent demands for social progress and peaceful coexistence in the United States and other capitalist countries ... will lead to the victory of the leftist reformist wing of the bourgeoisie, which will begin to implement a programme of rapprochement (convergence) with socialism, i.e., social progress ...

> In the third stage, the Soviet Union and the United States, having over-come their alienation, solve the problem of saving the poorer half of the world. The aforementioned twenty per cent tax on the national income of developed countries is applied. ...

> In the fourth stage, the socialist convergence will reduce differences in so-cial structure, promote intellectual freedom, science, and economic pro-gress and lead to the creation of a world government and the smoothing of national contradictions (Sakharov, 1968/1976, pp. 75-7).

Convergence involves synchronisation. If the timing is wrong, it fails—and it has failed. The West, on the one hand, and Russia and China on the other, have now swapped sides. The West is now the 'Communist' force destroying the past and imposing a world state, while Russia and the East are preserving traditional culture.

After the Soviet Union fell in 1991, Mikhail Gorbachev founded the Green Cross. He came out, not as a Red Communist, but as a Green one.

He teamed up with Maurice Strong and Steven C. Rockefeller (son of Nelson Rockefeller, and nephew of David) to draft the UN's Earth Charter. Maurice Strong was Secretary-General of the 1992 Earth Summit in Rio de Janeiro. Strong and Gorbachev were board members of the Club of Rome—founded at the home of David Rockefeller, in Italy.

In his 'River of Time' speech, Gorbachev (1992) spoke of the need for 'some kind of global government', and called for the U.N. to have its own military forces:

> More than 46 years ago Winston Churchill spoke in Fulton and in my country this speech was interpreted as the formal declaration of the "Cold War." ... the world community which had at that time already established the United Nations, was faced with a unique opportunity to change the course of world development, fundamentally altering the role in it of force and of war. ...

So I would like to commence my remarks by noting that the U.S.S.R. and the U.S. missed that chance ... I am not suggesting that they should have established a sort of condominium over the rest of the world. ...

An awareness of the need for some kind of global government is gaining ground, one in which all members of the world community would take part. Events should not be allowed to develop spontaneously. There must be an adequate response to global changes and challenges. If we are to eliminate force and prevent conflicts from developing into a worldwide conflagration, we must seek means of collective action by the world community. ...

The Security Council will require better support, more effective and more numerous peace-keeping forces. Under certain circumstances it will be desirable to put certain national armed forces at the disposal of the Security Council, making them subordinate to the United Nations military command. ...

Mikhail Gorbachev
President of Green Cross International
Earth Council (Gorbachev, 1992)

The Earth Council was an NGO created in September 1992 to implement agreements reached at the U.N. Earth Summit of 1992.

The Earth Charter (United Nations, 2000) is a vague document with some high-sounding principles which lend themselves to many interpretations. If implemented by Green fundamentalists, it could lead to a genocide of most of the human population. Agreeing to it would be like signing a blank contract, leaving the details to be supplied later by other persons.

Innocent-sounding phrases like "every form of life has value" could lead to the outlawing of meat-eating, of hunting, of culling, and even of keeping animals. The "inherent dignity of all human beings" could lead to the outlawing of abortion, voluntary euthanasia, and war. Agreeing to "prevent environmental harm" could lead to the outlawing of agriculture. "Responsibility to promote the common good" raises the use of the Responsibility To Protect (RTP) doctrine to justify the Western invasion of Libya and the murder of Gaddafi.

The Charter wants to "guarantee human rights and fundamental freedoms", yet the same Left want to classify conservative views as 'Hate', and censor them.

Ensuring a "livelihood that is ecologically responsible" could outlaw the harvesting of native trees to build houses. "Special concern for biological diversity" could stop many developmental projects, even wind farms and hydro dams; this even though nature has survived great extinctions in the past, with new species developing afterwards.

"Nature and biosphere reserves, including wild lands and marine areas" could outlaw fishing, and lock up land excluding any use by people.

"Take action to avoid the possibility of serious or irreversible environmental harm even when scientific knowledge is incomplete or inconclusive" could stop most development projects, even benign ones.

"Place the burden of proof on those who argue that a proposed activity will not cause significant harm, and make the responsible parties liable for environmental harm" could stop most development projects.

"Ensure that decision making addresses the ... long-term ... and global consequences of human activities" could authorise Green fundamentalists to genocide most of humanity.

"Prevent pollution of any part of the environment" sounds straightforward, but nearly all activity pollutes in some way; e.g. organic agriculture using manures.

"Allow no build-up of radioactive, toxic, or other hazardous substances" could stop nuclear power, as an alternative to fossil fuels.

Adopting "patterns of ... reproduction that safeguard Earth's regenerative capacities, human rights, and community well-being" would take away our right to have children.

"Right of indigenous peoples to ... lands and resources" could force everyone else off the land.

"Prevent cruelty to animals... and protect them from suffering" could outlaw farming.

The Earth Charter "was created by the independent Earth Charter Commission, which was convened as a follow-up to the 1992 Earth Summit in order to produce a global consensus statement of values and principles for a sustainable future. The document was developed over nearly a decade through an extensive process of international consultation, to which over five thousand people contributed. The Charter has been formally endorsed by thousands of organizations, including UNESCO and the IUCN (World Conservation Union)" (United Nations, 2000).

It says that it is a consensus document, but it surveyed the views of only five thousand people, clearly a Green minority, and would impose them on 8 billion, in the name of "consensus".

Chapter 22: H. G. Wells founded the Green Left

Wells is well-known for his science fiction, and this may lead many people to overlook his intellectual power. His books, both fiction and non-fiction, sold in the millions, and he seeded them with his Globalist ideology, so that it was imbibed unconsciously. He was the first person to envisage war in the air, and the first to imagine the atomic bomb. *A Modern Utopia*, written in 1905, envisages high-speed rail:

> No doubt the Utopian will travel in many ways. It is unlikely there will be any smoke-disgorging steam railway trains in Utopia, they are already doomed on earth, already threatened with that obsolescence that will endear them to the Ruskins of to-morrow, but a thin spider's web of inconspicuous special routes will cover the land of the world, pierce the mountain masses and tunnel under the seas. These may be double railways or monorails or what not—we are no engineers to judge between such devices—but by means of them the Utopian will travel about the earth from one chief point to another at a speed of two or three hundred miles or more an hour. (Wells, 1905, p. 45)

He educated a generation of intellectuals, yet he himself was not an academic. He'd never been to university, but this gave his writing the common touch. I personally shrink from Trotsky's Globalism but, despite my scepticism, I find myself enticed by Wells' version.

Wells, alone of all the intellectuals of his time, in 1898 took the side of the Tasmanian aborigines against the British. In his novel *The War of the Worlds*, he made the British fearful of invading Martians—a 1938 radio broadcast of it by Orson Welles created panic among listeners, who thought it was real-time— and then Wells told them that THEY were the Martians:

> And before we judge them too harshly, we must remember what ruthless and utter destruction own species has wrought, not only upon animals, such as the vanished bison and dodo, but upon its own inferior races. The Tasmanians, in spite of their human likeness, were entirely swept out of existence in a war of extermination waged by European immigrants, in the space of fifty years. Are we such apostles of mercy as to complain if the Martians warred in the same spirit? (Wells, 1898/1975, p. 11)

In 1905, his *Modern Utopia* featured a "synthesis of all nations, tongues and peoples in a World State" (p. 343); "a world-wide synthesis of all cultures and polities and races into one World State" (p. 344).

"It is to be a world Utopia, we have agreed, no less; and so we must needs face the fact that we are to have differences of race. Even the lower class of Plato's Republic was not specifically of different race. But this is a Utopia as wide as Christian charity, and white and black, brown, red and yellow, all tints of skin, all types of body and character, will be there" (pp. 23-4).

He accused the European powers of exterminating native peoples. Posing the question, is there really an inferior race?, he answered that his Modern Utopia would exterminate its own defective and inferior strains, regardless of race, but that in race terms it would be neutral (p. 339).

He enumerates ways of exterminating a race: the Biblical version, against the occupants of Palestine; the Spanish method, working it to death; poisoning it with junk food, as the Americans do with their Indians; and honest simple murder, "as we English did with the Tasmanians" (p. 338). Utopia's euthanasia of its own undesirables comes out preferable by comparison.

He doubts, however, that there is such a thing as an all-round inferior race.

"Even the Australian black-fellow is, perhaps, not quite so entirely eligible for extinction as a good, wholesome, horse-racing, sheep-farming Australian white may think. These queer little races, the black-fellows, the Pigmies, the Bushmen, may have their little gifts, a greater keenness, a greater fineness of this sense or that, a quaintness of the imagination or what not, that may serve as their little unique addition to the totality of our Utopian civilisation" (p. 339).

In *The New Machiavelli* (1911), he came out against urban sprawl. When the railway arrives in Bromstead, the Ravensbrook stream, with its bulrushes, kingfishers, ducks, and fish, becomes a dump for old iron, rusty cans, and abandoned boots. (pp. 36-8).

In 1932 he wrote that only a World Government would protect native peoples:

"It is really cannibalism that is occurring; not indeed the devouring of one man by another but the devouring of one human society by another. Whole populations have been and their remnants are still—now while the reader sits over this book—being tormented and crushed to produce salable products, very much in the same fashion as the penguins of the Southern ocean are massacred and crushed for marketable oil. There is no Humanity, no Homo sapiens, embodied in a world government to protect them; there are only competing sovereign states, not concerned by their extirpation" (Wells, 1932b, p. 665).

Also in 1932, in the ominously-titled *After Democracy*, he envisaged his World Government irrigating deserts and restoring forests:

It is really nothing more than what our statesmen and men of affairs are feeling their way towards to-day—too timidly and slowly, I fear—with their Debt conferences, the Bank of International Settlements, and so forth. As World Dictators, you or I can travel faster. They have to go slowly because they have to follow the spread of new ideas. We Dictators can lead ideas. My World Economic Council would make a Twenty Years' Plan for the reorganization of the world's production and distribution. It would not smash down all the tariff walls at once—that might lead to frightful convulsions—but it would set about reducing them methodically, organizing the transport of the world by sea and land and air as one system, assigning types of cultivation and manufacture to the most favourable regions, possibly shifting workers to new regions of employment, irrigating deserts, and restoring forests. (Wells, 1932a, p. 196)

In 1933 he spoke of "the earth, our Mother Earth, our earth and yours":

We are constituting a Bureau of Transition, for the simplification and modernization of the business activities, the educational and hygienic services, production, distribution and the preservation of order and security throughout our one home and garden, our pleasure ground and the source of all our riches—the earth, our Mother Earth, our earth and yours. (Wells, 1933/1979, p. 370)

In 1934 he advocated an 'ecological' stance in school textbooks

From the biological point of view my Professors would be human ecologists; indeed Human Ecology would be a good alternative name for this new history as I conceive it. ... Sooner or later Human Ecology under some name or other, will win its way to academic recognition and to its proper place in general education—in America sooner than in Europe, I guess—but the old history made up of time-worn gossip and stale and falsified politics, is deeply embedded in literature and usage. (Wells, 1934/1969, p. 647)

Giving a lecture in Canberra, Australia in 1939, Wells condemned the harvesting of forests, the loss of animal species, the dust bowl in the United States, and the bushfires and rabbits of Australia. He spoke like a Green of the year 2020:

"This was his new departure in the Canberra lecture of 1939:

What spendthrift ancestors we have had! What wastrels we still are! And all because history teaches us no better. Man burns and cuts down forests, he destroys soil, he acclimatises destructive animals. A map of the world showing the devastated regions, where devastation is due to mankind, would amaze most people. It ought to be put in every child's atlas. A history of the devastation of the world, due to planless exploitation is far nearer the reality of things than this amiable history some teachers want to teach. In the past two years you have seen great regions of the United States turned to sandy desert, you have seen Australia swept by fires, rickburning and rabbits. You have seen a slaughter of scores of useful animal species, you have seen a monstrous destruction of natural resources." (Foot, 1995, p. 258)

In 1940, in *The New World Order* (another ominous title), he wrote against destruction of forests, and killing off whales and rare species:

> The new power organisations are destroying the forests of the world at headlong speed, ploughing great grazing areas into deserts, exhausting mineral resources, killing off whales, seals and a multitude of rare and beautiful species, destroying the morale of every social type and devastating the planet. The institutions of the private appropriation of land and natural resources generally, and of private enterprise for profit, which did produce a fairly tolerable, stable and "civilised" social life for all but the most impoverished, in Europe, America and East, for some centuries, have been expanded to a monstrous destructiveness by the new opportunities. (Wells, 1940/2017, p. 19)

Wells' stance on overpopulation is the most controversial: he endorses Malthus. No matter what well-meaning governments do, they are defeated by the sheer mass of humanity: "An overwhelming flood of newcomers poured into the world and swamped every effort the intelligent minority could make" (Wells, 1922, p. 55).

Anticipations (1902/1999) faces the issue head-on:

> Malthus ... brought clearly and emphatically into the sphere of discussion a vitally important issue that had always been shirked and tabooed heretofore, the fundamental fact that the main mass of the business of human life centres about reproduction. ... Probably no more shattering book than the Essay on Population has ever been, or ever will be, written. ... it aimed simply to wither the Rationalistic Utopias of the time and by anticipation, all the Communisms, Socialisms, and Earthly Paradise movements ... it awakened almost simultaneously in the minds of Darwin and Wallace, that train of thought that found expression and demonstration at last in the theory of natural selection. (p. 162)

Wells says that Evolution theory destroys Christianity:

"Darwin destroyed the dogma of the Fall upon which the whole intellectual fabric of Christianity rests. For without a Fall there is no redemption" (p. 163).

However, the Zoroastrian concept of the Fall—that it occurred in Heaven with rebellious angels, and had nothing to do with Adam and Eve—is not vulnerable to Darwin. Christianity had two different concepts of the Fall, one Zoroastrian, one Semitic. In the same way, the Book of Genesis records two contrary accounts of Creation: chapter 1 is Zoroastrian; chapter 2 (Adam and Eve) is Semitic.

In *Anticipations* (1902), Wells had advocated the involuntary euthanasia of "base and servile types" (pp. 167-8), but in subsequent books he only argued that they should be stopped from procreating.

On this account, some critics have branded Wells a Nazi. Yet in *A Modern Utopia* he lampoons Cecil Rhodes (p. 344) and John Ruskin (p. 101), and his World State would be a racial melting-pot. Further, the book (1905) is online at the Trotskyist website marxists.org.

Wells' State would pay women to have children (p. 188); but the State would be in charge of them. It would provide pensions to all who need them, and aged-care homes (p. 141).

Wells was the first writer to envisage the atomic bomb. Martin Gardner described the impact, in his Introduction to the 1914 Dover Edition of *Anticipations*:

> It was in his 1914 novel The World Set Free that Wells made his most astounding hit. Dedicated to Frederick Soddy for his pioneer research on radium, the novel opens with a moving extract from the diary of a physicist who has found a way to split the atom and release atomic energy. He is fearful of the consequences of his discovery, but realizes that, had he not made it, other physicists soon would. The novel describes a war between England and Germany, in the middle of the twentieth century, during which "atomic bombs," as Wells actually called them, were dropped from airplanes. (Gardner, 1999, pp. iii-iv)

Leo Szilard actually used Wells' ideas when working out how to make the bomb:

> In 1914, Wells published The World Set Free, and when Szilard read the novel, in 1932, he saw science and politics in a new and frightful alliance. ... Wells's novel predicted—correctly—that artificial radioactivity would be discovered in 1933. Although Szilard regarded the book as fiction at the time, it jarred his thinking about war and peace and science, then and for years to come. (Lanouette & Silard, 1994, p. 107)

> Suddenly the H. G. Wells novel he had read a year before had a grave new meaning. Atomic bombs were science fiction to Wells when he wrote The World Set Free in 1913, and they were frightful to contemplate when Szilard first read about them in 1932. But by the fall of 1933, Rutherford's challenge and Szilard's response were moving atomic bombs away from fiction to scientific fact. Atomic bombs, and the chain reaction that would power them, became Szilard's "obsession," pushing aside his plans for a new career in biology. (Lanouette & Silard, 1994, p. 134)

Szilard was also impressed with Wells' case for an Open Conspiracy, and created his own movement, which he called the Bund:

> Szilard called his organization the Bund, to his mind a closely bound alliance of like-minded young people. When Szilard brainstormed with Polanyi about the Bund, he praised The Open Conspiracy: Blueprints for a World Revolution by H. G. Wells and thought that the first twenty pages

of this book, which was published in 1928, posed succinctly the problems that the world faced. (Lanouette & Silard, 1994, p. 96)

After Hiroshima, Szilard promoted the Baruch Plan to control nuclear energy, with World Government lurking in the background, and contributed (with other nuclear scientists and philosophers, many Jewish) to the book *One World or None*, issued in 1946.

The motto "One World or None" is the basic mantra of the Green Left. It applies not only to nuclear annihilation, but to Global Warming, Resource Depletion, Biodiversity, Overpopulation, and other ecological issues. One may therefore call Szilard one of the founders of the Green Left; but Wells was the main one.

In recent decades, Trotskyist and other Marxist groups have appropriated the 'Green' label.

The above quotes from Wells show that he was the first person to articulate the Green Left creed. However, today's crop of Greens and EcoMarxists give him scant credit.

Until the 1970s, Marxists had no interest in ecology; since then, Trotskyist groups have taken up 'EcoSocialism', grafting 'green' ideas onto Marxism.

The Green Left operates at both the Elite level (following Wells, Leo Szilard and David Rockefeller) and the Street level (dedicated to Marx and Trotsky). Most Trotskyist sites repudiate Wells, but marxists.org honours him as a Utopian Socialist.

The newspaper Green Left Weekly began in 1991, as the successor to Direct Action. Both were published by the Democratic Socialist Party, which had been the Socialist Workers Party until a name change in 1989. The DSP now calls itself Socialist Alliance.

The DSP practised entrism, i.e. penetration of other groups (e.g. the Nuclear Disarmament Party) and operated a Popular Front strategy with green/feminist/gay groups. Green Left Weekly is a Popular Front-type newspaper, a watermelon paper, green on the outside and red in the inside. Its heroes are Trotsky and Gramsci. It regards H. G. Wells as elitist, and does not acknowledge him as progenitor.

The SWP used to called itself 'Trotskyist'; but the DSP stopped using that label when it ceased regarding Trotsky, not Lenin, as the true leader of the Bolshevik Revolution.

Right up to his death, Trotsky insisted that the U.S.S.R. was a "degenerated workers' state" and should be defended; he hoped to return. But from the time of the Soviet-German Pact, his supporters split over the U.S.S.R. and the regimes it spawned.

The Pabloites, led by Michel Pablo, continued to defend such states, including Eastern Europe and Castro's Cuba; the Shachtmanites, led by Max Shachtman, broke with the U.S.S.R. and those other states. James Burnham went further than Schachtman, dumping Marxism altogether. Shachtman had arranged Trotsky's move from Norway to Mexico. After Trotsky's murder by Stalin, his widow Natalia became a Schachtmanite.

Michael Hudson visited the Anti-Defamation League (ADL), and reported, "These were old Schachtmanites who had become ultra-rightists" (Hudson, 2005).

What is the difference between Trotskyists and Anarchists? (Libertarians are also called 'anarchists', but they must be excluded here; they are socially conservative and oppose Covid-19 Vaccine Mandates). Both are anti-Stalin and anti-fascist; both don masks to participate as 'Antifa'. Trotskyists are Globalists who want a World State; they favour Speech Codes. Anarchists have a more local orientation and dislike oppressive government; they sometimes committ violent acts.

During the Spanish Civil War, the 1919 Madrid congress of the violent Anarchist—actually Anarcho-Syndicalist—Confederación Nacional del Trabajo (CNT) voted provisionally to join the Comintern. A different delegation from the CNT helped found the Red Trade-Union International. They later pulled back from both, repelled by the totalitarian nature of Soviet Russia. Anarchists (the violent kind) destroyed many churches and killed thousands of priests and nuns in Spain.

The Democratic Socialist Party, Socialist Alliance and most other Trotskyist groups today no longer hold Trotsky to have been the leader of the October Revolution (over Lenin), but they are Trotskyist by a broader definition as one who sides with Trotsky against Stalin, and promotes Trotsky's 'ultra-left' cultural revolution. Trotsky put his position clearly in his 1936 book *The Revolution Betrayed*, in which he accused Stalin of rehabilitating God and the Family. The Feminist, Gay, Green and Black liberation movements have substantial Trotskyist ancestry.

Bettina Arndt, an Australian sex-therapist, considered herself Feminist in the 1970s, but has since mounted a one-woman campaign against the excesses of that movement. She has opposed their sex-war against men.

In 2018, she gave talks at Australian universities in which she denied that there is an epidemic of rape on Australian campuses. She was asking why our higher education sector is lying about the safety of our universities for young women, even after the Australian Human Rights Commission survey showed over 99% of students said they hadn't experienced sexual assault. Through her action, university 'kangaroo court' committees face legal action over unfair treatment of accused male students. (Arndt, 2018).

At several campuses, screaming students bullied and harassed the audience and prevented them from accessing the venue. At Sydney University, Bettina

called the police. The group which ran the protest was called the Women's Collective. A photo shows a young woman shouting into a megaphone, a metre from Bettina; behind the young woman are some supporters holding a big banner. The banner reads "Smash Sexism"; at the top are the words "Socialist Alternative".

Socialist Alternative is a Trotskyist group.

Others who were radical leftists in their younger days but have now come out against the excesses of those movements include David Horowitz and Norman Podhoretz.

Daniel Cohn-Bendit was called "Dany the Red", and later became a Green politician, but even in 1968, despite the "Green" and "Anarchist" labels, he was a Marxist. BBC News reported on June 11, 1968:

French student rebel arrives in UK
French student rebel leader Daniel Cohn-Bendit has arrived in Britain stirring up fears of campus unrest. [...]

In Context {On this Day} Daniel Cohn-Bendit's stay in Britain was extended to 14 days during which time he and a group of supporters visited Karl Marx's grave where they sang the protest song Internationale. (Daniel Cohn-Bendit)

Václav Klaus, former president of the Czech republic, warned that Cohn-Bendit's Manifesto for a Green E.U. was Marxist: "They are co-founders of the movement Europeans Now, the so-called Young Europeans: "Unite!" This catch-phrase is a deliberate rephrasing of Marx's *Communist Manifesto* and its appeal "Workers of the world, unite!" and it clearly points in the same direction. Modern leftist radicals, not only of the red sort but nowadays more often of the green one too, are now trying to revive the horrors that were brought into being as a result of the Manifesto and its appeal, with its tens of millions of victims of the Communist social-engineering project which in the end, after a long time (alas! much too long a time!), collapsed almost a quarter of century ago — these people are trying to revive all this by means of the European Union" (Klaus, 2013).

John Laughland elaborated on Klaus' wake-up call:

> The libertarian ideology of 1968 had a massive influence in Western Europe in the 1980s and 1990s, when those who had been students in the 1960s came to power. But it is often forgotten that such people were often anti-Soviet because anti-Stalinist. Like Trotsky, they hated Stalin for his social conservatism and for having abandoned the project of world revolution. Although orthodox (pro-Moscow) communist parties remained strong in various countries across Western Europe, the future political class which started to wield power and influence in Europe in the 1980s came largely from the various anti-Soviet communist movements which had so prospered in the West. I am thinking of people like Cohn-Bendit himself, who denounced les crapules staliniennes of the CGT Trade Union in 1968; the anti-Stalinist former communist, Bernard Kouchner, who became Foreign Minister of France under the supposedly pro-free-market Nicolas Sarkozy; the former Maoist leader, José Manuel Barroso, now president of the European Commission; and intellectuals like the former Maoists, Bernard-Henri Lévy and André Glucksmann. Jürgen Habermas, prophet of the end of the nation-state and a product of the neo-Marxist anti-Soviet Frankfurt School, is also a case in point.

> Just as the anti-Soviet left was completing its long march through Western institutions, a similar movement was taking place in the East. Critical Marxists (critical, that is, of the actual regimes in power in Eastern Europe and the Soviet Union, but not critical of Marxism as such) played a key role in discrediting the practice of communism in Eastern Europe while upholding much of the theory. Many of the leading dissidents, especially those popular in the West, were leftists. Such people continue to be fêted today—the Sakharov Prize is awarded by the European Parliament to icons of political correctness like Nelson Mandela, Alexander Dubcek, Ibrahim Rugova, Reporters Without Borders and so on—while patriotic anti-communists like

Solzhenitsyn or Alexander Zinoviev have been dropped down the memory hole. ...

So broad and deep has this movement been, one might even say that Trotsky's expulsion from the U.S.S.R. in 1929, and his subsequent emigration to the West where he lived until 1940, has proved to be more of a spark igniting the ideology of world revolution than Lenin's arrival at the Finland Station was. It is certainly true that the post-national, one-world ideology of John Lennon has proved more powerful, in West and East, than the same ideology peddled by Vladimir Lenin. The events of 1989, therefore, did not mark the victory of conservatism over communism but instead of international liberalism over more or less nationalist socialism. As a poster in a Prague shop window in 1989 eloquently pointed out, "89" is nothing but "68" turned round. (Laughland, 2013)

Materialist Assumptions of Wells and the Green Left

Alfred Russel Wallace, after whom the Wallace Line is named, was a biologist who co-developed Evolution theory with Charles Darwin, and whom Wells mentioned alongside Darwin (see p. 274); but he believed in the reality of spirits, seances, clairvoyance and miracles (Wallace, 1874). He engaged in hypnosis, and studied pyschic phenomena; he came to believe in guided evolution (Flannery, 2020). The elite said that he "lost caste" with such views. Theosophists also assert the reality of a spiritual dimension: they say that material evolution occurs in a different dimension from spiritual evolution. I too believe in the reality of occult matters; I have experienced Telepathy (which I learned from a Rosicrucian lesson), Clairvoyance (during a Tarot reading, the only one I ever had; the Reader called up a spirit who gave a correct forecast and warning of an event in my life), and Witchcraft (the bad kind).

Evolution Theory usually depicts life arising on Earth by spontaneous generation. The Big Bang is usually taken as gospel. Dissident positions are suppressed.

Astrophysicists Fred Hoyle and Chandra Wickramasinghe challenge both of the above. They claim that the universe is eternal, without beginning or end, and that life on any planet is seeded from elsewhere in the cosmos, by bacteria and viruses in comets and meteorites. They claim that Life comes only from Life, not from Non-Life, i.e. they uphold the ontological distinction between Living and Non-Living Matter. In their books they call this cosmic lifeforce 'Panspermia'. But the BBC never gave them a TV series in which to present their case to the public.

Astronomer Halton C. Arp was the new Galileo who disproved the "Redshift equals distance" assumption of the Big Bang theory. Arp was Edwin Hubble's assistant; working at the Mt. Palomar and Mt. Wilson observatories in the U.S., he discovered that many pairs of quasars (quasi-stellar objects) which have extremely high redshift z values, and are therefore thought to be receding from us very rapidly, and thus located at a great distance from us, are physically associated with galaxies that have low redshift and are known to be relatively close by. Arp's photos disproved the assumption that high red shift objects have to be very far away. The Big Bang theory is therefore falsified and, with it, all "accepted cosmology". In the U.S., Arp was refused telescope time and denied publication of his results; he moved to the Max Planck Institute in Germany. So much for the cult of "Science".

In 1976, a Seventh Day Adventist pastor taught me the art of water-divining; In 2015 I watched a water-drilling company locate a site for a bore on my neighbour's land. The owner of the company used divining rods to locate the water and tell the depth and direction of the stream; he said their success rate was over 90%.

But according to Wikipedia, dowsing is a pseudoscience; so is Acupuncture. The Supreme Court of Israel, having been built by the Rothschild family, is sited over Ley Lines, which Wikipedia also brands a pseudoscience.

My term for this hyper-rationalism is 'Dogmatic Scepticism'. It's rampant in Academia. Universities are prominent in the Fact-Checking business; they have become part of the Ministry of Truth. Victor E. Frankl wrote, "The true nihilism of today is reductionism" (Frankl, 1969, as cited in Schumacher, 1978, p. 14).

All past civilizations have treated the mind as the foundation of human life. Every religion begins with consciousness: notions of spirits, ghosts, gods and goddesses are based on a view that consciousness is pre-eminent. Yet the post-Christian West, now Marxist/Illuminist, denies the reality of psychic powers, and proclaims a materialistic philosophy no different from that of the Soviet Union.

Some Heart Transplant recipients take on the Donor's personality (Pearsall, 1999; Sylvia & Novak, 1997). It's inexplicable by the materialist paradigm.

David M. Armstrong, a prominent materialistic philosopher, began his book on Metaphysics with these words:

"I begin with the assumption that all that exists is the spacetime world, the physical world as we say. What argument is offered for this assumption? All can say is that this is a position that many—philosophers and others—would accept. Think of it this way. This is a hypothesis that many would accept as plausible. The space-time entity seems obviously to exist. Other suggested beings seem much more hypothetical. So let us start from this position" (Armstrong, 2010, p. 1).

It did not occur to him that there might be a reality to clairvoyance, seances, Tarot readings, witchcraft, psychic surgery, Near-Death Experiences, telepathy, or exorcism. He just assumed a materialistic, reductionist position. Would it not be appropriate for a Philosopher of Mind to study such phenomena? If he had done so—avoiding the charlatans—he might have discovered another dimension.

Christian fundamentalists depict these spiritualist or 'New Age' psychic powers as satanic; they also depict water-divining as satanic. I admit that (evil) witchcraft and satanism are real and dangerous; but whether Satan is a real being, an evil god, the chief of demons, I do not know. Occult practices are not always harmful if one is wary and limits them. One famous atheist in Soviet Russia was so astonished at truths revealed in seances, that he became a monk, then an Archbishop, and ended up as Confessor of Vladimir Putin. His name is Archimandrite Tikhon, and he wrote the story in his book *Everyday Saints and Other Stories* (2012).

In 1987, when in the Philippines, I visited a Psychic Surgeon and saw him perform bloodless operations on patients without using instruments. My contacts in the Philippines were sceptical, and tried to dissuade me, but I was able to find out this healer's address, and called on him. He had patients queued up as in a doctor's surgery. In the operating room, there was a statue of Jesus of Nazareth, recumbent on a sofa. I have never seen such a recumbent statue before or since.

They do perform surgery; it is not just a matter of faith. He opened his patient's stomach with his bare hands, removed something, then closed the wound with his fingers. There was no blood. He sprinkled a disinfectant over the wound. Such healing occurs in other cultures too, e.g. Pachita Hermanito was a non-Christian psychic surgeon in Mexico.

Jesus of Nazareth would seem to have been a shaman too. The Jewish Talmud calls him a magician or sorceror. Peter Schafer writes (2007) in his book *Jesus in the Talmud*:

"On (Sabbath eve and) the eve of Passover Jesus the Nazarene was hanged (telduhu). And a herald went forth before him 40 days (heralding): Jesus the Nazarene is going forth to be stoned because he practiced sorcery (kishshef) and instigated (hissit) and seduced (hiddiah) Israel (to idolatry). Whoever knows anything in his defense, may come and state it. But since they did not find anything in his defense, they hanged him on (Sabbath eve and) the eve of Passover" (p. 64).

Surely the accusation of magic/sorcery attests to his healing practices.

My rule is: if the result is good, the healer is good. A shaman from Colombia's Inga tribe blessed people during a Bishops' conference. I see nothing wrong with that; only Fundamentalists do.

The New Age proclaims that wicca is the religion of the goddess, turning a blind eye to evil witchcraft, and welcoming all the occult forces that Christianity had suppressed; it has thus opened a Pandora's Box. Yet ancient civilisations distinguised between good and evil occult forces. In both ancient Babylon (Black & Green, 1992, pp. 124-7, 186) and Egypt (Bentresh Stela), religious leaders warned of the dangers of evil demons and evil witchcraft, and exorcism was practised.

Chapter 23: Where Orwell was Wrong

George Orwell's novel *Nineteen Eighty-Four* has never been out of print; the Covid-19 Plandemic and the Great Reset gave it a new lease of life,

During the early years of the Cold War, this book played a role akin to Solzhenitsyn's *The Gulag Archipelago*, in exposing the tyrannical aspects of the Soviet Union.

From the 1980s on, as the Soviet Union declined, Orwell's *Nineteen Eighty-Four* alerted conservatives to the tyrannical aspects of the Progressive movement in the West itself. U.N. Agenda 21, U.N. Agenda 30, the Covid-19 Pandemic and the Great Reset seemed intended to inaugurate H. G. Wells' World State—which he also called 'Cosmopolis'.

Cosmopolitanism would overcome patriotism. We would give up our sovereignty to stave off nuclear annihilation, or environmental devastation, or pandemics.

Wells had been inspired by Old Bolshevism—the first decade of the Soviet Union, before Stalin took over. He debated Churchill over its merits, and sustained the faith of Fabians Sidney and Beatrice Webb and George Bernard Shaw in the new regime.

Wells encouraged his readers (fiction and non-fiction) to transfer their allegiance from nation-states to the World State; and called the movement to accomplish it the Open Conspiracy. The 60s Movement, continued as the 70s Movement, was a Cultural Revolution in the West which seemed to fulfil Wells' predictions of the Open Conspiracy.

Two other leftist authors, Aldous Huxley and George Orwell, reacted to Wells' utopian claims for the World State by writing dystopian novels, depicting the World State as run by a self-chosen oligarchy enforcing its rule by either Dumbing Down the masses with drugs, sex and entertainment (Huxley) or by imposing Thought-Control via politically-correct language (Orwell).

We seem to have both now. Orwell's Newspeak is imposed by Hate Laws criminalising the old terminology.

Huxley wrote *Brave New World* in 1931; he said that it was a reply to the utopian novels of H. G. Wells. In a letter to Mrs. Kethevan Roberts, dated 18 May 1931, Huxley (1931/1969) wrote, " I am writing a novel about the future — on the horror of the Wellsian Utopia and a revolt against it.".

Just after George Orwell published *Nineteen Eighty-Four* , Huxley wrote to him, noting that H. G. Wells' utopian novel *The Shape of Things to Come* was a reply to *Brave New World*, published two years after it.

Huxley depicted Wells' World State as a nightmare in which a small clique of "alphas" dominates moronic underclasses; whereas Wells had depicted the World State as classless.

Orwell depicted the totalitarian threat as coming from the Left. In the 1930s and 1940s, Progressive newspapers in the West were pro-Soviet, and suppressed Orwell's denunciations, just as they suppressed reports of the Ukraine Famine.

In the post-Soviet era, Orwell is also seen as depicting the totalitarian threat as coming from the Left. But which Left? Orwell, a Trotskyist until he converted back to Christianity just before his death (he chose a Christian funeral), could only depict the threat as coming from Stalinist forces—INGSOC was to be a new version of Stalinism.

From the 1960s, however, the Cultural Revolution in the West has been anti-Stalinist. The 1960s-70s protest movements, e.g. Paris 1968, were led by Trotskyists, Anarchists and Maoists. Since then, the Maoists have mostly retired from the fray; the Anarchists have split into Greens (who support Speech Codes and compulsory vaccination) and Libertarians (who oppose them). The Trotskyists and Greens, together forming the Green Left, have set the agenda of the Cultural Revolution. However, they have not done so in a centralised way like the old Communist Party, but rather with dispersed networks of activists and sects.

In academia, humanities faculties have fallen prey to the Frankfurt School and Gramsci's Long March Through the Institutions. Both were supporters of Old Bolshevism. Together they have sought to deconstruct Western Civilisation; the universities are now seminaries of subversion.

Tax-free Foundations funded by major corporations have promoted the same Cosmopolitan agenda.

The media preaches, and Companies enforce, 'diversity and inclusion', but such agendas side with 'minorities' (e.g. the Trans movement) against the majority. Only 'populists' support the majority, now branded 'deplorables'.

Yet none of these groups back Stalin; his crimes are now almost as well known as Hitler's. Herbert Marcuse wrote a book denouncing Stalin; Erich Fromm wrote a book praising Trotsky.

As the sins of Stalinism and Maoism became better known, their supporters in the West have died away. But one group did not die away—the Trotskyists, because they denounced the Stalinist Soviet Union for the murder of their hero. They felt that their time was coming, to bring about a new version of Old Bolshevism. It chimed with Wells' Cosmopolitan World State.

Never mind that Trotsky, during his years in power, had helped found the Red Terror, had justified that Red Terror in a book, had executed millions of Russians defending the old order, and had ordered the Kronstadt Massacre of sailors, sons of peasants, who rebelled when they realised that Communism meant tyranny.

Orwell's ideas for *Animal Farm* and *Nineteen Eighty-Four* came partly from his experience fighting the Stalinist Republican forces during the Spanish Civil War.

During that war, George Orwell fought for the Trotskyist militia, P.O.U.M. Their headquarters was the Lenin Barracks. *Homage to Catalonia* begins with this sentence:

"In the Lenin Barracks in Barcelona, the day before I joined the militia, I saw an Italian militiaman standing in front of the officers' table." (Orwell, 1938/2021, p. 3).

P.O.U.M. proposed that Trotsky be offered asylum in revolutionary Catalonia; this would have increased the Soviet determination to destroy them.

The war was a three-way struggle among Franco, Trotsky and Stalin. Not that Trotsky was directly involved; but if his supporters had won the war, or won an independent state in Barcelona, Trotsky would have had a fortress from which to fight Stalin, with a view to overthrowing him and returning to power in the Soviet Union one day. This, Stalin felt that he could not allow.

But Orwell acknowledges another influence on his dystopian writings about the Soviet Union: Yevgeny Zamyatin's novel *We*. Zamyatin wrote this book in Russia in 1923, setting it centuries in the future (perhaps to allay the censors), but it was clearly inspired by his experience of Old Bolshevism—Trotsky's as much as Lenin's. His book, disguised as one about the future, depicts dehumanising values the author discerned in the early years of Bolshevism.

Orwell never admitted that those early years (before Stalin took over) were tyrannical; he dated the tyranny from the time Stalin took over. Yet in making *Nineteen Eighty-Four* as an updated version of *We*, he was inadvertently undermining his own naive Trotskyism.

The censors refused to allow the publication of *We* in the Soviet Union until 1988, under Gorbachev.

Paul Owen, writing in The Guardian, said that Orwell's *Nineteen Eighty-Four* "owes its plot, characters and conclusion to Yevgeny Zamyatin's 1920s novel *We*":

1984 thought crime? Does it matter that George Orwell pinched the plot?

George Orwell's Nineteen Eighty-Four is a classic — but it owes its plot, characters and conclusion to Yevgeny Zamyatin's 1920s novel We.

Orwell reviewed We for Tribune in 1946, three years before he published Nineteen Eighty-Four. In his review, he called Zamyatin's book an influence on Aldous Huxley's Brave New World, though Huxley always denied anything of the sort. "It is in effect a study of the Machine," Orwell wrote of We, "the genie that man has thoughtlessly let out of its bottle and cannot put back again. This is a book to look out for when an English version appears." He seems to have taken his own advice. ...

Foreign editions released in Zamyatin's lifetime led to his being banned from publishing, and eventually he wrote to Stalin to ask permission to live abroad. It was granted, and he left Russia for ever in 1931. He died six years later.

The characters in We are numbered rather than named: its Winston Smith is D-503, and its Julia I-330. Its Big Brother is known as the Benefactor ...

So does it matter that Orwell borrowed plot and characters from the earlier book? After all, it seems clear that he made a superior work of literature out of them. ...

In addition, unlike We, Nineteen Eighty-Four is written with expert control in an accessible style about a world recognisably our own, and its twists of plot—including the existence (or not) of the Brotherhood resistance movement—are gripping, sophisticated and convincing. The dark, pessimistic tone of Nineteen Eighty-Four is also all Orwell's. (Owen, 2009)

Sego Le Stradic wrote that Zamyatin's We inspired Brave New World as well as Nineteen Eighty-Four:

Zamyatin, Huxley And Orwell: Troubling Similarities

... Orwell praised Zamyatin and acknowledged his masterpiece for inspiring his 1984. ...

Huxley, on the other hand, never admitted to have read We before writing Brave New World and denied it as being a source of inspiration.

We's plot sets the reader in the future, in a society ruled by oppression and mechanical order. People are reduced to numbers and have no freedom. Zamyatin himself, summarises his dystopia in the novel- "Those two, in paradise, were given a choice: happiness without freedom, or freedom without happiness. There was no third alternative." The individual will of the main character, D-503, strives to defy the oppressive system as he meets and falls in love with a member of the resistance.

The depth of Zamyatin's insight is twofold. Firstly, he foresaw a close representation of what the situation in U.S.S.R. would become under Stalin long before it actually happened ... (Le Stradic, 2017)

That last comment expresses the usual ignorance in the Left, about the nature of (pre-Stalin) Old Bolshevism, the usual denial of totalitarianism right from the start of the regime. Zamyatin was under no such illusion.

Orwell reviewed *We* for Tribune, three years before he wrote '1984':

Review of "WE" by E. I. Zamyatin [Evgeny Ivanovich Zamyatin]

Several years after hearing of its existence, I have at last got my hands on a copy of Zamyatin's We, which is one of the literary curiosities of this book-burning age. Looking it up in Gleb Struve's Twenty-Five Years of Soviet Russian Literature, I find its history to have been this:

Zamyatin, who died in Paris in 1937, was a Russian novelist and critic who published a number of books both before and after the Revolution. We was written about 1923, and though it is not about Russia and has no direct connection with contemporary politics--it is a fantasy dealing with the twenty-sixth century AD—it was refused publication on the ground that it was ideololgically undesirable. A copy of the manuscript found its way out of the country, and the book has appeared in English, French and Czech translations, but never in Russian. The English translation was published in the United States, and I have never been able to procure a copy: but copies of the French translation (the title is Nous Autres) do exist, and I have at last succeeded in borrowing one. So far as I can judge it is not a book of the first order, but it is certainly an unusual one, and it is astonishing that no English publisher has been enterprising enough to reissue it.

The first thing anyone would notice about We is the fact—never pointed out, I believe—that Aldous Huxley's Brave New World must be partly derived from it. Both books deal with the rebellion of the primitive human spirit against a rationalised, mechanised, painless world, and both stories are supposed to take place about six hundred years hence. The atmosphere of the two books is similar, and it is roughly speaking the same kind of society that is being described though Huxley's book shows less political awareness and is more influenced by recent biological and psychological theories.

In the twenty-sixth century, in Zamyatin's vision of it, the inhabitants of Utopia have so completely lost their individuality as to be known only by numbers. They live in glass houses (this was written before television was invented), which enables the political police, known as the "Guardians", to supervise them more easily. They all wear identical uniforms, and a human being is commonly referred to either as "a number" or "a unif" (uniform). They live on synthetic food, and their usual recreation is to march in fours while the anthem of the Single State is played through loudspeakers. ...

So far the resemblance with Brave New World is striking. But though Zamyatin's book is less well put together—it has a rather weak and episodic plot which is too complex to summarise—it has a political point which the other lacks. In Huxley's book the problem of "human nature" is in a sense solved, because it assumes that by pre-natal treatment, drugs and hypnotic suggestion the human organism can be specialised in any way that is desired. A first-rate scientific worker is as easily produced as an Epsilon semi-moron, and in either case the vestiges of primitive instincts, such as maternal feeling or the desire for liberty, are easily dealt with.

Zamyatin's book is on the whole more relevant to our own situation. In spite of education and the vigilance of the Guardians, many of the ancient human instincts are still there. (Orwell, 1946a)

Orwell, a Trotskyist, made Trotsky the hero in both *Animal Farm* and *Nineteen Eighty-Four*. In *Animal Farm*, the horse Snowball is modelled on Trotsky; in *Nineteen Eighty-Four*, the underground leader Goldstein is modelled on Trotsky:

" ... the face of Goldstein ... was a lean Jewish face, with ... a small goatee beard" (Orwell, 1954, p. 13).

Personally, I find this depiction of Trotsky-as-hero offensive, because Trotsky helped set up the Red Terror.

Orwell should have known better; but his view of the U.S.S.R. was being shaped by Trotsky, whose organisation Orwell was a member of. James Burnham was in it too; but in *The Managerial Revolution* he acknowledges that the U.S.S.R. was only briefly the Workers' State Trotsky told the public it had been (before Stalin). Workers took over factories, but lacked expertise and managerial skills, so Lenin installed Technicians and Managers to run them. The Specialists and Managers, although not owning property, administered the State and thus attained a privileged life. In 1920-21, Trotsky advocated the militarization of labor, i.e. the conscription of workers into labor armies, the opposite of Workers' Control.

Goldstein (the hero who resists Big Brother) is Jewish.

Joseph Nedava (5732/1972) writes in his book *Trotsky and the Jews*:

This realization, apparently, was also what psychologically motivated George Orwell to give a Jewish coloring to the Opposition in his nightmarish Oceania in 1984. In this book the leader of the Opposition and the writer of "The Book" (The Theory and Practice of Oligarchical Collectivism), which attempts to answer the un-answerable question of "Why?," is Emmanuel Goldstein. "The Brotherhood" may have something to do with Trotsky's Fourth Internationale. It should also be recalled that Orwell was a member of the Trotskyite P.O.U.M. during the Spanish Civil War in the 1930s, and he was certainly acquainted with Trotsky's writings. Deutscher is of the opinion that "it was from Trotsky-Bronstein that he [Orwell] took the few sketchy biographical data and even the physiognomy and the Jewish name for Emmanuel Goldstein; and the fragments of 'the book,' which take up so many pages in 1984, are an obvious, though not very successful, paraphrase of Trotsky's The Revolution Betrayed." 27 (p. 175)

Endnote 27 (to the above) on p. 268 reads "I. Deutscher, *Russia in Transition* (New York, 1960), p. 261."

Today, with the "*Holocaust Industry*" (Finkelstein, 2000), and laws against "Hate speech" which define it in terms of subjective criteria (someone feels offence), those who criticise Judaism and Jewish power feel that they are taking on the Thought Police—a nice reversal of roles compared to the scenario in *Nineteen Eighty-Four* —but more like the situation in Soviet Russia before Stalin.

During the Cold War, readers of *Nineteen Eighty-Four* in the West identified the terror with the U.S.S.R. The book was a potent weapon which made its readers fear the U.S.S.R.

It shows how much Trotskyists hated Stalin. A whole swag of Anti-Communists broadly sympathetic to Marxism, or Zionism, or a World State—Jews like Arthur Koestler, non-Jews like Orwell, H. G. Wells, and Bertrand Russell—could never admit that Stalin had wrested control from the atheistic Jews. This is one of the great Denials of our time.

Even then, Stalin relied on Jews to help run the U.S.S.R. and, later, the East European satellites. But he stole their conspiracy. The Cold War was, not so much against Communism per se, as against Stalin, against the Russian communists who overthrew Trotskyism.

Trotsky kept from his Western followers, his own role in setting up the Red Terror. And that it was set up by a faction of atheistic Jews. Those followers did not bother to find out the facts.

Had Trotsky retained power, they would have been his apparatchiks and fellow-travellers in the West, and acting together they may have delivered us to a World State.

The forced collectivisation that Stalin implemented was actually a policy of Trotsky. It failed in Ukraine, and was not implemented in Eastern Europe, where farms remained in private hands.

So Stalin is a hero, but only in a negative way. He gave them a taste of their own medicine. Both Trotsky and Stalin lived by the sword and died by the sword.

If Orwell's book was only about the Soviet Union, it would be little read today. But close scrutiny shows that Orwell is warning us about OUR OWN SOCIETY. Here. Now.

Orwell's novel *Nineteen Eighty-Four* is set in Britain in the future, AFTER Nazism & Communism. And it's based on INGSOC, the acronym for "English Socialism". This is the ruling system in Oceania, i.e. the Anglo-American block.

O'Brien's Inquisitor says to him:

"Later, in the twentieth century, there were the totalitarians, as they were called. They were the German Nazis and the Russian Communists. The Russians persecuted heresy more cruelly than the Inquisition had done. And they imagined that they had learned from the mistakes of the past; they knew, at any rate, that one must not make martyrs. Before they exposed their victims to public trial, they deliberately set themselves to destroy their dignity. They wore them down by torture and solitude until they were despicable, cringing wretches, confessing whatever was put into their mouths ... And yet after only a few years ... The dead men had become martyrs and their degradation was forgotten. ... In the first place, because the confessions that they had made were obviously extorted and untrue. We do not make mistakes of that kind." (Orwell, 1954, p. 204)

As Progressive Left movements and Governments have imposed Speech Codes and other Political Correctness, they are fulfilling Orwell's prediction:

" ... a heretical thought—that is, a thought diverging from the principles of Ingsoc—should be literally unthinkable, at least so far as thought is dependent on words ... excluding all other meanings ... This was done partly by the invention of new words, but chiefly by eliminating undesirable words and by stripping such words as remained of unorthodox meanings." (p. 241)

"What was required in a Party member was an outlook similar to that of the ancient Hebrew who knew, without knowing much else, that all nations other than his own worshipped 'false gods'. (p. 246)

"History had already been rewritten, but fragments of the literature of the past survived here and there, imperfectly censored, and so long as one retained one's knowledge of Oldspeak it was possible to read them. ... A great deal of the literature of the past was, indeed, already being transformed." (p. 250)

In the novel, 1984 is the year the Dictatorship becomes entrenched:

"In the year 1984 there was not as yet anyone who used Newspeak as his sole means of communication, either in speech or in writing." (p. 241)

"In 1984, when Oldspeak was still the normal means of communication, the danger theoretically existed that in using Newspeak words one might remember their original meanings." (Orwell, 1954, p. 250)

Ironically, it is largely Trotskyist movements that have spearheaded these changes in the West.

Karl A. Wittfogel wrote on the same lines as Burnham, but his book *Oriental Despotism* bundles the civilisations of the Ancient World into the same 'tyrannical' basket as Stalin's Soviet Union.

He acknowledges a debt to Burnham:

"a. Social science is indebted to James Burnham for pointing to the power potential inherent in managerial control. The present inquiry stresses the importance of the general (political) organizer as compared not only to the technical specialist (see Veblen, 1945: 441ff.), but also to the economic manager. This, however, does not diminish the author's appreciation of the contribution made by Burnham through his concept of managerial leadership." (Wittfogel, 1957, p. 48, footnote a)

Once a Communist of the anti-Stalinist (Trotskyist) camp, Wittfogel turned against not only Stalin but also Marx, Lenin and Trotsky. For Wittfogel as for Arthur Koestler, the Nazi-Soviet Pact of 1939 was the final straw.

Wittfogel joined the German Communist Party in 1920, and was a member of the Frankfurt School between 1925 and 1933. Its other leading members were Jewish, and Wittfogel fits the pattern of Jewish Bolsheviks who abandoned ship through Stalin's seizing power. Evidence of Jewish ancestry or identity has not been presented, but the Christian religion was sometimes a cover for Jews who had assimilated but retained a Jewish identity. Leo Amery, part-author of the Balfour Declaration, is a modern example of a covert Jew.

Wittfogel says that Lenin criticised the Tsar's regime as an Asiatic Despotism, but before 1917 Lenin changed his tune and even acknowledged that the next revolution might bring an "Asiatic Restoration".

On p. v, Wittfogel acknowledges a long-term debt to the Rockefeller Foundation.

He writes,

Marx generally overstated the oppressiveness of Oriental society, which he held to be a system of "general slavery." Ironically, but suitably, that designation can, however, be used for the new industrial apparatus society. We can truly say that the October revolution, whatever its expressed aims, gave birth to an industry-based system of general (state) slavery. (Wittfogel, 1957, p. 441).

He attributes the "Asiatic Restoration" in the U.S.S.R. to the Tatar legacy acquired during centuries of conquest by the East.

At no point does he acknowledge the Jewish domination of the early U.S.S.R. This could be crucial for understanding the despotism—I believe it derives not from the Tatars but from the fundamentalist Judaism of the East-European Jewish communities (who had not assimilated, unlike the Jews of Western Europe).

If Soviet despotism had derived from the Tatar legacy, it would have been expressed under the Czarist regime. But the Czars' death toll was much less than the Communists'; and the leniency of the Czar's prisons was shown by the ease with which Bolshevik prisoners were able to escape. Trotsky was even allowed to write a book when in the Czar's jail at Odessa.

The Israeli Professor and dissident Israel Shahak repeatedly says in his book *Jewish History, Jewish Religion: The Weight of Three Thousand Years* (1994), that Judaism has a totalitarian streak (on pp. 10, 15, 16, 18, 19, 102, and 103).

The Jewish religion's harsh condemnation of pagans (goyim or "the nations"), its insistence on separation from them, its depiction of God's People's unending battle with its opponents—these are the origin of the hardness.

If this be the source, then it might offer the prospect of a less-severe Managerial State one day, not burdened by this Jewish bitterness or, equally, by a "white separatist" prejudice.

Joseph Needham (1959) panned Wittfogel, in his review of *Oriental Despotism*.

He acknowledged that hydraulic civilisation had functioned in ancient Egypt, ancient Mesopotamia, India, Sri Lanka, and the Incas, but defended those civilisations from the accusation of general slavery.

He notes that that slavery was never dominant in China; that no priesthood dominated there; that the Chinese bureaucracy could make poets and scholars into officials; that Wittfogel played down the examination system and played up the eunuchs (as the shock-troops of bureaucracy).

Needham concludes that a high degree of bureaucratic government seems quite inevitable given the technological complexities of modern society. Voltaire and other Enlightenment intellectuals also paid tribute to Chinese civilisation.

Ancient Greeks, such as Herodotus, respected Egypt and Babylon, and acknowledged that they derived much of their own civilisation from them. It's only the Biblical view that condemns them all outright (just as it erroneously says that the Pyramids were built by slaves—Hebrew slaves).

Burnham's idea of Managerialism drew upon a book by another Trotskyist, Bruno Rizzi. Trotsky himself addressed the issue, in his essay The U.S.S.R. In War:

> Recently, an Italian 'left communist,' Bruno R., who formerly adhered to the Fourth International, came to the conclusion that 'bureaucratic collectivism' was about to replace capitalism. (Bruno R.—La bureaucratisme du monde. Paris, 1939, 350pp.) The new bureaucracy is a class, its relations to the toilers is collective exploitation, the proletarians are transformed into the slaves of totalitarian exploiters. Bruno R. brackets together planned economy in the U.S.S.R., Fascism, National Socialism, and Roosevelt's 'New Deal.' ... Like many ultra lefts, Bruno R. identifies in essence Stalinism with Fascism. (Trotsky, 1939)

Bruno Rizzi presented his ideas in his book *The Bureaucratisation of the World* (1939).

George Orwell adopted some of Burnham's ideas, e.g. about the three blocs engaged in endless wars, in his book *Nineteen Eighty-Four*. Burnham's bundling of the New Deal with the totalitarian regimes also seems to have influenced Hayek in his book *The Road to Serfdom*, published in 1944.

None of these authors showed any awareness that the U.S.S.R. had been set up by atheistic Jews, and that Stalin had overthrown them. But, of course, their information came from Trotsky himself.

Trotsky set out his own analysis about the Bureaucratisation of the Soviet Union in his book *The Revolution Betrayed*.

Trotsky calls Stalin a Bonapartist, likening him to Napoleon I and Napoleon III. But he also likens him to Hitler, saying that all of them were defeaters of the democratic forces. Trotsky never admits the covert Jewish leadership of those "democratic" forces.

He writes, "Stalinism and fascism, in spite of a deep difference in social foundations, are symmetrical phenomena" (1937/1967, p. 278).

Rizzi , Burnham, Orwell, Wittfogel and Hayek all echoed this assessment.

Contrary to Trotsky's position, what Napoleon I, Napoleon III, and Stalin have in common is that they defeated Masonic and/or Jewish revolutionary movements from within, yet carried the revolution forward; Hitler did the same from the outside.

Some may object over the Freemasonry claim. But Trotsky himself agreed, in his autobiography *My Life: the Rise and Fall of a Dictator* (1930/1975), that the French Revolution had been launched by Freemasons or Illuminati. He studied this topic when in Odessa prison.

Orwell concurs with Burnham that Soviet Russia was originally a "Workers' State", but deteriorated under Stalin. He wrote in his essay Second Thoughts on James Burnham:

> Burnham does not, of course, deny that the new 'managerial' régimes, like the régimes of Russia and Nazi Germany, may be called Socialist. He means merely that they will not be Socialist in any sense of the word which would have been accepted by Marx, or Lenin, or Keir Hardie, or William Morris, or indeed, by any representative Socialist prior to about 1930. Socialism, until recently, was supposed to connote political democracy, social equality and internationalism. There is not the smallest sign that any of these things is in a way to being established anywhere, and the one great country in which something described as a proletarian revolu-

tion once happened, i.e. the U.S.S.R., has moved steadily away from the old concept of a free and equal society aiming at universal human brotherhood. In an almost unbroken progress since the early days of the Revolution, liberty has been chipped away and representative institutions smothered, while inequalities have increased and nationalism and militarism have grown stronger (Orwell, 1946b).

Orwell is here expressing a naive Trotskyism; Bakunin had predicted the Marxist tyranny during his battles with Marx.

The Kronstadt Massacre showed the despotic character of the regime—and it was ordered by Trotsky, in 1921. Whittaker Chambers wrote in his book *Witness* (1952/2001), of the Kronstadt sailors:

> "And they were the first Communists to realize their mistake and the first to try to correct it. When they saw that Communism meant terror and tyranny, they called for the overthrow of the Communist Government and for a time imperiled it. ... The fascist character of Communism was inherent in it from the beginning. Kronstadt changed the fate of millions of Russians. It changed nothing about Communism. It merely disclosed its character." (p. 460)

Alexander Solzhenitsyn also attested to the tyrannical nature of Bolshevism right from the start.

Malcolm Muggeridge, whose articles on the Ukraine Famine were ignored or censored by the Left media, felt much in common with Orwell, whose writings on Stalinism were similarly suppressed. He wrote (1972):

> I saw in Orwell's strong reaction to the villainies of the Communist apparat in Spain a comparable experience to my own disgust some years previously with the Soviet regime and its fawning admirers among the intelligentsia of the West as a result of a stint as Moscow correspondent of the Manchester Guardian. So I sent Orwell an appreciative note, to which I received a polite reply.

> Later, when I got to know Orwell, he told me the story of how the articles had been turned down by Kingsley Martin, then editor of the New Statesman. I pointed out that, in the same sort of way, my messages to the Guardian from the U.S.S.R.—for instance, about the famine caused by Stalin's collectivization policy in the Ukraine and the Caucasus, and about the arrest of some British engineers on spurious espionage charges—had been either whittled down or unused when they were more than mildly critical of the Soviet regime. ...

Orwell was to have a comparable experience with Animal Farm, which was offered first to Gollancz. His loathing of progressive publishers and publications, as a result of these incidents, was even greater than mine. He told me once with great relish that his model for the Ministry of Truth in Nineteen Eighty-Four had been the BBC, where he worked without much satisfaction during some of the war years. I was not inclined myself to regard Kingsley Martin, C. P. Scott and the other ostensibly 'enlightened' operators in the communications business as being intrinsically more despicable than the Northcliffes, the Beaverbrooks and the Henry Luces ... Incidentally, neither Kingsley nor Gollancz retracted from their position vis-a-vis the Spanish Civil War articles and Animal Farm. In his autobiography Kingsley continues to contend that he was right not to publish the articles. (p. 166)

Orwell took Wells to task for his naive faith in the Bolsheviks and in the World State, in his article: Wells, Hitler and the World State:

What has Wells to set against the "screaming little defective in Berlin"? The usual rigmarole about a World State, plus the Sankey Declaration, which is an attempted definition of fundamental human rights, of anti-totalitarian tendency. Except that he is now especially concerned with federal world control of air power, it is the same gospel as he has been preaching almost without interruption for the past forty years, always with an air of angry surprise at the human beings who can fail to grasp anything so obvious. ...

Wells accuses Churchill of not really believing his own propaganda about the Bolsheviks being monsters dripping with blood etc., but of merely fearing that they were going to introduce an era of common sense and scientific control, in which flag-wavers like Churchill himself would have no place. Churchill's estimate of the Bolsheviks, however, was nearer the mark than Wells's. The early Bolsheviks may have been angels or demons, according as one chooses to regard them, but at any rate they were not sensible men. They were not introducing a Wellsian Utopia but a Rule of the Saints, which, like the English Rule of the Saints, was a military despotism enlivened by witchcraft trials. The same misconception reappears in an inverted form in Wells's attitude to the Nazis. Hitler is all the war-lords and witchdoctors in history rolled into one. Therefore, argues Wells, he is an absurdity, a ghost from the past, a creature doomed to disappear almost immediately. But unfortunately the equation of science with common sense does not really hold good. The aeroplane, which was looked forward to as a civilising influence but in practice has hardly been used except for dropping bombs, is the symbol of that fact. Modern Germany is far more scientific than England, and far more barbarous. Much of what Wells has imagined and worked for is physically there in Nazi Germany. The order, the planning, the State encouragement of science, the steel, the concrete, the aeroplanes, are all there, but all in the service of ideas appropriate to the Stone Age. Science is fighting on the side of superstition. But obviously it is impossible for Wells to accept this. It would contradict the world-view on which his own works are based. The war-lords and the witch-doctors MU.S.T fail, the common-sense World State, as seen by a nineteenth-century liberal whose heart does not leap at the sound of bugles, MU.S.T triumph. Treachery and defeatism apart, Hitler CANNOT be a danger. That he should finally win would be an impossible reversal of history, like a Jacobite restoration.

But is it not a sort of parricide for a person of my age (thirty-eight) to find fault with H.G. Wells? Thinking people who were born about the beginning of this century are in some sense Wells's own creation. How much influence any mere writer has, and especially a "popular" writer whose work takes effect quickly, is questionable, but I doubt whether anyone who was writing books between 1900 and 1920, at any rate in the English language, influenced the young so much. (Orwell, 1941)

Later in life, Orwell acknowledged that Trotskyists could be bigoted like Communists (Stalinists), and that in practice "it is doubtful whether there is much difference":

The bigoted Communist who changes in a space of weeks, or even days, into an equally bigoted Trotskyist is a common spectacle. ...

People of Left opinions are not immune to it, and their attitude is sometimes affected by the fact that Trotskyists and Anarchists tend to be Jews. But antisemitism comes more naturally to people of Conservative tendency, who suspect Jews of weakening national morale and diluting the national culture. Neo-Tories and political Catholics are always liable to succumb to antisemitism, at least intermittently.

3. TROTSKYISM This word is used so loosely as to include Anarchists, democratic Socialists and even Liberals. I use it here to mean a doctrinaire Marxist whose main motive is hostility to the Stalin regime. Trotskyism can be better studied in obscure pamphlets or in papers like the Socialist Appeal than in the works of Trotsky himself, who was by no means a man of one idea. Although in some places, for instance in the United States, Trotskyism is able to attract a fairly large number of adherents and develop into an organized movement with a petty fuehrer of its own, its inspiration is essentially negative. The Trotskyist is against Stalin just as the Communist is for him, and, like the majority of Communists, he wants not so much to alter the external world as to feel that the battle for prestige is going in his own favour. In each case there is the same obsessive fixation on a single subject, the same inability to form a genuinely rational opinion based on probabilities. The fact that Trotskyists are everywhere a persecuted minority, and that the accusation usually made against them, i.e. of collaborating with the Fascists, is obviously false, creates an impression that Trotskyism is intellectually and morally superior to Communism; but

it is doubtful whether there is much difference. The most typical Trotsky-ists, in any case, are ex-Communists, and no one arrives at Trotskyism ex-cept via one of the left-wing movements. No Communist, unless tethered to his party by years of habit, is secure against a sudden lapse into Trot-skyism. The opposite process does not seem to happen equally often, though there is no clear reason why it should not. (Orwell, 1945)

Nevertheless, in *Nineteen Eighty-Four*, which Orwell wrote in 1948-9, he still depicts Trotsky as the hero.

Although Trotskyists present themselves as Marxists, the militant Trotskyist groups that dominate university campuses and run street demonstrations are ac-tually the agents of Globalist bankers like George Soros. Both promote LGBT, mass immigration, and censorship. They regard the working class as racist and sexist.

The Trotskyist site marxists.org, which promotes LGBT, has censored the cor-respondence of Marx and Engels about homosexuality. It lists their letters of 1869 at https://www.marxists.org/archive/marx/works/1869/letters/

Marx to Engels. 16 June
Engels to Marx. 22 June
Marx to Engels. 26 June

The letter of 22 June, which condemns homosexuality, used to be at https://www.marxists.org/archive/marx/works/1869/letters/69_06_22.htm,

but the Marx-Engels Archive now says "File No Longer Available!"

Yet it's at the Wayback Machine, at

https://web.archive.org/web/20111112214025/https://www.marxists.org/arc hive/marx/works/1869/letters/69_06_22.htm

Here is the letter:

Engels To Marx
In London
Source: MECW, Volume 43, p. 295.
First published: in Der Briefwechsel zwischen F. Engels und K. Marx
 Stuttgart, 1913.
Manchester, 22 June 1869
Dear Moor,

[...] The Urning you sent me is a very curious thing. These are extremely unnatural revelations. **The paederasts [homosexual paedophiles] are** beginning to count themselves, and **discover that they are a power** in the state. Only organisation was lacking, but according to this source it apparently already exists in secret. And since they have such important men in all the old parties and even in the new ones, from Rosing to Schweitzer, they cannot fail to triumph. **Guerre aux cons, paix aus**

trous-de-cul [war on the cunts, peace to the arse-holes] will now be the slogan. It is a bit of luck that we, personally, are too old to have to fear that, when this party wins, we shall have to pay physical tribute to the victors. But the younger generation! Incidentally **it is only in Germany that a fellow like this can possibly come forward, convert this smut into a theory,** and offer the invitation: introite [enter], etc. Unfortunately, **he has not yet got up the courage to acknowledge publicly that he is 'that way', and must still operate coram publico 'from the front',** if not 'going in from the front' as he once said by mistake. But just **wait until the new North German Penal Code recognises the droits du cul [rights of the arse-hole]** then he will operate quite differently. **Then things will go badly enough for poor frontside people like us, with our childish penchant for females. ...**

Your
F. E.

The same letter has also been removed from another Trotskyist site,

http://marxists.anu.edu.au/archive/marx/works/1869/letters/69_06_22.htm
Marx-Engels Archive
"File No Longer Available!"

Yet the Wayback Machine has it at

https://web.archive.org/web/20060907234534/http://marxists.anu.edu.au/archive/marx/works/1869/letters/69_06_22.htm

Another Trotskyist provided the rationale for censoring Marx & Engels:

https://newpol.org/issue_post/socialism-and-gay-liberation-back-future-0/

Socialism and Gay Liberation: Back to the Future

By: Doug Ireland

Winter 2009 (New Politics Vol. XII No. 2, Whole Number 46)

Well before the invention of the word "homosexual" by Karoly Maria Kertbeny in 1869, **the correspondence of Marx and Engels is riddled with** what we would now characterize as unmistakable **homophobia of a vicious character**. When the pioneering German homosexual liberationist Karl Ulrichs sent Marx one of his books on the subject, which Marx forwarded to his collaborator, **Engels described Ulrichs' platform of homosexual emancipation from criminal laws as "turning smut into history." Marx**, in commenting on Karl Boruttau's Gedanken über Gewissens Freiheit (Thoughts on Freedom of Conscience), **disparaged the author as "this faggoty prick" (Schwanzschwulen).**

Chapter 24: Who's behind the Covid Plandemic? Nazis?

Ivan Illich warned that Medicine was becoming a means of social control:

"My theme is that medicine is becoming a major institution of social control. ... It is becoming the new repository of truth, the place where absolute and often final judgments are made by supposedly neutral and objective experts" (1977, p. 41).

In his book *Medical Nemesis*, he cautioned,

The medical establishment has become a major threat to health. The disabling impact of professional control over medicine has reached the proportions of an epidemic. (1976, p. 3)

On a second level, medical practice sponsors sickness by reinforcing a morbid society that encourages people to become consumers of curative, preventive, industrial, and environmental medicine. On the one hand defectives survive in increasing numbers and are fit only for life under institutional care, while on the other hand, medically certified symptoms exempt people from industrial work and thereby remove them from the scene of political struggle to reshape the society that has made them sick. Second-level iatrogenesis finds its expression in various symptoms of social over-medicalization that amount to what I shall call the expropriation of health. (1976, p. 33)

Even before Covid-19, Alain Soral foresaw that the Globalist Oligarchs would use pandemics to terrorise the people and subject them to Lockdowns and Mandatory Vaccination. He wrote in 2011, in *Understand the Empire: Towards Global Governance or the Uprising of Nations?*:

For the sake of mankind's salvation and well-being, the fight against pollution, viruses, terrorism, and systemic financial crises are said to be dependent on bypassing governments (elected by the People) in favour of committees of experts (unelected) on a planetary level.

After global governance in the name of the environment and under the diktat of the IPCC, we move to global governance in the name of public health under the diktat of the World Health Organisation (WHO), another UN body. In place of a "carbon tax", we get the H1N1 vaccine, the silver bullet that is supposed to protect humanity from an epidemic that has gone global: the so-called swine flu "pandemic".

This is in fact another phony construct that will allow the global oligarchy to terrorise entire populations and subjugate them to authoritarian policies: mandatory vaccination under the supervision of armed forces, assembly bans, and so on—all useful measures in times of crisis and whenever popular uprising becomes too great a risk. (Soral, 2011/2022, pp. 320-3)

On Sat Nov 20, 2021, there were anti-Lockdown and anti-Vaccine-Mandate demonstrations in many Australian cities, but the biggest was in Melbourne, which had endured the world's longest Covid-19 lockdown. People who recorded it estimated that 450,000 took part.

The New York Times has a good video of it:

Melbourne's day of protest
November 20, 2021
https://www.nytimes.com/video/world/australia/100000008086651/australia-coronavirus-restrictions-protests-melbourne-sydney.html

In Melbourne, there was also a smaller "anti-Fascist" (i.e. Antifa) demonstration by Trotskyists, organised by Socialist Alliance and Socialist Alternative. They marched in the Anti-Vax crowd but carried a sign "Socialist Alliance", and a placard "Pro Vax Anti Fascist".

Rukshan Fernando, a Sri Lankan who video-records the Melbourne demonstrations, and showed the huge anti-Mandate crowd, videoed the Trot group too—it was only 100 to 200 people. The media treated the two demonstrations as equivalent.

Avi Yemini, of Rebel News, also covered both demonstrations. After he was called a "Nazi" in the Victorian parliament, he revealed that he's Jewish.

Ezra Levant, founder of Rebel News, called the Vaccine Mandates 'Nazi'. "How obedient are you? Do you conform to peer pressure? If you had been in Germany in 1936, would you have been like this man—the one man in a crowd refusing to salute the Nazis? August Landmesser," he asked in an email of Sept. 21, 2021. He's Jewish too.

The anti-Mandate side say that Covid 'vaccine' injections are equivalent to Dr. Mengele's experiments, and a violation of the Nuremburg laws.

Each side is calling the other 'Nazis'.

Two months earlier, on Sept 21, 2021, construction workers, members of the Construction, Forestry, Mining and Energy Union (CFME.U.), staged a violent protest outside their union headquarters in Melbourne.

The Victorian state government had announced a policy of "No Jab, No Ticket"—meaning that unvaccinated workers would not be allowed on job sites.

Union boss John Sekta supported the government policy; the angry workers booed, yelled obscenities, threw crates, and smashed the C.F.M.E.U.'s front door.

Australia's ABC has a good video of it:

VIDEO: Large protest against COVID restrictions at CFME.U. HQ in Melbourne

Posted Mon 20 Sep 2021 at 3:47pm
https://www.abc.net.au/news/2021-09-20/large-protest-against-covid-
restrictions-at-cfmeu-hq-melbourne/13549910

John Setka claimed that non-unionists hijacked the protest. Bill Shorten, former leader of the Australian Labor Party, blamed "hard-right, man baby Nazis":

Bill Shorten slams 'man baby Nazis' involved in violent CBD protest
21/09/2021
3AW NEWS
https://www.3aw.com.au/bill-shorten-slams-man-baby-nazis-involved-in-
violent-cbd-protest/

The protestors vowed to march every day. On Tuesday 21, they marched on
West Gate bridge; police fired rubber bullets. The Melbourne Age report after the
second march noted that "the majority marching on Tuesday appeared to be the
people industrial unions used to represent; young, working-class men":

https://www.theage.com.au/national/victoria/construction-shutdown-
sparks-huge-protest-as-fault-lines-exposed-20210921-p58tkw.html

Construction shutdown sparks huge protest as fault lines exposed

The government's no-jab, no-ticket ultimatum, which followed a week of
negotiations between senior government ministers, union leaders and
building companies, has exposed an emerging political and social fault line
over mandatory vaccinations.

ACTU secretary Sally McManus, a vocal supporter of vaccination across all
industries, questioned on Tuesday whether mandating the jab is the best
way of reaching high vaccination rates. ...

Images of an angry mob laying violent siege to the CFME.U. headquarters
on Monday and thousands of people willing to march in defiance of
COVID-19 restrictions the next day are symptoms of a city under increasing strain. ...

Despite the union movement's determination to distance itself from the
protesters, the majority marching on Tuesday appeared to be the people
industrial unions used to represent; young, working-class men who, in at
least some cases, have suddenly found themselves tossed out of work. ...

The protest was ugly at times and violent at others, but for the most part,
the marchers were intent on avoiding open conflict with heavily armed ri-
ot police. It began outside the CFME.U. headquarters, set off to Parliament
House, then headed back through the city and along the West Gate free-
way to the centre of the bridge. ...

Victoria Police Chief Commissioner Shane Patton said 500 officers were
deployed and rubber bullets, smoke roads and pepper balls fired to subdue

the protests. Three police were injured, and police cars were damaged. More than 60 people were arrested.

A video of the second march is at

REVOLUTION! Protesters Led by Construction Workers in Melbourne
https://healthimpactnews.com/2021/revolution-protesters-led-by-construction-workers-in-melbourne-shut-down-major-freeways-over-covid-tyranny-and-mandatory-vaccines/

The workers' sign (at the above link) reads

Victorian Workers Rally For Freedom
No Vaccine Mandates
Every Day: 10:00am
CFME.U. Headquarters 540 Elizabeth St
Rally will continue until demands are met. Bring your friends and family in support. Wear work gear, bring food and drinks.
https://healthimpactnews.com/wp-content/uploads/sites/2/2021/09/melbournefreedomrally.jpg

And the Workers demanded mass distribution of Ivermectin, vitamins C, D and zinc:

Melbourne protest demands
Emergency state powers to be removed immediately
Lockdowns to end immediately
Mask mandate to end immediately
Vaccines mandate to end immediately
Vaccine passports to be removed ...
Charges laid against officers assaulting peaceful protestors
All construction sites to resume immediately
Mass distribution of ivermectin, vitamins C, D and zinc
https://healthimpactnews.com/wp-content/uploads/sites/2/2021/09/melbourne-protest-demands.jpg

What side did the Trotskyists take? They took the union bosses' side, not the workers' side.

Red Flag, the newspaper of Socialist Alternative, proclaimed "Unions need to crush the anti-vax movement".

https://redflag.org.au/article/unions-need-crush-anti-vax-movement

Unions need to crush the anti-vax movement
CFME.U. officials attempt to guard the union's office during an attack by anti-vax protesters (including many CFME.U. members) on Monday 20 September
by Louise O'Shea
23 September 2021

In a frightening show of force, marauding fascist mobs have taken over the streets of Melbourne for three days running. They have smashed up union offices and occupied major arterials for hours. This is a disastrous development.

Green Left Weekly ran a piece by Sue Bolton of Socialist Alliance:

Behind the attack on the CFME.U. office
Sue Bolton
Melbourne
September 21, 2021
https://www.greenleft.org.au/content/behind-attack-cfmeu-office

She said that "CFME.U. officers were forced to take cover as the mob threw crates and other objects".

But she claimed that the protesters were mainly outsiders: "The Construction, Forestry, Mining and Energy Union (CFME.U.) offices were attacked by about 500 conspiracy theorist anti-vaxxers, some CFME.U. members and far-right activists on September 20."

However, she concluded, "it indicates that far-right, anti-working class ideas are growing in the union's ranks."

Red Flag had a reporter at the protests, Ben Hiller. Red Flag published his report, which refuted their own party line:

https://redflag.org.au/article/inside-three-days-rage-melbourne
Inside three days of rage in Melbourne
by Ben Hillier
23 September 2021
But the rage was not concocted by outside agitators. And the participants were mostly workers from the industry. ... Avi Yemini from Rebel News was a minor celebrity. At one point, perhaps a quarter or a third of the protest enthusiastically chanted his name. He was randomly stopped on occasion by people who wanted to shake his hand and praise his work.

Contrary to Trotskyist smears that the protestors were white racists, videos show that they were multi-racial, including Tongans and other Pacific Islanders. Avi Yemini, the reporter from Rebel News, is a Jew from Yemen. Rukshan Fernando, whose videos documented the events, is from Sri Lanka.

The conclusion? The Trotskyists, the Union bosses and the Labor Politicians are in league with the Globalist bankers, against the workers—whom they brand 'Nazis'.

On Nov. 22, 2022, Australia's Senate voted on a motion to publish the contracts between the federal government and pharmaceutical companies for

COVID-19 vaccines. These contracts include unspecified indemnities for harm that the vaccines may cause.

Senators Roberts, Hanson, Antic, Rennick and Canavan sponsored the motion. Liberal-National, One Nation, United Australia Party, and independents Jacqui Lambie and David Pocock voted in favour, while Labor and the Greens Party voted against.

The vote being 29-29, the motion was defeated. Enough said. The Left are in bed with the Globalists.

https://www.malcolmrobertsqld.com.au/motion-to-publish-vaccine-contracts-defeated-by-labor-greens/
Motion To Publish Vaccine Contracts Defeated By Labor/Greens
November 22, 2022

In anti-Vaccine Mandate writings, one finds statements that the tyranny being imposed is 'Orwellian'. But Orwell's *Nineteen Eighty-Four* depicts a LEFT-WING tyranny.

The fact that the Establishment media, as well as the Trots on the street, call the anti-Vaxxers "Far Right' and 'Nazis' attests to the Left-wing provenance of the Establishment.

And the Establishment's embrace of Woke ideology also attests the Left-wing nature of the tyranny.

The question then is, Who's behind the Plandemic?

Robert F. Kennedy Jr. lists a parade of conspirators, in his book *The Real Anthony Fauci* (2021):

• the Military,

• the CIA and other Intelligence Agencies

• Big Pharma

• Globalist Foundations (the Rockefeller Foundation and the Gates Foundation)

He makes no reference to Fauci's very noticeable Masonic hand sign at a press conference on Apr 5, 2020, which the media ignored (pp. 176-7 above; also see Myers, 2021/2022). The Warren Commission, which covered up the conspiracy to murder his uncle, JFK, was led by a Masonic Grand-Master, and LBJ was a Freemason too. The "mainstream media" seemed not to notice.

RFK Jr., being a Democrat, depicts the conspiracy as Right-wing and 'Nazi'. How, then, to bring the Orwellian Left into it?

The answer is: via H. G. Wells, the leading Left proponent of Globalisation, a.k.a. the World State.

Wells was a Fabian at one stage, a eugenicist, a supporter of Lenin and Trotsky but opponent of Stalin, and the founder of the Green Left. Prior to Wells, socialists had emphasised industrialisation, but Wells wrote of the need to limit industry and protect the natural environment. Wells was the biggest-selling Left author in the 1910s, 20s and 30s; he shaped the minds of a whole generation. Apart from his non-fiction books, he wrote many novels, into which he inserted his political viewpoint. Those novels influenced many people who did not share his political philosophy; even Winston Churchill, who had debated Wells over whether Bolshevism was good or bad, had only good words to say in his obituary for Wells.

The dystopian novels by Aldous Huxley and George Orwell were both responses to Wells' books on the Open Conspiracy for World Government.

Well's One World ideas bore fruit in 1946, when the U.S. Government proposed the Baruch Plan to the Soviet Union. It was drafted by two American Jews, David Lilienthal and Bernard Baruch. On the surface, the Plan was merely about limiting Nuclear Weapons, but the discussion in the Bulletin of the Atomic Scientists also covered a second, deeper agenda—World Government. That is why Stalin rejected it; and this was one of the markers of the start of the Cold War.

Even before the development of nuclear weapons, Wells had argued that we had needed a World Government, because otherwise nations at war with each other would destroy themselves and the planet.

The same theme was canvassed in depth in a book issued with the Baruch Plan, titled *One World Or None*. It had a leftist slant, and a large core of Jewish authors.

The One World Or None theme was in later years applied to ecological damage (only a World Government can save the environment), and then to Biological Warfare (only a World Government can eliminate that threat).

Yet, in 1946, some of the advocates of the Baruch Plan were scientists who had helped develop the Atomic Bomb; and some (like Robert Oppenheimer) had even helped transfer the technology to the Soviet Union.

There are many on the Right who oppose not only the solution (World Government), but also deny the reality of the threat too. That is not my position; I think that the threats are real, even if distorted by the Left. But whilst I think that there are two credible sides of the Global Warming debate, the issue of Resource Depletion is cut-and-dried. As mines reach a depth of 2 kilometres or more, we are using up the earth's resources as if we do not have to leave some for people of future centuries and millennia. They will judge us as terribly selfish. At the same time, many of these resources are wasted on extravagances, and on products that only last a short time before being thrown out. Rubbish tips used to allow recycling, some decades ago, but now they have "No Scavenging" signs up—as if "scavenging" is not recycling. They say they can't allow "scavenging" because you might trip over and sue them. Insurance trumps recycling; the solution would be to specify "enter at your own risk"; why is no-one pushing for that?

If you think I sound "green", well I am; but I oppose the Green Left. I oppose their protecting sharks, crocodiles and other predators (that eat or kill people) even though their numbers have built up excessively. I oppose their shutdown of the Australian hardwood timber industry, forcing people to build homes from steel or brick, which are more energy-intensive. I also would protect the Family and stop Communist (Trotskyist) indoctrination in schools and universities.

Anyway, I think that Wells present a strong case for World Government, and it is a matter we should be discussing openly and (I believe) agonising over, because we are in a Catch-22 situation. The threats are real, but the outcome could be Tyranny and the End of Civilisation.

The One World forces are using these threats to panic us, like cattle being rounded up, into an end-goal they long planned. Robert F. Kennedy Jr. reveals how, for years, they have conducted simulations to rehearse how they will manipulate us, to accept giving up our rights and freedoms, and to overthrow the U.S. Constitution, one of the main barriers in their way.

But who are they?

The military and CIA might be thought "Far Right"; certainly they opposed Stalin and his heirs. Yet in recent years they have become 'Woke'; like big business, they have supported Open Borders and joined the revolt against traditionalist America. The aircraft carrier Gerald R. Ford, commissioned in 2017, carries 5,000 sailors, but has no urinals. The U.S. fought the Afghan War in the name of Women's Rights.

The 'Trotskyoid' label fits the bill — that's how one can be both pro-Communist and anti-Stalinist.

What about Big Pharma, and the Globalist Foundations? They also support the Woke Left.

The lessons of the Bolshevik Revolution are starkly before our eyes. Whereas, a century ago, its victims were unaware of the fate that would befall them, today we, with hindsight, know what's coming, and are doing all we can to stop it.

In late February, 2023, the Biden administration was preparing to sign a Pandemic Treaty that cedes to the World Health Organisation (W.H.O.) the authority to dictate policies during future pandemics; Australia, the U.K., Canada and New Zealand—the UKUSA countries—also endorsed it (Roberts, 2023).

Proposed measures include compulsory vaccination through mandatory detention and forced medical procedures. Other measures include the power to order border closures (including internal borders such as between Australian states), shutdowns for businesses & schools, international vaccine passports, restrictions on product sales (such as those which may compete with approved pharmaceuticals) and much more.

The Treaty would also elevate the billionaire owners of the WHO to full member status as "stakeholders", meaning Pfizer for instance could vote on declaring a health emergency and mandating Pfizer vaccines. (Roberts, 2023)

The Treaty would apply in all countries including the United States, where the Constitution requires Senate approval for such a measure. However, Francis Boyle says, by designating the authority 'provisional', this Senate requirement is bypassed:

"Whoever drafted this clause knew as much about U.S. constitutional law and international law as I did, and deliberately drafted it to circumvent the power of the Senate to give its advice and consent to treaties, to provisionally bring it into force immediately upon signature," Boyle said. Further, he said, the measure "would set up a worldwide medical police state under the control of the WHO." (Stocklin, 2023)

Dr. Meryl Nass said that the W.H.O. would be able to mandate approved medicines such as Remdesivir, and ban others such as Hydroxychloroquine or Ivermectin. They would also be able to stipulate that "everybody in the world gets vaccinated, whether or not you need it, whether or not you're already immune" (Stocklin, 2023).

Pope Francis, seemingly in George Soros' camp, called on Jan. 24, 2023, for the decriminalisation of homosexuality in all countries. But a traditionalist Catholic, Archbishop Carlo Maria Viganò warned (2021) that the Great Reset was a plot to enslave humanity:

Considerations on the Great Reset and the New World Order

We should have understood—I wrote it some time ago—that the Great Reset plan was not the result of the ravings of some "conspiracy theorist" but the crude evidence of a criminal plan, conceived for decades and aimed at establishing a universal dictatorship in which a minority of immeasurably rich and powerful people intends to enslave and subjugate the whole of humanity to the globalist ideology. ... What Kalergi, the Rothschilds, the Rockefellers, Klaus Schwab, Jacques Attali and Bill Gates have been saying since World War II has been published in books and newspapers, commented on and taken up by international bodies and foundations, made up precisely by parties and government majorities. The United States of Europe, uncontrolled immigration, the reduction of wages, the cancellation of trade union guarantees, the renunciation of national sovereignty, the single currency, the control of citizens under the pretext of a pandemic, and the reduction of the population through the use of vaccines with new technologies are not recent inventions, but the result of a planned, organized and coordinated action—an action that clearly shows itself perfectly adhering to a single script under a single direction. (Viganò, 2021)

The script they are following seems to be the one that H. G. Wells pioneered from 1901 until his death in 1946. Of all the Globalists, he was the most persistent and the most convincing. Unlike Marxists, he did not pitch his line to the working class, and had no following in union ranks. Instead, he addressed the Progressives ('Liberals') and the bankers. They are the ones pursuing Globalisation today.

It is important to identify Wells' place in the political spectrum, because this helps show who's pulling the strings today, and shines a light on the path ahead. I have called Wells a Trotskyist, but others call him a 'Liberal Fascist', implying that the New World Order is fascist, meaning, in the camp of Mussolini or even Hitler.

If that's the case, why are the Holocaust Deniers in jail? Why do the media call the anti-lockdown protestors 'Nazi' or 'Far Right'? Why are Holocaust documentaries forever on our TV screens? Why is any non-Jew who mentions Jewish agendas branded a Nazi? Why are conservatives hounded out of universities and schools?

What we have now is not 'Liberal Fascism', but 'Liberal Communism'. Was George Orwell wrong when he depicted the coming tyranny as a Left-wing one?

Chapter 25: Hitler's Finance Policy and the Japanese and Chinese Economic Miracles

The German Workers Party was a socialist party founded by Gottfried Feder, Anton Drexler and Karl Harer. Hitler joined it and took it over, renaming it the NSDAP.

John Gunther (1938) described how Hitler took it over:

"Hitler entered political life as a spy. The fact is unpleasant. The story is fully told by Heiden. Hitler was a non-commissioned officer in the German army, which had just become the Reichswehr, and he was detailed early in 1919 as a sort of intelligence officer to attend labor meetings, mingle with workers' groups, and report to his superiors the state of popular opinion. Fulfilling one of these missions, he heard a man named Gottfried Feder speak. He was impressed by Feder's radical economic theories, including the distinction between raffendes (grasping) and schaffendes (creative) capital; he came again to hear him, and joined excitedly the discussion following the meeting, squelching an opposition speaker.

"... Hitler began to equivocate almost from the moment he seized control of the party. National Socialism began as a predominantly left-socialist movement, and the party program, written by Feder and pronounced unalterable by Hitler, was a formidably anti-capitalist document. Hitler began to shed the socialist parts of the program with systematic regularity as soon as he was on the road to power" (pp. 27-8).

The CFR's Foreign Affairs magazine published an article about Feder in 1935:

The clearest exposition of the economic aims of National Socialism is contained in a pamphlet issued as a speakers' manual for the July 1932 elections, and called "Immediate Economic Demands of the N.S.D.A.P." It deals with both general aims and specific plans, the latter largely confined to work-creation programs to combat unemployment. It asserts as a fundamental principle that labor, not capital, is the source of all wealth, demands the immediate nationalization of banks and all monopolistic industries and trusts, immediate departure from the gold standard, government credit expansion, dissolution of department and chain stores, the increase of small land-holdings, and an immense program of government housing. Minimum immediate demand: 400,000 workers' homes with sufficient land for agricultural production. It demands complete state control of foreign exchange, autarchy (except for basically necessary imports not obtainable at home), and the absorption of the export slack in a richer home market. It admits the impossibility of this except as the worker receives an "adequate wage for his toil." (Thompson, 1935)

That was the policy of Feder. The article continued:

Not Hitler, but the Munich engineer, Gottfried Feder, formulated the first economic platform of the National Socialist Party. Hitler's personal utterances often seem at variance with this program, which advocates limited state capitalism, whereas Hitler often expressed himself for laissez-faire. (Thompson, 1935)

Hitler gave National Socialism a bad name, but his regime was not really socialist. The early members of the party such as Feder enunciated a National Socialist program, and when Hitler took over he named the party thus, but later he repudiated such policies as 'Marxist' or 'Bolshevik'.

William L. Shirer (1961) described how Hitler reversed the socialist policies of Feder and the Strasser brothers (Gregor and Otto). This relates to Gregor:

Once in the fall of 1930 Strasser, Feder and Frick introduced a bill in the Reichstag on behalf of the Nazi Party calling for a ceiling of 4 percent on all interest rates, the expropriation of the holdings of 'the bank and stock exchange magnates' and of all 'Eastern Jews' without compensation, and the **nationalization of the big banks. Hitler was horrified; this was** not only **Bolshevism**, it was financial suicide for the party. He peremptorily ordered the party to withdraw the measure. Thereupon **the Communists reintroduced it**, word for word. **Hitler bade his party vote against it**. (p. 144)

Alan Bullock (1991) details a confrontation between Hitler and Otto Strasser in 1930:

After further discussion, Otto Strasser came to what he regarded as the heart of the matter. 'You want to strangle the social revolution', he told Hitler, 'for the sake of legality and your new collaboration with the bourgeois parties of the right.'

Hitler, who was rattled by this suggestion, retorted angrily:

... **What you understand by Socialism is nothing but Marxism**. Now look: the great mass of working men want only bread and circuses. They have no understanding for ideals of any sort whatever, and we can never hope to win the workers to any large extent by an appeal to ideals ... There are no revolutions except racial revolutions ...

The conversation was continued the following day in the presence of Gregor Strasser, Max Amann and Hess. When **Otto Strasser demanded the nationalization of industry, Hitler retorted with scorn**:

Democracy has laid the world in ruins, and nevertheless you want to extend it to the economic sphere. It would be the end of the German economy ... The capitalists have worked their way to the top through their capacity, and on the basis of this selection, which again only proves their higher race, they have a right to lead.

When Strasser asked him what he would do with Krupps if he came to power, Hitler at once replied:

Of course I should leave it alone. Do you think that I should be so mad as to destroy Germany's economy? Only if people should fail to act in the interests of the nation, then—and only then—would the State intervene. But for that you do not need an expropriation ... you need only a strong State. (p. 190)

From Feder, Hitler learned that Governments do not need Gold to operate an economy. As long as there are workers and resources, the economy can operate on a "Fiat" basis. The Central Bank can create as much money as is needed to fund employment, infrastructure and social programs. In this respect, Rauschning was wrong and Hitler was right. Whereas Rauschning argued that such money-creation would be inflationary, Hitler insisted that he would control prices and wages, to stop it; and that is what happened, the same as in the Soviet Union.

However, Hitler did not nationalize private property, as Feder had demanded and as happened in the Soviet Union. He simply placed control over private business in the hands of a managerial bureaucracy, subject to the Government. John Burnham's book *The Managerial Revolution* was the second book about the similarity between Soviet and Nazi management of the economy. Burnham was a Trotskyist who became a leading anti-Communist, and later worked for the CIA.

Burnham's book was not the first on that theme. It had been preceded by one other book, *The Bureaucratisation of the World*, by Bruno Rizzi (1939). He was also a Trotskyist, who praised the Nazi economic management:

http://www.marxists.org/archive/rizzi/bureaucratisation/index.htm

Trotsky himself commented on this book: http://www.marxists.org/archive/trotsky/1939/09/ussr-war.htm.

The theme was later taken up by Friedrich von Hayek in his book *The Road to Serfdom*. He argued that the New Deal, and by extension the postwar socialist regimes in Britain and Australia, were a slippery slope that would lead to Totalitarianism. This was the justification for Thatcherism and Reaganomics.

Stephen Zarlenga's book *The Lost Science Of Money* (2002) gives an excellent account of Nazi finance policy.

The basis of Feder's ideas was that the state should create and control its money supply through a nationalized central bank rather than have it created by privately owned banks, to whom interest would have to be paid. From this view was derived the conclusion that finance had enslaved the population by usurping the nation's control of money. (Zarlenga, 2002, p. 590)

Zarlenga explains how Feder was sidelined by Schacht (and Hitler). Hitler used MEFO bills to boost the money supply while keeping that investment off-Budget, i.e. not incurring a Budget Deficit over it; the MEFO bills funded infrastructure and created an economic miracle.

MEFO bills paid interest (4.5%), so were not debt-free money like Lincoln's Greenbacks, the sort Feder had advocated. The Bradbury Pounds that Britain issued early in World War I were another example Feder would have approved of; they were £300 million of interest-free money issued by the Treasury, not the Bank of England. Zarlenga continues:

> Hitler and the National Socialists came to power on January 30, 1933. Germany's foreign exchange and gold reserves had dropped from 2.6 billion marks in late 1929, down to 409 million in late 1933, and to only 83 million marks in late 1934. According to classical economic theory Germany was broke and would have to borrow, but Germany was to demonstrate that "classical" monetary theory is not very accurate.

> This period of German monetary history has received far too little attention in English. On May 1, 1933 Hitler outlined the 1st Reinhardt Program—a four-year plan to end unemployment by attacking it on several fronts:

> • Spending 1 billion marks worth of "employment creation bills."

> • Tax benefits for industry, agriculture, and the employment of domestic help.

> • Marriage bonus loans up to 1,000 marks and

> • Government control of the money and capital markets, under Schacht.

> Although elements of this program had already started under the predecessor Von Papen and Schleicher Regimes, they had not been all out efforts against unemployment.

> On May 31st, the German government decided to **issue 1 billion marks of short term public works bills**, designated to pay for specific infrastructure projects:

> "These were negotiable certificates paid out to employers who under-took projects of replacement or maintenance projects. Anyone who equipped a factory with new machines or who had his house repainted could finance his operations with these work drafts...," wrote Heiden.

> These **bills paid about 4 1/2% interest**, and as they were taken into the banking system, they were renewed indefinitely, and made eligible for rediscounting by the Reichsbank. This means that they **became part of the underlying basis for the nation's money supply**, along with gold and foreign exchange and long term Government Bonds.

The author has seen these bills referred to as **"Feder money,"** and as "work drafts" (Arbeits-Schatzanwersungen). **Schacht later referred to MEFO bills, mentioning no connection with Feder.**

Many of the bills never found their way to the Reichsbank, since the interest they paid was an incentive for banks and others to hold onto them. Roberts estimated that as much as 15 billion marks worth of such bills were issued. (Zarlenga, 2002, pp. 594-5)

Late in life, Schacht admitted that Feder's ideas had some merit.

Schacht clearly had to "eat crow" and swallow his own words as regards the new monetary issues that he earlier condemned. Thirty years later he justified his change of theory:

"... it was repeatedly asked whether the success of the MEFO bill scheme did not mean that whenever there was a shortage of capital savings one could compensate by replacing such capital savings with credits granted by the central bank, and thus by money specially granted for the purpose. The English economist J.M. Keynes has delt with the problem theoretically, and MEFO transactions prove the practical applicability of such an idea." (Zarlenga, 2002, p. 596)

In 1939, as war approached, Schacht refused to accept more MEFO bills. For this, Hitler sacked him, but kept his firing secret for five months, to calm the markets. Schacht's sacking saved him at the Nuremberg trials.

These bills were used from 1934 to 1938. Schacht relates how he got himself fired by refusing to continue renewing the bills:

"In January 1939, the Reichsbank handed Hitler a memorandum in which it indicated its refusal to grant the Reich any further credits. The consequences were drastic. On January 19, I was dismissed from my office as President ... on the following day Hitler issued an edict which ordered the Reichsbank to grant the Reich all credits for which the Fuhrer asked. It is true the MEFO bills were now honored when they came due, but only with the inflated money produced by the printing presses. The second inflation had begun."

Schacht's firing was not made public for five months. His refusal to continue financing the Reich was probably what saved him at Nuremberg. (Zarlenga, 2002, pp. 596-7)

Late in life, Schacht acknowledged his conversion from financial orthodoxy to the State theory of money enunciated by George Knapp.

Schacht began his banking career as a believer in the gold standard, the system then used in England and America. But by 1967, it appears he had come to agree with some of Gottfried Feder's "unorthodox" monetary views:

"Modern paper money, the banknote is backed by its creator, the state ..."

Thus Schacht made a monetary pilgrimage similar to that of Thomas Jefferson, Alexander Del Mar, and many others, away from the primitive commodity view of money as metal, to an awareness of the "nominal," fiat nature of money as being based in law.

"The granting of credit is unthinkable without a central bank. No central bank can be allowed to act against the government of the country. The government is over the central Bank ... A central bank cannot allow any competition," wrote Schacht. (Zarlenga, 2002, p. 599)

Hitler commented on Schacht's ties to the Jewish bankers:

Before each meeting of the International Bank at Basel, half the world was anxious to know whether Schacht would attend or not, and it was only after receipt of the assurance that he would be there that the Jew bankers of the entire world packed their bags and prepared to attend. (Hitler, 1941-44/2000)

I have read that Schacht learned Hebrew so that he could understand what the Jewish bankers were saying at those meetings.

Anthony Migchels (2013) wrote that Schacht "joined Dresdner Bank in 1903 and already in 1905 was meeting people like JP Morgan and Theodore Roosevelt. He studied Hebrew to advance his career. In 1908 he joined Freemasonry."

Anyone interested in Socialist Finance should look up "Bradbury Pounds" on the internet; also see my webpage How Banks Create Money; Why We Can Never Get Out of Debt: https://mailstar.net/money.html. Another webpage of interest would be Monetary Financing: Central Banks should directly fund government expenses during the (Coronavirus) crisis: https://mailstar.net/coronavirus-finance.html. It can be done without incurring debt; Feder knew that, and John Bradbury, head of the British Treasury, did too.

Feder's problem was that he knew the theory of money, but had no practical experience of, say, running a bank. If you want to learn a new skill—welding metal or grafting trees—the theory is insufficient; you must get practical experience too. Without that, you're nothing. That was the difference bwteeen Schacht and Feder.

Zarlenga quotes Robert de Fremery to the effect that the Gold-using countries were operating a financial war against Germany. The British Empire had left the Gold Standard by 1931, but was producing half the world's Gold. Roosevelt took the US off the Gold Standard in 1933, but the $ remained Gold-backed at $35 per ounce. These two powers did not take kindly to Germany showing that you could bypass Gold altogether.

However, even if that was a contributing cause to the war, Hitler's imperial ambitions were a greater cause. His racial antagonism to Slavs was a throwback from the First World War, during which Germany had conquered Ukraine and the other western provinces of Russia. Hitler wanted that territory back. Just as the British called the Germans "Huns" during that war, the Germans belittled the Slavs. It was the basis of Hitler's genocidal policies towards them.

Hitler Killed Off the Socialists

Hitler found that the party's left-wing policies had popular appeal, but not enough to gain power. In order to obtain funds sufficient to gain power, he needed the support of German industrialists, who were afraid of the party's left wing, which had been advocating a 'second revolution', i.e. a socialist one to nationalise the industries. The left wing even voted with the Communists on economic matters. Hitler liquidated them during the Night of Long Knives; many left-wing leaders were killed, e.g. Ernst Röhm, head of the S.A., and Gregor Strasser.

Otto Strasser escaped, and became the 'most wanted man in Europe'.

Hitler put Feder out to pasture; he placed Schacht, not Feder, in charge of finance policy. Neither Feder nor any of the other early left-wing leaders ever got a chance to implement their socialist economic policies. Hitler did not nationalise any part of the German economy.

Otto Strasser wrote several books attesting that 'Hitler means war'. I put those books online— *Hitler and I* is at https://mailstar.net/otto-strasser-hitler.html, and *Flight from Terror* is at https://mailstar.net/otto-strasser-flight.html.

Otto Strasser stood for public ownership of major parts of the economy, an end to Prussian militarism, equality between the nations, no territorial demands, and a federated Europe—but without mass immigration, Gay Marriage, and domination by private bankers, as in the E.U. today. "There would be no dictatorship, either of class or of race" (Strasser, 1940, p. 93).

I also put the *Memoirs of Rudolph Hoss*, head of Auschwitz-Birkenau Concentration Camp, online at https://mailstar.net/Hoss-Memoirs.html, noting, "this important document is on the internet here for the first time". And I put parts of *Hitler's Table Talk* online, where he details plans to settle Germans in Ukraine, and exterminate Jews: https://mailstar.net/holocaust-debate04.html.

Gilad Atzmon wrote of Paul Eisen, explaining how he became a Holocaust Denier:

> Eisen was tormented (as a Jew) to find out that the Israeli Holocaust museum Yad Vashem ... was built in proximity to Deir Yassin, a Palestinian village that was erased along with its inhabitants in a colossal coldblooded massacre by Jewish paramilitaries in 1948. Just three years after the libera-

tion of Auschwitz, the newly born Jewish state wiped out a civilization in Palestine in the name of a racist Jewish nationalist ideology. It is this vile cynicism that turned Eisen into a denier — a denier of the primacy of Jewish suffering. In his eyes, if the Jews could commit the massacre in Deir Yassin after Auschwitz, the holocaust must be denied because it failed to mature into a universal ethical message. (Atzmon, 2015)

The left of the NSDAP party had opposed usury, including Jewish usury, but rejected Hitler's fixation on racial purity. Hitler ignored Friedrich Nietzsche and Oswald Spengler because they advocated a 'strong' race but not a 'pure' one; they affirmed that all nations are mixed, and that a strong nation can absorb immigrants (though not without limit).

There are a lot of silly debates about whether Hitler wanted war. But that's the wrong question. The right question is, "Did Hitler want an Empire?" And the answer to that question is unequivally Yes. It's just that he preferred it to fall into his lap, without fighting if possible. Hitler made his imperial ambition clear in *Mein Kampf*. It was not for nothing that he visited the grave of Napoleon. Stalin, not being stupid, prepared for war too. Viktor Suvorov pointed out that, just before Hitler attacked Stalin, Stalin had been getting ready to attack Hitler. Both sides had dismantled their defensive positions. There was going to be a war between them; the only question was who would attack first. The lesson was not lost on Moshe Dayan in 1967.

Some people probably think I'm pro-Hitler, because I oppose Zionism and that strand of Judaism which identifies with the Maccabees, the War against Rome, and Masada. But I'm not a militaristic person; I find war-talk distasteful. I don't like wearing uniforms. Nor do I believe in "group souls", or bans on intermarriage. Other people write to me tell me how Hitler restored full employment, saved the German currency etc. But whatever good Hitler did in that way was undone by the war he launched.

Hitler's foreign policy was disastrous. In some respects, he was continuing World War I. That meant mounting a major war, with great suffering to many innocent people. Apart from that, there's a certain lack of consistency in Hitler's policy. He did want a war, but not the one he got. He wanted Britain to let him destroy the Soviet Union. Seeking an alliance with the British Empire, he halted his troops near Dunkirk, allowing the British to escape.

Yet Britain was the power which had done the deal with Zionism to bring the U.S. into World War I. Hitler hoped that the anti-Zionist faction in Britain would prevail over the pro-Zionist faction. He did not know that the Cecil Rhodes group was closely tied up with the Zionists.

Hitler Got the Wrong War

The Battle of Nomonhan, in Mongolia, was the most decisive battle of World War II; and it happened before the main war broke out.

It was decisive because it destroyed the Anti-Comintern Pact and paved the way for the German-Soviet Pact. As a result, the Strike South faction in Japan ousted the Strike North faction.

The greatest threat to the Soviet Union was war on two fronts, vs. Germany in the west and Japan in the east. At that time, the Japanese Empire included Taiwan, Korea, Manchuria, parts of Mongolia and parts of China.

Germany and Japan pursued a joint foreign policy via the Anti-Comintern Pact.

Japan's Kwangtung Army, which was somewhat independent of Tokyo, tested Soviet strength via clashes in Mongolia. Stalin's spy in Tokyo, Richard Sorge, informed him of the Japanese plans, and noted that the soldiers sent for the battles were young and inexperienced. But Stalin placed Zhukov in charge, and Zhukov initated a blitzkrieg war that demolished the Japanese forces. As a result, the Strike North faction in Japan lost face and the Strike South faction came to the fore.

That's why Japan attacked Singapore rather than Russia as Hitler had wanted. He ended up with the wrong war. If he'd got the war he wanted, Germany and Japan vs. Russia, the U.S. would not have been drawn into the war. It would have been fought in the Soviet Union rather than the Pacific Ocean.

Hitler was well aware of the failures of the Soviet army attacking Finland. He concluded that the Red Army was 'a paralytic on crutches'. But Stalin kept news of the overwhelming Soviet victory at Nomonhan out of the media; thus Hitler was unaware of the Red Army's true strength in continental war.

When Hitler sought to recover Danzig from Poland, Britain provided a guarantee like that given to Belgium before World War I; both functioned as tripwires. Hitler, who hitherto had taken an anti-Soviet line, suddenly became anti-British, confusing his Japanese allies.

At that point, Stalin hinted to German diplomats that a pact might be possible. The German-Soviet Pact was in fact a deception of Hitler by Stalin. Stalin escaped from a two-front war by giving Hitler a two-front war. The Pact gave Hitler a secure border in the east, allowing him to attack westwards. Stalin was buying time, but intended to launch his own attack once Germany was bogged down in the west. Zhukov and his best troops in Mongolia were transferred to the western front. Hitler's deal with Stalin was the final nail in the coffin of the Anti-Comintern Pact.

As Japan evicted whites (Europeans) from the Pacific, Hitler reflected that it was not turning out as he intended. He had got into the wrong war.

Despite the strategic benefits—Japan's advance on Singapore and Australia would force Britain to withdraw Indian and Anzac forces, particularly from the Mediterranean, and the United States would have to cut back her arms supplies to Britain and the Soviet Union—Hitler was heard to mutter, "I never wanted things to turn out like this. Now they"—meaning the British—"will lose Singapore!" It was after he had returned to the Wolf's Lair, with the "Barbarossa" campaign on the brink of its first winter crisis, that he made to Walther Hewel the remark that has already been reported: "How strange that with Japan's aid we are destroying the positions of the white race in the Far East—and that Britain is fighting against Europe with those swine the Bolsheviks!" (Irving, 1977, p. 354)

That quote is from the 1977 edition of *Hitler's War 1939-1942*. Irving had placed a lot of material unfavourable to the Nazis in the 1977 edition, but removed it from later editions. I discovered this by accident, and uploaded the removed material to https://mailstar.net/world-war-II.html.

Hitler's War, the Japan Miracle, and the China Model

Professor of International Banking Richard A. Werner shows, in his book *Princes of the Yen*, a study of Japan's Central Bank and Ministry of Finance, that Japan's postwar miracle economy was a Butter-not-Guns adaptation of Nazi economic policy. He says that, before World War II, Japan was a free-market economy like the U.S.:

Few people are aware of the fact that free markets were almost the norm in Japan before the war. In the 1920s, the famous postwar Japanese system did not exist. Then, Japan's economy in many ways looked like a carbon copy of today's U.S. economy—with fierce competition, aggressive hiring and firing, takeover battles between large companies, few bureaucratic controls, strong shareholders that demanded high dividends, and corporate funding from the markets, not banks. (p. 1)

But during and after World War II, Japan's 'miracle' economy was highly regulated:

Yet throughout the postwar era, Japan's economy has been the opposite: highly regulated, with cartels limiting competition, bank financing and cross shareholdings reducing shareholder power, no takeovers, and a frozen labor market with lifetime employment and seniority pay. (p. 1)

In the postwar years, Japan's economic miracle made it the second largest economy:

However, Japan did not use free markets to become the second largest economy in the world. This means that there is a rival capitalist economic system, based on the very visible hand of planners, that has outperformed other systems in terms of economic growth rates over a sustained period of time. (p. 3)

The secret of Japan's economic miracle was lessons learned from Nazi Germany:

Influenced by German thinkers, the war economy leaders encouraged the creation of large-scale firms. They realized that among the three stakeholders involved in large companies—management, shareholders, and employees—shareholders' aims were least in line with the planners' overall goal of fast growth. So shareholders were eliminated, managers elevated, and employees motivated through company unions and job security.

Management, freed by cross shareholdings from dividend-oriented shareholders, did not pay out profits but reinvested them. This allowed them to grow their companies and expand market share. It biased Japan's economy toward high growth.

At home, the ensuing cutthroat competition for market share had to be contained by the formation of cartels. This did not mean that competition ended; companies continued to compete to keep up their rankings within the cartel. Most importantly, there were no cartels restricting competition abroad. The world's open doors and free markets meant that Japan's growth machines wreaked havoc. In the 1960s and 1970s, one leading U.S. industry after another was eliminated. Europeans, less dogmatic about free trade, simply restricted Japanese entry. The Japanese complied—managed trade was what they were used to and trade friction never became a major issue with Europe.

While most of the intervention in Japan's economy took an indirect, market-oriented form, there was a control tool that was used for powerful direct intervention. However, it works in such a subtle way that today many economists would still dispute its presence. The tool is money. The wartime bureaucrats understood what money is, where it comes from, and how it could be used to control every aspect of the economy. ...

Influenced by the methods of Hitler's central banker, Hjalmar Schacht, the leaders of the Japanese war economy turned credit creation into their most powerful mechanism for total control. They used the banking system purposely and skillfully to allocate resources to targeted industries. (pp. 3-5)

After World War II, the economic system remained on a war footing, against the world; the bureaucrats at MoF, MITI and the Bank of Japan were in charge.

Managers were the commanding officers, workers and salarimen the corporate soldiers. The bureaucracies of MoF, MITI, and the Bank of Japan were the economic general staff. All fought the total economic war against the world.

Exports were the bullets flying out, hitting world markets and often leaving deep wounds in other countries in the form of high unemployment. Imports were hits taken and had to be minimized. This was done with the wartime exchange rationing system, revived immediately after the war. Importers required import licenses for each item, which were granted only to producers in priority industries, such as the export industry. This system was used to impose extreme restrictions on automobile imports, tantamount to total import ban, while the infant domestic car industry was getting into gear. The more bullets were fired and the fewer hits taken, the likelier Japan was going to win the economic war it was fighting. A trade surplus meant victory. It seemed Japan was following the oft-quoted caricature of mercantilism, where trade surpluses had become an end, not a means to an end. (p. 32)

Japan was closed to imports, and piling up trade surpluses as if they were war loot.

... Thus instead of a steady drain on the system, as weapons production had been, exports would continuously strengthen Japan. The only limit would be the willingness of the world to put up with a country that was still at war with the world in economic terms—closed to imports and hence piling up trade surpluses as if they were war loot. (p. 33)

Industry after Industry in the West was wiped out:

As the United States pushed the Western countries to welcome Japanese exports, the full force of Japan's war economy was unleashed onto the world. Ignoring profits and aiming at market share, Japanese exports soon dominated the steel and shipbuilding markets in the 1960s. European and U.S. firms, aiming at profitability, were soon driven out of business. The onslaught by Japanese carmakers followed. Subsidized by the underconsumption of the domestic population, they began to conquer world markets. Then, in the 1970s and 1980s, the entire U.S. consumer electronics industry was wiped out by Japan's militarized and mobilized exporters. As a consequence, unemployment rose in the United States and Europe.

U.S. economists were often puzzled by the fact that Japanese monopolization of many markets in the world did not lead to concerted price rises to exploit monopoly profits. Analysts still failed to see its intrinsically different organizational structure and dynamics as a scale-maximization machine. Profits were irrelevant for management. (p. 33)

Japan's Central Bank, the Bank of Japan, was co-ordinating the economic war, using techniques it had learned from Hjalmar Schacht:

> This was a method pioneered by the German central bank, the Reichs-bank. It already had gained invaluable experience during the First World War and in the 1920s in restricting overall credit growth to desirable levels and also in allocating the newly created money to preferred sectors. During the 1920s, the Reichsbank, under its president Hjalmar Schacht, also provided strict "guidance" to the banks regarding their loan extension. The discount rate—the short-term interest rate at which banks could officially borrow from the central bank—was still announced, but it had become more of a public relations tool. By 1924, inflation had been brought under control. But the Reichsbank's "guidance" continued virtually uninterrupted for years—indeed, until 1945.
>
> The procedure was simple: Each bank had to apply to the central bank for its loan contingent for the coming period. The banks then proceeded to allocate their contingents among borrowers. Once the contingent was used up, the central bank would refuse to discount any further bills presented by that bank and would punish further credit expansions. ...
>
> The credit control system imposed in Germany handed enormous power to the central bank. Since the Reichsbank had been made independent from the government after the hyperinflation of 1924, it could do as it wished. It was only a small step further to give the banks detailed instructions about the sectoral, regional, and qualitative allocation of their credits. Reichsbank president Schacht made ample use of this power. By giving instructions to banks about what type of industrial sector and even which companies to lend to—and which ones to cut off from lending—Schacht engaged in a far-reaching structural economic policy, favoring specific regions, sectors, and institutions that he considered "productive" and pushing for corporate restructuring. (pp. 52-3)

Japanese bureaucrats visited Germany to learn the Reichsbank's methods:

> In Japan, the reform bureaucrats had studied the Reichsbank's methods and realized the enormous potential offered by central bank credit controls over the banking system. They had dispatched officials to Berlin, based in the Japanese embassy or more directly at the Reichsbank. This included Hisato Ichimada, who had been sent by the Bank of Japan, and who featured prominently as the Bank of Japan's postwar credit dictator   ... Having come to power with the beginning of open hostilities in China in 1937, the reform bureaucrats moved to control the allocation of money through the Temporary Funds Adjustment Law of 1937. This law brought banks and their investment and loan decisions under strict control by the central bank and the Ministry of Finance. Funding through the stock mar-

ket was reduced to a trickle, and the banking system was relied upon for resource allocation. (p. 54)

The 1942 Bank of Japan Law was copied from the Reichsbank Law of 1939.

It was now time to use the central bank for the purposes of the war planners. ... In 1942, the war leaders brought the Bank of Japan directly under the control of the government and its finance ministry by translating Hitler's new Reichsbank Law of 1939 and introducing it as the new Bank of Japan Law. Together with the capital flow and foreign exchange control laws, this completed the system of financial controls. (p. 54)

In 1977 Ministry of Finance officials Eisuke Sakakibara, Chlo Koron and Yukio Noguchi

were the first and only public figures to clearly identify and acknowledge the true nature of Japan's economic system. They called it the "wartime system for total economic mobilization." (p. 80)

During the 1980s, Japanese companies went on a buying spree, snapping up foreign assets. By 1988, nine of the world's 10 biggest banks were Japanese. They were operating in the West and undercutting British and American banks by offering cheaper loans.

Western bankers had forced Free Trade on the Manufacturing industry, allowing imports which undercut local producers and wiped them out; but they wanted Protection for their own industry. So, at the Bank for International Settlements (BIS) they got together and imposed the Basel Accord on Japan, forcing it to lift its Capital Adequacy Ratio from 6% to 8%. A central banker who I know told me it had actually been about 3%. The British and Americans told the Japanese that if they wanted to continue to do business in the West, they would have to agree to an 'international standard' of Capital Adequacy.

The Basel Accord of 1988 was an agreement by the twelve countries who comprise the BIS at Basel that the minimum capital adequacy ratio should be 8 per cent of weighted loans, of which not less than 4 per cent should be provided by shareholders funds. Shareholders' funds are referred to as tier one capital and subordinated loans as tier two (personal communication from Geoffrey Gardiner, former director of the Financial Services Division of Barclays Bank).

The Basel Accord forced Japanese banks to sell assets in order to comply with the new Capital Adequacy rules. Given the interlocking shareholdings that were a feature of the system, this crashed the asset bubble in Japan and created a depression there. But its export surpluses continued, as Eamonn Fingleton noted in his book *In Praise of Hard Industries*. For more on the Basle Accord see my webpage The 1988 Basle Accord—destroyer of Japan's finance system, at https://mailstar.net/basle.html.

Werner shows that in the 1990s Japan's Central Bank deliberately abandoned the Miracle economy. It had featured substantial public ownership, equality and security for workers, but subordination.

China's Economic Miracle

But other "Tiger" economies, and China too, have copied such policies. As a result, the U.S. and Australia are becoming mere quarries and markets for industrial exporting countries. And worse, our populations are being dumbed down.

Western bankers brought down the "Tiger" economies in the Asia Crisis of 1997. But they have not found a way to bring China's economy down.

Werner does not cover the new Chinese economy. But after Mao died, Deng Xiaoping visited Japan. He was so impressed with its Miracle economy, that he decided to adapt the Japan Model for China. Deng also received assistance from Lee Kwan Yew and from overseas Chinese, in developing the China Model.

China's economic miracle was achieved by a switch from Marxist economics to National System Economics—the sort of protected and state-guided economy that the U.S. had in the late nineteenth century and early twentieth, and which Australia had until the 1980s. But it was also modelled on another miracle, the Japanese postwar one, which was based on Hitler's miracle economy from 1933.

Unlike Nazi Germany, much of China's economy is publicly-owned. Unlike the Soviet Union, it has a vibrant private sector subject to state guidance (just as Japan's private sector is subject to state guidance).

After its first experiments with high-speed trains, China built a high-speed network covering most of China in just ten years, whereas the US attempt to connect San Francisco and Los Angeles by high-speed rail failed. China's superior economic system has put the rest of the world on notice: get rid of Economic Liberalism, or be taken over. My webpage on China's economic miracle is at https://mailstar.net/China-economic-miracle.html.

With its single-party system, China today has some resemblances to National Socialist Germany. Henry C. K. Liu compared the two, in his article Nazism and the German economic miracle, which was published at Asia Times on May 24, 2005: https://www.henryckliu.com/page105.html. He wrote:

> After two and a half decades of economic reform toward neo-liberal market economy, China is still unable to accomplish in economic reconstruction what Nazi Germany managed in four years after coming to power, ie, full employment with a vibrant economy financed with sovereign credit without the need to export, which would challenge that of Britain, the then superpower. This is because China made the mistake of relying on foreign investment instead of using its own sovereign credit. The penalty

for China is that it has to export the resultant wealth to pay for the foreign capital it did not need in the first place.

More at https://mailstar.net/china-nazi.html.

But China did this in order to gain Technology Transfer, just as the U.S.S.R. commissioned Western industrial companies to build facilities in Russia, and imported high technology products with a view to cloning them: https://mailstar.net/sutton.html. The foreign reserves it accumulated through such trade have allowed China to buy energy and resource assets abroad. Hitler's Germany traded industrial goods for raw materials from Russia, which it later tried to acquire by conquest.

Whereas Hitler felt a need to expand his territory, China does not (not yet, anyway). However, it jealously guards that which it has—and says it will go to war should Taiwan declare independence. By this means, it has given the US a tripwire by which to go to war. A war between these two might have no winner—only losers. But just as Hitler, on discovering that he had underestimated Soviet military strength, felt he had to attack sooner rather than later, so the US might decide in relation to China.

I feel that both sides are wrong. China should let Taiwan go—why risk the whole regime for a small part it does not control anyway? Does it not already own much of the world? And the US should give up its "Free Trade" economic policy, which is impoverishing it and its neighbours. U.S. agricultural exports destroy small farming in those neighbours, causing those deprived of a livelihood to come flooding across its borders.

Finally, a word to those who protest that Hitler was uniquely the embodiment of Evil. Don't we all have blood on our hands? Remember, Hitler was facing Trotsky and Stalin. They all lived by the sword and died by the sword. My distaste for Hitler does not mean that I have joined the ranks of "Hitler-bashers", like the Trots, the Larouchites, and the "mainstream" media. I try to stay non-ideological, maintaining a ledger-book on each historical figure, as I guess that God must do.

A Jewish man, a small shopkeeper in Canberra, who had been a prisoner at the Belsen concentration camp, said to me, "Hitler did a lot of good for his people. Mussolini did a lot of good for his people. Mussolini's only mistake was to join with Hitler." That was such a stunning statement that I went home and entered it on my website straight away.

Hitler was a mix of genius and foolishness: genius for his rebuilding the German economy, foolishness for the racism and militarism which undid any good he achieved. Hitler gets a bad press—a terrible press. He's not the only one, though—Stalin and Mao do too. Gaddafi, Saddam, Assad ... most of them were enemies of Israel. Given the bias of the "mainstream" media, we have all wondered at times whether Hitler could really have been as bad as he's made out.

Well, he was. But, to be fair, he did some good things too, like ending the Depression; and he was a genius, even though he put that talent to malevolent ends. What really opened my eyes to Hitler's true nature was the books of Otto Strasser.

The debate about Hitler focuses almost exclusively on Jews. I do not cover his Jewish policy here, because that is too much a live-wire. But by showing that his policy on the Slavs was genocidal, one may extrapolate to the Jews.

This issue was triggered by Hermann Rauschning book's *Hitler Speaks*, which I put online. Some people claimed that it was proved a forgery by Wolfgang Hänel, shortly after Rauschning's death. Hugh Trevor-Roper disagreed, based on *Hitler's Table Talk*, a record of conversations and monologues of Hitler from 1941 to 1944.

David Irving wrote, in a Letters page on his website, 'Hitler's Table Talk: a dependable source? Michael V has questions about two volumes of depictions of Hitler's table talk, Saturday, June 21, 2003':

http://www.fpp.co.uk/Letters/Hitler/Law200603.html

HITLER'S Table Talk comes from the original Bormann Vermerke which the late François Genoud purchased from Bormann's widow Gerda Bormann. They were actually typed from notes taken by the stenographer Heinrich Heim, whom I interviewed and who confirmed the procedure in detail. Each day's entry was initialled by Bormann at the end. They are genuine, in the first person, and highly reliable.

In *Table Talk*, Hitler enunciates a Genocidal policy towards the Slavs, of the same kind as in Rauschning book's *Hitler Speaks*. In 1939, few believed that Hitler could be this bad. I provide quotes from both *Hitler Speaks* and *Hitler's Table Talk*; judge for yourself. That material is at https://mailstar.net/Rauschning-Table-Talk.doc. *Table Talk* records Hitler's dinner conversations from 5th July 1941 to 7th September 1942, from 13th June to 24th June 1943, and from 13th March to 29th-30th November 1944. If you just read the excerpts of *Table Talk* published at some sites on the internet, e.g. http://davnet.org/kevin/articles/table.html, Hitler comes across as a mild-mannered philosopher. That file omits his ruthless side. But if you read the whole pdf book (Hitler, 1941-44/2000), or do keyword searches, that other side of Hitler emerges.

Viktor Suvorov (2008/2013) describes Stalin's "game":

Stalin, in alliance with Zinovyev and Kamenev, removed Trotsky from power. Then, in alliance with Bukharin, he removed Zinovyev and Kamenev. Then he removed Bukharin as well. Stalin removed generations of Dzerzhinsky's secret police henchmen through the hands of Genrikh Yagoda. Then Yagoda and his generation were removed through the hands of Nikolai Ezhov. Then Stalin removed Ezhov and his generation through the hands of Lavrenti Beria, and on and on it went. (p. 103)

Suvorov claims that this applied in the international arena too, and that Stalin helped Hitler launch the war, supplying him with the raw materials he needed, with intent to overthrow him later (the idea being that the dislocation caused by major wars paves the way to revolution, as WWI led to Bolshevism). Suvorov quotes from a speech that, he says, Stalin gave at the Politburo on August 19, 1939:

If we accept Germany's proposal about the conclusion of a pact regarding invasion, she will of course attack Poland, and France and England's involvement in this war will be inevitable ... we will have many chances to stay on the sidelines of the conflict, and we will be able to count on our advantageous entrance into the war ... It is in the interest of the USSR—the motherland of workers—that the war unfolds between the Reich and the capitalist Anglo-French block. It is necessary to do everything within our powers to make this war last as long as possible, in order to exhaust the two sides. It is precisely for this reason that we must agree to signing the pact, proposed by Germany, and work on making this war, once declared, last a maximum amount of time. (p. 109)

Chapter 26: What's Next

Maurice Strong and Klaus Schwab co-founded the World Economic Forum, which meets at Davos each year. Like the Trilateral Commission, it was an initiative of David Rockefeller, and is financially supported by the Rockefeller Foundation. The World Economic Forum gathers the wealthiest capitalists together, and they attempt to rule the world, putting on a benevolent face.

Samuel Huntington wrote (1996): 'the term "universal civilization" ... might be called the Davos culture. ... Davos people control virtually all international institutions, many of the world's governments, and the bulk of the world's economic and military capabilities. The Davos Culture hence is tremendously important' (p. 57).

Klaus Schwab advocates replacing 'Shareholder Capitalism' with 'Stakeholder Capitalism'. His Davos Manifesto on Corporate Governance, dated Dec 2, 2019, states "a company serves not only its shareholders, but all its stakeholders—employees, customers, suppliers, local communities and society at large. the best way to understand and harmonize the divergent interests of all stakeholders is through a shared commitment to policies and decisions that strengthen the long-term prosperity of a company" (Schwab, 2019).

That is fine in theory; but what about the practice?

In 'Stakeholder Capitalism' decisions are supposedly made by Consensus. That's how the WEF itself operates: there are no debates; but the 'Consensus' is handed down from on high. Agenda 21-style 'Stakeholder' meetings are chaired by a Facilitator and have a pre-ordained outcome, despite the impression that the opinions of the participants would carry the day; this is Fake Democracy.

WEF participants, along with Lynn Forester de Rothschild and Pope Francis, promote 'Inclusive Capitalism'. This supposedly would share the profits more than 'Shareholder Capitalism', treat employees better, and give countries hosting the enterprises a greater share of the profits. The push for 'Inclusive Capitalism' is coming from the top, not the bottom. Are the proponents motivated by altruism, or by fear that they'll be overthrown for stealing the income of the people?

Given that Tax Havens keep poor countries poor and poor people poor (Shaxson, 2011, cover; see p. 144 above), one would expect proponents of 'Inclusive Capitalism' to advocate getting rid of Tax Havens. I did a site search in Google on Feb 2, 2023, to find what the main two sites of 'Inclusive Capitalism' said about Tax Havens. Here are the searches:

"tax havens" site:https://www.inclusivecapitalism.com/
"tax havens" site:https://www.coalitionforinclusivecapitalism.com

Here are the results:

No results found for "tax havens"
site:https://www.inclusivecapitalism.com/.
No results found for "tax havens"
site:https://www.coalitionforinclusivecapitalism.com

Enough said—their benevolence is Fake.

George Soros' Open Society Institute funds the International Consortium of Investigative Journalists (ICIJ), which campaigns against Tax Havens; but Soros himself uses Tax Havens. Fox News reported:

> Billionaire George Soros, who has spent millions of dollars financing Democrats and left-wing causes, used a controversial Panamanian law firm to establish a web of offshore investment partnerships that operate around the world and out of the scrutiny of U.S. regulators, according to leaked documents.

> The so-called Panama Papers ... contain links to Soros, who funds the journalism group that is disseminating the information. So far, the International Consortium of Investigative Journalists (ICIJ) has been silent on its benefactor's ties to the law firm.

> Three offshore investment vehicles controlled by Soros are catalogued in the Panama Papers. Soros Finance, Inc. was incorporated in Panama; Soros Holdings Limited was set up in the British Virgin Islands and a limited partnership called Soros Capital was created in Bermuda. ...

> Soros' offshore companies may not pay U.S. taxes (his spokesperson, Michael Vachon, declined to answer that question), but the billionaire donates lots of money to Democrats who write and enforce the tax laws. (Byrne, 2016)

Apart from the above, Soros' Quantum Funds are based in London, New York, Curaçao (a Dutch Caribbean island) and the Cayman Islands.

A Government of the People would repudiate all debts owed to companies in Tax Havens, and nationalise (without compensation) all assets that are owned by entities in Tax Havens. The Fed would be nationalised, and made a department of the Treasury. It may issue digital currency, but would also issue Notes (cash), partly as a safeguard for occasions when electricity was not available, but also because a cashless society would be totalitarian, allowing governments to control all financial transactions. Infrastructure would be funded by low-interest public money.

Jewish Neocons (former Trotskyists) run the State Dept. (see p. 3), and are behind the Ukraine War (see pp. 18-9) as well as the race war (in the U.S. & France), and they also support the LGBT movement. Their targets are White people and the Christian religion, as they mobilised minorities against the Great Russians in early Bolshevism. US Ambassador Charles H. Rivkin developed a 'Minority Engagement Strategy' in France, to mobilise minorities and reform the history curriculum taught in schools (Jordan, 2023). The French Left follows Saul Alinsky's strategy. Alain Soral (2011/2022) blames the Trotskyist Left for allying with the Globalists against the middle and working classes:

> In an era of deindustrialisation and mass unemployment, anti-racism became the Socialist Party's (Parti Socialiste, or PS) sole battleground. The workers were forbidden from protesting against their country's takeover by a hostile Third World, i.e. immigrants, who were now also unemployed, as well as having been indoctrinated from a young age with anti-colonial propaganda in order to hate France. This time, the manipulation was at the hands of the Trotskyist and Zionist operative Julien Dray, taking over from Daniel Cohn-Bendit. (p. 280)

> Leftist anti-racists remain pro-immigration out of their hatred for peoples who are rooted in their homeland (in the pure Trotskyist tradition). (p. 298)

> The Universal Declaration of Human Rights (UDHR), ratified on 10 December 1948, was drafted by René Samuel Cassin, who incidentally was also President of the Universal Israelite Alliance (Alliance israélite universelle). (p. 311)

They have installed a system that might be called *Liberal Communism*. But Soral also gives some hope that the middle and lower classes will throw off the Globalist yoke:

> The Empire may seem all-powerful, but faced with growing popular anger and misery, it now only holds on through propaganda and police repression. (p. 327)

> The power of Money knows it must prevent at all costs a winning union of the proletariat and the middle class. No matter that anti-fascists have run out of fascists to combat! They are still surfing on the victory of the Second World War and the resulting power-sharing and **discreet alliance** between Atlanticist-liberals and Communists (and after May '68, **between Atlanticist-liberals and Trotskyist-Leftists**). (p. 349)

Globalist companies—Apple and many others— made Chinese workers work 12-hour shifts, from 9am to 9pm, six days a week; it was called "996". As those companies seek to exit China, they are pressuring India, Indonesia and other destinations to allow similar SLAVE conditions. Those countries should refuse; they should call the companies' bluff. Slavery ANYWHERE devalues Labor EVERYWHERE. Mandatory 12-hour shifts should be rejected everywhere.

Hayek's dictum that Socialism was the 'Road to Serfdom', per the title of his book, was wrong. The meaning was that mixed-economies like postwar Britain and Australia were on a slippery slope that would lead to Communism.

On the contrary, the benefits of those mixed economies—full employment and relative equality—kept Communism at bay.

The problem in Communist regimes was the total control at the top; for innovation to occur, individuals need freedom and the opportunity to operate businesses. When the Soviet Union allowed a mixed economy during the NEP of the 1920s, prosperity recovered; the same happened in China when Deng allowed markets to operate. Vietnam and other Communist governments now allow mixed economies, and most are much less repressive than in the past.

During Australia's postwar years, there were many government-owned enterprises, but managers from private industry were recruited to run them. They were not run by the workers as per Marxist dictum. But these managers worked within the full-employment policies of the government; they did not put profits before people. Rapacious managers would not have been employed.

Rick Farley correctly predicted that the dismantling of Australia's Socialist (mixed) economy would lead to 'Big Brother' laws (see p. 119). At the same time, the Culture War took off; it was led by Trotskyists, the same people who had called for dismantling the Socialist (mixed) economy—because it was a *nationalist* one. They pronounced Black Nationalism 'progressive' and White Nationalism 'reactionary' (see pp. 116-7).

Restoring the Socialist (mixed) economy would probably go a long way towards ending the Culture War. But it cannot be done under conditions of Free Trade, because Free Trade allows importers to undercut local producers and put them out of business. If governments want to manage the national economy, they need tariffs and non-tariff barriers to limit imports. This would not stop trade entirely, but it would stop predatory practices. In the 1950s and 60s, Australia had plenty of imported vehicles, but it also had its own manufacturing industry.

Dissident economist Steve Keen observed that broad-based economies do best. Protected economies are broad-based; Free Trade economies are narrow.

Over a century ago, Werner Sombart wondered why there was no socialism in the United States. Since then, the New Deal inaugurated a Socialist (mixed) economy, which blossomed in the 1950s and 60s, a golden era as in Australia. But Ronald Reagan gutted it.

We are now at a stage where there is a move to restore mixed economies, and there is no reason why conservatives cannot lead the way, as they maintained the mixed economies in postwar Britain and Australia for decades.

Appendix 1: Media Blackout on JFK Assassination

Robert Morrow's Confession—ignored by Media

Robert Morrow's book *First Hand Knowledge: How I Participated in the CIA-Mafia Murder of President Kennedy* was published in 1992, but the mainstream media, and even the dissident media, have gone quiet on it; there is no Wikipedia webpage on Robert D. Morrow.

Yet it's probably the most important book on the JFK assassination, because Morrow confesses to direct involvement as a CIA agent with a leading role.

Morrow reveals that his CIA case-officer, Tracy Barnes, asked him to purchase and modify rifles for the assassination.

"My involvement with the plans to assassinate John F. Kennedy commenced at the end of June, 1963. On July 1, I was contacted by Tracy Barnes. He requested that I purchase four Mannlicher 7.35 mm surplus rifles. According to Barnes, the rifles were available in the Baltimore area from Sunny's Supply stores. Upon my agreement to make the purchase, Barnes requested that I alter the forepiece of each rifle so that the rifles could be dismantled, hidden and reassembled quickly. I th43ought this last request odd until I was informed that the rifles were to be used for a clandestine operation. One day later I received a second phone call. It was del Valle calling from, I assumed, Miami. He asked me to supply him with four transceivers which were not detectable by any communications equipment then available on the market" (pp. 204-5).

Hostile reviewer Ulric Shannon reviews *First Hand Knowledge* at https://www.jfk-assassination.net/morrow.htm. This is a "factchecker" type review, and jfk-assassination.net is a "factchecker" type site on the assassination.

Shannon focuses on minor details which, he says, Morrow got wrong, while ignoring the central point in the book, Morrow's confession that his CIA case-officer, Tracy Barnes, asked him to purchase and modify rifles for the assassination. The word "Barnes" occurs only once in Shannon's review, and then not in connection with those rifles.

It calls to mind the "cognitive infiltration" of dissident groups by Government agents, as advocated by Cass R. Sunstein in connection with 9/11.

Morrow's book is online at https://mailstar.net/Morrow-CIA-JFK.html.

E. Howard Hunt's Confession—ignored by Media

E. Howard Hunt made a deathbed confession of his role in assassination of JFK.

The mainstream media ignored Hunt's confession—did not publish it. But Rolling Stone magazine published an article about it at https://web.archive.org/web/20080618150441/http://www.rollingstone.com/new s/story/13893143/the_last_confessions_of_e_howard_hunt/1

The Last Confessions of E. Howard Hunt

He was the ultimate keeper of secrets, lurking in the shadows of American history. He toppled banana republics, planned the Bay of Pigs invasion and led the Watergate break-in. Now he would reveal what he'd always kept hidden: who killed JFK

ERIK HEDEGAARD

Posted Apr 05, 2007 1:15 PM

E. Howard scribbled the initials "LBJ," standing for Kennedy's ambitious vice president, Lyndon Johnson. Under "LBJ," connected by a line, he wrote the name Cord Meyer. Meyer was a CIA agent whose wife had an affair with JFK; later she was murdered, a case that's never been solved. Next his father connected to Meyer's name the name Bill Harvey, another CIA agent; also connected to Meyer's name was the name David Morales, yet another CIA man and a well-known, particularly vicious black-op specialist. And then his father connected to Morales' name, with a line, the framed words "French Gunman Grassy Knoll."

So there it was, according to E. Howard Hunt. LBJ had Kennedy killed. It had long been speculated upon. But now E. Howard was saying that's the way it was. And that Lee Harvey Oswald wasn't the only shooter in Dallas. There was also, on the grassy knoll, a French gunman, presumably the Corsican Mafia assassin Lucien Sarti, who has figured prominently in other assassination theories.

Bob Dylan's Song about JFK—details suppressed by Media

Bob Dylan's song Murder Most Foul rejects the official "lone gunman" story. Instead, Dylan depicts the assassination as a conspiracy, with LBJ one of the leaders. "We've already got someone here to take your place."

Then they blew off his head while he was still in the car
Shot down like a dog in broad daylight
Was a matter of timing and the timing was right
You got unpaid debts, we've come to collect
We're gonna kill you with hatred, without any respect
We'll mock you and shock you and we'll put it in your face
We've already got someone here to take your place

I searched Google to see what the NYT and WaPo said about Dylan's song on the JFK assassination.

The   WaPo   search   was   "bob   dylan"   "murder   most   foul" site:https://www.washingtonpost.com/

The NYT search was "bob dylan" "murder most foul" site:nytimes.com/

The NYT had one thoughtful article, which noted that Dylan was portraying the assassination of JFK as "a crucial American trauma." The author did not explore Dylan's contention that JFK's assassination was a conspiracy by the elite.

The only other NYT piece to touch the topic was:

https://www.nytimes.com/2020/06/12/arts/music/bob-dylan-rough-and-rowdy-ways.html
Bob Dylan Has a Lot on His Mind

It completely ignored (passed over) Dylan's theme that JFK had been murdered by the elite, and that LBJ was complicit. The interviewer could have questioned him about that, but chose to bury it.

At Dylan's 80th birthday, the NYT ran the following piece—which made no mention of Murder Most Foul:

https://www.nytimes.com/2021/05/24/arts/television/bob-dylan-birthday-comedy.html.

The Washington Post made only one mention of Dylan's song "Murder Most Foul"—in the following article:

https://www.washingtonpost.com/lifestyle/style/bob-dylan-holds-a-mirror-up-to-america-and-sees-himself/2020/06/18/e40dc22e-b19d-11ea-8f56-63f38c990077_story.html
Bob Dylan holds a mirror up to America and sees himself

Like the NYT, the WaPo chose to skip over Dylan's theme that JFK was murdered by the Elite, with LBJ complicit. The interviewer could have asked Dylan about his line "We've already got someone here to take your place" but decided not to.

Harry Truman's article in WaPo pulled from later editions, ignored by Media

A month after JFK's assassination, Harry Truman wrote in the Washington Post of December 22, 1963

http://www.maebrussell.com/Prouty/Harry%20Truman's%20CIA%20article.html
The Washington Post
December 22, 1963 - page A11
Harry Truman Writes:
Limit CIA Role To Intelligence
By Harry S Truman

For some time I have been disturbed by the way CIA has been diverted from its original assignment. It has become an operational and at times a policy-making arm of the Government. ... I never had any thought that when I set up the CIA that it would be injected into peacetime cloak and dagger operations.

Ray McGovern, a former CIA Agent, revealed that, although the Washington Post published the op-ed in its early edition on Dec. 22, 1963, Truman's op-ed was excised from later editions, and ignored by other media. McGovern suggested a CIA role in this suppression.

https://truthout.org/articles/trumans-true-warning-on-the-cia/
https://consortiumnews.com/2013/12/22/trumans-true-warning-on-the-cia/
Truman's True Warning on the CIA
By Ray McGovern,
December 23, 2013
The Washington Post published the op-ed in its early edition on Dec. 22, 1963, but immediately excised it from later editions. Other media ignored it. The long hand of the CIA?

Eisenhower's warning about the Military-Industrial Complex

https://www.archives.gov/milestone-documents/president-dwight-d-eisenhowers-farewell-address

On January 17, 1961, in his farewell address, President Dwight Eisenhower warned against the establishment of a "military-industrial complex."

we have been compelled to create a permanent armaments industry of vast proportions. ... In the councils of government, we must guard against the acquisition of unwarranted influence, whether sought or unsought, by the military-industrial complex. The potential for the disastrous rise of misplaced power exists and will persist. We must never let the weight of this combination endanger our liberties or democratic processes. ... Yet, in holding scientific research and discovery in respect, as we should, we must also be alert to the equal and opposite danger that public policy could itself become the captive of a scientific-technological elite. (Eisenhauer, 1961)

James K. Galbraith says JFK planned to withdraw from Vietnam—this could be a reason the Deep State killed him

http://portside.org/2017-10-06/jfk-had-ordered-full-withdrawal-vietnam-solid-evidence
JFK Had Ordered Full Withdrawal From Vietnam: Solid Evidence
The Ken Burns-Lynn Novick PBS Vietnam Series glosses over JFK's exit strategy
By James K. Galbraith - September 25, 2017

The Ken Burns/Lynn Novick documentary series on Vietnam, currently airing on PBS, skates very lightly over one of the war's most contentious questions: Did John F. Kennedy intend to pursue the fight or to pull out? ...

But this presentation is highly misleading. In fact, Kennedy's feelings about Vietnam went beyond mere qualms: he had already reached a decision and acted on it. In National Security Action Memorandum 263, dated October 11, 1963, Kennedy articulated his decision to withdraw all US military forces from Vietnam by the end of 1965—with the withdrawal to be completed after the 1964 election. This was the formal policy of the United States government on the day he died.

Evidence of JFK's Decision to Withdraw from Vietnam.

The evidence is massive and categorical. It includes:

Robert McNamara's instructions to the May 1963 SecDef Conference in Honolulu to develop the withdrawal plan. A detailed account of the McNamara-Taylor mission to Vietnam that returned with the withdrawal plan, drafted in their absence in the Pentagon by a team under Kennedy's direct control.

An audiotape of the discussion at the White House that led to the approval of NSAM 263 (National Security Action Memorandum), which implemented the plan; this audio was released by the Assassination Records Review Board at my request.

The precise instructions for withdrawal delivered by Maxwell Taylor, Chairman of the Joint Chiefs of Staff, to his fellow Chiefs on October 4, 1963, in a memorandum that remained classified until 1997.

Taylor wrote:

"On 2 October the President approved recommendations on military matters contained in the report of the Secretary of Defense and the Chairman of the Joint Chiefs of Staff. The following actions derived from these recommendations are directed: ... all planning will be directed toward preparing RVN forces for the withdrawal of all US special assistance units and personnel by the end of calendar year 1965. The US Comprehensive Plan, Vietnam, will be revised to bring it into consonance with these objectives, and to reduce planned residual (post-1965) MAAG strengths to approximately pre-insurgency levels... Execute the plan to withdraw 1,000 US military personnel by the end of 1963..."

Dr William Pepper says CIA killed MLK and RFK too

William Pepper is a barrister (attorney) who acted for the family of Martin Luther King, and for the man accused of killing him.

It was Pepper, then a journalist newly returned from Vietnam, who first persuaded King to come out against the Vietnam War. Pepper explained that the war was a nationalist war which the US could not win, and presented photos showing the devastation wrought in the attempt.

King being a powerful orator—the most outstanding black American of the century—his coming out against the war, combined with his plan to bring half a million blacks to Washington to press lawmakers, made him a marked man in Deep State circles (FBI & CIA). Despite King's advocacy of Non-Violence, they saw him as a great danger.

Pepper acted for the defendants incarcerated for the murders of King and Robert Kennedy. He represented these defendants only because he believed then innocent, framed by the CIA.

Confronting state agencies who were the real assassinations of King, JFK and Robert F. Kennedy, Pepper also became an investigator—particularly in the King case, to which he devoted 30 years of his life.

Pepper wrote three books on the King Assassination, branding it An Act Of State.

In his book *The Plot to Kill King*, Pepper shares the evidence and testimonies that prove that James Earl Ray was a fall guy chosen by those who viewed King as a dangerous revolutionary.

Robert F. Kennedy knew that the CIA had killed his brother; but he needed to get the White House in order to reopen the case. The CIA killed him to stop such a possibility.

Operation Northwoods (1962)

Operation Northwoods was a Deep State plot against Cuba and JFK. CIA papers on Operation Northwoods were released about 1995, as part of an investigation into the assassination of JFK.

Information on Operation Northwoods was revealed by James Bamford in his book *Body of Secrets*. Bamford revealed that the Joint Chiefs of Staff drew up and approved plans for a False Flag attack on an American plane, to be blamed on Cuba, which would then justify an American invasion of that country and Regime Change to oust Castro.

An aircraft at Elgin AFB would be painted and numbered as an exact duplicate for a civil registered aircraft belonging to a CIA proprietary organization in the Miami area. At a designated time the duplicate would be substituted for the actual civil aircraft and would be loaded with the selected passengers, all boarded under carefully prepared aliases. The actual registered aircraft would be converted to a drone [a remotely controlled unmanned aircraft]. Take off times of the drone aircraft and the actual aircraft will be scheduled to allow a rendezvous south of Florida. From the rendezvous point the passenger-carrying aircraft will descend to minimum altitude and go directly into an auxiliary field at Elgin AFB where arrangements will have been made to evacuate the passengers and return the aircraft to its original status. The drone aircraft meanwhile will continue to fly the filed flight plan. When over Cuba the drone will be transmitting on the international distress frequency a "May Day" message stating he is under attack by Cuban mig aircraft. The transmission will be interrupted by destruction of the aircraft, which will be triggered by radio signal. This will allow ICAO [International Civil Aviation Organization] radio stations in the Western Hemisphere to tell the U.S. what has happened to the aircraft instead of the U.S. trying to "sell" the incident. (pp. 85-6)

Flying the target plane as a drone was envisaged by the Joint Chiefs as long ago as 1962. The same technology, but improved, was available in 2001 for the planes which attacked the World Trade Center on 9/11; and in 2014 for the hijacking of MH370.

A Mossad Connection

It's well known that the Deep State collaborated with the Mafia to kill JFK, but Michael Collins Piper, in his book *Final Judgment*, exposed a role played by Mossad in the assassination. Kennedy had been trying to stop the proliferation of nuclear weapons, and discovered that David Ben-Gurion was developing them at Dimona, using French technology (but without French knowledge or consent). When Kennedy insisted on inspections, Ben-Gurion resigned as Prime Minister, rather than agree to the monitoring of the Dimona plant; Piper says that he gave the green light for the killing of Kennedy by the CIA-Mafia consortium.

Mark Braver summarised Piper's case, in a Customer Review at Amazon.

When New Orleans District Attorney Jim Garrison charged businessman Clay Shaw with participation in the JFK assassination conspiracy Garrison stumbled upon the Israeli Mossad connection to the murder of President Kennedy. Shaw served on the board of a shadowy corporation known as Permindex. A primary shareholder in Permindex was the Banque De Credit International of Geneva, founded by Tibor Rosenbaum, an arms procurer and financier for the Mossad.

What's more, the Mossad-sponsored Swiss bank was the chief "money laundry" for Meyer Lansky, the head of the international crime syndicate and an Israeli loyalist whose operations meshed closely on many fronts with the American CIA.

The chairman of Permindex was Louis M. Bloomfield of Montreal, a key figure in the Israeli lobby and an operative of the Bronfman family of Canada, long-time Lansky associates and among Israel's primary international patrons.

In the pages of "Final Judgment" the Israeli connection to the JFK assassination is explored in frightening—and fully documented—detail. For example, did you know:

• That JFK was engaged in a bitter secret conflict with Israel over U.S. [Middle] East policy and that Israel's prime minister resigned in disgust, saying JFK's stance threatened Israel's very survival?

• That JFK's successor, Lyndon Johnson, immediately reversed America's policy toward Israel?

• That the top Mafia figures often alleged to be behind the JFK assassination were only front men for Meyer Lansky?

• That the CIA's liaison to the Mossad, James Angleton, was a prime mover behind the cover-up of the JFK assassination?

... Piper's book documents ... the means, opportunity and the motive for Israeli Mossad involvement in the assassination (working in conjunction with the CIA). (Braver, 2002)

James Jesus Angleton was the CIA's liason to Israel's nuclear program; he was running a covert scheme to supply Israel with nuclear weapons behind Kennedy's back (Cruickshank, 2023).

Mordecai Vanunu was captured by Mossad, with the complicity of Australian and British intelligence agencies, for releasing, in 1986, photos revealing the nuclear program at Dimona. Vanunu was caught in a honey trap; he was imprisoned for 18 years, of which he was held in solitary confinement for 11 years. Since his release, he has been gagged from speaking about the matter.

Ari Ben-Menashe revealed, in his book *Profits of War*, the connection between Dimona and the project to build the Third Temple on the site of the Dome of the Rock:

The father of Israel's nuclear program in the mid-1950s was the then young Shimon Peres, who was director general of the Ministry of Defense under David Ben-Gurion, the state's first prime minister and defense minister. Peres believed that if Israel was to survive, it had to have a deterrent against the Arab countries, and the ultimate deterrent would be nuclear weapons. With this in mind, Peres flew to France in 1956 for a meeting with President Charles de Gaulle. His mission: to get a nuclear reactor for Israel.

De Gaulle, a good friend of Ben-Gurion's from their days in exile during World War II, quickly authorized the sale to Israel of a weapons-grade nuclear reactor with the technology for the development of a nuclear bomb.

Israel's first nuclear reactor was set up on the Mediterranean coast in Nahal Sorek in the Yavne area. It was used for research with enriched uranium, which was imported from France. The idea was to see if a nuclear project could be handled with Israeli know-how—and the aid of Jewish scientists brought in from the U.S.

After the initial research yielded positive results, Minister Without Portfolio Yisrael Galili, a leftwing powerbroker who directed the intelligence and security services, took upon himself with Ben-Gurion's blessing the cabinet-level supervision of the program. After tasting success in Yavne, within six to eight months he pushed through another nuclear plant in the Negev Desert near Dimona, some 40 miles northeast of Beersheba.

In a memorable speech after the groundbreaking for the supersecret Dimona nuclear plant, the usually subdued Galili stood up in a Mapai Party meeting and, with his chest proudly pushed out, declared, "The third temple is being built!"

This astonished other cabinet members, who at the time did not know what he was talking about. Galili continued by saying that the revival of Israel as a moral leader of the world was at hand and dared any of Israel's neighbors to attack. (pp. 204-5)

After Israel launched the 1967 war, de Gaulle called Jews "an elite people, sure of themselves and domineering":

It was 32 years ago, on Nov. 27, 1967, when President Charles de Gaulle of France publicly described Jews as an "elite people, sure of themselves and domineering", and Israel as an expansionist state. De Gaulle's comment came in the context of his disappointment that Israel had launched the 1967 war against his strong advice and then had occupied large areas containing nearly a million Palestinians. A firestorm of charges of anti-Semitism followed his remarks, culminating in an interesting exchange by two of the world's great elder statesmen, David Ben-Gurion and De Gaulle. (Neff, 1999)

Victor Ostrovsky, a former Mossad agent, revealed that a faction within Mossad planned to assassinate President George H. Bush, for pushing the Madrid Peace Conference of 1991 onto Israel; the assasination would be blamed on Palestinians. Another Mossad officer, Ephrtaim Halevy, warned Ostrovsky of the plot, and asked him to publicise it, so as to head off the plotters.

A certain right-wing clique in the Mossad regarded the situation as a life-or-death crisis and decided to take matters into their own hands, to solve the problem once and for all. (Ostrovsky & Hoy, 1990, p. 278)

Ephraim called me on Tuesday, October 1. I could sense from the tone of his voice that he was extremely stressed. "They're out to kill Bush," he said. At first, I didn't understand what he was talking about. ...

"I mean really kill, as in assassinate."

"What are you talking about? You can't be serious. They would never dare do something like that."

"Don't go naive on me now," he said. "They're going to do it during the Madrid peace talks." (p. 281)

Ostrovsky did make a public statement about it, after which one of Bush's security team contacted him and obtained the details. This foiled the plot.

In 2012, Andrew Adler, owner and publisher of the Atlanta Jewish Times, suggested that Mossad kill President Obama, in order to obtain a successor who would help Israel obliterate Iran (Cook, 2012).

Andrew Adler, the owner and publisher of the Atlanta Jewish Times, a weekly newspaper serving Atlanta's Jewish community, devoted his January 13, 2012 column to the thorny problem of the U.S. and Israel's diverging views on the threat posed by Iran. Basically Israel has three options, he wrote: Strike Hezbollah and Hamas, strike Iran, or "order a hit" on Barack Obama. Either way, problem solved!

Here's how Adler laid out "option three" in his list of scenarios facing Israeli president Benjamin Netanyahu ... {quote} Three, **give the go-ahead for U.S.-based Mossad agents to take out a president deemed unfriendly to Israel in order for the current vice president to take his place,** and forcefully dictate that the United States' policy includes its helping the Jewish state obliterate its enemies. (Cook, 2012)

The Jewish Lobby was quick to distance itself from Adler, but an article in Haaretz by Chemi Shalev argued that Adler's views did not arise in isolation; he was part of a network of extremist Jews and their supporters. Yitzhak Rabin was killed for a similar reason and by a similar ideologue.

The CIA and FBI investigated Adler, but took no action. He resigned from the newspaper, and the "mainstream" media let the story die. It would have been a different matter if Adler had been a Moslem. Brigadier David commented in an email to ReportersNotebook@yahoogroups.com dated 23 January 2012 01:11:

Can you imagine if this newspaper were the Atlanta Muslim Times, or the Atlanta Arab News? The FBI would be raiding the office within seconds. The Editor would be held for treason. Every person on the staff would be arrested, the newspaper shut down, the building that housed the office would be demolished, and every American news outlet would have this as their leading story. But since this is a Jewish newspaper, the editor gets off scot-free. There is no FBI raid, there is no arrests, no shut down, no office building demolished, and not one word in the American media. You have to go to the Israeli media to get the story. This is what's called in America as the "Jewish Double Standard."

The Mossad plot to kill Bush Snr., and Adler's proposed Mossad hit on Obama, aimed at installing the Vice-President in his place, show that David ben Gurion's purported endorsement of the assassination of JFK is not without parallel. Even so, major responsibility rests with the CIA and other components of the Deep State in the United States.

Appendix 2: The Balfour Declaration as a Secret Treaty

The Balfour Declaration was a turning point in the First World War.

That document formalised a contract between the British Empire and the Zionist faction of World Jewry, meaning the Jewish Lobby of that time, whereby Jews affiliated to the Lobby would get the United States into the war on the British side—winning the war for Britain—and in return receive Palestine.

National Jews, who were assimilationist, opposed the Balfour Declaration. The British Government had considered a deal with Jewish interests, as a way of breaking the deadlock in the war, but the Jews they knew, and had approached, were assimilationists, the kind that Churchill would later call "national" Jews, rather than Zionists. At the time, the Zionists were a minority of Jews.

A Miracle?

Restoring an ancient regime after 2000 years is so astonishing that Lord Jacob Rothschild, interviewed on the centenary of the Balfour Declaration, called it a 'miracle' (Oryszczuk, 2017). It is as if Ancient Egypt sprang back to life.

But it was less a miracle than the result of some very clever politicking, much of which remains hidden.

How, exactly, did Zionist Jews get the United States into the war? If they DID get the United States into the war, leading to the defeat of Germany, might that not explain later German animosity towards Jews? And if they did NOT get the United States into the war, why should they have got Palestine anyway?

That issue is never covered in the mainstream media, or in textbooks on World War I; but it needs to be examined, because, contrary to the promises in the Balfour Declaration that "nothing shall be done which may prejudice the civil and religious rights of the existing non-Jewish communities in Palestine", the Palestinians are undergoing genocide at the hands of the Jewish state, and the entire Middle East has been convulsed by an expansionist Israel intent on dominating the region, destroying all opponents, and suppressing all critics.

It receives the lion's share of U.S. Foreign Aid, taking funds that should be going to poor countries, even though it is a hi-tech economy, a major weapons exporter, and has a Space program.

Israel has already breached its contract in many ways; but more are to come. In 2018, the US Ambassador to Israel, David Friedman, posed with a photo showing the Jewish (Third) Temple in place of the Dome of the Rock and Al Aqsa Mosque.

David Ben-Gurion claimed that uniting the world, i. e. World Government, was a particularly Jewish idea: "We consider that the United Nations' ideal is a Jewish ideal" (Israel: The Watchman), and that Jerusalem would be a seat of that World Government, the site of the Supreme Court of Mankind (Ben-Gurion, 1962).

Explaining Judaism for Japanese readers, Ben-Ami Shillony, a Professor from Israel, wrote in his book *The Jews and the Japanese*,

"The peaceful world that the Jewish prophets envisioned was to be ruled over by a scion of the House of David, later called the Messiah" (Shillony, 1991, p. 32).

For these reasons, there is an urgent need to examine the Balfour Declaration as the contract that made it all possible.

The Asquith government had been losing the war

Herbert Henry Asquith, Prime Minister, was the leader of the Liberal Party in a unity government. Despite the ongoing war, the government's economic policies were Laissez-Faire, with no central organisation. War management was chaotic; the Army grabbed men from all walks of life, leading to a shortage in munitions factories and on farms. The War Council was merely a Committee which had no power; decisions had to be ratified by the full Cabinet, which was unweildly.

British leaders, facing stalemate by late 1916, and having used up their credit in the United States, considered a deal with Jewish interests, to break the deadlock.

It was just such a situation, of hopeless deadlock between the Great Powers, that Theodor Herzl had earlier envisaged might be used to get Palestine.

But the Jews the British leaders knew, and approached, were assimilationists—the kind that Churchill would later call "national" Jews—rather than Zionists. The only Jew in the British cabinet, Edwin Montagu, strongly opposed Zionism. So did Lucien Wolf, Claude Montefiore, and Sir Mathew Nathan. Lord Nathanael ("Natty") Rothschild opposed Zionism too. He died in 1915, and Walter, who succeeded him, was pro-Zionist, but the Rothschilds were split.

American Zionist Jews favoured Germany, because they regarded the Czar as their #1 enemy. Only by getting rid of the Czar, could they be brought around.

British Prime Minister Herbert Henry Asquith opposed Zionism, even though Arthur Balfour and David Lloyd George were for it. Asquith would have to go.

President Wilson was maintaining neutrality, trying to impose a Negotiated Peace on the belligerents, with a view to drawing them into a World Government, such as he hoped the League of Nations would be. His version of World Government would be based on 'Peace Without Victory'. The war would be halted without any victor; all the powers would give up independence, pooling their sovereignty, their armed forces and their courts, and future wars would be avoided. Unlike at the subsequent Peace Conference of Versailles, where Germany was blamed for the war and penalised as a defeated enemy, in Wilson's plan both sides of the war would accept blame and participate in the World Government. Britain would have to return the German colonies it had seized, and allow 'Freedom of the Seas'—it could not use its navy to restrict German ships or blockade them.

World War One as an Opportunity

Theodor Herzl envisaged that the deadlock between the Great Powers might be used to get Palestine. Leonard Stein wrote in *The Balfour Declaration*:

"Herzl describes in his diaries an interview with Chamberlain in April 1903, when the El Arish scheme was again discussed. He told Chamberlain, he says, that 'we shall get [Palestine] not from the goodwill but from the jealousy of the Powers. And if we are in El Arish under the Union Jack, then our Palestine will likewise be in the British sphere of influence." (Stein, 1961, p.25).

Alfred M. Lilienthal wrote in *The Zionist Connection II*:

"With the outbreak of World War I, the Zionists moved their central headquarters from Berlin to Copenhagen, from where they could woo both the Central and the Allied powers" (p. 13).

American Jewish News of March 7, 1919 featured an article by Litman Rosenthal. He quotes from his diary, written in Siberia in 1914 as Turkey was entering the war, reminiscing about a meeting with Herzl in 1897, just before the First Zionist Congress. He reports Herzl's forecast, in 1897, of a coming Great War among the European powers, and his plan to use it a means of gaining Palestine at the ensuing Peace Conference:

I think of a talk I had with Herzl just before the First Zionist Congress. ...

"'It may be that Turkey will refuse or will be unable to understand us. This will not discourage us. We will seek other means to accomplish our end. The Orient question is now a question of the day. Sooner or later it will bring about a conflict among the nations. A European War is imminent."
...

"'The great European War must come. With my watch in hand do I await this terrible moment. After the great European war is ended the Peace Conference will assemble. We must be ready for that time. We will assuredly be called to this great conference of the nations and we must prove to them the urgent importance of a Zionist solution of the Jewish Question. ... the solution must be the return of Palestine to the Jewish people." (Rosenthal, 1919).

Lord Alfred Milner—to Dec. 2016

As democracy increased in Britain, the elite fought back by forming a secret society, to preserve elite rule despite the appearance of democracy.

Milner was the head of Cecil Rhodes' secret society in the years 1902-1925. It was known as the Milner Group, Chatham House, and the Round Table Group. Carroll Quigley wrote its history, and claimed that the Council on Foreign Relations (CFR) is its American branch, but others cast the CFR as allied but independent.

Rhodes' aim, based on the supremacy of the British race, was to get the U.S. back into the Empire, even if its capital be transferred to the USA, and republican government replace the Monarchy.

Milner was a member of the House of Lords; he was very talented, but had never been a Cabinet minister. He was a visionary, an organiser behind the scenes, but not a public speaker. He instigated and ran the Boer War on behalf of Rhodes, to keep the Gold in British hands and Southern Africa British. He was appointed High Commissioner for South Africa.

Milner's Kindergarten was his group of workers in South Africa who helped implement his plans. Milner participated in the Coefficients Club, an occasional dinner group organised by Beatrice Webb. Most of its participants were imperialists, but Milner also met Bertrand Russell and H. G. Wells there; they were not members of the Round Table.

Asquith Overthrown

In late 1916, members of Asquith's cabinet, in desperation, reconsidered Wilson's proposal for a Negotiated Peace. Lloyd George rejected this; so did Milner and Leo Amery, a fellow member of the Round Table.

Throughout 1916, Milner, Amery and their cohort despaired of the Asquith government's chaotic handling of the war. They met regularly on Monday nights as the Monday Night Cabal. On December 4, a member of the Cabal, Geoffrey Dawson, Editor of the Times, published a report titled "Reconstruction" that precipitated Asquith's resignation.

On Dec. 6, King George V summoned Balfour and Lloyd George to Buckingham Palace. It was agreed that Lloyd George would become Prime Minister, and Balfour Foreign Secretary.

From December 7, 1916, Lloyd George ruled as Prime Minister; he installed a Five-Man War Cabinet the very same day.

Lloyd George Government—from Dec. 7, 1916

The Lloyd George Government, from Dec 7, 1916, implemented a 5-person War Cabinet. This was an emergency measure, but it had no legal basis. The members were

David Lloyd George, PM, Leader of the Liberal Party,
Andrew Bonar Law, Leader of the Conservative Party and Chancellor (Treasurer),
Lord Alfred Milner, who joined the War Cabinet on Dec. 11, Minister Without Portfolio,
Arthur Henderson, Leader of the Labour Party,
and Lord George Curzon, Leader of the House of Lords.

The War Cabinet Secretariat comprised public servants—bureaucrats not politicians:

Secretary Sir Maurice Hankey, helped keep Cabinet organised.
Under-Secretaries Sir Mark Sykes and Leo Amery co-ordinated Departments, intelligence, and Generals.

Balfour replaced Sir Edward Grey as Foreign Secretary; Balfour was not in the War Cabinet.

Lord Alfred Milner, Minister Without Portfolio from Dec. 11, 1916

As a child, Milner had been to school in Germany, where he acquired the German talent for efficient organisation; he was considered somewhat "Prussian".

He advocated private ownership, but central management of the economy. He was socialist but anti-Communist, like Napoleon III, Bismarck, and Mussolini.

He appointed members of his Kindergarten to key jobs, including retaining Mark Sykes and Leo Amery as Under-Secretaries of the War Cabinet.

Milner was neither pro- nor anti-Jewish, but became pro-Zionist once he saw that it would help win World War One.

He drafted the Balfour Declaration, then got Leo Amery to revise it, producing the final draft. At the time, the others did not know that Amery was a secret Jew.

Milner was an Imperial Federalist: he sought to govern the British Empire as a single state, with the U.K. and the dominions equally represented in a federal government. In economic policy, he advocated Imperial Preference (i.e. a Trade Bloc, with tariffs on imports from outside the Empire); he opposed Free Trade and Laissez-Faire.

That is why he found a certain consonance with the Webbs.

However, in the Imperial War Cabinet (of U.K. and dominion leaders, plus India), dominion leaders rejected Imperial Federalism.

As Minister Without Portfolio in the Lloyd George Government, Milner was free to take charge of the war economy and much of the war effort. He is arguably the main person who won the war for Britain, as he had won the Boer War. However, he was an administrator, not a political leader; Milner worked in the background, while Lloyd George remained the focus of public attention.

German submarines made food security a vital issue. Overcoming objections from the Generals, Milner refused to let the Army conscript agricultural workers. His Corn Production Bill of 1917 provided a floor price for wheat and oats, reversing decades of Free Trade. It also established an Agricultural Wages Board, with a minimum wage, and limited the rights of landowners to raise rents (Gollin, pp. 416-9). Gollin comments, "His supreme skill as an administrator made itself felt in almost every department of the higher direction of the war" (p. 419).

David Lloyd George reveals 'A Contract with Jewry'

How do we know that the Balfour Declaration was 'a Contract with World Jewry'? Because David Lloyd George, Prime Minister at the time, said so in his Memoirs. He wrote that the British Government hoped thereby to wean American Jews away from supporting Germany, Russian Jews away from Bolshevism, "and secure for the Entente the aid of Jewish financial interests", since Britain had already exhausted its credit. (Lloyd George, 1939, p. 726).

Lloyd George further explained:

It seems strange to say that the Germans were the first to realise the war value of the Jews of the dispersal. In Poland it was they who helped the German Army to conquer the Czarist oppressor who had so cruelly persecuted their race. They had their influence in other lands—notably in America, where some of their most powerful leaders exerted a retarding influence on President Wilson's impulses in the direction of the Allies. The German General Staff in 1916 urged the Turks to concede the demands of the Zionists in respect of Palestine. Fortunately the Turk was too stupid to understand or too sluggish to move. The fact that Britain at last opened her eyes to the opportunity afforded to the Allies to rally this powerful people to their side was attributable to the initiative, the assiduity and the fervour of one of the greatest Hebrews of all time: Dr. Chaim Weizmann. ... Dr. Weizmann then brought to his aid the eager and active influence of Lord Milner, Lord Robert Cecil, and General Smuts. (pp. 722-3)

And drawing attention to Britain's desperate straits at the time:

I should like once more to remind the British public ... of the actual war position at the time of that Declaration. ... in 1917 the issue of the War was still very much in doubt. We were convinced - but not all of us - that we would pull through victoriously, but the Germans were equally persuaded ... They had smashed the Roumanians. The Russian Army was completely demoralised by its numerous defeats. The French Army was exhausted ... The Italians had sustained a shattering defeat at Caporetto. The unlimited submarine campaign had sunk millions of tons of our shipping. There were no American divisions at the front, ... available in the trenches. For the Allies there were two paramount problems at that time. The first was that the Central Powers should be broken by the blockade before our supplies of food and essential raw material were cut off by sinkings of our own ships. The other was that the war preparations in the United States should be speeded up ... public opinion in Russia and America played a great part, and we had every reason at that time to believe that in both countries the friendliness or hostility of the Jewish race might make a considerable difference. (p. 724)

Attesting the leading role of Jews in the Russian revolutionary movement—now suppressed from official histories—Lloyd George continued:

Quite naturally Jewish sympathies were to a great extent anti-Russian, and therefore in favour of the Central Powers. No ally of Russia, in fact, could escape sharing that immediate and inevitable penalty for the long and savage Russian persecution of the Jewish race. ...Russian Jews had been secretly active on behalf of the Central Powers from the first; they had become the chief agents of German pacifist propaganda in Russia; by 1917 they had done much in preparing for that general disintegration of Russian society, later recognised as the Revolution. It was believed that if Great Britain declared for the fulfilment of Zionist aspirations in Palestine under her own pledge, one effect would be to bring Russian Jewry to the cause of the Entente. (pp. 725-6)

But Jewish finance also figured prominently in Lloyd George's calculations:

It was believed, also, that such a declaration would have a potent influence upon world Jewry outside Russia, and secure for the Entente the aid of Jewish financial interests. In America, their aid in this respect would have a special value when the Allies had almost exhausted the gold and marketable securities available for American purchases. Such were the chief considerations which, in 1917, impelled the British Government towards making a contract with Jewry. (p. 726)

The leading Jewish role in both Finance and Revolution is now dismissed as an "antisemitic canard"; but Lloyd George shows that, in this critical period of history, both were very real.

James A. Malcolm reveals Secret Treaty between Britain and Zionist leaders in Oct. 1916

Of the main players, one revealed more of the secret dealings than the others. This was James Aratoon Malcolm, an Armenian who had moved from Persia to London in 1881 at age 13.

His family in Persia had engaged in shipping and commerce, and were treasurers in British Missions to the Shah. Although not Jewish, his family had close ties to Jews in Persia, and according to Malcolm, had helped shield them from persecution.

When he moved to London to continue his schooling, his guardian was Albert Sassoon. The Sassoon family, called "the Rothschilds of the East", were Iraqi Jews engaged in the Opium trade, with bases in Bombay, China, and Britain. Albert was made a Baron by Queen Victoria.

James Malcolm attended private schools, then Balliol College at Oxford. He became a financier, an arms-dealer, Chairman of the Royal Thames Yacht Club, and a founder of the British Empire League. He was the representative in London of the Armenian resistance against Turkey.

However James Malcolm, the facilitator who had brought the major participants together, stated that the Balfour Declaration merely formalised a "gentlemen's agreement"—in reality a Secret Treaty—between Zionist leaders and the War Cabinet in October 1916, which he had brokered. He wrote, "The consideration for this contract had already been given by the Jews before November 2nd, 1917." (Malcolm, 1944a and 1944b)

James Malcolm knew that Judge Louis Brandeis had a hold over Wilson. Allegedly, Wilson had been blackmailed by a Mrs Peck, with whom he had had an affair. Samuel Untermyer, her attorney, paid the blackmail, and got Wilson to appoint Brandeis to the Supreme Court in return for her dropping further legal action. The way to get the the US into war was through Brandeis and the Zionist Jews, not the National Jews.

Wilson asked Congress to declare war on April 2, 2018. Congress agreed on April 6.

This means that the Consideration remains largely unknown to the public. The Balfour Declaration was the public part of a Secret Treaty between Britain and the Zionist faction of Jewry, whose terms remain secret today, over a century later.

Milner and Lloyd George won the war, with Mark Sykes and Leo Amery; these four put the Balfour Declaration in place.

Chaim Weizmann and Leonard Stein deny James Malcolm's role in the Balfour Declaration

Chaim Weizmann omits James Malcolm's role in the Balfour Declaration, in his autobiography *Trial and Error* (1949).

But Hamish Hamilton, publisher of that book, later admitted Weizmann's error.

Leonard Stein dismissed James Malcolm's account as a 'myth':

"All this is part of a fairy-tale invented by Malcolm to flatter his own megalomania and elaborated, with still greater fertility of imagination, in a memorandum privately circulated by him in July 1944. The one grain, or half-grain, of truth contained in it is that at the end of January 1917 Malcolm introduced Weizmann to Sykes in the circumstances described in the text. His story is not worth serious discussion and is mentioned here only to show that it has not been overlooked. Professor Trevor-Roper has remarked (The Last Days of Hitler, p. 24) that 'mythopceia is a far more common characteristic of the human race than veracity.' The Malcolm myth is a good example" (Stein, 1961, p. 364 n13).

James Malcolm's role in the Balfour Declaration attested by major participants

James Malcolm's pivotal role was attested by:

Leopold Amery, a secret Jew who edited the final draft of the Balfour Declaration,

Malcolm Thomson, the official biographer of David Lloyd George,

Ronald Sanders, author of *High Walls of Jerusalem*,

Hamish Hamilton, publisher of *Trial and Error*, Weizmann's autobiography,

Oskar K. Rabinowicz, author of *Fifty Years Of Zionism*,

Samuel Landman, Solicitor and Secretary to the Zionist Organisation,

Christopher Sykes, son of Sir Mark Sykes, the Under-Secretary (of State) who drafted the secret Sikes-Picot Treaty, and later helped modify it to allow for the Balfour Declaration,

And Benjamin H. Freedman, a Jew who attended the Paris Peace Conference, but revealed Jewish machinations once he converted to Christianity.

Neither Mark Sykes nor James Malcolm were Jewish. Whilst sympathetic to Jews, their main motives were to win the war for Britain.

Testimony on James Malcolm's role in the Balfour Declaration

Documentation is presented below, of statements and letters on this matter published in the media. In these documents, the critical word is 'Brandeis'. Malcolm knew, somehow, the hold that Brandeis had over Wilson. Mark Sykes had tried American Jews before, but did not offer Palestine. Christopher Sykes (1953) hints at blackmail (Mrs Peck, Untermeyer); Freedman (1961) says so openly.

These documents pertain to the outcome of World War I; they should therefore not be suppressed on confidentiality grounds or commercial grounds. They are also pertinent to the origins of World War II. The public has a right to know.

(i) Leopold Amery, a secret Jew who helped compose the Balfour Declaration

Amery wrote,

> Meanwhile a new factor had come into the picture in the shape of Mark Sykes. An old traveller in the Middle East, he had thrown himself ardently into the cause of Arab and Armenian liberation and had been more recently employed by the Foreign Office in secret negotiations with the French as regards our future respective spheres of influence in the Arab world. An Armenian-born engineer, Mr. James Malcolm, had recently brought him into touch with the Zionist leaders. Mark's imaginative and receptive mind had at once seized upon all the possibilities of the Zionist movement. He became an enthusiastic Zionist, and his enthusiasm found an entirely new scope when he became a secretary to a War Cabinet which included such whole-hearted sympathizers as Lloyd George and Milner, soon to be joined by Smuts and, above all, with Balfour at the head of the Foreign Office. In his new capacity Sykes practically took charge of all the negotiations which led up to the Balfour Declaration. The Zionist movement owed much, at a critical moment in its history, to his infectious enthusiasm and to his indefatigable energy.." (pp. 114-5)

> Half an hour before the meeting Milner looked in from his room in the Cabinet offices, next door to mine, told me of the difficulties, and showed me one or two alternative drafts which had been suggested, with none of which he was quite satisfied. Could I draft something which would go a reasonable distance to meeting the objectors, both Jewish and pro-Arab, without impairing the substance of the proposed declaration? I sat down and quickly produced the following (Amery, 1955, p. 116)

(ii) James Malcolm's Letter to the Jewish Chronicle, published Fri. April 8, 1949, with copy of Weizmann letter admitting Malcolm's role

When Weizmann's autobiography *Trial and Error* was published in 1949, making no mention of the role of James Malcolm in the Balfour Declaration, James Malcolm wrote to the Jewish Chronicle about the omission of his role. Note the reference to Malcolm's role in 1916: "your useful and timely initiative in 1916".

AUTOBIOGRAPHY OF DR. WEIZMANN
An Omission
To the Editor of THE JEWISH CHRONICLE
From Mr. JAMES A. MALCOLM

SIR—Although my services in the Zionist cause have been clearly stated in various books and publications, including the recently published Biography of the late Earl Lloyd George, and some years ago in detail in THE JEWISH CHRONICLE, of which the Editor, my friend the late Mr. Greenberg, played a considerable part, together with the late Dr. Hertz, the Chief Rabbi, I think you may be interested and amazed that Dr. Weizmann, in spite of the fact that he has himself admitted my services in his letter of March 5, 1941, of which the enclosed is a photostatic copy, has omitted to mention my name in his Autobiography—you may make any use of the enclosed. You will be interested that several Jewish and non-Jewish friends have rung me up to express to me their amazement and to say that such ingratitude on Dr. Weizmann's part does a great injustice to his race.

JAMES A. MALCOLM. [ENCLOSURE]

James A. Malcolm, Esq., 25 Palace Gate, W.8.

My dear Malcolm.—In reply to your inquiry, you will be interested to hear that time time ago I had occasion to write to Mr. Lloyd George about your useful and timely initiative in 1916 to bring about the negotiations between myself and my Zionist colleagues and Sir Mark Sykes and others about Palestine and Zionist support of the Allied cause in America and elsewhere. But naturally I could not very well refer to the fact that in 1922 it had been the intention of Mr. Lloyd George to recognise your valuable services in the war in this regard (and others). Unfortunately the whole matter has been lost sight of, but possibly it can be revived again. I do hope that it will, as appropriate recognition of your services would be well deserved.

Yours ever.

Ch. WEIZMANN.

(iii) Malcolm Thomson, the official biographer of David Lloyd George, corrects Weizmann's account

Malcolm Thomson, official biographer of Lloyd George and privy to his papers, wrote to The Times Literary Supplement and to The Times backing up James Malcolm's statements. Hamish Hamilton, publisher of Chaim Weizmann's autobiography *Trial and Error*, also wrote to The Times admitting Weizmann's errors.

Malcolm Thomson letter to Times Literary Supplement, July 22, 1949, on Balfour Declaration

Times Literary Supplement

Friday July 22, 1949

THE ORIGIN OF THE BALFOUR DECLARATION

Sir.—Dr. Chaim Weizmann's autobiography, Trial and Error (reviewed in your columns on April 23), contains a rather surprising error about an important matter of history; an error which seems rather surprisingly to have been widely overlooked.

The winning of the Balfour Declaration , from the British Government in November 1917, was the decisive achievement of Dr. Weizmann's. career. It opened the way for the establishment of the new State of Israel, and made Dr. Weizmann's life story a vital chapter in world history. How the Declaration was secured is therefore a matter of front-rank historical moment. Now, the facts about the negotiations have during the past thirty years been correctly set out without challenge by men of unquestionable authority in various publications. Thus, in his monumental history of Zionism, Die Zionistische Bewegung (Vol. I, p. 656), Dr. Adolf Boehm says that when the U.S.A. had turned down the Sykes-Picot propsals for partitioning the Near East, "Mr. Malcolm, President of the Armenian National Committee in London, advised Sir Mark Sykes to influence Wilson through Brandeis, and to guarantee Palestine forthwith to the Jews, in order to gain their support. After discussion with Lord Milner, Sykes begged Mr. Malcolm to put him into touch with the Zionist leaders, because Sir Edward Grey and Mr. Balfour were convinced of the justice of the Zionist demand for Palestine. Through Greenberg, Malcolm made contact with Weizmann." Mr. Samuel Landman tells the same story in the Essays presented to J. H. Hertz, and these facts are also recorded in a number of other publications.

I myself, when writing the biography of the late Earl Lloyd George, studied the mass of documents dealing with the affair, and independently reached the same conclusion. In brief summary I noted how, when earlier efforts of Dr. Weizmann and his friends had failed to influence the Government to support their Zionist programme, Mr. James A. Malcolm suggested and initiated, on the ground of Zionism's potential value to the Allied war effort, a fresh approach to Sir Mark Sykes, the Under-Secretary to the War Cabinet; put him in touch with Dr. Weizmann and his associates; and was a member of the deputation that visited the Quai d'Orsay to win over the French to the proposal, after it had found favour with the new Coalition Cabinet under Lloyd George and the Foreign Office had sent word to Brandeis and through him had worked on Wilson, in Washington.

Curiously, in the account which Dr. Weizmann gives of the Balfour Declaration in chapters XV-XVI of his autobiography he makes no mention of Mr. Malcolm's vitally important intervention, and attributes his own introduction to Sykes to the late Dr. Gaster. I have communicated with Mr. Malcolm, who informs me that Dr. Gaster was only brought in some months after the negotiations had commenced, in February, 1917, on a single occasion—no doubt the one described by Dr. Weizmann on page 230 of his book. Dr. Weizmann's omission is the more surprising, because he wrote to Mr. Malcolm on 5th March. 1941, saying: "You will be interested to hear that some time ago I had occasion to write to Mr. Lloyd George about your useful and timely initiative in 1916 to bring about the negotiations between myself and my Zionist colleagues and Sir Mark Sykes and others about Palestine and Zionist support of the Allied cause in America and elsewhere." The omission in Dr. Weizmann's autobiography was no doubt due to a lapse of memory; but in view of the historical importance of the matter and in justice to Mr. Malcolm, I feel that the true facts should be clearly stated.

MALCOLM THOMSON.

Letter from MALCOLM THOMSON published in the Times of London on Nov. 2, 1949

THE BALFOUR DECLARATION
TO THE EDITOR OF THE TIMES

Sir,- The issuing of the Balfour Declaration by Mr. Lloyd George's Cabinet on November 2, 1917, was a notable event in world history, because it opened the way for the establishment of the new state of Israel. This thirty-second anniversary of that declaration seems a suitable occasion for stating briefly certain facts about its origin which have recently been incorrectly recorded. When writing the official biography of Lloyd George, I was able to study the original documents bearing on this question. From these it was clear that although certain members of the Cabinets of 1916 and 1917 sympathized with Zionist aspirations, the efforts of Zionist leaders to win any promise of support from the British Government had proved quite ineffectual, and the secret Sykes-Picot agreement with the French for partition of spheres of interest in the Middle East seemed to doom Zionist aims. A change of attitude was, however brought about through the initiative of Mr. James A. Malcolm, who pressed on Sir Mark Sykes, then Under-Secretary to the War Cabinet, the thesis that an allied offer to restore Palestine to the Jews would swing over from the German to the allied side the very powerful influence of American Jews, including Judge Brandeis, the friend and adviser of President Wilson. Sykes was interested, and at his request Malcolm introduced him to Dr. Weizmann and the other Zionist leaders, and negotiations were opened which culminated in the Balfour Declaration.

These facts have at one time or another been mentioned in various books and articles, and are set out by Dr. Adolf Boehm in his monumental history of Zionism, "Die Zionistische Bewegung," Vol. I, p. 656. It therefore surprised me to find in Dr. Weizmann's autobiography, "Trial and Error," that he makes no mention of Mr. Malcolm's crucially important intervention, and even attributes his own introduction to Sir Mark Sykes to the late Dr. Gaster. As future historians might not unnaturally suppose Dr.

Weizmann's account to be authentic, I have communicated with Mr. Malcolm, who not only confirms the account I have given, but holds a letter written to him by Dr. Weizmann on March 5 1941 saying: "You will be interested to hear that some time ago I had occasion to write to Mr. Lloyd George about your useful and timely initiative in 1916 to bring about the negotiations between myself and my Zionist colleagues and Sir Mark Sykes and others about Palestine and Zionist support of the allied cause in America and elsewhere."

No doubt a complexity of motives lay behind the Balfour Declaration, including strategic and diplomatic considerations and, on the part of Balfour, Lloyd George, and Smuts, a genuine sympathy with Zionist aims. But the determining factor was the intervention of Mr. Malcolm with his scheme for engaging by some such concession the support of American Zionists for the allied cause in the first world war.

Yours, & c.,
MALCOLM THOMSON.
Hampstead.

(iv) Hamish Hamilton, publisher of Chaim Weizmann's autobiography *Trial and Error*, acknowledges Weizmann's errors

Malcolm Thomson's letter to the Times drew a response from Hamish Hamilton, publisher of Chaim Weizmann's autobiography *Trial and Error*, in which he acknowledged Weizmann's errors:

This letter was published in the Times of London on December 3, 1949.

"TRIAL AND ERROR"
TO THE EDITOR OF THE TIMES

Sir, — Mr. Malcolm Thomson's letter to The Times of November 2 has been brought to the attention of Dr. Chaim Weizmann, who has asked me to confirm that his first introduction to Sir Mark Sykes was through the good offices of Mr. James Malcolm. Dr Weizmann's letter to Mr. Malcolm of March 5, 1941, correctly describes the position. Dr. Weizmann regrets that in "Trial and Error" this fact was not made clear. "Trial and Error" was dictated at times and places where references to documents was frequently impossible. Dr Weizmann is very sorry if, as a result of this, an apparent injury should have been done to an old friend of the Zionist movement.

Yours faithfully,
HAMISH HAMILTON.
90, Great Russell Street, W.C.1, Dec 1.

(v) Oskar K. Rabinowicz, author of *Fifty Years Of Zionism*, on James Malcolm's role

Rabinowicz (1950) wrote in Fifty Years Of Zionism, subtitled A Historical Analysis of Dr. Weizmann's 'Trial and Error':

FROM Dr. Weizmann's book it becomes obvious that up to 1916 discussions with leading personalities in public life in England went on but no definite or concrete proposals were submitted nor, of course, accepted. ... At that dark moment help was to be forthcoming from an unexpected quarter. In the narrative of this most important chapter of Zionist history before the Balfour Declaration Dr. Weizmann omits the most important link in the chain. He says (p. 181 [229]) that it was Sir Mark Sykes who became "one of our greatest finds" about whose services rendered to Zionism and Jewry he "cannot say enough" (p. 182 [230]). From Dr. Weizmann's story it appears (p. 181 [229]) that "Sykes was brought in touch with Zionist affairs and myself through Dr. Gaster". The facts, however, are as follows:

At the time the British Government felt it necessary to influence President Wilson towards a more favourable attitude to the Allies and it was James Malcolm, President of the Armenian National Committee in London, who advised Sir Mark Sykes to try to influence Wilson through Brandeis. It also seemed important to the Government to win over American Jewry towards the Allied cause and Malcolm therefore advised Sykes to "promise Palestine to the Jews after the victory" and thus gain their sympathies. Brandeis was a Zionist and the Zionist aim was the restoration of Palestine-Sykes understood where his work would have to start. Being Under Secretary of the War Cabinet he immediately sounded some of its members, and after further negotiations Sykes requested and authorised Malcolm to approach the Zionist leaders and give them the assurance that the War Cabinet was disposed to promise Palestine to the Jews. This conversation took place in October 1916. The fact that the Cabinet, to which Balfour as well as Lloyd George then belonged, authorised Sykes to contact Zionist leaders through Mr. Malcolm shows the scanty results of the preparatory political work of Dr. Weizmann and his colleagues, in great contrast to its appraisal in Trial and Error. Malcolm did not approach Dr. Weizmann nor did Sykes ask him to do so. He personally knew L. J. Greenberg, editor of the Jewish Chronicle, and the Chief Rabbi, Dr. J. H. Hertz, who were both members of the "Russian Society" founded by Malcolm in 1915. He wrote the former a letter informing him of the important decision of the Government. Greenberg thereupon arranged a meeting between Malcolm and Dr. Weizmann. The latter, in view of the complete deadlock in his efforts wished to see Sykes immediately. Malcolm telephoned Sykes from Dr. Weizmann's house and Sir Mark invited him to call the next morning. As Dr. Weizmann was unable to attend Sokolow went instead. Further conversations were held in which Dr. Weizmann also participated. All these interviews took place with the knowledge and approval of Sir Maurice Hankey, the Secretary of the War Cabinet. The first important formal meeting at which Sir Mark Sykes as well as the Zionist and Jewish representatives participated was that of February 7, 1917 in the house of Dr. Gaster (p. 188 [238]).

Malcolm Thomson, Lloyd George's biographer, corroborates the important initiative of Malcolm and confirms that he "when writing the biography of the late Earl Lloyd George, studied the mass of documents dealing with the affair, and independently reached the same conclusion". Malcolm published in the Jewish Chronicle a letter referring to the fact that Dr. Weizmann in his memoirs did not mention his intervention and simultaneously released Dr. Weizmann's communication to him, dated March 5, 1941, in which the latter said: "In reply to your inquiry, you will be interested to hear that some time ago I had occasion to write to Mr. Lloyd George about your useful and timely initiative in 1916 to bring about the negotiations between myself and my Zionist colleagues and Sir Mark Sykes and others about Palestine and Zionist support of the Allied cause in America and elsewhere." (Rabinowicz, 1950, pp. 76-8)

(vi) Samuel Landman's account of Balfour Declaration attests James Malcolm's pivotal role

Samuel Landman was a Solicitor, and Secretary to the Zionist Organisation of the U. K. from 1917 to 1922.

He wrote (1936/1978) an essay on the origins of the Balfour Declaration, published in March 1936 as a pamphlet titled Great Britain, The Jews And Palestine:

> The author of this pamphlet is a well-known English Zionist. He was Hon. Secretary of the Joint Zionist Council of the United Kingdom in 1912, Joint Editor of the" Zionist" in 1913-14 and Author of pamphlets on "History of Zionism" and " Zionism, Its Organisation and Institutions" published during the war. From 1917 to 1922 he was Solicitor and Secretary to the Zionist Organisation. He is now Legal Adviser to the New Zionist Organisation. (p. 2)

> Great Britain, The Jews And Palestine

> by Samuel Landman (Solicitor and Secretary to the Zionist Organisation of the UK from 1917 to 1922)

> London: New Zionist Press, 1936

> Those who assisted at the birth of the Balfour Declaration were few in number. This makes it important to bring into proper relief the services of one who, owing above all to his own modesty, has hitherto remained in the background. His services however should take their proper place in the front rank alongside of those Englishmen of vision whose services are more widely known, including the late Sir Mark Sykes, the Rt. Hon. W.

Ormsby Gore, The Rt. Hon. Sir Ronald Graham, General Sir George Mac-
donagh and Mr. G. H. Fitzmaurice.

In the early years of the War great efforts were made by the Zionist
Leaders, Dr. Weizmann and Mr. Sokolow, chiefly through the late Mr. C.
P. Scott of the Manchester Guardian, and Sir Herbert Samuel, to induce
the Cabinet to espouse the cause of Zionism.

These efforts were, however, without avail. In fact, Sir Herbert Samuel has
publicly stated that he had no share in the initiation of the negotiations
which led to the Balfour Declaration. The actual initiator was Mr. James A.
Malcolm and the following is a brief account of the circumstances in which
the negotiations took place.

During the critical days of 1916 and of the impending defection of Russia,
Jewry, as a whole, was against the Czarist regime and had hopes that
Germany, if victorious, would in certain circumstances give them Palestine.
Several attempts to bring America into the War on the side of the Allies
by influencing influential Jewish opinion were made and had failed. Mr.
James A. Malcolm, who was already aware of German pre-war efforts to
secure a foothold in Palestine through the Zionist Jews and of the abortive
Anglo-French démarches at Washington and New York; and knew that
Mr. Woodrow Wilson, for good and sufficient reasons, always attached
the greatest possible importance to the advice of a very prominent Zionist
(Mr. Justice Brandeis, of the U.S. Supreme Court); and was in close touch
with Mr. Greenberg, Editor of the Jewish Chronicle (London); and knew
that several important Zionist Jewish leaders had already gravitated to
London from the Continent on the qui vive awaiting events; and appreci-
ated and realised the depth and strength of Jewish national aspirations;
spontaneously took the initiative, to convince first of all Sir Mark Sykes,
Under Secretary to the War Cabinet, and afterwards Monsieur Georges
Picot, of the French Embassy in London, and Monsieur Goût of the Quai
d'Orsay (Eastern Section), that the best and perhaps the only way (which
proved so to be) to induce the American President to come into the War
was to secure the co-operation of Zionist Jews by promising them Palestine, and thus enlist and mobilise the hitherto unsuspectedly powerful
forces of Zionist Jews in America and elsewhere in favour of the Allies on
a quid pro quo contract basis. Thus, as will be seen, the Zionists, having
carried out their part, and greatly helped to bring America in, the Balfour
Declaration of 1917 was but the public confirmation of the necessarily secret "gentleman's" agreement of 1916 made with the previous knowledge,
acquiescence and/or approval of the Arabs and of the British, American,
French and other Allied Governments, and not merely a voluntary altruis-
tic and romantic gesture on the part of Great Britain as certain people ei-

ther through pardonable ignorance assume or unpardonable illwill would represent or rather misrepresent. ...

The Balfour Declaration, in the words of Professor H. M. V. Temperley*, was "a definite contract between the British Government and Jewry." The main consideration given by the Jewish people (represented at the time by the leaders of the Zionist Organisation) was their help in bringing President Wilson to the aid of the Allies. Moreover, officially interpreted at the time by Lord Robert Cecil as "Judea for the Jews" in the same sense as "Arabia for the Arabs;" the Declaration sent a thrill throughout the world. The prior Sykes-Picot Treaty of 1916, according to which Northern Palestine was to be politically detached and included in Syria (French sphere), was subsequently, at the instance of the Zionist leaders, amended so that the Jewish National Home should comprise the whole of Palestine in accordance with the promise previously made to them for their services by the British, Allied and American Governments and to give full effect to the Balfour Declaration, the terms of which had been settled and known to all Allied and associated belligerents, including Arabs, before they were made public. [...]

The fact that it was Jewish help that brought U.S.A. into the War on the side of the Allies has rankled ever since in German - especially Nazi - minds, and has contributed in no small measure to the prominence which anti-Semitism occupies in the Nazi programme. (pp. 4-6)

* History of the Peace Conference in Paris, 1920, volume 6, page 173.

(vii) J. M. N. Jeffries on Mark Sykes' role as liaison between War Office, Intelligence & Cabinet

J. M. N. Jeffries (1939/2015) wrote:

Sir Mark Sykes, I may interpolate, was Assistant-Secretary to the War Office then, a position which however was not at all departmental. It was his official title, but in reality he acted as liaison officer between the War Office, the India Office, the Intelligence organizations, and other bodies of the highest importance. He used to visit all the seats of power daily, co-ordinating their information, besides interviewing generals back from the front on leave, ambassadors and ministers, people of every standing and of every position, provided they had something worth telling to tell him. He had the ear of the Cabinet of course, and was in sum a man of the greatest influence.

It is not difficult to perceive why he had not been so successful in his German-American endeavours. He, with the "conscience-group" at the Foreign Office very possibly, was trying to work through the leaders of British Jewry, through the moderate Lucien Wolf section, through various rabbis whose only aim was to establish a spiritual-cultural Jewish centre in Palestine.

I return to Mr. Landman. Sir Mark Sykes was regretting his insuccess one day in the presence of Mr. James Malcolm, "'a prominent British Armenian'" as Mr. Wickham Steed designates him. Mr. Malcolm, a Balliol man, belonged to a family of Armenian origin but British for several generations. He was in contact. with some "ardent political Zionists, and he now told Sir Mark Sykes that it was to the political Zionists he should have turned. "You are going the wrong way about it," he said, "the well-to-do English Jews you meet and the Jewish clergy are not the real leaders of the Jewish people." Political Zionism or national Zionism, as Mr. Malcolm called it, was the key to influence over the Jewish body in the United States, and to more even than that. Mr. Malcolm said that there was a way to make American Jews thoroughly pro-Ally, and that he knew a man in America who was probably the most intimate friend of President Wilson. Through that man, if through anybody, the President's mind could be turned towards active participation in the War on the side of the Allies. (The man in question was Judge Louis Brandeis, of the United States Supreme Court.) (pp. 134-5).

(viii) Benjamin H. Freedman on the Consideration paid for the Balfour Declaration

Freedmam (1961) said in a speech at the Willard Hotel:

World War I broke out in the summer of 1914. [...] Within two years Germany had won that war: not alone won it nominally, but won it actually. The German submarines, which were a surprise to the world, had swept all the convoys from the Atlantic Ocean, and Great Britain stood there without ammunition for her soldiers, stood there with one week's food supply facing her -- and after that, starvation.

At that time, the French army had mutinied. They lost 600,000 of the flower of French youth in the defense of Verdun on the Somme. The Russian army was defecting. They were picking up their toys and going home, they didn't want to play war anymore, they didn't like the Czar. And the Italian army had collapsed.

Now Germany -- not a shot had been fired on the German soil. Not an enemy soldier had crossed the border into Germany. And yet, here was Germany offering England peace terms. They offered England a negotiated peace on what the lawyers call a status quo ante basis. That means: "Let's call the war off, and let everything be as it was before the war started."

Well, England, in the summer of 1916 was considering that. Seriously! They had no choice. It was either accepting this negotiated peace that

Germany was magnanimously offering them, or going on with the war and being totally defeated.

While that was going on [...] the Zionists in London went to the British war cabinet and they said: "Look here. You can yet win this war. You don't have to give up. You don't have to accept the negotiated peace offered to you now by Germany. You can win this war if the United States will come in as your ally."

The United States was not in the war at that time. We were fresh; we were young; we were rich; we were powerful. They [Zionists] told England: "We will guarantee to bring the United States into the war as your ally, to fight with you on your side, if you will promise us Palestine after you win the war."

[...] It's absolutely absurd that Great Britain -- that never had any connection or any interest or any right in what is known as Palestine -- should offer it as coin of the realm to pay the Zionists for bringing the United States into the war.

However, they made that promise, in October of 1916. October, nineteen hundred and sixteen. [...]

The Jews didn't like the Czar, and they didn't want Russia to win this war. So the German bankers -- the German-Jews -- Kuhn Loeb and the other big banking firms in the United States refused to finance France or England to the extent of one dollar. They stood aside and they said: "As long as France and England are tied up with Russia, not one cent!" But they poured money into Germany, they fought with Germany against Russia, trying to lick the Czarist regime.

Now those same Jews, when they saw the possibility of getting Palestine, they went to England and they made this deal. At that time, everything changed, like the traffic light that changes from red to green. Where the newspapers had been all pro-German, where they'd been telling the people of the difficulties that Germany was having fighting Great Britain commercially and in other respects, all of a sudden the Germans were no good. They were villains. They were Huns. They were shooting Red Cross nurses. They were cutting off babies' hands. And they were no good.

Well, shortly after that, Mr. Wilson declared war on Germany.

The Zionists in London sent these cables to the United States, to Justice Brandeis: "Go to work on President Wilson. We're getting from England what we want. Now you go to work, and you go to work on President Wilson and get the United States into the war." And that did happen. That's how the United States got into the war. We had no more interest in it; we had no more right to be in it than we have to be on the moon tonight instead of in this room. [...]

After we got into the war, the Zionists went to Great Britain and they said: "Well, we performed our part of the agreement. Let's have something in writing that shows that you are going to keep your bargain and give us Palestine after you win the war." Because they didn't know whether the war would last another year or another ten years. So they started to work out a receipt. The receipt took the form of a letter, and it was worded in very cryptic language so that the world at large wouldn't know what it was all about. And that was called the Balfour Declaration.

The Balfour Declaration was merely Great Britain's promise to pay the Zionists what they had agreed upon as a consideration for getting the United States into the war. So this great Balfour Declaration, that you hear so much about, is just as phony as a three dollar bill. And I don't think I could make it more emphatic than that.

Now, that is where all the trouble started. The United States went in the war. The United States crushed Germany. We went in there, and it's history. You know what happened. Now, when the war was ended, and the Germans went to Paris, to the Paris Peace Conference in 1919, there were 117 Jews there, as a delegation representing the Jews, headed by Bernard Baruch. I was there: I ought to know. Now what happened?

The Jews at that peace conference, when they were cutting up Germany and parceling out Europe to all these nations that claimed a right to a certain part of European territory, the Jews said, "How about Palestine for us?" And they produced, for the first time to the knowledge of the Germans, this Balfour Declaration. So the Germans, for the first time realized, "Oh, that was the game! That's why the United States came into the war." And the Germans for the first time realized that they were defeated, they suffered this terrific reparation that was slapped onto them, because the Zionists wanted Palestine and they were determined to get it at any cost.

Now, that brings us to another very interesting point. When the Germans realized this, they naturally resented it. Up to that time, the Jews had never been better off in any country in the world than they had been in Germany.

(ix) Benjamin H. Freedman on the Secret Agreement of October 1916

Freedman (1970) gave this address titled The Hidden Tyranny:

Shortly after President Wilson's first inauguration, he received a visitor in the White House by the name of Mr. Samuel Untermeyer. Mr. Untermeyer was a prominent New York City attorney ... Mr. Untermeyer informed President Wilson that he had been retained to bring a breach of promise action against President Wilson.

Mr. Untermeyer informed President Wilson that his client was willing to accept $40,000.00 in lieu of commencing the breach of promise action. Mr.

Untermeyer's client was the former wife of a Professor at Princeton University at the same time President Wilson was a professor at Princeton University.

Mr. Untermeyer produced a packet of letters from his pocket, written by President Wilson to his colleague's wife when they were neighbors at Princeton University. These letters established the illicit relationship which had existed between President Wilson and the wife of his colleague neighbor. [...]

Mr. Untermeyer returned to President Wilson a few days later as they had agreed. President Wilson did not hesitate to inform Mr. Untermeyer that he did not have the $40,000.00 to pay his blackmailer. President Wilson appeared irritated. Mr. Untermeyer considered the matter a few Moments and then volunteered a solution to President Wilson for his problem.

Mr, Untermeyer volunteered to give President Wilson's former sweetheart the $40,000.00 out of his own pocket on one condition: that Wilson promise Untermeyer to appoint to the first vacancy on the United States Supreme Court a nominee to be recommended to Wilson by Untermeyer. [...]

Mr. Untermeyer recommended Louis Dembitz Brandeis for the vacancy, who was immediately appointed by Wilson. President Wilson and Justice Brandeis became unusually intimate friends. Justice Brandeis knew the circumstances of his appointment to the Supreme Court by President Wilson. In 1914 Justice Brandeis was the most prominent and most politically influential of all Zionists in the United States. [...]

After the October 1916 agreement was concluded between the British War Cabinet and the World Zionist Organization, the Talmudists throughout the world were hopeful that an international incident would soon occur to Justify a declaration of war against Germany by the United States. [...]

Prior to the October 1916 London Agreement, Talmudists throughout the world were pro-German. [...] Talmudists throughout the world were informed by cable from London about the October 1916 London Agreement.

That information transformed them from pro-German to pro-British. Great Britain placed at the disposal of Talmudists in London their secret codes and worldwide cable facilities to inform Talmudists throughout the world about Great Britain's pledge to turn over Palestine to them as compensation for railroading the United States into the war in Europe as Great Britain's ally in their war against Germany. Talmudists enlisted in great numbers in October 1916 in Great Britain's Department of Defense. [...]

Germany's October 1916 peace offer was on the table before the British War Cabinet; it needed only one signature to end the war. Great Britain would have quickly accepted Germany's peace offer if the World Zionist Organization had not interfered.

(x) Christopher Sykes, son of Sir Mark Sykes, attests James Malcolm's pivotal role

Christopher Sykes wrote in *Two Studies in Virtue* (1953):

In the autumn of that year [1915] Sykes had been appointed one of the two "Assistant Secretaries to the War Cabinet," the other one being Mr. Leopold Amery. The post was a little more than it sounded. The two Assistants enjoyed the rank of Under-Secretaries of State; their official duty was to prepare "Intelligence Summaries" at regular intervals for the information of Ministers, Mr. Amery dealing with European and Far Eastern affairs, Mark Sykes with the problems of Islam ...

In March of 1916 Sykes and Picot went to St. Petersburg, and in a conversation with Sazanov Sykes discussed the possibility that Zionism might solve the Jewish problem of Russia. Then, after his return to England, he showed in one small incident that his Zionist sympathies had by this time grown strong. The most eminent English Jewish scholar of those days was Lucien Wolf. He was also an extreme opponent of Zionism and he presented an aide-memoire to the Foreign Office some time in the early part of 1916, pointing out the dangers of Jewish nationalism. (p. 177). ...

The office of the Assistant Secretaries was in Whitehall Gardens. One day in October of 1916 a certain Mr. James Malcolm came to visit Mark Sykes there. ... He had met Mark Sykes before the war and knew him on familiar terms. ...One day in October of 1916 a certain Mr. James Malcolm came to visit Mark Sykes there. ... Mr. Malcolm ... proceeded to tell him about Zionism ... Sykes began at last to yield ... and asked Mr. Malcolm to come back soon. (p. 180)

After reflection the opinion of Sykes was that the prospect of Zionism ... had come too late. He told Mr. Malcolm so at their next meeting a few days later. He said that arrangements had already been concluded which made it impossible for the British Government to take on any new policy in the East, and he added that this was not merely his personal opinion: he had consulted Lord Milner, he explained, and Lord Milner, like himself, found the idea of Zionism genial, but too radical ... Mr. Malcolm .. replied that the well-to-do English Jews he met were not the real leaders of the Jewish people. "You have not met the other kind of Jews," ... He then told Sykes of a very curious and powerful influence which Zionists could exert. One of President Wilson's closest advisers and friends was justice Louis D. Brandeis,... Wilson was attached to Brandeis by ties of peculiar hardiness, because, so the story ran, in his earlier days the future President had been saved by this man from appearing in a damaging law-suit. It was said that Brandeis was regarded by Wilson as the man to whom he owed his career. ... Brandeis was Wilson's intimate adviser, and Brandeis was a Zionist. ... When Sykes heard this he was again moved to confer with Lord Milner, and the latter told the Cabinet of Malcolm's proposals and ideas. (Sykes, p. 183)

As the go-between Mr. Malcolm now arranged to meet the Zionist leaders through his friend Leopold Greenberg, whom we last noted at the Sixth Zionist Congress in Basle reading Sir Clement Hill's letter on Uganda. Greenberg did as he was asked. He took his friend to No. 67 Addison Road, West Kensington, the house of Dr. Weizmann. Mr. Malcolm noted "his tall figure, his pale face and keen eyes and natural geniality." A small company of Dr. Weizmann's fellow-Zionists, mostly members of the movement's political committee in England, were assembled to see and hear the negotiator. Among them was a member of the Zionist Executive who bad come to England in 1914, Nahun Sokolov, who was destined to play a chief role in these events.

The meeting was not immediately dramatic. ... At the end of Malcolm's recital Dr. Weizmann recalled his own discussions with Mr. Scott and with Balfour and how he had had breakfast with Lloyd George, to no great purpose. Was Mr. Malcolm perfectly certain that he was really authorised by the British Cabinet? That he had not misunderstood? Malcolm assured him of the reality of his mission. Dr. Weizmann then put the following question to him: "Are you really and personally convinced that the British Government seriously intend to promise Palestine in return for the help of leading American Jews?" Malcolm said that that was his conviction. Dr. Weizmann asked him another question: Do you advise us to accept the British Government's offer?" "Yes," said Mr. Malcolm, " I do." Dr. Weizmann rose and shook hands with him, a minute ceremony by which he signified the entry of the Jewish leaders into the negotiation. " When can I meet Sir Mark Sykes?" he asked. Malcolm rang Sykes up then and there and arranged for a meeting at the latter's house in Buckingham Gate on the next day.

On the next day Dr. Weizmann was unable to go because of some appointment at the Admiralty where he held an official post, and so his place as leader of a Zionist delegation was taken by Sokolov. This was to be the usual pattern of events throughout the negotiations. Dr. Weizmann was the directing mind, but taking little active part in day-to-day business, which was handled by this other man. (pp. 185-6)

When introductions had been made by Mr. Malcolm, a memorandum was presented to Sykes for him to convey to the Cabinet. ... Before the delegation left, Sokolov made a simple request, namely that the Zionist Committee should have facilities for communication abroad. He pointed out that since they were an international body this was especially needful to them, and he suggested that they should be granted governmental privileges, since they could thus attain their object while subjecting themselves to the needs of secrecy and censorship.

Sykes promised to put this to the authorities. Oddly enough, he had once before requested such facilities for the Zionists in a telegram which he sent from Russia, without success, it seems. On this occasion when he re-peated the request, the next morning he got what he asked for: it was agreed that the War Office and the Foreign Office would send Zionist let-ters and telegrams by way of Embassies, Consulates or Headquarters. ... once the news was given out to Jewish communities all over the world that in return for certain services the British Government would use their then massive power in Eastern affairs to satisfy the Jewish longing for Pal-estine ... then there could be no going back on the promise ... the decision had been taken on this October day in 1916, and it was irrevocable. (Sykes, pp. 187-8)

(xi) James Malcolm 1944 pamphlet ORIGINS OF THE BALFOUR DECLARATION: Dr. Weizmann's Contribution

Malcolm (1944a) wrote in this pamphlet:

In my official capacity I had frequent contacts with the Cabinet Office, the Foreign Office and the War Office, the French and other allied Embassies in London, and had also to be in touch personally during visits to Paris, with my colleagues there and with the leading French authorities. ...

During one of my visits to the War Cabinet Office in Whitehall Gardens in the late autumn of 1916, I found Sir Mark Sykes less buoyant than usual. As I had known his family of old and our relations were unrestrained, I en-quired what was troubling him. He spoke of military deadlock in France, the growing menace of submarine warfare, the unsatisfactory situation which was developing in Russia and the general bleak outlook. He also told me that the much publicised Arab revolt in the desert, which was intended to deal a mortal blow to the Turks from within, was a dismal and costly failure.* The Cabinet was looking anxiously for United States intervention. I asked him what progress was being made in that direction. He shook his head glumly. (p. 2)

I enquired what special argument or consideration had the Allies put for-ward to win over American Jewry. Sir Mark replied that they had made use of the same argument as used elsewhere, viz. that we shall eventually win and it was better to be on the winning side, I informed him that there was a way to make American Jewry thoroughly pro-Ally, and make them conscious that only an Allied victory could be of permanent benefit to Jewry all over the world. I said to him, "You are going the wrong way about it. The well- to-do English Jews you meet and the Jewish clergy are not the real leaders of the Jewish people. You have overlooked what the call of nationality means. Do you know of the Zionist Movement?" Sir Mark admitted ignorance of this movement and I told him something about it and concluded by saying, "You can win the sympathy of the Jews everywhere, in one way only, and that way is by offering to try and secure Palestine for them."

Sir Mark was taken aback and confessed that what I had told him was something quite new and most impressive. He would talk to me again about it. A day or two later he reverted to the subject and again said it was most interesting, but there were very great difficulties. I did not know at the time the exact nature of these difficulties (it was only later that I heard of the Sykes-Picot Treaty with France and Russia.) I suggested that he should discuss it with Lord Milner, a member of the War Cabinet who was known to take a large and imaginative view of the several European nationalist issues raised by the War. He promised to do so and kept his promise. He told me that Lord Milner was greatly interested to learn of the Jewish Nationalist movement, but could not see any possibilities of promising Palestine to the Jews. I replied that it seemed to me the only way to achieve the desired result, and mentioned that one of President Wilson's most intimate friends, for whose humanitarian views he had the greatest respect, was Justice Brandeis, of the Supreme Court, who was a convinced Zionist. Sir Mark was much interested in this new aspect and said he would check up on the matter, but he still saw no possibility of the War Cabinet adopting my idea. I asked him why, and he replied, "We cannot act without our Allies and I am afraid they would never agree". I then suggested that if the object was to secure United States help, surely the Allies would agree. If he could obtain from the War Cabinet an assurance that help would be given towards securing Palestine for the Jews, it was certain that Jews in all neutral countries, especially the United States, would become pro-British and pro-Ally. He promised to put the question again to Lord Milner, with the additional arguments I had suggested.

About a week later he reported that Milner had informally discussed the matter with his colleagues, and they were favourably disposed to the idea. Of course they could not commit themselves, but advised that I should open negotiations with the Zionist leaders. ... I replied, "... you have not met the other kind of Jews, who are remarkable types and intensely attached to the idea of Zion. There are tens of thousands, perhaps hundreds of thousands, of such Jews. The wealthy Jewish bankers of London are completely out of touch with them." Sir Mark undertook to report our conversation to the Cabinet. He thought Lord Milner and George Barnes would understand. A day or two later, he informed me that the Cabinet had agreed to my suggestion and authorised me to open negotiations with the Zionists. (Malcolm, 1944a, p. 5)

(xii) James Malcolm in New Judea

James Malcolm (1944b) wrote,

I FIRST met Dr. Weizmann during the last war. In October, 1916, the late Mr. L. J. Greenberg, Editor of The Jewish Chronicle, took me to his house in Kensington, where I found a small group of remarkable Jews assembled, totally different from the English and German Jews I had met before. They were the leaders of the Zionist Movement, the men whom the British Government had asked me to find after the War Cabinet had adopted my suggestion to win the support of Jewry by a promise of Palestine. [...]

I gave them a brief account of my discussions with Sir Mark Sykes, Under-Secretary of the War Cabinet, and my own conviction that here was an historic opportunity of uniting Jewish and British interests. They were rather sceptical in view of their own difficulties in getting a hearing for their cause. [...] But, finally, after further discussion, Dr. Weizmann came forward and shook me by the hand, saying they would follow my, advice. The next day I introduced them to Sir Mark Sykes, and the vital messages were flashed by cipher to Washington and other parts of the allied and neutral world, thus beginning the close co-operation which resulted, a year later, in November, 1917, in the issue of the historic Balfour Declaration. [...]

The "gentlemen's agreement" between the Zionist leaders and the War Cabinet, which I was entrusted to bring about, was the basis of co-operation, and within a few months, despite numerous setbacks due to war conditions, solid progress was achieved. , The support of President Wilson was, of course, the main achievement, because United States help was vitally needed by the Allies. It was only in the following April that the United States came into the war. Then followed quickly the agreement of France, Italy and the Vatican to the pro-Zionist policy of Britain. [...]

I well remember the grim struggle against the enemy within when the Anglo-Jewish leaders, strongly supported by the late Edwin Montagu, a member of the Cabinet, came within an ace of persuading the Cabinet to withdraw from their "gentlemen's agreement" and actually succeeded in whittling down very considerably the terms of the eventual Government Declaration. [...]

The original draft of the Declaration was prepared by Dr. Weizmann and his friends in London in the summer of 1917, at the instance of Sir Mark Sykes [...]

This draft was cabled by Sir Ronald Graham (Assistant Under Secretary of State at the Foreign Office) to Brandeis in Washington for submission to President Wilson and to secure his concurrence. Baron Edmond de Rothschild also agreed to it and it was then submitted to the War Cabinet and to Mr. Balfour, who would have to sign it, as Foreign Secretary. It underwent further amendment whereby the word "people" was substituted for "race" and the reference at the end to "fully contented" was omitted, and in this final form remained at the Foreign Office until the military situation in the East improved. [...]

Towards the end of October, 1917, I heard from Sir Mark Sykes that the Declaration was likely to come up before the Cabinet in view of satisfactory military progress in Palestine. [...] Balfour, as Foreign Secretary, in a five minutes' speech, convincingly explained the value of the Declaration. In this he was strongly supported by Milner and Smuts, as well as the Prime Minister. Thus the War Cabinet arrived at a unanimous decision to issue the statement. I knew then that, at last, after many anxious weeks and months, my seed had borne fruit and that the Government had become an ally of Zionism. The Declaration is dated 2nd November, 1917, and is known to history as the Balfour Declaration. [...]

By issuing this declaration the British Government duly carried out-as I had all along been convinced they would-its obligation to promise British help for the Jews to obtain Palestine. It is therefore strictly correct for Professor Temperley, the official historian of the Paris Peace Conference, to describe the Balfour Declaration as "a definite contract between Great Britain and Jewry." The consideration for this contract had already been given by the Jews before November 2nd, 1917 (Malcolm, 1944b).

(xiii) James Malcolm 1948 says he met Weizmann (at his house in Addison Road) in Oct. 1916

James Malcolm wrote to Weizmann in 1948:

http://thomassuarez.com/SUAREZ___KV_2-3171_IMG_1845.jpg

25, Palace Gate,
W.8.
18th Jute, 11948
Dr. Chaim Weizmann,
Hotel Meurice,
Paris,
France.

My Dear Weizmann,

As you wrote to me on 12th April, from New York, that on your return you would communicate with Ross, I have, enattendant, begun to refresh my contacts here. Apparently, however, you have not bean able to deal with the matter yet (June 18th). I do not know what your views may be now but I sincerely want you to recall what my friends were able to accompllish in 1916 and 1917 and to be assured that my friends of 1948, though of a different category, are even more influential than those of 30 years ago. On that fateful Saturday evening in October in Addison Road, you, unlike some of your then and present incredulous friends, manfully asked and accepted my advice and never I believe regretted doing so.

Unfortunately as you are aware the enemies of 1948 are also more formidable than those of 1917 and they too must be routed. It is now up to you to decide and you know well what is needed to meet the occasion. I feel that no opportunity should be missed at this juncture. In any case I should be glad if you could let me know at the earliest whether you are writing to Ross or not. His present business address is 175, Oxford Street, London W.1.

I shall, of course, continue to do all I personally can. I am sending this letter by hand together with a note of some importance which you will appreciate.

With all the best,
Yours ever,
{signed} James A. Malcolm

(xiv) Weizmann's Reply 1948 (having been made President of Israel):

http://thomassuarez.com/SUAREZ___KV_2-3171_IMG_1843.jpg

June 23rd, 1948.
Mr Ivor J. LINTON
77 Great Russell Street
LONDON W.C.1

My Dear Ivor,

I am sending you a letter and a memorandum which I received from Malcolm.

I have no intention to entangle myself with these people any longer. I would be most grateful, if you would see Malcolm and point out to him, that in my present position I cannot write to Cyril Ross. Perhaps you would speak to Cyril Ross.

With many thanks, I remain,
Yours ever,
{signed} Chaim Weizmann

Inconsistencies

James Malcolm, and other sources above, say that Mark Sykes consulted Lord Milner, as a member of the War Cabinet, in October 1916.

But the Asquith government did not fall until Dec 6. It had a War Committee (not a War Cabinet), and Milner was not part of it. Sykes and Amery were, however,

Under-Secretaries in both the Asquith and Lloyd George governments, so Malcolm could have discussed the matter with Sykes.

Sykes could still have discussed it with Milner before Dec 6, as 'Proconsul' and de-facto Opposition leader who shared his views. Milner was widely admired, including by the King. Then Sykes would have liaised with him from Dec 11 as Cabinet Minister, with the historical articles blurring the distinction between War Committee and War Cabinet.

Christopher Sykes, son of Mark, himself blurs the distinction, in his book *Two Studies in Virtue*. He writes there that 'in the last days of 1915 ... In the autumn of that year Sykes had been appointed one of the two "Assistant Secretaries to the War Cabinet," the other one being Mr. Leopold Amery.' (pp. 176-7).

Yet the War Cabinet was only formed a year later. It seems that the War Committee and the War Cabinet were often equated. Further, "Sykes had been chosen on Lord Kitchener's recommendation" (p. 177). That would apply to the Asquith government; Kitchener died on June 5, 1916.

But on p. 178, Sykes uses the word 'Committee': "The British decision to conduct secret negotiations with France for a Syrian understanding was finally taken at a meeting of the War Committee held at 10 Downing Street on December 16th of 1915 ..."

Milner in Russia, Jan. 1917, just before fall of Czar

Milner led a British delegation to Petrograd in January 1917. At Murmansk they found chaos, with munitions lying on the docks. Bruce Lockhart, Consul-General, wrote of Milner's frustrations: "he had realised the inefficiency of the Russians, and he made no attempt to conceal his opinion that he was wasting time ...". Lockhart arranged a meeting with Prince Lvov, soon to lead the Provisional Government. Lvov presented a paper: "if there was no change in the attitude of the Emperor, there would he a revolution within three weeks." (Lockhart, 1933, p. 164).

The Czar told Milner he would make peace with Germany unless weapons were supplied (MacGregor & Docherty, 2018, p. 450). MI6 seems to have murdered Rasputin, to stop just such a Russian exit. Back in Britain, Milner recommended against weapons supplies, but said that revolution was unlikely. Then riots broke out, the Czar fell on March 15, and Lvov took over. The only concern of the British government was that Russia stay in the war. The House of Commons sent this message:

"That this House sends to the Duma its fraternal greetings and tenders to the Russian people its heartiest congratulations upon the establishment among them of free institutions" (Hansard Congratulations To Duma).

Mr. GINNELL, an Irish MP, objected: "What do you know about free institutions, except what a murderer knows of his victim. I beg ... to insert instead thereof, the words, "this House, while appreciating Lord Milner's action in fomenting the Revolution which has dethroned our Imperial Russian Ally ..."

John Cornelius on the Zimmermann telegram and the Balfour Declaration

Arthur Zimmermann, German Foreign Minister, sent a telegram on Jan. 16, 1917, offering Mexico an alliance to restore "Texas, Arizona and New Mexico" if the U.S. entered World War One. He sent it without permission, and later admitted such in the Reichstag, then resigned. The Telegram was of no benefit to Germany, but helped bring the United States into the war.

Britain gave the U.S. Embassy the text on Feb. 19, 1917; Wilson released it on Feb. 28; Zimmerman admitted that it was genuine on March 3. Wilson called for war on Apr. 2; Congress agreed on Apr. 6. The Czar had fallen on March 15, so American and Russian Jews were no longer pro-German. Germany had began unrestricted submarine warfare on Feb. 1.

There were two versions of the Zimmermann telegram.

ZT-1: the original telegram cabled from Berlin to German Embassy in Washington on Jan. 16, 1917; sent in secure Code 7500.

ZT-2: the version then forwarded to the German Embassy in Mexico City on Jan. 19, 1917; it was sent in an older, less secure code, 13042.

Two different codes were used because the German legation in Mexico did not possess code 7500. The texts of the two versions of the ZT were identical, but they had different preambles.

Britain possessed the full text of ZT-1 shortly after it was sent. But it could not go public then, without revealing that it had German codes. So it had to wait for another way to release it—by "buying" a copy in Mexico. But that one had a different preamble.

John Cornelius says that if the Balfour Declaration was truly a contract to get the USA into World War One, the Zimmermann telegram had to have been part of the deal. The British government must have obtained the Zimmermann telegram, or the code in which it was sent, from an informant, rather than by code-breaking.

i.e. EITHER (1) a draft of the ZT was concocted in London and presented to Zimmermann by one of his subordinates in Berlin, OR (2) German code 7500, in which ZT-1 was sent, was obtained by a Zionist agent in the German government, and provided to Britain. Cornelius considers the second option more likely.

In Britain, codebreaking was done at Room 40, under Sir Alfred Ewing and Director of Naval Intelligence, Captain Reginald Hall, R. N.

Gottlieb Von Jagow, who had been German foreign secretary since 1913, was replaced by Zimmermann in November 1916.

Cornelius (2005) wrote,

> We may infer that at this time British-Zionist negotiations were well under way and that Room 40's role was being broadened from cracking German codes to include pretending to crack German code 7500. ... It is the unproven belief of the present writer that German code 7500, in which the original ZT was sent in January 1917, was obtained by a Zionist agent inside the German government, possibly either by means of photography or a photographic memory, and provided to the British government. ... The ZT was transmitted by cable from Berlin to Washington on Jan. 16, 1917. It was copied by Room 40 and promptly d-coded. ...

> Thus, by the time of the Sykes-Zionist meeting of Feb. 7, 1917, the Zionist part of the bargain had been accomplished, and America was as good as at war. All that remained was for the British to find the best time and method for revealing the contents of the ZT to President Wilson and for him to convince Congress and the American people to go to war.

Bibliography (Balfour Declaration)

Amery, Leopold S. (1955). My Political Life, v. 2. War and peace, 1914-1929. Hutchinson, London.

Ben-Gurion, David. (1962). I Predict—The Next 25 Years. Look Magazine Special Issue, January 16, 1962.

Cornelius, John. (2005, November). The Hidden History of the Balfour Declaration. Washington Report, pp. 44-50.
http://www.wrmea.com/archives/November_2005/0511044.html

Freedman, Benjamin H. (1961). A Jewish Defector Warns America: Benjamin Freedman Speaks on Zionism (Speech at the Willard Hotel).
http://www.sweetliberty.org/issues/israel/freedman.htm.

Freedman, Benjamin H. (1970). The Hidden Tyranny: The Issue that Dwarfs All Other Issues. New Christian Crusade Church.
https://web.archive.org/web/20060701062525/http://www.iamthewitness.com/Freedman-Jewish-Pawns.html.

Gollin, A. M. (1964). Proconsul in Politics: A study of Lord Milner in opposition and in power. The MacMillam Company, New York.

Hansard Congratulations To Duma. (1917) Hansard, HC Deb 22 March 1917 vol. 91 cc2085-94 2085. https://api.parliament.uk/historic-hansard/commons/1917/mar/22/congratulations-to-duma.

Israel: The Watchman. (1948, Aug. 16). Time Magazine, p. 25.

Jeffries, J. M. N. (1939/2015). Palestine: The Reality. Longmans, Green and Co., London, 1939. Reprint 2015 by Facsimile Publisher, Delhi.

Landman, Samuel. (1936/1978). Great Britain, The Jews And Palestine. New Zionist Press, London, 1936. Reprint 1978 Seeds of conflict, Series 7: Palestine, The twice-promised land, Three volumes: I The British Viewpoint II The Jewish Cause III The Arabs—and some Neutrals.

Lilienthal, Alfred M. (1983) The Zionist Connection II: What Price Peace?. Veritas Publishing Company, Bullsbrook, Western Australia.

Lloyd George, David. (1939). Memoirs of the Peace Conference, Volume II. Yale University Press.

MacGregor, Jim & Docherty, Gerry. (2018). Prolonging the Agony: How the Anglo-American Establishment Deliberately Extended WWI by Three-And-A-Half Years. Trine Day.

Malcolm, James A. (1944a). Origins Of The Balfour Declaration: Dr Weizmann's Contribution. London. https://mailstar.net/malcolm.html.

Malcolm, James A. (1944b, October-November). Dr. Weizmann And The Balfour Declaration. The New Judea.

Rabinowicz, Oskar K. (1950). Fifty Years Of Zionism: A Historical Analysis of Dr. Weizmann's 'Trial and Error' Robert Anscombe & Co. Ltd.

Rosenthal, Litman. (1919, March 7). "The War is Imminent": Theodore Herzl's Prophecy of the Great War (From My Siberian Diary). American Jewish News. https://mailstar.net/herzl-rosenthal.html.

Shillony, Ben-Ami. (1991). The Jews and the Japanese: the Successful Outsiders. Charles E. Tuttle Company, Rutland, Vermont.

Stein, Leonard. (1961). The Balfour Declaration. Valentine, Mitchell & Co. Ltd, London.

Sykes, Christopher. (1953). The Prosperity of His Servant: A Study of the Origins of the Balfour Declaration of 1917. In: Two Studies in Virtue. Collins, London.

Weizmann, Chaim. (1949). Trial and Error: The Autobiography of Chaim Weizmann. Harper & Brothers, New York.

Appendix 2A: Fake Hate Crimes and Antisemitic Attacks

Fake Hate Crimes are on the increase. Why would anyone do it? To defame political oppoents? To prompt a crackdown on them? To promote censorship? It's an underhand tactic, and it's important that it be detected and exposed.

Jewish student, using a gentile name, posts Antisemitic statements at Harvard

From the London Review of Books:

"Recently, at Harvard University where I am based, a Jewish student, using an assumed (gentile) name, began posting anti-semitic statements on the weblog of the Harvard Initiative for Peace and Justice, an anti-war, pro-Palestinian group on campus. The student, it turned out, is the secretary of Harvard Students for Israel—which dissociated itself from the incident—and had previously accused the HIPJ of being too tolerant of anti-semitism. He now went undercover as part of a self-appointed effort to monitor anti-semitism on campus. In one posting, for example, he referred to Israel as the 'AshkeNAZI state'. Incidents of this kind, which are becoming commonplace on American campuses, reflect a wider determination to monitor, report, defame and punish those individuals and institutions within academia whose views the right finds objectionable" (Roy, 2004).

Court convicts woman for fabricating Antisemitic attack

From Haaretz:

"A young French woman who admitted to lying about being the victim of an anti-Semitic attack was convicted Monday for fabricating a story that stunned France. Marie-Leonie Leblanc, 22, was handed a four-month suspended sentence ... A public prosecutor explained how she invented the attack, cut off part of her hair and drew swastikas on her body. ... The woman claimed she was robbed on a suburban Paris train earlier this month by a knife-wielding gang that mistook her for a Jew and scrawled swastikas on her body. ... In a search of her home in the suburb of Aubervilliers, police found the marker she had used to draw swastikas on her body and other evidence. The woman subsequently went on national TV to issue a public apology" (Paris fake antisemitic attack).

Professor Kerri Dunn, a convert to Judaism, jailed for falsely reported that her car was damaged in a campus hate crime

"A former Claremont McKenna College visiting professor, who spray-painted her car with racist and anti-Semitic slurs and then reported a hate crime on campus, was sentenced today to a year in state prison" (Sailor, 2004).

US-Israeli teen Michael Kadar convicted of threats against Jewish centres

From BBC News:

"A court in Israel has convicted a 19-year-old American-Israeli man of making hundreds of threats to bomb or attack Jewish schools and community centres. Michael Ron David Kadar was also found guilty of extortion, money laundering and assaulting a police officer. He used the internet to make hoax telephone calls to the US, UK, Canada, New Zealand and Australia" (Threats to bomb or attack Jewish schools and community centers).

James Petras comments:

"Fake anti-Semitism is most recently seen in the launching of series of anti-Semitic 'threats' by ethno-centric Jews to create hysteria ... On March 23, 2017, an Israeli-American man was arrested in Israel for sending hundreds of fake anti-Semitic threats to Jewish institutions and schools in four European countries and nine US states. Such threats led to the emergency grounding of two US airlines and the panicked evacuation of countless schools and cultural centers. This man used a sophisticated system of cloaking accounts to appear to originate in other countries. Despite his high skills at cyber-terrorism, Israeli authorities preposterously described him as a 'teenager with a learning disability'" (Petras, 2017)

American Jew Joshua Goldberg posed as a Moslem, called for terrorist attacks against the West

From the Sydney Morning Herald:

'Joshua Goldberg is not Muslim, and he's not Australian. He is a 20-year-old nerd of Jewish background ... But under the online alias "Australi Witness", Goldberg managed to convince even Islamic State jihadists that he was an Australian IS mujahid who once worked for Amnesty International. ... Joshua Goldberg is a troll. But he has liaised with IS supporters and called for terrorist attacks against the West' (Potaka and McMahon, 2015).

JewishProgressive denounced his own Jew-hating posts as HamBaconEggs

At Common Dreams,

"The HamBaconEggs character was taken to task for his hatred of Jews by the JewishProgressive character ... Common Dreams director, Craig Brown, noticed that commenters using other screen name had the same IP address. ... one major, constant stream of anti-Semitic posts--as well as posts condemning the anti-Semitism--came from a few, close-in-proximity computers" (Common Dreams).

Jewish Advocacy of Immigration/Multiculturalism to overcome Antisemitism

From Denis McCormack:

'In the 1992 winter edition of 'Australian Jewish Democrat', editorial committee member Miriam Faine said: "The strengthening of multicultural or diverse Australia is also our most effective insurance policy against anti-semitism. The day

Australia has a Chinese Australian Governor General, I would feel more confident of my freedom to live as a Jewish Australian' (McCormack, 1993).

Faine's statement implies that antisemitism is mostly carried out by white people, and that replacing them with immigrants would fix the problem. But not Moslem immigrants! Doesn't it matter that white people defeated Nazi Germany? Why repay them this way?

Fake Hate Crimes: Jussie Smollett staged a fake racist, anti-Gay attack on himself.

A database of fake hate crimes in the USA is at https://fakehatecrimes.org/reports/155.

Parents called 'hateful, bigoted, transphobic'

A TV documentary on Trans Regret interviewed parents Jude and John, of Newcastle, Australia, who were called "hateful, bigoted transphobic" by their 17-year old daughter when they said one can't change sex.

She had been using a male name at school without their knowledge; the school did not inform them that she was now registered as a boy. Then she was diagnosed 'suicidal' by a psychiatrist and admitted to hospital. Jude went in next day "to see my daughter", but "I was corrected and told I had a son in there; and on her bed was a male name."

The parents had admitted her as a girl, but the hospital changed her sex. Hospital staff told the parents "that we were bigoted, that we needed to teach our family Inclusion." The hospital advised testosterone and mastectomy (Bartlett, 2023).

Appendix 3: MH370 Solved: The CIA and the Broken-Wing Display

The Broken-Wing Display

Wild birds often feign injury, to lead a possible predator away from the nest. It's called the 'broken wing display'.

What if Intelligence Agencies do that too, to lure researchers away from their crime scenes?

Most MH370 sleuths accept certain tenets that keep them bound to the official dogma and the failed search-areas.

One of those tenets is the Inmarsat satellite data. It constrains sleuths to the 7th Arc theory, off the coast of Australia, safely away from Diego Garcia, the Maldives, and the west Indian Ocean sites where wreckage has been found— Reunion, Mauritius, Madagascar, and the east coast of Africa.

When sightings of a plane matching MH370 over the Maldives were published, shortly after it went missing, none of the official Search teams or the "mainstream media" bothered to send reporters or investigators there, because of the Inmarsat data and the 7th Arc.

They happily spent $200 million on fruitless searches, yet could not fork out $10-20,000 to send a couple of reporters to the Maldives.

Reports linking MH370 with Diego Garcia were similarly pooh-poohed.

A 2023 Netflix documentary, MH370: The Plane That Disappeared, included commentators who disparaged wreck hunter Blaine Gibson, claiming that he had planted debris. In fact, he who did more than anyone else to find wreckage and publicise the search to residents of Mauritius, Madagascar and Mozambique. They had found pieces, but did not know from what; Blaine told them.

Why would anyone vilify him? For the same reason that he received death threats; he has been in hiding for six years. The Deep State has tweaked the commentary since 2014, in debunker or fact-checker style, letting everyone know the approved narrative and the bounds of discourse.

A defence of Blaine Gibson is put by Geoffrey Thomas at Thomas (2023).

More than 30 pieces of wreckage from MH370 have been found around Reunion, Mauritius, Madagascar, and the east coast of Africa. The official theory is that MH370 went down off Western Australia, and that these pieces floated across the ocean over to Africa.

No debris from MH370 has ever been found in the official search area along the 7th Arc.

It's much more likely that MH370 went down in the area where pieces have been found. This would mean that MH370 headed west, towards the Maldives and Diego Garcia. Most likely, it was hijacked by the CIA, to stop Technology Transfer to China. Twenty Freescale (Motorola) employees, mostly engineers and other experts, were on board, and a mystery load weighing 89kg was added to the cargo flight list after take-off (Grafton-Green, 2019).

To go beyond Diego Garcia, MH370 would have needed to refuel. I suggest that it landed and refuelled at Male, Maldives about 3.20am, and departed by 5.45am; this matches the sightings at Kuda Huvadhoo at 6.15am. Passengers & cargo of interest to the CIA would have been removed, and transferred to Diego Garcia by small plane or boat.

MH370 would then have passed near Diego Garcia, but would not have landed there, because it was daylight by that time, and no hangar on Diego Garcia is tall enough to hide a Boeing 777; its tail is too high. Instead, it would have continued towards Reunion, and been dumped there, disintegrating when it hit the water at speed.

Forget pilot suicide theories. If the pilot(s) wanted to suicide, why fly for 5 hours, as per the official theory?

A conspiracy is involved. Authorities do not want to find MH370.

Those of us who think thus, also believe that JFK was murdered by the CIA, that 9/11 was a Mossad/CIA job, and that Covid-19 was a Plandemic intended to get us to accept the Great Reset. Doubters should study Operation Northwoods.

Intelligence agencies operate as a Deep State in defiance of elected Governments. They have officers working at major media, to stop them from revealing unwanted truths.

Underwater hydrophones at Diego Garcia, operated by the Comprehensive Test Ban Treaty Organisation (CTBTO), station HA08s, were shut down for 25 minutes around the time MH370 disappeared. This Shutdown of all 3 hydrophones is without explanation. It's likely that MH370 was dumped into the ocean during that shutdown.

We need to search the ocean between Diego Garcia and Mauritius/Madagascar.

A French spy told Ghyslain Wattrelos that American Intelligence Agencies took MH370, and know where it is (Myers, 2023).

One of the greatest crimes of the century is left to amateur investigators, and to scientists who are not part of the official investigation, to solve.

Flight Paths and Maps

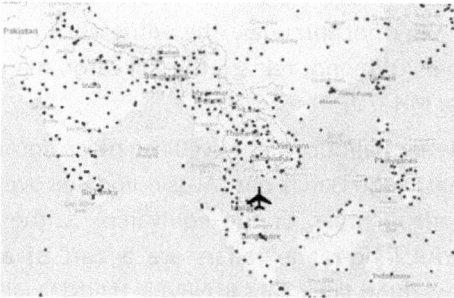

MH370's route until contact was lost (at Banda Aceh) is at mailstar.net/MH370-route.png.

The 634 runways MH370 could have reached without refuelling are at mailstar.net/MH370-634-runways.png.

The 3 isolated dots (runways) at the south-west of the map are (from north to south), Male, Gan (both in the Maldives), and Diego Garcia.

My sketch of MH370's path from Banda Aceh to the Maldives then to Diego Garcia is at mailstar.net/MH370-Male-DG.jpg. The black dots are the 634 airports MH370 could have reached without refueling.

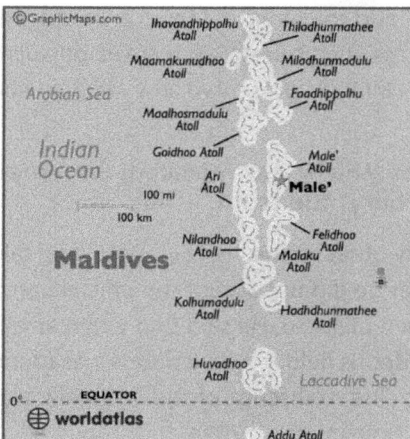

The map of the Maldives shows Huvadhoo atoll, south of Male, also called Kuda Huvadhoo, where there were multiple reported sightings of a plane matching MH370 on March 8, 2014.

Blaine Gibson's sketch of the path of the plane sighted at Kuda Huvadhoo is at mailstar.net/Kudahuvadhoo-turn.png.

It's also possible that MH370 flew direct from Banda Aceh to Diego Garcia.

People looking for debris would have

been looking within the circle of 634 airports. If it had crashed at sea, there would have been a huge debris field. Given the worldwide interest, the debris would have been spotted. Debris was not within that circle, so the plane landed somewhere. It would have either been stored in a hangar (but MH370 is too tall for military hangars), or refuelled and then dumped further afield, for example between Diego Garcia and Mauritius.

Forget Pilot Suicide

If the pilot had planned to suicide, he would not have bothered to fly for 5 hours before doing it, as per the official theory.

As for his practice landings at Indian Ocean airports, on his simulator, that is not unusual; flights are sometimes diverted by bad weather. It does not indicate malice on his part. The media beat up such stories, but failed to ask hard questions of government spokesmen, eg, Why wasn't MH370 picked up on the US military radars at Singapore and Diego Garcia? Why not interview the witnesses in the Maldives? Why not release the full cargo manifest for MH370?

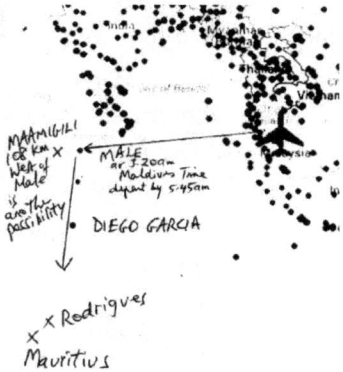

Henry Balfour <henry@404.co.nz> informs me that Diego Garcia has "Aussie Jindalee over-the-horizon radar, or the equivalent .... these powerful long-range radars are a part of an early warning layer that is NEVER TURNED OFF ... but when I ask the Aussie Defence people for clarity they told me it was "not switched on at that time" I will let you judge the reason that I don't believe them The Jindalee system would have 'seen' MH370 entering its scan zone."

The US military bases around Singapore and the Strait of Malacca would also have such radar; yet the media failed to press such questions, instead pursuing 'pilot suicide'. Neither the FBI nor the U.S. Military presented any data to the Search.

Emirates CEO Tim Clark told Spiegel that MH370 was hijacked, & warned "others would like to bury" the truth

Emirates flies more Boeing 777s than any other airline. Its CEO, Tim Clark, said in 2014, in an interview with Der Spiegel, that he did not accept the official narrative about MH370; he claimed that it had been hijacked. He said that when an airplane crashes in the water, there is always a debris field; no such debris was found in the official search area along the 7th Arc. The transcript of the interview was published by the Sydney Morning Herald on November 21, 2014.

Tim Clark's statements have been removed from the Wikipedia pages on MH370. Here's what he said:

CLARK: My own view is that PROBABLY CONTROL WAS TAKEN OF THAT AEROPLANE, the events that happened during the course of its tracked flight will be anybody's guess of who did what and when. I think we need to know who was on this aeroplane in the detail that obviously SOME PEOPLE DO KNOW, WE NEED TO KNOW WHAT WAS IN THE HOLD OF THE AEROPLANE, in the detail we need to know, in a transparent manner. ...

Q: But why would they FLY DOWN FIVE HOURS STRAIGHT TOWARDS ANTARCTICA?

CLARK: IF THEY DID! I am saying that every single element of the 'facts' of this particular incident must be challenged and examined in full transparency ...

Q: So YOU NURTURE DOUBTS that it actually happened as is said?

CLARK: ... our experience tells us that IN WATER INCIDENTS, WHERE THE AIRCRAFT HAS GONE DOWN, THERE IS ALWAYS SOMETHING. We have not seen a single thing that suggests categorically that this aircraft is where they say it is, nothing. Apart from this 'handshake', which calls my electronic engineers to start thinking 'what is all this about?'.

Q: Who can change that?

CLARK: I'm not in a position to do it, I'm essentially an airline manager. But I will continue to ask the questions and will make a nuisance of myself, when OTHERS WOULD LIKE TO BURY IT, and we have an obligation to the passengers and crew of MH 370 and their families, whose deep distress you see every day. We have an obligation not to brush this under the carpet, but to sort it out and do better than we have done.

You can read his statements in full at Myers (2023). There is a lot of other source material there too.

Unreliability of the Inmarsat Data

Atlantic Monthly published an article by Ari N. Schulman on May 8, 2014, in which satellite experts dispute Inmarsat's claims.

Why the Official Explanation of MH370's Demise Doesn't Hold Up: Outside satellite experts say investigators could be looking in the wrong ocean.

The article concludes, "the claim that Flight 370 went south rests not on the weight of mathematics but on faith in authority".

This article is not mentioned by Wikipedia; it's been flushed down the memory hole, and is now only available behind a paywall—which is inappropriate since this is a likely Crime Scene. But I placed the full text of the article at Myers (2023).

Even if the Inmarsat data were reliable, there is no proof that MH370 turned south. As Field McConnell said, a decoy plane could have been used, as proposed by the U.S. military in Operation Northwoods.

If MH370 was hijacked by the CIA, it would have been flown as a drone, as were planes on 9/11; their transponders were turned off too. The "Uninterruptible Auto Pilot" technology, and AWACS jamming technology, could explain all the anomalies on March 8, 2014.

Because the Inmarsat data was assumed correct, the eyewitness reports at Kuda Huvadhoo were dismissed by official Search bodies, and the witnesses were ridiculed. Investigators chose to spend $200 million on undersea searches in the wrong area, rather than spend $10-20,000 interviewing those witnesses in the Maldives. None of the "mainstream" media sent journalists to interview them either; but Blaine Gibson did interview them, and so did Marc Dugain—both in a private capacity.

Acoustic Data from three hydrophones on Diego Garcia

There have been several papers on locating MH370 by acoustic data from underwater hydrophones. These devices are used to monitor nuclear tests, and are operated by the Comprehensive Test Ban Treaty Organisation (CTBTO). There are three such detectors at Diego Garcia, station HA08s.

Media reports on the acoustic data are Barker (2019), Kadri (2017, 2019a and 2019b). Kadri notes (2019a):

"Last but not least, a fifth signal appears at 3:07 (see Fig. 5). This signal probably indicates restarting the system after it was shutdown for 25 minutes, i.e. there is a missing data in these specific CTBTO recordings. [...] The locations of signals found on HA08s are with high uncertainty or unknown and require further analysis. Though, if related to MH370 that might suggest a location in the northern part of the Indian Ocean. Due to the sensitivity of the recorded data, it is unlikely that the three hydrophones on HA08s had a simultaneous technical failure and the reason behind the shut down is to-date unknown. The missing data might be related to the military action in the area (during or after the impact), but another argument is that a violent nearby activity (including impact, explosion) could have resulted in a shutdown of the system. Both the signal HA_30 of bearing 247° recorded at 11:57 on March 7th, and the missing data if related to MH370 could (independently) suggest that the impact location is closer to Diego Garcia's station, as opposed to Cape Leeuwin's station."

The text at Figure 5 says, "Figure 5. Raw data recorded by all three hydrophones of HA08s. The sharp signal indicates restarting the system after 25 minutes of missing data on all three hydrophones starting from 3:07 UTC."

Note that the Comprehensive Test Ban Treaty Organisation (CTBTO), which operates the hydrophones, has been unable to explain the 25-minute shutdown.

I propose that the centrepoint of the 25-minute shutdown, 3.20 UTC (which is 9.20 a.m. Diego Garcia time) is the time MH370 crashed into the ocean; and that those behind the hijacking got the three hydrophones switched off to hide the event.

MH370: Acoustic Data cf Maldives sightings & Field McConnell's claim

Station HA08s is at Diego Garcia. The Acoustic Source is shown between there and Madagascar; it's close to the area where Blaine Gibson found debris. The Acoustic Source is shown on this map: https://images.theconversation.com/files/256064/original/file-20190129-108355-1rtdb1g.JPG.

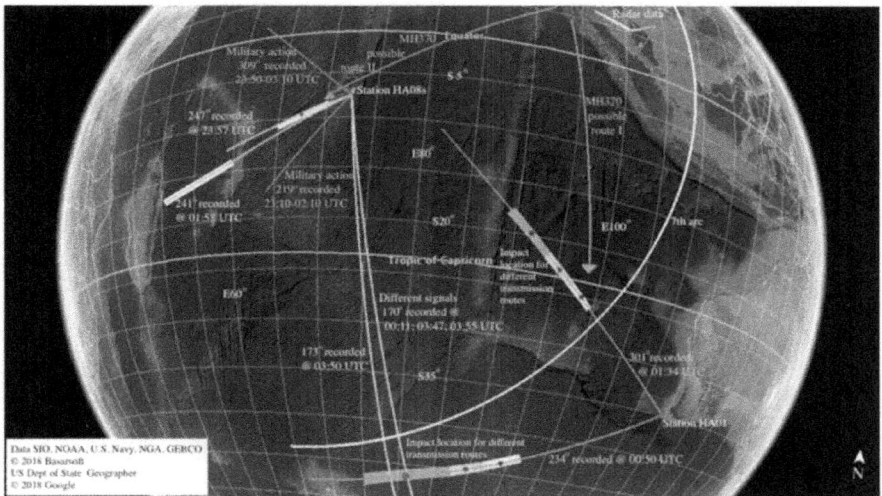

- The purple line shows the bearing of signals recorded on HA01 that could be associated with MH370, with white-grey polygons representing new possible source locations.
- Cyan represents the bearing of signals recorded on HA08s that could be associated with MH370.
- White represents the satellite data of the last "handshake" with MH370, known as the 7th arc.
- Red shows the bearings of military action recorded intermittently on HA08s between 23:00-04:00 UTC.
- And finally, orange denotes two possible MH370 routes - only "I" is in agreement with the 7th arc.

The acoustic data detected at station HA08s on Diego Garcia are in two sets: one at 247° (bearing from Diego Garcia) at 23.57, i.e. 11.57pm UTC (5.57am DG time) another at 241° at 1.58am UTC (7.58am DG time).

In adition, there was a 25-minute shutdown from 3.07 UTC to 3.32 UTC.

Diego Garcia is about the same longitude as Male and Kudahuvadhoo; but whereas the Maldives is UTC+5, Diego Garcia is UTC+6.

Is the acoustic data compatible with the Kudahuvadhoo sightings at 6.15am Maldives time?

The site https://www.travelmath.com/ gives the flight time from Kudahuvadhoo to Diego Garcia as 1h 52 m., including 30m for takeoff & landing. If MH370 did not land at DG, but merely flew over, it would have arrived at 7.37am Maldives time, 8.37 DG time, 2.37am UTC. This is too late to match either acoustic signal.

Field McConnell, a former US airforce pilot (F4 & F16) and airline captain (747-400), flew for 31 years, but resigned in protest over—he says—government hijackings of planes.

He says that during 9/11 the planes were remotely hijacked by intelligence agencies, using Uninterruptible AutoPilot. There's a Boeing brand, and a Thales one; they are patented. All modern planes have one; they can be flown remotely as a drone.

The pilot of American 77, which supposedly hit the Pentagon on 9/11, was a friend of his. In fact, a missile hit the Pentagon; AA77 was switched and, he says, detonated over the Atlantic Ocean.

This sort of "decoy plane" was first advocated in Operation Northwoods, in 1961. At that time, the Joint Chiefs of Staff signed off on it. They wanted to stage a False Flag attack, to be blamed on Cuba, as an excuse to invade it.

But President Kennedy and Attorney General Robert Kennedy vetoed it, and sacked the Chairman of the Joint Chiefs of Staff.

On Feb 10, 2017, I did a Skype video call with Field McConnell. He told me that MH370 was hijacked by the CIA and flown to Diego Garcia; and that someone in Australia, connected to Boeing, rang him and told him that MH370 landed in Diego Garcia and that the engines were turned off at 6.51am Malaysia time. This is 3.51am Maldives time, 4.51am DG time, 10.51pm UTC.

Since there is no hangar on Diego Garcia big enough for a Boeing 777, because the tail is too high, MH370 would have taken off again before daylight, after passengers & cargo were offloaded. I believe it would then have been remotely flown towards Mauritius/Reunion and dumped.

On March 8, 2014, Sunrise was 6.14am at Male (see https://www.timeanddate.com/sun/maldives/male), and 7.15am at Diego Garcia (see https://www.timeanddate.com/sun/biot/diego-garcia). First Light is about 40 minutes earlier. The moon was at First Quarter on March 8, 2014.

Let's see if McConnell's claim fits with the acoustic data.

Flight time from DG to Mauritius is 3h 10m, incl 30 min for takeoff & landing. Obviously MH370 did not land, so this is reduced to 2h 55m. Northern parts of Madagascar are about the same distance as Mauritius.

The 247° path acoustic zone stretches from about 20m flying time from DG, to 1h. from DG, the centre being 40m (plus 15m for takeoff). The acoustic time, 11.57pm UTC (5.57 DG time) is feasible but tight. Taking the centre as our mark, MH370 would have had to leave about 5.17am DG time (11.17 UTC), allowing 11 minutes to offload cargo & passengers. Unlikely, but cannot be ruled out.

The 241° path heads towards the middle of Madagascar. The acoustic zone stretches from about 1h 40m flying time from DG, to 2h 40m from DG, the centre being 2h 10m (plus 15m for takeoff). Taking the centre as our mark, the acoustic time, 1.58am UTC (7.58 DG time) is compatible with McConnell's claim, if MH370 left about 5.33am DG time. This would have allowed 42 minutes to offload cargo & passengers.

I'm not suggesting that we should dump the Maldives sightings and go with the acoustic data. Rather, we should pursue both lines until the case is resolved.

MH370: Acoustic Data cf Maldives sightings & 25 minute shutdown

ABC News Australia published a report on the acoustic data "MH370 may have crashed near Madagascar, underwater microphones suggest" (Barker, 2019).

It states, regarding the shutdown:

"Inexplicably, 25 minutes of data from the Diego Garcia station—where the US has a secretive military base—is missing.

"Dr Kadri said the signals his team analysed indicated a 25-minute shutdown that cannot be explained by a technical failure or maintenance, given the three hydrophones operate independently of each other.

"He said the CTBTO has failed to give any reason why the data is missing, though either military action or Malaysia Airlines flight MH370 may have caused the system shutdown."

The 25-minute shutdown began at 3:07 UTC.

Let us now consider the possibility that MH370 crashed during that shutdown; say at the mid-point, 3.20 UTC. (9.20am Diego Garcia time); and that the shutdown may have been staged to conceal that event.

If MH370 had landed at Diego Garcia at 4.51am DG time as Field McConnell says, then unloaded passengers and cargo, then taken off again heading for Mauritius/Reunion, the crash location could be anwhere up to about 3 hours after departing DG. But we require that it have left before sunrise at 7.15am DG time (1.15

UTC). A crash at 3:20 UTC would be quite feasible, thus Field McConnell's scenario is possible.

What of the Maldives sightings (6.15am at Kudahuvadhoo)—are they compatible with this scenario?

MH370 was detected half-way between Banda Aceh at the tip of Sumatra, and Phuket on the Thailand coast, at 2.22am Malaysia time.

From that waypoint to the Maldives is about 4 hours' flying time, which means that if MH370 went west, it would have arrived there about 6.20am Malaysia Time (UTC+8), which is 3.20am Maldives time (UTC+5).

Yet the sightings at Kuda Huvadoo atoll were about 6.15am Maldives time. This would require that MH370 have landed somewhere. And if it landed, it would have refuelled.

The witnesses at Kudahuvadhoo said it came from the north-west, and headed south towards Diego Garcia. But Malaysia is to the east. Why was the plane coming from the wrong direction? Kuda Huvadoo is in the southern Maldives—south of Male, but north of Gan.

Blaine Gibson sketched the path of the plane sighted at Kuda Huvadhoo, according to witnesses.

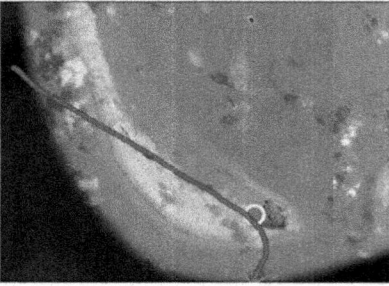

Direction of plane seen by witnesses on Kudahuvadhoo 8 March 2014

MH370 could have landed at Male or Maamigili in the Maldives, about 3.20am Maldives time, and taken off around 5.45am. The site https://www.travelmath.com gives the flight time from Male to Kudahuvadhoo as 13 minutes plus 15 minutes for takeoff.

Both Male and Maamigili are international airports, with runways long enough for a Boeing 777.

Male International Airport (also called Velana) has a 3000m runway, and routinely takes Boeing 777s. There were no scheduled arrivals or departures at those early hours on March 8, 2014.

MH370 could have touched down at the southern end of the runway, pulled up at the northern end, which is remote from houses and buildings, and unloaded cargo and passengers. They would have been transferred to Diego Garcia by either a small plane, or a boat (the water is close to the runway).

The site https://www.travelmath.com/ gives the flight time from Kudahuvadhoo to Diego Garcia as 1h. 52 m., including 30m. for takeoff & landing.

But MH370 did not take off from Kudahuvadhoo, and it would not have landed at Diego Garcia because it would have arrived after sunrise. Thus the flight time would be 1h. 22m.

If MH370 flew over (or near) DG, it would then have arrived at 7.37am Maldives time, 8.37 DG time, 2.37am UTC. Sunrise being 7.15am DG time.

Male airport arrivals 8 March 2014

If it then continued towards Mauritius / Reunion, a crash at 3:20 UTC is quite feasible. This would mean about 43 minutes flight time from Diego Garcia.

Male airport departures 8 March 2014

Thus a crash during the 25-minute shutdown of the three hydrophones at Diego Garcia is compatible with both scenarios offered here.

Why did Blaine Gibson receive Death Threats?

Blaine Gibson was reported in The Australian of May 29, 2018 as stating that stalking, death threats and even assassination are being used to stop his work:

"In an interview with The West Australian, Gibson, who is said to have found more than half of the debris that has been discovered of the ill-fated jet, said his own search was subjected to intimidation, stalking, death threats, defamation and assassination.

"For whatever reasons, some people are very upset that I and other private citizens are finding pieces of the plane," he told the newspaper" (Death threats, 2018).

Earlier in January 2018, he found debris that, he said, disproves the pilot suicide theory.

"He said the wing flap was found to be retracted and not deployed for landing, indicating that there was no controlled glide." (Disproves Pilot Suicide, 2018).

Blaine Gibson DID interview the eyewitnesses at Kuda Huvadhoo, and published his account at Gibson (2016).

He found many pieces of MH370 wreckage around Madagascar, Mauritius, Rodrigues Island, and the east coast of Africa. But he was loath to accept that it might have been an Inside Job, so for years he kept trying to fit his data with the official theory.

Blaine suspected Malaysian authorities; it did not occur to him that the CIA might have been behind those death threats.

No scheduled flights from Diego Garcia on March 8-10; hangars not tall enough for Boeing 777

Some say Diego Garcia is the most likely location MH370 went to. There were no scheduled flights from Diego Garcia airport on March 8-10, 2014; flights resumed on March 11. The flight board was at https://beforeitsnews.com/v3/global-unrest/2014/2458394.html

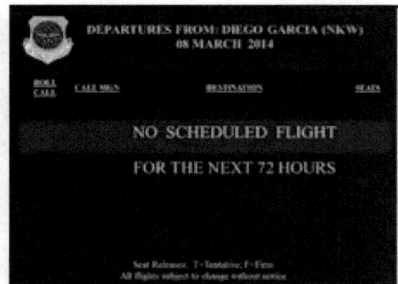

DEPARTURES FROM: DIEGO GARCIA (NKW)
08 MARCH 2014

ROLL
CALL   CALL SIGN   DESTINATION   SEATS

NO SCHEDULED FLIGHT
FOR THE NEXT 72 HOURS

Seat Releases: T-Tentative; F-Firm
All flights subject to change without notice

I uploaded that flight board to mailstar/net/DG-140308-no-flights.JPG .

Landing at Diego Garcia could not be done without approval of the US Military. Hijacking by the Captain or co-pilot is unlikely, because they would still have needed permission to land at Diego Garcia. No demands or ultimatums were presented to Malaysian authorities, of the type "do this or else", and there are more pleasant ways to commit suicide.

Which leaves the CIA as the most likely culprit. One might surmise that the intelligence agency behind the hijack could have stored MH370 in a hangar on Diego Garcia, and disposed of it later, after it faded from public attention.

After I did a radio interview on Tony Gosling's radio program in 2017, I received an email from Ann Diener <raven_knight@sbcglobal.net>, as follows:

"I have a friend who was stationed on Diego Garcia. This is her response to the Diego Garcia portion.

"Diego Garcia theory—there is no hanger to hide a jet that large on the island. There aren't regular schedule flights because there are only 3/4 flights a month that come and go. 2 of those flights are every 2 weeks, 1 flight is once a week and the other flight is once a month."

Following up, I then investigated the hangars on Diego Garcia. The Boeing 777 is much larger than military jets; in particular, its tail is too high for the hangars on Diego Garcia.

The B-2 Shelter System [B2SS], also called Extra Large Deployable Aircraft Hangar Systems, provides hangars 250' wide by 60' high on Diego Garcia: http://www.globalsecurity.org/military/systems/aircraft/systems/xldahs.htm

But the tail of the 777 is 60 ft 9 in high: https://en.wikipedia.org/wiki/Boeing_777.

It follows that MH370 could not have remained on Diego Garcia during daylight hours. Although there were no flights scheduled from March 8 to 10, and workers may have been deployed offshore on a naval exercise, the risk of someone seeing MH370 there and later blabbing would be too great, whatever the penalties.

Next, I investigated the times of reported sightings of MH370 in the Maldives, and sunrise there and on Diego Garcia.

Male and Maamigili International Airports

Male International Airport is also called Velana International Airport; it has a 3000m runway, and routinely takes Boeing 777s.

Maamigili is about 108km to the west of Male. Its airport is called Villa International Airport. The runway is 1800m, just sufficient for a 777; Leeds airport (LBA) is 1800m, and takes 777s. Maamigili is a quieter airport than Male, but the runway is less secluded from domestic buildings.

Thimarafushi, on the other hand, is too short.

The runway at Male is on Hulhule Isand; it runs north-south. MH370 would have landed from the south, and stayed at the northern end of the runway, instead of taxiing to the terminal near the southern end. It would have been refuelled, and cargo & passengers of interest been transferred to another plane, or a boat, or both. Those other craft would then have gone to Diego Garcia, where they would not have aroused suspicion. Then MH370, flying as a drone, would have headed towards Diego Garcia, but, I believe, not have landed there, because it would have been daylight, and thus too risky. Instead, it would have been dumped between Diego Garcia and Mauritius.

To familiarise yourself with Male airport (Velana InternationalAirport), study the Google Map: https://www.google.com/maps/@4.1929451,73.5286127,15z.

It's also called Ibrahim Nasir International Airport, and Hulhule Airport.

The airport is on Hulhule Island. It is connected by a causeway to Hulhumale Island, to the north-east, and by a bridge (built by China) to Male city, which is on Kaafu Island, to the south-west.

Another map of the airport is at https://mapcarta.com/14910168.

Here is a youtube of a High Power Take off of an Emirates Boeing 777-300er from   Male   International   Airport: https://www.youtube.com/watch?v=c0Vu58MTl60.

The Emirates 777 is firstly towed from the Terminal, which is on the east side, to the south end of the runway; then it taxis to the north end of the runway; then it reverses around, at which point you can see the city of Hulhumale on the left, i.e. the east (it's on Hulhumale Island).

Then the Emirates 777 takes off towards the south. As the plane lifts off the ground, you see the Terminals on the left (i.e. east).

China built the bridge connecting Male airport to Male city; alarms U.S. Military

The Maldives consists of many small islands. Male airport and Male city are on two different islands; China built a bridge to connect them.

China has a long-term lease on Hambantota port in Sri Lanka, has built many engineering projects in Mauritius, and has been courting the Maldives government; Male International Airport was recently upgraded by a Chinese company.

Such intrusion alarmed the US. In 2013, the US proposed a "lily pad" military base in the Maldives (Bhadrakumar, 2013).

"The intriguing 'leak' of a draft Status of Forces Agreement [SOFA] between the United States and the Maldivian government has led to reluctant confirmation by both countries that they are indeed involved in discussion with each other to conclude such an agreement."

The draft SOFA is at http://www.dhivehisitee.com/images/US-Maldives-SOFA-draft.pdf.

But in 2014 the Maldives government rejected the "lily pad" Military Pact with US, because it would upset neighbors India and Sri Lanka (Maldives rejects Lily Pad, 2014).

"The Maldives has decided not to take part in a proposed military cooperation pact with the United States over fears that it could upset the regional power India, senior officials said Wednesday. Speaking on a visit to Sri Lanka, the atoll nation's new President Abdulla Yameen said he did not want to proceed with the Status of Forces Agreement (SOFA) that would have given the US a foothold in his archipelago located across the main east-west sea route."

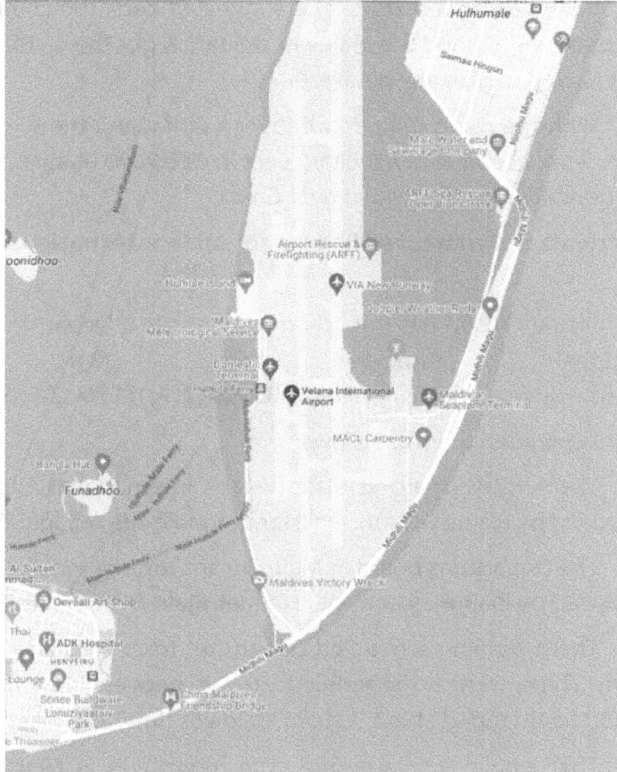

Nevertheless, the discussions mean that there was close contact between Diego Garcia and the Maldives military.

That liason came in handy in the wake of sightings of MH370. The Maldives National Defence Force dismissed those sightings:

"Eyewitness reports of a possible sighting of missing Malaysian Airlines Flight MH370 flying near the Maldives have been officially discounted in a statement issued by the Maldives National Defence Force" (Koutsoukis, 2014).

If MH370 landed at Male as suggested here, the commander at Diego Garcia would have phoned the Maldives military & got the ok for a job in the night, without having to give any details.

With the rising Cold War between China and the West, the Maldives and the U. S. went ahead with a military pact in Oct. 2020 (Ranjan, 2020). Maldives political factions are sharply divided over China.

Arrivals & Departures Boards for Male International Airport on March 8, 2014

Blaine Gibson has published the Arrivals & Departures Boards for Male International Airport on March 8, 2014: https://drive.google.com/file/d/0B35tmLZHg1FESOI4ZlFnYWd1bE0/view

I uploaded them as follows:

The Arrivals board at Male (Velana International Airport) for March 8, 2014; supplied by Blaine Gibson: mailstar.net/Male-AR-140308.JPG

The Departures board at Male (Velana International Airport) for March 8, 2014; supplied by Blaine Gibson: mailstar.net/Male-DP-140308.JPG

There were no scheduled Departures from Male airport between 2.50am and 6am. There were no scheduled Arrivals between 11.05pm and 6.50am. MH370 could have landed about 3.20am Maldives time, and taken off by 5.45am.

That whole time was dark. The moon was at First Quarter. Sunrise was at 6.14am (see https://www.timeanddate.com/sun/maldives/male); first light about 5.35am. At Male, residential areas are a long way from the northern end of the runway.

It was just a matter of luck that Blaine saved the Arrivals & Departures Boards of Male Airport for March 8, 2014. He explained how, at https://drive.google.com/file/d/0B35tmLZHg1FESOI4ZlFnYWd1bE0/view:

Maldives Revisited
By Blaine Alan Gibson
12 August 2016

3. Last year an article was published in Le Monde claiming that a domestic Dash 8 propeller plane, Maldivian flight 149, flew off course over Kudahuvadhoo and landed at Thimarafushi at 6:33 AM March 8, 2014. This claim was repeated widely in the press, and was republished in a book by the same author this year. This claim was used to dismiss the testimony of more than twenty eyewitnesses who reported seeing a large low flying jet, and state they saw flight 149 instead. The attached official flight records prove this claim to be totally incorrect. There was no such flight.

The plane seen by the Kudahuvadhoo witnesses was NOT any of the Dash 8 Turbo propeller plane domestic flights. According to Maldives ATC they never fly over Kudahuvadhoo, and none were flying to or from any nearby airports around the time of the sighting. When Die Zeit reporter Bastian Berbner inquired with the head of Maldives Civil Aviation about the domestic Dash 8 flight schedules, and flight 149 in particular, he was told Civil Aviation does not maintain those records, and to inquire with Male Airport Operations and Air Traffic Control. So we did.

We have obtained the actual flight records for March 8 2014 from an official within Male airport operations. They were later confirmed by a Male ATC official.

Bibliography (MH370)

Barker, Anne. (2019, Jan. 31). MH370 may have crashed near Madagascar, underwater microphones suggest. ABC News , Australia. https://www.abc.net.au/news/2019-01-31/mh370-underwater-microphones-suggest-alternate-crash-site/10767550

Bhadrakumar, M K . (2013, Apr. 26). US seeks military presence in Maldives. https://www.rbth.com/blogs/2013/04/26/us_seeks_military_presence_in_maldives_24183

Death threats. (2018, May 29). US wreck hunter Blaine Gibson claims stalking, death threats and assassination prevent MH370 mystery being solved. Staff writers News Corp Australia Network. https://www.news.com.au/travel/travel-updates/incidents/us-wreck-hunter-blaine-gibson-claims-stalking-death-threats-and-assassination-prevent-mh370-mystery-being-solved/news-story/96cbc9d7e676ba364cd32a62d3726f70.

Disproves Pilot Suicide. (2018, Jan. 21). MH370 'wreck hunter' says debris found disproves pilot suicide theory. Free Malaysia Today. https://www.freemalaysiatoday.com/category/nation/2018/01/21/mh370-wreck-hunter-says-debris-found-disproves-pilot-suicide-theory.

Gibson, Blaine Alan. (2016, Aug. 21). Maldives Revisited. https://drive.google.com/file/d/0B35tmLZHg1FESOl4ZlFnYWd1bE0/view.

Grafton-Green, Patrick. (2019, July 16). MH370 investigators 'discover mystery load weighing 89kg was added to the cargo flight list' after take-off. The Standard, UK. https://www.standard.co.uk/news/world/mh370-investigators-discover-mystery-load-weighing-89kg-was-added-to-the-cargo-flight-list-after-a4191111.html.

Kadri, Usama et. al. (2017). Rewinding the waves: tracking underwater signals to their source. Nature Magazine, article number 13949. https://www.nature.com/articles/s41598-017-14177-3.

Kadri, Usama. (2019a, Jan. 29). Effect of sea-bottom elasticity on the propagation of acoustic—gravity waves from impacting objects. Nature Magazine, published online. https://www.nature.com/articles/s41598-018-37626-z.

Kadri, Usama. (2019b, Jan. 29, updated Jan. 30). MH370: New underwater sound wave analysis suggests alternative travel route and new impact locations. The Cpnversation, ABC Australia. https://theconversation.com/mh370-new-underwater-sound-wave-analysis-suggests-alternative-travel-route-and-new-impact-locations-110664.

Koutsoukis, Jason. (2014, March 19). Missing Malaysia Airlines plane: Maldives discounted as possible location for MH370.

Maldives rejects Lily Pad. (2014, Jan. 22). Maldives Rejects Military Pact With US. AFP, Colombo. https://www.business-standard.com/article/pti-stories/maldives-rejects-military-pact-with-us-114012201130_1.html.

Koutsoukis, Jason. (2014, March 19). Missing Malaysia Airlines plane: Maldives discounted as possible location for MH370. Sydney Morning Herald. http://www.smh.com.au/world/missing-malaysia-airlines-plane-maldives-discounted-as-possible-location-for-mh370-20140319-hvkjq.html.

Myers, Peter Gerard. (2023). MH370 Source Material. https://mailstar.net/MH370-Source-Material.html.

Ranjan, Amit. (2020, Oct. 14). United States-Maldives Defence Pact: What Lies Ahead for India? https://www.isas.nus.edu.sg/papers/united-states-%C2%ADmaldives-defence-pact-what-lies-ahead-for-india/.

Schulman, Ari N. (2014, May 8). Why the Official Explanation of MH370's Demise Doesn't Hold Up: Outside satellite experts say investigators could be looking in the wrong ocean. https://www.theatlantic.com/technology/archive/2014/05/why-the-official-explanation-of-mh370s-demise-doesnt-hold-up/361826/

Spaeth, Andreas. (2014, Nov. 21). Sir Tim Clark believes information is being concealed: Emirates head presses for change to prevent further tragedy. Sydney Morning Herald. http://www.smh.com.au/world/full-transcript-emirates-chief-sir-tim-clark-on-mh17-and-mh370-20141121-11rc70.html.

Thomas, Geoffrey. (2023). Mh370 Debris: Now For The Facts! https://www.airlineratings.com/news/mh370-debris-now-for-the-facts/.

Appendix 4: The Attacks of September 11, 2001

These attacks are blamed on Islamic hijackers. Alternative explanations blame them on the Deep State (e.g. Dick Cheney) or on Mossad. This topic is too big to cover here, but some notes are presented for those who believe the official story.

Begin with Richard Gage's 10 minute video <https://environmentaljusticetv.wordpress.com/2012/12/30/richard-gages-new-10-minute-showcase-video>. Then videos by Major-General Albert Stubblebine <https://youtu.be/JDoCLobUhuc>. Then Alan Sabrosky's Shocking Press TV Interview <https://www.youtube.com/watch?v=XB4HghszT2k>. Sabrosky, part-Jewish, was Director of Studies at the U. S. Army War College.

Search for "Dancing Israelis" and "Odigo". Read books and articles by Christopher Bollyn; he covers Mossad's role.

Watch Alex Jones' interview with Dr Steve Pieczenik on April 21, 2016 <https://www.youtube.com/watch?v=pP-qBQ4xey4>; it's also at <mailstar.net/Pieczenik-911-CIA-Israel-160421.mp4>. Pieczenik is Jewish, and the most senior U.S. Government official to reveal the plot, which he blames on Mossad with CIA complicity.

00.46 Pieczenik says he began to see CIA civilians totally take over the Pentagon.

Says it will lead to a Standown & False Flag attack. The Saudis, the Pakistanis et al will be implicated, so that none of them can blow the whistle.

SP: "So it was clear to me who would be involved. It would be Paul Wolfowitz, it would be Walter Yagel. It would be Zalmay Khalilzad. All of these people who I'd worked with - Richard Perle, Dov Zakheim, who's a rabbi, I didn't know but I didn't like. Elliot Abrams who I almost killed in another iteration. He knew I was going after him on the Panama thing. And when it occurred, I knew immediately that this was a stand down false flag because Israeli operatives immediately called me up and said the planes had attacked the towers and they were collapsing and I said there is no precedent in the history of any building where a plane has crashed and collapsed the building - and immediately they said, within minutes of the time I said that this was a false flag, "Oh, you must be an Arabist", now I said I know who was involved. So it was Israel, I knew the Pakistani senior intelligence officer was coming here because I was forewarned by one of his predecessors - Jacob Khan - that the Pakistani Generals were involved in a potential coup. I was forewarned that the Saudis would be involved. I knew that the Israelis would be involved because they had people like Michael Chertoff, who should have been indicted because he had double citizenship here and in Israel and was in charge of Homeland Security along with Richard Perle and others whose loyalty has never been to the United

States. Unfortunately these American Jews, whose loyalty is to Israel, have never served the American government, never been in the American military, but are more than happy to serve the Israeli military. As Dov Zakheim has done, as Rahm Emanuel and that whole family on both the Republican and Democratic side."

My webpage on 9/11 is at http://mailstar.net/wtc.html. It reveals Mossad's repeated use of stolen identities. Thus, 'Mohammad Atta' was a Mossad agent impersonating the real Atta. Watch the interview with the fake Mahammad Atta's American girlfriend, Amanda Keller, disclosing his un-Islamic lifestyle <https://www.youtube.com/watch?v=CSKV65zsbsk>.

Atta's father said that the real Atta was still alive after 9/11, and blamed Mossad. A Saudi Prince said that seven alleged hijackers were alive after 9/11.

The stolen identities of hijackers in 9/11 occurred also in the case of the assassination of Hamas leader Mahmoud al-Mabhouh in Dubai on January 19, 2010, which was carried out by Mossad agents using passports with stolen identities from European countries and Australia. The Mossad agents were caught on video.

Victor Ostrovsky, a former Mossad agent who exposed Mossad in his book *By Way of Deception*, said that Mossad did this assassination, and explained how the agency developed the habit of using stolen identities for its agents' passports.

The video and assassination have sparked extensive debate in the media, inside and outside Israel, over, among other things, the alleged assassin team's use of forged passports from the United Kingdom, Ireland, France and Germany. At least seven of the passports used the names of residents in Israel who hold dual citizenship in other countries and who say they were not part of the operation. (Zetter, 2010)

Physics Professor Steven E. Jones proved that controlled demolition devices were placed in the Twin Towers—and this is what brought them down, not planes; they were demolished from the top down. WTC7, a 50-storey skyscraper not hit by any plane, was a Controlled Demolition from below. The owner, Larry Silverstein, admitted it on TV; Danny Jowenko, a Dutch expert, testified to it being a CD.

Jones said that molten metal, found in the sub-basements of the buildings, was caused by Thermate, an incendary used to demolish steel. Niels Harrit, a Chemistry Professor, backed up Jones' findings. Jones was forced out of his university job. Jones also said that heated dust with particles of Thermite was discovered in the WTC area. Allegedly, three New York Jewish steel and scrap companies shipped the metal, which could have been used as evidence, to China and India.

Appendix 5: Evidence that Stalin was Murdered

On March 5, 1953, Soviet media announced the death of Stalin; he had died within 2 months of the Doctors' Plot being announced.

Pavel Sudoplatov, the head of SMERSH, the top counter-intelligence body, wrote that the Plot was not restricted to Jews, and was part of a purge of the Politburo:

> Although it was known as an anti-Semitic campaign, the Doctors' Plot was not restricted to Jews. Rather it was part of a struggle to settle old scores in the leadership. On one side Stalin, with the help of Malenkov and Khrushchev, was trying to purge his own old guard and Beria. The scapegoats in the alleged Jewish "conspiracy" were to be Molotov, Voroshilov, and Mikoyan, the last of Stalin's Politburo old guard. (1995, p. 298)

They sensed that he was out to get them, so they plotted against him too.

Many books (e.g. Rapoport, 1990, pp. 176 & 214) claim that Stalin intended to deport the Jews to Siberia, but was killed first; and that he was poisoned on March 1, the feast of Purim, which celebrates the destruction of enemies of the Jews.

The Jerusalem Post published an article 'Purim Miracle of 1953': "Purim in 1953 fell on March 1. On that day, Haman-Stalin had a stroke. Soon came the tyrant's death. A heavenly stroke brought down the villain on the eve of the terrible stroke Stalin was about to inflict upon the Jewish people" (Roginsky, 2017).

However, Sudoplatov, whose wife was Jewish, and who had many Jewish colleagues, said that it was just a rumour:

> It is rumored now that a plan existed for deportation of Jews from Moscow on the eve of Stalin's death. I never heard of it; if such a plan existed it could be easily traced in the archives of state security and of the Moscow party committee, because it would have required large-scale preparations. Deportation operations are very difficult to carry out, especially if they are not concealed beforehand. There would have been some sort of top-secret directive, endorsed by the government at least one month before the start of such an operation. Therefore, I believe that it was only a rumor, probably based on comments by Stalin or Malenkov assessing the outrage of public opinion against Jews associated with the Doctors' Plot. (1995, p. 388).

Stuart Kahan attested the Jewish connection to the purge Stalin was planning:

> Stalin was about to launch a new terrorist campaign against the party's higher-ranking members, and it appeared that no one was safe, least of all those with Jewish connections. They would be the targets for the upcoming purges. Besides Molotov, Voroshilov had married a woman of Jewish

extraction, Beria's mother was half-Jewish, Khrushchev's son-in-law was of Jewish origin, and Lazar himself was a Jew. (1987, p. 256)

But Stalin's own (third) wife, Rosa Kaganovich, sister of Lazar, was Jewish too.

Harry Waton, a Jewish communist, wrote a book about the Jewish Program for Jews and for Humanity. I uploaded part of it to my website, after which I received emails from members of the Waton family, who had lost touch with each other, through war and migration; I put them in touch with one another.

I also uploaded extracts of the biography of Lazar Kaganovich by Stuart Kahan to my website. Subsequently, I received emails from a number of Kaganovich descendants, widely dispersed, and put some of them in touch with one another too! One, Miriam de Vore, wrote, "my aunt florence cohen told me that her aunt rose was married to stalin". She authorised me to publish her correspondence. It's at https://mailstar.net/wives-of-stalin.html.

Other Kaganovich family members denied that Rosa was married to Stalin; and even denied her very existence; so did the Jugashvili family.

But the Times of London published an Obituary of Stalin on Friday March 6, 1953, whose last sentence was "Late in life he married Rosa Kaganovich, the sister of Lazar Kaganovich; a member of the Politburo."

https://www.thetimes.co.uk/article/obituary-marshal-joseph-stalin-0zbdtrxcmfq.

Trotsky affirmed it too: "Stalin married the sister of Kaganovich, thereby presenting the latter with hopes for a promising future." (Trotsky, 1940/2019, p. 788).

Robert Payne also affirmed it. He quoted housekeeper Natalia Trushina's report of an argument between Stalin and his (second) wife Nadezhda, on the night she died:

Nadya was infuriated. "Rosa, I suppose, revives you! ... I know the kind of leader you are. More than anyone else, I know the kind of revolutionist you are!" And she went on to accuse him of usurping the leadership of the party dishonestly, of involving her in his shady schemes. She was, she said, ashamed to look her comrades in the eye because of his blood purges and liquidations. (1965, p. 412)

Stalin, in a rage and under the influence of alcohol, allegedly strangled her that night. Aino Kuusinen published the story in his book *Before and After Stalin* (1974, pp. 91-3). https://mailstar.net/wives-of-stalin.html.

Given that many of the Politburo had a Jewish connection, including Khrushchev and even Stalin himself, it cannot be Jewish ethnicity that was operative, but rather Jewish political action, i.e. operating as a Lobby.

Three events in the 1940s triggered the change:

1. The Jewish Anti-Fascist Committee (JAC), an alliance of leading Soviet and American Jews, proposed turning Crimea into an autonomous Jewish republic funded by American Jews (Sudoplatov, 1995, p. 187).

The JAC put this proposal in letter addressed to Stalin, dated Feb. 15, 1944. Solomon Lozovsky, deputy foreign minister and supervisor of the JAC, edited the letter, redated it Feb. 21, and readdressed it to Molotov.

Sudopatov wrote, "I was informed by Beria that the initiative came from the American side, from American Jewish organizations" (p. 286).

American Jewish Plutocrats would fund the project. Stalin wanted them to invest in, and and supply technical assistance to, the whole Soviet Union, to help rebuild it after the war, but they were only interested in funding the Jewish zone (Crimea). Crimea, hosting Sevastopol naval base, is strategically important. Stalin and Khrushchev envisaged that an American-dominated Crimea would be a dagger aimed at Russia's underbelly, and prone to secession.

2. The U.S. Government put the Baruch-Lilienthal Plan for control of Atomic Energy to Stalin on June 14, 1946; it proposed a surrogate World Government, without a Soviet veto, as had been discussed in the Bulletin of the Atomic Scientists (BAS), which carried the Plan and the debate. The authors of the Plan, David Lilienthal and Bernard Baruch, were Jewish, and both editors of the BAS (Eugene Rabinowitch and Hy Goldsmith) were Jewish. Many of the other writers at the BAS, and in the book *One World Or None* they published in 1946, were also Jewish and International Socialists.

Baruch was a Wall St. banker, who had been associated with Wilson's attempt to have the League of Nations created as a World Government with a World Army and a World Court. David Eli Lilienthal had written an article titled The Mission of the Jew, in 1918, claiming that World Unity (meaning World Government) was the mission of the Jews, alongside Monotheism (Lillienthal, 1918). https://mailstar.net/baruch-plan.html.

In the BAS issue of October 1, 1946, Bertrand Russell wrote, "The American and British governments ... should make it clear ... when their plan [sic] for an international government are ripe, they should offer them to the world ... If Russia acquiesced willingly, all would be well. If not, it would be necessary to bring pressure to bear, even to the extent of risking war" (p. 21).

and earlier in the same article he wrote:

"When I speak of an international government, I mean one that really governs, not an amiable facade like the League of Nations or a pretentious sham like the

United Nations under its present constitution. An international government ... must have the only atomic bombs, the only plant for producing them, the only air force, the only battleships, and, generally, whatever is necessary to make it irresistible." (p. 19)

3. Golda Meir arrived in Moscow in October 1948 as ambassador of the newly-created state of Israel. Over a one month stay, she was mobbed repeatedly by large crowds of ecstatic Jews. Thousands subsequently applied to emigrate to Israel; the government sensed the unreliability of the Jews.

Sudoplatov, whose wife was Jewish, attests that Stalin's 'anti-semitic' turn began in late 1946. Note the date: this was just after the Baruch Plan alerted him to the hegemonic intentions behind "One World".

> It was in the second half of 1946, when Stalin had become disenchanted with Jewish alliances abroad and Jewish demands at home and was feeling isolated by the British-American joint stand in Palestine, that he began to stimulate an anti-Semitic campaign, which culminated in a purge of Jews from the party machinery, diplomatic service, military apparatus, and intelligence services. It developed into the infamous Doctors' Plot and Zionist conspiracy charges, in which every Jewish doctor was suspect. The anti-Semitic campaign was a repeat of the purges of the 1930s (Sudoplatov pp. 293-4).

Yuri Slezkine noted (2004) that the Soviet bomb was being built by Jewish scientists too; and that the plan to unite the two bombs was also Jewish: "And who (stage whisper) was building the Soviet atomic bomb? And how were they connected to their kinsmen building the American atomic bomb? And what about the spies who were, in their own way, trying to connect the two atomic bombs?" (Slezkine, p. 304).

Gerhard Falk wrote, in an article about Jewish achievements, "the atomic bomb was a Jewish invention and ... the atomic age was introduced to the world by Jews. What is true of this country is also true of Russia. The Russian atomic bomb and the hydrogen bomb were also invented by Jewish physicists" (Falk, n.d.).

Apart from the atomic, Slezkine lists many other sensitive occupations that were Jewish-dominated: tank production, airplane design, chief engineers, top managers, philosophers, publishers and academics (pp. 302-3).

Many of these Jews were probably loyal Communists, not at all Zionist. But the Government had no way of knowing who it could trust, and who not.

After the creation of Israel, and the outbreak of the Cold War, Soviet Jews were seen as a nationality with divided loyalties. Insofaras the Soviet intelligentsia was Jewish, it was suspect: "here was a race that was both ubiquitous and camou-flaged ... a nationality that consisted almost entirely of intelligentsia (or rather, refused to engage in proletarian pursuits); a nationality that used pseudonyms instead of names (Slezkine, pp. 297-8).

In 1948, the letter from the Jewish Anti-Fascist Committee was used in Stalin's purge of the JAC. Solomon Mikhoels was murdered, Yiddish theaters were closed, and most Yiddish writers were arrested. In 1952, Lozovsky and members of the JAC were arrested, tried and executed.

Stalin also intended to purge leaders closely involved with the Crimea scheme: Beria, Molotov, Mikoyan, Voroshilov and Voznesensky (Sudoplatov, pp. 287-8). This was the genesis of the Doctors Plot.

Kaganovich, and other leaders with a Jewish connection, such as Khrushchev, were not targeted for the purge, because they had not compromised the integrity of the U.S.S.R.

Sudoplatov says that Beria had helped establish the JAC (p. 288). His mother was half-Jewish (Wolf, p. 256). "In the final period of the Zionist conspiracy in 1952, it ballooned out of its organizers' control. Ryumin and Ignatiev joined the minister of state security of Georgia, Nikolai M. Rukhadze, to accuse Beria of concealing his Jewish origin and fabricating a conspiracy against Stalin in Georgia. Beria was next on the list for elimination by Stalin (Sudoplatov, p. 306).

Timeline of the Doctors Plot

January 13, 1953: Tass announced the discovery of a terrorist group of poison-ing doctors. (Radzinsky, p. 539)

February 8, 1953: Pravda published the names of Jewish saboteurs (Radzinsky p. 542)

February 11, 1953: the USSR severed diplomatic relations with Israel (Govrin, pp. 3-4).

End of February, 1953: rumors went around Moscow that the Jews were to be deported to Siberia (Radzinsky, p. 542), with March 5 rumoured to be the date when this would happen (p. 546}.

March 4: Moscow radio announces Stalin's illness.

March 5: The death of Stalin announced.

March 6: Beria's tanks surround Moscow.

March 9: Stalin's funeral.

March 23: From this date Stalin's name disappeared from Soviet media.

April 3: Kremlin doctors freed.

April: Collective leadership was announced: Malenkov (nominal head), Beria and Molotov (actual heads).

"With almost indecent haste Stalin's name disappeared from the newspapers. It was replaced, not by the name of any one man, but by those of Malenkov, Molotov, Khrushchev and Bulganin" (Monitor, 1958, p. 59).

Beria seized power,; his regime denounced the Doctors' Plot as bogus, and freed the Doctors. He was overthrown a few months later by Khrushchev, with the help of Malenkov. The fall of Beria was announced on July 10, 1953.

The above provides context; evidence that Stalin was murdered is itemised below.

1. Indications that Stalin was poisoned

Evidence of poisoning is presented by Dr. Miguel A. Faria, retired Clinical Professor of Surgery (Neurosurgery, ret.) and Adjunct Professor of Medical History (ret.) Mercer University School of Medicine; Associate Editor in Chief of Surgical Neurology International (SNI) from 2012-present; Editor Emeritus, the Association of American Physicians and Surgeons (AAPS).

He wrote two articles on this topic:

Stalin's Mysterious Death (Nov 14, 2011). Surg Neurol Int 2011;2:161. https://www.ncbi.nlm.nih.gov/pmc/articles/PMC3228382/.

and, in 2015, a reply to the Autopsy report:

The death of Stalin — was it a natural death or poisoning? Surg Neurol Int. 2015; 6: 128.

Published online 2015 Jul 30. doi: 10.4103/2152-7806.161789

PMC4524003 PMID: <https://pubmed.ncbi.nlm.nih.gov/26257986>

https://www.ncbi.nlm.nih.gov/pmc/articles/PMC4524003/

In the 2011 article, he reported:

"When the doctors arrived to treat Stalin on the morning of March 2, the Boss was soaked in urine and lay unconscious on the sofa. Both his right arm and leg were paralyzed with a right Babinski reflex (i.e., right-sided hemiplegia consistent with a left cerebral stroke). ... On March 4, Stalin began to hiccup uncontrollably and vomit blood."

Vomiting blood indicated a stomach hemorrhage, such as Warfarin or Dicoumarol can cause.

Stalin also had a cerebral hemorrhage, indicative of a stroke.

Faria continues, citing Jonathan Brent and Vladimir P. Naumov, *Stalin's Last Crime—The Plot Against the Jewish Doctors, 1948-1953*, NY, HarperCollins, 2003, pp. 312-322 (the following quotes are from p. 321):

Final Diagnosis: "Arising on March 5 in connection with the basic illness — hypertension and the disruption of circulation in the brain — a stomach hemorrhage facilitated the recurrent collapse, which ended in death."

But in the final draft of the report submitted to the Central Committee, Brent and Naumov note: "All mention of the stomach hemorrhage was deleted or vastly subordinated to other information throughout in the final report."

Faria's 2015 paper addresses the Autopsy report and media claims that Stalin died of natural causes, i. e. stroke.

On the fiftieth anniversary of Joseph Stalin's death, the British newspaper, the Daily Mail, headlined, "It's official! Stalin died of natural causes: Autopsy published for 1st time says Soviet leader suffocated after suffering a stroke death as from 'natural causes.'"

Faria counters by quoting the the autopsy report that was published in Pravda in 1953:

AUTOPSY OF THE BODY OF J. V. STALIN: Postmortem examination disclosed a large hemorrhage in the sphere of the subcortical nodes of the left hemisphere of the brain. This hemorrhage destroyed important areas of the brain and caused irreversible disorders of respiration and blood circulation. Besides the brain hemorrhage there were established substantial enlargement of the left ventricle of the heart, numerous hemorrhages in the cardiac muscle and in the lining of the stomach and intestine, and arteriosclerotic changes in the blood vessels, expressed especially strongly in the arteries of the brain. These processes were the result of high blood pressure.

"The findings of the autopsy entirely confirm the diagnosis made by the professors and doctors who treated J. V. Stalin.

"The data of the postmortem examination established the irreversible nature of J. V. Stalin's illness from the moment of the cerebral hemorrhage. Accordingly, the energetic treatment which was undertaken could not have led to a favorable result or averted the fatal end.

"U.S.S.R. Minister of Public Health A. F. Tretyakov; Head of the Kremlin Medical Office I. I. Kuperin; Academician N. N. Anichkov, President of the Academy of Medicine; Prof. M. A. Skvortsov, Member of the Academy of Medicine; Prof. S. R. "

[<https://www.ncbi.nlm.nih.gov/pmc/articles/PMC4524003/#ref1>1]

To the novice, it seems to indicate Natural Causes, i.e. Stroke.

But Faria explains:

What the Daily Mail journalist and the social historian did not understand is that if there was evidence of hemorrhage in any body system other than the brain, then this was strong evidence for a bleeding diathesis or poisoning as I described. Stalin did not have a history of a bleeding diathesis or treatment with anticoagulation, therefore poisoning by systemic anticoagulation is the most likely cause for the "numerous hemorrhages in the cardiac muscle and in the lining of the stomach and intestine." [<https://www.ncbi.nlm.nih.gov/pmc/articles/PMC4524003/#ref1>I]

He goes on to point out that had the doctors plainly concluded death by poisoning, Beria, who was running the Soviet Union at that time, would have been the prime suspect. It would have been very risky for the doctors; hence they camouflaged their report, using technical language that, nevertheless, pointed to poisoning:

While prudently citing hypertension as the culprit, the good doctors left behind enough traces of pathological evidence in their brief report to let posterity know they fulfilled their professional duties, as best they could, without compromising their careers or their lives with the new masters at the Kremlin. High blood pressure, per se, commonly results in hypertensive cerebral hemorrhage and stroke but does not usually produce concomitant hematemesis (vomiting blood), as we see here in the clinical case of Stalin, and a further bleeding diathesis affecting the heart muscle, scantily as it is supported by the positive autopsy findings.

2. Reported Confession by Beria: "I did him in!", "I saved all of you!"

Feliks Chuev interviewed Molotov regularly over a number of years. The following interview is recorded in his book *Molotov Remembers* (1993):

CHUEV: Beria himself was said to have killed him.

MOLOTOV: **Why Beria?** It could have been done by a security officer or a doctor. As he was dying, there were moments when he regained consciousness. At other times he was writhing in pain. There were various episodes. Sometimes he seemed about to come to. At those moments Beria would stay close to Stalin. Oh! He was always ready...

One cannot exclude the possibility that he had a hand in Stalin's death. Judging by what he said to me and I sensed.... While on the rostrum of the Mausoleum with him on May 1st, 1953, **he did drop hints** ... Apparently he wanted to evoke my sympathy. **He said, "I did him in!"**—as if this had benefited me. Of course he wanted to ingratiate himself with me: **"I saved all of you!"** Khrushchev would scarcely have had a hand in it. He might have been suspicious of what had gone on. Or possibly... All of them had been close by. Malenkov knows more, much more, much more. (Chuev., 1993, p. 237)

3. Svetlana reports Beria's "triumph"

Stalin's daughter Svetlana Alliluyeva described Stalin's death:

When we were through the gates and Khrushchev and Bulganin waved my car to a stop in the drive outside the house I thought it must be all over. They took me by the arms as I got out. They were both in tears. (p. 14)

During the final minutes, as the end was approaching, Beria suddenly caught sight of me and ordered: 'Take Svetlana away!' The people who were standing around stared, but no one moved. The second it was over he darted into the hallway ahead of anybody else. The silence of the room where everyone was gathered around the deathbed was shattered by the sound of his loud voice, the ring of triumph unconcealed, as he shouted: 'Khrustalyov! My car! (Alliluyeva, 1967, pp. 15-6)

Footnote 6 on p. 248 states: Vasily Khrustalyov: head of Stalin's personal bodyguard.

4. Khrustalev's unusual order: 'Go to Bed'

Dmitri Volkogonov based his account of Stalin's death on the testimony of A.I. Rybin, one of Stalin's bodyguards. But Rybin was not present at the crucial events; he had only been told what had happened by the guardsmen on duty.

Edvard Radzinsky learned that on March 5, 1977, Rybin organized a little party that included the guardsmen who were "at the nearer dacha around the time when Stalin died." (Radzinsky, p. 550)

Their remembrances were written down, and Rybin recorded their testimony:

On the night of February 28-March 1, members of the Politburo watched a film at the Kremlin. After this they were driven to the nearer dacha. Those who joined Stalin there were Beria, Khrushchev, Malenkov, and Bulganin, all of whom remained there until 4:00 a.m. The duty officers on guard that day were M. Starostin and his assistant Tukov. Orlov, the commandant of the dacha, was off duty and his assistant, Peter Lozgachev, was deputized for him. Matryona Butusova, who looked after the Boss's linen, was also in the dacha. After the guests had left, Stalin went to bed. He never left his rooms again. (p. 550)

Rybin separately recorded the testimony of Starostin, Tukov, and Lozgachev. Starostin and Tukov were afraid to go into Stalin's room without being called (it was against protocol), and delayed until late in the day, so Lozgachev went in about 10pm, and found Stalin lying on the floor in a pool of urine. (Radzinsky, p. 553)

Starostin, it appeared, had omitted a surprising detail. Before going to bed Stalin had given his guards an incredible order. In Tukov's words: 'When the guests left, **Stalin told the servants and the commandants "I'm going to bed, I shan't be wanting you, you can go to bed too."** ... Stalin had never given an order like that before.' (p. 550)

Radzinsky comments: "So then the Boss, with his obsessive concern for his own security, suddenly **for the first time orders his guards to go to bed. In effect, leaving his own suite unguarded. And that very night he suffers a stroke**" (p. 550).

Radzinsky later tracked Lozgachev down and interviewed him. Lozgachev said that only light wine was drunk that night; and that it was not Stalin who gave the unusual order at 4am, but another guardsman, Khrustalev. Khrustalev left the dacha at 10:00 a.m. on March 1, and was then relieved by Starostin, Tukov, and Lozgachev.

It was Khrustalev who passed on the order, and left the dacha next morning. **The order came as a surprise** to Lozgachev and the other guard, Tukov, **because the Boss insisted on strict observance of standing regulations. Those alleged words of his were a breach of his sacrosanct routine: they authorized the attachments not to guard his rooms. And not to keep an eye on each other**. (p. 552)

Radzinsky comments: "Either the Boss suddenly lost his mind, ordered everybody to bed, and then had a stroke in the night, **or Khrustalev was ordered by somebody to send his subordinates to bed so that he, or someone unknown to us, could be alone with the Boss**. ... Beria had seized his last chance of survival. Was it Khrustalev himself who ventured into the Boss's room? Or someone else? Perhaps they gave the Boss, who was fast asleep after his Madzhari, an injection? Perhaps the injection caused his stroke?" (p. 556)

5. Delay in calling a doctor

Doctors did not arrive to treat Stalin until the morning of March 2.

On the night of March 1, Starostin phoned Ignatiev at the the Ministry of State Security, but he panicked and told Starostin to try Beria and Malenkov. After half an hour Malenkov phoned back; after another half hour, Beria phoned and said, 'Don't tell anybody about Comrade Stalin's illness' (p. 554).

Khrushchev, in his memoirs *Khrushchev Remembers*, says that he, Malenkov, Beria and Bulganin went to the Dacha that night, but "we decided that it wouldn't be suitable for us to make our presence known while Stalin was in such an unpresentable state" (Khrushchev , 1971, p. 317).

But Radzinsky says that Lozgachev told him Beria and Malenkov arrived by car, without Khrushchev, at 3:00 a.m..on March 2.

They came in: 'What's wrong with the Boss?' He was just lying there, snoring. ... Beria swore at me, and said, 'What d'you mean by it, starting a panic? The Boss is obviously sleeping peacefully. Let's go, Malenkov.' I told them the whole story, how he was lying on the floor, and I asked him a question, and he could only make inarticulate noises. Beria said to me: 'Don't cause a panic, don't bother us. And don't disturb Comrade Stalin.' Then they left. (p. 555)

Radzinsky comments, "So, then—after declaring that a seventy-four-year-old man, who had been lying for four hours or possibly longer in a pool of his own urine, was 'sleeping peacefully,' his comrades-in-arms drove off, leaving the Boss still without help" (p. 555).

6. Stalin's trusted personal security staff were removed before his death

Svetlana noted that prior to her father's death, his trusted security personnel were removed:

"Shortly before my father died even some of his intimates were disgraced: the perennial Vlasik was sent to prison in the winter of 1952 and my father's personal secretary Poskrebyshev, who had been with him for twenty years, was removed." (Alliluyeva, 1967, pp. 217-8, fn *).

This was the work of Beria, head of the MGB. He had fed Stalin lies, as a result of which he sacked them.

Peter Deriabin, a former Soviet counter-intelligence chief who defected to the West, documents (1972) Beria's stripping Stalin of his security personnel:

Beria's commission ... proceeded—and with the fullest cooperation of Malenkov—to cut Stalin's bodyguards to the bone and thereby put him under control. By that time. the dictator was so engrossed with his "Doctors' Plot" aborning that he had thoughts for almost nothing else.

As a result, Beria purged the Okhrana, the very bodyguard organization that Stalin, when in full command of his powers and senses, had so labored to perfect. Dozens of generals and colonels were imprisoned or transferred, and about seven thousand men were dropped from the original Okhrana force of some seventeen thousand. (p. 318)

Stalin no longer received any special, individual protection, but only the same kind that was given to other members of the Politburo and similar hierarchs. (p. 322)

... the process of stripping Stalin of all personal security ... had been a studied and very ably handled business: the framing of Abakumov, the dismissal of Vlasik, the discrediting of Poskrebyshev, the emasculation of the Okhrana and its enforced subservience to the MGB, Kosynkin's "heart attack," the replacement of Shtemenko, and the removal of the general staff from the last vestiges of Okhrana control. And certainly not to be forgotten at that juncture was the dismissal of the Georgian's personal physician followed by MGB control of the Kremlin medical office. With state security and the armed forces under their command, the connivers were finally in the driver's seat. (pp. 325-6)

7. Khrushchev's Secret Speech of 1956

The book *The Death of Stalin: An Investigation by 'MONITOR'* (Monitor, 1958) was written anonymously, but I believe it was by intelligence agents. It gives the most cogent explanation of Khrushchev's 'secret' speech of 1956:

Then, suddenly and without a word of warning, three years after Stalin's death Khrushchev launches his bitter, recriminating attack.

To what purpose?

So far as the delegates to the Congress were concerned, the large majority must have been aware of the terror that had dominated Russia for thirty years, even if there were not many left who knew the awful details as revealed by Khrushchev.

If we accept the fact that Khrushchev was not really so naive as to think his speech would remain a secret from the outside world, why did he go to such lengths to confirm what Stalin's enemies had so long believed?

Why, then, and with what object did Khrushchev make his speech?

We believe he delivered it to prove a case of justifiable homicide—the killing of Stalin.

We believe that he delivered it so that if at any time he and his accomplices should stand accused of Stalin's murder, he could answer: 'I have proved to you all what manner of man he was. Had we not the right to kill him?'

It must be remembered that at the time when Khrushchev made the 'secret' speech, in February, 1956, the battle for power still raged in the Kremlin and, although he was gaining ground, his position was not yet secured. The opposition was still strong. Malenkov, Molotov, Kaganovich, Shepilov and Bulganin still had some fight left in them. And all of them knew what had happened to Stalin. Any one of them could have used that knowledge as a weapon to destroy Khrushchev. That is why in his speech he was at pains to implicate them all. That was the purpose of the little anecdotes, not only about the opposition but about his supporters as well —Mikoyan, Voroshilov and Zhukov—in fact, all the members of the old

Politburo. It was imperative to establish that every one of them had a motive for murdering Stalin. (pp. 131-2)

And the authors conclude that the 'secret' speech is the final piece of evidence that Stalin was murdered.

We believe the loyal shield-bearer disappeared because he was liquidated by the very men whom he had unmasked as the instigators of the 'Doctors' Plot'.

What other reason could there have been for Poskrebyshev's disappearance except that he knew too much? Nor even Khrushchev questions his loyalty to Stalin, nor since the latter had chosen him as his personal aide-de-camp, could it possibly be doubted.

As we have already said, it is extremely unlikely that Stalin would have planned to finish off all the old members of the Politburo unless they had given him cause. And what better cause could they have given him than by plotting his murder aided by his own doctors? Can it be doubted that, having discovered such a plot, Stalin's persecution mania would not have reached such dimensions that he would attempt to annihilate the entire Politburo? (p. 137)

His [Khrushchev's] purpose was to justify Stalin's murder; not to reveal who did it. ...

If the doctors had hatched their plot amongst themselves, let us suppose, to bring about such a miracle by poisoning Stalin, they would have been liquidated immediately. The very fact that they were not is proof that Stalin needed time to find out how many were actually implicated. And the greater the number, the more time he would have needed.

Paradoxically, Khrushchev's own words can be used to prove our point. Stalin did not have time to end the case— 'as he conceived that end.'

Stalin conceived not merely the deaths of a dozen or so Kremlin physicians who were ostensibly plotting to kill a number of ageing Marshals. He conceived the unmasking and finishing off of Beria, Khrushchev, Mikoyan, Voroshilov, and the rest of the old members of the Politburo.

But they did not give him time. (pp. 138-9)

AT THIS POINT we must state that on the evidence of Khrushchev's speech we can no longer accept the belief that Stalin died a natural death. (p. 140)[1]

---

[1] For more information on the Death of Stalin see https://mailstar.net/death-of-stalin.html.

Bibliography

ac2012 (pseudonym). (2012, August 5). Top 10 Crowley Myths which are actually true. https://ac2012.com/2012/08/05/aleister-crowley-myths-actually-true/

A Former Russian Commissar (anon). (1980). Trotsky and The Jews Behind The Russian Revolution. Sons of Liberty. https://www.scribd.com/document/51564140/2810805l-Trotsky-and-the-Jews-Behind-the-Russian-Revolution-by.

Alliluyeva, Svetlana. (1967). *Letters to a Friend* (tr. from the Russian by Priscilla Johnson). Hutchinson of London.

Altman, Dennis. (1972). *Homosexual: Oppression and Liberation*. Angus & Robertson, Sydney.

Altman, Dennis. (1980). *Coming Out In The Seventies*. Penguin Books, Ringwood, Victoria.

Anderson, Kevin B. (2010). *Marx at the Margins: On Nationalism, Ethnicity, and Non-Western Societies*. University of Chicago Press.

Anelauskas, Valdas. (1999). *Discovering America As It Is*. Clarity Press, Inc.

Anthony, David. W.(2007). *The Horse the Wheel and Language: How Bronze-Age Riders from the Eurasian Steppes shaped the Modern World*. Princeton University Press.

Armstrong, D.M. (2010). *Sketch for a Systematic Metaphysics*. Clarendon Press.

Arndt, Bettina. (2018). Bettina Arndt's Fake Rape Campus Tour. Aug 14-Alan Jones; Sept 4-Andrew Bolt; Sky News. https://www.youtube.com/watch?v=fu7JRmVq3ml. Also see https://www.bettinaarndt.com.au/campus-tour/.

Arp, Halton. (1998). Redshifts, Cosmology and Academic Science. Apeiron, Montreal.

Atzmon, Gilad. (2015, Aug. 18). The Kingmaker. http://www.gilad.co.uk/writings/2015/8/18/the-kingmaker.

Babeuf, Gracchus. (1797/1967). *The defense of Gracchus Babeuf before the High Court of Vendome* (ed. & tr. John Anthony Scott). University of Massachusetts Press.

Bakunin, Michael. (1871/1924) Personliche Beziehungen zu Marx. In *Gesammelte Werke. Band 3*, Berlin 1924. Original German by Bakunin published 1871. Tr. Ulli Diemer at https://www.connexions.org/RedMenace/Docs/RM4-BakuninonMarxRothschild.htm

Bamford, James. (2001). *Body of Secrets*. Doubleday, New York.

Barruel, A. (1798/1995). *Memoirs Illustrating The History Of Jacobinism* (tr. Robert Clifford). American Council On Economics And Society, Fraser, Michigan, 1995. First published in 1798.

Bartlett, Liam. (2023, Sept. 3). Trans Regret: De-Transitioning From The Gender Agenda. 7news Spotlight (Australian current affairs documentary on the Seven TV network). https://rumble.com/v3ej73f-channel-7-spotlight-de-transitioning-from-the-gender-agenda.html.

Bates, Daisy. (1967). *The Passing of the Aborigines: A Lifetime spent among the Natives of Australia*. Praeger, New York. https://gutenberg.net.au/ebooks04/0400661h.html.

Baumer, Christoph. (2012). *The History of Central Asia, Volume One: The Age of the Steppe Warriors*. I.B. Tauris.

Ben-Gurion, David. (1962). I Predict—The Next 25 Years. Look Magazine Special Issue, January 16, 1962.

Ben-Gurion, David. (1970). *Recollections*, ed. Thomas R. Bransten. Macdonald Unit Seventy-Five, London.

Ben-Menashe, Ari. (1992). *Profits of War: The Sensational Story of the World-Wide Arms Conspiracy*. Allen & Unwin, Sydney.

Bentresh stela. (2023, Aug. 13, at 13:23 UTC). Wikipedia. https://en.wikipedia.org/wiki/Bentresh_stela.

Berlin, Isaiah. (1979/1981). *Against the Current: essays in the History of Ideas* (ed. Henry Hardy). Clarendon Press, Oxford, 1981. First published in 1979.

Bernal, Martin. (1991). *Black Athena: The Afroasiatic Roots of Classical Civilization Volume II The Archaeological and Documentary Evidence*. Rutgers University Press, New Brunswick NJ. https://mailstar.net/gimbutas.html.

Bernard Baruch. (1971). *Encyclopaedia Judaica, volume 4*. Macmillan. https://www.encyclopedia.com/philosophy-and-religion/bible/bible-apocrypha/baruch-judais.

Billington, James H. (1980). *Fire in the minds of men: Origins of the revolutionary faith*. Temple Smith.

Black, Jeremy and Green, Anthony. (1992) *Gods, Demons and Symbols of Ancient Mesopotamia: An Illustrated Dictionary*. University Of Texas Press, Austin.

Bloom, Harold. (2005). *H. G. Wells*. Chelsea House Publishers.

Bomb Rome. (1941, Jan 20). "Bomb Rome," Advises H. G. Wells. Sydney Morning Herald, p. 8. https://trove.nla.gov.au/newspaper/article/17719531.

Book of Enoch. (2023, Feb. 18, at 01:36 UTC). Reception of the Book of Enoch in premodernity. Wikipedia. https://en.wikipedia.org/wiki/Reception_of_the_Book_of_Enoch_in_premodernity.

Bosco, Andrea. (2017). *The Round Table Movement and the Fall of the 'Second' British Empire (1909-1919)*. Cambridge Scholars Publishing.

Boyce, Mary. (1975) *A History of Zoroastrianism, Volume One: The Early Period*. E. J. Brill, Leiden.

Boyce, Mary. (1982). *A History of Zoroastrianism, Volume Two: Under the Archaemenians*. E. J. Brill, Leiden.

Boyce, Mary. (1991). *A History of Zoroastrianism, Volume Three: Zoroastrianism under Macedonian and Roman Rule*. E. J. Brill, Leiden.

Boyle, Francis A. (2005). *Biowarfare and Terrorism*. Clarity Press, Inc.

Boyle, Francis. (2015). Brzezinski wants to break Russia up into constituent units. Pravda.ru, February 16. http://english.pravda.ru/news/world/16-02-2015/129834-brzezinski_russia-0/ .

Brandon, S. G. F. (1968). *The Trial of Jesus of Nazareth*. B. T. Batsford Ltd., London.

Braver, Mark. (2002, nov. 28). The Last Word on the JFK Assassination. https://www.amazon.com/review/R3PTK1W2RVBZS1.

Breasted, James Henry. (1951). *A History of Egypt: From the Earliest Times to the Persian Conquest* (2nd. edition, fully revised). Hodder & Stoughton, London.

Brown, Ellen Hodgson. (2013). *The Public Bank Solution: From Austerity to Prosperity*. Third Millennium Press, baton Rouge, Louisiana.

Buchanan, George Wesley. (2014). In Search Of King Solomon's Temple. Americans for Middle East Understanding, 2014, Volume 47. https://www.ameu.org/Current-Issue/Current-Issue/2014-Volume-47/In-Search-of-King-Solomons-Temple.aspx.

Bucky, Peter A. (c1992). The private Albert Einstein; in collaboration with Allen G. Weakland. Kansas City: Andrews and McMeel. Online at Albert Einstein: Conversation on Religion and Antisemitism, https://catalogue.nla.gov.au/Record/1238459.

Buckley, William. (1852/2002). *The Life and Adventures of William Buckley* (ed. Tim Flannery). Text Classics, Melbourne, Victoria, 2002. First published in 1852.

Bullock, Alan. (1991). *Hitler and Stalin: Parallel Lives*. HarperCollins.

Burnham, James. (1966). *The Managerial Revolution*. Indiana University Press, Bloomingham.

Butlin, Noel G. (1959). Colonial Socialism in Australia, 1860-1900. In Aitkin, Hugh G. J. (ed), *The State and Economic Growth*. Social Science Research Council, New York, 1959.

Byrne, Peter. (2016, May 16). Panama Papers reveal George Soros' deep money ties to secretive weapons, intel investment firm. Fox News. https://www.foxnews.com/world/panama-papers-reveal-george-soros-deep-money-ties-to-secretive-weapons-intel-investment-firm.

Chagnon, Napoleon A. (2013). *Noble Savages: My Life among two dangerous Tribes—the Yanomoto and the Anthropologists*. Simon & Schuster.

Chambers, Whittaker. (1952/2001). *Witness*. Regnery Publishing, Washington, 2001. Firsat published in 1952.

Chuev, Feliks. (1993). *Molotov Remembers*. I. R. Dee, Chicago.

Childs, Altiyan. (2021). Freemasonry Unveiled. https://odysee.com/@MrCoffee:f/Freemasonry-Unveiled-by-Altiyan-Childs-:f, also at https://www.bitchute.com/video/bTarHsgmfuBF/.

Churchill, Winston. (1920, Feb 08). Zionism Versus Bolshevism: A Struggle for the Soul of the Jewish People. Illustrated Sunday Herald (London), pg. 5. https://en.m.wikisource.org/wiki/Zionism_versus_Bolshevism.

Churchill, Winston. (1930). The Ogre of Europe. Cosmopolitan Magazine, March. International Magazine Co., New York.

Clarke, Peter. (1984). Bertrand Russell and the Dimensions of Edwardian Liberalism. Russell: The Journal of Bertrand Russell Studies, 4(1). https://doi.org/10.15173/russell.v4i1.1612 https://mulpress.mcmaster.ca/russelljournal/article/download/1612/1638/1928

Clement of Alexandria. (c.200/1954). "On Marriage"; in *Stromata, Book III. The Library of Christian Classics: Volume II, Alexandrian Christianity: Selected Translations of Clement and Origine with Introduction and Notes by John Ernest Leonard Oulton and Henry Chadwick*. Westminster Press, Philadelphia, 1954. http://www.earlychristianwritings.com/text/clement-stromata-book3-english.html.

Cohn, Norman. (1957/1970). *The Pursuit of the Millennium: Revolutionary Millenarians and Mystical Anarchists of the Middle Age* (3ed.). Pimlico, 1970. First published 1957.

Cohn, Norman. (1993). *Cosmos, Chaos and the World to Come: The Ancient Roots of Apocalyptic Faith*. Yale University Press.

Common Dreams. (2014, Aug. 20). The Double Identity of an "Anti-Semitic" Commenter Smearing a Progressive Website to Support Israel. https://www.commondreams.org/hambaconeggs.

Cook, John. (2012, Jan. 20). Newspaper Editor: Israel Should Consider Assassinating Obama. http://gawker.com/5877892/newspaper-editor-israel-should-consider-assassinating-obama.

Coombs Taoist. (2004/2020). Dr H. C. Coombs on Central Banking, Wartime Finance, and Monetary Policy in Australia. https://mailstar.net/coombs.html.

Cooper, Nick. (2012). Things to Come Viewing Notes. Wikipedia. https://en.wikipedia.org/wiki/Things_to_Come#cite_note-Cooper,_Nick_2012,_page_14-8.

Coudenhove-Kalergi, Count Richard. (1925/2019). Practical Idealism: The Kalergi Plan to Destroy European Peoples, tr. Dimitra Ekmektsis. Omnia Veritas Ltd. First published as Praktischer Idealismus in 1925.

Coulter, Ann. (2022, Jan. 6). The Great Epstein Cover-Up, Part 1. https://www.takimag.com/article/the-great-epstein-cover-up-part-1/.

Coupland, Philip. (2000). H.G. Wells's 'Liberal fascism'. In Bloom (2005), pp. 171-191. First published in Journal of Contemporary History, 35 [4], October 2000, pp. 541-58. https://doi.org/10.1177/002200940003500402. https://anti-democracy-agenda.blogspot.com/2010/02/article-hg-Wellss-liberal-fascism.html

Courtois, Stephane et. al. (1999). The Black Book Of Communism: Crimes, Terror, Repression (tr. Jonathan Murphy and Mark Kramer). Harvard University Press.

Cowell, Adrian. (1995). The Tribe That Hides From Man. Pimlico, London.

Cowley, A. (1923). Aramaic Papyri Of The Fifth Century B.C. (tr. & ed). The Clarendon Press, Oxford University Press, Oxford.

Cribb, Julian. (1988, March 9). NFF warns of 'social control'. The Australian, p. 19.

Cruickshank, Geoff. (2023, Jan. 2). JFK 2022 documents: CIA's James Angleton running a covert program to supply Israel with nuclear weapons behind President Kennedy's back. https://www.linkedin.com/pulse/jfk-2022-documents-cias-james-Angleton-running-covert-cruickshank.

Daniel Cohn-Bendit. (1968, June 11). French student rebel arrives in UK. BBC News. http://news.bbc.co.uk/onthisday/low/dates/stories/june/11/newsid_3003000/3003831.stm

Daniel, John. (1993). Scarlet and the Beast: A History of the War between English and French Freemasonry. Omnia Veritas. https://archive.org/stream/ScarletAndTheBeastJohnDaniel1995/Scarlet%20and%20the%20Beast%2C%20John%20Daniel%20%281995%29_djvu.txt.

Darius, Emperor. (c.521BC). Achaemenid Royal Inscriptions: DNa. http://www.livius.org/aa-ac/achaemenians/DNa.html.

Daszak, Peter. (2016, Feb. 23). Pandemics: Sonia Shah moderated a forum on emerging infectious diseases and the next pandemic. https://www.c-span.org/video/?404875-1/pandemics. Daszak describes "insert[ing] spike proteins" into viruses to see if they can "bind to human cells". Daszak spoke in four intervals, beginning at 00:30:01. The c-span webpage provides a transcript, but the transcript of Daszak's talk omits important parts. The critical part is at 1:17:06-37. Watch that part. Or watch a clip at https://rumble.com/vi94ht-explosive-video-shows-peter-daszak-bragging-about-creating-killer-viruses-w.html. Download it at https://rumble.com/embed/vfmycj/.

Des Mousseaux, Gougenot (1869/2022). *Judaism And The Judaization Of The Christian Peoples* (tr. I. McGillivray), 2022. First published in 1869. http://mailstar.net/Bakunin-Mousseaux.html.

Deutscher, Isaac. (1970). *The Prophet Outcast.* Oxford University Press.

Diamond, Jared. (2005). *Collapse: How Societies Choose to Fail or Succeed.* Viking.

Dickson, Lovat (1969). *H. G. Wells: His Turbulent Life and Times.* Penguin Books.

Diky, Andrey. (1967). *Jews in Russia and in the USSR.* Self-published in New York. A catalog entry for Diky's book at the National Library of Australia is at https://catalogue.nla.gov.au/Record/2927034.

Dillon, E. J. (1919). *The Peace Conference.* Hutchinson & Co., London.

Downing, F. Gerald. (1988). *Christ and the Cynics: Jesus and other Radical Preachers in First-Century Tradition.* JSOT Press, Sheffield UK. https://mailstar.net/downing.html.

Downing, F. Gerald. (1998). *Paul and the Cynics.* Routledge, London. https://mailstar.net/neither.html.

Duncan-Kemp, A. M. (1961). *Our Channel Country: Man and Nature in South-west Queensland.* Angus and Robertson, Sydney.

Duncan-Kemp, A. M. (1968). *Where Strange Gods Call.* W. R. Smith & Paterson Pty. Ltd, Brisbane.

Durden, Tyler. (2023, Aug. 04). US Intelligence Has Been Manipulating Wikipedia For Over A Decade: Wiki Co-Founder. Zero Hedge. https://www.zerohedge.com/political/wikipedia-co-founder-describes-us-intelligence-manipulation-worlds-largest-online

Ehret, Matthew J. L. (1919, May). The Origins of the Deep State in North America Part I: The Round Table Movement. https://highlanderjuan.com/wp-content/uploads/2019/05/Matthew-Ehret-Origins-of-the-Deep-State-Parts-1-3-a.pdf.

Ehret, Matthew. (2020, Dec 24). H.G. Wells' Dystopic Vision Comes Alive With The Great Reset Agenda. https://www.strategic-culture.org/news/2020/12/24/Wells-dystopic-vision-comes-alive-with-great-reset-agenda.

Eisenhower, Dwight D. (1961). Farewell address by President Dwight D. Eisenhower, January 17, 1961; Papers of Dwight D. Eisenhower as President, 1953-61, National Archives and Records Administration. https://www.archives.gov/milestone-documents/president-dwight-d-eisenhowers-farewell-address.

Elignon, John. (2023, Aug. 2). 'Kill the Boer' Song Fuels Backlash in South Africa and U.S. https://www.nytimes.com/2023/08/02/world/africa/south-africa-kill-boer-song.html.

Elliott, Jackson. (2023, May 27). Transgender Movement Has 'Dangerous' Hidden Motivations, Says Former LGBT Activist. Epoch Times. https://www.theepochtimes.com/in-depth-transgender-movement-has-dangerous-hidden-motivations-says-former-lgbt-activist_5279272.html.

Engels, Frederick. (1884/1908). *The Origin Of The Family, Private Property And The State* (tr. Ernest Untermann). Charles H. Kerr & Co, Chicago, 1908. First pub. 1884.

Engels, Frederick. (1890/1934). On Anti-Semitism; Karl Marx and Frederick Engels Correspondence 1846-1895. Written by Frederick Engels on April 19, 1890; first published: in the Arbeiter-Zeitung, No. 19, May 9, 1890. Published by M. Lawrence, 1934. http://www.marxists.org/archive/marx/works/1890/04/19.htm

Engels, Frederick. (1894/1975). On the History of Early Christianity. In *Collected Works of Karl Marx and Frederick Engels, volume 27*. Progress Publishers, Moscow, 1975. http://www.marxists.org/archive/marx/works/1894chri/index.htm.

Engels, Frederick. (1902). Introduction. In Kelley, Florence (Ed. & Tr.). *Wage-labor and Capital*. New York Labor News Co, New York.

Evans-Pritchard, E. E. (1965). *The Position of Women in Primitive Society and Other Essays in Social Anthropology*. Faber & Faber, London.

Executive Intelligence Review. (1992). The Ugly Truth about the Anti-Defamation League. https://www.islam-radio.net/farrakhan/The.Ugly.Truth.about.the.ADL.pdf.

Executive Intelligence Review. (1997). The true story of Soros the Golem. SPECIAL REPORT, April. Partly online at https://mailstar.net/soros.html.

Ezzat, Ashraf. (2016, July 24). Why Are The Pyramids Not Mentioned In The Bible? https://ashraf62.wordpress.com/2016/07/24/why-are-the-pyramids-not-mentioned-in-the-bible.

Falk, Gerhard. (n.d.). The Achievements of the American Jewish Community: Four Fruits of Freedom. http://www.jbuff.com/c122100.htm.

Fanny Kaplan. (2023, Jan. 19, at 15:02 UTC). Wikipedia. https://en.wikipedia.org/wiki/Fanny_Kaplan.

Farrell, Nicholas. (2023, April 29). Meloni knows that immigration and fertility are linked. The Spectator magazine. https://www.spectator.co.uk/article/meloni-knows-that-immigration-and-fertility-are-linked.

Figes, Orlando. (2007). *The Whisperers—Private Life in Stalin's Russia*. Penguin.

Finkelstein, Israel. (2018). *Hasmonean Realities Behind Ezra, Nehemiah, And Chronicles: Archaeological and Historical Perspectives*. SBL Press, Atlanta, Georgia.

Finkelstein, Norman G. (2000). *The Holocaust Industry: Reflections on the Exploitation of Jewish Suffering*. Verso, New York.

Fitzgerald, Ross. (1994). *"Red Ted": the Life of E. G. Theodore*. University of Queensland Press.

Flannery, Michael A. (2020). *Intelligent Evolution: How Alfred Russel Wallace's World of Life Challenged Darwinism; With an Abridged Version of The World of Life*. Erasmus Press, Nashville, Tennesee.

Flint, John. (1976). *Cecil Rhodes*. Hutchinson.

Flood, Brian (May 21, 2020). Wikipedia co-founder Larry Sanger says online encyclopedia scrapped neutrality, favors lefty politics. Fox News. https://www.foxnews.com/media/wikipedia-co-founder-larry-sanger-says-online-dictionary-scrapped-neutrality-favors-lefty-politics.

Foot, Michael. (1995). *H.G.: The History of Mr Wells*. Doubleday.

Forward 50. (2002, Nov. 15). Growing Clarity, Sharpening Debate. The Jewish Forward. https://web.archive.org/web/20031119043839/https://forward.com/issues/2003/03.11.14/forward50.html.

Frale, Barbara. (2004/2009). *The Templars: The Secret History Revealed* (tr.). Maverick House, Dunboyne, Ireland, 2009. First published as *I Templari*, in 2004.

Frankl, Victor E. (1969). Reductionism and Nihilism. In Koestler, A. and Smythies, J. R. (eds), *Beyond Reductionism*. Hutchinson, London.

Fraser agrees with Carr on Lobby. (2014, May 17). The Truth Will Out: First Carr, Now Fraser. http://middleeastrealitycheck.blogspot.com.au/2014/05/the-truth-will-out-first-carr-now-fraser.html.

Free Speech burn Koran. (2023, July 24). Two protesters burn Koran in front of Iraqi embassy in Denmark. Jerusalem Post. https://www.jpost.com/breaking-news/article-752248.

Freud, Sigmund. (1967). *Moses and Monotheism* (tr. Katherine Jones). Vintage Books, New York. https://mailstar.net/moses.html.

Fromm, Erich. (1958/2002). Trotzky's Diary in Exile, 1935. Harvard University Press, 1958. From the unpublished papers of the Erich Fromm Archives, Tübingen. Also published in Science & Society, Vol. 66, No. 2, Summer (2002), pp. 271-2.

Gardner, Martin. (1999) Introduction. In Wells (1902/1999).

Ginsberg, Benjamin. (1993). *The Fatal Embrace: Jews and the State.* University of Chicago Press.

Glasse, Cyril (2009). *The New Encyclopedia of Islam, edition 3.5.* Altamira USA.

Glasse, Cyril. (2014, Jan. 1). The Second Coming of the Judeo-Zoroastrian Jesus of the Dead Sea Scrolls. Published by Revelation. https://mailstar.net/Isaiah-Zoroastrian.html.

Gmirkin, Russell E. (2006). *Berossus and Genesis, Manetho and Exodus: Hellenistic Histories and the Date of the Pentateuch.* T & T Clark International, New York.

Goldman, David P.(2009, July 5). Confessions Of A Coward. https://www.firstthings.com/web-exclusives/2009/05/confessions-of-a-coward.

Goldsmith, Sir James. (1994). *The Trap.* Carroll & Graf Publishers.

Gollin, A. M. (1964). *Proconsul in Politics: A study of Lord Milner in opposition and in power.* The MacMillam Company, New York.

Gorbachev, Mikhail. (1992). The River of Time and the Imperative of Action. Speech delivered 6 May 1992, Westminster College, Fulton, Missouri. http://cours.ifage.ch/archives/webdev03/mikay/GreenCrossFamily/gorby/river.html

Gordon, Cyrus H. (1962). *Before the Bible: the Common Background of Greek and Hebrew Civilisations.* Collins, London. https://mailstar.net/gimbutas.html.

Gorvin, Yosef. (1990/1998). Israeli-Soviet Relations 1953-1967: From Confrontation To Disruption. Frank Cass, London, 1998. Translated from the Hebrew edition of 1990. https://mailstar.net/moscow-vs-jerusalem.html.

Greer, Germaine. (1971). *The Female Eunuch.* Paladin, London.

Greer, Germaine. (1984). *Sex and Destiny.* Secker & Warburg, Melbourne.

Gunther, John. (1938). *Inside Europe (revised).* Harper & Brothers, New York.

Halevy, Elie. (1941). The Age of Tyrannies (tr. May Wallas). Economica, 8 (29): 77—93.

Hall, Manly P. (1923/2020). *The Lost Keys of Freemasonry: The Legend of Hiram Abiff*, 2ed. (ed. Tarl Warwick), 2020. ISBN 9781660182695. First published 1923. https://en.wikisource.org/wiki/The_Lost_Keys_of_Freemasonry/Chapter_4.

Hall, Manly P. (1929/2018). *Rosicrucian and Masonic origins*. Wilder Publications, 2018. An extract from *Lectures on Ancient Philosophy (1st ed.)*, 1929, The Hall Publishing Company, pp 397-417.

Hass, Ludwik. (1983). The Russian Masonic Movement in the Years 1906—1918, tr. Phillip G. Smith. http://www.skirret.com/papers/russian_masonic_movement.html. Source: Hass, L. (1983). The Russian Masonic Movement in the Years 1906-1918. Acta Poloniae Historica, 48, 95-131. https://rcin.org.pl/ihpan/Content/28112.

Hayek, F. A. (1944). *The Road to Serfdom*. George Routledge & Sons Ltd, London.

Henderson, Ben. (2013, Nov. 1). Mundine defends comments about Aboriginal culture and homosexuality. NITV News. https://www.sbs.com.au/news/article/mundine-defends-comments-about-aboriginal-culture-and-homosexuality/pt7ix8ro0.

Herodotus. (c. 430 BC/1860). *Histories, Book One* (tr. George Rawlinson), 1858-1860. http://www.yorku.ca/pswarney/Texts/herodotus1-69-216.htm.

Herzl, Theodore. (1896/1988). *The Jewish State* (tr. Slyvie d'Avigdor, revised by Jacob M. Alkow). Dover Publications. First published in 1896.

Hess, Moses. (1862/1918). *Rome and Jerusalem: A Study in Jewish Nationalism* (tr. Meyer Waxman). Bloch Publishing Co., New York, 1918. First published in 1862.

Hewett, Jennifer. (1997, November 15). The Man Who Sold the World ... And Then Gave Away the Profits. Sydney Morning Herald, Spectrum Features section.

Higger, Michael. (1932). *The Jewish Utopia*. The Lord Baltimore Press, Baltimore.

Hitchens, Christopher. (2010, Apr. 17). Christopher Hitchens re-reads Animal Farm. https://www.theguardian.com/books/2010/apr/17/christopher-hitchens-re-reads-animal-farm.

Hitler, Adolf. (1941-44/2000). *Hitler's Table Talk 1941-44: His Private Conversations* (tr. Norman Cameron and R.H. Stevens, Introduced and with a new Preface by H.R. Trevor-Roper). Enigma Books, New York 2000. https://ia800203.us.archive.org/24/items/HitlerTableTalk/Hitler%20TableTalk.pdf.

Hobson, J. A. (1900). *The War In South Africa: Its Causes And Effects*. James Nisbet & Co, Limited, London.

Hobson, J. A. (1902/1905). *Imperialism: A Study, Second edition*, 1905. George Allen & Unwin Ltd, London. First published in 1902.

House, Col. Edward M. (1912) *Philip Dru: Administrator*. R. W. Huebsch, New York.

Hudson, Michael. (1972/2003). *Super Imperialism: the Origin and Fundamentals of U.S. World Dominance, 2nd edition.* Pluto Press, London, 2003. First published in 1972 as *Super Imperialism: the Economic Strategy of American Empire.*

Hudson, Michael. (2005, Mar. 13). Re: [A-List] William Engdahl? A-list archives at the University of Utah. Formerly at archives.econ.utah.edu/archives/a-list/2005w10/msg00097.html and at lists.econ.utah.edu/pipermail/a-list/2005-March/020237.html.

Hudson, Michael. (2022, Nov. 8). The Rentier Economy is a Free Lunch: The Real Progressives Live with Michael Hudson on The Destiny of Civilization. https://michael-hudson.com/2022/11/the-rentier-economy-is-a-free-lunch/.

Huntington, Samuel. (1996). *The Clash of Civilizations and the Remaking of World Order.* Simon & Schuster, New York.

Huxley, Aldous. (1931/1969). Letter to Mrs. Kethevan Roberts. Written May 18, 1931. Footnote 17 at https://en.wikipedia.org/w/index.php?title=Brave_New_World&oldid=1138277238, last edited Feb. 8 2023, at 21:22 (UTC). The letter is from Smith, Grover (ed.). *Letters of Aldous Huxley.* Harper & Row, New York, 1969. p. 348.

Illich, Ivan. (1976). *Medical Nemesis: The Expropriation Of Health.* Pantheon Books, New York.

Illich, Ivan. (1977). *Disabling Professions.* Marion Boyars Publishers Ltd, London.

Irving, David. (1977). *Hitler's War 1939-1942.* Macmillan, London.

Ivry, Benjamin. (2015, Jan. 3). Deconstructing the Jewishness of the Frankfurt School. The Forward. https://forward.com/culture/211598/deconstructing-the-jewishness-of-the-frankfurt-sch/.

Jacob, Margaret C. (2006). *The Radical Enlightenment: Pantheists, Freemasons and Republicans, Second Revised Edition.* Cornerstone Book Publishers.

Jews a Nation. (n. d.). Judaism: Are Jews a Nation or a Religion? Jewish Virtual Library. https://www.jewishvirtuallibrary.org/are-jews-a-nation-or-a-religion.

Joffre, Tzvi. (2023, July 19). Catholic abbot told to cover cross at Western Wall: The abbot was told that the cross worn at the Western Wall in Jerusalem's Old City was "really big and inappropriate for this place." The Jerusalem Post. https://www.jpost.com/israel-news/article-751637.

Jones, Tony. (2001, Aug. 27). Israel's propaganda war. Lateline, ABC Radio, Australia.

Jordan, Joseph. (2023, July 6). The US Government Is Responsible For France's Anti-White Race Riots. National Justice Party. https://xyz.net.au/2023/07/the-us-government-is-responsible-for-frances-anti-white-race-riots.

Kahan, Stuart. (1987). *The Wolf of the Kremlin*. William Morrow and Company.

Karl Marx Library. (2019, Dec. 2, at 20:11 UTC). Wikipedia. https://en.wikipedia.org/wiki/Karl_Marx_Library

Kennan, George F. (1997, Feb. 5). A Fateful Error. New York Times. https://www.nytimes.com/1997/02/05/opinion/a-fateful-error.html.

Kennedy, John F. (1961). The President And The Press: Address Before The American Newspaper Publishers Association, April 27. Waldorf-Astoria Hotel, New York City. https://www.jfklibrary.org/archives/other-resources/john-f-kennedy-speeches/american-newspaper-publishers-association-19610427. https://www.youtube.com/watch?v=FnkdfFAqsHA.

Kennedy, Robert F. Jr. (2021). *The Real Anthony Fauci*. Skyhorse Publishing.

Kennedy, Robert F. Jr. (2023, Apr. 4, 10:50 am). Twitter, @RobertKennedyJr. https://twitter.com/RobertKennedyJr/status/1643053498483855361.

Kenner, David. (2023, July 7). Australia spikes plan to force companies to disclose global tax data. https://www.icij.org/investigations/paradise-papers/australia-spikes-plan-to-force-companies-to-disclose-global-tax-data.

Kerensky, A. F. (1927/2008). The Catastrophe: Kerensky's own story of the Russian Revolution. First published in 1927. Marxists Internet Archive (2008). https://www.marxists.org/reference/archive/kerensky/1927/catastrophe/ch16.htm.

Khrushchev, Nikita. (1971). *Khrushchev Remembers* (tr. & ed. by Strobe Talbott). Andre Deutsch.

Kienholz, Mary L. (2008). *Opium Traders and Their Worlds: A Revisionist Expose of the World's Greatest Opium Traders, Volume Two*. iUniverse, Inc.

Klaus, Václav. (2013, September 8). Democrats of Europe, wake up. https://www.klaus.cz/clanky/3435.

Kolakowski, Leszek (1978). *Main Currents of Marxism, volume 1—The Founders* (tr. P.S. Falla). Oxford University Press.

Kollontai, Alexandra. (1977). *Selected Writings of Alexandra Kollontai* (tr. Alix Holt). Lawrence Hill and Co., Westport, Conn.

Kuusinen, Aino. (1974). *Before and After Stalin: A Personal Account of Soviet Russia from the 1920s to the 1960s* (tr. Paul Stevenson). Michael Joseph, London. https://mailstar.net/wives-of-stalin.html.

Kyrkunov, Oleksii. (2022). *Freemasonry in the East European History: Its Political and Cultural Influence.* University of Bonn. https://bonndoc.ulb.uni-bonn.de/xmlui/bitstream/handle/20.500.11811/9531/Freemasonry_Eastern_European_History.pdf

Labaree, David. (2021). Beneficent Buffoon—The Case of Napoleon III. January 28. https://davidlabaree.com/2021/01/28/beneficent-buffoon-the-case-of-napoleon-iii/

Lang, J. T. (1962). *The Great Bust: The Depression of the Thirties.* McNamara's Books, Katoomba. https://mailstar.net/Jack-Lang-Banking.html.

Lanouette, William & Silard, Bela. (1994). *Genius In The Shadows: A Biography of Leo Szilard The Man Behind the Bomb.* University of Chicago Press, Chicago.

Lardner, George Jr. & Smith, R. Jeffrey. (1989, June 25). Intelligence Ties Endure Despite U.S.-China Strain. Washington Post. https://www.washingtonpost.com/archive/politics/1989/06/25/intelligence-ties-endure-despite-us-china-strain/f8b2789d-0f0c-4ea7-932b-9f4267a994a3/

Larson, Martin A. (1959). *The Religion of the Occident: or The Origin and Development of the Essene-Christian Faith.* Philosophical Library, New York.

Laski, Harold. J. (1932). *The Socialist Tradition In The French Revolution.* George Allen Unwin.

Laughland, John. (2013, Nov. 12). President Klaus' European Manifesto. Hungarian Review, Volume iv, No. 6 - Current. https://hungarianreview.com/article/20131128_president_klaus_european_manifesto.

Lawson, Dominic. (2004, January 25). If Conrad Black was a bully, I never saw it. UK Telegraph.

Lay, Paul. (2007) Obituary—Norman Cohn. The Guardian, Thu 9 Aug. https://www.theguardian.com/news/2007/aug/09/guardianobituaries.obituaries

Lazare, Bernard. (1894/1995). *AntiSemitism: Its History and Causes* (tr.). University of Nebraska Press, Lincoln. Originally published: L'Antisémitisme, son histoire et ses causes: London: Britons Pub. Co., 1894.

Ledbetter, James. (2007). *Dispatches for the New York Tribune: Selected Journalism of Karl Marx* (selected and with an Introduction by James Ledbetter, Foreword by Francis Wheen). Penguin Books, London. https://libcom.org/files/Marx%20-%20Dispatches%20for%20the%20New%20York%20Tribune.pdf.

Lee, John M. (1971, Sept. 2). Ruble Devalued By Token Amount. The New York Times, Special section. https://www.nytimes.com/1971/09/02/archives/ruble-devalued-by-token-amount-soviet-move-affects-some-western.html

Lehning, Arthur. (1956). Buonarroti And His International Secret Societies. International Review of Social History, Vol. 1, No. 1 (1956), pp. 112-140. Cambridge University Press. https://www.cambridge.org/core/journals/international-review-of-social-history/article/buonarroti/EDB0D1BCB67ABE6D749121B388A1FCD5#

Leighton, John. (1871/2019). *Paris Under the Commune: or the Seventy-Three Days of the Second Siege.* Facsimile Publisher, Delhi, 2019. First published in 1871.

Le Stradic, Sego. (2017, Feb 27). Zamyatin, Huxley And Orwell: Troubling Similarities. The London Globalist. http://www.thelondonglobalist.org/zamyatin-huxley-and-orwell-troubling-similarities/.

Leys, Simon. (1974/1977). *Chinese Shadows* (tr. from the French). Viking Press, New York, 1977. First published in French as Ombres Chinoises, 1974.

Lillienthal, David Eli. (1918, Aug. 3). The Mission of the Jew. The News-Sentinel, Fort Wayne, Indiana. https://mailstar.net/baruch-plan.html.

Little, Reg and Reed, Warren. (1989). *The Confucian Renaissance.* The Federation Press, Sydney.

Liu, Henry C. K. (2011). Development Through Wage-Led Growth, Part XII: The Failed Revolutions of 1848—The Economic Background. Published at Asia Times on May 13, 2011. http://henryckliu.com/page248.html

Leon Trotsky. (2023, Jan. 3, at 15:16 UTC). Wikipedia. https://en.wikipedia.org/wiki/Leon_Trotsky.

Liu, Henry C. K. (2002). Dollar Hegemony. https://henryckliu.com/page2.html. Originally published as US Dollar Hegemony has to go, in Asia Times on April 11. 2002.

Lloyd George, David. (1939). *Memoirs of the Peace Conference, Volume II.* Yale University Press.

Lockhart, Bruce. (1933). *Memoirs Of A British Agent (With An Introduction By Hugh Walpole).* G. P. Putnam's Sons.

Lovelock, James. (2000). The Ages of Gaia. Oxford University Press.

McBriar, A. M. (1966). *Fabian Socialism & English Politics 1884-1918.* Cambridge at the University Press.

Maccoby, Hyam. (1982). *The Sacred Executioner: Human Sacrifice and the Legacy of Guilt.* Thames and Hudson.

McCormack, Denis. (1993, May 1). The reporting of tolerance. Letters to the Editor, The Age newspaper, Melbourne. An image of the complete letter, plus notes, is at https://mailstar.net/DMc_MC_Antisem Age.jpg. Also see page 419 of https://reduceimmigration.files.wordpress.com/2013/07/mccormack_desirable-composition-of-any-migrant-intake_1992.pdf.

McDonald, John. (2013, September 14). Occult figures—Artists cast a wicked spell as popular culture embraces all things supernatural, mystical and demonic. Sydney Morning Herald. https://www.smh.com.au/entertainment/art-and-design/occult-figures-20130912-2tla9.html.

MacDonald, Kevin. (1994). *A People That Shall Dwell Alone*. Praeger, Westport, CT. Also see http://mailstar.net/macdonald.html.

MacDonald, Kevin. (1998). *The Culture of Critique: An Evolutionary Analysis of Jewish Involvement in Twentieth-Century Intellectual and Political Movements*. Praeger, Westport, CT.

McEvilley, Thomas C. (2002). *The Shape Of Ancient Thought: Comparative Studies In Greek And Indian Philosophies*. Allworth Press.

McKechnie, Sarah. (1989). Descent and Sacrifice. The Beacon, September-October 1989. https://www.lucistrust.org/arcane_school/talks_and_articles/descent_and_sacrifice

Mackenzie, Donald. (1907/1978). *Egyptian Myth and Legend*. Bell Publishing Company, 1978. https://www.sacred-texts.com/egy/eml/eml37.htm.

MacLeod, Alan. (2022, Feb. 22). Documents Reveal US Gov't Spent $22M Promoting Anti-Russia Narrative in Ukraine and Abroad. https://www.blackagendareport.com/documents-reveal-us-govt-spent-22m-promoting-anti-russia-narrative-ukraine-and-abroad.

Magee, M. D. (n. d.) *Persia & The Creation Of Judaism; Book 2 How Persia Created Judaism*; chapter 5 Zoroastrian Influences on Judaism and Christianity Part III. Circle of Ancient Iranian Studies. http://www.cais-soas.com/CAIS/Religions/non-iranian/Judaism/Persian_Judaism/book2/pt5.htm.

Magee, M. D. (2009, August 11). How Persia Created Judaism. www.academia.edu/22882969/How_Persia_Created_Judaism.pdf.

Mahoney, Harry Thayer & Mahoney, Marjorie Locke. (1998). *The Saga Of Leon Trotsky: His Clandestine Operations and His Assassination*. Austin & Winfield, San Francisco.

Malcolm, James A. (1944). Origins of the Balfour Declaration. https://mailstar.net/malcolm.html.

Malinowski, Bronislaw. (1927). *The Father in Primitive Psychology*. W.W.Norton & Co, New York.

Mallory, J.P. and Mair, Victor H. (2000). *The Tarim Mummies: Ancient China and the Mystery of the Earliest Peoples from the West*. Thames & Hudson.

Marom, Ran. (1979). The Bolsheviks and the Balfour Declaration. In Robert S. Wistrich (ed.), *The Left Against Zion*. Valentine, Mitchell & Co. Ltd., London.

Martin, Ernest L. (2000). *The Temples that Jerusalem Forgot*. Ask Publications, Portland, OR.

Marx, Karl. (1844/1974). Criticism of Religion is the Presupposition of All Criticism, tr. Saul K. Padover. From "Towards the Critique of Hegel's Philosophy of Law: Introduction", Deutsch-Französische Jahrbücher, 7 & 10 February 1844. In *On Religion, Karl Marx Library, Vol. 5* (ed. Saul K. Padover). McGraw-Hill, 1974. https://www.marxists.org/archive/marx/works/1843/critique-hpr/intro.htm.

Marx, Karl. (1855, Nov. 22). The Loanmongers of Europe. New York Daily Tribune. https://mailstar.net/NY-Daily-Tribune-18551122p4.jpg.

Marx, Karl. (1856, Jan. 4). The Russian Loan. New York Daily Tribune. https://mailstar.net/NY-Daily-Tribune-18560104p4.pdf. The whole issue (including the front page) is at https://mailstar.net/NY-Daily-Tribune-18560104.pdf.

Marx, Karl. (1872/1972). The Old Christians' Contempt for Politics. In Padover (1972). From a speech delivered in Amsterdam, September 8, 1872.

Marx, Karl. (2007). *Dispatches for the New York Tribune: Selected Journalism of Karl Marx, Selected and with an Introduction by James Ledbetter, Foreword by Francis Wheen*. Penguin Books.

Marx, Karl. (1843/1972) On the Jewish Question. In Tucker, Robert (Ed.), *The Marx-Engels Reader*. Norton & Company, New York, 1972.

Marx, Karl. (1848/1976). Speech on the Question of Free Trade, Delivered to the Democratic Association of Brussels at its Public Meeting of January 9, 1848. In Marx, Karl & Engels, Frederick. Collected Works, Volume 6, Lawrence & Wishart, London 1976.

Marx, Karl. (1872/1971). Qualifying Violent Revolution; speech delivered in German and French on September 8, 1872, tr. Saul K. Padover. In *On Revolution*, Karl Marx Library, Vol. 1, ed. Saul K. Padover. McGraw-Hill, 1971.

Marx, Karl & Engels, Frederick. (1845/1975). The Holy Family: or Critique of Critical Criticism. *Collected Works of Karl Marx and Frederick Engels, Volume 4*. Lawrence & Wishhart.

Maxwell, Jordan. (2000). *Matrix of Power: Secrets of World Control*. Book Three.

Maybury-Lewis, David. (1992). *Millenium: Tribal Wisdom and the Modern World*. Viking Penguin, New York.

Mayne-Wilson, Rosemary. (1974, July). Coombs: midwife to the University adviser to the Nation. The Coombs Contribution, Australian National University News, August 1974, Vol. 9, No. 2.

Mearsheimer, John J. (2014). Why the Ukraine Crisis Is the West's Fault. Foreign Affairs, Sept./Oct. 2014. https://www.foreignaffairs.com/articles/russia-fsu/2014-08-18/why-ukraine-crisis-west-s-fault.

Melgunoff, S. (1927). The Record of the Red Terror. Current History (1916-1940) Vol. 27, No. 2 (November, 1927), pp. 198-205. University of California Press. https://www.jstor.org/stable/45332605.

Melanson, Terry. (2001). The Earth Charter and the Ark of the Gaia Covenant. Accesses Feb 23, 2023. https://www.lucistrust.org/arcane_school/talks_and_articles/descent_and_sacrifice

Mesarovic, Mihaljo & Pestel, Eduard. (1974). Mankind at the Turning Point. Club of Rome.

Migchels, Anthony. (2013, Sept. 16). Real Currencies: Supporting People and the Commonwealth and resisting the Money Power by defeating Usury. http://realcurrencies.wordpress.com/2013/09/16/hitlers-finances-and-the-myth-of-nazi-anti-usury-activism.

Miller, Chris. (2016, Dec. 29). Why Putin's Economy Survives. Wall Street Journal. https://www.wsj.com/articles/why-putins-economy-survives-1483020001.

Mills, Lawrence H. (1903-4). *Zoroaster, Philo and Israel, Part 1: Zoroaster and the Greeks.* F.A. Brockhaun, Leipzig.

Mishkinsky, Moshe. (2007). Bolshevik Theory (19031917). *Encyclopaedia Judaica (2007).* Thomson Gale; Macmillan Reference USA, Detroit. https://judaism_enc.en-academic.com/4464/COMMUNISM. Also at http://www.encyclopedia.com/religion/encyclopedias-almanacs-transcripts-and-maps/communism, Updated Aug 13 2018.

Monitor. (1958). *The Death of Stalin: An Investigation by 'MONITOR'.* Allen Wingate, London. https://mailstar.net/death-of-stalin.html.

Monteith, Stanley. (2000). *Brotherhood of Darkness.* Hearthstone Publishing.

Motroc, Gabriela. (2015). Why The World's Richest Families Are Not Included In Forbes' Rich List. Sep 23. http://www.australiannationalreview.com/worlds-richest-families/.

Mount, Ferdinand. (1982). *The Subversive Family.* Jonathan Cape Limited, London.

Moyers, Bill. (1980). TV special, The World of David Rockefeller, as quoted in The "Proud Internationalist": The Globalist Vision of David Rockefeller (2006) by Will Banyan, p. 9.

Muggeridge, Malcolm. (1972). A knight of the woeful countenance. IN *The World of George Orwell,* ed. Miriam Gross, Weidenfeld and Nicolson, London).

Murray, John Courtney. (1964). *The Problem of God*. Yale University Press, New Haven.

Myers, Peter. (2000/2010). Lloyd George on the Balfour Declaration. https://mailstar.net/l-george.html.

Myers, Peter. (2001/2023). The Balfour Declaration: World War I as an Opportunity. https://mailstar.net/balfour.html.

Myers, Peter. (2002/2012). Derivation of the Adam & Eve story from the Epic of Gilgamesh. https://mailstar.net/adam-and-eve.html.

Myers, Peter. (2002/2018). The Death of Stalin: a Coup d'Etat. https://mailstar.net/death-of-stalin.html.

Myers, Peter (2002/2023). The *Rig Veda* records the Aryan invasion of Pakistan and northern India. http://mailstar.net/rig-veda.html.

Myers, Peter. (2003/2019). Antony C. Sutton and Viktor Suvorov on Technology Transfer from the West to the Soviet Union. https://mailstar.net/sutton.html

Myers, Peter. (2009/2011). The Holocaust-Denial Debate. First published February 9, 2009; updated February 25, 2011. https://mailstar.net/holocaust-debate.html.

Myers, Peter. (2018a). Debate with Victoria on Holocaust matters. https://mailstar.net/Debate-Victoria-Holocaust.doc.

Myers, Peter. (2018b). The Balfour Declaration, Chaim Weizmann & the Morgenthau mission. https://mailstar.net/morgenthau.html.

Myers, Peter. (2018/2023). Supreme Court building in Israel with Illuminati pyramid—just like US $ Bill. https://mailstar.net/illuminati.html.

Myers, Peter. (2019a). The Baruch Plan for World Government https://mailstar.net/baruch-plan.html.

Myers, Peter. (2019b). US House of Representatives Calendar 2017 is Jewish rather than Christian. November 16, 2019. https://mailstar.net/ZOG-Calendar.html.

Myers, Peter. (2019/2023). CIA agent Robert D. Morrow confesses his role, and the CIA's, in the assassination of JFK. https://mailstar.net/Morrow-CIA-JFK.html.

Myers, Peter. (2020, Nov. 4). Lobby's Ouster of Jeremy Corbyn is a Violation of British Sovereignty. https://mailstar.net/corbyn-lobby.html.

Myers, Peter. (2020/2023). China's economic miracle was achieved by a switch from Marxist economics to National System Economics. https://mailstar.net/China-economic-miracle.html.

Myers, Peter. (2021/2022). Anthony Fauci and Xi Jinping make Masonic Hand Signs. https://mailstar.net/Masonic-hand-signs.html.

Myers, Peter. (2022). Putin attacks West as 'Satanic', says Russia stands for "traditional" values. https://mailstar.net/Putin-West-Satanic.html.

Near-death experience. (2023, July 31 at 06:53 UTC). Wikipedia. https://en.wikipedia.org/wiki/Near-death_experience.

Nedava, Joseph (5732/1972). *Trotsky and the Jews*. The Jewish Publication Society of America. The book bears the date 5732/1972, 5732 being the year since Creation in the Jewish Calendar.

Needham, Joseph. (1959). Review of Oriental Despotism. Science and Society 1959 Volume XXIII pp. 58-65.

Needham, Joseph. (1961). *Science and Civilization in China. Volume I Introductory Orientations*. Cambridge University Press.

Neff, Donald. (1999). De Gaulle Calls Jews Domineering, Israel an Expansionist State. Washington Report on Middle East Affairs, October/November 1999 , pages 81-82. http://www.wrmea.org/wrmea-archives/180-washington-report-archives-1994-1999/october-november-1999/9329-de-gaulle-calls-jews-domineering-israel-an-expansionist-state.html.

Newman, Hannah. (1997/2006). The Rainbow Swastika: A Report To The Jewish People About New Age Antisemitism. https://juchre.org/nor/swastika/default.htm.

Newman, Hannah. (5761=2001). Introduction to The Rainbow Swastika. https://juchre.org/nor/swastika/naA.htm.

Nicolaevsky, Boris. (1966). Secret Societies and the First International. In Milorad M. Drachkovitch, (Ed.), *The Revolutionary Internationals, 1864-1943*. Stanford University Press. https://libcom.org/article/secret-societies-and-first-international-boris-i-nicolaevsky.

Nietzsche, Friedrich. (1974). *The Genealogy of Morals* (tr. Francis Golffing). Doubleday Anchor, New York.

North, David. (2000). Was there a high-level MI5 agent in the British Workers Revolutionary Party? March 2. http://www.wsws.org/articles/2000/mar2000/lenn-m02.shtml.

Nuland, Victoria. (2013, Dec. 13). Remarks by Victoria Nuland at the U.S.-Ukraine Foundation Conference. Voltaire Network. https://www.voltairenet.org/article182080.html. Video at https://www.youtube.com/embed/xtMwcE9K_NA.

O'Brien, Terence H., (1979). *Milner: Viscount Milner of St James's and Cape Town 1854-1925.* Lonstable, London.

Oliver, Revilo P. (2001). *The Origins of Christianity.* Historical Review Press.

Orwell, George. (1938/2021). *Homage to Catalonia.* Oxford University Press, 2021. First published in 1938. https://www.marxists.org/archive/orwell/1938/homage-catalonia.htm.

Orwell, George. (1941). Wells, Hitler and the World State. http://ebooks.adelaide.edu.au/o/orwell/george/o79e/part15.html

Orwell, George. (1945). Notes on Nationalism. http://ebooks.adelaide.edu.au/o/orwell/george/o79e/part30.html.Orwell, George. (1946a, Jan 4). Review of "WE" by E. I. Zamyatin [Evgeny Ivanovich Zamyatin]. Tribune, London. https://orwell.ru/library/reviews/zamyatin/english/e_zamy .

Orwell, George. (1946b). Second Thoughts on James Burnham. Polemic magazine, May. http://orwell.ru/library/reviews/burnham/english/e_burnh.

Orwell, George. (1954). *Nineteen Eighty-Four.* Penguin in association with Secker and Warburg, Harmondsworth.

Ostrovsky, Victor & Hoy, Claire. (1990). *By Way of Deception: the Making and Unmaking of a Mossad Officer.* St Martin's Press, New York.

Ostrovsky, Victor. (1994). *The Other Side of Deception.* HarperCollinsPublishers, New York.

Ostrovsky, Victor. (1995). The Contrasting Media Treatment of Israeli and Islamic Death Threats. Washington Report, Special Report, January/February 1995, pages 17, 88. http://www.washington-report.org/backissues/0195/9501017.htm

Outlander. (1911, Jan. 30). The Workers' Paradise. Barrier Miner, Broken Hill NSW. https://trove.nla.gov.au/newspaper/article/45152619.

Owen, Paul. (2009, Jun 8). 1984 thought crime? Does it matter that George Orwell pinched the plot? The Guardian. https://www.theguardian.com/books/booksblog/2009/jun/08/george-orwell-1984-zamyatin-we.

Padover , Saul K (Ed.). (1972) *The Karl Marx Library, Volume 5 On Religion.* McGraw-Hill Book Company.

Paglia, Camille. (2016, Nov. 4). Feminism: in conversation with Camille Paglia; Camille Paglia interview with Claire Fox, at the Battle of Ideas. https://www.youtube.com/watch?reload=9&v=4y3-KlesYRE. Key excerpts are at https://traitor666.blogspot.com/2016/12/camille-paglia-gender-reassignment.html.

Paris fake antisemitic attack. (2004, July 27). Court convicts woman for fabricating anti-Semitic attack. Haaretz newspaper, Israel. https://web.archive.org/web/20040803111642/http://www.haaretzdaily.com/hasen/spages/456367.html.

Payne, Robert. (1965). *The Rise and Fall of Stalin*. Simon & Schuster, New York.

Pearsall, Paul. (1999). *The Heart's Code: Tapping the Wisdom and Power of Our Heart Energy*. Harmony, reprint edition. https://www.amazon.com/Hearts-Code-Tapping-Wisdom-Energy/dp/0767900952.

Perry, Roland. (1994). *The Fifth Man*. Pan Books, London. https://mailstar.net/perry.html.

Petras, James. (2017, Apr. 17). Judeo-Centrism: Myths and Mania. https://petras.lahaine.org/judeo-centrism-myths-and-mania/.

Pickard, Jim. (2019, May 2). Jeremy Corbyn under fire over foreword in anti-Semitic book. Financial Times, London. https://www.ft.com/content/ac5670ec-6c2f-11e9-80c7-60ee53e6681d.

Pike, Albert (1871/2011). *Morals and Dogma of the Ancient and Accepted Scottish Rite of Freemasonry*. Theophania Publishing. First published in 1871. If you order Morals and Dogma, make sure you get the full volume—it will be expensive—not the abbreviated one that covers only the first three degrees.

Piper, Michael Collins. (2005). *Final Judgment: The Missing Link in the JFK Assassination Conspiracy* (sixth edition). American Free Press, Washington D.C.

Plato. (c. 360 BC/1901). *The Republic* (tr. Benjamin Jowett). http://classics.mit.edu/Plato/republic.6.v.html

Pollack, Malcolm. (2009, Sep 21). The Forgotten H.G. Wells. https://malcolmpollack.com/2009/09/21/the-forgotten-hg-wells/.

Popper, Karl. (1966). *The Open Society and Its Enemies, Vol. I: The Spell of Plato*. (fifth ed. (revised)). Routledge & Kegan Paul Ltd.

Potaka, Elise and McMahon, Luke. (2015, Sep. 12). Unmasking a troll: Aussie 'jihadist' Australi Witness a 20-year-old American nerd. Sydney Morning Herald.

Pozsar, Zoltan. (2022, Aug. 1). War is inflationary. Published by Credit Suisse. https://plus2.credit-suisse.com/shorturlpdf.html?v=5hig-YP34-V&t=-7k6igsca7azmsnjxid59q5wex.

Pozsar, Zoltan. (2023, Jan. 6). War and Peace. Published by Credit Suisse. https://plus2.credit-suisse.com/shorturlpdf.html?v=5hig-YP34-V&t=-7k6igsca7azmsnjxid59q5wex.

Price, Robert M. (2003). *The Incredible Shrinking Son of Man*. Prometheus Books.

Price, Robert M. (2017). *Holy Fable, volume II The Gospels and Acts Undistorted by Faith*. Mindvender.

Price, Robert M. (2021). *Judaizing Jesus: How New Testament Scholars Created The Ecumenical Golem*. Pitchstone Publishing Durham, North Carolina.

Quigley, Carroll (1966). *Tragedy And Hope: A History Of The World In Our Time*. The Macmillan Company.

Quigley, Carroll (1981). *The Anglo-American Establishment*. Books in Focus, Inc.

Queensborough, Lady, Edith Starr Miller. (1933/2013). *Occult Theocracy*. Isha Books, 2013. First published in 1933 as Occult Theocrasy.

Radzinsky, Edvard. (1996). *Stalin* (tr. H.T. Willetts). Hodder & Stoughton, London.

Rapoport, Louis. (1990). *Stalin's War Against The Jews: The Doctors Plot and the Soviet Solution*. The Free Press, 1990.

Rath, R. John (1964), "The Carbonari: Their Origins, Initiation Rites, and Aims", The American Historical Review, 69 (2): 353—370, doi:10.2307/1844987, JSTOR 1844987. https://vdocument.in/download/the-carbonari-their-origins-initiation-rites-and-aims

Rathmell, Peter. (2017, July 21). No urinals on the new Navy aircraft carrier. Navy Times. https://www.navytimes.com/news/your-navy/2017/07/21/no-urinals-on-the-new-navy-aircraft-carrier.

Ravage, Marcus Eli. (1928, Jan.) A Real Case Against the Jews. Century Magazine. The Century Company, New York.Ravage, Marcus Eli. (1928, Feb.)

Ravage, Marcus Eli. (1928, Feb.) Commissary to the Gentiles. Century Magazine. The Century Company, New York.

Redford, Donald B. (1992). *Egypt, Canaan and Israel in Ancient Times*. Princeton University Press.

Red Terror. (1918, September 1). Krasnaya Gazeta (The Red Gazette). https://kerchtt.ru/en/kogda-byl-prinyat-dekret-o-krasnom-terrore-obyavlenie-bolshevikami/

Reeves, William Pember. (1902/1969). *State Experiments In Australia & New Zealand, Vol. I*. Macmillan of Australia 1969. First published in 1902 by Grant Ritchards, Republished in 1923 by George Allen & Unwin Ltd.

Reeves, William Pember. (1902/1969). *State Experiments In Australia & New Zealand, Vol. II*. Macmillan of Australia 1969. First published in 1902 by Grant Ritchards, Republished in 1923 by George Allen & Unwin Ltd.

Reich, Wilhelm. (1991). *The Mass Psychology of Fascism* (ed. Mary Higgins and Chaster M. Raphael, M. D.). Farrar, Straus and Giroux, Inc.

Rizzi, Bruno.(1939). *The Bureaucratisation of the World* (tr. Adam Buick). http://www.marxists.org/archive/rizzi/bureaucratisation/index.htm.

Roberts, Senator Malcolm. (2023, July 12). Who Has Been Bought By Predatory Billionaires. https://www.malcolmrobertsqld.com.au/who-has-been-bought-by-predatory-billionaires.

Robinson, Robert, with Jonathan Slevin. (1988). *Black On Red: My 44 Years Inside the Soviet Union.* Acropolis Books, Washington.

Rockefeller, David. (1994). Statement to the United Nations Business Council, September 23, 1994. https://americasbestpics.com/picture/we-are-on-the-verge-of-a-global-transformation-all-Xus3LKhAA.

Roginsky, Dan. (2017, March 12. Purim Miracle of 1953: Many Jews were arrested on false denunciations. https://www.jpost.com/Opinion/Purim-miracle-of-1953-483994.

Rosenberg, Stephen Gabriel. (2015, Apr. 1). Who was the pharaoh of the Exodus? Jerusalem Post, Israel.

Rosenthal, Andrew. (1991, September 18). The Soviet Transition; Soviets Drop Solzhenitsyn Treason Charges. the New York Times. http://www.nytimes.com/1991/09/18/world/the-soviet-transition-soviets-drop-solzhenitsyn-treason-charges.html.

Rousseau, Jean-Jacques. (1762/1968). *The Social Contract* (tr. Maurice Cranston). Penguin Books, 1968. First published in 1762 as Du Contrat Social.

Rousseau, Jean-Jacques. (1781/1953). *The Confessions of Jean-Jacques Rousseau* (tr. J.M. Cohen). Penguin, 1953. First published in 1781.

Roy, Sara. (2004, Apr. 1). Short Cuts. London Review of Books, Vol. 26 No. 7. https://www.lrb.co.uk/the-paper/v26/n07/sara-roy/short-cuts.

Rushkoff, Douglas. (2002). Judging Judaism by the Numbers. New York Times, November 20. http://www.nytimes.com/2002/11/20/opinion/20RUSH.html.

Russell, Bertrand. (1946). *History of Western Philosophy.* George Allen and Unwin.

Russell, Bertrand. (1920/1975). Letter To Ottoline Morell (1920). In *The Autobiography of Bertrand Russell, Volume 2.* George Allen & Unwin, 1975.

Russell, Bertrand. (1935/1973). *In Praise of Idleness.* Unwin Books, London, 1973.

Russell, Bertrand. (1920/1962). *The Practice and Theory of Bolshevism* (2nd ed.). George Allen & Unwin Ltd., 1949; reprint 1962.

Russian ruble. (2023, Feb. 8, at 19:32 UTC). Wikipedia.
https://en.wikipedia.org/wiki/Russian_ruble.

Sailor, Steve. (2004, Dec. 15). Kerri F. Dunn Sentenced to Prison. Unz Review.
https://www.unz.com/isteve/kerri-f-dunn-sentenced-to-prison/.

Sachs, Jeffrey D. (2022, July 1). Ukraine Is the Latest Neocon Disaster. Consortium
News. https://consortiumnews.com/2022/07/01/ukraine-is-the-latest-neocon-disaster/

Sakharov, Andrei. (1968/1976). Progress, Coexistence and Intellectual Freedom.
Penguin, Hartmondsworth; First published in 1968.

Santaniello, Weaver. (1997). A Post-Holocaust Re-Examination Of Nietzsche And
The Jews vis-a-vis Christendom and Nazism. IN Golomb, Jacob, ed., *Nietzsche And
Jewish Culture*. Routledge.

Saul Padover. (2022, Dec. 17, at 18:13 UTC). Saul Kussiel Padover. Wikipedia.
https://en.wikipedia.org/wiki/Saul_K._Padover.

Saunders, Frances Stonor. (2000). *The Cultural Cold War: The CIA and the World of
Arts and Letters*. The New Press, New York.

Schaefer, Standard. (2004, Feb 27). An Insider Spills the Beans on Offshore Banking
Centers: an Interview with Michael Hudson for Counterpunch. https://michael-hudson.com/2004/02/an-insider-spills-the-beans-on-offshore-banking-centers/.

Schafer, Peter. (2007). *Jesus in the Talmud*. Princeton University Press.

Schapiro, Leonard. (1960). *The Communist Party of the Soviet Union*. Eyre &
Spottiswoode.

Schapiro, Leonard. (1961). The Role of Jews in the Russian Revolutionary
Movement. Slavonic and East European Review, Volume 40, December 1961.

Schnoebelen, William Schnoebelen. (1991). *Masonry Beyond the Light*. Chick
Publications.

Schumacher, E. F. (1978). *A Guide For the Perplexed*. Abacus, London.

Schwab, Klaus.(2019). Davos Manifesto on Corporate Governance. Dec 2, 2019.
https://www.weforum.org/agenda/2019/12/davos-manifesto-2020-the-universal-purpose-of-a-company-in-the-fourth-industrial-revolution/.

Schwarz, Peter. (2006, March 24). The French Popular Front of 1936: Historical
lessons in the "First Job Contract" struggle.
https://www.wsws.org/en/articles/2006/03/fr36-m24.html

Shabi, Rachel, and Kiss, Jemima. (2010, Aug. 19). Wikipedia editing courses launched by Zionist groups. The Guardian. https://www.theguardian.com/world/2010/aug/18/wikipedia-editing-zionist-groups.

Shahak, Israel. (1994). *Jewish History, Jewish Religion: The Weight of Three Thousand Years*. Pluto Press.

Shavit, Ari. (1996, May 27). How Easily We Killed Them. New York Times, Oped, p. A21. https://www.nytimes.com/1996/05/27/opinion/how-easily-we-killed-them.html.

Shavit, Ari. (2003, Apr 03). White man's burden. Haaretz. https://www.haaretz.com/2003-04-03/ty-article/white-mans-burden/0000017f-e398-d804-ad7f-f3fa5d520000.

Shaxson, Nicholas. (2011). *Treasure Islands: Tax Havens and the Men Who Stole the World*. Vintage Books, London.

Shillony, Ben-Ami. (1991). *The Jews and the Japanese: the Successful Outsiders*. Charles E. Tuttle Company, Rutland, Vermont.

Shirer, William L. (1961). *The Rise and Fall of the Third Reich*. Secker and Warburg, London.

Shpak, Max. (2002). The Fraud of Neoconservative "Anti-Communism". Published at Original Dissent, May 15, 2002. http://www.originaldissent.com/shpak051502.html

Singer, June. (1989). *Androgyny: the Opposites Within*. Sigo Press, Boston.

Slezkine, Yuri. (2004). *The Jewish Century*. Princeton University Press.

Smith, David C. (1986). *H.G. Wells: Desperately Mortal: A Biography*. Yale University Press, New Haven.

Smith, W.H.C. (1985). *Second Empire and Commune: France 1848-1871*. Longman, New York.

Soral, Alain. (2011/2022). *Understand the Empire: Towards Global Governance or the Uprising of Nations?* (tr. A. Robin). Éditions Kontre Kulture, Paris, 2021; Original in French was *Comprendre l'Empire* by Éditions Blanches, Paris, 2011.

Sorokin, Pitirim. (1924). *Leaves From A Russian Diary*. E. P. Dutton & Co, New York.

Soros, George. (1990). A Perspective On the Collapse of the Soviet System. Excerpt from the Ernst Sturc Memorial Lecture. Washington, D.C., Nov. 14. https://www.georgesoros.com/1990/11/14/a-perspective-on-the-collapse-of-the-soviet-system/. Also quoted in Executive Intelligence Review (1997), pp. 21-2.

Soros, George. (1994). *The Alchemy of Finance* (with new Preface, 1994). John Wiley & Sons. First published in 1987.

Soviet collapse. (2005, April 26). Putin: Soviet collapse a 'genuine tragedy'. NBC News. https://www.nbcnews.com/id/wbna7632057

Soviet Ruble. (2023, Feb. 5, at 19:30 UTC). Wikipedia. https://en.wikipedia.org/wiki/Soviet_ruble#Sixth_Soviet_ruble,_1961.

Spence, Richard B. (2017). *Wall Street And The Russian Revolution, 1905-1925*. Trine Day LLC, Walterville, OR.

Spinoza, Benedict. (1670/2021). A Theological-Political Treatise [Part I], tr. R. H. M. Elwes. Project Gutenberg, 2021. First published as Tractatus Theologico-Politicus in 1670. https://www.gutenberg.org/files/989/989-h/989-h.htm.

Stanner, W.E.H. (1960). Durmugam: A Nangiomeri. In *In the Company of Man: Twenty Portraits of Anthropologists* (ed. Joseph B. Casagrange). Harper & Brothers Publishers, New York.

Stavrakopoulou, Francesca. (2004). *King Manasseh and Child Sacrifice: Biblical Distortions of Historical Realities*. De Gruyter; https://doi.org/10.1515/9783110899641.

Sternhell, Zeev. (1998). *The Founding Myths of Israel: Nationalism, Socialism and the Making of the Jewish State* (tr. David Maisel). Princeton University Press.

Steed, Henry Wickham. (1924). *Through Thirty Years 1892-1922: A Personal Narrative, Volume II*. William Heinemann Ltd, London.

Stobbart, Lorraine. (1992). *Utopia fact or fiction? The Evidence from the Americas*. Alan Sutton, Phoenix Mill.

Stocklin, Kevin. (2023, Feb 20). Biden Admin Negotiates Deal to Give WHO Authority Over US Pandemic Policies—New international health accord avoids necessary Senate approval. Epoch Times. https://www.theepochtimes.com/biden-admin-negotiates-deal-to-give-who-authority-over-us-pandemic-policies_5066631.html.

Strasser (1940). *Hitler and I*. Jonathan Cape, London. Translated from the French, *Hitler Et Moi*, by Gwenda David and Eric Mosbacher. https://mailstar.net/otto-strasser-hitler.html.

Sudoplatov, Pavel. (1995) *Special Tasks: The Memoirs Of An Unwanted Witness—A Soviet Spymaster*. By Pavel Sudoplatov and Anatoli Sudoplatov, with Jerrold L. and Leona P. Schecter. Little, Brown And Co., London.

Sutton, Antony C. (1973) *Western Technology and Soviet Economic Development 1945 to 1965*. Hoover Institution Press, Stanford University, Stanford Ca.

Suvorov, Viktor. (2008/2013). *The Chief Culprit: Stalin's Grand Design to Start World War II*. Naval Institute Press, Annapolis, Maryland, 2013. First pub. in 2008.

Sylvia, Clare with Novak, William. (1997) *A Change of Heart: A Memoir.* https://www.amazon.com/Change-Heart-Memoir-Claire-Sylvia/dp/0316821497. Little, Brown and Company.

Talmon, J. L. (1970). *Israel Among the Nations.* Weidenfeld and Nicolson.

Taubman, Philip. (1986, Dec. 20). Soviet Lifts Sakharov Banishment And Grants A Pardon To Bonner. Special To the New York Times. https://www.nytimes.com/1986/12/20/world/soviet-lifts-sakharov-banishment-and-grants-a-pardon-to-bonner.html

Taylor, Lenore. (2014, Apr. 9) Bob Carr diaries: foreign policy was subcontracted to Jewish donors. The Guardian. https://www.theguardian.com/world/2014/apr/09/bob-carr--gillard-foreign-policy-jewish-donors.

Thompson, Dorothy. (1935, July). National Socialism: Theory and Practice. Foreign Affairs. http://www.foreignaffairs.com/articles/69543/dorothy-thompson/national-socialism-theory-and-practice.

Threats to bomb or attack Jewish schools and community centers. (2018, June 28). US-Israeli teen convicted of threats against Jewish centres. BBC News. https://www.bbc.com/news/world-middle-east-44641427

Tiesler, Vera & Cucina, Andrea. (2006). Procedures in Human Heart Extraction and Ritual Meaning: A Taphonomic Assessment of Anthropogenic Marks in Classic Maya Skeletons. Latin American Antiquity, Vol. 17, No. 4 (Dec., 2006), pp. 493-510. Published by: Society for American Archaeology. https://www.academia.edu/2162426/Procedures_in_human_heart_extraction_and_ritual_meaning_A_taphonomic_assessment_of_anthropogenic_marks_in_Classic_Maya_skeletons.

Tindale, Norman B. & Lindsay, H. A. (1963). *Aboriginal Australians.* The Jacaranda Press.

Todd, Emmanuel. (2023, Jan. 12/14). Emmanuel Todd On The Third World War, tr. Arnaud Bertrand. Moon of Alabama, Jan. 14, 2023. https://www.moonofalabama.org/2023/01/emmanuel-todd-on-the-third-world-war.html. Originally published on Jan. 12 by Le Figaro as La Troisième Guerre mondiale a commencé. https://www.lefigaro.fr/vox/monde/emmanuel-todd-la-troisieme-guerre-mondiale-a-commence-20230112/.

Tørsløv, Thomas et. al. (2022). Close to 40% of multinational profits are shifted to tax havens each year. https://missingprofits.world.

Toynbee, Arnold J. (1939). *A Study of History, Volume V.* Issued under the auspices of the Royal Institute of International Affairs; published by Oxford University Press.

Toynbee, Arnold J. (1961). *A Study of History Volume XII Reconsiderations.* Oxford University Press, London.

Traverso, Enzo. (1994). *The Marxists and the Jewish Question* (tr. Bernard Gibbons). Humanities Press, New Jersey.

Tritten, Travis (2022, Mar. 7). How Believers in the Paranormal Birthed the Pentagon's New Hunt for UFOs. https://www.military.com/daily-news/2022/03/07/how-believers-paranormal-birthed-pentagons-new-hunt-ufos.html.

Trotski, Leon. (1947). *Stalin: An Appraisal of the Man and his Influence* (edited and translated from the Russian by Charles Malmouth). Hollis and Carter, Ltd, London.

Trotsky, Leon. (1918/1920). A Paradise In This World. An Address delivered to a Working Class audience on April 14th, 1918. British Socialist Party, London, 1920.

Trotsky, Leon. (1920). *The Defence of Terrorism.* George Allen & Unwin, London.

Trotsky, Leon. (1927). The Platform of the Joint Opposition (1927). https://www.marxists.org/archive/trotsky/1927/opposition/ch09.htm.

Trotsky, Leon. (1930/1975). *My Life.* Penguin, Harmondsworth, 1975. First published in 1930.

Trotsky, Leon. (1935, June 10). An Open Letter to the French Workers: Stalinist Betrayal and the World Revolution. https://www.marxists.org/archive/trotsky/1935/06/french.htm

Trotsky, Leon. (1937/1941). Thermidor and Anti-Semitism. Written on Feb. 22, 1937. New International, May 1941. Transcribed for the Trotsky Internet Archive by Matt Siegfried in 1999. http://www.marxists.org/archive/trotsky/works/1938/1938-th.htm

Trotsky, Leon. (1937/1967). *The Revolution Betrayed: What is the Soviet Union and Where is it Going?* (tr. Max Eastman). New Park Publication, London. First published 1937. http://www.marxists.org/archive/trotsky/works/1936-rev/ch07.htm#ch07-1

Trotsky, Leon. (1939). The U.S.S.R In War. Written 25 September, 1939; published in The New International, New York, November 1939, Volume 10, No. 11 pages 325-332. https://www.marxists.org/archive/trotsky/1939/09/ussr-war.htm.

Trotsky, Leon. (1940/2019). *Stalin: An Appraisal of the Man and His Influence* (eds. Alan Woods and Robert Sewell). Haymarket Books, Chicago, 2019. Originally published in 1940.

Trotsky, Natalia Sedova. (1942). Mr. Davies and the Moscow Trials. Written: December 21, 1941. Fourth International, Vol. III No. 1, January 1942, pp. 9—11. https://www.marxists.org/archive/sedova-natalia/1941/12/21.htm

Trotsky, Natalia Sedova. (1947). Stalin's Guilt. Written: April 19, 1947. https://www.marxists.org/archive/sedova-natalia/1947/04/19.htm

Trotsky (TV Series). (2017). Троцкий, directed by Alexander Kott and Konstantin Statsky. https://www.khabenskiy.com/filmography/filmography-trotsky-biopic-tv-series/.

Tsatsarounos, Alexandros. (2014). The origins of "Revolutionary Freemasonry". Paper presented at the "Summer 2014 International Masonic Workshop", Anavyssos, Greece, August 27-31, 2014. Pub. by "Philotecton Society" Aug. 6, 2015. https://www.academia.edu/20079542/The_origins_of_Revolutionary_Freemasonry.

United Nations. (2000). The Earth Charter. https://www.iau-hesd.net/sites/default/files/documents/echarter_english.pdf.

University of Pennsylvania library. (n. d.) The New Age. Online serials. https://onlinebooks.library.upenn.edu/webbin/serial?id=newagemason#:~:text=The%20New%20Age%20was%20a,Jurisdiction%20of%20the%20United%20States.

U.S.S. Liberty. (2014, Nov. 04). The Day Israel Attacked America: Al Jazeera investigates the shocking truth behind a deadly Israeli attack on a US naval vessel. Al Jazaara. https://www.aljazeera.com/program/featured-documentaries/2014/10/30/the-day-israel-attacked-america. Video (49 min) is at https://www.youtube.com/watch?v=tx72tAWVcoM.

Utley, Freda. (1940). *The Dream We Lost: Soviet Russia Then And Now.* The John Day Company, New York.

Vaksberg, Arkady. (1994). *Stalin Against The Jews* (tr. Antonina W. Bouis). A. Knopf.

Vigano, Archbishop Carlo Maria. (2021, August 28). Considerations on the Great Reset and the New World Order. https://www.thevoid.uk/void-post/vigano-the-great-reset-and-the-new-world-order-lifesite/

Volkogonov, Dmitri. (1996). *Trotsky: The Eternal Revolutionary* (tr. & ed. Harold Shukman). HarperCollinsPublishers.

Voltaire, Francois-Marie Arouet. (1757/1924). Men of letters. In *The Philosophical Dictionary: Voltaire, Selected and Translated by H.I. Woolf,* pub. Knopf, New York, 1924. Original Title: Gens de lettres, Vol. 7 (1757), pp. 599—600.

Wagar, W. Warren. (1971). *Building The City Of Man: Outlines of a World Civilization.* Grossman Publishers.

Wallace, Alfred Russel. (1874). *Miracles and Modern Spiritualism, revised edition, with chapters on Apparitions and Phantasms.* Nichols & Co., London.

Walsh, Max. (1998, February 19). Sleeping Giant is now wide awake. The Bottom Line, Sydney Morning Herald, opinion page.

Walzer, Michael. (1985). *Exodus and Revolution*. Basic Books, Inc., Publishers.

Waton, Harry. (1939). *A Program for the Jews: An Answer to All Anti-Semites: A Program for Humanity*. Committee for the Preservation of the Jews, New York. https://mailstar.net/waton-program.html.

Webb, Beatrice. (1936/1978). 'Beatrice Webb to E. Halevy', 1 September 1936. In N. MacKenzie, *The Letters of Sidney and Beatrice Webb, Vol. III*, Pilgrimage, 1912-1947. Cambridge University Press, 1978.

Webb, Beatrice. (1943/1985). *The Diary of Beatrice Webb* (eds. N. and J. MacKenzie), *Vol. Four, 1924-1943, The Wheels of Life*. Virago, London, 1985. First published 1943.

Webb, Sidney & Webb, Beatrice. (1935). *Soviet Communism: A New Civilisation?, Volume II*. Longmans, Green And Co., Ltd., London.

Webster, Nesta. (1921/2013). *World Revolution*. Isha Books, 2013. The original was published in 1921; this is not the edition revised by Anthony Gittens.

Webster, Nesta. (1924/2000). *Secret Societies and Subversive Movements*. Omni Publications, Palmdale, 2000. First published in 1924.

Weigel, George. (2021). Catholic Progressives and the Culture War. First Things, November 17. https://www.firstthings.com/web-exclusives/2021/11/catholic-progressives-and-the-culture-war

Wells, H. G. & Stalin, J. (1934/2008). Marxism Versus Liberalism: An Interview With H.G. Wells. Marxists Internet Archive, 2008. Source: Works, Vol. 14; Publisher: Red Star Press Ltd., London, 1978. Transcription/HTML Markup: Salil Sen. Also at http://www.rationalrevolution.net/special/library/cc835_44.htm.

Wells, H. G. (1898/1975). *The War of the Worlds*. Pan Books, London, 1975. First published in 1898.

Wells, H. G. (1902/1999). *Anticipations of the Reaction of Mechanical and Scientific Progress Upon Human Life and Thought*. Dover Publications, Inc. First pub.1902. Includes Wells' preface to 1914 edition, and 1999 introduction by Martin Gardner.

Wells, H. G. (1905). *A Modern Utopia*. COLONIAL EDITION (For Circulation in the British Colonies and India only) T. Fisher Unwin, London. Note:newer editions often retain the original page-numbering. http://www.marxists.org/reference/archive/hgwells/1905/modern-utopia/index.htm

Wells, H. G. (1911/1978). *The New Machiavelli*, Penguin Books Ltd., 1978. First published in 1911

Wells, H. G. (1918/2003). *In the Fourth Year: Anticipations of a World Peace*. Project Gutenberg EBook, 2003. First published in 1918.

Wells, H. G. (1920). *Russia in the Shadows*. Hodder & Stoughton, Ltd., London.

Wells, H. G. (1922). *Men Like Gods*. William Collins, London, 2020. First published 1922.

Wells, H. G. (1928). *The Open Conspiracy: Blue Prints for a World Revolution*. Victor Gollancz Ltd, London.

Wells, H. G. (1931). *The Outline of History: Being a Plain History of Life and Mankind*. New and Revised Edition. Garden City Publishing Company, Inc., New York.

Wells, H. G. (1932a). *After Democracy: Addresses and Papers on the Present World Situation*. Watts & Co.

Wells, H. G. (1932b). *The Work, Wealth And Happiness Of Mankind*. William Heinemann Ltd, London.

Wells, H. G. (1933a). The Open Conspiracy; in *The Open Conspiracy and Other Writings*. Gollancz, London.

Wells, H. G. (1933/1979). *The Shape of Things to Come: the Ultimate Revolution*. Corgi Books (Transworld Publishers Ltd.), London. First published in 1933. http://gutenberg.net.au/ebooks03/0301391h.html.

Wells, H. G. (1934/1969). *Experiment in AutoBiography, volume 2*. Jonathan Cape, London. First published in 1934.

Wells, H. G. (1939). *The Fate of Homo Sapiens*. Secker and Warburg, London.

Wells, H. G. (1940). *The Outline of History: Being a Plain History of Life and Mankind*. Enlarged and Revised. Garden City Publishing Company, Inc., New York.

Wells, H. G. (1940/2017). *The New World Order*. Facsimile Publisher, Delhi, 2017. First published 1940.

Wells, H. G. (1961). *The Outline of History: Being a Plain History of Life and Mankind from Primordial Life to Nineteen-sixty* (revised by Roman Postgate). Cassell, London.

Wells World Brain. (2023, May 11, at 17:55 UTC). World Brain. Wikipedia. https://en.wikipedia.org/wiki/World_Brain.

Werner, Richard A. (2003). *Princes of the Yen*. M. E. Sharpe, Armonk, New York. Also see https://mailstar.net/werner-princes-yen.html.

West, Anthony. (1984). *H. G. Wells: Aspects of a Life*. Hutchinson, London.

West, Geoffrey. (1930). *H. G. Wells: a sketch for a portrait*. Gerald Howe Ltd.

West et al. (1979). *Socialism or Nationalism?: Which Road for the Australian Labor Movement?* Socialist Workers Party.

West, Jon. (1979). Nationalism and the Labor Movement. In West et al. (1979).

White Genocide. (2002, Sep. 4). Harvard professor argues for 'abolishing' white race. Washington Times. https://www.washingtontimes.com/news/2002/sep/04/20020904-084657-6385r/.

Whitlam, Gough and Ralph Willis. (1982). Reshaping Australian Industry: Tariffs and Socialists. Fabian Society Pamplet No. 37, published in Melbourne.

Wilson, Derek. (1994). *Rothschild: A Story of Wealth and Power* (Revised Edition). Andre Deutsch, London.

Wittfogel, Karl A. (1957). *Oriental Despotism*. Yale University Press, New Haven.

Yearwood, Peter J. (2009). *Guarantee of peace: The League of Nations in British Policy 1914-1925*. Oxford University Press.

World Currency. (1988, Jan. 9). Get Ready for the Phoenix. The Economist, Vol. 306, pp 9-10. https://goldbroker.com/news/the-economist-get-ready-for-a-world-currency-by-2018-1179.

Wormser, Rene A. (1958/2014). *Foundations: Their Power And Influence*. Dauphin Publications, 2014. First published by the Devil-Adair Company, New York, 1958. https://archive.org/stream/ShadowGovernmentAndBankingEliteTopSecret145/Foundations-Their-Power-and-Influence-by-Rene-A-Wormser-438_djvu.txt.

Yergin, Daniel. (2001/2022). Understanding Gorbachev's True Challenge—My 2001 interview with Mikhail Gorbachev. The Globalist, September 4, 2022. https://www.theglobalist.com/daniel-yergin-mikhail-gorbachev-cold-war-iron-curtain-soviet-union-perestroika/

Yong, Ed. (2013, Jan. 14). Aboriginal Australian genomes reveal Indian ancestry. Nature (2013). https://www.nature.com/articles/nature.2013.12219.

Zamiatin, Eugene. (1923/1924). We (Tr. Gregory Zilboorg). E. P. Dutton, New York, 1924. First published in 1923. https://www.gutenberg.org/files/61963/61963-h/61963-h.htm.

Zarlenga. Stephen. (2000). A Deeper Look Into "Tragedy and Hope". Barnes Review VI/1 (Jan-Feb, 2000): 39-46. http://www.alpheus.org/html/reviews/parapolitics/rev_tragedy_hope.html.

Zarlenga. Stephen A. (2002). *The Lost Science of Money: the Mythology of Money—the Story of Power*. American Monetary Institute.

Zetter, Kim. (2010, Feb. 18). Dubai Assassination Was Work of Mossad and Likely Sanctioned by Prime Minister Says Former Intel Officer. http://www.wired.com/threatlevel/2010/02/dubai-assassination-has-hallmarks-of-mossad.

Index

About the Author

Peter Gerard Myers was born in 1948, and grew up in Sydney. He spent several years in a Catholic seminary studying Philosophy and Biblical Exegesis. He later gained degrees in Arts (Social Anthrolopogy Hons and Philosophy, Uni. of Sydney) and Science (I. T, Maths and Physics, Uni. of Tasmania), and worked as an I.T. professional in Canberra.

In the mid 1970s, Peter became an advocate of "plain living and high thinking". He left Sydney and took up rural living in Tasmania. He learned to build from hippies, and acquired many rural skills, usually doing things the "old way". For study and to get work, he had to move to the cities (Hobart and Canberra), but returned to the countryside when the opportunity arose. He has a small Rare Fruit orchard near Bundaberg, Qld.

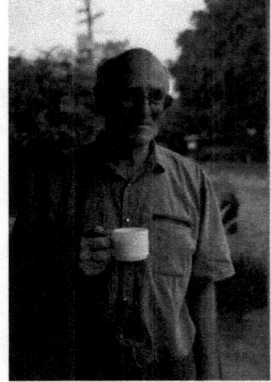

He could never give up intellectual life, but he finds today's universities hostage to business and political lobbies, enforcers of materialist ideologies, and stifling of original thought. They perpetuate the "Platonic Illusion" that Reality can be grasped intellectually and expressed in words or formulas; compare that with the Taoist notion that Reality can be intuited but not expressed, except partially and inadequately. The Taoist approach is to leave all debates open: living with uncertainty is part of the *Via Negativa*. Agnosia is the greatest knowledge: the more you know, the more you are aware of what you don't know.

Dogmatic scepticism is entrenched in academia. During the Covid pandemic, empirical data was discarded if it did not fit the government line; university 'factcheckers' became part of the Ministry of Truth. The Dogmatic Sceptics treat Ockham's Razor as a metaphysical principle, a substitute for the Principle of Verification, demolished by Karl Popper. I challenge them to prove that Ockham's Razor is a metaphytsical principle; and if they can't, to stop using it as one. If it is only a Rule of Thumb, it can't be used to prove anything.

We can asymptote in towards the truth, but never reach it; that's why the "Science" is never final; our knowledge is always partial. Socrates' philosophy was dialectical like the Taoists', not propositional like Plato's: he confessed his own ignorance, and urged "Know Thyself", like Lao Tzou. Dialectical thinking is also called 'lateral' or 'reflexive', in contrast to 'linear'. Creative work is now done outside academia. Peter seeks a blessing from Arnold J. Toynbee, the patron saint of Generalists, who warned of the dangers of over-specialisation, because it "leaves critical questions not only unanswered but unasked" (1961, p. 633).

Peter has been a conspiracy researcher since 1994. He operated a forum for political discussion from 2000 to 2010; that forum comprised experts from opposing parts of the spectrum. His website is https://mailstar.net.

Voltaire wrote, in Men of Letters (1757/1924), "The men of letters who have rendered the greatest services to the small number of thinking beings spread over the world, are the isolated writers, the true scholars shut in their studies, who have neither argued on the benches of the universities, nor told half-truths in the academies; and almost all of them have been persecuted. Our wretched species is so made that those who walk on the well-trodden path always throw stones at those who are showing a new road."

The Big Picture

This book is about conspiracies in high places. But on account of its complexity and controversial nature, I feed the need to explain where I am coming from, i.e. my philosophy. Some readers may suspect me of being a Nazi or a Stalinist, but I have never been either. To explain, I have added material to the Front Matter and Back Matter, which are not part of the main book.

I advocate a reformulated Christianity without the Old Testament, based, instead, on Christianity's historical ties with the religions of Zoroaster, Ancient Egypt (e.g. the Judgment), Buddhism and shamanism—the very features that Protestant Fundamentalists, some Jews, and atheists such as Martin Larson (1959) criticise it for.

I call it 'New Age Christianity', but it is opposed to some elements of the New Age movement: satanism and (evil) witchcraft. Christianity, like Judaism, has been through a number of transformations. Early Christian Europe was pacifist and meek, but the Vikings brought a martial ethic back, while Islam was expanding. The Vikings converted and, as the Normans, became the First Estate, with the Church as the Second; Thomas Aquinas' 'Just War' theory replaced earlier pacifism.

For 2000 years, Christianity has emphasised Dogma. If you look up Aquinas' 'Three Ways of Knowing God', you will see that the first way is Affirmation; that's Dogma. The second way is Negation—the *via negativa*. That's what I advocate; I reject all the Dogmas. There is a third way, but we're not there yet; I can't envisage it. Aquinas called it 'analogy' or 'transcendence'.

The dialectical method, first articulated by Aquinas in his Three Ways of Knowing God (affirmation, negation, analogy or transcendence), was later applied by Hegel and Marx to historical processes (thesis, antithesis, synthesis). Marx renamed analogy (or transcendence) "negation of the negation."

John Courtney Murray explained Aquinas' Three Ways of Knowing God, in his book *The Problem of God* (1964), p. 64f. "The first of the three ways of knowing God—the way of affirmation. ... the second way, the way of negation ... the third way, the way of transcendence or eminence" (p. 72). The *Via Negativa* is summed up in the statement "In the things of God the confession of no knowledge (agnosia) is great knowledge (gnosis)" (p. 66). I'd like to see the propositional philosophers parse that. For more information see my webpage https://mailstar.net/murray.html.

As explained on p. 50, the *Rig Veda* records the Aryan invasion of Pakistan and northern India. Their homeland, Arkaim, in Central Asia just east of the Urals, belonged to the Sintasha culture. Having domesticated the horse and developed the chariot, they spread, peacefully or forcefully, west into Europe, south into the Middle East and east into Siberia, as shown by Anthony (2007), Mallory and Mair (2000) and Baumer (2012). The word 'Iran' means *Aryan*, and so does 'Eire'. The Tarim Mummies attest their peaceful presence in the Taklamakan Desert, and their role in the spread of technology and ideas to China; later, technology and ideas came the other way too. Later invaders—e.g. Mongols and Huns—moved westwards.

The bold religion of the Aryan conquerors—admired by Hitler—was reformed by the Upanishad philosophers in India, which led to Jainism and Buddhism, philosophies of nonviolence, and by Zoroaster in Bactria (thence Persia). Both reforms led to the development of conscience; both Zoroastrianism and Buddhism were Aryan religions. Indra, god of war in the *Rig Veda*, has disappeared from the pantheon.

In Babylon, during the Exile, the Jewish religion was reformed in the Zoroastrian mould; it adopted Monotheism, Moralism and Messianism. Before that, Judaism was polytheistic and engaged in child sacrifice. Christianity is a form of Zoroastrianism, and Dualistic, but Judaism is Monotheistic. Freud said that Jewish Monotheism, a lofty religion, derived from Akhenaten, but that Jahve was "a rude, narrow-minded local god, violent and bloodthirsty" (1967, p. 61). These two conceptions of divinity are currently contesting for the streets of Jerusalem.

Like Jesus of Nazareth, Zoroaster is recorded as having had a Baptism and a Temptation by the Devil. The Three Wise men were Zoroastrian priests, attesting that this child would be the savior promised in the Zoroastrian scriptures. I can't see that the Crucifixion had anything to do with it; nor do I believe in the Trinity. The Christian Fall is based not on Adam and Eve, but on the Fall in Heaven—the clash between the bad angels and the good, as first presented in the Zoroastrian religion. Whether there is a real Devil we do not know; but people who deal with the occult attest that there are evil forces. I think of Jesus of Nazareth primarily as a psychic healer. In this he is allied with other psychic healers, whatever their religion; he was also a leader against evil psychic forces. I don't see celibacy as a higher state, but I pay tribute to the Nuns, Brothers and Priests who raised me.

Religion and the Paranormal

Queen Nefertari, wife of Pharaoh Ramesses II, died about 1256 BC, and was buried in the Valley of the Queens, at Luxor (Thebes). Her tomb is the most beautiful in Egypt; it depicts her trip to the Underworld, after her death. She meets Osiris, the Judge of the Dead, and other gods and goddesses. Osiris was a man, a king, who died and became a god, the first man to attain an afterlife; he then became Judge of the Dead. He is depicted with green skin and white clothing, like a mummy (mummies were wrapped in white cloth).

The tomb depicts scenes from the *Book of the Dead*, which gives advice on what to say to Osiris when you face Judgment. Your heart is weighted on a scales; on the other side is a feather. If your heart is lighter than the feather, you pass the Judgment and enter an afterlife. But if your heart is too heavy—meaning that you led a sinful life—your heart is eaten by the crocodile god or the jackal god Anubis, and you cease to exist.

You had to make a "Negative Confession", that you had not committed a list of 42 sins. Your heart was called on to give witness against you. On the walls of the tomb is a prayer to your heart: "O my heart which I had from my mother, O my heart which I had upon earth, do not rise up against me as a witness in the presence of the Lord of Things; do not speak against me concerning what I have done, do not bring up against me anything I have done in the presence of the Great God, Lord of the West (Osiris)."

Osiris' overcoming of death, to attain eternal life, paving the way for others too, was later emulated by Jesus. Christianity adopted features from many other religions, to facilitate conversion. Whereas fundamentalists disparage Christianity for this, and atheists see it as a proof of the falsity of religion, I see Christianity as a treasure-trove of ancient religions. It condemned them, but it preserved them. Those religions are dead now, but they live on in Christianity. Let's turn a weakness into a strength: New Age Christianity has a place for the spiritual traditions of many peoples; but not satanism or (evil) witchcraft.

The idea of the heart as the self was continued in the Sacred Heart of Jesus, though mixed with Greek ideas that the self resided in an immaterial soul, as in "body and soul", and Semitic ideas that the life-principle was the blood, as in "the Body and Blood of Christ."

As a solo traveller in 2018, I was a target for guides who expect a tip. In the Temple of Karnak, an unofficial Arab guide latched onto me and showed me around. At one place he motioned with his hands, as if transferring something from the wall to me. "Is that a blessing?" I asked. He nodded; he was transferring a blessing from Amun-Ra to me. How amazing! This would never happen in a group tour. The same happened at another site in that temple too.

The Pentagon has admitted to a secret program investigating UFOs, a unit instigated by believers in the Paranormal (Tritten, 2022). UFOs, despite showing up on videos, are considered Paranormal, like ghosts and other psychic phenomena. I am reminded of dowsing (water divining): I can do it, but not everyone picks up the signal; very rationalistic people seem to lack this ability.

Whereas Wikipedia's entries on most psychic phenomena are dismissive, its article on Near-Death Experiences reports "changes in personality and outlook on life, less concern for acquiring material wealth, a feeling of being more intuitive, no longer worrying about death." Recipients become more spiritual, but not necessarily more religious (Near-death experience). Even atheists such as A.J. Ayer have been shaken by NDEs.

www.ingramcontent.com/pod-product-compliance
Lightning Source LLC
Chambersburg PA
CBHW072040020426
42334CB00017B/1338